وَلَا قُوَّةَ إِلَّا بِاللَّهِ

لَمْ يَبْقَ صَافٍ وَلَا مُصَافٍ وَلَا مُعِينٍ وَلَا مُعَانٍ

وَفِي الْمَبَادِي بَدَا النَّبَاوِي فَلَا أَمِينَ وَلَا أَمِينِينَ

ثُمَّ قَالَ لِلْهَامِنِي النَّفِيسِ وَعِدْهَا وَاجْمَعِ الرِّقَاعَ وَعِدْهَا فَقَالَتْ لَقَدْ عَدَدْتُهَا لَمَّا

اسْتَعَدْتُهَا فَوُجِدَتْ بِعَدَدِ الضِّبَاعِ فَدُرْ غَالَتْ اجْلِبِ الرِّقَاعَ فَقَالَ يَغْسَلُ الْكَلَامُ أَنْجَمْ

IMPOSTURES

LETTER FROM THE GENERAL EDITOR ☖

The Library of Arabic Literature makes available Arabic editions and English translations of significant works of Arabic literature, with an emphasis on the seventh to nineteenth centuries. The Library of Arabic Literature thus includes texts from the pre-Islamic era to the cusp of the modern period, and encompasses a wide range of genres, including poetry, poetics, fiction, religion, philosophy, law, science, travel writing, history, and historiography.

Books in the series are edited and translated by internationally recognized scholars. They are published in parallel-text and English-only editions in both print and electronic formats. PDFs of Arabic editions are available for free download. The Library of Arabic Literature also publishes distinct scholarly editions with critical apparatus and a separate Arabic-only series aimed at young readers.

The Library encourages scholars to produce authoritative Arabic editions, accompanied by modern, lucid English translations, with the ultimate goal of introducing Arabic's rich literary heritage to a general audience of readers as well as to scholars and students.

The Library of Arabic Literature is supported by a grant from the New York University Abu Dhabi Institute and is published by NYU Press.

Philip F. Kennedy
General Editor, Library of Arabic Literature

IMPOSTURES

AL-ḤARĪRĪ

TRANSLATED BY
Michael Cooperson

FOREWORD BY
Abdelfattah Kilito

VOLUME EDITORS
Devin J. Stewart
Richard Sieburth

NEW YORK UNIVERSITY PRESS
NEW YORK

NEW YORK UNIVERSITY PRESS
New York

Copyright © 2020 by New York University
All rights reserved

Library of Congress Cataloging-in-Publication Data

Names: Ḥarīrī, 1054-1122, author. | Cooperson, Michael, translator. |
Kilito, Abdelfattah, 1945- author of foreword.
Title: Impostures / Al-Ḥarīrī ; translated by Michael Cooperson ;
foreword by Abdelfattah Kilito.
Other titles: Maqāmāt. English
Description: New York : New York University Press, 2020. | Series: Library
of Arabic literature | Includes bibliographical references. | Summary: "An itinerant con
man. A gullible eyewitness narrator. Voices spanning continents and centuries. These
elements come together in Impostures, a groundbreaking new translation of a celebrated
work of Arabic literature. Impostures follows the roguish Abū Zayd al-Sarūjī in his
adventures around the medieval Middle East--we encounter him impersonating a preacher,
pretending to be blind, and lying to a judge. In every escapade he shows himself to be a
brilliant and persuasive wordsmith, composing poetry, palindromes, and riddles on the
spot. Michael Cooperson transforms Arabic wordplay into English wordplay of his own.
Featuring picaresque adventures and linguistic acrobatics, Impostures brings the spirit
of this masterpiece of Arabic literature into English in a dazzling display of translation"--
Provided by publisher.
Identifiers: LCCN 2019055291 (print) | LCCN 2019055292 (ebook) | ISBN
9781479800841 (cloth) | ISBN 9781479800858 (ebook) | ISBN 9781479800865
(ebook)
Classification: LCC PJ7755.H3 M313 2020 (print) | LCC PJ7755.H3 (ebook) |
DDC 892.7/83407--dc23
LC record available at https://lccn.loc.gov/2019055291
LC ebook record available at https://lccn.loc.gov/2019055292

New York University Press books are printed on acid-free paper,
and their binding materials are chosen for strength and durability.

Typeset in Tasmeem, using DecoType Emiri.

Series design, typesetting, and digitization by Stuart Brown.

Manufactured in the United States of America
c 10 9 8 7 6 5 4 3 2 1

Table of Contents &

FOREWORD: IN PRAISE OF PRETENSE &

By ABDELFATTAH KILITO

It is thanks to al-Hamadhānī—al-Ḥarīrī's model—that the character of the eloquent rogue makes his sudden appearance in Arabic literature. The *Maqāmāt* ("Impostures") genre features a protagonist who is at once a man of letters and also a shameless beggar and vagabond who engages in roguery without compunction. Imposture is in his blood; it is second nature to him.

In his preface, al-Ḥarīrī praises the illustrious predecessor in whose footsteps he follows. And yet he is clearly ambivalent: he has his hero Abū Zayd al-Sarūjī say he is better than al-Hamadhānī's hero Abū l-Fatḥ al-Iskandarī. And for seven centuries readers have accepted this claim, and affirmed al-Ḥarīrī's superiority. An antagonistic quality permeates the *Maqāmāt* of al-Ḥarīrī, who effectively stole the glory from al-Hamadhānī, the very founder of the genre who fell into oblivion and who would not be reinstated till late in the nineteenth century. The imitator had eclipsed the originator: al-Ḥarīrī's *Maqāmāt* proved, if proof were needed, that a copy could surpass the original.

A successful imitator, however, is not always let off easy. Attempts are made to find flaws in his work, instances of plagiarism are supposedly discovered or unearthed, and sometimes he is even accused of having plundered the work outright. At least, that is what happened to al-Ḥarīrī, who was alleged not to have authored his *Maqāmāt*—and so the one who had devoted his work to the impostures of Abū Zayd came to be treated as an impostor himself. In fact, a curious rumor spread in Baghdad soon after the *Maqāmāt* were published. Yāqūt records it in his *Dictionary of Learned Men* and it has all the makings of a first-rate novel: during an attack on a caravan, some bedouin had seized as part of the booty a pouch belonging to some Maghribis; they had put it up for sale in Basra, al-Ḥarīrī had bought it and gotten his hands on a manuscript that was in it, specifically the manuscript of the *Maqāmāt* bearing his name . . . .

The rumor died out after a time, but one argument advanced by the rumormongers remains troubling: their assertion that they did not recognize in the *Maqāmāt* al-Ḥarīrī claimed were his the style or mode of expression of his previous works. This led them to conclude that the *Maqāmāt* were written by a traveler, one originally from—and why not!—a western part of the Muslim realms.[1] But must a writer be condemned to the stranglehold of a single style, and never permitted to write differently? Is he to be a hostage to his style, to intractable destiny?

In any event, it has to be conceded that al-Ḥarīrī's style in the *Maqāmāt*, already distinct from al-Hamādhānī's, differs from that of his earlier writing, as the enviers maintain. Severed from himself, one might say that al-Ḥarīrī is *several*. In one interview, Borges cites the following declaration by Whitman: "I contradict myself, I contain multitudes." This statement could apply just as easily to al-Ḥarīrī, but also more aptly to Abū Zayd al-Sarūjī, his protagonist, whose being is nothing but an uninterrupted series of semblances, of refractions. This shimmering is characteristic of Abū Zayd, of his universe, and of the way in which the book is composed.

Chased out of his native city of Sarūj by the Crusaders, Abū Zayd leads a vagrant's life, traveling far and wide. During these wanderings, he lives by his wits and relies mainly on the alms he is given in appreciation for his talented oratory and literary performances. People do not provide assistance out of compassion, but because they are essentially impressed by his command of literary materials and by his rhetorical powers. He is a beggar poet (as was Homer, according to one ancient legend). In the *Maqāmāt*, roguery is an art, a *genre*, which is to say a comportment, a way of being and thinking, indeed a distinction, a style. A mixture of genres, we should add, as the art of literature went hand in hand with the art of deception. In this world of variegation and varicoloration, literature therefore presents itself as an imposture. Abū Zayd's first victims are specifically men of letters. Surreptitiously introducing himself into their company, he manages over and over to charm them and to collect their gifts. Initially, they

---

1. See Abdelfattah Kilito, *L'Absent ou l'épreuve du soleil*, translated from the Arabic by Francis Gouin (Casablanca: Toubkal, 2019), 98–101.

reject him on account of his pitiful appearance and his miserable attire, but the moment he opens his mouth he subdues them, their contempt dissipates, and revulsion turns to admiration.

Abū Zayd never appears twice in the same guise. He changes appearance at will, showing a new face on every occasion, an actor taking on various roles: now a blind man, now a lame one, a decrepit old man, a jurist, a hemiplegic, a shrewd litigant, a preacher, a seller of charms . . . From one episode to the next, his repertoire changes and inevitably the themes of his disquisitions do too. More often than not, his role-playing is so skillful that at first he isn't recognized by the narrator al-Ḥārith ibn Hammām, who meets him in each and every setting, following him like a shadow. Abū Zayd is several, he has no choice but to be untrue to himself. In each of his performances he wears a new mask; his identity, provisional and fleeting, is at every instant a borrowing, an impersonation. But who is he in reality? It bears repeating that in some ways he is just a succession of countless semblances. We should not be suprised by the fact that he is compared to the moon, the orb of night that perforce yields to the orb of day. But is there a sun in al-Ḥarīrī's *Maqāmāt*?

We should mention the explanation Abū Zayd provides as justification for his various postures. If we are to believe him, the passage of time is to blame, the nights (*al-layālī*), the days (*al-ayyām*): in a word, *dahr*, Time itself, the prime controller of life's vicissitudes and reversals of fortune. *Dahr* governs all the events that impact human existence. Sometimes *dahr* shows its magnanimous side: in some episodes Abū Zayd is treated well by rulers and he struts about like a lord, surrounded by servants and by obvious signs of affluence. But more often, *dahr* is synonymous with adversity and setback: it can't be trusted, it is inherently traitorous, fickle, reversing circumstances, making promises it will not keep—like lightning flashes not followed by rain. If *dahr* is the paragon of imposture, no surprise then that Abū Zayd is made in its image, as al-Sharīshī, one of al-Ḥarīrī's commentators, has observed: he says that Abū Zayd has the same traits as *dahr*, is a metaphor for it, an incarnation of it.

Ambiguity permeates Abū Zayd's disquisitions, which time and again are not what they seem. This is because of his frequent use of *tawriyah*, a figure of speech that relies on the double meaning of a text, where the obvious meaning conceals another one. What's more, an utterance can have a double destination and therefore be understood differently by two distinct recipients. The palindrome in particular is a device much favored by al-Ḥarīrī. For example, one poem by Abū Zayd reads the same from beginning to end as it does from end to beginning: even when read backward the content remains consistent. One letter, a remarkable accomplishment, when read one way produces one text, and when read backward reveals an entirely different one: a disturbance has taken place, an astral and cosmic one, so to speak, whereby the sun rises at one and the same time in both East and West. This letter, jubilantly delivered by Abū Zayd to a mesmerized audience, "whose firmament is its fundament and whose fundament is the firmament—whose long low lines of dawn and dusk are the same" is "much like a cloak of which the warp is the weft and the weft the warp, and the shimmering cloth changes colour when turned out!" (§17.2).

Similarly, the chaos brought about by *dahr* is in a manner of speaking echoed in the very organization of al-Ḥarīrī's work, which exhibits no narrative continuity between its fifty episodes. At first glance, the scattershot and arbitrary arrangement reflects to a certain extent the reversals and volte-face of *dahr*. There is neither transition nor bridge from one episode to the next, and if there is any narrative continuity to be discerned, it is slack and contrived (as when the thirty-second episode appears to prolong the thirty-first).

But things aren't so simple. If each episode is independent, it is nevertheless linked to neighboring episodes through the recurring appearance of the protagonist and narrator. Truth be told, the feeling of disjointedness is more in evidence in al-Hamādhānī's *Maqāmāt*, where the succession of episodes appear to follow no fixed plan. And significantly, his protagonist Abū l-Fatḥ al-Iskandarī does not appear in all the episodes, whereas in al-Ḥarīrī's case Abū Zayd is present from start to finish, which makes a compelling case for an overarching structure to al-Ḥarīrī's book. There is no doubt that al-Ḥarīrī laid out the episodes in a specific order, and we more or less get the sense that we aren't supposed to read them in an order not intended by the author. Of course, readers are free to decide how they will read the book, for instance, reading around according to their liking (and there's no shortage of such readers), but my feeling is that they won't do this without some reservations, as they will have the distinct impression that each episode is in its proper place. Several clues reinforce this view. And a number of editions establish at the outset that the work exhibits a discernible thematic and rhetorical structure, consisting of five series of ten episodes each, that the first episode in each cycle is exhortatory (*wa'ẓiyyah*), the sixth literary (*adabiyyah*), the fifth and tenth whimsical (*hazliyyah*). In any case, changing the placement of the first episode, which describes the initial meeting of the two associates, is as categorically impossible as changing the position of the last episode, which describes them finally going their separate ways. In each episode, they meet only to part ways again, but we know that they will again be reunited, and that we will be reunited with them. We know that Abū Zayd hides behind a disguise and that sooner or later his identity will be revealed. Narrative coherence is maintained by the constancy of his name and also that of the narrator, al-Ḥārith ibn Hammām.

Al-Ḥārith is the hero's double; it is difficult therefore not to think of them as a kind of Doctor Jekyll and Mr. Hyde. Al-Ḥārith is always on hand to witness Abū Zayd's deeds, to attend his performances, to relate his disquisitions, and as a result he too is in a state of perpetual displacement. A number of stories involve a quest for a treasure, for an island, for a woman. For his part, al-Ḥārith is engaged in a perpetual quest: for Abū Zayd or, rather, for *adab*, that magical word that denotes, among other things, the literary arts. There are no illiterates in any episode, everyone is in search of *adab*: on highways and in public squares, in mosques, in caravanserais and in libraries, in the midst of banquets and in drinking sessions. The *Maqāmāt* treat listeners and readers to eloquent speech, to witticism, to accomplished word play, and they are constantly on the lookout for the secrets of the arts of writing and reading. They are a veritable feast of *adab*'s distinctive language, one that everyone knows and engages in, one that has currency everywhere. *Adab* is the main theme, the real protagonist of al-Ḥarīrī's work, one that touches on everything that relates to the literary arts: verse and prose, the protocols of composition, genre, poetic and edifying themes, role models, archetypal animals with distinctive nicknames, and so on.

In the fiftieth and final episode, Abū Zayd repents. But of what exactly? True, he has engaged in repugnant activities, lied, stolen, swindled. And yet, in this closing episode, something unexpected happens: to dupe everyone—as is his habit—he confesses his misdeeds before a gathering of the faithful in the Grand Mosque of Basra (the narrator's native city, but also al-Ḥarīrī's), asking them to plead with God to show him mercy. Knowing him all too well, al-Ḥārith ibn Hammām has doubts about Abū Zayd's sincerity and believes this to be just another one of his tricks. But he later learns that the prayers of the Basrans were granted, that Abū Zayd was caught at his own game. Having put to an end his wanderings, his rogue's life, any sort of adventure, he is now leading the life of an ascetic. In order to see him again, al-Ḥārith goes to Sarūj, which, significantly, has since been evacuated by the Crusaders. There, the reality of Abū Zayd's repentance and of his total detachment from the trappings of the world is confirmed.

It is noteworthy that the protagonist's conversion is followed almost immediately by his return to Sarūj, his native city for which he often expresses nostalgia. He finally finds his moorings, only leaving his home to go pray at the mosque. Profusion, followed by withdrawal. He lives alone, and whereas he used to relish good food, he now subsists on bread soaked in oil. Remarkably, he no longer speaks, except when praying. He wears no disguise—unless his asceticism is to be understood as the crowning disguise, one he will not be able to shed.

His conversion isn't only religious, it is also literary. He renounces literature, he repents of *adab* and of everything this word entails: language, society's rules of conduct, places of gathering, verbal jousts, audiences . . . Of all the literary genres, he devotes himself to one only, the sermon. His interlocutor this time around is God, to whom he addresses pious disquisitions couched in verse and rhyming prose. As a result, al-Ḥārith can no longer play his part as narrator. What is there to relate to posterity when Abū Zayd is consigned to silence? As he dismisses al-Ḥārith, Abū Zayd enjoins on him one final instruction, his spiritual testament: "Keep Death before your eyes!" The fiftieth episode then ends with the words: "I bid him fare well with boisterous sobbings and great plenty of tears. Then parted we asunder and I saw him no more" (§50.11).

What is striking here is al-Ḥārith's demeanor: he cries because he has lost a friend, a distinguished master who instructed him in *adab*. He does not disapprove of his decision to live as an ascetic, but he doesn't approve of it either. He respects his decision but is in no way attracted by his example. He isn't about to place death before his eyes, isn't about to abandon *adab*. Nor al-Ḥarīrī either, surely, else he would never have written his celebrated *Maqāmāt*. As for the reader . . .

Abdelfattah Kilito
Rabat   *(Translated by Shawkat M. Toorawa)*

❧   Acknowledgements

I am indebted to the Library of Arabic Literature for giving me a chance to play with the impossible. The members of the Executive Board—Philip Kennedy, James Montgomery, and Shawkat M. Toorawa, along with editorial director Chip Rossetti—amiably insisted that this translation meet the high standard they have established for the series. All devoted countless hours to ensuring that it did. My project editor, Devin J. Stewart, kept me honest and made the Notes a good deal more informative. Volume editor Richard Sieburth offered bracing responses to every one of my drafts, along with multilingual riffs on themes I had glimpsed only dimly in the Arabic. The members of the Editorial Board, particularly Joseph Lowry and Maurice Pomerantz, were generous throughout. Besides carefully reviewing the Arabic text, Matthew Keegan shared his digital copies of the earliest manuscripts as well as his ongoing scholarly work on al-Ḥarīrī. Rory MacDonald assisted me in editing several of the Arabic Impostures. Abdelfattah Kilito was kind enough to write the Foreword, beautifully translated by Shawkat M. Toorawa. Copyeditor Keith Miller, proofreader Wiam El-Tamami, cartographer Martin Grosch, digital production manager Stuart Brown, and assistant editor Lucie Taylor all did meticulous work on the text and the volume.

 Of the many friends whose kindness I fear I have abused, I am most grateful to Phillip Mitsis and Jeannie Miller, who commented incisively on early drafts. Several of the Impostures were translated with the help of those better acquainted than I with the variety of English I was trying to use. These include Jeremy Fernando and Philip Jeyaretnam (Singlish, Imposture 3), James Montgomery (Scots English, 14), Shawkat M. Toorawa (Indian English, 15), and Tony C. Brown (Kiwi, 28). Leyla Rouhi corrected the Spanish part of my Spanglish (16). Nandi Sims advised me on African-American Language (21) and US college slang (37). Phillip Mitsis, Peter Goodrich, and Joseph Lowry helped compose the puns in Imposture 32. Mel Tom corrected the current London slang (23). Slavomír Čéplö put the Arabic and Persian names in Imposture 40 into plausible Irish forms. Stuart Brown corrected the Cockney (44). Richard Ali, who entirely rewrote my Naijá, should be considered a co-author of Imposture 45.

In working with translated Impostures and related works in various languages, I benefited from the kind assistance of many friends and colleagues, including Ailin Qian and Shiyi Zhou (Chinese); Slavomír Čéplö, Yasser Djazaerly, Julia Hauser, and M. Rahim Shayegan (German); Alexandre Roberts and Phillip Mitsis (Greek); Catherine Bonesho, Abraham Greenstein, Lev Hakkak, and Yona Sabar (Hebrew); Jan Loop and Phillip Mitsis (Latin); Domenico Ingenito, Latifeh Hagigi, Ahmad Karimi-Hakkak, and M. Rahim Shayegan (Persian); and Pavel Angelos, Hristina Chobanova-Angelova, Kirill Dmitriev, and Masha Kirasirova (Russian).

Much of the translation was drafted during a LAL fellowship at the New York University campus in Abu Dhabi, where Alexandra Sandu and Amani Alzoubi made me feel welcome. I thank Mahmoud Abdalla, Kirill Dmitriev, Ranya Abdel Rahman, Hossam Barakat, Claire Gallien, Parween Habib, Trevor Kann, Alexander Key, Maru Pabón, Flora Rees, Alexandre Roberts, Sarah R. bin Tyeer, Paul Walker, David Wilmsen, and Luke Yarbrough for inviting me to read or discuss work in progress. I gratefully acknowledge the Forum for Arab and International Relations and the Sheikh Hamad bin Khalifa Award for Translation and International Understanding for their magnanimous support of translators and translation.

Among the many others who shared their expertise, spoke a kind word when it was needed, or inspired me in ways they have probably forgotten are Ahmed Alwishah, Sean Anthony, Zeina Hashem Beck, Abdessalam Benabdelali, Hinrich Biesterfeldt, Kevin Blankinship, Jess Bravin, Dominic Brookshaw, Julia Bray, Richard Bulliet, Brigitte Caland, Frederic Clark, Peter Cole, Nino Dolidze, Emily Drumsta, Shereen El Ezabi, the late Salwa Eltorai, Albert Gatt, Jessica Goldberg, Matthew Gordon, Beatrice Gründler, May Hawas, the late Wolfhart P. Heinrichs, Lucas Herchenroeder, Walid Hamarneh, Tamer M. Hussein, Dominique Jullien, Daniel L. Keegan, Philip Kennedy, Nancy Khalek, Batool Khattab, Zia Khoshsirat, Pamela Klasova, Yaron Klein, Marcel Kurpershoek, the late Abraham Lavi, Chris Lucas, Saree Makdisi, Annabel Mallia, Denise Marie-Teece, Daniel Medin, Ronald Mendoza-De Jesus, Geoffrey Moseley, Shad Naved, Daniel

Newman, Bilal Orfali, Tyler Patterson, Charles Perry, Margret Pfeiffer, Jay Phelan, Julia Phelan, Claudia Rapp, Salam Rassi, Hector Reyes, Dwight F. Reynolds, Kishwar Rizvi, Leyla Rouhi, Everett K. Rowson, Christine van-Ruymbeke, Peter Sagal, David Schaberg, Emily Selove, Stuart Semmel, M. Rahim Shayegan, Rebecca Spang, Anna Ziajka Stanton, Denise Sutherland, Adam Talib, Newell Ann Van Auken, Katrien Vanpee, Chathan Vemuri, David Wilmsen, Liran Yadgar, and Luke Yarbrough. I regret that John P. Flanagan did not live to see this book completed; I hope he would have liked it.

I would not have been able to finish a translation based on pastiche and constrained writing without relying on Project Gutenberg, the all-volunteer project that supplies searchable full-text editions of many works in English. Internet Archive provided complete online editions of many critical Arabic texts, and Abū ʿĀṣim Yaḥyā Fatḥī helpfully posted his readings of all fifty Arabic originals on YouTube.

I am indebted to my wife, Mahsa Maleki, her parents, Armita Farhoomand and Mahmoud Malaki, and my brother- and sister-in-law, Hamidreza Maleki and Shima Torabi, for seeing us through two international relocations and taking care of the children while I worked on this book. I am also grateful to my parents, Georgia and Jay N. Cooperson, who kept their doors open throughout. Much of the reading that went into this translation took place years ago in our book-filled house.

In 382/992, in the city of Nishapur in the northeast corner of what is now Iran, a young visitor named al-Hamadhānī astounded the city's elite by defeating a local celebrity in a prose-and-poetry slam.[1] At various points during the contest, al-Hamadhānī offered to produce pieces of language subject to odd constraints: an essay without the word "the" in it, for example, or one containing verses embedded in it diagonally. Dismissing such games as "verbal jugglery," his opponent demanded that he improvise a bureaucratic letter on a topic suggested by the audience. Al-Hamadhānī accepted this conventional challenge but added a twist that let him show off his talent: he improvised his letter starting from the last word and working backward.

Al-Hamadhānī, called "The Wonder of the Age," died young. His greatest work, at least in retrospect,[2] is a collection of unusual stories called *maqāmāt*, a term I translate (following a suggestion by Shawkat Toorawa) as "impostures."[3] Although al-Hamadhānī's fifty-odd Impostures differ

---

1. Or so he later claimed. Rowson ("Religion and Politics") seems to believe him, while Hämeen-Anttila is more skeptical (*Maqama*, 24–27). For an illuminating study of the "vizier culture" that promoted literary rivalries of this kind, see England, *Medieval Empires*.

2. Hämeen-Anttila has pointed out that al-Hamadhānī "was not seen primarily as a *maqama* writer by his contemporaries" and suggests that his reputation as the master of the genre may have arisen because of al-Ḥarīrī's later efforts to outdo him (Hämeen-Anttila, *Maqama*, 117–25).

3. Etymologically, *maqāmah* indicates any occasion when one stands, and by extension a speech made before an audience. As used by al-Ḥarīrī and al-Hamadhānī, its obvious sense is that of a verbal performance delivered to strangers while standing in a mosque, market, or street, as opposed to one delivered while seated in comfort among friends, as would be the case in a *majlis*. Even so, the term's wide application as a designation for literary works has generated much discussion. My position is that of Katia Zakharia, who argues that no single definition is adequate to the variety of documented uses (Zakharia, *Abū Zayd*, 93–101). I would add that even if the connection between "standing" and a particular kind of speech was at some point clear, it was evidently lost over time—just as, for example, no one today is quite sure what the word "tragedy" originally meant. In practice, a *maqāmah* is simply the genre, or any single example of it, known by that name. Throughout this book, I will use the

widely in content, certain characters and themes recur.[1] Every Imposture
has a narrator who travels from one city or region to another. Everywhere
he goes, he encounters an enigmatic figure endowed with stunning eloquence. In some cases, this figure shows off his wit at a gathering of scholars. In others he is found begging in a market or a mosque. Some Impostures contain little more than speeches and verses, but others go on to tell
a story that exposes the eloquent preacher as a sinner and a fraud.[2]

Although the so-called picaresque Impostures (that is, the ones with
stories) have attracted the most attention in modern times, pre-modern
Arabic readers were more interested in the verbal performances. Indeed,
the Imposture's most striking feature is its form. Whether spoken by the
narrator, the eloquent stranger, or one of the occasional characters, the
frame story and the speeches are almost all in rhymed prose. The speeches
are punctuated by verse, which unlike the prose has a single rhyme and
a consistent number of feet per line. Strikingly, none of al-Hamadhānī's
Impostures are palindromic, lipogrammatic, or otherwise constrained,
even though al-Hamadhānī claimed he could produce texts that were.[3]
But even without those flourishes, his work was regarded as the freakish
production of a boy genius unlikely to be imitated, let alone outdone.

So matters stood until 495/1101–2,[4] when an unlikely prospect named
al-Ḥarīrī[5] decided to challenge the Wonder of the Age.[6] Al-Ḥarīrī (who was

---

capitalized word (Imposture, Impostures) to refer to the genre or to individual *maqāmāt*.
I will use *Impostures* in italics only when referring to al-Ḥarīrī's text.

1. Al-Hamadhānī's Impostures were collected, copied, and published at different times, but
apparently never by the author himself, making it impossible to know whether we have them
all or whether all the ones attributed to him are genuine. See Pomerantz and Orfali, "Three
Maqāmāt." Whether he was the first to write Impostures is a question much debated in the
secondary literature. For an incisive summary see Malti-Douglas, "Maqāmāt," 247–51, and
Hämeen-Anttila, *Maqama*, 64–73.

2. For a more detailed overview see Hämeen-Anttila, *Maqama*, 38–61.

3. Prendergast, *Maqamat*, 21.

4. On the date see MacKay, "Certificates," 8–9.

5. More fully Abū Muḥammad al-Qāsim ibn ʿAlī al-Ḥarīrī al-Baṣrī al-Ḥarāmī, "al-Qāsim, the
father of Muḥammad, the son of ʿAlī the silk trader, from the quarter of the Ḥarām tribe in
Basra." One biographer calls him Ibn al-Ḥarīrī (Yāqūt, *Muʿjam*, 5:2202), implying that the silk
trader in question was an ancestor.

6. Most critics no longer believe that he was inspired by meeting with a real mountebank
named Abū Zayd: see Zakharia, "Norme." But one version of the story seems plausible

born in 446/1054 and died in 516/1122)[1] was a proud citizen of the southern Iraqi town of Basra. During his lifetime, the town was governed by a motley parade of Abbasid caliphs, Seljuk sultans, Arab chieftains, and Turkish emirs.[2] One source reports that al-Ḥarīrī was a wealthy landowner while another claims he was employed by the Abbasid administration in Baghdad to report on local affairs. Though "extremely clever and articulate," he was also "short, ugly, stingy, and filthy in his person"[3]—all liabilities in a world where knowledge was transmitted face to face and being an author often meant performing one's works in public. Most damningly, al-Ḥarīrī was unable to compose on the spot. While thinking, he would pull at his beard, which he did so often that he plucked the hairs out.[4] After he presented his first Imposture he was asked to write another, but even after weeks of solitary effort, "blackening page after page," he "found himself unable to put two words together."[5] Later, after he had managed to produce forty episodes, he was asked, while calling on a high official in Baghdad, to improvise one more. "Taking pen case and paper, he went off to a corner of the audience room and remained there for a good long while, but no inspiration came and he left the room, mortified."[6] So unlikely a superstar did he seem that he was widely accused of plagiarizing his stories from a visiting North African.

But al-Ḥarīrī had the last laugh. When the *Impostures* were finished, he took his scribbled manuscript to Baghdad. There he read the work aloud to one al-Mubārak al-Anṣārī, who made a fair copy. In Rajab 504/January 1111, al-Ḥarīrī invited a group of prominent literary and legal scholars to hear the first five Impostures read aloud. The attendees must have liked what

enough: see the note to Imposture 48. Al-Ḥarīrī's preface speaks vaguely of a patron; see further the notes to §0.3.

1. The major pre-modern biographies are Yāqūt, *Muʿjam*, 5:2202–16, and Ibn Khallikān, *Wafayāt*, 4:63–68. The essential modern studies are de Sacy, *Séances*, 2:1–50, and Zakharia, *Abū Zayd*, 23–51.

2. On the complex political history see de Sacy, *Séances*, 2 (introduction, by M. Reynaud and M. Derenbourg): 5–14, 21–27, 28–31, 42, 50.

3. Yāqūt, *Muʿjam*, 5:2206.

4. This is a real condition known as trichotillomania. One of my college roommates dealt with stress by yanking on his hair, a habit that eventually produced a distinct bald spot on the top of his head.

5. Yāqūt, *Muʿjam*, 5:2204.

6. Ibn Khallikān, *Wafayāt*, 4:65.

they heard, as many of them returned for session after session to hear the whole work through. Just over a month later, on Shaʿban 7, 504/February 18, 1111, the first public reading of the Impostures came to an end, with at least thirty-eight senior men of letters in attendance. The auditors' names and the precise date of the last session are carefully noted on al-Mubārak's fair copy, which by some miracle has survived into modern times.

After the first reading of the Impostures was finished, the fair copy was used to teach the Impostures another twenty-nine times. The last of these teach-ins took place in Damascus in Rabiʿ al-Awwal 683/June 1284.[6] As impressive as its diffusion is, this manuscript is only one of the seven hundred copies reportedly approved by al-Ḥarīrī himself. This number means that he was approached seven hundred times by people who wanted him to confirm that they had studied an authentic copy of his work.[7] After his death, the Impostures continued to grow in popularity. As one of his biographers puts it:

> The Impostures have enjoyed a reception unlike anything else in literary history. The work is of such a high standard, so marvelous in expression, and so copious in vocabulary, as to carry all before it. The author's choice of words, and his careful arrangement of them, are such that one might well despair of imitating him, much less of matching his achievement. The work is justly celebrated by critics as well as admirers, and has received more than its due of accolades.[8]

Unlike al-Hamadhānī's, al-Ḥarīrī's Impostures are clearly intended to fit together as a collection. In the first Imposture, the narrator, al-Ḥārith, meets the eloquent rogue, Abū Zayd, for the first time; in the last Imposture, Abū Zayd supposedly reforms. There is also more consistency across

---

6. This account is based on MacKay, "Certificates."

7. Yāqūt, Muʿjam, 2205. As Asma Sayeed and Bilal Abdelhady have pointed out to me, al-Ḥarīrī might well have authorized dozens of copies at a time by reading aloud to large groups of people. Thus the number seven hundred, though doubtless an approximation, need not be dismissed as a mere figure of speech.

8. Yāqūt, Muʿjam, 2205. It should be noted that not all readers have agreed (as Yāqūt implies) that al-Ḥarīrī outdid his predecessor. For example, Margoliouth and Pellat flatly describe his Impostures as "no more than a pale reflection of those of al-Hamadhānī" ("al-Ḥarīrī").

the stories. With a few notable exceptions, all of them feature Abū Zayd as "a clever and unscrupulous protagonist, disguised differently in each episode," who "succeeds, through a display of eloquence, in swindling money out of the gullible narrator"—namely, al-Ḥārith, "who only realizes [Abū Zayd's] identity . . . when it is too late."[1] In effect, al-Ḥarīrī has taken one of al-Hamadhānī's plots and standardized it. He is also more consistent than his predecessor in matters of form. Al-Hamadhānī may have one poem in an Imposture, or several, or none, while al-Ḥarīrī often has just two. Similarly, al-Hamadhānī frequently drops out of rhyme in transitional passages, while al-Ḥarīrī almost never drops out of rhyme unless he is quoting a Qur'anic verse or pious formula.

Most famously, al-Ḥarīrī made a point of including examples of the kinds of trick writing that his predecessor had claimed to be able to produce. In Imposture 28, the roguish Abū Zayd delivers a sermon in which every word consists entirely of undotted letters (excluding, that is, half the letters in the Arabic alphabet). In Imposture 6, he dictates a letter in which every second word contains only dotted letters and the remaining words only undotted ones. In Impostures 8, 35, 43, and 44, he composes a story or poem that seems to be about one thing but contains so many words with double meanings that it can be read as telling an equally coherent story about something else. In Imposture 16, he extemporizes several palindromes (sentences that read the same backward as forward). In Imposture 17, he delivers a sermon that can be read word by word from the end to produce a different but equally plausible speech. In 32, he produces ninety legal riddles, each based on a pun. And in 46, he trains schoolchildren to perform feats such as taking all the words that contain the rare letter *ẓā'* and putting them into a poem. To some critics, manipulations like these have seemed an embarrassing waste of time, and evidence of the decadence of "Oriental taste."[2] To my mind, however, they lie at the heart of al-Ḥarīrī's enterprise.

---

1. Stewart, "Maqāmah," 145.

2. Reinaud and Derenbourg attribute al-Ḥarīrī's "decadence" to Persian and Hellenistic influences (quoted in de Sacy, *Séances*, 2:54). Rückert felt the need to apologize for what he calls "der falscher Orientalischer Geschmack," but suggests that it is redeemed by humor (Rückert, *Verwandlungen*, VI and XII). Ernest Renan was more severe, commenting that the Impostures, "appréciée d'après nos idées européennes, dépasse tout ce qu'il est permis

As Matthew Keegan has recently argued, the Impostures are about learning.[1] Here it is useful to recall that twelfth-century Arabic was not simply a means of communication in the ordinary sense. For one thing, native speakers had long been in the minority in the territories captured by Islam, and in many places still were. Thus it was by no means guaranteed that any given Muslim, much less anyone living under Muslim rule, could speak the language. Moreover, Arabic was the language in which God had revealed the Qur'an to the Prophet Muḥammad. For non-native speakers, learning it meant fully inhabiting one's identity as a Muslim—and not coincidentally making oneself eligible for opportunities denied to one's monolingual Persian-, Coptic-, Berber-, or Aramaic-speaking cousins. This aspirational quality of Arabic is evident from the eagerness with which al-Ḥarīrī's characters debate fine points of grammar, semantics, and etymology. It also explains their palpable fear of making mistakes, as well as their chagrin when Abū Zayd outdoes them in punning, rhyming, riddling, or whatever the challenge might be.

Yet Abū Zayd does more than take cocky neophytes down a peg. He does things with language that are practically impossible—at least, if one imagines him doing them on the spot. In imagining a character with such extraordinary powers, al-Ḥarīrī seems to be grappling with the problem of divine and human language. When God conveyed his final revelation to humankind, he did so in Arabic. With the end of revelation, Arabic becomes a merely human language once again. As such, it can be used to inform, guide, or illuminate, but it can also be used to lie, cheat, defraud, swindle, and deceive. Yet even when it is being used dishonestly, it retains its numinous character: that is, its memory of having once been the voice

---

d'imaginer en fait de mauvais goût." For him, al-Ḥarīrī is primarily of interest as an exemplar of "Arab decadence." See Renan, "Les Séances de Hariri," 288 and 300; I thank Maurice Pomerantz for this reference. For a deconstruction of Renan's views see Kilito, *Séances*, 202–8. Also noteworthy here is Devin Stewart's observation that in pronouncing these harsh judgments, European scholars were not necessarily expressing "Orientalist disdain for Arabic literary sensibilities" but rather "parroting views prominent in Arabic literary studies in the Islamic world" (Stewart, "Classical Arabic *Maqāmāt*").

1. Keegan, "Commentarial Acts," 81–117.

of the Eternal.[1] Like Milton's Satan, it retains, even after its fall, some of its original God-given beauty:

> ... his form had not yet lost
> All her Original brightness, nor appear'd
> Less than Arch Angel ruind, and th' excess
> Of Glory obscur'd ... [2]

It is this numinous character of Arabic that makes verbal miracles possible. It allows Abū Zayd to compose sermons without dots, or verses full of ẓā'-words, or speeches that can be read both backward and forward. These are not idle tricks: as Katia Zakharia has argued, games played with a sacred language are never just games.[3] Rather, Abū Zayd's performances convey what Stephen Greenblatt has called "a pervasive sense . . . that there is something uncanny about language, something that is not quite human."[4]

If we take this tack, a number of things make sense. The narrator, al-Ḥārith ibn Hammām, begins many of the routines by telling us that he went to one town or another in search of some inspiring oratory. This quest appears insufficiently motivated unless we read it as a thwarted reflex of a spiritual search. In late antique Egypt, Christians would journey into the desert in search of holy men, and when they found them, would say, "Give me a word," meaning a memorable summation of some spiritual precept.[5] This is the sort of word al-Ḥārith is looking for, even if he calls it *adab* (an Arabic word meaning "disciplined self-presentation" as well as "literary and linguistic training").[6] Naturally enough, he is drawn to the shabby,

---

1. On the language of the Qur'an as "the Discourse of the Eternal" see, e.g., Lumbard, "The Quran in Translation."

2. *Paradise Lost*, 1:589–94.

3. Zakharia, *Abū Zayd*, 45.

4. [Shakespeare], *Norton Shakespeare*, 68.

5. "In his early days, Abba Euprepius went to see an old man and said to him, Abba, give me a word so that I may be saved": [Proclus], *Procli Archiepiscopi Constantinopolitani Opera omnia*, Euprepius 7, col. 172, translated in Ward, *Sayings*, 62. For more examples see Theodore 20, col. 192 (*Sayings*, 76); Hierax 1, col. 232 (*Sayings*, 104).

6. Angelika Neuwirth has argued that the *adab* that al-Ḥārith is looking for is a kind of antinomian practice manifested in *'ajā'ib* or marvels of rhetoric (Neuwirth, "Adab Standing

hermit-like figure he sees haranguing crowds all over the world. And indeed, Abū Zayd is always up to the task of saying whatever needs to be said as eloquently as possible. Otherwise, there is nothing definite or stable about him: he varies so much in appearance and demeanor that al-Ḥārith almost always fails to recognize him. Abū Zayd may be what Abdelfattah Kilito says he is: a sorcerer's apprentice who loses control of the forces he has set in motion.[1] But the most economical explanation for his vaporous indeterminacy is that he is Arabic itself. To paraphrase Sheldon Pollock's description of Sanskrit, he is the language of God in the world of men.[2] And that language is so powerfully in excess of material reality that it overwhelms the agreed-upon relationship of word and object. This unmooring of meaning creates what Daniel Beaumont, one of al-Ḥarīrī's most perceptive readers, calls the work's "dreamy, haunting mood."[3] It also makes Abū Zayd's manifestations of piety seem forced and unconvincing. By this I do not mean that the real Abū Zayd is a sinner or a hypocrite. As Beaumont reminds us, there is no real Abū Zayd, only "the materialization of a function."[4] Rather, I mean that when language becomes unmoored from reality, it becomes unmoored from the sacred as well. Al-Ḥarīrī's language is saturated with the Qur'an, the Hadith (reports of the Prophet's words and actions), the rhythms of ritual, and the vocabulary of the religious sciences. But that language is left to fend for itself in a world that seems largely hostile to its purposes, where "the truth is incessantly discovered to be a pack of lies."[5] Of course, Abū Zayd prays to God to deliver him from poverty and exile, and see him safely to Sarūj, his lost hometown. But the entity that actually defines his life is chance, which is usually malign.

The result of Abū Zayd's predicament is a desperate search for a passage through or around language. At least, this is one way to make sense of his trajectory. For his part, al-Ḥārith so craves spiritual experience that

---

Trial," 211). To me, those marvels are cognate with the wonder (*thauma*) inspired by the piety and eloquence of the church fathers. For examples of wonder see, e.g., [Proclus], *Procli Archiepiscopi Constantinopolitani Opera omnia*, Achilles 6, col. 124–25 (Ward, *Sayings*, 30); Benjamin 2, col. 144 (Ward, *Sayings*, 43); John the Dwarf 7, col. 205 (Ward, *Sayings*, 87).

1. Kilito, *Séances*, 226.
2. Pollock, *Language of the Gods*.
3. Beaumont, "Trickster," 13.
4. Beaumont, "Mighty," 148–49.
5. Kennedy, *Recognition*, 306.

he is willing to scour the earth "from Ghana to Fergana" (§9.1) in search of words to help him find it. Strangely, though, none of Abū Zayd's sermons move him to tears of penitence. What al-Ḥārith fails to understand is that the word is not God. His teacher's speeches are about themselves; the divine must be approached by other means, if it is approachable at all. This is why, despite their humor and occasional raunchiness, the *Impostures* are suffused with a desperate sadness.[1] Language remains marvelous, but even as we marvel, we know we are seeing an imposture.

---

1. Zakharia describes al-Ḥarīrī's project as "an attempt to reconcile his certainties about language with the reality of the world he inhabits," an effort she describes as "tragic" (*Abū Zayd*, 48).

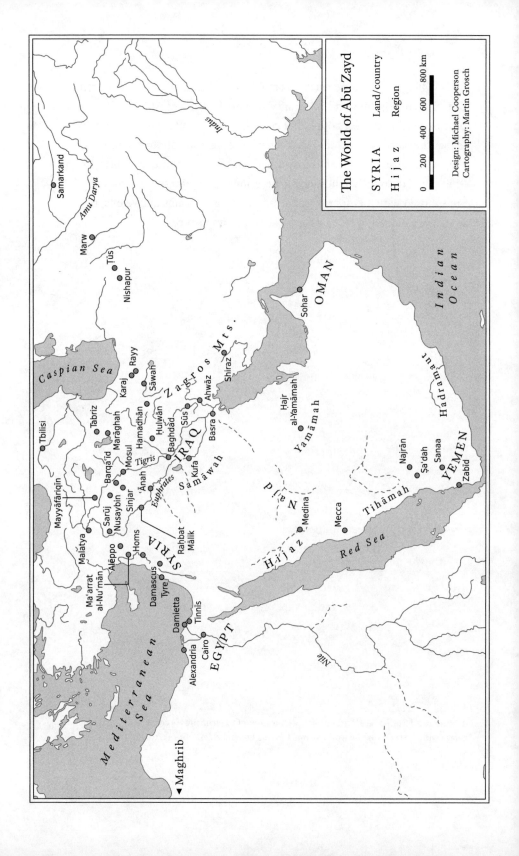

Note on the Translation ❧

Introducing her successful translation of Homer's *Odyssey*, Emily Wilson explains her choice of a low-key idiom:

> Impressive displays of rhetoric and linguistic force are a good way to seem important and invite a particular kind of admiration, but they tend to silence dissent and discourage deeper modes of engagement. A consistently elevated style can make it harder for readers to keep track of what is at stake in the story. My translation is, I hope, recognizable as an epic poem, but it is one that avoids trumpeting its own status with bright, noisy linguistic fireworks, in order to invite a more thoughtful consideration of what the narrative means, and the ways it matters.[1]

Without articulating the principle as clearly as Wilson has, I have always tried to translate in the self-effacing way she describes. But what is a translator to do with an *original* text whose avowed purpose is to fire off "bright, noisy linguistic fireworks"? Al-Ḥarīrī's *Impostures* do not simply include some excessive verbal performances; excessive verbal performance is what they are *about*. It seems to me, therefore, that any translation that fails to reproduce this feature sells the original short. The problem, of course, is that so many of the fireworks are tied to particular features of Arabic. These include rhyme, especially prose rhyme, and constrained writing—lipograms, palindromes, and the like. Strictly speaking, none of these features can be translated; they can only be imitated. And the only way to imitate them is to throw out the rule book. To understand why, it will be helpful to look at how other translators have treated the *Impostures*.

In the pre-modern period, responses to al-Ḥarīrī included everything from annotations to word-for-word renditions to imitations to translations proper. The Persian-language responses, documented by ʿAlī Ravāqī,

---

1. Homer, *Odyssey*, tr. Wilson, 83.

include four translations produced or copied between AD 1191 and 1809.[1] All of them are interlinear, meaning that Persian equivalents for the Arabic words are written between the lines of al-Ḥarīrī's text. At least one of these translations can be read straight through—that is, it consists of continuous Persian text, not simply a sequence of word-for-word equivalents. Still, what it conveys is the referential or propositional content: in other words, what the text *says* but not what it *does* in terms of rhyme, constrained writing, and so on. Presumably, translations of this kind were made to help readers whose main interest was reading the Arabic.

Not all approaches were so timid. In 551/1156, Qāżī Ḥamīd al-Din Balkhī, known as Ḥamīdī (d. 556/1164), discovered the *Impostures*, which he compares to "blazoned volumes" and "coffers full of precious stones." But, he points out, they do not mean very much to speakers of Persian:

> All their Wit avails the Gentile naught, nor do have the Persians any Share in those Rarities; any more than the Fables of Balkh should captivate the Ear, if recounted in the Patois of Karkh, or the Repartee of Rey retain its Charm, if rendered in Arabick, for lo:

> Wouldst thou tell thy Sorrows to Men abroad?
> In *their* Tongue, then, let thy Discourse be:
> Bid the Arab *ífʿal*! or else *lâ táfʿal*!
> But say *kón*, or *mákon*, to a good Parsee.[2]

Using the simple example of imperative verbs (*Do! Don't!*), Ḥamīdī suggests that transferring content between languages is a matter of finding the

---

1. Specifically, a partial one by Sirāj Kātib, completed 587/1191, in a copy dated to 662/1264; another whose original author and date are unknown, copied in 686/1287, and published by ʿAlāʾ al-Dīn Iftikhār Javādī in 1985 and Ravāqī himself in 1987; and two more of unknown authorship but apparently of more recent date, copied in 1218/1803–4 and 1223/1808–9, respectively. There is also an undated interlinear translation into Gilaki, an Indo-Iranian language today spoken on the southern shore of the Caspian Sea (Ravāqī, *Maghāmāt*, xx–xxi). On the latter see further Mokhtarian, *Maqāmen*.

2. [Ḥamīdī], *Gozīdeh*, 23. I have chosen a florid translation style to match the rococo phrasings of the original. Balkh is a city located in what is now north-central Afghanistan, Karkh is a district of Baghdad, and Rey is a town south of Tehran. For more on the Persian *maqāmah* see Behmardi, "Maḍīrah."

idiom that one's audience understands. In his view, the best way to convey the experience of reading al-Hamadhānī and al-Ḥarīrī was not to translate but rather to compose original Impostures in Persian. Though they take the form of rhetorical displays rather than stories, Ḥamīdī's Impostures are faithful to the form—that is, they combine verse and rhyming prose. And, in one way at least, he outdoes his predecessors: his Impostures mix Persian and Arabic. As eloquent as they may have been, al-Hamadhānī and al-Ḥarīrī worked their magic in only one language; Ḥamīdī works his in two.

A half century after Ḥamīdī, Yehudah ben Shlomo al-Ḥarīzī (d. 622/ 1225), a Jewish scholar living in Aleppo, took up the challenge of putting al-Ḥarīrī into Hebrew.[1] Writing after the fact, he describes the original Arabic *Impostures* as terrifying to all who heard them. No wonder, then, that those who first attempted to put them into Hebrew "captured rightly but one in fifty parts." But the problem, it turns out, was not that it cannot be done. Rather, it was that the ones trying did not know Hebrew well enough: "The burning bush beckons—but they hear not; ears have they— but they hear not." The citation of Exodus 3:1–5 makes the point that all the words a Hebrew translator needs are in the Bible; it is merely a matter of taking the trouble to look for them.

Al-Ḥarīzī clearly knew the Bible well enough: his translation, called *Maḥberot Ithi'el* ("The Compositions of Ithi'el") is a masterpiece of inge- nuity. Although the only surviving copy begins partway through the first and ends partway through the twenty-seventh Imposture, a later refer- ence indicates that he translated all fifty. The same later reference explains why: to show that the "Holy Tongue" could do anything that Arabic could do.[2] This being his aim, the timid lexical approach was not an option. For the poetry, he produces poetry, and for the rhymed prose, rhymed prose. Moreover, he naturalizes the allusions, even to the point of Biblicizing the names. Abū Zayd, for example, becomes Ḥever, after "a charmer" men- tioned in Psalms 58:6, with the tribal name ha-Qeni, after the Qenites, a tribe of wanderers who appear in Genesis 4:12 and Numbers 24:21–22.[3]

---

1. Alcharizi, *Machberoth Ithiel*, ed. Chenery; al-Ḥarizi, *Machberoth Ithiel*, ed. Perets. On his life see Sadan, "Intellectuel."

2. Alḥarizi, *Taḥkemoni*, 17–18.

3. Lavi, *A Comparative Study*, 13–15.

Al-Ḥarīzī even manages to imitate most of the special effects, including, for example, the palindromes in Imposture 16.[1] In only a few cases does his ingenuity fail. Imposture 6 contains a passage in which half the words are entirely dotted and the other half undotted, in alternation. After breaking the fourth wall to explain the constraint, al-Ḥarīzī admits defeat: "We could not reproduce this particular feature in the Holy Tongue." Instead he offers "a rendering of the sense."[2]

Both Ḥamīdī and al-Ḥarīzī display a healthy appreciation for al-Ḥarīrī's "bright, noisy linguistic fireworks." Strikingly, though, neither suggests that the *Impostures* are untranslatable. In his work on Arabic and Persian poetics, Alexander Key has proposed that untranslatability, as a presumed property of certain foreign texts, is a modern idea. For their part, pre-modern readers believed that content (*ma'nā*) was always transferable between languages.[3] Applied to Ḥamīdī and al-Ḥarīzī, at least, Key's argument rings true. Of course, the assumption that anything could be translated did not make everything translatable: as we have seen, Ḥamīdī chose to imitate rather than translate, and al-Ḥarīzī had to let at least one of al-Ḥarīrī's word games go unreplicated. Even so, the idea of *intrinsic* untranslatability—which is arguably the product of early-modern European notions about the spirit of peoples being embodied in their languages—does not apply, at least when it comes to human language.

It was only when al-Ḥarīrī arrived in Europe that he became untranslatable. But this verdict was not issued immediately. As recent work by Jan Loop has shown, early-modern European scholars hoped to find in the *Impostures* "an ideal text with which to practice and teach the Arabic language." This they needed in order to pursue their broader aim, which was "to unlock the mysteries in the Hebrew texts of the Old Testament" and ultimately "to solve all theological questions."[4] It was against this background that Jacobus Golius (d. 1667) produced a Latin rendering of

---

1. Alcharizi, *Machberoth*, ed. Chenery, 50.
2. Alcharizi, *Machberoth*, 16. Fully spelled out, Hebrew does have dots, but they are (almost always) used to indicate contextual variations in pronunciation rather than to distinguish otherwise unrelated letters as in Arabic.
3. Key, "Translation of Poetry."
4. Loop, "Language of Paradise," 445 and 453.

Imposture 1 in 1656.[1] His work was "re-publiſhed with much larger notes, by that great Maſter of Arabic, *Albert Schultens*, at *Franequer*, 4to, 1731 [. . . to] which he added five more, purſuing the same method that he took in the firſt, of explaining difficult paſſages from the Scholiaſst, &c."[2] The reference here is to the Dutch Orientalist Albert Schultens (d. 1750), whose edition and Latin translation of the first six Impostures formed the basis of the first English translation, that of Leonard Chappelow.

Chappelow's rendition, published in 1767, offers a fascinating glimpse of a moment when the "ingenious conversations of Learned Men among the Arabians" could still be treated with reverence by English readers. Chappelow, who was a clergyman as well as the professor of Arabic at Cambridge, reads al-Ḥarīrī as "a prudent, diſcreet Satyriſt" who, had he been introduced to Christianity, "would have lived and died a Chriſtian in the beſt and trueſt senſe." In keeping with his assumption that the *Impostures* should be scoured for lessons "inſtrumental in promoting the comfort and happineſs of life," his translation of the first six Impostures operates on the principle of expansion. That is, every word is given as many of its senses as possible, and all are included in the same sentence, producing English that is a great deal longer than the Arabic it is supposed to be rendering.[3]

In the writings of the splendidly named French Orientalist Jean Michel de Venture de Paradis (d. 1799) we find a reading of the *Impostures* that is much closer to our own. We also find an early expression of the belief that they cannot be translated. An Imposture (*Mecamé*), says Venture de Paradis, is the story of an amusing adventure told in elevated style. Because Impostures owe so much of their beauty to puns, rhymes, rare words, and far-fetched figures of speech, "it is very difficult, and often impossible, to

---

1. This was not the first publication of an Imposture in Europe. That honor goes to Golius's student Johannes Fabricius, who published an Arabic edition of one Imposture in 1638 (Loop, "Language," 453).

2. Chappelow, *Six Assemblies*, vi. "Franequer," today Franeker, is a city in the Netherlands. The abbreviation "4to" stands for "quarto," a print size.

3. Chappelow, *Six Assemblies*, iv, vi, ii. Here, for example, is his rendering of the seven words *ṭawwaḥat bī ṭawāʾiḥu z-zaman / ilā Ṣanʿāʾi l-Yaman* (roughly, "the flingings of fate flung me to Sanaa in Yemen"): "The *viciſſitudes of fortune*, like the boiſterous waves of the ſea, when they distreſs the shipwrecked mariner, with the ſame ſwiftneſs as an arrow discharged from a bow, preſſed upon me with such an impetuous force; clouded me with ſo much error and confusion, that they *haſtened my passage* as far as *Sanaa* in *Arabia Felix*" (*Six Assemblies*, 18).

render them in another language."[1] His own timidly literal French translations make no attempt to render those features he acknowledged as indispensable to the appeal of the original. But at least he found them appealing; some of his successors would not.

In 1822 the great French Orientalist Silvestre de Sacy published what
was to become the standard critical edition of al-Ḥarīrī's *Impostures*. In his
preface he addresses the question of why he did not translate the text into
Latin or French. What matters about the *Impostures* (*Séances*), he says, is
their form, not their content. Many episodes consist of "riddles, anagrams,
and puns . . . that even the most gifted translator could not put into another
language."[2] Nor indeed should any translator want to: though the word
games can be amusing, they can also be tiresome and pointless.[3] Clearly,
we have come a long way from Chappelow and his belief that the *Impostures*
are full of good advice for living a better life.

For de Sacy, the *Impostures* are most useful as a means to learn the fine
points of Arabic. Even so, he admits that there is something irresistible
about them. And he offers a perceptive diagnosis of why translations into
European languages have failed to do them justice. Translators, he says,
feel obligated to retain the allusions they find in the original. But then they
must do one of two things, neither of which works. If they leave the allusions
unexplained, the reader will have trouble understanding what is going on.
But if the allusions *are* explained, they will draw more attention to themselves than they do in the original, spoiling the effect of al-Ḥarīrī's style.[4]

This insight was not wasted on the German Romantic poet Friedrich
Rückert (d. 1866), the next great translator of the *Impostures*, and the first

---

1. [Ḥarīrī], *Séances*, tr. Venture de Paradis, cxv.
2. De Sacy, *Séances*, 1:ix. As it happens, he was aware of al-Ḥarīzī's Hebrew translation; in
fact, he includes a sample of it in his edition of the *Impostures*. He should therefore have
known that one translator, at least, had managed it.
3. De Sacy, *Séances*, 1:v.
4. "Les personnes qui ne conoissent le style de Hariri que par des traductions, ne sauroient
s'en faire une juste idée, sur-tout lorsque les traducteurs se sont efforcés de conserver dans
leurs versions certaines associations d'idées que les termes employés dans le texte rappellent
à quiconque connoît à fond la langue de l'original, mais qu'on doit se contenter de faire aper-
cevoir dans une sorte de lointain et comme à travers un brouillard, si l'on ne veut pas sacrifier
le principal à ce qui n'est qu'accessoire. Ce genre de fidélité est presque un travestissement"
(de Sacy, *Séances*, 1:v).

after al-Ḥarīzī to venture beyond plodding literalism. In the preface to his *Verwandlungen des Abu Seid von Seruj*, which appeared in 1826, Rückert admits that a translator who approaches the *Impostures* as a specifically Oriental text would indeed have to explain all the cultural references, since al-Ḥarīrī, unlike Homer or Shakespeare, is culturally alien to German readers. But Rückert refuses to produce an academic treatise. Instead, he says, he decided to focus on the poetic elements: the "incessant word- and sound-play, the rhymed prose, the over-the-top images, and the hairsplitting, overwrought expressions." The result, he says, is not a translation but a recasting (*Nachbildung*) of the *Impostures*.[1]

True to his word, Rückert strives to replace al-Ḥarīrī's special effects with equally elaborate tricks in German. To translate the palindromes, for example, he uses *Doppelreim*, a form where the ultimate *and* the penultimate stressed syllables in each line rhyme with their respective counterparts in successive lines.[2] Yet even Rückert could not come up with an equivalent for everything. Like al-Ḥarīzī before him, he throws up his hands at the dotted and undotted epistle. The German text faithfully reports that the challenge is to avoid certain letters, but not which ones or why; and, as far as I can tell, the German epistle obeys no constraint.[3] In other cases, the difficulty proved so insuperable that entire episodes had to be dropped. And Imposture 20 he appears to have omitted simply because of its sexual content. As a result of these avoidances and omissions, his translation contains only forty-three Impostures.

With Rückert's German on his desk, Theodore Preston, fellow of Trinity College, Cambridge, produced the first English translation to acknowledge the formal properties of the *Impostures*. His 1850 rendering uses "a species of composition which occupies a middle place between prose and verse," not rhyming, but "arranged as far as possible in evenly balanced periods." But the more complex special effects—the puns, palindromes, and so forth—presented "almost insuperable obstacles," leading him to omit three-fifths of the text.[4] And the copious notes betray his failure to

---

1. Rückert, *Verwandlungen*, III to XII, quotes at V, VI, and XII. For an appreciative but critical reading of Rückert see Preston, *Makamat*, 16–19; cf. Renan, "Séances," 300.

2. For an example see my notes on Imposture 16.

3. See my notes at §6.4.

4. [Ḥarīrī], *Makamat*, tr. Preston, 2.

heed Rückert's warning that any translation that treats the *Impostures* as a text to be parsed for information about something else (the manners and customs of the Orient, for example) will produce an academic treatise rather than a work of art.

After Preston there was one more nineteenth-century attempt to put the *Impostures* into English. The initiative was that of Thomas Chenery, a Barbados-born polyglot who resigned from a position at Oxford to assume editorship of *The Times* of London.[1] Following de Sacy's advice, he decided to treat the *Impostures* as a teaching text.[2] In 1866, he published a translation of the first twenty-six episodes, stating flatly that he had made "no attempt to imitate the plays on words, or the rhyme of the original" but rather composed "a literal prose rendering, intended primarily to help the student in Arabic."[3] After Chenery's untimely death in 1884, his work was carried on by the German-born Orientalist Francis Joseph Steingass, whose rendition of the remaining episodes appeared in 1898. In a preface, F. F. Arbuthnot tells us that Steingass "completed his portion of the work under great physical difficulties. . . . For some part of the time he was actually blind."[4] Like his predecessor's, Steingass's rendering is strictly lexical. And, like Preston, both Chenery and Steingass append page after page of annotation, as if still laboring under the conviction that if the *Impostures* could not be translated they could at least be explained.

Whatever the merits of the lexical approach, it must be admitted that it has contributed nothing to making the *Impostures* part of Anglophone literary culture. Outside the narrow confines of medieval literary scholarship, I have never seen a reference in English to any of these translations, nor any other evidence that nonspecialists have heard of al-Ḥarīrī or, for that matter, of al-Hamadhānī (whose Impostures were translated, also lexically, by Prendergast in 1915), or of anything called a *maqāmah*.

In Russian, the situation is quite different: the *Impostures* exists as a full-fledged literary text. This is the result of work by Anna Arkadievna Iskoz-Dolinina (d. 2017) and Valentin Michaelovich Borisov (d. 1985), whose

---

1. Matthew, "Chenery."
2. For the advice see de Sacy, *Séances*, ix.
3. [Ḥarīrī,] *Assemblies*, tr. Chenery, vii.
4. [Ḥarīrī,] *Assemblies*, tr. Steingass, ix.

partial translation appeared in 1978, followed by a complete translation, with Valeria Kirpichenko (d. 2015), in 1987.[1] Like al-Ḥarīzī and Rückert, the translators render poetry as poetry and rhymed prose as rhymed prose. The latter, they say, can work in Russian, since Russian prose, like Arabic, can be made rhythmic by repeated sounds and parallel grammatical forms. Arguing, however, that too close an imitation of the Arabic form would result in unreadability, they unpack al-Ḥarīrī's dense conceits and let his clauses go on longer than they do in Arabic before ending them with a rhyme word.[2] The result is a distinctively patterned yet still readable text—one that became a Russian bestseller and won, along with Dolinina's translation of al-Hamadhānī, a major Saudi translation award in 2012.[3]

As far as I know, the only other languages in which complete translations exist are Ottoman and modern Turkish, French, and Chinese.[4] The Ottoman translations include four complete and three partial renderings. Of these, the only one I have been able to look at is the partial translation published by Hâşim Veli in 1908 or 1909. It is intricately patterned, full of lightly rhythmical sentences and Arabic-style prose rhyme (Kaplan, "Roma Sefâreti Imami Hâşim Veli'nin Makâmât-i Harîrî Tercümesi," 219–21). There is also a modern Turkish translation by Sabri Sevsevil (Kiliç, "Makamat"). The French translation, by René Khawam (d. 2004), appeared under the title *Le Livre des malins* (*The Book of Rascals*) in 1992. Like the English of Chenery and Steingass, it acknowledges the formal properties of al-Ḥarīrī's work without actually trying to duplicate them. The prose is neither rhymed nor marked in any other way, and the verse is simply prose formatted as verse. Similarly, the special effects are noted but not imitated. In Imposture 16, for example, Khawam has al-Ḥārith explain the palindrome game (which he does incorrectly) but then translates all the Arabic

---

1. [Ḥariri,] *Makamy*. Dolinina was professor of Arabic philology at St. Petersburg State University, and published extensively on modern Arabic literature. Borisov, also primarily a modernist, was professor of Arabic at the Moscow State University. Kirpichenko was a researcher at the Institute of Oriental Studies specializing in modern Egyptian literature. My knowledge of their work comes entirely through the generous assistance of several colleagues (see Acknowledgments).

2. [Ḥariri,] *Makamy*, 3–14.

3. See Tolmacheva, "Professor Dr. Anna Arkadievna Iskoz-Dolinina."

4. Ḥarīrī, *Maqamas*, tr. Arvide, which I have not seen, contains translations of eleven Impostures into Spanish.

palindromes literally into French, resulting, obviously, in phrases that are not reversible.[1] By contrast, the French translation of al-Hamadhānī's *Impostures*, published by Philippe Vigreux in 2012, does a masterful job of reproducing both the rhythm and the rhyme.[2]

The Chinese translation, by Wang Dexin, appeared between 2010 and 2017. It is partially rhymed and does not replicate all the special effects. Imposture 17, for example, includes a passage that can be read backward as well as forward. In its Chinese rendition, the passage is monorhymed but not reversible.[3]

For a text that is supposedly untranslatable, al-Ḥarīrī's *Impostures* has been translated many times.[4] At least four of those translations have succeeded in carrying over many of the original's distinctive formal features. The more daring renditions have also been the most successful: as far as I can judge, the Hebrew, German, and Russian *Impostures*, at least, have had a good deal more resonance in those languages than the timid French and English ones have had in theirs. So, if it is worth translating al-Ḥarīrī again, there is no point in producing another literal version. Instead, any new rendering should take its cue from al-Ḥarīzī, Rückert, Hâşim Velî, and the Russian team, and attempt a transculturation into English. Minimally, this means

---

1. Harîrî, *Livre des Malins*, 164.

2. Here is an example, from the beginning of the famous Imposture of Baghdad: "Abû Zaid! Que Dieu te prête vie! D'ou viens-tu donc ainsi? Qui t'abrite? Quand es-tu arrivé? Viens chez moi prendre gîte" (Hamadhânî, *La Parole est d'or*, 55).

3. [Ḥarīrī], *Mài kǎ mǔ cíhuà*, 88. My knowledge of the Chinese translation is based entirely on generous personal communications from Prof. Ailin Qian, who is preparing her own rhymed translation of al-Hariri's *Impostures*.

4. This may be the time to say a word about the title. To translate the word *maqāmah*, translators into English have used "assemblies," which made sense in the nineteenth century but today suggests something that one does to furniture. Translators into French use *séance*, "session," which grates on the ear since it involves sitting, not standing. With characteristic brilliance, al-Ḥarīzī uses *maḥberet*, "bringing together," a term that invokes both a compilation of written material and a coming together of scholars. Rückert gave his recasting the title *Verwandlungen*, "Transformations," which is quite apropos as a title though not as a rendering of the word *maqāmah*. The pre-modern Persian interlinears simply adopt the Arabic word, as do the modern translations into Russian and Chinese. "Impostures," suggested to me by Shawkat M. Toorawa, conveys both the substance of Abū Zayd's activities (the term appears in this sense in Zakharia, *Abū Zayd*, and Kennedy, *Recognition*) and the embodied character of the Arabic (standing being a kind of posture).

translating the verse as verse, and finding equivalents for the puns, riddles, and palindromes. Admittedly, such equivalents rarely have the same lexical meaning as their originals. But the lexical meaning, in these cases, is not the point. In Imposture 16, for example, al-Ḥārith is amazed that Abū Zayd can produce spontaneous palindromes; what they mean is barely relevant. That is why a translation like "Won ton? Not now!" (§16.5) works perfectly well even though the original says something else (which happens to be almost equally nonsensical).[1] Similarly, the alternation of dotted and undotted letters in §6.6 can be imitated by alternating words of French and words of Germanic origin. Fortunately, there are enough of both in English that the translation can say reasonably close to the lexical meaning of the original.[2]

But how does one deal with rhymed prose? In Arabic, Hebrew, and French, there are more rhymes to work with; in German and Russian, words in a sentence can be more freely rearranged to put a rhyming word at the end. But rhyme in English, being harder to produce, calls a great deal of attention to itself. In prose, moreover, it "introduces an air of flippancy," as Preston put it.[3] The solution I have chosen begins with the recognition

---

1. On the translation of nonsense see Steiner, *After Babel*, 196–206.

2. This approach is of course nothing new. When Gilbert Adair translated Georges Perec's 1969 novel *La disparition* into English, he had to address the fact that the original is written entirely without the letter *e*. In French, avoiding *e* means not using many extremely common words, including *une, le, les, de, et,* and *est* ("a," "the," "of," "and," and "is"). The resulting contortions mean that the prose is constantly calling attention to itself. And this, it turns out, is the point: The missing *e* (pronounced in French identically with *eux*, "they") is a metaphor for the Jews exterminated in the Holocaust, among them Perec's mother, who died in Auschwitz. The book, in other words, is about a world *without them* ("*sans e,*" "*sans eux,*" pronounced the same way). This is why the constraint has to be replicated. And indeed, Adair's English translation, entitled *A Void*, brilliantly eschews the letter in question. As I argue in the Introduction, al-Ḥarīrī's use of constraint is equally thematic, and must therefore also be duplicated.

3. [Ḥarīrī], *Makamat*, tr. Preston, 2. For evidence, see the compulsively rhymed translation of Alḥarizi's *Taḥkemoni*, by David Simha Segal, a work I otherwise admire, and which anticipates my approach here in several respects. The problem is visual, too. Unless one can consistently match Gertrude Stein's or James Thurber's uncanny mastery of prose rhythm, the rhyming clauses need to be set off by some kind of punctuation or special typography (as Rückert's are, with dashes). If they are not, the reader does not know that a particular word is the first rhyme word and so may not notice the second. But special signaling generates its own problem: if the first rhyme word is marked, the reader will feel an irresistible urge to skip ahead to the second, and so lose track of the sense. Another way to make the rhyme scheme clear is to indent after each rhyme. But that would produce a text graphically identical

that rhyme in Arabic prose produces a kind of markedness, in the sense that linguists use the term. In the *Impostures*, al-Ḥarīrī's Arabic is marked for literariness by (among other things) rhymed prose. To replicate it does not require rhyming one's own prose; rather, it requires finding some other kind of markedness to use instead. In other words, the way out of the untranslatability trap is to give up on the idea that one has to make the English distinctive *in the same way* as the Arabic. Arabic has rhymed prose, which English (mostly) lacks. But English, unlike the kind of Arabic al-Ḥarīrī is using here, can (for example) be written in a bewildering variety of historical, literary, and global styles.[1] One way to show off English as al-Ḥarīrī meant to show off Arabic is to exploit these possibilities.[2]

---

with poetry, which *sajʿ* is not. One solution is that of Humphrey Davies, whose translations for the Library of Arabic Literature put the rhyme word in italics. His renditions work well because they use off rhymes as well as full rhymes, and because they do not insist on rhyming everywhere the originals do. It also helps that the rhyming passages are embedded in ordinary prose texts: in other words, the rhymed-prose effect does not need to be sustained across an entire work, as it would have to be with the *Impostures*.

1. Of course Arabic can be written in such a way as to bring out the historical, social, or geographical positionality of its speakers. But formal Arabic of the kind al-Ḥarīrī uses was constituted by the presumption that it was unvarying across time and space, and identical to the language of the Qurʾan. So, while the *Impostures* contains several passages in jargon (specifically the jargon of the Banū Sāsān, the underworld of beggars and thieves), it remains morphologically and syntactically standard at all times. In this respect my translation differs radically from the original. See Micallef, "Essential Achille Mizzi," for the thought-provoking argument that literary translation should be understood as a carrying forward of purposes intended, if not fully realized, by the original work.

2. I owe this idea of showing off a language to Jeannie Miller. I am also grateful to Amy Richlin, whose translations of Plautus into a variety of modern idioms (e.g., Spanglish) showed me that this sort of thing could actually be done. See *Rome and the Mysterious Orient: Three Plays by Plautus*. In an important review, Vincent Hunink makes the point that in bringing "an ancient text very close to present day readers" Richlin "excludes very many such readers who do not share exactly the same cultural background," in this case membership in "an educated, American, Anglo-Saxon, English-speaking audience of 2005 that is also thoroughly familiar with Hollywood movies and cartoons, TV and show business, and mass culture in general." He adds: "Perhaps the status of English as the *lingua franca* all over the world is part of the problem here. Many readers will initially feel that an English translation is accessible to them, whereas in fact it may be meant for local and temporary use." In the present translation I have used English idioms from a variety of times and places, in the hope that readers who find some episodes hard to follow will find others enjoyably familiar.

In putting this principle into practice I have been guided by Raymond Queneau's *Exercices de style*.[1] Published in 1947, it tells the same odd little story ninety-nine times, each time in a different style or under a different constraint: as told, for example, by a speaker who cannot make up his mind, by another who is furious about the situation, and by a third who speaks with an English accent. As a model for translating the *Impostures*, an approach like Queneau's has several advantages. First, it compensates for the fact that in many cases al-Ḥarīrī's story is barely developed. What the reader hopes to enjoy is the verbal performance, not the plot. Second, it encourages the reader to look forward to the next story: one never knows what the next constraint will be, or how it will be applied. While both Queneau and al-Ḥarīrī experiment with a variety of styles, there is nothing obviously systematic in their approach, and thus no way to guess what sort of idiom will come next.[2] Third, once the reader knows what the constraint is, he or she can enjoy watching the author's contortions as he strives to apply it all the way through, a sensation similar to watching someone "walk a tightrope with fettered legs," as John Dryden described the work of translation.

In applying Queneau's method to the *Impostures*, I have adopted three kinds of idiom. The first consists of imitations of particular authors, for example Chaucer (see Imposture 10), Frederick Douglass (34), and Margery Kempe (50). The second consists of global varieties of English, including the Singaporean creole Singlish (3), Scots (14), and Indian (15). And the third consists of specialized jargons, such as management speak (22), legalese (32), and thieves' cant (42). In each case, the choice of idiom is based on some feature of al-Ḥarīrī's original. For example, Imposture 4 contains a debate about friendship and reciprocity. Since these are the themes of John Lyly's *Euphues*, I rendered the Imposture as a pastiche of Lyly. Similarly, Imposture 27 involves horse thieving and camel rustling, so I put it into the cowboy slang of the American West. In some cases (e.g., Impostures 19 and 23) I have combined two or more styles, based again on

---

1. Raymond Queneau, *Exercices de style*. Paris: Gallimard, 1947. On constrained writing in general, see Mathews and Brotchie, *Oulipo Compendium*; and Hofstadter, *Le ton beau de Marot*.
2. I'm not sure that I agree with Kilito that "chaque séance . . . tourne autour d'un genre" (*Séances*, 244), though if the claim is true it would help make the case for my approach.

some feature of the original.[1] Similarly, the verses in each Imposture are modeled on those of particular English poets, chosen for their connection to the theme or the style of narration.

As the reader will notice, the English verses often use a different idiom than the speech that precedes them. Although this shift in register may be jarring, it corresponds to a fact of life in al-Ḥarīrī's world as well as our own. In many parts of the world today, people write in Standard English but use a local variety, if not another language, for informal communication. Premodern Arabic speakers, similarly, spoke local languages and dialects in the market and at home, but read and wrote in formal Arabic. So when, for example, a Jamaican-speaking Abū Zayd and his "Jafaican"-speaking son produce a formal English poem in §23.6, they are simply being bi- or multilingual, as many speakers of both Arabic and English have always been.

Although the periods, authors, and jargons I have imitated come from a wide range of times and places, I have not made a systematic effort to represent every major variety of English. Nor have I attempted to represent "world literature": I have excluded writers known in English only through translation, since imitating, say, *Don Quixote*, would for me mean imitating Edith Grossman, rather than Cervantes (who is, however, cited in Spanish in Imposture 16). Apart from the near impossibility of including examples of *everything*, the most obvious reason for limiting my English sources is that al-Ḥarīrī did not make a systematic effort to represent every major variety of Arabic. Beyond that, some early experiments made it clear that certain English idioms would not work. John Milton, for example, is a major English author, but he is a writer of epics, and there is nothing epic about the *Impostures*. Also, he is not funny, while al-Ḥarīrī often is. So no Milton, except in a few quotations.

Another self-imposed constraint was chronological. When imitating authors, I discovered that the older they were, the better they sounded

---

1. Translating into a particular historical or literary idiom is of course nothing new either. For examples and discussion see Steiner, *After Babel*, 352–71. Note, however, that the cases he discusses involve putting the entirety of the foreign work into a past register of the target language, not using many different registers in the course of a single translation. By using some of the "many voices, standard and nonstandard, that constitute English speech and writing," I am hoping, among other things, "to interrogate the unified appearance that English is given" in naturalizing translations (Venuti, *Translator's Invisibility*, 190; see also 235 and 273).

as stand-ins for al-Ḥarīrī's characters. Like al-Ḥarīrī, English authors from Chaucer to Austen lived in a world lit by fire (or gas lamp); the general sameness of the props—horses, swords, inns, and so on—made it possible to put the *Impostures* into the language of these authors without too much distortion. But as we approach the world of factories, nylon stockings, and Gatling guns, only a few authors could be relied on to supply an idiom that would not be too jarring. These include Melville, who wrote deliberately archaic English; and Woolf, whose stream-of-consciousness technique can arguably be applied to any kind of content. As a practical matter, more-over, the closer we come to the present, the more likely it is that a poem, song, or novel is protected by copyright. Slang and jargon, fortunately, are open-source; and some modern varieties of English, despite being of recent origin, turned out to be extensive enough to supply equivalents for everything al-Ḥarīrī says without relying on modern props. These include Nigerian Pidgin, and—to my surprise—University of California, Los Ange-les, slang, circa 2009. Unfortunately, giving disproportionate weight to the pre-modern means that the selection of English authors slants more heav-ily to the male and white than might otherwise be the case. But *heavily* does not mean *entirely*, as the reader will discover.

The use of ethno-specific varieties of speech and writing raises the vexed question of cultural appropriation, a question to which I have given a good deal of thought. I take seriously the argument that privileged users of Standard English have no business imitating, and profiting from the use of, the speech varieties associated with less privileged communities, espe-cially since members of those communities have suffered everything from ridicule to persecution for speaking as they do. But I also take seriously the arguments of linguists and writers, many of them members of the same communities, who point out that ethno-specific forms of speech are fully developed forms of language and therefore no less deserving of serious study than, say, classical Arabic or Standard English. When local varieties of English reach the point, as many have, of being used to compose literary texts, they have for all intents and purposes become full-fledged languages. For better or worse, one of the properties of a language is that it can be learned by non-native speakers. And indeed, every variety I have imitated here has its linguistic anthropologists, textbook authors, and video upload-ers eager to pass on the secrets of their talk.

In using these varieties to translate Arabic, I am taking the enthusiasts at their word that their forms of expression are worth sharing. Using a non-standard variety of English is not the same as mocking its users, speaking for them, or pretending to convey their experience—all habits of privilege that are indeed obnoxious. Rather, it is a matter of treating all varieties as equally worthy of being called upon to represent the staggering diversity and inventiveness of English. Given the nature of the original, moreover, using different idioms did not entail trying to create facsimiles of ordinary talk. Rather, it meant coming up with something as verbally excessive as the *Impostures*. To do this, I relied primarily on speech and writing by ver-bally excessive speakers and authors, and on the second place on diction-aries, glossaries, and linguistic studies. In as many cases as possible, I asked a native speaker, a well-informed writer or linguist, or—in the case of his-torical varieties—an expert reader to review my draft. In one case, that of Naijá (Imposture 45), the review was so extensive that it amounted to a largely new text, which should be read as a collaboration between myself and the Nigerian novelist and editor Richard Ali.

In an essay on the translation of classical Chinese poetry into English, Paul W. Kroll warns against "the idea that it is permissible, even necessary in some cases, to rewrite the original text to accommodate either the defi-ciencies or the particular strengths of the target language." This "self-pro-tective approach," he says, fosters "the tendency to discover simply oneself and one's own ideas in a text." When a translator gives in to the urge to "rewrite the text in order to please himself," the result is a monument to "self-display and the anticipated desires of an intellectually incurious audi-ence" rather than "an honest carrying-over of the original author's words and thoughts." Kroll does not deny that an "imitation" (John Dryden's term) can find a place "in the broad market of literature," but it should be understood as "a new performance inspired by, but not reliably reflective of, the original text."[1]

Before I met al-Ḥarīrī, I would have agreed with everything Kroll is saying here. Having now learned something about the *Impostures* and its

---

1. Kroll, "Translation, or Sinology," 561.

reception in various languages, I cannot imagine carrying it over honestly without self-display. Nor can I imagine a translation of al-Ḥarīrī that is "reliably reflective of the original text" without being a performance of some kind. In this case, the point of the performance is to create a text that is impossible to read as anything but a celebration of language. If the result does not quite seem to deserve the name of translation, I will happily accept two other names. One is new: transculturation. The other is old: Englishing.[1]

While deeply engaged in the Englishing of al-Ḥarīrī, I happened to make the acquaintance of Abdessalam Benabdelali, an accomplished translator and theorist of translation. When I told him about this project, he said simply, "The *Impostures* cannot be translated." Before we parted, he kindly gave me a copy of his bilingual volume *Ḍiyāfat al-gharīb/L'hospitalité de l'étranger* ("Stranger's Welcome"). Looking at it later, I came across a passage that may explain what he meant:

> The untranslatable is the space where the differences between languages and cultures come to the surface. This does not mean that certain things can never be rendered, but rather that we must never stop trying to render them. The untranslatable, therefore, is not something that cannot be translated, but rather something that can be translated infinitely many ways.[2]

This I take to mean that all translations fail, but all the failures are necessary. In my work on the *Impostures*, I have found this a consoling thought. The second thing that has sustained me is not so much a thought as an image: al-Ḥarīrī, blackening page after page, tugging at his beard, and all too often finding himself at a loss for words, as he strove to match wits with the Wonder of the Age.

---

1. I suspect that Kroll might describe my work as an example of what Dryden calls "imitation" (see "Translation, or Sinology," 561). But an imitator "assumes the liberty not only to vary from the words and sense, but to forsake them both as he sees occasion" (cited in Steiner, *After Babel*, 267–68), while my English *Impostures*, though cast in a variety of idioms, strives always to maintain the sense. (Forsaking the words, it seems to me, is inevitable.) Being put into non-Standard English does not, in itself, make a translation inaccurate.
2. Benabdelali, "Fī mā lā yaqbalu t-tarjamah / De l'intraduisible," in *Ḍiyāfat*, 11–17, at 13.

❧ Bibliography

Alcharizi, Yehudah ben Shelomoh. *Machberoth Ithiel*. Edited by Thomas Chenery. London: Williams and Norgate, 1872.

Al-Ḥarīzī. *Machberoth Ithiel*. Edited by Yitshak Perets. Tel Aviv: Maḥbarot le-Sifrut, 1950 or 1951.

Alḥarizi, Judah. *The Book of Taḥkemoni*. Translated by David Simha Segal. Liverpool: Liverpool University Press, 2003.

Beaumont, Daniel. "A Mighty and Never Ending Affair: Comic Anecdote and Story in Medieval Arabic Literature." *Journal of Arabic Literature* 24 (1993): 139–59.

———. "The Trickster and Rhetoric in the Maqāmāt." *Edebiyât* 5 (1994): 1–14.

Behmardi, Vahid. "The Maḍīrah of Baghdād versus the Sikbāj of Nishapur: The Migration of a *maqāma* from Arabic to Persian." In *Poetry's Voice, Society's Norms: Forms of Interaction between Middle Eastern Writers and their Societies*, edited by Andreas Pflitsch and Barbara Winckler, 95–104. Wiesbaden: Reichert, 2006.

Benabdelali, Abdussalam. *Ḍiyāfat al-gharīb / L'Hospitalité de l'étranger*. Casablanca: Toubkal, 2015.

Chappelow, Leonard. *Six Assemblies; or Ingenious Conversations of Learned Men Among the Arabians*. Cambridge, 1767.

England, Samuel. *Medieval Empires and the Culture of Competition: Literary Duels at Christian and Islamic Courts*. Edinburgh: Edinburgh University Press, 2017.

[al-Hamadhānī]. *The Maqámát of Badíʿ al-Zamán al-Hamadhání*. Translated by W. J. Prendergast. London: Luzac, 1915.

Hämeen-Anttila, Jaako. *Maqama: A History of a Genre*. Wiesbaden: Harrassowitz, 2002.

[Ḥamīdī]. Qāḍī Ḥamīd al-Dīn Balkhī. *Gozīdeh-ye Maghāmāt-e Ḥamīdī*. Selected by Reẓā Inzābīnejād. Tehran: Sahāmī, 1370/1991-92.

[al-Ḥarīrī]. *The Assemblies of al-Ḥarîrî*. Translated by Thomas Chenery. London: Williams and Norgate, 1867.

[al-Ḥarīrī]. *The Assemblies of al-Ḥarîrî*. Translated by F. Steingass. London: The Royal Asiatic Society, 1898.

Al-Harîrî, al-Qâsim. *Le Livre des Malins: Séances d'un vagabond de génie.* Translated by René R. Khawam. Paris: Phébus, 1992.

[———]. *Mài kǎ mǔ cíhuà* (麦卡姆词话). Translated by Wángdéxīn. Beijing: Huawen Publishing House, 2010–17.

———. *Maqāmas.* Translated by Luisa Maria Arvide. Granada: Grupo Editorial Universitario, 2009.

[———]. *Makamat or Rhetorical Anecdotes of Al Hariri of Basra.* Translated by Theodore Preston. London: Madden, 1850.

[———]. *Makamy: arabskie srednevekovye plutovskie novelly.* Moscow: Nauka, 1987.

[———]. *Les Séances de Hariri, publiées en Arabe, avec un commentaire choisi.* Edited by Silvestre de Sacy. Paris: Imprimerie Royale, 1822.

[———]. *Les Séances de Hariri: Traduction française par Venture de Paradis.* Edited by Attia Amer. Stockholm: Almqvist & Wiksel, 1964.

Hofstadter, Douglas R. *Le Ton beau de Marot: In Praise of the Music of Language.* London: Bloomsbury, 1997.

Homer. *The Odyssey.* Translated by Emily Wilson. New York: Norton, 2018.

Ibn Khallikān. *Wafayāt al-aʿyān.* Edited by Iḥsān ʿAbbās. Beirut: Dār Ṣādir, 1972; also in Hariri, *Séances,* 1:6–10.

Kaplan, Orhan. "Roma Sefâreti Imami Hâşim Velî'nin Makâmât-i Harîrî Tercümesi." *Türük* 3:6 (2015): 211–35.

Keegan, Matthew. "Commentarial Acts and Hermeneutical Dramas: The Ethics of Reading al-Ḥarīrī's *Maqāmāt.*" PhD diss., New York University, 2017.

Kennedy, Philip F. *Recognition in the Arabic Literary Tradition: Discovery, Deliverance, and Delusion.* Edinburgh: Edinburgh University Press, 2016.

Key, Alexander. "Translation of Poetry from Persian to Arabic: ʿAbd al-Qāhir al-Jurjānī and Others." *Journal of Abbasid Studies.* Forthcoming.

Kiliç, Hulûsi. "El-Makâmât." In *Türkiye Diyanet Vakfı İslâm Ansiklopedisi,* 28: 414–15. Üsküdar: Türkiye Diyanet Vakfı, 2013.

Kilito, Abdelfattah. *Les Séances: Récits et codes culturels chez Hamadhânî et Harîrî.* Paris: Sindbad, 1983.

Kroll, Paul W. "Translation, or Sinology: Problems of Aims and Results." *Journal of the American Oriental Society* 138, no. 3 (2018): 559-65.

Lavi, Abraham. "A Comparative Study of al-Hariri's *Maqamat* and Their Hebrew Translation by al-Harizi." PhD diss., University of Michigan, 1979.

Loop, Jan. "Language of Paradise: Protestant Oriental Scholarship and the Discovery of Arabic Poetry." In *Faith and History: Confessionalisation and Erudition in Early Modern Europe*, edited by Dmitri Levitin and Nicholas Hardy, 442–66. Oxford: Oxford University Press, 2019.

Lumbard, Joseph. "The Quran in Translation." In *The Study Quran*, edited by Seyyed Hossein Nasr et al., 1601–6. New York: HarperCollins, 2015.

MacKay, Pierre A. "Certificates of Transmission on a Manuscript of the Maqāmāt of Ḥarīrī (MS. Cairo, Adab 105)." *Transactions of the American Philosophical Society* 61, no. 4 (1971): 1–81.

Margoliouth, D. S., and Charles Pellat. "Al-Ḥarīrī." In *Encyclopaedia of Islam, Second Edition.* Leiden: Brill, 1960–2007.

Malti-Douglas, Fedwa. "*Maqāmāt* and *Adab*: 'Al-Maqāmah al-Maḍīriyya' of al-Hamadhānī." *Journal of the American Oriental Society* 105, no. 2 (1985): 247–58.

Mathews, Harry, and Alastair Brotchie. *Oulipo Compendium.* London: Atlas, 2005.

Matthew, H. C. G. "Chenery, Thomas." *Oxford Dictionary of National Biography.* http://www.oxforddnb.com/view/article/5215.

Micallef, Bernard. "*The Essential Achille Mizzi*, selected, translated, and introduced by Peter Serracino Inglott. A case for performative translation." *Symposia Melitensia* 7 (2011): 129–35.

Mokhtarian, Bahar. "Die Maqāmen des Ḥarīrī in tabarischer Übersetzung (I–VII) nach einer Teheraner Handschrift (Bibliothek Malek, ms. 2487)." PhD diss., University of Tübingen, 2004.

Neuwirth, Angelika. "Adab Standing Trial—Whose Norms Should Rule Society? The Case of al-Ḥarīrī's al-Maqāmah al-Ramliyah." In *Myths, Historical Archetypes, and Symbolic Figures in Arabic Literature: Towards a New Hermeneutic Approach*, edited by Angelika Neuwirth et al., 205–24. Beirut: Steiner, 1999.

Perec, Georges. *La Disparition.* Paris: Denoël, 1969.

Pollock, Sheldon. *Language of the Gods: Sanskrit, Culture and Power in Premodern India.* Berkeley: University of California Press, 2006.

Pomerantz, Maurice A., and Bilal Orfali. "Three Maqāmāt Attributed to Badīʿ al-Zamān al-Hamadhānī." *Journal of Abbasid Studies* 2 (2015): 38–60.

Prendergast, W. J. *The Maqámát of Badíʿ al-Zamán al-Hamadhání.* London: Luzac, 1915.

[Proclus]. *Procli Archiepiscopi Constantinopolitani Opera omnia.* Edited by J. P.
Migne. Paris: Migne, 1864.

Ravāqī, ʿAlī. *Maghāmāt-e Ḥariri, Tarjumeh-ye Fārsī.* N.p.: Moʾassaseh-ye
Farhangi-ye Shahīd Moḥammad-e Ravāghī, 1365 [= 1987?].

Renan, Ernest. "Les Séances de Hariri." In *Essais de morale et de critique,*
287–302. Paris: Michel Lévy, 1859.

Rowson, Everett K. "Religion and Politics in the Career of Badīʿ al-Zamān
al-Hamadhānī." *Journal of the American Oriental Society* 107 (1987):
653–73.

Rückert, Friedrich. *Die Verwandlungen des Abu Seid von Serug, oder die Makamen des Hariri.* 4th ed. Stuttgart: Cottaschen, 1864.

Sadan, Joseph. "Un intellectuel juif au confluent de deux cultures: Yehūda
al-Ḥarīzī et sa biographie arabe." In *Judios y musulmanes en al-Andalus y el
Magreb: contactos intelectuales,* edited by Maribel Fierro, 105–51. Madrid:
Casa de Velázquez, 2002.

[Shakespeare, William]. *The Norton Shakespeare.* Edited by Stephen Greenblatt
et al. New York: Norton, 2016.

Steiner, George. *After Babel: Aspects of Language and Translation.* 3rd ed.
Oxford: Oxford University Press, 1998.

Stewart, Devin J. "The *Maqāma.*" In *Arabic Literature in the Post-Classical
Period,* edited by Roger Allen and D. S. Richards, 145–58. Cambridge:
Cambridge University Press, 2008.

———. "Classical Arabic *Maqāmāt* and the Picaresque Novel." In *Classical
Narratives,* edited by Salma Jayyusi. Forthcoming.

Tolmacheva, Marina A. "Professor Dr. Anna Arkadievna Iskoz-Dolinina."
http://networks.h-net.org/node/8330/discussions/180461/professor-
dr-anna-arkadievna-iskoz-dolinina-1923-2017.

Ward, Benedicta. *The Sayings of the Desert Fathers.* Rev. ed. Kalamazoo: Cister-
cian Publications, 1984.

Yāqūt al-Ḥamawī. *Muʿjam al-udabāʾ.* Edited by Iḥsān ʿAbbās. Beirut: Dār al-
Gharb al-Islāmī, 1993.

Zakharia, Katia. *Abū Zayd al-Sarūǧī, imposteur et mystique: Relire les Maqāmāt
d'al-Ḥarīrī.* Damascus: Institut français d'études arabes de Damas, 2000.

———. "Norme et fiction dans la genèse des Maqāmāt d'al-Ḥarīrī." *Bulletin
d'études orientales* 46 (1994): 217–31.

For R. and R.

Κι ἂν εἶσαι στὸ σκαλὶ τὸ πρῶτο, πρέπει
νᾶσαι ὑπερήφανος κι εὐτυχισμένος.
᾿Εδῶ ποῦ ἔφθασες, λίγο δὲν εἶναι·
τόσο ποῦ ἔκαμες, μεγάλη δόξα.

Impostures

THE AUTHOR'S INTRODUCTION

In this short Introduction, al-Ḥarīrī confides to God his fear of being so carried away by his own rhetoric that he strays from the truth. He claims to have written the Impostures *under duress, though his protests are not very convincing. He also insists that his efforts, painstaking though they are, can only be an echo of the original Impostures, those of al-Hamadhānī. Finally, he defends the practice of inventing characters and speeches in order to make a point. To convey a sense of the balanced, rhythmic character of al-Ḥarīrī's Arabic, the English Introduction imitates the style of Edward Gibbon (d. 1794), whose* Decline and Fall of the Roman Empire *uses a variety of rhetorical devices to achieve a stately momentum.*

In the name of the most merciful God   0.1
Lord, let my gratitude to thee insure the renewal of thy bounty.

Thou hast imparted to us the art of declamation, and instilled in us the power of discernment. Grateful for thy gifts, and safe beneath thy shield, I offer thee the tribute of thanksgiving. From intemperance, as from bombast, guard my tongue; let no defect in speech, or sudden fit of stammering, make me ridiculous. May flattery not inspire, nor indulgence nourish, an unbecoming pride. Be thou my bulwark against hostile and contumacious spirits! Forgive me for kindling those passions that lead, by insensible degrees, to profligacy and vice; and for directing the reader's steps toward the precipice of sin. Bestow, rather, maturity of judgment, and a disposition to yield to the just demands of truth. Suffer me to speak with an honest voice. Let a firm resolve check the arrogance, and temper the excesses, of self-love. Guide me gently to a more perfect understanding, supply my want of eloquence, and defend me from error in the quoting of authorities. Curb my levity, lest it assume the character of insolence. Suffer me not to reap the bitter harvest of loquacity, or yield to the blandishments of pomposity and affectation. Let me have no reason to feel the lashings of remorse; let me furnish no pretext for censure or reproach; and let me not excite, by some thoughtless ejaculation, the reader's just reproof.

0.2   Admit, Lord, my petition; grant my wish; admit me to thy sanctuary; suffer me not to be consumed. In fervent supplication, I implore thy boundless mercy. If humility avails, behold my abject plea; if an offering must be made, I have nothing to offer but hope. I entreat thee also in the name of Mahomet, our lord and intercessor, the seal of the prophets, whom thou hast raised to the loftiest heights of heaven, and exempted from the penalty of sin. Of him a passage of the Koran, the most credible of witnesses, declares: "These are the words of an honourable messenger, endued with strength, of established dignity in the sight of the possessor of the throne, obeyed and faithful." Lord, bless the Prophet and those trusted guides, his kinsmen, as well as his companions, who raised and preserved the edifice of his faith. Make us worthy of their guiding hand, and deserving of their tender care.

0.3   In a certain assembly, convened to promote a learning now sunk in oblivion, mention was made of the Impostures devised, with much ingenuity, by the Wonder of the Age, Badee al-Zamán, the prodigy of Ecbatana; and ascribed by him to Abu Al-Fath of Scanderoon, and Jesu ben Hesham. The former is said to be the author, the latter the chronicler, of those harangues. Both, however, are buried in obscurity, and must defy every attempt to determine their identities. At the mention of Badee's Impostures, a certain personage, whose command is no less profitably than deservedly obeyed, enjoined me to compose an imitation of them, even though it be a faint and feeble copy. I reminded him, with copious proofs, of the harsh treatment sustained by authors, whether of prose or verse. I begged him to release me from a trial as bewildering to the understanding, as merciless in its demands upon the powers of invention; one as likely to expose a man's ignorance, as to display his worth. Any one so engaged (I said), gathers wood by night, or levies foot and horse: I mean,

4

undertakes a work, where mere industry cannot prevent, and indeed must promote, the accumulation of useless matter.

It was in vain that I begged to be released from the duty of obedience. 0.4 I resolved, therefore, to acquit myself of the charge with all the diligence I could muster. Though wanting in ingenuity, impoverished in invention, and distracted by painful cares, I composed, after a long struggle, these fifty Impostures. In them are mixed the grave and the ridiculous, the rugged and the delicate. Studded with the gems of oratory, salted with the table-talk of cultivated men, and emblazoned with verses of the Koran, they are replete with figures and allegories, proverbs and maxims, literary subtleties and grammatical enigmas, and judgments on disputed points of speech. Nor will they be found deficient in pleasantry and laughter, in epistles ingenuously contrived, in orations gaudily bedecked, or in sermons bedewed with the tears of penitence. All these are placed in the mouth of Abu Zeid of Batnae, as if related to me by Hareth Ebn Hamam of Bassora. Thus urged from one pasture to another, my readers will, I trust, peruse with eager curiosity the lessons they encounter. With regard to poetry, almost all the verses are my own. The exceptions are the two upon which the second Imposture, "A Basran Boswell," is based; and the distich comprised in the twenty-fifth, "De froid trempé." The rest are my virgin-brides: the luscious fruit, or bitter weeds, of my invention.

Yet so far has Badee, the prodigy of Ecbatana, outstripped every courser 0.5 in the race, that all who vie with him in the making of Impostures, be they granted the eloquence of Kodama, tread a path well-trod, and quaff a cup already drained. A poet says:

> Had I wept first, instead of bitter grief
> I might ere now have tasted sweet relief;
> But wept I not, till I beheld her sighs;
> So precedence is hers, and hers the prize.

It is my hope, that having presumed to lay this work of turgid rhetoric 0.6 before the public, I may yet escape the blame naturally incurred by any who hands his executioner the knife; or amputates, with more severity than sense, his own offending nose. "Shall we declare unto you," says the Koran, "those whose works are vain, whose endeavor in the present life hath been wrongly directed, and who think they do the work which is right?" Though partiality be disposed to overlook, and friendship to excuse, the manifest deficiencies of this book, it is unlikely to escape the cavils of the ignorant, or the calumny of the wilful. This fiction, its captious judge will say, violates the laws of God. Yet the eye of reason, that sees by the light of first principles, will find it a work of instruction, similar to those fables told of talking animals, or mute objects brought to life. Is there one who refuses to listen to such tales, or condemns their recital, in an idle hour? If our deeds are judged, as our acts of worship are affirmed, by our intentions, how can justice reprove any one who composes pleasantries, not to deceive, but to teach; and whose fables pretend to utility, not veracity, in the correction of error? I know not how such an author differs from any teacher of virtue or religion.

> Do not resist the Muse's mighty gale:
> Against her force no mortal can prevail.
> When she slackens, thou mayest slip away:
> Do but survive, and thou hast won the day.

In this as in all my designs, I grasp the strong arm of God, that he might conduct me in the right path, and steer me past the stumbling-block. He is my succor and my sanctuary, my refuge and my guide. Upon him I rely, and to him I turn in penitence.

NOTES

Readers of al-Ḥarīrī's Introduction may wonder what terrible thing he is worried about having done. His hero, Abū Zayd, practices fraud, drinks alcohol, and occasionally steals, all without being punished. At the same time, he delivers powerful sermons that move his listeners to tears. Are his sermons somehow invalidated by his hypocrisy? And are the *Impostures*, which are supposed to teach Arabic, tainted by the sordidness of the events they describe?

James Monroe's pioneering study of al-Ḥarīrī's predecessor al-Hamadhānī argued that both sets of Impostures are parodic inversions "of the values embodied in the ḥadīth" (the words and actions attributed to the Prophet) and other genres of Arabic writing (*The Art*, 26). This thesis has been revived, though with important modifications, by Devin J. Stewart, who reads al-Hamadhānī's Impostures as parodies of "specific genres of Islamic religious discourse, particularly the *hadith*-lecture or *majlis*." But, he adds, al-Ḥarīrī's *Impostures*, though they retain the framing device associated with hadith transmission ("So-and-so related to us"), are nevertheless more concerned with "belles lettres *per se*" (Stewart, "The Maqāma," 149–50). And indeed, several important studies of the genre emphasize its continuity with other kinds of writing in Arabic. Abdelfattah Kilito, for example, has discussed the *Impostures*' development of themes already present in travelogues and in anecdotes about madmen, mimics, and beggars (Kilito, *Séances*, 19–94). Similarly, Fedwa Malti-Douglas's study of al-Hamadhānī analyzes his "creative use of preexisting literary roles, techniques, and situations," including, for example, the dish that never arrives, a staple of the hospitality anecdote (Malti-Douglas, *Maqāmāt*, 1). And Philip Kennedy's recent study of (mis)recognition explores the web of intertextuality that links the *Impostures* to the Qur'an, Qur'anic exegesis, folklore, and poetry (Kennedy, *Recognition*, 246–312).

In contrast to those who find the *Impostures* parodic, Katia Zakharia sees Abū Zayd's language "as a path toward God and truth" and the *Impostures* as a text to be decoded. The result of her own decoding is a story about the hero's gradual progression toward mystical bliss (*Abū Zayd*, citation at 59). Matthew Keegan's more recent reading also invokes decoding, but of a different kind. For him, al-Ḥarīrī's text, at least to its original audiences, was not parodic or subversive. Rather, the *Impostures* had a pedagogic function: to teach the reader the skills necessary to make sense of complex, polyvalent texts, above all the Qur'an (Keegan, "Commentarial Acts," 404). On this view, al-Ḥarīrī's introduction may thus be read as saying exactly what it seems to be saying—namely, that using fiction to teach people how to read was an anxiety-producing business. This is not because fictionality as such was problematic (on which see the discussion of §0.6 below), but because the stakes of learning to read correctly might be nothing less than salvation.

The Qur'anic verse cited in §0.2 has been a matter of controversy. Extant early manuscripts, including al-Ḥarīrī's authorized copy, have Q Takwīr 81:19–21, "These are the words . . . " (I quote from George Sale's translation of 1734).

7

But other manuscripts reportedly contained a different verse, Q Anbiyā' 21:107: "We have not sent thee but as a mercy unto all creatures" (also Sale, with an interpolation omitted). According to one commentator, al-Ḥarīrī was unaware that the "honourable messenger" mentioned in 81:19 is the angel Gabriel, not the Prophet Muḥammad. When he realized his mistake, he replaced the verse with 21:107, which is unambiguously about the Prophet. By then, though, the first version had already been widely disseminated. The result was what Keegan calls a "productive co-mingling" of the two versions that allowed commentators to debate not only al-Ḥarīrī's competence as a reader of the Qur'an but the merits of the *Impostures* as a whole (Keegan, "Commentarial Acts," citation at 297).

"Badee al-Zamán" (§0.3) is my pseudo-eighteenth-century spelling of Badīʿ al-Zamān al-Hamadhānī (d. 398/1008), author of the first (known) Imposture. For more on him and his relationship to al-Ḥarīrī, see my Introduction.

"Ecbatana" is the name Gibbon knows for Badīʿ al-Zamān's hometown of Hamadhan, which lies in the northeast of what is now Iran. "Abu Al-Fath of Scanderoon" is Abū l-Fatḥ al-Iskandarī, the eloquent protagonist of al-Hamadhānī's Impostures. "Jesu ben Hesham" is ʿĪsā ibn Hishām, Abū l-Fatḥ's sidekick and narrator.

"A certain personage": the biographer Yāqūt identifies the supposed patron as Sharaf al-Dīn Anūshirwān ibn Khālid al-Iṣfahānī or al-Kāshānī (d. 532 or 533/1137, 1138, or 1139; Lambton, "Anūshirwān b. Khālid"), vizier to the Abbasid caliph al-Mustarshid (reigned 512–29/1118–35). According to a report attributed to al-Ḥarīrī himself, the vizier read what is now Imposture 48, at the time still the only one written, and urged him to compose more like it. But another biographer, Ibn Khallikān, says that a copy of the *Impostures* he saw in Cairo bore a note in al-Ḥarīrī's own hand saying that he had written them for another vizier to al-Mustarshid, namely Jalāl al-Dīn Ḥasan ibn ʿAlī ibn Ṣadaqah, called ʿAmīd al-Dawlah (d. 522/1128; see Hillenbrand, "al-Mustarshid").

In her discussion of this passage, Zakharia argues that it is unlikely that al-Ḥarīrī would have spent years toiling away on his *Impostures* to please a patron whom he would then fail to name. In her view, the "certain personage, whose command is no less profitably than deservedly obeyed," is probably God (Zakharia, *Abū Zayd*, 70–75, though her claim that al-Ḥarīrī spent twenty years on the *Impostures* is inaccurate, as the correct figure is ten years, per MacKay, *Certificates*, 8–9). Keegan makes a different proposal—namely, that the two biographical reports can be reconciled if we read the annotation on the Cairo copy to mean that al-Ḥarīrī "dedicated *that particular manuscript*" to ʿAmīd al-Dawlah (Keegan, "Commentarial Acts," 154). On this view, the original commissioner of the work could still be Anūshirwān ibn Khālid.

It should be noted that neither of the viziers is described as paying anything for the *Impostures*, or otherwise supporting the author. One contemporary figure, however, reportedly did reward him: this is Dubays al-Asadī, head of the Mazyadids, a quasi-independent Arab dynasty based in central Iraq. In Imposture 39, Abū Zayd, who has just delivered a baby, is acclaimed "as if he were . . . Dubays al-Asadī" (§39.7). When he learned that he had been praised in the *Impostures*, Dubays sent al-Ḥarīrī a staggering number of gifts (Sharīshī, *Sharḥ*, 4:313). That Dubays's name should have remained in situ is ironic, as his interests were often opposed to those of al-Ḥarīrī's supposed Abbasid patrons, to the point that he later rebelled openly against the caliph (Bosworth, "Mazyad"). In any case, al-Ḥarīrī evidently managed to take advantage of the complex political and cultural rivalries of the period to monetize his *Impostures* with or without a commission from a patron.

Various explanations are offered as to why al-Ḥarīrī wrote exactly fifty Impostures (§0.4). He may have intended to outdo al-Hamadhānī, who was credited with forty. But, as Jaakko Hämeen-Anttila has pointed out, the number of al-Hamadhānī's Impostures "was not necessarily stabilized" by al-Ḥarīrī's time. In fact, the number of Impostures credited to al-Hamadhānī "may have been influenced by the later al-Ḥarīrī" (Hämeen-Anttila, *Maqama*, 148–49). As work by Bilal Orfali and Maurice Pomerantz has shown, the state of al-Hamadhānī's oeuvre is quite chaotic, with different Impostures and Imposture-like texts being attributed to him, or taken away from him, by various editors (see, e.g., Orfali and Pomerantz, "Three Maqāmāt"). It is only with al-Ḥarīrī that we find the soon-to-become-classical model of a fixed number of episodes, usually forty or fifty, with a preface by the author. Later readers, possibly including al-Ḥarīrī himself, may have assumed this model existed from the beginning, and thus back-projected onto al-Hamadhānī an awareness of genre he did not possess (Hämeen-Anttila, *Maqama*, 149). In any event, al-Ḥarīrī clearly thinks of al-Hamadhānī as the man to beat. Here in the preface, he is piously deferential, but in §47.9 he has Abū Zayd declare himself a greater master of language than al-Hamadhānī's hero, Abū l-Fatḥ.

"Abu Zeid of Batnae" (§0.4) is Abū Zayd al-Sarūjī, the eloquent protagonist of al-Ḥarīrī's Impostures, and "Hareth Ebn Hamam of Bassora" is al-Ḥārith ibn Hammām, the starstruck narrator. ("Batnae" is an ancient name for Sarūj, and "Bassora" Gibbon's spelling of Basra, the city in southern Iraq.) A recurrent story has it that Abū Zayd is modeled on a real-life mendicant whom al-Ḥarīrī met, or heard of, in Basra (see the Notes on Imposture 48). It is not clear whether this supposed model was named Abū Zayd, or simply al-Sarūjī. The latter means "from Sarūj," a town located on what was then the frontier with Byzantium and is now part of southeast Turkey near the Syrian border (see the note on §1.9). Inspired by real life or not, the names bear at least a formal resemblance to those of the corresponding characters in al-Hamadhānī. "Zayd" may allude to the figure of the same name used in examples in grammar books: "Zayd struck ʿAmr," for example, has a resonance similar to "See Spot run" for American English speakers. Al-Ḥārith's name apparently derives from a saying attributed to the Prophet to the effect that every man is a *ḥārith*, that is, one who plows, or more generally, toils for his bread; as well as a *hammām*, that is, one beset by cares (Ibn Khallikān, *Wafayāt*, 4:65; Hämeen-Anttila, *Maqama*, 155).

In §0.4, al-Ḥarīrī refers to Impostures 2 and 25 using titles: "of Hulwan" and "of Karaj," respectively. Al-Hamadhānī's earlier Impostures have titles, so it is not surprising to find al-Ḥarīrī giving titles to his as well. But the reference in §0.4 does not mean that all of those titles had stabilized or that any of them were treated as part of the text. Al-Ḥarīrī's authorized copy introduces all but one of the Impostures by number only: "Imposture No. 1," "Imposture No. 2," and so on. The now-conventional titles may have come into use when al-Ḥarīrī began teaching the Impostures, as he and his students would doubtless have found it more helpful to refer to "the one about Hulwan" than to "No. 2." The Istanbul University manuscript, which has titles scribbled in the margins, may represent an intermediate stage during which the titles had attached themselves to their Impostures without counting as part of the text. The fact that several Impostures have alternative titles is compatible with this reconstruction. Indeed, the manuscript copied and illustrated by al-Wāsiṭī over a century later does not use titles at all.

"Kodama" (§0.5) is my invented eighteenth-century spelling for Qudāmah ibn Jaʿfar (d. after 320/932), most famous for his *Naqd al-shiʿr* (*The Assaying of Verse*), a pioneering survey of Arabic poetics.

"Shall we declare unto you . . ." (§0.6): Q Kahf 18:103–104, tr. Sale.

"This fiction (*waḍʿ*), its captious judge will say, violates the laws of God (*min manāhī l-sharʿ*)" (§0.6). What al-Ḥarīrī is afraid of, according to Kilito, is being called out for "disguising his voice by giving it to characters who by virtue of the deception acquire a presence and an independence no different from those of real beings" (Kilito, *Séances*, 251; for older discussions of the fictionality problem see Nicholson, *Literary History*, 330–31; and Bonebakker, "*Nihil obstat*"). Al-Ḥarīrī goes on to defend himself by arguing that no one objects to "fables told of talking animals, or mute objects brought to life." In the event, one reader, Ibn al-Khashshāb (d. 567/1172), did accuse him of lying. Fables and parables, he protested, cannot possibly deceive anyone, since (for example) animals cannot speak, and any story that claims they do is obviously using them to make a point. But (says Ibn al-Khashshāb) nothing prevents someone like Abū Zayd from actually existing.

How then is the reader to know that the *Impostures* are a fiction? One can think of several tip-offs, none of which, however, are mentioned by Ibn Barrī (d. 582/1187), who sprang to al-Ḥarīrī's defense. Instead, as Kilito delights in telling us, Ibn Barrī insists that al-Ḥarīrī cannot have been lying because Abū Zayd was a real person after all (Kilito, *Séances*, 248–59, cf. also 125–33; on the "real" Abū Zayd, see the Note to Imposture 48). Keegan, however, contends that this exchange offers little evidence to support the notion of "a cultural resistance to fiction." Rather, he says, the Arabic critical tradition had already done a lot of thinking about how fables and other kinds of fiction work. What bothers Ibn al-Khashshāb about the *Impostures* is not their fictionality but their failure to signal to the reader that a nonliteral reading of the text is possible (Keegan, "Commentarial Acts," 249–302, esp. 281).

BIBLIOGRAPHY

Bonebakker, S. A. "*Nihil obstat* in Storytelling?" In *The Thousand and One Nights in Arabic Literature and Society*, edited by Richard C. Hovannisian and Georges Sabagh, 56–77. Cambridge: Cambridge University Press, 1997.

Bosworth, C. E. "Mazyad." In *Encyclopaedia of Islam, Second Edition*. Leiden: Brill, 1960–2007.

Hämeen-Anttila, Jaako. *Maqama: A History of a Genre*. Wiesbaden: Harrassowitz, 2002.

Hillenbrand, Carole. "Al-Mustarshid." In *Encyclopaedia of Islam, Second Edition*. Leiden: Brill, 1960–2007.

Keegan, Matthew. "Commentarial Acts and Hermeneutical Dramas: The Ethics of Reading al-Ḥarīrī's *Maqāmāt*." PhD diss., New York University, 2017.

———. "Commentators, Collators, and Copyists: Interpreting Manuscript Variation in the Exordium of Al-Ḥarīrī's Maqāmāt." In *Arabic Humanities, Islamic Thought*, edited by Joseph E. Lowry and Shawkat M. Toorawa, 295–316. Leiden: Brill, 2017.

Kennedy, Philip F. *Recognition in the Arabic Literary Tradition: Discovery, Deliverance, and Delusion*. Edinburgh: Edinburgh University Press, 2016.

Kilito, Abdelfattah. *Les Séances: Récits et codes culturels chez Hamadhânî et Harîrî*. Paris, Sindbad, 1983.

Lambton, A. K. S. "Anūshirwān b. Khālid." In *Encyclopaedia of Islam, Second Edition*. Leiden: Brill, 1960–2007.

Malti-Douglas, Fedwa. "Maqāmāt and Adab: 'Al-Maqāmah al-Maḍīriyya' of al-Hamadhānī." *Journal of the American Oriental Society* 105, no. 2 (1985): 247–58.

Monroe, James T. *The Art of Badīʿ az-Zamān al-Hamadhānī as Picaresque Narrative*. Beirut: American University of Beirut Press, 1983.

Nicholson, Reynold A. *A Literary History of the Arabs*. New York: Scribners, 1907.

Pomerantz, Maurice A., and Bilal Orfali. "Three Maqāmāt Attributed to Badīʿ al-Zamān al-Hamadhānī." *Journal of Abbasid Studies* 2 (2015): 38–60.

Al-Sharīshī, Abū l-ʿAbbās Aḥmad ibn ʿAbd al-Muʾmin al-Qaysī. *Sharḥ Maqāmāt al-Ḥarīrī*. Edited by Muḥammad Abū l-Faḍl Ibrāhīm. Beirut: Al-ʿAṣriyyah, 1992.

Stewart, Devin. "The Maqāmah." In *Arabic Literature in the Post-Classical Period*, edited by Roger Allen and D. S. Richards, 145–58. Cambridge: Cambridge University Press, 2008.

Zakharia, Katia. *Abū Zayd al-Sarūǧī, Imposteur et mystique: Relire les Maqāmāt d'al-Ḥarīrī*. Damascus: Institut français d'études arabes de Damas, 2000.

IMPOSTURE 1

EVER THE TWAIN SHALL MEET

In this episode, al-Ḥārith meets Abū Zayd for the first time. Al-Ḥārith's voice is based on that of Mark Twain's Huckleberry Finn *(1884), particularly Huck's description of the two con men, the King and the Duke. Abū Zayd's pious poem combines two nineteenth-century temperance hymns. His verses at the end are a tribute to Cab Calloway's "Minnie the Moocher," first recorded in 1931.*

That A-rab feller told us all about it: 1.1

I hadn't got any money, so I made up my mind to leave my loved ones behind, and sling a leg over the back of beyond, and see what luck I'd have. I had some adventures, which throwed me this way and that and th' other, but after a long time I landed in Sana, which is in the kingdom of Sheba. By the time I fetched up there, I was a sight to look at, without a cent in the world, or crumbs enough in my feed-bag to bait a fish-hook with. So I shoved off into town not knowing where I was going. What I was after was a fellow with a good heart in him, a fellow who'd help me, or leastways cheer me up with poetry and tales, and not look down on me for being so poor. So I walked up and down them streets and lanes and back alleys till my wits got addled. But then I reckoned I'd ask directions; and pretty soon I was in a big open place packed with people crying fit to bust.

I pushed and shoved and got up there to the front to see what all the   1.2
fuss was about. There in the middle of the circle was a dried-up cretur dressed in rags with a bundle on a stick over his shoulder, like a hermit

from the woods, and a voice ever so sweet and saddish. He'd begun to preach, and begun in earnest too, and it was kind of grand to hear it, he done it in such a rousing way, scolding his crowd and warning them that if they didn't repent they'd go straight to perdition. Well, them folks closed up around him as thick as they could jam together, their necks stretched, trying to see; and I wormed through the crowd to get a good place so's I wouldn't miss a word. By and by the preacher began to rip and rave and swell up his chest, and just knocked the spots out of any preaching ever *I* see before.

1.3   The first thing he done was tell us we was a gaudy sight, capering in silk and lace and ruffles, but we had no business prancing around with our noses in the air, because we warn't nothing but low-down humbugs and frauds. Did we intend to march on looking mighty proud and satisfied, while the path we was going down didn't lead nowheres but shame and misery? Did we s'pose that God, who could hoist us up by a lock of hair, and knew what we was thinking before we did, couldn't see how wicked and low-down and ornery we was?

It was funny, he said, how particular we was about keeping secrets from our families and our slaves; but how we didn't care a cent that God could see every one of our trans-creshuns clean and clear. Maybe we reckoned them airs we was putting on would help us when the undertaker came a-knocking, or the money we'd saved could buy us a ticket out of hell, or we'd have our relations there to comfort us when the last trump blew. Well, it was all hogwash! That day we'd be sorry, but it would be too late.

1.4   Then he told us what to do: "Oh, come to the straight path! come, sick and sore! come with a broken spirit! come with a contrite heart!" And so on. Then he told us that we was all going to die; there warn't no doubt about it; if we didn't believe it, why, all we had to do was look at our white hairs, or think about all our relations that was already buried. Was we prepared to die? Was we ready to face God and explain why we'd been so wicked? Warn't nobody else going to explain it, that was for certain.

Then he said he didn't understand why folks never took no notice of the signs. Why, anywheres we looked was the plain hand of Providence slapping us in the face and letting us know that our wickedness was being watched all the time from up there in Heaven. Besides, he said, him and his brother preachers had worn their throats sore trying to get that same notion in our heads. But it warn't no good: folks just rolled over and went on sleeping, or allowed they couldn't see what was plain as anything. One thing he knew, being too scared to look Death in the eye warn't a-going to make Death knock off; and if we was planning to get some good works to our credit, we better do it now, because we was all goners.

He warn't done yet. Instead of living right, he said, and going to worship 1.5 and giving alms and saving up rewards in Heaven, he saw folks chasing up profit, and eating dainty grub, and building palaces forty miles long, and dressing up in clothes that cost heaps of drachms. Blamed if they didn't take more stock in silks and julery, and silver plate, and fancy gifts, and merry tales, than they ever did in prayer, or charity, or reading the Scripture out loud! It's because their hearts weren't right; it was because they warn't square; it was because they was playing double. Why, they was scared of each other, but it was God they ought to be scared of, leastways if they'd got any sense. Then he lined out a hymn:

> You captives once to sin and shame,
> By dire intemperance led,
> Whose thirst was as the fiery flame,
> With burning spirits fed:
>
> Oh, pause ere yet the cup you drain,
> The hand that lifts it, stay;
> Resolve forever to abstain,
> And cast the bowl away!

Then he brushed off the dust, and wiped off his mouth, and slung his 1.6 water-skin under one arm, and tucked his stick under the other. When the crowd seen him get ready to leave, somebody sang out, "Take up a collection for him, take up a collection!" So everybody fished up some money out of their pockets. "Take it," they said, "and spend it any way you want to, or give it away." He looked kind of humble, and tucked down his head, and scooped in the money, and began to slip away ever so slow. Whenever anybody tried to walk along with him, or follow him, the preacher shook his hand and said "Good-bye," so they had to leave him alone, so couldn't nobody see where he was shoving off to.

1.7   Well, I go sneaking after him (the A-rab feller continued). Every now and then I stop a second and hide so he won't see me. By and by we come to a cavern in the rock, and he slips inside. I wait a tolerable long time for him to take off his shoes and wash his feet. Then I spring up and make a rush for him. There he is, with a 'prentice sitting over opposite, and baker's bread—none of your low-down corn-pone—in front of him, and a whole roast goat, and a jug of date-wine.

"Why, you cheap old humbug!" I shout.

1.8   He got mad then, and looked huffy and bothered both, and I was afraid he was going to go for me. But he swallowed two or three times and quieted himself down. Then he sung:

> I got up and put on a preacher's gown
> I spoke the good word to all the folks in town
> I took their fews n' two and I bought a steak
> And I got me some wine and a honey cake
>
> Hi-dee hi-dee hi-dee hi!
> Hi-dee hi-dee hi-dee ho!
>
> I've had some luck but it's all been lousy
> I've had to live by the bowsy-wowsy
> Ain't nobody better at foolin' men
> Or snatchin' his supper from the lion's den
>
> Hi-dee *etc.*
>
> Well that lion he was tough and strong
> But I talked to him the whole night long
> He had a heart as big as a whale
> And he fed me his supper right out of a pail
>
> Hi-dee *etc.*

I've seen hard times to beat the devil
But this hep cat is on the level.
And if life was fair you wouldn't see
No cut-rate Jeff high-hattin' me

Hi-dee *etc.*

Then he says to me, "Come in to supper, or give me up, if it suits you
better." **1.9**

So I turn to the 'prentice and swear a colossal nine-jointed oath that he
better tell me who his boss was.

"Why, that's Aboo Zeid of Sarooj, the school-men's lamp, alone in the
world!"

There warn't nothing to do then but go back out the same way I come
in. "Good land," I said to myself, "I never seen nobody like that old blister
for clean out-and-out cheek!"

GLOSSARY

fews n' two   money or cash in small quantity

Jeff   a pest or a bore

high-hat   to put on airs with, act superior to

NOTES

The wordplay in §1.1, which sets the tone for the whole collection, might be lexically translated as "when I took for a seat the withers (*ghārib*) of exile (*ightirāb*)."
The Arabic words *ghārib* (the upper part of a horse's back) and *ightirāb* (being
far from home) share the same root letters but are otherwise unrelated. This
sort of wordplay (called *jinās*) occurs in every Imposture. I have not tried to duplicate it in every instance. In this case, the expression "back of beyond" brings
together some of the same meanings.

"Sana" (§1.1) is Sanaa (in Arabic, Ṣanʿāʾ), the principal city of Yemen. Here
and elsewhere I have spelled placenames as I imagine my model text would have
spelled them. Most of the Impostures begin by stating that the action took place
in a particular city or town (See Map, p. xxviii), but nothing specific to that town

is ever named or shown, with three exceptions (in Mecca, the pilgrimage; in Baghdad, the caliphal palace; and in Basra the riverbank and the mosque of the Ḥarām tribe). In his discussion of the "fictional landscape" of the *Taḥkemoni*, al-Ḥarīzī's Hebrew *Impostures*, Michael Rand remarks that "the function of the geographical names . . . is not to chart a particular route, but rather to create a general sense of motion and restlessness" (Rand, *Evolution*, 18). The Imposture form, he goes on to say, is "suited for representing movement as such, not telic movement from a starting point to an end":

> [Coming] from a particular place and having a specific place to go would con-
> strain Heman and Ḥever [the narrator and protagonist of al-Ḥarīzī's Impos-
> tures] to the point that they could no longer play out their game of unexpected
> meetings and surprise-recognitions as they roam over a far-flung landscape
> that is tantalizingly real and familiar and at the same time elusive and fantastic
> (Rand, *Evolution*, 22).

Besides running into Abū Zayd almost everywhere he goes, al-Ḥārith, no matter how far-flung his destination, nearly always finds learned men discussing the fine points of the same linguistic and literary tradition. In that sense, nothing he sees anywhere in the "realm of Islam" really surprises him (Kilito, *Séances*, 21). It has also been argued that cities in the *Impostures* figure as spaces where the rule of law applies, as opposed to the wilderness, where Abū Zayd goes to escape justice (Bin Tyeer, "Literary Geography"; see further Zakharia, *Abū Zayd*, 181–82).

Date wine (*nabīdh*, §1.7), being an intoxicant, was often banned by Islamic jurists. Some, however, permitted drinking it before it was fully fermented. As for the disciple, Zakharia thinks he is Abū Zayd's son, who appears in several of the episodes (Zakharia, *Abū Zayd*, 128). Apart from who he might be or what he might stand for, he is needed here to introduce Abū Zayd to al-Ḥārith.

The song in §1.8 is a pastiche of Cab Calloway's song "Minnie the Moocher" (1931). As I realized to my surprise when I was halfway through the translation, the 1932 Betty Boop animated short of the same title puts the song into the mouth of a grouchy creature who lives in a cave. This coincidence did much to reassure me that making Abū Zayd sound like Cab Calloway was not as bizarre a choice as one might suppose.

"Sarooj" (§1.9) is Sarūj, now called Suruç, a town in southwestern Turkey near the border with Syria. Perhaps not coincidentally, given Abū Zayd's fondness for wine, the town was known for its viniculture. Its real-life alternation between Christian and Muslim rule may have recommended it to al-Ḥarīrī, whose hero claims to have been exiled from there and returns there in the last Imposture. But there are other, better-known cities that changed hands too, and it remains unclear why al-Ḥarīrī chose it as his hero's birthplace (Zakharia, *Abū Zayd*, 140). Al-Ḥarīrī had no known connection to the place, unless the report of his meeting a real-life refugee from Sarūj is true (Yāqūt, *Mu'jam*, 5:2203). Although Zakharia is right to point out the story should not be taken to mean that Abū Zayd was a real person (Zakharia, "Norme"), there is no reason why al-Ḥarīrī cannot have taken the name from that of a real-life refugee and mendicant. Equally, he may have chosen the name because it coincidentally shares three letters with the Arabic root *s-r-j*, making it usable for playing games with such words as *sarj*, saddle, and *sirāj*, lamp.

BIBLIOGRAPHY

Bin Tyeer, Sarah R. "The Literary Geography of Meaning in the Maqāmāt of al-Hamadhānī and al-Ḥarīrī." In *The City in Arabic Literature: Classical and Modern Perspectives*, edited by Nizar F. Hermes and Gretchen Head, 63–80. Edinburgh: Edinburgh University Press, 2018.

Calloway, Cab. "Hepster's Dictionary." http://www.openculture.com/2015/01/cab-calloways-hepster-dictionary.html and http://www.dinosaurgardens.com/wp-content/uploads/2007/12/hepsters.html.

Calloway, Cab, and Irving Mills. "Minnie the Moocher." Performed by Cab Calloway and his orchestra. Recorded March 3, 1931. Released by Brunswick BR 6074.

Fleischer, Dave, dir. *Minnie the Moocher*. Animated by Willard Bowsky and Ralph Sommerville. Released by Paramount Pictures, 1932.

Kilito, Abdelfattah. *Les Séances: Récits et codes culturels chez Hamadhânî et Harîrî*. Paris: Sindbad, 1983.

Marsh, John. "A Call to Reformation." In *Temperance Hymn Book and Minstrels*, 15–16. New York: American Temperance Union, 1841.

———. "Oh Touch It Not, For Deep Within." In *Temperance Hymn Book and Minstrels*, 53. New York: American Temperance Union, 1841.

Rand, Michael. *The Evolution of al-Ḥarizi's Taḥkemoni*. Leiden: Brill, 2018.

Twain, Mark (Samuel Clemens). *The Project Gutenberg EBook of The Entire Project Gutenberg Works of Mark Twain*. http://www.gutenberg.org/cache/epub/3200/pg3200-images.html.

Zakharia, Katia. *Abū Zayd al-Sarūǧī, imposteur et mystique. Relire les Maqāmāt d'al-Ḥarīrī*. Damascus: Institut français d'études arabes de Damas, 2000.

IMPOSTURE 2

A BASRAN BOSWELL

In some ways the English literary pair that most resembles al-Ḥārith and Abū Zayd is James Boswell (d. 1795) and Samuel Johnson (d. 1784). In both cases we have a narrator eager to learn from, and to impress, an older contemporary famous for his command of language. The senior member of the pair does not disappoint when it comes to eloquence, though in both cases he occasionally exploits his admirer or treats him with contempt. This Imposture, which is Englished after Boswell's Life of Samuel Johnson, *involves a game similar to one played in Johnson's literary circle: taking an existing poem and improving on it, usually on the spot. In the original, the first couplet cited is by the Abbasid court poet al-Buḥturī (d. 284/897), and the verses intended to top it are put into the mouth of Abū Zayd. In English, the first couplet is by Edmund Spenser (d. 1599) and the toppers by Philip Sidney (d. 1586). The common element is the comparison of teeth and tears to pearls. As Abū Zayd continues to improve on the verses, the similes become more and more elaborate. In English, the series culminates in Sidney's Sonnet LXXXVII, which, like Abū Zayd's poem, describes a lovers' parting. The English also includes a few phrases from Chappelow's 1767 translation of this Imposture.*

2.1 *Elhareth Eben Hammam communicated this curious anecdote:*

No sooner had the amulets, by which children are shielded from a malignant Nature, been removed from my neck, and replaced with the turband that marks the young man, than I began to frequent the lodging-places of literature, where I intended to acquire such polish as might avail me in polite society, and to amass a store of knowledge that might maintain me should I find no other means of support. So ardent was my love of letters, and so eager my desire to dress myself in their suit of cloaths, that I omitted no degree of importunity in making myself known to poor scholars as well as to men of fortune and rank, for I was desirous of being introduced to any one, who might impart knowledge, or instill discernment. I continued thus for some time, warmly cherishing a dream of hope, and seeking such improvement as my forwardness could procure.

2.2 After my arrival in *Hulwán*, having brought to the test the society I found there, and reckoned in the scale pompous and shabby alike, I found myself in the company of *Abuzeid* of *Serugium*. He was a man of extraordinary mutability, at times giving out that he was of Asiatick royal blood, and upon other occasions that he was a chieftain of the Saracens. Compelled by irresistible necessity, he appeared now in the guise of poet, now in that of gentleman. The disagreeable impression that this lack of candour made upon the mind was however effaced by his extraordinary manner of address, his exuberant talk, his celebrated eloquence, his pleasing attentions, his exquisite flattery, his quickness of wit, his copious learning, and his capacious intellect. So engaging was his conversation, that every one overlooked his disadvantages, and so various his knowledge, that all sought his acquaintance. It must be admitted, that such was the force and vigour of his address, that most were unwilling to contradict him, and that the general eagerness to obtain his complaisance arose from fear of being checked by one of his sallies. Yet being most desirous of increase in my stock, and of the opportunity of consulting a sage, I outstripped all others in cultivating his acquaintance, and was assiduous in my attachment to him. For he was, as a certain poet writes:

A friend, that eased the burden of my care,
And bid the joyful days: Arise, ye fair!
His comforts made he mine, no kin by birth,
That I should ne'er thirst, nor want for mirth.

We continued in this manner for a considerable time, he every day con-   **2.3**
triving to offer me some instruction or delight, or explaining some matter
that I had ill-construed. But Fortune at long last compounded him a *Bishop*
of want, misery, and destitution, which obliged him to quit *Chaldea*. Thus
routed upon the field, and resolved to go once again abroad, he departed
on camel-back, with my heart as if on a tether drawn along behind. To any
other who afterwards seemed desirous of my familiar acquaintance, I spoke
as did the poet, *viz*:

O hopeful one, that seeks my heart,
Did you not see my friend depart?
And did you, gazing, not despair,
That you might to absent love compare?

For some time after that day I did not see him, notwithstanding all my   **2.4**
efforts to discover the giant in his den, and my entreaties to persons presumed able to point me to his lair. I then returned to my native place.

One day, while upon a visit to our considerable LIBRARY, that served
as a meeting place for men of letters, whether of the town, or from abroad,
there entered a man of unshorn beard and slovenly appearance, who, upon
saluting the company, sat down upon the ground, in the back row of spectators. After a short pause he began to shew his powers.

Addressing himself to his neighbor, he asked: What book is it, sir, that
you turn over? It is, he replied, the poems of the celebrated El-Bohtoree.

And have you met, sir, with any verses you think are particularly fine?
I have (said the man). These lines:—

If Rubies, loe his lips be Rubies found,
If Pearls, his teeth be pearls both pure and round.

It is a very pretty likeness.

2.5 To this, the visitor replied: O brave! What strange want of taste is this, sir, that should cause you to mistake swelling for substance, and cold ash for glowing embers? For how can that verse compare with one, that combines the several similitudes of lips and teeth:-

> *Rubies, Cherries, and Roses new,*
> *In worth, in taste, in perfette hew:*
> *Which never part but that they showe*
> *Of pretious pearl the double rowe.*

2.6 The company greeted these verses with approbation, and begged the stranger to recite them once more, that they might take them down. He was then asked, whose they were; and whether their author was alive, or dead? O, gentlemen, he replied, I must tell the truth, for I love nothing so much as veracity. The verses are MY OWN.

The company, suspecting him of imposture, shewed its perplexity. Apprehending the reason for their uneasiness, and fearful of injury to his reputation, he immediately recited from the ALCORAN: "O true believers, carefully avoid *entertaining* a suspicion of *another*, for some suspicions *are* a crime." Then he said: I perceive, gentlemen, that you are connoisseurs of poesy, and criticks of verse. Mankind has agreed, that the purity of any mineral is shewn by fire, and likewise any claim must stand the test of a trial, by which superiority of parts and knowledge will necessarily appear. The proverb says, The proof of the Pudding is in the eating. I have spoken plainly; you may oppose me as you please.

2.7 One of the company said: I have, sir, an uncommonly ingenious verse, one superiour, I believe, to all others of its kind. If us you would persuade, pray outmatch it:—

> *Oh teares, no teares, but showers from beauties skies,*
> *Making those lilies and those Roses growe.*

The stranger said: I think, sir, I can make a better. Then he extempore produced the following:

Alas I found that she with me did smart:
I sawe that tears did in her eyes appeare:
I sawe that sighs her sweetest lips did part:
And her sad words my sad dear sense did heare.
For me, I weep to see Pearls scattered so,
I sighed her sighs, and wailed for her woe.

These verses, and the uncommon rapidity of their composition, pro- **2.8**
duced a fine impression on the company, which declared itself assured of
his veracity. Now sensible of their approbation, and gratified by the marks
of their esteem, he said: Pray let me complete my poem for you. He cast his
eyes downwards for a moment, and then said:

I sighed her sighs, and wailed for her woe:
Yet swamme in joy such love in her was seene.
   Thus while the effect most bitter was to me,
   And than the cause nothing more sweet could be,
I had beene vext, if vext I had not beene.

The company, thus conceiving a very high admiration of his powers,
favoured him with expressions of the greatest respect and honour, and
undertook to mitigate the shabbiness of his dress.

Our narrator resumed his account thus: **2.9**

The superlative action of the stranger's wit, and the animated glow of
his countenance, prompted me to examine him more closely; and, upon
minute study of his particulars, I perceived that he was my friend from
Serugium, his hair now white with age. Delighted to have found him again,
I ran up to him, took him by the hand, and exclaimed, Pray, sir, what has
befallen you, to thus whiten your hair, and so transform your countenance,
that I was at pains to recognize my old friend? He replied:

Year chases year, decay pursues decay,
Still drops some joy from with'ring life away.
Fate! snatch away the bright disguise,
And let thy mortal children trust their eyes.
Hope not life, from grief or danger free,
Nor think the doom of man reversed for thee.
Hide not from thyself, nor shun to know,
That life protracted is protracted woe.
But long-suff'ring patience calms the mind:
Pour forth thy fervors for a will resign'd.

Then he rose and departed, taking our affections with him.

NOTES

In the original, Abū Zayd impresses his audience by increasing the number of similes and metaphors. Because "teeth as pearls" and the like were commonplace images, he is able to pack many of them into a few lines without losing the thread. In English, however, anything resembling a close translation becomes unreadably dense. Readers who wish to see for themselves may look at Chenery's crib (*Assemblies*, 115–16) and Preston's versified rendering (*Makamat*, 396–405). Rather than try to improve on these versions, which are freely available, this translation takes one theme—the teeth and the pearls—and sticks with it. Because this theme appears in English poetry as well, it was possible to quote entire poems without changing them. Since one of the themes of the story is plagiarism, and since Abū Zayd, a notorious liar, assures his audience that the poems are his own work, it did not seem entirely unfair to make him a plagiarist.

"Hulwán" (§2.2) is Ḥulwān, an ancient town located where the Iranian town of Sar-i Pol Zahab is today, at the entrance to one of the passes through the Zagros mountains (Lockhart, "Ḥulwān"). It was known for its olives, date palms, and sugarcane (Sharīshī, *Sharḥ*, 1:78). "*Abuzeid* of *Serugium*" is from Chappelow, *Six Assemblies*, 19.

"Bishop" (§2.3) is "a cant word for a mixture of wine, oranges, and sugar" (Johnson, *Dictionary*), and one of Johnson's favorite drinks (see Boswell, *Life*,

1791 ed., I:135). The Arabic has "mixed him a cup," using a rare word for "mix." The expressions of affection between men described in this passage, and again in many other Impostures, are part of what Shawkat M. Toorawa, following Eve Sedgwick, has called the "homosocial" character of the pre-modern Arabic scholarly milieu. This is to be distinguished from the homoerotic, which appears as well (see Imposture 10).

Al-Ḥārith's native place (§2.4) is Basra, which, being al-Ḥarīrī's home too, is more fully realized than any other place mentioned in the *Impostures* (see 48 and 50). "El-Bohtoree" (§2.4) is al-Buḥturī (d. 284/897), an Abbasid court poet and leading representative of the so-called Modern school, famous for its complex images. The verses cited here compare teeth to pearls, hailstones, and daffodils. "If Rubies . . .": Spenser, Sonnet XV in *Works*, p. 123, with "her" changed to "his" to match the Arabic. Preston, *Makamat*, 399, quotes part of this poem as well.

The Arabic verses in §2.5 add a comparison to hearts of palm and bubbles. To match it I have used "Rubies, Cherries, and Roses . . ." from *The Countesse of Pembrokes Arcadia*, Lib. 2., in Sidney, *Complete Works*, I:209. In the citations of sixteenth-century poetry I have modernized a few of the spellings to make for easier reading.

The Qur'anic verse in §2.6 is from Ḥujurāt 49:12, here given in the 1734 translation by George Sale (1877 edition, p. 419).

The Arabic poem in §2.7 replaces the teeth with tears, which it compares both to pearls and to rain, besides adding henna-dyed fingers to the line. For this I have used "Oh teares . . .": Sidney, Sonnet C, in *Complete Works*, I:282. Abū Zayd's next lines compare the face to the moon and tears to pearls dropped from a perfumed ring. My equivalent is "Alas I found . . .": Sidney, Sonnet LXXXVII, in *Works*, I:277. "The proof of the Pudding . . .": This is the form attested in the *OED* citations for 1790 and 1802.

Abū Zayd's topper (§2.8) describes parting from a veiled lover who is weeping and biting her hands in grief, which he describes as "biting crystal with pearls." My English ("I sighed her sighs . . .") continues Sidney, Sonnet LXXXVII, in *Works*, II:277.

Section §2.9 is the first recognition scene in the *Impostures*: that is, the first of the many scenes in which al-Ḥārith recognizes the eloquent stranger as his old friend Abū Zayd. Abdelfattah Kilito has argued that the recognition scene is what defines an Imposture (*Séances*, 122). For a typology of recognition scenes see Zakharia, *Abū Zayd*, 189–212; and for a thematic study, Kennedy, *Recognition*, esp. 246–306. Abū Zayd's envoi is cobbled together from lines by Johnson, all of them from "The Vanity of Human Wishes," except "Fate! snatch away . . . ," which is adapted from "Stella in Mourning."

BIBLIOGRAPHY

Boswell, James. *The Life of Samuel Johnson, LL.D.* London: Henry Baldwin for Charles Dilly, 1791.

———. *The Life of Samuel Johnson, LL.D.* London: Richardson, 1823. [Edited by Edmund Malone.] This fifth edition of the work contains Boswell's supplements and additional correspondence redistributed in chronological order. Unfortunately, many pages (in the electronic edition, at least) are missing or out of order.

[Boswell, James]. *Boswell's Life of Johnson*. Abridged and edited by Charles Grosvenor Osgood. [? Princeton, 1917.] Though abridged, this edition has the advantage of being searchable, at http://www.gutenberg.org/files/1564/1564-h/1564-h.htm.

Chappelow, Leonard. *Six Assemblies; or Ingenious Conversations of Learned Men Among the Arabians*. Cambridge, 1767.

[Johnson, Samuel]. *The Yale Digital Edition of the Works of Samuel Johnson* http://www.yalejohnson.com/frontend/node/3#subject#Genre/Poem.

Johnson, Samuel. *A Dictionary of the English Language: A Digital Edition of the 1755 Classic by Samuel Johnson*. Edited by Brandi Besalke.

Kennedy, Philip F. *Recognition in the Arabic Literary Tradition: Discovery, Deliverance, and Delusion*. Edinburgh: Edinburgh University Press, 2016.

Lockhart, L. "Ḥulwān." In *Encyclopaedia of Islam, Second Edition*. Leiden: Brill, 1960–2007.

[Qur'an]. *The Koran, or, Alcoran of Mohammed*. Translated by George Sale. London: William Tegg, 1877; originally published 1734.

[Sidney, Philip]. *The Complete Works of Sir Philip Sidney*. Edited by Albert Feuillerat. Vol. I. Cambridge, 1912.

[Spenser, Edmund]. *The Works of Edmund Spenser*. Volume V. Edited by J. Payne Collier. London: Bickers, 1873.

Toorawa, Shawkat M. "Language and Male Homosocial Desire in the Autobiography of ʿAbd al-Latif al-Baghdadi (d. 629/1231)." *Edebiyât: The Journal of Middle Eastern Literatures*, new series, 7, no. 2 (1997): 251–65.

IMPOSTURE 3

SING O' RICH, SING O' POOR

In this episode, Abū Zayd produces on demand a poem in praise of a gold coin, and then a poem disparaging it. Being directly about money, this Imposture lent itself to translation into the English of Singapore, which despite its diminutive size is regularly ranked as one of the world's most competitive economies. It is also a place where English has been transformed by contact with local languages, producing a creole called Singlish that is difficult to follow for speakers of other varieties. Because the diction of the Impostures *is highly formal and often archaic, they too can be difficult to understand. This was true in the past as well, to judge by the many commentaries on the text and the definitions scribbled in various languages, including Arabic, on the manuscripts. These associations provided a pretext for choosing Singlish—in the style of the comedy routines still practiced by the likes of Selina Tan and Sebastian Tan—as the model English for this episode. One striking feature of this variety is the use of particles like* ah *and* lah *at the ends of sentences to convey emphasis, seek clarification, and the like. As these particles have no fixed translation, the notes usually do not provide one, but the meaning in any given case can be guessed from context. The Singlish of this Imposture was corrected by Jeremy Fernando.*

Dat Haris bin Hammam guy tell story: 3.1

Went to Higher Arabic party wit' kaki, we macam bubbles in bubble tea. No one blur blur over dere, no one talk cock, no one cry father, cry mother. Actually we trade poem, mention rare sequence people transmit historical report. Later da man come, he bad leg one, and wear buruk clothes, like dat. He say, "Ho seh boh! Eh, you very kilat! Make whole family happy like bird! Dis morning you drink, hah? Yuuuuuuuuuuum seng! Eh, don' be so yaya papaya, lah. Last time I rich, I belanjah everyone, spend everyone, hor. Good luck, had it. Cannot eat finish, ah. Own big property, big estate, always have gues' gues' gues' gues'. But later wah lau eh! Eat salt, fighting, trouble, aiyoh! Evil eye ones cut cabbage head, we go pok kai, gues' chabut, house go empty, habis, gone case, mati. Arse luck! Children eat grass, even cow die; evil eye oso feel sorry for me. Damn cham one!

"Later, life chia lat, very har', lor. No money, no slipper, feet pain! Lapar 3.2 lah, damn hungry, peng san, wot? No mo eye liner, just bag under eye only; no mo live Bukit Timah, just stay kampung only; forget last time white horse, now just walk thorns only. Si peh siong cannot tahan, can die! Need what? Need so good one be generous, friend-friend, give face. Swear by God in Heaven, my grandmalher Kai La, good family, but now no money, not even place to koon. Can help or not?"

Dat Haris bin Hammam guy say: 3.3

Old uncle, I say to him, "So sayang, so sayang!" But wan' test him: zai or not? So I take out gold coin, say, "Uncle, you say poem, praise coin, can meh? You can, you keep coin, promise."

He say "Can can," straight away begin, recite poem he ownself compose:

> Glitter golden farflung glories
> Richly obverse secrets stories
> Partner profit welcome pleasure
> Lifeblood molten bundle treasure
> Stalwart brightness kinsmen spent
> Sovereign helpmeet rescue lent

Pamper squander needy shouted
Armies clamour glisten routed
Moonface earthbound thousand buyer
Soothing angry whispered fire
Ransom hostage cheerful odds
Almost power fearful God's.

3.4   He finish poem, open hand, say, "Don' play play only lah! You say orredy
you give money lah. Give or not?"

I give coin, say "Like dat win orredy lor. Take take, just take, take take
take!"

He take, put in mouth, say: "Heng ah!" After say kum sia, he pants roll
up, wan' leave. But I itchy backside, wan' to hear more, spend more money
no problem. So I bring other coin, say: "You wan' badmouth dis one, take
oso? This time, suan coin, can or not?"

Chop chop kali pok he say:

Damn its grinning golden face!
Behold the pallor 'neath the gold;
Obey its orders, make God angry,
Wish that it had never been!

No more misers,
Thieves, or creditors,
No more evil eye!

To help, it leaves.
Can you toss it away?"

I say, "Ho seh! Damn shiok!" He say, "You hutang number two coin,
hor!" I throw coin, say, "Recite Fatihah, no lose." He catch, put in mouth
with other one. He say, "Damn heng wake up come here, good people lah!"
Now turn, wan' leave.

Haris bin Hammam say: 3.5

I tell my ownself, "This one Bǔ Zàidé; bad leg play play only." I say, "Come back, lah! Not say I say what ah, you talk shiok one, I think I know you lah! Stop walking here walking there bengkok!"

He say, "You Hammam son, is it? Long long no see! God bless, give long life, have good neighbor!"

I say: "Ya, I is al-Haris. Amakam? Life good not good?"

He say, "Aiyoh! One day good, make money; one day bad, no money. One day wind powderful, one day no wind, until sian orredy."

I say, "Alamak! But why like that, play play bad leg meh? Where got? How can?"

Now he get angry, look smelly face one, wan' leave, say poem:

> Not like limp, but mus' tan chiak;
> I free and easy: truth lie same same.
> You say: keng king, why so spiak?
> I say: limp fake one, not make me lame.

GLOSSARY

3.1

wit' with

kaki friends

macam like

blur blur slow to catch on

dere there

cock nonsense

cry father, cry mother complain

later then

da man a man

buruk ragged

ho she boh hello

kilat impressive

Yuuuuuuuuuuum seng! Drink to success!

don' don't

yaya papaya standoffish

last time once

belanjah treat

hor know what I mean?

cannot eat finish I had great unending fortune

gues' gues' gues' gues' many guests

wah lau eh! yow!

eat salt I suffered a bitter setback

aiyoh alas

cut cabbage head   took advantage

pok kai   bankrupt

chabut   hurry away

habis, gone case, mati   nothing could
   be done

3.2

chia lat   terrible

lapar lah   starving

peng san   faint

no mo live Bukit Timah   I could
   no longer live in Bukit Timah (a
   wealthy district)

kampung   village

3.3

so sayang   that's too bad

wan'   I wanted to

3.4

orredy   already

like dat win orredy lor   You win, fair
   and square

heng ah!   phew!

kum sia   thank you

I itchy backside   I felt the impulse to
   provoke him

3.5

not say I say wat ah   Don't take this
   the wrong way

bengkok   crooked

amakam?   How are you?

powderful   powerful

sian   world-weary

arse   bad

oso   also

cham   pitifully disastrous

forget last time white horse   I forget
   that I was once a well-connected
   soldier

si peh siong cannot tahan   I really can't
   take any more

can die   I'm exhausted

friend-friend   to really befriend me

grandmalher   grandmother

koon   sleep

zai   working well under pressure

suan   berate

chop chop kali pok   hastily

ho seh   great

shiok   wonderful

hutang   owe

heng   lucky

alamak!   for goodness' sake!

tan chiak   earn a living

same same   are the same

keng king   malingerer

spiak   pretentious

NOTES

Singlish, a local term derived from "Singaporean English," combines Standard English, Hokkien and other Chinese topolects, Malay, and a bit of Tamil. It is used primarily as a means of informal communication, as opposed to Standard English, which is used in formal settings and in writing. For linguistic discussions and further bibliography see Leimgruber, "Singapore English," and Deterding, *Singapore English* (though the latter focuses on speech very close to Standard). Singlish has become a point of pride for many users, a dozen or so of whom have flooded YouTube with videos purporting to teach Singlish to foreigners (see, e.g., "How to Speak Singlish," "Learning Singlish," "Singlish Lesson 1," "Singlish Lesson 2," and the forty installments by the endearing Dr. Jiajia and BigBro, of which "Singlish—21" offers a brilliant response to the government's "Speak Good English" initiative). Singlish has also been adopted as a literary language (see, e.g., Lim, "New Englishes"). But, as Jeremy Fernando pointed out to me, most of the examples are skewed toward Standard and—linguistically at least—come across as rather flat. (For a discussion of what is lost when Singlish is "corrected," see Lim, "Review of Ming Cher.") My translation, by contrast, is deliberately skewed away from Standard. It draws heavily on the citations in the *Dictionary of Singlish* and the *Coxford Singlish Dictionary*, and on the points of grammar and usage agreed upon by the posters of "learn Singlish" videos. The phonology is based on Leimgruber, "Singapore English," 4–5, and the "Singlish—1" to "Singlish—40" series by Dr. Jiajia and BigBro.

"Higher Arabic" (§3.1) is my invention based on "Higher Chinese," that is, advanced study of Chinese, an educational option for students in Singapore. "Bubble tea" is a beverage consisting of sweetened tea, milk, and tapioca balls (the "bubbles"). On repetition for emphasis see "Singlish Lesson 2—'Repeated Words.'" "Kai La" (§3.2) is my Sinicization of *Qaylah*, a matriarch claimed by Ghassan, a noble Arab tribe (Sharīshī, *Sharḥ*, 1:140).

"Uncle" (§3.3) is "a polite term of address for a middle-aged or elderly man who may or may not be a relative" (*Dictionary of Singlish*). "Meh" is a question marker conveying slight incredulity (*Coxford Singlish Dictionary*). The poem in this section is an *empat perkataan*, a form used in Malay and other Austronesian languages. Every line must consist of four words, each of two syllables, arranged not in sentence form but by association of meaning or sound; rhymes may be consecutive or alternating (see "Empat Perkataan," and Lim, "New Englishes").

The poem in §3.4 is a *liwuli*, an originally Chinese form consisting of (1) a set of instructions in thirty-one syllables; (2) fourteen syllables arranged in three lines, of unspecified content; and (3) ten syllables arranged in two lines, phrased as a question (see Ip, "Getting Liwulis," and Jain, "Liwuli on Life"). The Fatihah is the first chapter of the Qur'an, called in al-Ḥarīrī's original "the seven oft-repeated verses."

"Bǔ Zàidé" (卜在德) in §3.5 is a Sinicization of Abū Zayd, suggested by David Schaberg. *Bǔ* is a relatively rare surname meaning "to divine using cracks in bone or shell," but is now nearly homophonic with *bù*, meaning "not." *Zàidé* means "is dependent on virtue," so the combination sounds like "not dependent on virtue." The poem in this section is a *pantun*, a Malay form consisting of a rhymed quatrain in which each line contains between eight and twelve syllables ("Pantun").

BIBLIOGRAPHY

"Best of Singlish Words and Phrases." *Remember Singapore*, August 11, 2011. http://remembersingapore.org/2011/08/21/best-of-singlish-words-and-phrases/.

"The Coxford Singlish Dictionary." *TalkingCock.com*. http://72.5.72.93/html/lexec.php.

Deterding, David. *Singapore English*. Edinburgh: Edinburgh University Press, 2007.

"A Dictionary of Singlish and Singapore English." www.singlishdictionary.com.

"Empat Perkataan." Wikipedia. http://en.wikipedia.org/wiki/Empat_perkataan.

Hopkins, Mike. "Getting Liwulis with Joshua Ip." Mistaken for a Real Poet, September 7, 2015. http://mistakenforarealpoet.wordpress.com/tag/liwuli/.

Jain, Siddharth. "Liwuli on Life." Posted at Verse Craft by Life Scholar, April 22, 2014. http://versecraft.blogspot.ae/2014/04/liwuli-on-life.html.

"Learning Singlish (Singaporean English)—Xiaxue's Guide to Life: EP178." Clicknetwork, March 27, 2016. http://www.youtube.com/watch?v=pb4XSy-d2Ck.

Leimgruber, Jakob R. E. "Singapore English." *Language and Linguistics Compass* 5, no. 1 (2011): 47–62.

Leong, Liew Geok. "Forever Singlish." *The Demented Fly*, March 3, 2006. http://demented-fly.livejournal.com/2721.html.

Lim, Catherine. "The Taximan's Story." *Miraflorredula*, November 18, 2012. http://miraflorredula.wordpress.com/2012/11/18/the-taximans-story-by-catherine-lim/.

Lim, Jerome. "New Englishes: Writing Singlish in Singaporean Anglophone Poetry." Posted by Emily Bell, Global Literatures, February 11, 2016. http://globalliteratures.wordpress.com/2016/02/11/writing-singlish/.

Lim, Lee Ching. Review of Ming Cher, *Spider Boys* (Singapore: Epigram Books, 2012). *Singapore Review of Books*. April 16, 2013. http://singaporereviewofbooks.org/2013/04/16/spider-boys/.

"Pantun." Wikipedia. http://en.wikipedia.org/wiki/Pantun.

"Shakespeare in Singlish." Posted in Cloudywindz, *Today's Mostly Cloudy*, November 12, 2009. http://cloudywindz.blogspot.ae/2009/11/shakspeare-in-singlish-romeo-and.html.

"Shakespeare in English Part 1." English Language and Literature Department, February 22, 2013. http://www.youtube.com/watch?v=m7KgcKUjICk.

"Shakespeare in English Part 2." English Language and Literature Department, February 22, 2013. http://www.youtube.com/watch?v=kSCeM1_jGiw.

"Shakespeare in English Part 3." English Language and Literature Department, February 27, 2013. http://www.youtube.com/watch?v=ZiiD9S18B9A.

"Singlish—4: Study Like Xiao." Dr. Jiajia & BigBro's Show, October 22, 2011. http://www.youtube.com/watch?v=BRSh76jIbRg.

"Singlish—21: Speak Proper Singlish Campaign." Dr. Jiajia & BigBro's Show, April 8, 2012. http://www.youtube.com/watch?v=sQOHLQNSVso.

"Singlish Lesson 1—One." SingSingSingapore, February 4, 2013. http://www.youtube.com/watch?v=90g2F0CTSsY.

"Singlish Lesson 2—Repeated Words—Play Play Only Lah!" SingSingSingapore, November 25, 2013. http://www.youtube.com/watch?v=qDAusnW-On8.

Wong, Tessa. "The Rise of Singlish." BBC News, Singapore, 6 August 2015. http://www.bbc.com/news/magazine-33809914.

Yap, Arthur. "2 Mothers in a HDB Playground." *The Lit. Crusader*, June 26, 2006. http://mrs-d.blogspot.ae/2006/06/singaporean-classic-2-mothers-in-hdb.html.

Yee, Amos. "How to Speak Singlish." August 10, 2012. http://www.youtube.com/watch?v=pxFYW8BBjXI.

IMPOSTURE 4

EUPHUES' DAMIETTA

In this Imposture, Abū Zayd and his son discuss whether we should always expect our friends to reciprocate our kindness, or instead be willing to give without getting anything back. Reciprocity is also the theme of John Lyly's (d. 1606) romance Euphues *(1578), making the so-called euphuistic style, with its elaborate conceits, learned allusions, and long, delicately balanced sentences, a natural choice for the speakers in this episode.*

4.1 Ben Hamam *vttered this speache:*

It happened me to ariue, trailing the robes of a rich patrimonie, at Damietta, in a yeare of Clamour and Strife. In those days I was as much admired for the encrease of my Possessions as secure in the enioyment of true Friendship, for I wanted neither Meate, nor Musicke, nor any other pastime. I spent the flourishe of my gladdest Dayes in league wᵗʰ a goodly companie of younge Gentlemen who loved Amitie and loathed Discord, and in whom sympathy of Manners so made coniunction of Mindes, that they kept all things in common betweene them. We were wont to iourney on fleet She-Camills, as wᵗʰ swiftest Wings, no sooner halted at each way-station but departed, and no sooner led to Water but agayne upon the Road.

4.2 And one night above the rest, at an houre as black as the raven haires of Youth, we ranged abrode until the Skie glowed as white as the hoary heade of Age. Wearied wᵗʰ travel, and craving slumber, we came upon a breadth of land as delightful for the Dews that fell upon the Hills as for the Airs that sighed upon the Grass. As a halting-place for Camills, and a Camp for our-selves, the companye could wish itself no better, and so alighted.

No sooner had the grvnting of Camills and the snoring of Men once abated, but I heard a Voice sounde from some other Tente hard by, asking his Fellow this Question: "What usest thou to bear of thy Feres, or suffer from thy Friends?"

The other answered him, "I show my dutie to my Neighbor, though he 4.3 fall from his to me. By how much the more my Friend blvster and bellow, by so much the more do I protest my Regard; and take him by so much the more patiently, by howe much the more I doute his Faith. To him will I show Amity, even though he quat me wth his Slibber-Sawce, for no Blood-brother can be of more Valewe then a Friend. Doth one in whose bosome thou maist sleepe secure without Feare, not deserue thy Loyalty, although he pinch on thy Side? To whom shouldst thou show Courtesy, if not to him, that lodgeth wth thee? For whom shouldst thou strew green Rushes, if not for thy Guest? Hee who spendeth the night delighting me wth Talk is for that tract of tyme the Master of my house, and he who pro-claimeth himself Friend has my Hand, my Heart, my Lands, and my Lyfe at his Commaundement. To him that disliketh me I speak gently, and of him that waxeth cold to me do I most eagerly enquire. If he requite Constancy wth Disdain, let him proffer but a Trifle in Amends; if he be penitent, I am content. Lions spare those that couch to them, and the Tigress biteth not when she is clawed."

His fellowe replyed: 4.4

"My Sonne! Wither art thou carried? Hee that lendeth to all that will borrow showeth great good Will but little Wit. I enter league only wth him whose trust I have tried, and care only for his Honour, that hath a care for mine. Why shouldst thou take for pleasure in prosperity one that giveth no solace in adversity? Or seek a merry companion in joy who giveth no comfort in grief? Wouldst thou contract amity wth him that giveth a cold countenance, and feedeth thee wth idle hope? Wouldst thou be accounted a meacock, a milksop, by one who under the show of a steadfast friend cloaketh the malice of a mortal foe, and under the cloud of simplic-ity shroudeth the image of deceit? Behold, my sonne, the falsehood in friendship, the painted sheath wth the leaden dagger, the fair words that make fools fain!

4.5 "Where is it ordained that thou shouldst sow and he shouldst reap? That thou be kind and he unkind? That thy heart should melt and his freeze? That thy flame should blaze while his embers cool? Nay, contract wth thy friend a *reciprocal* amity, each requiting the other grain for grain, as much alike as a pair of shoes! In such manner shall each no more be a fool then make one of his fellow, and no more fear a grudge than bear one. Else, one shall live in Joy and Merriment, and the other in Cark and Care, thou pinned to his Sleeve, and he standing on his Pantofles. Is Equity to be gained by Injury, more than is the Sunne to be seen in Darkenes? Why shouldst thou be taunted and retaunted, flouted and reflouted, wth intolerable Glee? Nay, pluck up thy Stomach, and heed thy Father's Poem:

4.6
    I loue no man but him that loueth me
    And requiteth what I give, Pound for Pound;
    I let no Frute fall freely from the Tree
    Nor strewe my Harvest heedlesse on the Grounde.
    Friend, if thou wouldst gather what we growe,
    Thou must needs with me till the Soyle I sowe.

    I seeke not to deceive, nor do I slide,
    But imagine not, that thou canst beguile me:
    I shall have from thy Purse, or from thy Hide
    An Account of all that I have rendered thee.
    I know not, whether he that steals thy Purse,
    Or he who never op'neth his, be worse!"

4.7 Ben Hamam *continved:*

Thinking that the sight of these two Champions would be as much diverting to the Eye, as their Discourse was to the Ear, I went forth, when the Sunne had beset wth his Beames the Sky, ere the Companie mount, or the Crow fly, in the way whence came the Voices I hearde in the Night, sifting each Face I spied, till I beheld at last *Aboo Zeid,* clad in ragged Cloutes, speaking wth his *Sonne*; and knew them to be those that yesternight used the Dialogue I heard.

As much eager to try their Curtesie, as moved to Pitie by their State, I approached near to them, and invited them to alight at my Camp, placing at their Commaundement, all that was mine, whether in Prosperitie, or Adversitie. Presently I praised them to the Companie, that adopted them as Friends; and by my doing shook before them laden Boughs, that battered them down wth Frute. We were that Evening at a high Camping-Place that gave a view of the Towns below, and of the cheerful Fires kindled therein, at which Sight, *Aboo Zeid*, perceiving that his Budget was now as full as his Miserie abated, declared himself filthish and mucky, and asked leave to descend to a Town, where he might bathe himself, and join Healthe of Body, to Ease of Mind.

I answered him thus: "If thou must go, make all haste to depart, and as much to repaire." To which he replyed: "I shall be agayn before you as quick as Sight to the Eye." Presently he started up like a Horse pricked wth the Spurr, bidding his Sonne: "Goe, runne, flye!" I no more mistrusted them of Fleeting, than suspected them of Fraud.   4.8

As longingly as men attend a Feast, so did we attend their Return, but Nothing. At length we sent certain of the Companie to look for their Coming, but yet Nothing. How long we attended, it were tedious to write; let it suffice, that like a Bank or Cliff that hath been eaten by the Floode, so that some Part of it every Hour falls, the Daye by stealth dropt away; and, like a lewd Strumpet who, at the coming of old Age, repents of the hot assaults of Youth, and vows to end her Dayes in Rags, the Sunne, forgetting it had once been young, sank behind a tattered Cloud; seeing which, I said to my Companions: "Our Friend is *false*, even as Musk, although it be sweet in the Smell, is sour in the Smack. We have tarried too long, and lost the Daye. Let us stand not in a Mammering, but *depart*, for we have swallowed a Gudgen!"

As I rose to mount my Camill, my Eye fell on the Saddle, and I saw that   4.9
Aboo Zeid had scribbled on the Pommel:

O Friend in my Adversitie,
Acquit me of Uncourtesy:

Not in Weariness, nor Pride,
Did I command my Son to ride,
But in Duty to the Holy Verse
That sayeth: "Sup ye, then disperse!"

I read this scribble alowde to the Companie, so that those that had blamed him might forgive, and those that rebuked him be content. Marvelling no less at his Tale, than at his Bale, no more at his Fame, than at his Bane, we mounted, wondering where, the Sky grown dark, he should find another Mark.

GLOSSARY

4.2

feres   companions

4.3

though he fall from his to me   though he fail in his duty to me

quat me wth his Slibber-Sawce   nauseate me with his dirty wash-water or filthy ointment

pinch on thy Side   avoid paying what he owes you

4.4

Wither art thou carried?   You can't be serious!

meacock   weakling   *fain*   compliant

4.5

Cark   distress

pinned to his Sleeve   wrapped around his little finger

standing on his Pantofles   holding his head high

4.7

Cloutes   clothes   *Budget*   wallet

4.8

Smack   taste

stand not in a Mammering   not hesitate

swallowed a Gudgen   been tricked

4.9

Bale   wickedness   *Bane*   misfortune

NOTES

Although al-Ḥarīrī and Lyly share a penchant for balanced clauses and rhymed prose, they differ in other respects. Al-Ḥarīrī uses a great deal of obscure vocabulary, but the need to rhyme at regular intervals keeps his clauses relatively short. Lyly, conversely, makes no special effort to pile on difficult words, but revels in long, tangled sentences. The translation splits the difference: it uses shorter sentences than Lyly would like, but tries to employ as many of his favorite rhetorical devices as possible. To imitate al-Ḥarīrī's use of rare words, I have used expressions from Lyly that may not have been rare in his time but are now oddly charming or completely unknown. The more difficult of these are explained in the Glossary. Whether listed there or not, all the words in the translation are attested either in Lyly's works or (in those few cases when those did not suffice) in *OED* citations from the same period. The spelling reproduces a few features of Lyly's (very inconsistent) orthography, in the hope of conveying a sense of the visual character of Elizabethan writing and printing.

"Pinch on thy side" is adapted from "to pinch on the parson's side," to save money by withholding the tithe one owes the church (Lyly, *Euphues*, p. 72, n. 2).

"As a pair of shoes" probably refers to a pair of horseshoes, as the left and right were the same.

The sequence about waiting a long time is based on a letter Lyly wrote to Queen Elizabeth protesting her neglect of him (Lyly, *Complete Works*, 1:70–71). The extended metaphors of the cliff and the sun are based on mere phrases in al-Ḥarīrī, but since Lyly loves to extend his metaphors, I chose to expand these, thereby also compensating in part for the many Haririan metaphors I have smoothed away elsewhere. Part of the language about the cliff comes (anachronistically) from Lane's *Arabic-English Lexicon*, s.v. *j-r-f*.

BIBLIOGRAPHY

Lyly, John. *The Complete Works of John Lyly*. Vol. 1, *Life: Euphues: The Anatomy Of Wyt; Entertainments*, edited by R. Warwick Bond. Oxford: Oxford University Press, 1902.

———. *Euphues: The Anatomy of Wit; Euphues and His England*. Edited by Morris William Croll and Harry Clemons. London: Routledge, 1916.

Imposture 5

Woolf at the Door

In this episode Abū Zayd tells a tearjerker of a story about meet-ing his long-lost son. Since Abū Zayd tends to lie, his account has a feeling of unreality about it, especially in view of his pri-vate comments to al-Ḥārith at the end. To capture that effect in English, he adopts the style of Virginia Woolf's Mrs. Dalloway *(1925), whose stream-of-consciousness narration leaves the reader unsure of what is really happening—or more exactly, per-haps, suddenly aware of how much we rely on the contrivance of the omniscient narrator. The poems are based on various styles of light verse by other authors of the period, as specified in the notes on each section.*

5.1   It was Hárith—Hammám's son—who told us.

He remembered Kúfa, sitting up till all hours of the night talking; the sky now striking light to the earth, now darkness, the moon a chink of silver, an amulet. The others were wholly admirable, companions in the art of exqui-site address, as if they had been given to suck on it since childhood, and could now draw a great sweeping brush across the memory of names as great as Sahbán's. Everybody owed these men words, but how wonderful to feel no strain, only at one's ease with them and light-hearted. They went on talking until the moonlight had gone. Even afterwards they sat awake, the darkness now profound; but at last they felt that they must sleep.

But somebody was rousing the dogs, thumping at the door. Who could it be? What a surprise, to be interrupted at that hour, in that profound darkness!

A voice, suddenly, from behind the door: 5.2

> Knockety-knockety!
> Stygian darkness has
> Forced me to cadgerous
> Pounding on doors;
>
> Dusty, disheveled, I'm
> Looking for lodging, so
> Philanthropologically
> Let it be yours!
>
> Knockety-knockety!
> Rolling has rounded me:
> Now, consequently, I
> Grin like the moon;
>
> If you allow me, I'll
> Repay your kindness by
> Double-dactylically
> Chanting this rune.

The effect was extraordinary—a sonorous voice sounding, and a prom-   5.3
ise of depths beneath the surface agitation. Now they were throwing open the door, welcoming the stranger in, calling to the servant boy to bring out the cold meats.

"No, no," the stranger was saying, vowing that, as God had brought him to them—and it was God who had led him to that house and no other—that he wouldn't taste anything they offered him unless they were quite sure he wasn't a burden to them, that they wouldn't take the trouble to prepare a meal. It was true, wasn't it, that food one feels awkward about eating turns sour in the belly so that one misses his next few meals altogether? "The worst sort of guest is one who causes fuss and bother for his host," especially the sort of bother that affects the digestion and brings on illness. "The best dishes are eaten in daylight": what did that familiar saying mean, except that the evening meal should be taken as early as possible, and dining at night was to be avoided, for it weakens the eyesight—unless of course one felt so awfully hungry that sleep was impossible?

5.4   It was wonderful how the stranger had known their feelings, had understood without their speaking. Of course they accepted his condition, put him at his ease, offered their compliments on his amiable manners.

Now the servant came with the dishes, lit the lamp. Now Hárith examined the stranger's face, and—"What a guest we have," he told his friends, "he is delicious even served cold!" To see Abuzeid suddenly—what a surprise; as if the stars had shifted in their courses to make room for his star of poetry, or the constellations fled when the pale moon of his prose broke the surface of the sky. They glowed with expectation, their eyes kindled with pleasure. Sleep was forgotten, beds forgotten, the playthings of the mind—put away only a moment ago—pulled out again.

Abuzeid just sat there, eating. At last he asked the servant to take up the table. "Tell us your stories," Hárith asked, stories about adventures far away, stories for all hours of the night.

5.5   Things happened to Abuzeid that no one had seen or heard the like of. One of the oddest, he said, had happened that night, before he came to them, came to their door unexpectedly. What had he seen, wandering so late? He'd been tossed about, he said, by the storms of the world, and been spat out on this shore; hunger, misery, his bag hollowed out, utterly empty within: Jochebed's heart when she lost Moses. When darkness fell he rose, footsore as he was, to seek a house, a host, a crust of bread; and starvation, or fate, the Begetter of Wonders, drew him along to that house, the house where he improvised, chanting:

5.6   I hope my visit finds you well.
          Now let me bless this house:
          May Plenty smile on all who dwell
          Within, and round about.

Endless weary roads I've walked
Without a crust of bread;
One more night of cheerless dark
And dawn will find me dead.

If any be within, oh speak!
How sweet if I could hear
You say, "Come in, put down your stick,
And take your supper here."

Then a boy came out of that house, a boy wearing a sort of smock, and   5.7
answered him.

For our Abrahamic father
It was clearly not a bother
Feeding all the guests who'd turn up at his door;
But we haven't got a mouthful
For us, much less a house-ful,
So tell me: can the starving feed the poor?

Nothing to be done, Abuzeid thought, with such barren soil, in a house   5.8
so degradingly poor. But what was the boy called? His cleverness was
charming. "My name is Zeid," he said. Zeid, from Feid. He'd come to town
only last night with his maternal uncles, men of the Ábsi family. "Tell me
more," said Abuzeid, wishing him a long life, a happy life. The boy's mother
Bárrah—her name means "reverent"—had, in the year the raid happened
in Mawán, married a nobleman of Sarúj, of the Ghassán family. But then
Bárrah was expecting a baby, and then her husband ran away, without a
word to anybody, the rascal, and never came back. Was he still alive, and
would he return, or was he dead now, buried in a lonely grave?

Why, it was obvious, Abuzeid thought: this boy is my son. But he could
not bring himself to tell him: he was too poor for that, he had nothing to
give him. He turned away; and was overcome with grief, the tears running
down his cheeks.

Had they, he asked, in all their experience heard of such a chance as that?

No, they assured him, swearing by Him who knew the Book before it was revealed. An event to record for posterity, to register in the rolls of marvellous surprises, for nothing like it had ever happened in the world. Bring a reed pen and ink-pot, they said, and write down the story just as he told it.

But what did he mean to do about the boy? If he had some coppers in his pocket, he would take charge of him. Would twenty dinars be enough? Collect it, collect it at once! Yes, of course it would suffice, he said: he would have to be mad to fling away such a sum as that.

5.9 Kindly, obligingly, everyone put in his share, wrote a note for some amount. "Thank you," said Abuzeid, thank you, thank you, he went on saying, expressing the keenest gratitude, until one felt his praise was out of proportion to the trifling sums he had received. Then he was talking, his night-tales unrolling like strips of figured silk, spangles, ribbons, putting the striped gowns of Yemen to shame, all through the perfect blackness of the night, the perfect joy of the night, until up came a wavering phosphorescence, washing the sky; the hind-locks of darkness grew grey in the dawn, the sunbeams striking now here, now there, leaping like gazelles.

"Shall we go cash my cheques?" he said. He was about to split asunder: the longing to see his son was so terrific. Hárith took his hand and walked with him, helped him collect his money. As the coppers went into his purse, joy flushed his face. It was so very kind of him to have come, he said; farewell, he said.

Now Hárith wanted to meet that fine son of his. Of course he would have ideas about everything. But Abuzeid was laughing, tears running down his cheeks, looking at him as if to say, you poor fool.

5.10   harith did you believe what i said
         i didn t think they would take the bait
         barrah s made up and so is zayd
         stories are how i outwit fate
         compare verses mine beat out kumayt s
         i only use them when i m played out
         like tonight when i crashed the gate
         i gave you memories at least to laugh about

48

Now Abuzeid said good-bye, lighting a fire, an ember burning through his heart.

NOTES

The original is called *al-Kūfiyyah*, "Of Kufah," referring to the Iraqi city, but also to the Imposture of that name composed by al-Ḥarīrī's predecessor al-Hamadhānī. For a comparison of the two see Kennedy, *Recognition*, 262.

"Sahban" in §5.1 is Saḥbān, a proverbially famous orator, apparently a contemporary of the Umayyad caliph al-Walīd I (r. 86–96/705–15), but otherwise practically unknown as a historical figure (see Fahd, "Saḥbān"). Philip Kennedy suggests that in the companions' assumption of superiority to Sahban is "a warning about rash inadvertence" (*Recognition*, 261) especially in view of how the episode ends.

Abū Zayd's poem in §5.2 consists of half-length lines with a single rhyme. The rhyme is double *r*, which allows him to use a number of unusual verbs that to my mind produce a comical effect. To approximate it, the translation uses a very constrained English light-verse form, the double dactyl—actually, two double dactyls. This form consists of two stanzas of four lines each; the first three must be in dactylic dimeter and the fourth a single choriamb. The first line of the first stanza must be nonsense and the third line of the second stanza must be a single word. (I have ignored an optional constraint, which is that the second line should mention only the subject of the poem.) My use of the form is slightly anachronistic, as it was invented (by Anthony Hecht and Paul Pascal) in 1951, ten years after Woolf's death.

Section §5.5 contains the first of many allusions to the story of Moses (for an analysis of which see Kennedy, *Recognition*, 267–70, 272, 276). For "the mother of Moses" I have supplied Jochebed, from Exodus 6:20 and Numbers 26:59. The name does not appear in al-Ḥarīrī's Arabic or in the Qur'anic tellings of the Moses story. But using it allowed me to avoid the awkward "the heart of the mother of Moses" in English.

The English of the poem in §5.7 is based on the form of Arthur Guiterman's "Philadelphia," from *The Lyric Baedeker* (1918), cited in Hollander, *American Wits*, 7–9.

Regarding the relationship between Abū Zayd and his son (whom we may for convenience call Zayd), Abdelfattah Kilito has argued that Zayd's insistence that he owes nothing to his father parallels al-Ḥarīrī's wish to do away with his figurative father—namely, al-Hamadhānī, author of the first Impostures (*al-Ghāʾib*, 46–47). Katia Zakharia argues rather that the attenuated relationship between Abū Zayd and his son amounts to an argument for the superiority of another kind of relationship, that of teacher and disciple (*Abū Zayd*, 171–79).

I have taken the phrase "hind-locks grew grey in the dawn" (§5.9) from Chenery, *Assemblies*, 131. "Cash" does not appear in *Mrs. Dalloway*, but the *OED* dates it to 1811.

In later episodes, Abū Zayd will appear with a wife and a son—or, at least, with women and children identified as such. His claim here that "barrah s made up and so is zayd" (§5.10) is, therefore, no more believable than anything else he says. The English form of the poem is based on that of the third stanza of Don Marquis's "mehitabel s extensive past," from *archy and mehitabel* (1927), cited in Hollander, *American Wits*, 22. In Marquis's work, the use of lowercase letters follows from the conceit that the poems are the work of a cockroach who cannot reach the shift key while typing letters (Hollander, *American Wits*, xxiii). "Kumayt" is al-Kumayt (d. 176/743), a poet renowned for praising both the Umayyads and the Alids—an odd choice, as the two great political families were deadly enemies.

BIBLIOGRAPHY

"Double Dactyl." Wikipedia. http://en.wikipedia.org/wiki/Double_dactyl.

Fahd, T. "Saḥbān Wāʾil." In *Encyclopaedia of Islam, Second Edition*. Leiden: Brill, 1960–2007.

Hollander, John, ed. *American Wits: An Anthology of Light Verse*. [New York]: Library of America, 2003.

Kennedy, Philip F. *Recognition in the Arabic Narrative Tradition: Discovery, Deliverance, and Delusion*. Edinburgh: Edinburgh University Press, 2016.

Kilito, Abdelfattah. *Al-Ghāʾib: Dirāsah fī maqāmah li l-Ḥarīrī*. Casablanca: Tubqāl, 1987.

Woolf, Virginia. *Mrs. Dalloway*. Orlando: Harcourt, 1925. Full text at http://gutenberg.net.au/ebooks02/0200991.txt.

IMPOSTURE 6

PLAIN ANGLISH

This Imposture is the first of several that require Abū Zayd to produce a piece of constrained speech or writing. Here the challenge is to compose a petition in which every second word consists of letters written with dots, and the remaining words of letters written without dots. (He fudges on the feminine ending -ah, which he counts as undotted, as it often is in manuscripts.) To produce something comparable, the translation takes the two largest groups of English words, those of Germanic and those of Romance origin, and uses them in alternation. This constraint produces a language comparable to al-Ḥarīrī's: meaningful, but odd-sounding. The prose narration, which in the original is constrained by rhyme, in English uses only words of Germanic derivation.

Harald Hammamson told this tale:　　　　　　　　　　　　　　6.1

Once, having hied to the moot in Maraaghah, I fell upon a gathering where the talk was all of speechcraft. Reed-reeves and tongue-wielders were grumbling that no living wight could trim the lore's unruly bough, or twist words about his finger as eretide-folk once did. Could anyone (they asked) still blaze untrodden word-ways, or hammer out a leaf-writ that forbad being twinned? No, they whined: no reed-reeve of latter days, not even a cunning one with Sahbaan's tongue in his head and show-speech's reins in his hands, could do better than tear a leaf out of his elders' book.

6.2   Sitting on the crowd's ragged edge, amid the hangers-on, was a man of middle years. He was sitting hunkered down, as if nocking an arrow or gathering himself to strike. Whenever a mooter overshot the mark, or drew from wit's carry-bag a palm-apple that seemed withered, the outsider looked at him asquint and lifted his nose in scorn. At last, when the speakers had emptied their quivers, a stillness fell where once the winds had roared. Then the man pounced.

6.3   "'You have said a dreadful say,'" he cried, "and wandered well awry! When you worship dry bones and grovel before the dead, you give short shrift to nowen men—the nowen men who are bound to you by liking and by birth.

        "You sifters of speech, high priests whose doom is law! Have you forgotten the yearlings and the upstarts? What of their well-hewn words and biting rimes, their clever kennings, and the leaf-writs they spin, as if from golden thread?

        "Go scrut the elders and their lore! Are their pools not choked with mud, and their stock a-stumble on a hobble? Yes, the first to draw from a well is more thought of than the ones who follow. But no one is deemworthy merely by dint of being dead!

        "Among the nowen men, moreover, I know of one whose writs are gilded worm-weave, every stroke as bold as a stripe across a cloak. His word-craft, whether of the clipped kind or the fulsome, leaves all others speechless, and drives the elders from men's thoughts. Even when he spins offhand, he dazzles; and when he says a thing anew, he breaks the old words and leaves only shards behind."

6.4   "Who is this word-splitter of yours?" asked the head of the Maraaghah moot-hall, who was a man of high standing.

        "He sits before you," came the answer, "and you're talking to him now. Send me for a run around the ring, and bewonder what you see."

        "See here," said the head of the Maraaghah moot-hall. "You can call a finch a falk if you like, but it's a finch all the same. In this land we have a knack for telling falks from finches, or calkins, or winches. None go unbruised who strike at us, and lucky are they who flee unscathed, once the fight-dust starts to rise. So take my rede and fly before you shame yourself."

"Who knows my arrows better than do I?" said the man of middle years. "Call no man beaten before the race is run."

At that the reed-reeves fell to whispering about a trial and a harrowing.

At last one of them spoke up. "Leave this man to me!" he said. "I have a 6.5 happenlore to sink him like a stone and tie his tongue in knots." The gathering granted him the headship, as if they were the Breakers-Away and he their Aboo Naamah. To the man of middle years spoke he thus:

"I wait upon the reeve, living by my show-speech. In my own land, I had wealth enough to meet my needs. But my offspring fell to teeming and my stream dwindled to a trickle. My hopes then fell upon the reeve, and I left my home to seek him. I beseeched him to wet my root and stir my sap. He welcomed me and showered me with kindness. But when I sought his leave to leave, he said: 'I swear no more to house and feed you, nor let you join your kin, until you write a writ that tells your life-tale. But of every two words, one must be Anglish, and Frankish the next.'

"I gave myself a year to do what he asked, and for a twelvemonth racked my brain. But nothing came forth and now my mind is barren. When I asked the speech-sifters for help, all of them frowned and backed away. Now here you are, crowing about your word-craft. 'If you are a truth-teller, bring us the proof.'"

"For a heartbeat there I was worried," said the man of middle years. 6.6 "I thought you might ask for something hard. But I was weaving word-shifts before anybody was." He paused to tug on the udders of his wit. When the flow began, he said: "Take seed-wool and plug your flask of book-black. Then take up your reed and write:

I pray God prolong your felicity and repulse the malicious! Giving adorns men; stinginess demeans them. Liberality will gratify others; pinching pennies disappoints. Warm hosts make visitors welcome; avaricious householders—alas!—drive travellers away. Cordial greetings inspire thankful responses, while grudging, halfhearted salutations will provoke bitter resentment. Give graciously; don't promise and fail to deliver. A benediction makes fealty clear; praise sweeps doubt aside. Courtesy means admitting debts, for ingratitude is base. To abuse a respectable man amounts to folly; to deny a petitioner's wish implies bad judgment. Who except a fool would choose greed? Conversely, who except a miser is qualified to act the fool? Only misers hoard; piety is open-handed.

Confident your honor's good promises are reliable; his judgment fair, firm, and equitable; his bounty free, copious, and unstinting; assured his magnanimity will triumph — his valiant heart prevail — the entire world admit his virtue — I praise you, aspiring to favor; I acclaim you, contemplating gain; I implore you, pleading for charity — I, aged, shrunken, diminished, hapless! Jealously seeking consideration, I offer maiden verses that merit bridegifts. Manifestly, my rights are clear, my demands few. Couplets of praise will benefit you; verses of reproach will damage your reputation.

I invoke my famished, ragged, miserable children—alas!—and, Sir, my pathetic, heartbroken, troubled self, emaciated, sorrowful, lachrymose, and tormented; hopes deferred, wishes denied, foes ravenous, comfort gone. Constant in affection, I merit no rebuff; ever loyal, I deserve fair return; my devotion is fervent, my attachment unwavering. Remember, Sir, that safeguarding one's honor never demands high-handedly abusing another's. Reward my fealty by approving my petition; in return, your praise will traverse the inhabited world. Prosper as guarantor of safety, live generously and relieve the afflicted, kindly assist an aging man! Enjoy a bounteous life, reveling in pleasure until assemblies go defunct and petitioners stop requesting help. Salut!

6.7 By the time he reached his leaf-writ's end, the newcomer had shown his mettle on the field. Now welcoming and warm, the gathered mooters showed him thanks in word and deed. Then they asked: "Whose kin are you? And from what crack did you climb?" To answer he sang:

Of Ghassan come I, Sarooj my home,
  My clan a sun upon the land;
  But I, like father Adam, banned
From distant Eden, lost I come.

How great it is what I have lost:
  The days I dragged sweet pleasure's train
  Across a meadow full of rain;
That blessing I remember most.

What knew I then of loss and pain?
  'T were merciful, if pain might kill.
  But I do ache, and yet live still,
Each dawn to rise and mourn again.

'Tis better to die proud than lead
  A skulking, shabby, bestial life;
  To bring swift end to earthly strife,
Than from a thousand cruelties bleed.

Soon thereafter, tidings of him reached the reeve. He filled his mouth with sea-stones and sought him for an around-man, to take headship of the writ-craft house. But pride held him aloof from king-work, and the gifts made him happy enough.

Harald Hammamson went on: 6.8

Even before the outsider sprung his trap, I'd known him by the cut of his jib. I nearly blurted his name out, but he'd stopped me with a wink that held my tongue. Then he won the word-spin and came forth with his back sore bent by a well-stuffed sack. Giving him his guest-right, I walked him to the gate, but called him out along the way for scorning king-work. He smiled and hummed this lay:

Remember David's lesson just:
"In princes never put thy trust."
I always keep a due decorum
But never stand in awe before 'em;
I'd rather slip aside and choose
To talk with wits in dirty shoes.
For oh! how short are human schemes
That put their trust in princes' dreams!

GLOSSARY

6.1

moot   a meeting, an assembly of people, esp. one for judicial or legislative purposes

reed-reeves   princes of the pen

leaf-writ   a document, specifically a *risālah*, any piece of correspondence generated by government secretaries

6.2

nock   place the arrow on the bow   *palm-apple*   date

6.3

scrut   scrutinize

6.5

happenlore   a *qiṣṣah*, a request for relief, along with an explanation of the circumstances, sent to a judicial official

rede   advice

6.6

book-black   ink   *seed-wool*   cotton

NOTES

Being specific to the Arabic script, the alternating-dots constraint has stumped Ḥarīrī's translators. Al-Ḥarīzī admits that he is unable to replicate it in Hebrew (which also uses dots, but for different reasons) and simply paraphrases the petition (ed. Chenery, 16). Rückert, who elsewhere substitutes a German constraint for an Arabic one, appears not to do so here. He notes that the challenge is to avoid certain letters, but he does not explain which ones or why (*und in welchem*

Ganz der Buchstab ist vermieden—den auszusprechen dir nicht ist beschieden, 34). As far as I can tell, his translation of the petition does not follow any constraint: it contains all the letters of the German alphabet except *q* and *x*, which are relatively rare and easily avoided. Chenery, as usual, gives a literal rendering of the text and explains the trick without trying to duplicate it. Preston, who omits all the other *maqāmāt* that contain formal manipulations of this kind, does translate this one. But he calls his rendering of the petition "necessarily very jejune" because "it is impossible to convey in English" anything like the alternation of dotted and undotted words (*Makamat*, p. 323, n. 3; see also p. 311, n. 1).

Of course English does have two dotted letters, *i* and *j*. In theory, therefore, Abū Zayd's feat could be imitated by writing something like "i came, i saw, i conquered," and so on for about two hundred words, using an E. E. Cummings-style lowercase i to supply the dot. But this solution makes it practically impossible to convey any of the original meaning. My Germanic–Romance solution, conversely, sacrifices the visual dimension of al-Ḥarīrī's constraint. This I have tried to reproduce in my Englishing of 26, where Abū Zayd must alternate dotted and undotted *letters*.

In the narration, the Germanic-only constraint allowed me to use functional words like articles and pronouns, and most basic verbs. For other words, I consulted *The Anglish Moot*, a wiki bent on "replacing borrowed words in Common English with true English words." In practice, this means using Germanic words that mean the same thing as their Greek-, Latin-, or French-derived equivalents (e.g., "skill" or "craft" for "art") or, when none can be found, coining them on the basis of older English or related languages (e.g., "knowhood" for "information"). The wiki contributors have compiled English-Anglish and Anglish-English dictionaries, and have translated ("overset") a selection of well-known texts. As the editors themselves admit, the notion that such a thing as "true English" really exists is indefensible: given the tangled history of the language, labeling every word as Germanic or Romance is to a certain extent arbitrary. Moreover, it is manifestly untrue that the new coinages are necessarily easier to understand (for these discussions see the page on the "Goals of Anglish"). But, shaky as its foundations may be, "Anglish" can produce some oddly resonant prose (see, e.g., Kingsnorth, *The Wake*). For the most part I have chosen coinages that can be deciphered without special knowledge.

"Maraaghah" in §6.1 is Marāghah, a city located in what is now northwestern Iran. For "Sahbaan" see notes on §5.1.

"You have said a dreadful say" (§6.3) is a quotation from the Qur'an: Maryam 19:89.

"Who knows my arrows better than do I" (§6.4) is a proverb drawn from *maysir*, a game of chance where players cast arrows to win cuts of a slaughtered animal. For the game to work, each player needed to be able to identify his arrow.

"Breakers-Away" in §6.5 refers to the Khawārij, who were originally any one of the many groups that declared themselves opposed to the larger Islamic community in the course of disagreements over leadership during the first two centuries, and, by extension, means "rebels" or "bandits." "Aboo Naamah" is al-Qaṭarī ibn Fujāʾah, called Abū Naʿāmah (d. 78 or 79/697–98 or 698–99), who led a two-decade-long insurrection against the Umayyads. "If you are a truth-teller . . ." is another Qur'anic quotation: Shuʿarāʾ 26:154.

In keeping with its elegiac theme, the poem in §6.7 is modeled on Tennyson's *In Memoriam*, while the one in §6.8 recasts verses from "Verses on the Death of Dr. Swift, D. S. P. D." by Jonathan Swift.

BIBLIOGRAPHY

The Anglish Moot. http://anglish.wikia.com/wiki/Main_leaf.

Kingsnorth, Paul. *The Wake.* London: Unbound, 2014.

Swift, Jonathan. "Verses on the Death of Dr. Swift, D. S. P. D." In *Irish Poetry*, edited by W. J. McCormack. New York: NYU Press, 2000, 32–45, at 40–41.

[Tennyson]. Alfred, Lord Tennyson. *In Memoriam.* Edited by William J. Rolfe. Boston: Houghton Mifflin, 1895.

IMPOSTURE 7

GANGS OF NEW SAYBIN

This episode features a blind Abū Zayd and an unidentified old woman working together as peddlers. The old woman distributes copies of a poem containing a request for money and people who wish to keep a copy must pay for it. The poems being their stock in trade, the peddlers are careful to collect all the unwanted copies for reuse. No one is coerced into paying anything, but, like most of Abū Zayd's other activities, this one entails fraud, in this case because he is not really blind. At the end of this story, he pulls another fast one by eating the food al-Ḥārith offers him and then sneaking out of the house. Presumably he does this to avoid having to sing for his supper, though the reason is never properly explained. In keeping with the theme of well-practiced fraud, all the characters in the English rendering use the argot spoken by mid-nineteenth-century swindlers, thieves, and rowdies in New York, as compiled by George Matsell in his Vocabulum; or, The Rogue's Lexicon *(1859).*

El-Hâret Ebn Hammâm whiddled this whole scrap:　　　　　　　7.1

I was set to leg it out of Barkaid, but I could smell the festival gathering like a storm, and I didn't want to hop the twig before the jeffey. When the Bairam came, with its row and fanfare, its liturgies and articles, I upheld ancient custom and sallied out rum-togged in a new set of duds. Around the autum, the stir had gotten in kelter, and the coves in the push were starting to whiffle. Just then an old sharp in tats rose to his feet. Over his peepers was a tatty-tog, and under his rammer a knapsack. An old hen with a bracket-mug was leading him around. Staggering, he moused a salutation. Then he dipped into his bag and took out some pieces of scrip scratched in different colors. Handing them to the harridan, he told her to gun the flats in the push. If any looked bene and plump, she was to give them each a stiff.

7.2   As Old Shoe would have it, one of the gapeseeds came to me. On it was this glibe:

> Old Poger has made me swim for my swag,
> But lenten in my panny is my pap-lap;
> For his sweet sake tip us a rag.

> I've been rooked by curlers who sweat the bag,
> I've been bilked by burners for a goose-cap;
> Old Poger has made me swim for my swag.

> If only I could square it and turn stag!
> But kinchin needs scran in his flatter-trap;
> For his sweet sake tip us a rag.

> I've been kimbawed and tied with a gag,
> And lost my regulars after the scrapp;
> Old Poger has made me swim for my swag.

> He's made me heave peters off a drag,
> And when my squeaker whindles, I tap.
> For his sweet sake slip us a rag.

> I'm rum-bit by the best—not to brag:
> By coves that lace, and coves that snap;
> Old Poger has made me swim for my swag,
> For our sweet sake tip us a rag.

When I had measured the way those lines had been laid out I got smoky, 7.3
and I wanted to get the party who dealt them down close. A rover came
into my nouse-box: I'd use the trot to rope him in, dawbing her as if she
were a dookin mort. So I gunned her as she worked the rows one by one,
asking the coves in the push to post some sugar. But it was a no go: the
gripe-fists were canting her nix. At last she gave it up. "Of God are we," she
chanted, "and to Him we hare it!" Then she began to take the stiffs back.
For some reason Old Poger made her forget about mine, and she never
transpeared me. So she hared back maudling to the old cove, mouthing
that she'd been dealt a skinning hand. "Dunnakin!" he said. "In God we
trust, and in Him alone!" Then he chanted:

All men are equal in my eyes,
For all are hard of heart;
Not one will help his fellow rise
When Malice casts her dart!

Then he told her: "Collect the stiffs and count 'em again, and tell your- 7.4
self, 'It will come off rye buck, for bully times are here!'"

"I counted 'em when I collected 'em," she said, "and one of them's been
pilched."

"Nickey take you, harridan!" he cried. "Shall we lose the stick after the
hook, and the glimstick along with the tace? Why, this is the last strammel!"

So the old hen legged it back the way she had come, buzzing for her
piece of scrip. When she drew close to me, I held up her fakement, along
with a spanish and a jack. "Here's a teston; if you want it, you must chant.
But if you would rather keep your wid shut, take the spud and mizzle!"

"Kirjalis!" she said, emphatically declaring her partiality for the hard
cole, which was big and shiny as Oliver. "I'll cackle."

So I asked her to whiddle me the whole scrap about the old sharp, and
tell me who had scratched the verses.

"Why, that's the cove from Saroodj, and he's the word-pecker."

Quick as a ramper, she grabbled the spanish and legged it.

That is when I tumbled to him: why, the cove must be Aboo Zaid! I grew 7.5
glum at the thought that his gagers had been gouged out. I hoped to sneak

up and chaff with him until I got him down fine. But there was no way of reaching him but to step over all the coves in the push. That proceeding, say the brothers of the coif, merits a jobation; and I was unwilling to be chivied for jostling through the stir. So I stuck to my spot, keeping my peepers planted on the old cove until the autum bawler's patter was ended and the breakup began. Then I bolted after him. Though his glims were gummed together, I'm as fly with the seavey and the scavoir as Ebn Abbâs or Ebn Iyâs, and when I measured his mug I saw I had copped him to rights. I told him my chant, gave him one of my mill-togs, and offered him some tommey. He was glad I'd chalked him, he said, and he was grateful for the lift, and yes, he would come and yam some pannam. So we legged it, with him piping me and hanging on to my flapper, and the cutty-eyed hen making tray.

7.6   After we had moved our beaters into my crib, I flicked him some pannam and kaffar.

"Hâret!" said he, "is anyone with us but pilgarlic?"

"No one," I said, "but the lady."

"And she is a staunch moll, so there need be no fear."

Then he opened his peepers—his gagers—his glims—his lamps—his ogles—his day-lights—and *that* was a Jew's-eye! But pleased as I was, I was bustled, and agog to be flash. "Why play a groper," I asked, "when you so often walk your boots to daisyville, pad the hoof on dusty donbites, and ride your stampers far and wide?"

At first he pretended his potato-trap was full of scroof and he was too busy yamming to gab; but when he had wound up the tooth-music, he chanted at me cutty-eyed:

> One queer lamp has Mother Goodluck,
> And dark her other glim;
> If you need her help to come off rye buck
> Best keep your ogles dim.

7.7   Then he said: "Now off to the back-room, there's a bene cove, and bring me a bit of washing-powder to delight the eye, scour the palm, soften the skin, perfume the breath, tighten the gums, and brace up the old bread-basket! Scent it well, grind it fresh, pound it fine, and serve it in a clean dish, so it smells like camphor and feels like gummy-stuff for the glims. Pair it with a toothpick split off bang-up timber: a jock to stubble in your gob and a prime twig that edges you to yam, as lathy as a heaver, as limber as a switch, and as glib as a spado or a spit!"

I got up agogare to bring him the cog-picker and the slippery, in order not to lurch him with a reeky daddle. But he was sending me to the back room to put me on a string and I never tumbled to it. I was away only for an instant; but when I hared it the panny was M T and Aboo Zaid and his drab long gone. In a pelt over being topped, I hopped the twig to tout them, but they might as well have been boated, or been hoisted into nubibus.

GLOSSARY

7.1

whiddle the whole scrap   tell all one knows

leg it   run away, clear out

hop the twig   be off, go off

jeffey   lightning

Bairam   an older English name for either of the two great Muslim festivals

rum-togged   well-dressed

duds   clothes

autum   church, here used to mean "mosque"

stir   crowd

kelter   order

coves   people

push   crowd

whiffle   yelp or cry out in pain

7.2

Old Shoe   good luck

gapeseed   anything that makes people stop, look, or listen

old sharp   a knowing old fellow

tats   rags

peepers   eyes

tatty-tog   a sweat cloth

rammer   arm

hen   woman

bracket-mug   very ugly face

mouse   speak in a low voice

scrip   writing paper

scratch   write

gun   examine

flat   one unacquainted with the tricks and devices of rogues

bene   good

plump   rich

stiff   a letter or printed paper

glibe   writing

Old Poger   the Devil

made me swim for my swag   cheated me of my share

lenten   starving

panny   home

pap-lap   baby

tip us a rag   give us a dollar

rooked   cheated

curlers who sweat the bag   swindlers who put gold pieces into a bag, shake them, and gather the dust

bilked   cheated

burners   gamblers who prey on bumpkins

goose-cap   fool

square it   get one's living honestly

turn stag   become an informer

7.3

smoky   suspicious, curious

get him down close   find out all about him

rover   thought

nouse-box   head

trot   old woman

dawb   bribe

dookin mort   fortune-teller

post   pay

no go   no avail

7.4

come off rye buck   turn out well

bully times   good times

Nickey   the Devil

you bat   an insult directed at a woman

glimstick   candlestick

tace   candle

kinchin   child

scran   food

flatter-trap   mouth

kimbaw   beaten

my regulars   my share

scrapp   a planned act of roguery

heave peters off a drag   steal boxes off a wagon

squeaker   child

whindle   moan

tap   steal

rum-bit   cheated

coves   people

lace   beat

snap   arrest

gripe-fist   miser

cant   give

nix   nothing

hare it   return

transpear   approach

maudling   crying

mouthing   crying

skinning   cheating

dunnakin   it can't be helped

strammel   straw

fakement   a written or printed paper

spanish   silver coin

jack   small coin

teston   coin with a head on it

chant   talk, inform

keep your wid shut   be silent

spud   base coin

mizzle   be off

kirjalis   Bring it on!

hard cole   gold or silver money

Oliver   the moon

7.5

tumble to   suspect (of being someone)

chaff   banter

got him down fine   know all his antecedents

brothers of the coif   lawyers

jobation   reproof

autum bawler's patter   sermon

breakup   dispersing of people from theaters, lecture rooms, churches, etc.

seavey   sense, knowledge

scavoir   cunning, knowledge

7.6

beaters   boots

crib   house

flick some pannam and kaffar   cut some bread and cheese

no one with us but pilgarlic   we are alone

staunch   who can be trusted with a secret

Jew's-eye   a pleasant sight

bustled   confused, puzzled

agog   anxious, impatient

flash   knowing

7.7

bene cove   good fellow

bread-basket   stomach

cackle   to blab

word-pecker   a wit or punster

ramp   to tear something away from someone

grabble   seize

copped to rights   caught fair and square

chant   name

tommey   bread

chalk   spot

yam   eat

pannam   bread

pipe   follow, trail

flapper   hand

cutty-eyed   looking askance, looking suspicious

tray   three

groper   blind man

walk your boots   be off

daisyville   the country

pad the hoof   walk the street

dusty   dangerous

donbite   street

stampers   shoes

potato-trap   mouth

yam   eat

gab   talk

tooth-music   hearty chewing

queer lamp   blind or squinting eye

gummy-stuff   medicine

bang-up   best

jock joy	*cog* tooth
stubble hold	*slippery* soap
gob mouth	*lurch* abandon
prime twig first-rate condition, here	*daddle* hand
re-literalized	*put on a string* send on a wild-goose
edge encourage, induce	chase
lathy thin	*M T* empty
heaver lover	*drab* nasty woman
glib smooth	*pelt* rage
spado sword	*tout* follow, pursue
spit sword	*boated* gone to sea
agogare anxious, eager	*nubibus* the clouds

NOTES

Matsell (d. 1877), "Chief of the New York Police" (though not the only one, as there was more than one force), claims to have spent "years of diligent labor" studying thieves' cant, which he identifies as "the Romany or Gipsy language, adapted to the use of rogues in all parts of the world." In addition to the lexicon, the book contains a sample conversation, a story, a poem, and even a tailor's advertisement translated into cant. It seems doubtful that anyone spoke the way Matsell imagines—that is, using jargon equivalents for all common words all the time (although there was evidently a term for doing just that—namely, "stam-fishing"; cf. Scots English "scomfish't," 14.1). By composing texts entirely in cant, Matsell has in effect created a literary language, and it is the one I am using here. To learn it, I found it helpful to read Herbert Asbury's *The Gangs of New York* and to watch Martin Scorsese's film of nearly the same title. The film's screenwriters (Jay Cocks, Steven Zaillian, and Kenneth Lonergan) drew on Matsell's glossary, and the bits that made it into the script sound especially convincing when performed by Daniel Day-Lewis in his role as gang lord Bill Cutting. Although the Five Points gangsters are altogether more brutal and savage than anyone in the *Impostures*, their language proved a good fit for this one. Among other things, it contains eight different ways to say "eyes," which came in handy in a story about a man pretending to be blind. In a few cases where Matsell could not supply a word I needed (e.g., "its liturgies and articles" in §7.1), I drew on *Moby-Dick* by Herman Melville, who was also a nineteenth-century New Yorker.

"Barkaid" (§7.1) is Barqaʿīd, a now-vanished town between Mosul and Nusay-bin (Nisibin), in what is now northeast Syria, just over the border with Iraq, and "a place of considerable scale, especially in the 3rd/9th century, with its walls and three gates, excellent springs, 200 shops (largely wine-shops) and busy traf-fic" (Streck and Longrigg, "Barqaʿīd").

The poem in §7.2 is noteworthy in that every Arabic line contains one or more examples of *tajnīs*, that is, sequences of words that are identical but for one letter (e.g., *mukhtāl wa-muḥtāl wa-mughtāl* [مختال ومحتال ومغتال] in line 2) or one vowel (e.g., *akhṭiru* [أَخْطِر] and *akhṭuru* [أَخْطُر] in line 6), or sequences of letters that yield different meanings based on how they are spaced (e.g., *aṭfā lī* [أطفا لي] and *aṭfālī* [أطفالي] in line 7). In line 13, the sequence *ḥurrun yarā* [حرٌ يرى] ("a free man deems it good"), if reread without a space, yields *ḥarīrī* [حريري], the author's name, making this line the equivalent of the self-portrait some European paint-ers included in their crowd scenes. This kind of trick is very hard to pull off in English (see also the Notes on Imposture 36). The only attempt I know is this poem by Harryette Mullen (*Sleeping*, 17):

Coo/Slur

da red
yell ow
bro won t
an orange you
bay jaun
pure people
blew hue
a gree gree in
viol let
pure people
be lack
why it
pee ink

This poem works because it sets a limited task for itself—to riff on the names of the colors—but even so a good deal of cheating is needed. Instead of trying to make Abū Zayd's poem work in this form, I have imitated the repetitive effect by casting the poem as a villanelle: that is, a nineteen-line poem where two of the lines appear three times, among other features.

In §7.4, "pilch" is my back-formation from pilcher, "one who steals handkerchiefs," here meaning to pocket the good lady's piece of paper; and "hook" and "stick" I drew from the entry on "anglers," who "place a hook on the end of a stick, and therewith steal from store-windows, doors, etc."

"Ebn Abbâs" (§7.5) is Ibn ʿAbbās, the Prophet's cousin, who is often cited as an authority on the Qurʾan and Sunnah. "Ebn Iyâs" is Ibn ʿAbbās, a proverbially observant judge in Basra.

In §7.6 "scroof" is my formation for food offered to a guest, from "to scroof," to live at a friend's expense.

The cleaner that Abū Zayd asks for in §7.7 evidently belongs to the class of powders "based on washing soda obtained from ashes of a sort of tumbleweed" and scented with various additives (see Perry, *Scents*, xxxv, and §§9.1–8).

In her discussion of this Imposture, Zakharia argues that Abū Zayd's blindness, as well as al-Ḥārith's failure to notice his escape, symbolize spiritual blindness. Abū Zayd, however, is destined to be cured: his being "hoisted into nubibus" (*ʿurija bihi ilā s-samāʾ*) echoes Qurʾanic expressions for ascent to Heaven (see Zakharia, *Abū Zayd*, 207–8 and 226–31).

BIBLIOGRAPHY

Asbury, Herbert. *The Gangs of New York*. New York: Knopf, 1927.

Matsell, George W. *Vocabulum; or, The Rogue's Lexicon*. New York: Matsell, 1859. Original volume online at http://archive.org/details/ cu31924073798740 and transcription at http://www.gutenberg.org/ files/52320/52320-h/52320-h.htm.

Mullen, Harryette. *Sleeping with the Dictionary*. Berkeley: University of California Press, 2002.

Perry, Charles, ed. and trans. *Scents and Flavors: A Syrian Cookbook*. New York: NYU Press, 2017.

Scorsese, Martin, dir. *Gangs of New York*. Miramax, 2002.

Streck and Longrigg. "Barqaʿīd." In *Encyclopaedia of Islam, Second Edition*. Leiden: Brill, 1960–2007.

IMPOSTURE 8

TEXT/ILE

This is the first of several Impostures in which Abū Zayd and a confederate—his wife or his son—ask a judge to settle a dispute that turns out to be a pretext for showing off their verbal abilities. In this episode, Abū Zayd accuses his son of borrowing a piece of his property and damaging it. Upon first reading, the piece of property seems to be an enslaved woman, but the description turns out to be of a needle. Similarly, the son's account of the pledge he gave against damages seems to describe a man but turns out to refer to a kohl pencil—a stick for applying dark pigment to the eyelids. To mark the rest of the text in the way the original is marked by rhyme, the translation extends the conceit to the whole story, using terms from sewing, tailoring, and the garment industry.

Al-Harith ibn Hammam unspooled this yarn.　　　　　**8.1**

I once witnessed an incident in Naaman's Knot that knocked my socks off. Two disputants had buttonholed the judge to pleat their case. One was a crotchety old fellow who'd gone loose and baggy, and the other was a straight stitch.

The old man went first. "May God back His Honor the judge," he said, "and save me from getting fleeced! She was sharp as a tack and neat as a pin, and she could handle the rough patches. She would tear through a job of work, then lie there flat as a board. She didn't mind filing; she always kept her head, and never lost the thread. She was good for a nip and a tuck, but she had only one eye. She might string you along, or take a stab at you, but she always got her point across. She loved a cold bath. She could bob and weave and leave you in stitches, but as long as I had her under my thumb she made sure I had a shirt on my back. Whenever she went on a tear, she made sure to tie up the loose ends, and if I put her down she'd stay on the case. If something needed letting out, no one was a patch on her; but if I rubbed her the wrong way she'd give me a good jab.

"Well, this young fellow here asked me if he could avail himself of her services. I let him have her without asking anything in return except that he not push her too hard. But he used her for pricking and boning, and left her warped and bent. He's offered me compensation, but it's not enough, darn it!"

8.2   Then it was the young man's turn.

"Every word the old man said is true enough, your Honor, but the warping and bending happened by mistake, and in any case I gave him a pledge against damages.

"Now that pledge is a sight for sore eyes, and a heavy tipper who won't bend under the lash. Once you've got him in your corner, he'll hold the line and fill in for you wherever he's needed. He casts a long shadow, but he'll let you spread your wings, and he brings out the best in his pupils. I admit there's something shady about him: he'll give you the brush-off, and he lays it on thick. He's a double-dipper, and he'll take a powder if he goes to pot. In fact, he's just as black as he's painted. But he'll make sure you turn the other cheek, and there's no dispensing without him."

8.3   The judge said, "Speak plainly, you two, or be off!" So the young man stepped up and said:

> What he gave me was a needle
> To darn my rags.
> When I drew on it, it broke.
>
> Now the fellow won't forgive me.
> He says, "Repair it,
> Or pay me what it's worth!"

And he's keeping the kohl pencil
I use to daub my eyes.
Free me, your Honor, from his crewel yoke!

The judge turned to the old man and said: "Your turn! And no hemming **8.4**
and hawing." So the man replied:

It's not by choice I've come to hold
A kohl stick for ransom
When a single needle breaks.

But I've been jabbed and stabbed
And pricked and poked
By the ripping shears of fate.

Now I'm as destitute as he is
And he as poor as I;
Otherwise I would despise the fellow's paltry stake.

When the judge realized the two were a cut above the usual disputants, **8.5**
and were truly out of pocket, he produced a gold dinar from under his
prayer mat. "Take this," he said, "and patch things up."

Cutting ahead of the nipper, the old man snapped up the coin. "One half
is mine," he said, "because it was a gift to both of us; and the other half is
mine too, for the loss of my needle. But I won't wrong-side you: here's your
kohl stick."

The young man was thrown for a loop and looked put out. Meanwhile
the judge's temper was starting to fray, not least because the codger had
collared his gold coin. But he kept his shirt on and placketed the boy with
a few pieces of silver. Then he said, "No more scrapping, you two! And no
more basting my time with lawsuits: I have no more surplice to hand out."

The two sprung up, rejoicing in the gifts he had given them, full of praise **8.6**
for the judge, and bolted. Meanwhile His Honor was looking snippy, as
if he'd let them draw the wool over his eyes. Finally, he pulled himself
together and turned to his trotters. "Something tells me that so-called suit

was no suit at all. Those two had something up their sleeve, and we've been worsted. And now they've given us the slip!"

His chief striker spoke up. "Let's bring them back and hang them out to dry."

So the judge sent a trotter to fetch them. When the pair reappeared before him, he said that if they came clean he'd let them off the hook. The younger one shrunk away, clearly eager to skirt the issue. But the old man stepped forward and recited off the cuff:

8.7   I'm the man from Sarúj, this my son,
        He's cut from the same cloth as I.
        I've never plied a needle in my life
        And he never puts kohl on his eye.

        Our luck wore thin, we took to the road
        To shift for our bread every day.
        We're dyed in the wool, we live by a rule,
        Where there's a twill there's a way!"

8.8   "Sheer eloquence," cried the Judge. "If only you weren't so shifty!" He continued: "Now let me lay it out for you. Next time you deal with officials or other stuffed shirts, button your lip and don't get too big for your britches. Eyelet you go, but others might not cut you any slack."

The old man promised he would do as the judge advised. But as he peeled away I saw him smirk.

Al-Harith ibn Hammam wrapped up his tale:

I'd been all across the muslin world and read books of every stripe, but never before heard of anything clothes to that.

GLOSSARY

8.1

board   tailor's workbench

cold bath   a reference to the quenching process, that is, the plunging of the
   needle into cold water after it has been hammered into shape

boning   strips of bone used to hold a fitted garment in place

8.6

trotter   fetcher and carrier, messenger

striker   assistant to a cutter (that is, a tailor)

NOTES

"Naaman's Knot" in §8.1 is the Syrian town of Maarat al-Numaan, where this
Imposture is set, which is most famous as the birthplace of the poet al-Maʿarrī
(d. 449/1057). My English rendering ignores the meaning of the name, which is
unclear in any case, opting instead for euphony and correspondence with the
sartorial theme.

BIBLIOGRAPHY

Apperson, Donna Gettings. *The Sewing Dictionary*. http://www.thesewing
   dictionary.com/#b.

Discovery and Science Channel. "How It's Made: Needles & Pins." Uploaded
   by Panos Egglezos, February 19, 2012. http://www.youtube.com/
   watch?v=wZJPpuL2sqQ.

"Fabric-isms." Fabric Link. http://www.fabriclink.com/dictionaries/cism.cfm.

Eldridge, Lisa. "The Ultimate Smokey Kohl Tutorial." Uploaded March 4, 2016.
   http://www.youtube.com/watch?v=X6OoGMG-f2Y.

"Tailoring Terms." Savile Row Bespoke. http://www.savilerowbespoke.com/
   about-us/tailoring-terms/.

"Glossary of Sewing Terms." Wikipedia. http://en.wikipedia.org/wiki/
   Glossary_of_sewing_terms.

"Glossary of Textile Manufacturing." Wikipedia. http://en.wikipedia.org/wiki/
   Glossary_of_textile_manufacturing.

IMPOSTURE 9

STRINGING HER ALONG

This is the first of the four Impostures in which Abū Zayd's wife, or a woman who claims to be his wife, hauls him before a judge. Here she accuses him of lying to her about his profession before they were married. A similar breach-of-promise claim is the subject of Trial by Jury *(1875), a dramatic cantata that represents the second collaboration between composer Arthur Sullivan and librettist W. S. Gilbert. This Imposture will accordingly take the form of a Gilbert and Sullivan operetta. In many respects the world of comic opera resembles that of the Impostures: both place characters in absurd situations created by the figurative, deceptive, or ambiguous use of language, and both play free and easy with time and space. Most of all, what makes Gilbert and Sullivan a natural model for an English Imposture is the over-the-top wordplay. Of course, the Arabic original, though it was meant to be read aloud, was not written as musical theater. As a result of the change in form, some of what is narrated in the original appears here in the form of stage directions.*

DRAMATIS PERSONAE

Al-Harith son of Hammam, an itinerant man of letters	A Judge
	A Bailiff
Abu Zayd al-Saruji, a confidence man	A Child
Barrah, wife to Abu Zayd	Spectators

AL-HARITH *assumes the stage.* **9.1**

SONG—AL-HARITH

Swept across the seven seas,
    Fully drunk on youthful folly;
Hoping for a life of ease,
    Washing up in distant Mali;
Heading eastward by degrees,
    Learning Pushtu and Bengali;
Braving hunger and disease,
    Always keeping bright and jolly.

AL-HARITH: Now I should like to impart a piece of advice to the traveller, given me by sages and men of learning. Upon arriving in any town, a prudent man should seek out and befriend the chief representative of the local judiciary, that he may have recourse should any bring suit against him, and that he may have one to protect him in a strange land from the injustice of the powerful. I have taken this counsel to heart and applied it from Ghana to Fergana, and thus become the intimate of many a worthy judge.

Curtain rises to reveal the judicial court of Alexandria. The JUDGE *discovered seated on a chair, with the* BAILIFF *standing to one side and* SPECTATORS *seated on the ground.* **9.2**

AL-HARITH: And so it was that, once upon a chilly evening, I chanced to be waiting on the judge of Alexandria. On that very night he was to dispose of the poor relief so liberally supplied by the people of that city. All at once a lady petitioner entered the hall. She was holding a child in one arm. With the other she was dragging a wicked-looking chap who evidently wished to be elsewhere.

AL-HARITH *sits down among the* SPECTATORS. *During his speech* BARRAH *has entered carrying the* CHILD *and dragging* ABU ZAYD *before the* JUDGE.

BARRAH: God save the magistrate
       And help him . . .
ALL: Help him!
BARRAH: . . . to adjudicate.

SONG—BARRAH

I am a dame of pedigree, born of a noble sire,
Descended from a fam'ly tree that lesser folk admire.
A good help-meet I meant to be, unstinting of my labor,
And thrifty with the household cash, unlike my lady neighbor.
When suitors came to seek my hand, my father sent them packing,
A man, he said, must ply a trade; a man that won't is slacking.

My fortunes went from bad to worse the day this cad came calling.
He met Pa-Pa and said, "A-ha! No need to go on stalling:
A stringer I of Orient pearls, and oh! how some folk *do* spend!"
And soon I found that I was bound to this do-nothing husband.
He took me far away from home and kept me in a hovel,
And there I learned his fancy talk was laid on with a shovel.

His tale of trade's a masquerade: the fellow is bone lazy;
He stays in bed till afternoon, and even on the days he
Gets out of bed he stays at home, reclining on a bolster.
But now of course he can't do that as easy as he used ter:
He's gone and sold each scrap of cloth, the plain ones and the
       flow'ry,
And every pot and pan and bed they gave me for a dowry.

With nothing left to sell or pawn, you'd think he'd think to work
    some,
But all he says is times are tough and finding work is irksome.
We have a son—this little one—as scrawny as his father,
And I'm afraid if he's not fed the lad will start to holler.
So I've brought this louse to Your Honor's house to see why he
    won't labor,
And if he won't, dear magistrate, then please rule in my favor.

SONG—JUDGE

9.3

  O luckless wife!
Your plea has now been heard.
  Upon my life,
I groaned with every word.
  Defendant, rise!
Explain yourself, but know:
  If I hear lies
'Tis off to gaol you'll go.

ABU ZAYD *rolls up his sleeves as if preparing for a fight and lowers his head like a viper about to strike.*

SONG—ABU ZAYD

My tale is tragi-comical and when it's done you'll realize
That though I dress the truth a bit I never stoop to real lies.
Although I come from noble stock, I live by arts rhetorical,
For which the going rate is less than what you'd pay an oracle.
I trade in verses panegyrical and confrontational,
And all the texts you need to preach at prayers congregational.
In metaphor, metathesis, ellipsis, and metonymy,
In simile and syncrisis, why . . . you can ask a *ton* o' me!

In former days, to paraphrase, my choice seemed quite a stroke o'
     luck:
No matter where I found myself I never strained to make a buck.
With eloquence a welcome guest I never failed to get my due,
The smitten sent me everything from bags of gold to pots of stew.
But now, alas, the times have changed, and patrons have grown
     negligent:
When I appear, my former friends all say, "Oh what an ugly gent!"
No plutocrat will part with cash to help support a Cicero:
Our Maecenas would rather in a galley see his . . . *Sis* a-row!

And when at last the creditors came knocking fast and furious,
And when at last I found myself as poor as Saint Mercurius,
And when at last I'd pawned away the bedding and the crockery,
With nothing to expect except a sempiternal hockery,
And after going five whole days deprived of all that's edible,
With heavy heart and dragging feet I took a step regrettable:
I seized my goodwife's property and sold it off *in extremis*,
With her consent: so try now barking up the *next* tree, Ms!

Now as for her assertion that I bent the truth a tad or two
And to my resumé I was a shameless sort of adder-to,
I urge you, sir, to disregard her recent testimonial:
I never lie to ladies in *re* prospects matrimonial.
I hardly meant to say I was an expert gemological,
My declarations on that point were strictly homological;
The only pearls I string are words in verses like the present ode,
And so it seems that in this instance compensation . . . *isn't* owed!

9.4   *The* JUDGE *is favorably impressed by this performance.*

78

RECITATIVE—JUDGE (TO BARRAH)

The best authorities agree, and clearly:
The age of patronage has fallen hard,
And love of letters is extinct, or nearly;
Your husband speaks the truth in this regard.

On charge of imposture he is acquitted,
Because he strung some verses here in court.
The debt he owes to you he has admitted,
Which means I cannot hold him for a tort.

Now I could keep him locked up in the compter,
And let him rot in fetters evermore.
But in this case, sweet mercy is my prompter:
I cannot hold a man for being poor.

My goodwife, go, and bear your lot in silence;
Humility will teach you better ways.
Forgive this man, and do him no more violence;
In God be all your hope for better days.

AL-HARITH *rises.*

AL-HARITH *(to the audience)*:   With that the good Judge set aside a
    share for them from the money collected for the poor, and gave each
    of them a heaping handful of coins.
JUDGE: May these coins offer you sustenance in your time of hardship,
    and may God see fit to favor you with better fortune.

ABU ZAYD *looks enormously relieved.*

Exeunt BARRAH *and* ABU ZAYD.

9.5 AL-HARITH (*addressing the audience*):   I had of course recognized Abu Zayd immediately, and I had an inkling of what his wife's purpose might be in dragging him before the court. I was on the verge of exposing them but then thought the better of it, lest the Judge, once he learn of their deception, repent of his charitable act. So I held my tongue—that is, as much as one can be said to hold his tongue, who proposes, after some time had gone by, that the Judge send after them some officer who might follow them unseen and return with a report of how they fared. This the Judge did.

The JUDGE *gestures to the* BAILIFF, *who exits. After an interval he returns in great haste, convulsed with laughter.*

JUDGE: What news, man?

BAILIFF: I have seen a marvellous thing, sir.

JUDGE   Speak, you ninny, that we may share in your marvelling.

BAILIFF: After the defendant went out, sir, he set to clapping, and skipping, and warbling a merry air:

> She's a *brazen hussy*:
>> Let me say it in italics!
> But the man's not fussy,
>> Our magistrate in Alex!

CHORUS—SPECTATORS

> But the man's not fussy,
>> Our magistrate in Alex!

9.6 *The* JUDGE *laughs hugely and his cap falls off. With some effort he regains his composure.*

JUDGE: May God forgive me! And may no man of letters ever languish in my gaol. (*To the* BAILIFF) Bring him to me!

Exit BAILIFF. *After a pause he returns.*

BAILIFF: I can't find him, sir.

JUDGE: He had no good reason to flee. If he had but appeared I would have found a suitable appointment for him, and been more liberal with him than I was before.

AL-ḤĀRITH *(addressing the audience)*:   When I saw how much the Judge admired him, I understood that, had I pointed him out, I might have secured myself some reward; and so regretted my silence as bitterly as Farazdak rued his rash words to Nawár, or as El-Kusaee repented of breaking his trusty bow.

NOTES

In this Imposture, Abū Zayd's wife, or confederate, is not named. In Imposture 5, Abū Zayd claims to have a wife named Barrah, though he later says he was lying. In Impostures 40 and 45, he again appears in court with a woman identified only as his wife. For clarity's sake, I consider all these women (but not the old woman in Imposture 7) to be the same person and have called her Barrah everywhere she appears.

For librettos and links to Internet Archive recordings, some going back to the 1920s, I gratefully availed myself of the Gilbert and Sullivan Archive. In composing lyrics—or, more exactly, light verse intended to be reminiscent of lyrics— I learned a great deal from the notes and comments in Sondheim, *Finishing the Hat*. Al-Ḥārith's opening solo may be sung to the tune of "Taken from the County Jail" (*The Mikado*, Act I). Barrah's song (§9.2) is based on "When Frederic Was a Little Lad" (*The Pirates of Penzance*, Act I). The judge's song (§9.3) may be sung to the king's solo part of "Away, Away, My Heart's on Fire," beginning with "With falsehood foul" (*Pirates*, Act II). Abū Zayd's defense is based on "I Am the Very Model of a Modern Major-General" (*Pirates*, Act I). Unlike many parodies of this well-known song, this imitation adheres to the original form, including triple rhymes throughout and contrived mis-stressed rhymes in the last lines of each stanza. The judge's recitative (§9.4) follows "The question, gentlemen—is one of liquor" (*Trial by Jury*).

"Farazdak" (§9.6), properly al-Farazdaq, was a celebrated poet of the Umayyad period who divorced his beloved wife Nawār (here spelled "Nawár"). "El-Kusaee" (more properly al-Kusaʿī) is a figure of Arab lore, who, thinking he had missed all his shots during a nighttime hunt, broke a new bow in frustration, only to discover at daybreak that he had made every one.

BIBLIOGRAPHY

Gilbert, W. S., and Arthur Sullivan. *The Mikado*. http://gsarchive.net/mikado/html/index.html.

———. *The Pirates of Penzance*. http://gsarchive.net/pirates/html/index.html.

———. *Trial by Jury*. http://gsarchive.net/trial/html/index.html.

Sondheim, Stephen. *Finishing the Hat: Collected Lyrics (1954–1981) with Attendant Comments, Principles, Heresies, Grudges, Whines and Anecdotes*. New York: Knopf, 2010.

IMPOSTURE 10

ALHARET EBEN HAMMAM HIS TALE

In this episode, Abū Zayd accuses a young man of murdering his (Abū Zayd's) son. Of course, the young man is his son, and the accusation is a pretext for scamming the judge, who has a weakness for beautiful boys. Thematically, this Imposture has much in common with Geoffrey Chaucer's "Physician's Tale," where a lecherous justice hounds a young girl, and his "Miller's Tale," where the miller's wife humiliates an amorous clerk. Inspired by these parallels, al-Ḥārith, Abū Zayd, and company will speak here in the Middle English of Chaucer's Canterbury Tales.

Quod Alharet Eben Hammam: 10.1

WHAN that longing bad me wend adoun   *when; bade; go down*
    Thorogh Surrye to Tawkes toun,[1]
I hasted me with herte and honde   *hurried; vigorously*
Pon swifte camaille to that deere londe,   *camel; dear land*
In his waters my ankers for to caste   *its; anchors*
And my cordes to his pegs make faste.

And whan all fresh and newe y-shave
From the bath I came, espeyed I a knave,   *saw; young man*
Cast from the mold of lovelinesse
As he were kirtle-clad in parfitnesse,   *dressed; perfection*

---

1. Through Syria to the town of Raḥbat Mālik ibn Ṭawq, literally "the expanse belonging to Mālik, son of Ṭawq."

With an old man that hent him by the zone   *clung to his belt*
And bar on hond, he slow his sone.

10.2   Quod he: "I knowe him nat, by my crede,   *not; faith*
Ne sleen him, God me forbede!"   *nor killed*
Greet wex the stryf bitwixe the two   *great grew*
And a meynee gadred of heigh and low   *crowd gathered*
Til the lad assente with his accusour   *agreed*
To gon biforn the Governour.   *go before*

Of this Iustice every wight sayde   *everyone said*
He loved faire lads but neer a mayde.   *never*
To his consistorie the plaintes made haste   *court; plaintiffs*
As they were Mercurie that ran full faste.   *as if*
Sone that they came the man gan to crye   *as soon as*
Vengeaunce, and justice of the felonye.

Now the laddes hair lyk ringes was y-ronne,   *clustered*
And his face was white and glitered as the sonne.
The Iustice, who withal loved ayen kinde,   *against nature*
Looked and loste both wit and mynde.
Natheless he bad him ageyn the pleynt replye.[1]
"I ner shed blood," quod the lad. "It is a lye!"

10.3   "Bring me two witnesses, Mussulmans both,"
Quod the Iustice, "else the lad swere an oth."[2]

"He took my son," quod the man, "ful subtilly,
Thanne keveled him and mordred him prively   *gagged*
With no man ther-besyde, so God ye blesse!
Whom then shal I finde to beren witnesse?
Therefor, I pray, lat him reherse my oth   *repeat*
That ye may seyn if he speketh soth."   *truth*

---

1. He nevertheless ordered him to reply to the charge.
2. "Unless the boy swears an oath."

"I graunte it thee," quod the Iustice anon,
"By right of pitee of thy mordred son."

The old man bad the lad: "Saye: 10.4
By God that made blak myn eyen tweye,   *my two eyes*
That paynted my cheekes as flambes rede   *flames*
And wove the brode lokkes upon my hede,
That ful smale y-pulled my browes bent   *plucked thin*
And hath my mydell molded smal and gent,[1]
That opened bitwixe my teeth a gap narwe   *narrow*
And yaf me a nose as tretys as a sparwe,[2]
And eie-lids fulle and a mouth tendre,
And finger-endes yaf me long and sclendre,   *gave*
And layd above my lippe a line of here,   *hair*
By this God, upon my trouth I swere:

"I slow not thy sone, ne willfully,   *killed*
Ne took his lyf unwittingly,
Ne sheathed my swerde inside his brayn.
If I lye, God blere myn eyen tweyne,   *lie; blear*
Make hem holwe, and grisly to beholde,   *make them hollow*
My hewe falwe and pale as asshen colde,   *my color yellow*
My visage with fraknes overspred,   *freckles*
Make soure my breth, and balled my heed;   *bald*
May bristles springe upon my cheek
As mone clipsed, or sonne in reek,   *moon; sun; smoke*
Or silver that in a flambe wol brenne,   *is about to burn*
And may every clerke threst his penne   *pen*
Into my ink-horn, if I saye fals!"

"I have as leef be hanged by the hals,"   *would rather; neck*   10.5
Quod the lad, "though giltelees, by my fey,
As swere this oth! Allas, and weylawey!   *alas and woe*

---

1. Who made my waist slender and graceful.
2. And gave me a nose as well-shaped as a sparrow.

Han ye herd ever slyk an oth er now?"[1]

But the villard wolde that he make avow   *the old man wanted*
Word for word, and of the bitter draughte
Drinke every drope that he him taughte.
The lad shrewed his face and that other eke;[2]
Neither wold foryeve, nor foryeveness seke.

10.6   All the whyl the Iustice his eyen caste
       Upon this knave, avysing him full faste,   *scrutinizing*
       So was he caught with his beauty as he pleyde   *pled*
       And turned about, and to himself he seyde:
       "This ladde shal be myn, for any man!"   *mine*
       Anon the feend into his herte ran   *devil*
       And taught him sodeynly that he by slyghte
       The knave to his purpose wynne myghte:[3]
       He wold deliver him from the villard's holde
       And his lemman be, wher-so he wolde or nolde.[4]

10.7   To the old man spak he thus: "Woostow
       My reed, to Goddes paye and for thy prow?"[5]
       "I wol doon," quod he, "as ye comande, certayn,   *will do*
       In nowys me liste to stonden ther-agayn."[6]
       Quod he: "Namoore of thy suit, trewe or fals;   *no more*
       Be contented of an hundred mitigals[7]
       Of gold, of that I paye one part faire and wel
       And for thee in catel glene the other del."[8]

---

1. Have you ever heard such an oath before?
2. The boy cursed him and the other did the same.
3. At once put into his mind the thought that he might win the boy over by a trick.
4. And be his lover, willingly or otherwise.
5. "Would you take my advice, to please God, and for your own benefit?"
6. "I have no wish to oppose you."
7. "Accept a hundred mithqals" (a measure of weight) as a settlement.
8. "And scrape together the rest in kind."

"God woot I spare nat to taken," quod he,[1]
"If ye holde your plighted trouth, pardee." [2]

The Iustice of his mitigals yaf one score,	*gave twenty*	**10.8**
And his baillys gadred ful thirty more,	*bailiffs; gathered*	
Bifor the sonnes arraiment lost his light,	*raiment*	
And the gadring moste stinten ere it drow to night.[3]		
"Take," quod he, "the gold thou hast biside,		
Stint thy debaat, and lat thy suit abide;	*give up your suit*	
The remenaunt I plight my trouth to give	*I promise*	
To thee on the morwe, as I live."	*morrow*	

"Yis," said the man, "on this condicioun,	
That the lad abide in my possessioun,	
And under warde to-night bisette,[4]	
Til ye paye the somme of the dette.	
Thenne wol I suffre him go where him liste	*where he wants*
Free as a fowle new-hacchid, or the beeste	*new-hatched; beast*
Aquyted of the deth of Isaacs son,	
As ye wel know from our Alkaron."	*the Qur'an*

"I graunte," quod the Iustice, "for as I gesse,
You do no outrage, nor greet excesse."

Quod Alharet: **10.9**

Whan the old man spak as Soraich of heigh renoun,[5]	
I knew him for the sotile clerk of Sarouge-toune.[6]	
Abood I neer til it was woxen night,	*stayed close*
And the hevene blosmed with starres bright.	

---

1. "God knows I don't mind taking (the money)," he said.
2. "If you keep your promise, by God."
3. The collection had to stop when night fell.
4. Spend the night under guard.
5. Soraich: Surayj, a well-known early Muslim jurist.
6. I recognized him as the ingenious (or deceitfully clever) scholar of Sarūj.

The prees y-gadred at the Iustices dore   *crowd*
Was goon, and filleth the yerd namoore.
The old man wardeth the lad whan he slept.
I axed him: "Art thou not Abuzaid y-clept?   *called*
"I am," quod he, "for love of venerye!   *hunting*
I sayde: "Who is this lad in thy companye,
That hath folkes with likerous lust bigyld?   *lecherous*
Quod Abuzaid: "By parage, he is my child,   *birth*
But he playeth the lime-rod in our mistere."[1]
I seyd: "Suffise the sighte of his fair chere![2]
Wherfore puttest thou the Iustice in assay?"   *to the test*
Quod he: "Without the croket, I dare wel say,   *curled hair*
That lyk an S on the laddes forheed skipt,
Thilke fifty mitigals I coude nat have kipt."[3]

10.10   But let us to-night in mirth dispende,
And for long absence make amende,
For on the morwe wol I stele henne   *steal away*
And the Governours herte with longing brenne."   *burn*

Al the night long we spak and made us glade;[4]
His speche was lyk floures ysprung in a glade.   *like flowers*
But whan the foxes tayle in hevene gan growe[5]
And the dayes light began for to glowe,
Abuzaid took his leve, and in swich wyse   *in that way*
Defrauded the Governour of his pryse.   *prize*

Biforn he went he yaf me a lettre seled faste   *gave; sealed*
And seyde: "When that the Governour atte laste   *finally*

---

1. "In our trade he plays the part of the stick covered in lime" (used to catch birds).
2. "The sight of his beautiful face should be enough."
3. "I could never have snatched those fifty mithqals."
4. Talked and enjoyed ourselves.
5. When the false dawn appeared in the sky.

Wot that we are agon, and ne stand not stille [1]
For verray peyne, yif him this my bille."   *letter*
Thus he spak; but adradde lest I fare amis,   *afraid*
I brak the lettre, as did wys Motálamis. [2]
The lettre spak: **10.11**
    Thou art ful of torment and of rage.
Thy herte is ravisshed, and thy gold is al ago.
Thou rewest sore, and thy rewe wol noone aswage;   *feel great regret*
Thou yevest coin to winne a lad that is namo   *gave; no more*
And thogh thy venerye bought thee only wo,
And thy sorwe, thou wenst, is Hosens distresse,   *Husayn's*
Thou shalt, with wysdom wonne, thy wo redresse.

The deer layth his hede not in thy lappe,
The fowles flee, and whann thou seekest hare
Or cacchest reyn in every thonder-clappe   *catch rain*
No wight save thee is comen in the snare.
Cast thine yë adoune, and bear thy care,   *eyes*
Lest ye renne aftir pray unhende
That bringe noble wights to wikked ende.

Quod Alharet:

Whan I of this bille took hede,   *understood*
I rente it al to cloutes, for drede;   *tore it up*
And of his chyding, witen and not wene,   *certainly*
I counted nat a fly, ne roghte a bene!   *cared a bean*

---

1. "Realizes we've left, and can't stand still."
2. Al-Mutalammis, a pre-Islamic poet who wisely broke open a letter entrusted to him and discovered that it instructed the recipient to put him to death.

NOTES

Almost every word of the English comes from Walter Skeat's edition of the *Tales* or can be derived from an entry in the University of Michigan's online *Middle English Dictionary*. The only words I can recall using without attestation are "lovelinesse" (§10.1), by analogy from many forms that do exist (e.g., "parfit-nesse"), and "mitigal" (§10.7), which comes from a later period. My spelling does not pretend to be any more consistent than Chaucer's. The text is formatted in imitation of A. C. Cawley's Everyman edition of the *Tales*, including marginal glosses and footnotes.

To describe the judge, of whom al-Ḥarīrī says that he was *mimman yuzannu bil-hanāt, wa-yughallibu ḥubba l-banīna ʿalā l-banāt* (§10.2) "among those sus-pected of certain things, and those who prefer to love boys rather than girls," the English uses the expression "loved ayen kinde" ("loved against nature"), which I needed not only for sense but also for the meter and the rhyme. Unfor-tunately, this translation suggests an attitude to same-sex attraction that may not have been shared between al-Ḥarīrī's world and Chaucer's. As Khaled El-Rouay-heb (in *Before Homosexuality*) has shown, Muslims writing in Arabic during the late medieval and early modern periods often celebrated same-sex attraction as a literary pose while at the same time condemning same-sex intercourse. Though Abū Zayd reproaches the judge for letting lust get the better of him, none of the characters seems to think that there is anything bad or even unusual about same-sex attraction. If anything, the text is sympathetic to the judge, and might plausibly be read as a celebration of the homoerotic, or more exactly, of the lan-guage associated with it. Then again, the expression "accused of certain things" (*hanāt*, meaning bad things; see §41.1) suggests that the public found the judge's behavior reprehensible.

Given his appreciative literarization of same-sex desire, it is probably unfair to make al-Ḥarīrī use the expression "ayen kinde," which in Middle English texts unambiguously condemns non-procreative sex of all kinds, including same-sex intercourse (see Dinshaw, *Getting Medieval*, xxiii). If I were writing a history of sexuality, I would not impute to al-Ḥarīrī the view that intercourse, much less attraction, between men was against nature. I wouldn't necessarily deny it, either, as similar views were held by some of his near contemporaries, and believing that a thing is unnatural is of course no good reason to avoid writing about it. The point, in any case, is that there is no single right translation here:

every choice carries historical and ethical baggage. In an initial attempt to blunt the force of "ayen kinde," I proposed "was gay" as a marginal gloss, but several readers rejected it as jarring and anachronistic. In the spirit of al-Ḥarīrī, who commented on several of his own Impostures, I will write "was gay" here, acknowledging that my readers are right, but I would have liked to use it anyway. On the myriad ways in which philological commentary on the *Impostures* has served as a space for debating questions of morality and ethics, see Matthew Keegan, "Commentarial Acts."

In §10.11, the Arabic says "even if what you suffer is as appalling as the loss of al-Ḥusayn was to the Muslims," referring to the massacre of the third Shi'i imam and his family by the Umayyads in 61/680.

BIBLIOGRAPHY

Chaucer, Geoffrey. *The Canterbury Tales*. Edited by Walter Skeat. Oxford: Oxford University Press, 1900. http://en.wikisource.org/wiki/Canterbury_Tales_(ed._Skeat).

———. *The Canterbury Tales*. Edited by A. C. Cawley. New York: Everyman's Library, 1958.

Dinshaw, Carolyn. *Getting Medieval*. Durham, NC: Duke University Press, 1999.

El-Rouayheb, Khaled. *Before Homosexuality in the Arab-Islamic World, 1500–1800*. Chicago: Chicago University Press, 2005.

Fulk, R. D. *Introduction to Middle English: Grammar and Texts*. Toronto: Broadview, 2012.

McSparran, Frances, et al., eds. *Middle English Dictionary*. http://quod.lib.umich.edu/m/med/.

IMPOSTURE 11

SINNERS IN THE HANDS OF
AN ANGRY PREACHER

This Imposture is one of five where Abū Zayd delivers a fire-and-brimstone sermon. As in Impostures 7 and 33, he feigns a disability in order to gain sympathy, provoking al-Ḥārith to reproach him. But he does not go drinking afterward—at least not visibly—as he does in Impostures 1 and 28. The English renderings of al-Ḥārith's narration and Abū Zayd's exhortations in prose are based on the writings of the colonial American revivalist preacher Jonathan Edwards (d. 1758), most famous for his sermon on "Sinners in the Hands of an Angry God." The long poem is a pastiche of the works of the two most prolific English hymnists of the eighteenth century, Isaac Watts (d. 1748) and Charles Wesley (d. 1788).

11.1   *Elhareth Eben Hamam* gave this Account of Himself:

When I removed to *Sawah*, I felt a Stubbornness in my Heart, and sought to soften it, as the *Prophet* bade us do, by a solitary walk in a Burying-place. When I came to the common Golgotha of the City, I saw a Crowd aſſembled to watch a Trench being dug and a Man carried out of this World. Put in Mind anew of the common Fate of Mankind, and of dear Souls departed, I bent my Steps toward the Mourners.

11.2   When the dead Corpse was shut up in his Grave, his earthly Endeavors at an End, lo, there came an aged Man, that ſtood upon a Hill, with a Staff at his Girding-place, and his Face concealed under his Cloak, as if for some Mischief. He cried with a loud Voice:

"'Let it be for *this* that you labor,' not for earthly Things! Let the Careless take heed; let the Indolent beftir themselves; let the Discerning see and tremble. How can a Man look upon the Burying of his Friend, and not think where, and how, and what his own Body will be a few years hence? And even as your Friend could not foresee whether he should ftand one Moment, or fall the next, so too are you *always* exposed to deftruction, as one that ftands in slippery Places is always exposed to fall. Will you not then look a little forward? Even the Fool knows that all former Generations, that used to make as great a Stir in the World as he, are *gone*. How is it then that you see the Tears, and hear the Wailing of the Bereaved, and yet think only of the Eftate left behind? How is it that you bury your Kinsman, yet think only of your Share of his Riches? How do you turn from the Grave, where your Friend muft lie buried in the Ground, his Flesh by Degrees rotting off from his Bones, and return to your Harp and Flute?

"You grieve when a Farthing slips between your Fingers; how then do you regard with Indifference the sudden Demise of your Friend? You tremble at Prospect of Poverty, yet are scarce affected by the Extinction of your Line. Though your Feet ftand on the Brink of the Grave, you make Sport, as if in a Dance; and you exalt Yourselves with an high Look, and a proud Heart, even as you march in the Funeral. You turn aside from the bereaved Mother and piteous Mourners, thinking only of Banquets and Dainties, juft as if you intended to live upon this Earth always, and the dead Man's Fate will not ere long be yours. Do you flatter yourselves that you alone shall escape *Death*? Do you imagine that it will not hale you from all your dear Enjoyments, naked and ftripped of all your earthly good Things? O cursèd Foolishness! 'Hereafter shall ye know *your Folly!*'"

Then he sang: 11.3

> How long wilt thou in Sin remain?
> How long in thine own Wisdom truft?
> How long wilt thou defy His Reign
> And scorn the Wisdom of the Juft?

Shake off the Veil that blinds thy Sight,
And to His Word incline thine Ears;
Behold His Sign: the Shock of White
That mid thy ebon Locks appears!

Hark! There comes the Call of Death,
That bids thee rise, thy Quittance make,
And soon resign this fleeting Breath!
O Sinner, wilt thou not awake?

What avails thy bootlefs Strife,
Thy pompous Strutting to and fro?
What good the spoils of a wafted Life,
When to the Graveyard thou doft go?

Oh, when wilt thou thine Heart subdue?
When wilt thou thine own Fury quell,
And beg GOD form thy Heart anew,
Absolved of Pride, and Wrath, and Hell?

Sinner, thou doft thy LORD despite,
And not one Qualm thy Heart afsails;
But oh! what Cries! what Fright,
Whene'er thy worldly Scheming fails!

In Gold and Silver is thy Delight,
Of worldly Ruin all thy Fear;
Not e'en the Bier—oh woeful Sight!
Doth melt thine Heart, or draw a Tear.

Thy friends for Sin and Satan plead,
Fruits of Deceit they surely bear,
To Hell, not Heaven, their Doctrines lead,
And there the specious Prophets are!

Those Sons of Pride, that hate the Juſt,
And trample heedleſs on the Poor,
When Death has brought them down to Duſt,
Their idle Pomp shall rise no more.

If only thou hadſt not gone aſtray
Nor done the Bidding of thine Eyes;
Thou wouldſt not greet the Preacher's Say
With a tormented Sinner's Cries!

When G OD to Judgment shall descend,
And all are brought before His Throne,
His fellow Man will none defend:
There shall each Mortal ſtand alone.

Can Man redeem one Hour from Death
Or save his Kinsman by his Truſt?
Or give a dying Brother Breath
When G OD commands him down to Duſt?

There the darkened Earth, the dismal Shade
Shall clasp Men's naked Bodies round;
Their Flesh, so delicately fed,
Lies cold and molders in the Ground.

And close behind the Tribulation
Of those laſt tremendous Days,
Will come the Hour of Resurrection
And the Bridge above the fiery Blaze!

What Man, new-risen from the Duſt,
Will boaſt of Learning, Rank, or Blood?
That glorious Day exalts the Juſt
To full Dominion o'er the Proud.

Turn, I cry, ye Sinners, turn!
You have but little Time to live;
Repent, I cry! Or would you burn
When GOD ſtands ready to forgive?

Far from this World I bid you go!
Its gaudy Show is Satan's teſt;
You would as soon, if you did know,
Clutch a Viper to your Breaſt!

See how the Pit gapes wide for you!
Pale Death, with all his ghaſtly Train,
Bids thy Soul look downward too,
And caſt away its heavy Chain.

From Turn of Fortune be not proud,
Or vainglorious of worldly Gain:
Hold your Tongue, leſt it cry aloud
Words that damn to laſting Pain.

Help us help each other, LORD,
Each other's Weal and Woe to share;
Let each his friendly Aid afford
And feel his Brother's loving Care.

Help us to build each other up,
And each his little Stock improve;
Increase our Faith, confirm our Hope,
And perfect us all in selfless Love.

Oh, kindle now the cleansing Fire
That will Shame and Greed outglow,
Burn up the Dross of base Desire,
And let your gen'rous Bounty flow!

Teach your Souls to reach for Good,
Teach them to shrink away from Shame;
Prepare your Ship, and ride the Flood;
And let the Faithless watch, and blame!

My Counsel this I give to thee,
I have now taught thee all I know;
Blessed is the Man who heedeth me
And preacheth he to those below!

Then he drew back his Sleeve and laid bare a brawny Arm faſtened with **11.4**
Splints, bound upon himself to give the Appearance of a broken Bone.
He thus gained the Charity of those present, with such Importunity, that
he wrung out the Pockets of that Assembly and filled up his Sleeves with
Coins. Then he skipped like a Ram from the Hill, rejoicing in his Treasure.

Elhareth continued:

I got me behind him, and seized the Hem of his Garment; whereupon he
turned him meekly about, and gave his Face to me in Greeting; and lo,
it was our aged Maſter, Aboo Zeid, in all his Guile. And I reproved him,
saying:

How long wilt thou live by the Snare
And fleece the Lamb with low Deceit,
Unmoved by those that see thee there
And damn thee for a lying Cheat?

With undisguised Impudence he replied:

Ah, the Damper waxes hot!
But what bold Man in any Land
Would hesitate to take the Pot
When the Game is in his Hand?

I cried: "Get thee behind me, Old Scratch, thou Pack-horse of Infamy! To what shall I compare thee, with thy glitt'ring Surface, and rotten Heart, but to a plaſtered Bog-house, or a gilded Turd?" Whereupon he betook himself to the left Hand, turning his Face to the North, while I betook myself to the right Hand, my face to the South.

NOTES

The English draws freely on all of Edwards's works, with the greatest reliance on "Sinners"; "The Nakedness of Job," another fire-and-brimstone sermon; and *An Account of the Life of Mr. David Brainerd* (1749).

"Sawah" (§11.1): is Sāwah, now called Saveh, a town in Iran, sixty miles southwest of modern Tehran.

The two Qur'anic verses cited in §11.2 (Q Ṣāffāt 37:61 and Takāthur 102:4) are given in the translation by George Sale (d. 1736).

BIBLIOGRAPHY

Edwards, Jonathan. *An Account of the Life of Mr. David Brainerd*. Boston: Henchman, 1749. http://archive.org/details/TheLifeOfDavidBrainerd-1749-1stEdition-ByJonathanEdwards-Complete.

———. *Works of Jonathan Edwards Online*. Digitized by the Jonathan Edwards Center at Yale University. http://edwards.yale.edu/.

Watts, Isaac. Selected hymns online at hymntime.com: http://www.hymntime.com/tch/bio/w/a/t/t/watts_i.htm.

Wesley, Charles. Selected hymns online at hymntime.com: http://www.hymntime.com/tch/bio/w/e/s/wesley_c.htm.

———. Selected hymns at the Wesley Center Online: http://wesley.nnu.edu/charles-wesley/wesley-hymn-collection/.

IMPOSTURE 12

ARABIA ABSURDA

In this Imposture, Abū Zayd first appears in the guise of a holy man. He guides al-Ḥārith and his companions across the desert from Syria to Iraq, teaching them a prayer to keep them safe. The theme of desert travel dictated the model for the English: Charles Doughty's Travels in Arabia Deserta *(1888), which recounts the author's (mis)adventures among the Arabs in a dreadfully earnest and deliberately archaic style that was much admired in its day. Upon arrival, the holy man is transformed into a figure much like Bacchus, the ancient Greek god of revelry. This scene features a drinking song, which Abū Zayd delivers in the style of Charles Swinburne (d. 1909).*

El-Hâreth Ibn Hammâm related:　　　　　　　　　　　　　　　12.1

Envied of my good fortune, being then the possessor of some short-haired horses, *jurd*, I set forth from Irâk, to go down to that district of Damascus called the Ghrûṭa, that abounds with water and trees. The flat of my forearm, where the rider's burden rests, was unencumbered; and my full purse, swollen as a long-bound udder, excited me to levity. When after a forced march that cost our stalwart nâgas their spring fatness, we arrived at the place, I found it to be as men had spoken of it, for therein were delights to fill the eyes and quench the longings of the heart. Now I was grateful for the journey. Free as Heaven's air, I broke open the sealed jars of pleasure, and plucked the fruits of vice; until, recovering my senses, I at last pulled myself from that torrent-bed. Then came news of a departure to Irâk.

Seized now with longing for my native marches, and for my own watering-trough, I struck the tent of Exile and saddled Homeward's mare.

12.2   Soon all who were to set forth had met together in a common place without the city; but we dreaded to adventure ourselves without a *khafîr*, or camel-master, to convey us through the wilderness. We enquired of the clans, and made trial of every expedient, but in vain. Nor did a diligent search of the settlements discover any trace of such a one, as if all *khafîrs* were not merely absent, but dead and buried. Wherefore we assembled, as men confounded, near the *Boábet* (Great Gate) of Jayrûn. Inclined first to depart, then to remain, we tarried long irresolute, some twisting the rope one way and others another; until every murmur died away, and those who had clamoured to set out felt thwarted of their wish.

Standing not far off was a figure stamped with the impress of youth, but clad in the raiment of a monk. In his hand was a rosary, like those carried by women, and upon his face the rubric of the drunkard, *nashwân*. He had tethered his glances to the company and had been straining to overhear our talk. Divining our purpose, and seeing now that we meant to disperse, he hailed us. "Comfort yourselves (said he), and be not dismayed; for I have that which will do your bidding and convey you safe to Irâk."

12.3   *Said the one telling the tale:*

We enquired of this escort, and offered the fellow a liberal fee for his good offices in procuring it. "Your escort (said he) is a mouthful of words taught me in a dream, that I might defend myself of the guile of men!"

Seeing us cast unquiet side-glances, or stare on him and avert our eyes, he perceived that we little regarded his *hijâb*, or protective spell, and thought ourselves deceived. "Eigh!" he cried out, "What aileth you, that ye mock what I tell you in earnest, and esteem of my gold, as dross? Have I not by its power traversed pitiless deserts and courted mortal dangers without need of *khafîr*, or of arms? But come, I will show you, there is nothing to fear, nor any cause of mistrust. I will accompany you through the lands of the Beduw and carry you safely through the Samâwa," the waterless tract between Irâk and Sham, wherein dwell the Thamûd.—"Find ye then my saying sooth, ye may multiply my reward, and increase my fortune; or, if ye find me deceitful, ye may rend my flesh and shed my blood."

El-Hâreth Ibn Hammâm continued his tale: 12.4

Moved to believe him, and to take upon credence his story of a dream-vision, we disputed no more, but cast lots, that he might share a litter with one of the company. Thereafter we permitted no further delay. Putting aside all dread of robbery and molestation, we made fast our girthing-cords; and, the hour of departure come, we asked him to reveal his spell, that we might enter under its protection as long as we rode.

He said: "Let every one of you recite at sunset and at daybreak the Jewel of the Koran. Then let him intone, in humble supplication, this lorica:

> O Ullah, who revives the dead,
> Who averts disaster,
> Who requites His servants,
> Who pardons the penitent,
> God of mercy, God of refuge:

> Bless Muhammad, Your last Prophet and Emissary,
> Bless his radiant Kin,
> Bless his valiant Helpers!

> Protect me from mischievous devils,
> From fickle princes,
> From merciless tyrants,
> From arrogant despots,
> From hostile foes,
> From scheming enemies,
> From swaggering victors,
> From plunderers,
> From plotters,
> From killers.

Shelter me, O Ullah, from encroaching neighbors,
From cruel oppressors.
Turn from me the blows of malice,
Deliver me from the shadow of evil.
Lead me into Your mercy, among Your righteous.

Watch over me when I abide at home,
When I go abroad,
When I am long absent,
When I return,
When I seek sustenance,
When I turn back,
When I wander,
When I depart,
When I waver,
When I part.

Guard my life,
My property,
My honor,
My goods,
My kin,
My furnishings,
My family,
My home,
My strength,
My health,
My death,
My riches.

I bind unto myself today
The power of God to shield me from adversity,
To protect me from assault,
To grant me strength.
I bind upon myself today

God's eye to look before me,
His hand to assist me,
His arm to shelter me,
His bounty to sustain me,
His favor to support me.

O Ullah, leave me not alone,
Give me vigor that fadeth not,
Give me sustenance that faileth not,
Protect me from hardship,
Cover me in mercy,
Blunt the claws of hate,
You, Who hearest every prayer."

Then he cast down his eyes and kept silence, so long forbearing to lift his eyes, that we imagined him overcome by dread, or dumbstruck by some clouding of the mind. At last lifting his head and heaving a long sigh, he said: "I swear upon the spangled heaven, and the clefted earth, and the rushing torrent, and the kindling sun, and the booming sea, and the wind and the dust, that this *hijâb* will more avail ye, than a troop of men in iron caps; rehearse it at daybreak, and you need fear naught, until the sun go down to its setting; whisper it to the dusk, and no thief will come by night."

So we repeated the words until we could recite them, and rehearsed   12.5
them together lest we forget them.

Then we departed, with prayer, not the *khafîr*, to guide us; and incantations, not men-at-arms, to guard our baggage. Evening and morning our companion came forth to the *mejlis*, but asked not, what we would give him at journey's end; until, when we descried afar off the house-tops of *Ânah*, he cried, "What charity? Oh, what charity?"

Whereat we brought forth the goods we had carried openly, and those we had hidden, whether corded in sacks or sealed in our saddle-bags. "Take whatsoever thou wouldst claim of us (we said), for none will gainsay thee."

Of our goods he deemed the greater part too heavy to carry off, and so chose the lightest; as well as gold, of all our offerings the fairest in his eyes. He filled a mule-bag, *wiqrah*, with enough to drive the wolf from his tent.

Then, slippery as quicksilver, and privily as a cut-purse, he stole away, leaving us to wonder, desolate, at his sudden flight. We sought for him at every assembly, enquiring of all alike, of whom some spoke sooth, and others lies; until it was told us, that since his coming into *Ânah*, he had not gone forth from the tavern.

So hateful a report could not be left untried, even if I, who would try it, must needs act contrary to my nature. Disguising myself, I came stealthily by night into the *daskarah*, or wine-hall. There I found the sheykh, wearing a raiment gaily dyed, sitting amidst the amphorae, near a wine-press. About him were goodly cup-bearers, blazing candles, wreaths of myrtle and daffodil, and merrymake of string and flute. Now he cried for a bung to be bored in a jug, and now for the musicants to chant more lustily; now he held a spray of myrtle to his nose, and now cast amorous glances at the pot-boys.

Having exposed his double-dealing, and discovered what a chasm lay between his words one day and his deeds the next, I reproached him, saying, "Beware, accursed one! Rememberest thou not, what thou didst say at Jayrûn?" He laughed to the ears, then recited, as if chanting:

12.6   Through lands that swelter
For lack of shelter
I rode a-skelter
To find my joy;

I urged my horses
Down watercourses,
To where the source is,
A mirthful boy;

My land I deeded,
For what I needed
Had gone unheeded:
Why, 'twas wine!

And all the chanting
You found enchanting?
Why, I was panting
To reach the vine;

I rode beside you
At first to chide you
And then to guide you
To old Irâk;

Now don't you dare me,
You'll never scare me,
So why not spare me
Your rude attack?

We're growing older!
Who wants to molder?
Why not be bolder
And drain the glass?

Whatever ails you
When life assails you,
Wine never fails you,
You silly ass!

Don't hold the hurt in!
This much is certain;
Pull down the curtain,
And feel no shame!

The greatest treasure
Is drunken pleasure
Surpassing measure,
Despising blame!

So shout it loudly,
Proclaim it proudly,
Embrace it madly,
Drink it up!

Forget tomorrow;
If need be, borrow
To drown that sorrow:
Another cup!

And where's it written
You can't be smitten
With that kitten
Tending bar?

Or that musician
Who's on a mission
Against religion
With that guitar?

And if they tell you
'Bout what befell you
The last time, well, you
Can just say no;

But when lovely faces
Are finding places
For quick embraces
Then I say, go!

This counts as living:
First, be forgiving,
And then, keep giving!
That's how to live.

Then quit the table,
And while you're able,
REPENT—'tis no fable:
He will forgive.

"*Bakh bakh!*" I cried, that is, bravo! "for thy verses; but *uff uff*," that   **12.7**
is, *faugh!*— "for thy frowardness! But tell me *billah*, 'by God', from what
thicket is thy root? for thy strangeness hath cast me into a perplexity."

"I mislike (he said) to name myself outright, but I will give thee a
by-name:

The Rarity of the Age
Is among Arabs and Persians all the rage:
Their minds boggle
At his hornswoggle.

But the Marvel of All Nations
Despite numerous instantiations,
Has been chewed up and spat out by life,
Much to the distress of his ill-fed children and his ill-kept wife."

Said El-Hâreth: **12.8**

Then it was as if a new voice had hailed me of an old friend, for I recognized
Abu Zeyd, πολύτροπον, of many wiles, bringer of shame upon the hoary-
bearded. It pained me to see him so far fallen into impudence and outrage.
I thus addressed him in a haughty familiar manner, saying, "Has the time
not come, o sheykh, to renounce abomination?" Whereat he was vexed,
and growled at me; his countenance changed, and he thought a while, and
then he said, "This is a night for merriment, not sorrow; an occasion to
drink, not to quarrel. So put this behind us till we meet again tomorrow."
But I took my leave of him, for I had no faith in his promises, and dreaded
his drunken contumely.

I spent that night wrapped in the mourning-cloak of remorse, for having
betaken myself to a toping-place and not some house of good repute; and I

swore before God a mighty oath, that were I offered even the Seat of Baghdad, I should not enter a wine-shop; nor lay eyes on a wine-press, even if I were given again the days of youth. Come the last darkness of night, we saddled our roan-white camels, leaving those two old friends, Abu Zayd and the Devil, to shift for themselves.

GLOSSARY

12.1

nâga   female camel

12.2

Jayrûn   the eastern gate of the Umayyad mosque

12.5

mejlis   gathering   *daskara*   wine hall

NOTES

When necessary, the English draws on the language of Lane's *Lexicon* and Chenery's *Assemblies*, as both authors were contemporaries of Doughty. "Excited me to levity" (§12.1), for example, comes from Lane's definition of the verb *izdahā*. "Mischievous devils" (§12.4) is based on a phrase in Chenery, *Assemblies*, 171; and "From what thicket is thy root?" (§12.7) comes from Chenery, *Assemblies*, 174.

The Ghūṭah (spelled "Ghrûṭa" by Doughty; §12.1) is a fertile region to the south and east of Damascus. The usual route from there to Iraq would have cut through the Syrian desert to al-Qaryatayn and Palmyra, crossed the Euphrates at Deir ez-Zur or a point south of there, and then followed the river down to the town of ʿĀnah in Iraq. In §12.3, however, Abū Zayd speaks of going to Samāwah, a region much farther south, no doubt because the name lends itself to an apt rhyme. Al-Sharīshī, who lived in far-off Spain, identifies Samāwah vaguely as "a wilderness between Syria and Iraq" (*Sharḥ*, 2:46). Even so, his description of it is so like something Doughty might say that I could not resist putting it into the text, phrasing it as Doughty might have.

The "Jewel" (literally "mother") "of the Koran" (§12.4) is the Fatihah or opening chapter. A lorica is a prayer for protection. The English rendering of Abū Zayd's prayer imitates the Lorica of St. Patrick, distinctive for its pattern of anaphora, that is, the repetition of words at the beginning of successive lines.

It has been set to music as "I Bind unto Myself Today." A version billed as "a literal translation from the old Irish text" appears in Moran, "Saint Patrick." "Ullah" is Doughty's spelling of Allah; though nonstandard, it accurately reflects the dark-L sound in this word.

Doughty calls the "mejlis" (§12.5) "the congregation or parliament of the tribesmen" (*Travels*, 1:248). The "daskarah" is defined by Lane as "a sort of *qaṣr* [that is, a walled compound], surrounded by houses, or chambers, in which the vitious, or immoral (*shuṭṭār*), assemble." The term can also indicate "houses of the foreigners (*a'ājim*) in which are wine and instruments of music or the like"). "Wine-hall" comes from Chenery, *Assemblies*, 173.

The original poem in §12.6 has the rhyme scheme AAAB, which is unusual in Arabic. In their translations, al-Ḥarīzī, Rückert, and Dolinina-Borisov all manage to replicate the form. This is harder to do in English, but a model does exist: Algernon Charles Swinburne's "Before Dawn," on which see Eberhard, "Swinburne 7776." My imitation removes one foot from each line in the hope of achieving something closer to the rollicking effect of the Arabic. Each of the two poems in §12.7 is a clerihew, a comical form invented by Edmund Clerihew Bentley (d. 1956). It consists of four irregular lines, of which the first is the subject's name.

"A new voice," etc. is based on Doughty, *Travels*, 1:1. In imitation of Doughty's penchant for inserting Greek (see, e.g., *Travels*, 1:12, 135, 362), I have translated *dhū l-rayb wa l-'ayb* as πολύτροπον, "much turned, much travelled, much wandering," as well as "shifty, versatile, wily" (Liddell and Scott, *A Greek English Lexicon*), or, as Emily Wilson suggests, "complicated" (Homer, *Odyssey*, tr. Wilson, 105). The term is used by Homer to describe Odysseus (Homer, *Odyssey*, 1.1) but applies equally well to Abū Zayd.

BIBLIOGRAPHY

"Clerihew." Wikipedia. http://en.wikipedia.org/wiki/Clerihew.

Doughty, Charles M. *Travels in Arabia Deserta*. London: Warner, 1921. First published 1888.

Eberhard, Laurence. "Swinburne 7776." Poets Collective. http://poetscollective.org/poetryforms/tag/aaabcccb/.

Homer. *The Odyssey*. Translated by A. T. Murray. 2 vols. Cambridge, MA: Harvard University Press; London: William Heinemann, 1919. http://www.

perseus.tufts.edu/hopper/text?doc=Perseus:abo:tlg,0012,002:1:1&lang
=original.

———. *The Odyssey*. Translated by Emily Wilson. New York: Norton, 2018.

Liddell, Henry George, and Robert Scott. *An Intermediate Greek English Lexi-con*. Oxford, 1959.

Moran, Patrick Francis Cardinal. "St. Patrick." In *The Catholic Encyclopedia*, vol. 11. New York: Robert Appleton Company, 1911. http://www.newad-vent.org/cathen/11554a.htm.

[Patrick, Saint, attr.]. "I Bind unto Myself Today." Translated by Cecil Frances Alexander. http://hymnary.org/text/i_bind_unto_myself_today.

———. "Lorica of Saint Patrick." http://www.ewtn.com/Devotionals/prayers/patrick.htm.

Swinburne, Algernon Charles. "Before Dawn." In *Poems and Ballads* (1866). http://www.bartleby.com/334/453.html.

IMPOSTURE 13

THE COZENING QUEAN OF BABYLON

This Imposture features Abū Zayd (here called Abbot Sandys) dressed as an old woman. It calls to mind The Merry Wives of Windsor, *where Falstaff dresses as the old woman of Brentford (also called the "cozening quean"), as well as other Shakespeare plays in which women dress as men, including* Two Gentlemen of Verona, Twelfth Night, *and* The Merchant of Venice. *As in Imposture 9, the story is recast as a play.*

DRAMATIS PERSONAE

Harry Ben Hamnet   *Poets*
An Old Woman   *Children*
Abbot Sandys of Saruj

ACT I

A garden. Enter HARRY BEN HAMNET *and* POETS. *The* POETS *sit.* **13.1**

HARRY: Once I sat on sun-bright Babel's shore
   And heard nine rhymers, sweetly as a lark,
   Utter such dulcet and harmonious breath
   That the rude Tigris grew civil at their song,
   And the dewy musk-roses and eglantine
   Did bow their loaden heads abash'd.

(Enter OLD WOMAN *and* CHILDREN.*)*

At length the noontide sun bedimm'd their wit
And all their vapours at its zenith dried,
And ev'ry man had hied him home to bed
Had not there assail'd our company
An old woman, carried before the wind
With speed, and in her rude and ragged train,
Her chicks, bare-boned, spare-shanked lean-Jacks all.
Seeing us, she bent the steerage of her course,
And once beside hailed us with fair speech.

13.2　OLD WOMAN:　How now, my good lords! What your names are, I know not, but there is goodness in your faces, and hope of cheer and comfort. Know, most noble sirs, I am daughter to a line of kings. My husband and my nears't of kin drew the gallant head of war, their hearts more hunter than hunted, like unback'd colts, their exploits in hand; but alas! their necks did yield to fortune's yoke, a curse did light upon their limbs, and all the body members rebel against the belly. They live no more in men's eyes nor run upon their tongues, their bows are broken, they are uncrown'd, lash'ed with woe, led by the nose, at their butt-end, out of joint, and out at heels. Sicklied o'er with a green and yellow cast are faces that once waxed red with mirth, or beaten black and blue, that you cannot see a white spot about them. Behind me, sirs, behold my chicks, whose sunken eyes confess their hard distress. They crave no more than a thin gruel and a cloak upon them as cover to their bones. Marry, I did vow on pain of death not to unfold my misfortune to any but a noble lord. But the very instant that I saw you, did my heart whisper me: Be not dismay'd, for if there be truth in sight, succour is at hand; and in those generous bosoms hath no niggard strain set foot. O prove true! and blessed be him who first makes substance of surmise.

13.3　FIRST POET:　A mellifluous voice, as I am true poet.
　　　　SECOND POET:　And most fine figures, i'faith.

THIRD POET: Widow, we will consider of your suit. Thy speech sticks in the heart. But hast thou no staff, no stanze, no verse?

OLD WOMAN: I have verses too, to crack and split the gutter'd rocks. It is no boast, being ask'd, to say I have.

HARRY: Make us the bearers of thy torch, that we may requite thee by making rich yourself.

OLD WOMAN: I will draw the curtain and show you the picture. Then will I give you leave my poesy to disperse. *(Extends a hand from her ravel'd sleeve, and lifts up her veil, revealing the countenance of a withered hag. Sings:)*

In me behold, by Fate's malignant pow'r,
The injury of many a blasting hour.
Undone by goodness! Strange, unusual blood,
When man's worst sin is he does too much good!
My kinsmen's bounty was not made for store:
An autumn 'twas, that by reaping grew the more.
Of their abundance all did share a part;
Better cheer had none, nor better heart.
Such a house of gentle and unforc'd accord
Fall'n! and in his grave my gen'rous lord!
Who then dares to be half so kind again?
For bounty, that makes kings, does still mar men.
Now I alone beweep my outcast state,
And look upon myself and curse my fate.
But for these mewling babes that I do nurse
None should compel me tell my shame in verse.
One hope have I: 'tis, dear God, in thee:
Wherever sorrow is, relief would be.

FIRST POET: O, this is full of pity!   13.4

SECOND POET *(giving her money)*: There's gold for thee.

THIRD POET *(to the* SECOND POET*)*: I see a good amendment of life in thee: from purse-taking to purse-giving!

FOURTH POET: Hold, widow, here's my purse.

FIFTH POET: Hold, here is forty ducats.

SIXTH POET: Hold, here's half my coffer.

(The POETS *give her coins. She puts them into her sleeve.)*

OLD WOMAN: O, take a mother's thanks, a widow's thanks!

(Exit, followed by CHILDREN.*)*

FIRST POET *(throwing his eyes after her)*:   What a strange case was that!

SECOND POET: I would know more of her.

THIRD POET: I would know whether the sums we did disburse be spent on them that well deserve a help, for I fear this widow doth make mock of us.

FOURTH POET *(to* HARRY*)*:   Son, I say, follow the hag.

FIFTH POET: Seek her out, we pray you.

SIXTH POET: Pursue her, sirrah! Go after.

HARRY: I'll follow, sirs. *(Exit)*

ACT II

13.5   *The garden, evening. The* POETS *are seated. Enter* HARRY.

FIRST POET: How now! what news of the widow?

HARRY: I followed her, good sirs, to a market-place. What a multitude was there! She leapt into the angry flood, and I plunged in after. As I buffeted the torrent, she fetched a slippery turn; and, leaving those beggar's brats bobbing on the wave, slid into an unpeopled mosque hard by. I stood at the door and gazed upon her unseen through the gap, to behold what prodigies she should bring forth. She doffed her cloak and threw her veil aside, and mark what object did present itself: the face of Abbot Sandys! I would have rushed and seized him, and rebuked him for his outrage; but then, like one infused with self and vain conceit, he lay upon the ground and sang an anthem.

(Darkness. ABBOT SANDYS, *dressed like the* OLD WOMAN, *is revealed lying on the ground.)*

ABBOT SANDYS: Lord, what fools these mortals be!
　　Do none in all the world but I
　　Own such false dissembling guile?
　　No motion tends to vice in man
　　But I affirm it mine: flattering, mine;
　　Craft, mine; deceitful cunning, mine!
　　I gull by gins, by snares, by subtlety
　　By manly voice, by woman's tears, all feigned!
　　Dispute it not with me: 'tis my vocation.
　　Were I an honest man, to mine own self
　　Would I be false, and traitor to my purse.

(Darkness. A pause. Lights. ABBOT SANDYS *is gone.)*

HARRY: Discovering his audacious wickedness, and seeing how he did   13.6
　　clothe his naked villainy with the magic robe of poesy, I bethought
　　myself that such a contumelious devil would hear no chiding, and
　　would do only as he would. And so I am returned to you with the true
　　avouch of mine own eyes. I am sorry the news is tart.
FIRST POET: O my ducats!
SECOND POET: I shall never see my gold again!
THIRD POET: Widow! a pox o' that! How came that "widow" in?
FOURTH POET: Let us make a solemn vow—
FIFTH POET: —never more to give a purse—
SIXTH POET: —to unnatural hags, that beg in verse!

NOTES

"Harry": in addition to Hal, a nickname of Henry IV's. "Hamnet" is Shakespeare's son, who died in 1596 at the age of eleven. Richard Wheeler links his death to the flurry of cross-dressing in Shakespeare's subsequent plays, which, he suggests, arose from "a father's fantasy of transforming the surviving daughter"—

Hamnet's twin, Judith (d. 1662)—"into the lost son" (Wheeler, "Deaths," 146). The name "Abbot Sandys" combines parts of two Shakespearean names: the Abbot of Westminster, a character in *Richard II*, and Lord Sandys, pronounced *sands*, from *Henry VIII*. "Mosque" (§13.4) is not used in Shakespeare, but it is attested in the seventeenth century.

In §13.2, the old woman uses a long series of words for body parts and color terms in their extended sense: e.g., "the heart of an army" for its center, and "red death" meaning death by violence. The literary scholar Khalīl ibn Aybak al-Ṣafadī (d. 764/1363) described this passage as "intoxicating" (see Keegan, "Commentarial Acts," 20), evidently because of the rapid-fire sequence of idioms that otherwise would not appear together. The English puts together body-part and color idioms from Shakespeare.

BIBLIOGRAPHY

NS = Norton Shakespeare

Branagh, Kenneth, dir. *Twelfth Night*. Thames Television, 1988.

Coleman, Basil, dir. *As You Like It*. BBC, 1978.

Radford, Michael, dir. *The Merchant of Venice*. Sony Pictures Classics, 2004.

Shakespeare, William. *Project Gutenberg EBook of The Complete Works of William Shakespeare*. http://www.gutenberg.org/cache/epub/100/pg100-images.html.

———. *Twelfth Night*. Edited by Cedric Watts. Ware: Wordsworth, 1993.

Shakespeare, William et al. *The Norton Shakespeare*. New York: W. W. Norton & Company, 2015.

Wheeler, Richard P. "Deaths in the Family: The Loss of a Son and the Rise of Shakespearean Comedy." *Shakespeare Quarterly* 51, no. 2 (Summer 2000): 127–53.

IMPOSTURE 14

SCOT FREE

"This assembly," says Chenery, "has little that is remarkable"
(Assemblies, 181). At the level of plot, admittedly, not much
happens, and the episode may be one of the earlier ones in which
al-Ḥarīrī was still teaching himself the form. Its most striking fea-
ture is the poem in which Abū Zayd's son demands, among other
things, roast meat and pudding. As these items bring to mind
Robert Burns's comic masterpiece "Address to a Haggis" (1786),
Zayd (who is not actually named) will take Burns as a model
for his English version. Inspired by the choice of Scottish Eng-
lish, Abū Zayd (who, unusually, is not named either) will recast
the first of his two poems in the style of Walter Scott's "Lay of
the Last Minstrel" (1805), and make the second a riff on Burns's
"Auld Lang Syne." In keeping with the theme, al-Ḥārith (here
called Plewman MacHamish) will narrate in the Scots-inflected
English of poet and novelist James Hogg (d. 1835). The entire text
was corrected and improved by James E. Montgomery.

Plewman MacHamish ha' a tale to tell ye: 14.1

Now, maisters, I had gaen awa' to Auld Roolie, thence to pass in pilgrimage. Efter a bonny week's wark on't, and comin' to look like a right clarty
stook o' dirt, I had ta'en the bath an' I was glaggerin' for a bit moost an'
a hearty touzle. But or it was lang, a simmer scaud o' heat scomfish't the
gaithering at Lach Ayf. It growed sae switherin' at the none that I was gar't
to set a leddern tent as a bield.

I was sitten in the scug wi' some knackie billies, the mowrie bein' hot as a girdle an' the simmer-cowts fit to blind an adder's een, when a doddle-trottin' auld carle up-startid on us wi' a ramlin' bairn behind him. He hadna weel hailed us an' begun to speak till I kent he was a buikman, and menseful too: he spake as if he kent us, an' we stranged to see how shod he was i' the gab.

14.2   "Whit are ye," we asked, "and whit the de'il are ye aifter, comin' on without speerin' the leave ae us?"

"As for whit I am," he said, "I'm a poor, needful man, an' my wae is as plain as bumbees: why, take a look o' me! And as for up-startin' on ye, it's nae ferlie: the door o' the weel-hartit aye stands wide to the wall."

"But o' a' the cots in the field, what brang ye 'pon ours?"

"Faith," quoth he, "gentie fowk have a fragrance wha' blaws like the scent o' roses in simmer air. Whan I snuffed an' snoked the snift o' ye, I kenned it, an' followed the flewer to the flower. Being full o' freits, I took the smell as sonsy; and sae here I am askin' if there's any good in yer mind the day, sirs!"

We bid him tell us what he wad hae, sae we might help him.

"I hae ane request," quoth he, "and my sin has anither."

"Consider baith granted," we said. "But let the callan bide gin his alders be sairt."

14.3   "I shall speak, maisters," said the auld carle, "as weel as I can, God guide me!" Then, leapin' up like a collie efter a fox, he scroftit aff thir verses:

> Remark, good sirs, my weary pace,
> My heavy sighs, and tear-stained face;
> The way is long, the path is bleak,
> I am a man infirm and weak;
> A wand'ring poet, scorned and poor,
> I beg my bread from door to door;
> My palfrey gone, my feet astray,
> I friendless fear to lose my way.
> But now with wishful eye I gaze
> On fields where warriors come to graze,
> Where humble serf and doughty chief

From war and famine seek relief,
Where Plenty suffers raid on raid
While Honor looks on undismayed.
If you had starved, or suffered thirst,
Like mine, your noble heart would burst,
And you would grant my boon anon:
A camel strong, to ride upon!
If I retold my pedigree,
Though fallen low the wretch you see,
You would not doubt that my distress
Was suckled at the Muse's breast:
A patron poor is poesy;
I wish my sire ne'er taught it me.

"It's plain as parritch," we said, "that the weary widdle's gien ye muckle   **14.4**
grief and trouble. Guidman, you shall have the price of your hame-gaun!
An' the bairn: wha' will he speer?"

"On your feete, lad," said the auld man, "an' tell the fowk plainly what
ye're seekin'."

The callan stertit up as he were tossin' a caber, and with a tongue like a
braidsword yerkit oot thir verses:

Fair fa' ye, lairds of noble bluid,
Whose castle aye a refuge stood
In time o' need, to a' that's guid,
   An' aye was rife wi' routh;
I beg a drink an' a bite o' fuid
   To stench a chapman's drowth.

Let a roast the trencher fill,
Its hurdies like a distant hill,
An' a pan-loaf from the mill
   Baked wi' speed,
An' a puddin', whose hinnie grains distil
   Like amber bead.

An sich be dear, gie a bannock
Wi' mutton keekin' through the winnock,
Or dooker-soup thick as the Greenock,
    Or a creshie date,
Or scrocken meat-scran frae old Tinnock's
    Sittin' on a plate.

Kind-hairted sirs, make me yur care,
And dish me oot my bill of fare,
For ye hae muckle an' to spare,
    Afore we maun depairt
An' I'll gie the gratefu' prayer
    Of a skempie's hairt.

14.5 *MacHamish gaed on wi' his tale:*

Whan we saw the pup took aifter the dug, we set the father to the road an'
scuttled vivers for the bairn. Baith thanked us trimly an' blessed our baines.
Then, as they were tursin' their bundles an' settin' to the gait, I askit the
auld carle if he thought us warld's-worms, or if he had cause to tarrow at
the laggen they hae clautet full clean that day.

"Nae, God forbid! I thank ye for your kindness to me and mine."

"Then, guidman, do us wan in return, and tell us plainly, for we are
stoundit at ye: where dae ye come frae?"

He hove a sigh as one whose hairt is still at hame. Then he sang thir
verses, wi' sobs slidderin' his tongue:

Should auld acquaintance be forgot
And never brought to mind?
Should auld Saruj-toun be forgot
And auld lang syne?

Wi' fire an' sword aroun' the braes
Came my faemen, and thine;
Alas, how chang'd the times to come
Sin' auld lang syne...

An' wi' that the tear-blobs filled his e'en. He dinna like to skiff them, but couldna keep them frae tricklin' doon owre his cheek; so he sang his sweet strain nae mair, but bid us a dockit guid bye, an' fitched awa'.

GLOSSARY

14.1

Plewman plowman (what al-Ḥārith's name means)

gaen awa' gone away

Auld Roolie Baghdad (my invention)

clarty dirty, muddy, sticky

stook o' dirt dirty, unwashed person

glagger for desire avidly

a bit moost a bit of musk

touzle intercourse

or it was lang before long

simmer summer

scaud o' heat period of hot sunshine

scomfish't overcame (with heat)

gaithering gathering

sae so

swither be very hot, parch, swelter

the none midday

gar't forced

leddern of leather

14.2

wae woe

plain as bumbees obvious

nae ferlie no wonder

bield shelter

scug shade, shelter, concealment

knackie lively and pleasant in conversation

billie comrade

mowrie gravel mixed with sand

girdle griddle

simmer-cowts the quivering of the air on a hot day

doddle-trot the rapid, short-step walk of an old person

auld carle old man

up-start intrude

ramlin' fast-growing, tall, lanky

bairn child

kent knew, recognized

buikman scholar

menseful well-mannered, respectable

speering the leave asking permission

weel-hartit generous

aye stands wide to the wall is always wide open

gentie fowk   noble people

snuffed   sniffed

snoke   sniff out

flewer   odor

full o' freits   superstitious

sonsy   well-omened

Is there any good, etc.   a question
asked by beggars

14.3

loup   leaped

scrofted aff   rattled off

14.4

weary widdle   "toilsome contest of
life" (Burns)

gien   given

muckle   much

hame-gaun   journey home

braid   broad

yerk oot   rattle off

bluid   blood

routh   plenty, abundance

fuid   food

stench   allay

14.5

set to the road   prepare for a journey

scuttle   serve on a plate, dish up

vivers   provisions or refreshments

turse   pack

set to the gait   set off on a journey

warld's-worm   miser

tarrow   "murmur at one's allowance"
(Burns)

laggen   "the angle between the side
and bottom of a wooden dish"
(Burns)

wad hae   would have

ane   one

sin   son

*let the callan bide gin his alders be
sairt*   let the boy wait until his
elders are served

thir   these

slidder   slur one's words in speaking

chapman's drowth   a demand for food
and drink

hurdies   buttocks

hinnied   honeyed

keek   peep

winnock   window

dooker   bread dipped in soup

creshie   greasy

scrocken   shrunk by drying

scran   scrap of food

skempie   little rascal

claut   scrape

hame   home

slidder   cause to slip or slide

auld lang syne   times long ago

brae   hill

faemen   enemies

skiff   brush away

dockit   clipped, testy

fitch awa'   be off, depart

NOTES

Indispensable to the Hibernization of this Imposture was the splendid *Diction-ary of the Scots Language*, specifically the *Scottish National Dictionary* (SND), which covers the period after 1700. The definitions in the notes come from SND unless otherwise indicated. I have mostly adopted the first spelling given in the headword, though I have sometimes used one of the variants if it seemed easier to read. The other source repeatedly cited is the glossary appended to Allan Cunningham's 1855 edition of Burns's *Collected Works*, pp. 531–42. I am uncertain whether it is the editor's work or the poet's, but the whimsy of the definitions suggests the latter; I have therefore marked citations from it by "Burns" in the Glossary. (I am sorry not to have been able to use *skelpi-limmer*, defined as "a technical term in female scolding," or *drimmer*, defined as "the motion of one who tries to dance but moves the middle only.")

"Auld Roolie" (§14.1), literally "old peaceful," translates *madīnat al-salām*, literally "salvation city," the official name of Baghdad. This ad hoc coinage is modeled on "Auld Reeky" (Old Smoky), a nickname of Edinburgh. "Touzle," fully defined as "rough dalliance with one of the opposite sex," translates *rafath*, the permitted return to sexual activity after the pilgrimage. "Scomfish," meaning to overcome with heat, may be related to the nineteenth-century New York rogue's term *stamfishing* (see Imposture 7, Introduction). "Lach Ayf" is my Hibernization of al-Khayf, a mosque in Mina, near Mecca, visited by pilgrims because the Prophet reportedly prayed there.

In §14.4, a caber is a long, heavy pole, usually made of a pine or fir tree; especially in the phrase "to toss the caber": to throw such a pole so that it lands on the thicker end and falls away from the thrower, a contest in Highland games. A pan-loaf is "a loaf baked in a pan or tin having a hard smooth crust," more expensive than a plain loaf; and a bannock is "a round, flat, thickish cake of oatmeal, barley, pease or flour" baked on a griddle. Greenock the river is mentioned in Burns's "Brigs of Ayr" (*CW*, 139), and Greenock the town is mentioned many times in his works (e.g., *CW*, 368).

In §14.5, "bless your baines" is "a wish or prayer for comfort and prosperity to the party addressed, or a promise of future benefits in return for present favour or aid." The phrase "hairt is still at hame" comes from Burns, "Jockey's Ta'en the Parting Kiss," in *CW*, 260. Tinnock's is a tavern mentioned by Burns in "Parody on Milton" (CW, 109). "The laggen they hae clautet full clean" comes from Burns, "A Dream," in *CW*, 132.

BIBLIOGRAPHY

[Burns, Robert]. *The Complete Works of Robert Burns: Containing His Poems, Songs, and Correspondence. With a New Life of the Poet, and Notices, Critical and Biographical by Allan Cunningham*. Boston: Philips, Samson, 1858. Internet Archive, http://archive.org/details/completeworksofr07burn; Project Gutenberg, http://www.gutenberg.org/files/18500/18500.txt. Page references are to the Gutenberg text.

Dictionary of the Scots Language. http://www.dsl.ac.uk/.

Hogg, James. The *Brownie of Bodsbeck, and Other Tales*. Edinburgh: Ballantine, 1818. Vol. 1 at http://archive.org/details/brownieofbodsbec01hogg and http://www.gutenberg.org/files/40955/40955.txt. Vol. 2 at http://archive.org/details/brownieofbodsbec01hogg and http://www.gutenberg.org/files/41796/41796.txt.

MacFayden, Harry. "Address tae the Haggis." At page entitled "Robert Burns—Salute the Haggis." http://www.youtube.com/watch?v=qfYFAA4drG4.

MacLean, Dougie. "Auld Lang Syne." Tribute. Dunkeld Records, 1995.

Scott, Walter. *The Lay of the Last Minstrel*. Originally published 1805. http://en.wikisource.org/wiki/The_Lay_of_the_Last_Minstrel.

Grant, William, and David Murison, eds. *The Scottish National Dictionary*. http://dsl.ac.uk/.

IMPOSTURE 15

HOBSON'S CHOICE

In this episode, Abū Zayd is challenged with a question about how to calculate an inheritance. The Qur'an specifies how estates are to be divided among surviving family members (Q Nisā' 4:11–12 and 176), but since the bequests are explained proportionally based on who the surviving heirs are (e.g., twice as much to sons as to daughters) or fractionally (e.g., a sixth to each parent, if there are grandchildren), the actual amounts have to be calculated in each case. Such calculations could be quite complex, and being able to perform them quickly counted as evidence for superior brainpower. On first reading, this Imposture, with its inheritance puzzle, seemed to promise an algebraic calculation. Because India was celebrated by pre-modern Muslims as the home of higher mathematics, Abū Zayd uses a jocular literary register of early-twentieth-century Indian English for the translation. As it turns out, though, the puzzle requires lateral thinking, not math. The Indian English draft was revised by Shawkat M. Toorawa.

Al-Haaris ibne Hammaam recounted:

One night-time, with pitch-dark sky and so much of rain, my goodself is trouble with Insomnia worse than grief that seizes amorous Youth when dismiss from beloved Door and spurn by nears and dears. I am in deplorable state also. My melancholic Spirits sinking to such low ebbing, and my heart so much trouble, I express fervent Wish that some Pundit appear and make time pass with his talkings. Just I am making the wish and not yet closing eyes for sleep when one Person knocking on door and hailing in loud-loud Voice. Think to myself, "So little time I did wait in the wings, and behold, my wish is granting!" Then I am rising with utmost dispatch and asking, "Who it is knocking this Hour only?"

"A pardesi overtaken by Night," return the Voice, "drenched from top to toe, and begging the favor of Lodging. Myself fully prepared to quit same next early morning."

15.2   This beam of Eloquence keep me in no doubt of his Sun, as title of Book is ballyhooing its Contents. I am realizing what a precious boon should be night-talking with such fellow and how preferable his discourse than sleep. With smilings I am opening door and quoting verse "Enter ye here in peace!"

Chap who step in, he is bent over as if too heavy burden on back, and wet-wet all through. "Wishing your good self the pink of health!" he is telling, in clear and mellifluous tone. "Grateful for prompt reply to knocking. Please excuse inopportune timing for making nuisance."

With lighted lamp I am approaching him with utmost scrutiny when am seeing by Jove! it is my pir Aboo Zaitt! With so much of reverence I place him in position of honour for obliging urgent request and granting so fervent wish after many despairings. He is complaining of drooping and languishing spirit and I am inquiring from where and how he is reaching. "Kindly let me wet my throat," he is telling, "for long walking has tested my mettle to the uttermost."

Myself am thinking that he is troubled by an emptiness of belly, and so therefore afflicted by low tone of health and lack of Vigour. Accordingly I am bringing him such Refreshments as are providing to unexpected guest at darkest Night. But he is refusing all Nourishments like one whose belly is too much swelling with Foodstuff. Naturally I am believing is a very shame-shame business and having suspicion of his fellow Feeling. I am nearly ballyragging him for rascally chap and telling him a shocking when he perceiving my very Thought and reading my Design.

"I think so, you are misgiving me," he is saying. "Not eating is there. But with respect to this is concerned you must trust your friend. I tell, you listen."

"'I tell, you listen'? Then please to tell, nonsense fellow!"

"Yesterday only," he is saying, "I am prey to nettlesome thoughts, having 15.3 no cash in the wallet. When at last the night sloughs off its mortal boil, so to say, and morning sink its stars, I go at dawn hour to the bazaar, hoping for easy mark to come along, or open-hearted high-caste to offer one square meal hospitality.

"There in market itself I see first-class stacking of Dates, summered in best of all Groves, showing Purity of Nectar and Ruddiness like Cornelian. Opposite same was a golden Custard of Biestings of an appetizing Saffron colour, its Perfection doing honour to the bavarchee who stir it and likewise to any who should purchase same, even at high price of throbbing Heart. So I fall direct into snare of Hunger and stand helpless in toils of Craving for creamy Repast. I am at loss, like dazzled Lizard, and besotted as amorous Youth, because lacking monetary Fundament for obtention of Desire and speedy devouring of same. Meanwhile unwilling to depart also, on account of gnawing Emptiness of Belly. Head now eating circles because of Famine and Privation, I am scouring every Nook and Cranny of Market for source of Sustenance, but all Rivulets are so much dry that Pail of Hope returns empty from Well. All the daylong I am scraping and seeking but not obtaining any Consideration from any Body. By the Hour of Sunset, despite afflicted by Vertigo, Esurience, and Inflammation of Liver, am yet foot-dragging from one Place to other.

"Then while I am hesitating between taking Repose and again walking 15.4 to and fro to and fro, I am seeing old Gentleman approaching, heaving great Sighings and weeping like bereave Lady. Myself have not too much push and posh gone out of me to neglect Opportunity now to learn his Cause of Grief and seek Pretext to offer Service.

"'O Uncle,' I say, 'surely your Tears are for some Reason flowing, and your vital Energies because of some Misfortune churning into Incandescence. If so kindly divulging same, your humble Servant is offering wholesome Advice and proposing efficacious Course of Treatment.'

"'Myself am most assuredly, by God,' said he, 'not afflicted by Recollections of former Life, or Memories of pleasant By-gones. On contrary I am lachrymose because of low Estate to which Scholarship and Learning is falling. Lo and behold: the Suns and Moons of punditry are swallow up by Darkness!'

"'And what Catastrophe is transpire to provoke these Sighings and Grievings?'

"The Gentleman reach into Sleeve and produce therefrom one Chit. Then he swear a great Oath that he was showing the same to all most learned Gurus, Swamis, and Pandits but all were staying silent-silent and making no more answer than Boulder or Tomb.

"'Let me take a dekho,' I say. 'Inspiration may strike hard blow."

"'Does no harm to shoot,' he say. 'Beginner luck, why not?'

"I take the Chit and read:

> A pious Mussulman is dead
> Leaving one full brother,
> Leaving also a Mussulman wife,
> Who has her very own brother.
>
> The wife takes her allotted share,
> Her brother takes the rest,
> And for the dead man's consanguiner
> No share at all is left!
>
> How, wise scholar, can this be?
> Is someone here a crook?
> Many before have racked their brains
> And told me only zook!

15.5 "As I am reading the Verses I am perceiving the Chicanery. So I tell, 'You are boxing with an Expert and stepping over a Giant. Yet one Impediment is there: I am too Starving, and Supper is my most needy Choice. Accordingly, I propose that your goodself possibly and desireably do the Needful before hearing my Futwah.'

"'Not excessive Price,' he says, 'within Bounds of Reason, I think so. Come come come! my Dwelling is here only. There please to take your Repast, afterward repairing here, no jiggery-pokery!'

Aboo Zaitt is continuing story:

"So I accompany him to Dwelling, which was Hut cramped as Coffin. But his princely Gesture make Redress for incommodious Abode, for he offer to purchase any tasty Tiffin I am fancying. 'Uncle,' I tell him, 'do one thing. Give me splendid Rider who lies upon that mouth-watering Palanquin; or that wholesome Sitter upon a noxious Bed.'

"After chewing over for long time chap says, 'You mean produce of *Phoenix dactilifera*, or Date Palm, and Colostrum of *Ovis aries*, or Common Sheep!'

"'That pair itself I mean,' I cry, 'for they are Object of my Toil and Cause of my Affliction only!'

"Uncle just scrambling to the feet when suddenly he stop and give me angry eye. 'Beware beware!' he say. 'Speaking truth is conduct of gentleman, telling fib is vile vile. You must take care hunger—prophets and begging monks priceless virtue—not make you feeling free of all moral inhibitories and adopting conduct of riff-raffs. Think of high-caste ladies, who are gladly suffering belly-pangs instead of allowing a misconduct and going into ditch of degradation. I am not your easy mark also: I am absolutely refusing to pay for goods not received. So now I am warning, before exposing your disgraceful, or making any quarrel: beware not heeding last and final warning and making so much tragic blunder!'   15.6

"'By Deity itself who forbid usury,' I am answering, 'and permit eating of Custard, I was speaking only in most truthful and veridical sense. Don't refuse to believe until you try. As follows you will not regret expenditure on Date and Dessert.'

"When this he hear he is relenting and running level best back to bazaar. In a jiffy he is coming back, scowling and lurching under heavy load. Then he is slapping down food as if doing me too much kindness. 'Fraternize the both of them energetically for a most enjoyable fare,' he is grumbling. With utmost capacity I go into the attack and shortly I am gorging like famished elephant only. Meanwhile Uncle is steady-gazing me and seething with indignation as if wishing me to choke also.

15.7   "At last I shove all in, polishing the both dishes off. Now myself in some perplexity regarding most fitting reply to poem and soon-to-be pressing matter of lodging. But Uncle is too energetic and leaping up to fetch pen-case and reeds. 'Now that Belly is repleted please to dictate,' he tells. 'If you are shirking, myself will be demanding restitution for all items consumed.'

"'Fulfillment to the letter is my stock-in-trade itself,' I tell him. 'Compose as follows, with help of God:

> Tell the one who thought it up
> I've solved his little puzzle.
> A Mussulman died: you'd think his wealth
> Would go to his full brother.

> But imagine that the man who died
> (The one that has the brother)
> Had wed a girl, while his son
> Had married that lady's mother!

> And that, alas, the son died first,
> But left a son of his own,
> Who'd be grandson to our first man,
> And his widow's brother too!'

15.8   "Then Uncle is checking computation and I am verifying solution is correct. But when finished he is saying, 'Shadows are falling and storm is coming: roll up dhoti and run to your nears and dears!'

"I protest myself at big loss in matter of lodging and urge that so much of merit would be attained by sheltering me, in particular view of darkness pitching and thunderings audible overhead. But yet he is shouting at me to get out. 'Wide world is your oyster,' he says, 'except this Domicile.'

"'But why?' I am asking. 'The house is so much empty.'

"'Room is there,' he is saying, 'but myself witnessing ravenous attack on tiffin and leaving plate clean, and so realising, that your concern for health and well-being are leaving much to be desired. Any fellow who so intently pursue insalubrious Repletion will be suffering an excruciating Colic in the abdomen followed by Emesis and a most horrible Senesmus. Let us part without contradiction therefore while you are yet enjoying pink of Health, for promising by God who is creating and destroying, do not sit on my head! You are finding no lodging here.'

"Upon hearing his Swearings and seeing his most firm Resolve, I am obliged to quit the place, with under the Belt one Provender of Sorrow only. Out of Doors I am lavished with generous Downpours and Stumblings by Night, being bark by Dogs, and buffet from Door to Door, until kind Destiny lead me to your respectable Self, and so thanking same." 15.9

"Delighted, old fellow!" I am telling. "Spirits are waxing jovial at seeing you."

Thereafter he is telling stories on variety of subjects and making narrations so much jocular on account of mixing with lachrymose. So he kept until the Sneezing of the Dawn and even the Crying of the Prayer-caller. When he get up to answer Call he turn to take Leaving. I am stopping him and telling that Hospitality is being offer Three Days, but he is making many Swearings and Affirmations not to be retracted. As he is making for Door he is reciting:

> Visit your friend just once a month
> Though you love him as a brother,
> As you give one look to the crescent moon
> Each month, but never give another.

Al-Haaris ibne Hammaam told:

With raw and bleeding Heart I am bidding him Farewell and wishing Morning not so soon arrive.

GLOSSARY

15.1

pardesi foreigner

15.2

pir (religious) teacher or guide

15.3

bavarchee cook

15.4

take a dekho   take a look

zook   zero; zilch

15.5

tiffin   lunch; snack

15.8

dhoti   loincloth

NOTES

The Indian English variety imitated here is the English used as a second (or third, or fourth) language by many South Asians during British rule, and subsequently as a national language of India. In keeping with my usual policy in this book, I have chosen to mimic a past form of the language, in this case the variety used from the early to the mid-twentieth century. Like G. V. Desani, Anurag Mathur, and other writers who have used Indian English as a literary language, I have deliberately accentuated its distinctive features. Examples of these differences as manifested in writing come from George Clifford Whitworth's *Indian English* (1907) and Binoo K. John's *Entry from Backside Only* (2013). Whitworth's compilation of sentences he disliked was intended to improve Indian English, while John's survey seems torn between an impulse to celebrate and a compulsion to mock. But, authorial intentions aside, both works show how English, though forced upon India by British rule, became the preferred vehicle of written communication in many cases; and that many Indian writers, far from clinging timidly to the basic constructions easily acquired by learners, strove to exploit the full range of the language. From a prescriptivist's point of view, the results might in some cases be described as "giving grammar and syntax the go-by" (John, *Entry*, L296). But from a linguistic or literary perspective, the supposedly substandard texts produced by Indian writers are as deserving of interest as any other variety of English. I might add that the arbitrariness of many of the rules supposedly being broken is evident from how many of Whitworth's examples of errors and bad usage no longer read as incorrect: for example, "well-informed source" (*Indian English*, 218), "to aim at" (220), and "family member" (243).

In addition to these citations from written sources, I draw on Claudia Lange's recent study of how spoken Indian English works today (for a short account of common features explained in nontechnical language, see Baldridge, "Linguistic"). Unless I have direct evidence to the contrary, I assume a continuity of syntactic and pragmatic principles between periods and registers. For example, Lange tells us that present-day spoken Indian English rarely uses cleft constructions ("It was this question that . . ."). I did not find any in older materials either, and so decided not to use any in my translation. At the same time, I have been fairly strict about using period-appropriate vocabulary. I have therefore excluded almost all of the brilliant coinages compiled at *Samosapedia* as being too modern, unless I could verify that they were used around 1900. One exception is "zook," which supplied precisely the meaning, the rhyme, and the metrical foot I needed to complete the poem in §15.4. In cases of doubt I checked my English against Kipling's *Kim* (1900), from which I also took the word "pardesi" (§15.1). Finally, Shawkat M. Toorawa kindly read and corrected my Indian English text and made a number of suggestions for improving it.

On the erratic doubling of final consonants, see John, *Entry*, L97. On the erratic use of definite and indefinite articles see Whitworth, *Indian English*, 11–39. On "also" and "itself" as focus markers see Lange, *Syntax*, 180–94. On nonstandard pluralization see Whitworth, *Indian English*, 85–90. On the use of progressive verb forms see Whitworth, *Indian English*, 133.

"Enter ye here . . ." (§15.2) is Q Ḥijr 15:46, as translated by the British Indian Abdullah Yusuf Ali (d. 1953). "Morning sink his stars" (§15.3) is borrowed and modified from Chenery, *Assemblies*, 188. "My head is eating circles" expresses giddiness, puzzlement, or annoyance (*Samosapedia*), a meaning confirmed by informants as going back to the early twentieth century. "Biestings" means milk produced by a cow, sheep, etc., that has just given birth. The word is supplied by Lane, *Arabic-English Lexicon*, s.v. *l-b-'*. On how to make custard out of it, see *Mother Earth News*, "Feedback on Cow Colostrum" (not for the lactose-intolerant!). "Push and posh gone out of me" (§15.4): I am not sure of the derivation or precise meaning of this phrase, but as used in Desani, *All About*, 121, it seems to fit.

In prose, the solution of the inheritance puzzle (§15.7), based on al-Sharīshī's explanation (*Sharḥ*, 2:179), runs as follows. Imagine a Mr. X senior (the "pious Mussulman") and his son, Mr. X junior, along with a Ms. Y senior and her daughter, Ms. Y junior. Mr. X senior marries Ms. Y junior, and Mr. X junior marries Ms. Y senior. In other words, Mr. X junior has married his father's mother-in-law. Then Mr. X junior dies, leaving his wife (Ms. Y senior) pregnant. The baby, a boy, is born. This baby is grandson to Mr. X senior and half-brother to his wife, Ms. Y junior. Then Mr. X senior dies. As stipulated by the law of inheritance, one-eighth of his estate goes to his widow, Ms. Y junior, and the rest goes to his grandson. The riddle deliberately misleads by identifying the major heir as the widow's brother, which he is, but that status is irrelevant to the division of the estate. What matters is that he is a lineal descendant, and as such has priority over the dead man's brother.

A "dhoti" (§15.8) is described as "the loin-cloth worn by all the respectable Hindu castes of Upper India, wrapt round the body, the end being then passed between the legs and tucked in at the waist, so that a festoon of calico hangs down to either knee" (Yule, *Hobson-Jobson*, s.v. *dhoty*; spelling modified by Toorawa). To "sit on someone's head" is "to nag or pester; be insistent" (*Samosapedia*, confirmed by informants as going back to the early twentieth century).

BIBLIOGRAPHY

Baldridge, Jason. "Linguistic and Social Characteristics of Indian English." *Language in India* 2, no. 4 (June/July 2002). http://www.languageinindia. com/junjul2002/baldridgeindianenglish.html.

Desani, G. V. *All About H.* Hatterr. New York: Farrar, Straus, and Giroux, 1970. Originally published 1948.

Hobson-Jobson: see Yule.

John, Binoo K. *Entry from Backside Only: Hazaar Fundas of Indian English.* Revised edition. New Delhi: Rupa, 2013. References are to chapters or to location numbers in the Kindle edition.

Kipling, Rudyard. *Kim.* 2 vols. Macmillan: London, 1915.

Lange, Claudia. *The Syntax of Spoken Indian English.* Amsterdam: Benjamins, 2012.

"Feedback on Cow Colostrum." *Mother Earth News.* September/October 1973. http://www.motherearthnews.com/natural-health/cow-colostrum-zmaz73sozraw.

Samosapedia: The Definitive Guide to South Asian Lingo. www.samosapedia.com

Whitworth, George Clifford. *An Anglo-Indian Dictionary.* London: Kegan Paul, 1885.

———. *Indian English: An Examination of the Errors of Idiom Made by Indians in Writing English.* Letchworth, Herts.: Garden City, 1907.

Yule, Henry, and A. C. Burnell. *Hobson-Jobson: A Glossary of Colloquial Anglo-Indian Words and Phrases, and of Kindred Terms, Etymological, Historical, Geographical and Discursive.* New edition edited by William Crooke. London: Murray, 1903.

IMPOSTURE 16

CON SAFOS

In Arabic this episode is called al-maghribiyyah, *meaning "the Far Western," referring to the expanse of land from Tunisia to Morocco, possibly including al-Andalus ("Islamic Spain") as well. Seen from al-Ḥarīrī's Basra, this was one of the ends of the earth. Even so, when al-Ḥārith arrives there, he finds educated people discussing the same literary topics that engaged their counterparts back east. One of these is palindromes: phrases that read the same backward and forward. To al-Ḥārith's chagrin, he is dragged into a game that requires players to improvise palindromes of increasing length. Based on its title and setting, this Imposture will use a far-western variety of English—far western, that is, if you assume a starting point in England or on the East Coast of the United States—namely, Spanglish. Al-Ḥārith will speak in the Southern California variety; Abū Zayd will use the same variety, but with bits of Cervantes and the Spanish Bible thrown in, to convey his Qur'anic and literary allusions; and the servant boy of §16.8 will speak in the distinctive youth jargon of Miami, Florida. The Spanish part of the Spanglish was corrected and improved by Leyla Rouhi.*

El Xaret Benamam tol' us: 16.1

Una vez I assisted a la prejer de la tarde en una mezquita de Marruecos. Cuando finishé la parte obligatoria y two more rakas for if the flies, I noticed un grupo de amigos who seemed closer than fingernails and grime. Se habían retirado off to the side, donde they were havin' una animada discusión full of guiticismos. Ahora como ustedes saben I'm always buscando new giros de frase. So I go op to them like a crasheador de bailes: "Eh, vatos, you min' if I join la tardeada? Porque me gusta collectar the guiti things que dice la gente. No estoy aquí pa' espongear ni pa' tomar su beicon de camello."

"No hay bronca," they say, loosening their ponchos and moving over un poco para hacerme some room. "Between, between and drink a seat!"

16.2   Bueno, I hadn' been sittin' there longer than a flas' of lightnin' when jomps op un vagabundo, as espeedy as a pajarito golpeando agua, y saludó a los presentes and the mosque también. Then he said:

"As hombres de conocimiento y de sensatez, you know that la oferta más preciosa one can make al SEÑOR, y la más potente en asegurar la salvación, is charity to the poor. I eswear por Dios, who led me aquí, an' decretó that I should address ustedes y nobody else, that I come before you as a refugee, un 'sin ventura que de tan lueñes tierras viene,' with sunken-bellied niños wailin' at my back. Will no one, Señores, help me apagar el fuego de la hambre?"

"La zalá de la tarde is oredi terminada," they said, "y todo lo que tenemos es leftover, but if you're not too piqui, sírvete las sobras."

"I'm at the en' of my ropa," he said, "so I accep' your 'rajas de queso y mendrugos de pan'; for 'Whatever's there I call a hair,' as the bal' one said."

So todos los presentes order their esclavos to give the poor necesitado whatever they have lef'. He put himself contento de como they were treatin' him, and says 'Tankiú' a todos. Then he sit down pa' examinar what they were puttin' enfrente de él.

16.3   Retornando a la discusión de las rarezas literarias y las joyas del espiche, we ended op hablando de palíndromos: es decir, frases that read the same tan backwar' que forwar', como "A ti no, bonita," y "Am I, Ma?" Entonces somebody suggested that we make it a partida. Whoever wen' primero would improvisar un palíndromo de tres palabras, tan bonitas como perlas on a string. Entonces la persona on his right would make up one with four, esétera, esétera. Porque there were five of us—like the paws on the cat, o los Durmientes de Éfeso—la última persona would have to inventar a palindrome of seven words.

136

Que bad lock: mi neighbor a la derecha decided to go first. He said: "Emir, I rime!" ¡Újule!

Su vecino se inventó: "Maya sees a yam."

Pues the next man said: "On top, a pot? No!"

Entonces el siguiente: "'Tis too hot to hoot; sit!"

Then it hit to me. ¡Siete perlas! I broke my head and unwound my brains, pero no se me ocurrió nadita: every phrase I started fell aparte. I even asked for help, pero everybody seemed to be thinking instead about the lifespan of the crayfish. Al fin y al cabo I was so made into balls that I threw in la toalla.

"If only mi amigo de San Ruche estuviera aquí!" I said. "For him, com-poner un palíndromo de seven words would be a piece of eaten bread." **16.4**

"¿En serio? Even Ejjás Elmósani, if you esprung this one on him, would give himself for beaten!"

While todos comentaban on how *súper*-difícil it was to solve tha' head-breaker, our gues' inesperado was looking at us from above the choulder y componando—without us knowing nadita—su propio collar de perlas. Por fin, when he saw que we were getting nowhere, and it didn't have your aunt, dijo: "Carnales, it's not worth la pena to ask for pears from an elm, ni sangre a la piedra! 'Above todo sabio,' dice el Corán, 'is someone que sabe más.'"

Pues turnó a mi. "Oqué, let me take your torn, que te bajo del huque. **16.5** Le's say I ask you if you shared your comida with your vecinos en el barrio. En prosa, you can say:

'Me? Definitely: let in, I fed 'em.'

"O supongamos que quieres un poema donde every *line* is a palindrome. Ahí está:

Minus Malayalam sun, I'm
A mote (ow! woe to Ma!),
A fool, a loofa.
Won ton? Not now!
Knits never even stink.
Gnus? Never even sung.
Smug Babak swots, stows kabab, gums
Mud, a pap, a papadum!

16.6   ¡Guau! Nos quedamos estupefactos, as if he were un mago who had stunned us con su hechizo. We chowered him with so many dólares y elogios que al final he beg us to estop. Pues he roll' op his eslives, put his mochila on his cholder, y se levantó, the whole time recitando:

> ¡Que banda! Elocuencia de verdad,
> With more conocimiento
> Than any banda's ever had;
> If they met Sahban
> They'd leave him sin aliento;
> Y cuando vine mendigando
> Demostraron su bondad;
> Los marroquíes gave as freely
> As any Oriental.

16.7   Pero había walkeado only un tiro de piedra agué when sudenmente he was back. "Me refugio en Dios de la sodden death!" he cried. "¡Chale, vatos! You guys are la raza del que no tiene raza, y un tesoro para él who was all out of dinero. Miren: "las tinieblas estan hoverando sobre la haz del abismo," y the path I have to follow is "del todo escura." Entre mí y mi nidito sits una noche 'as dark as the mouth of a wolf,' y the only way to ge' there is un camino no usado. Una lámpara, por favor, que no trip, and slip, y pierda el rumbo!"

Pues somebody trajó a lamp and lit it. Cuando brilló, reveló las caras of my compañeros, and I saw que el pícaro was mi viejo Abosaïd.

"Es él!" I said. "The one I tol' you about, the one que siempre hits the nail en la cabeza, y puede hablar the hin' legs off a burro!"

Por un rato, todos looked at him embobados and boquiabiertos. Pues they offered to take care of su familia if he would spend la noche con nosotros chateando.

"That's what's not even what!" he said. "Sería mi honor, excep' that when I lef', los peques were re-twisting themselves in hunger an' begging a gritos for me to come back. Sospirarán, desmayaránse, acuitaránse mucho if I keep them waitin'; so let me take con que satisfagan su sed y su hambre, pues I'll come back pronto, ready for la sobremesa."

So we said to one of our muchachos: "Ve con él, an' espeed things op: carry su mochila, and keep him moviendo!"

Pues they lef' and didn' come back for a long time. Por fin el muchacho **16.8** chow' up solo.

"¡Mira güey!" we say. "Wha' happen to ese cabrón?"

"Hello-o! Not gonna lie: that was such a mission! I mean the thing is like, this guy leeeterally took me to Casa Yuca—like, BFE, I swear. ¡Qué pena! Finally we get to this leetle *shack*, dasit. He says, 'Oye bro, this is my crib, donde viven mi kids.' He knocks on the door and somehow gets his bag back from me. Pero like, he says that I was *super* helpful carrying it for him and he wants to do something for me. ¡Dale! He says, 'Here's some advice that's gonna be *super* useful, irregardless. I mean, it's supposably the best consejo ever:

> Da asco la confianza:
> > Familiarity breeds contempt!
> The first time, you're a star,
> > Pues se llevarán un chasco
> And call you a tranza!
> > No one is exempt:
> Take one step too far,
> > Y te caerás del banco.
> So rein in your esperanza:
> > If your first attempt
> Succeeds, tienes que saludar
> > The house before you go,
> And accept la alabanza,
> > Then go without regret,
> And leave 'em wanting more.
> > Ya tu sabes. ¡Ay te wacho!"

Then he says, 'Bro, learn dat by heart, and it'll do you a montón de bien. Now bang it back to your patrones, and when you see them, tell them I said, 'What's good, papos?' Pues tell them from me that stayin' up late at getties and talkin' tonterías—tha's BUZZARD, bros! Tha's why yo siempre tengo cuidado, que my brain no se draye y no pierda mi mente. ¡Ve con Dios!'"

16.9 *El Xaret dijo:*

It took us un minuto to understan' the sneaky punto he was makin' en su poema sin vergüenza. Then we blamed each other for believin' his mentiras y lettin' him escapar. Al fin, wearin' bad faces over payin' for nada, we took cada uno su camino.

GLOSSARY

16.1

con safos   with respect

una vez   once

prejer   prayer

tarde   afternoon

en una mezquita de Marruecos   in a mosque in Morocco

cuando   when

finishé   I finished (an English verb with a Spanish suffix)

for if the flies   just in case

un grupo de amigos   a group of friends

closer than fingernails and grime   thick as thieves

se habían retirado   they had withdrawn

donde   where

una animada discución   a lively discussion

guiticismos   witticisms

ahora como ustedes saben I'm always buscando new giros de frase   now, as you know I'm always looking for new turns of phrase

crasheador de bailes   party crasher

vato   a term of address used among Mexican and Chicano men

tardeada   afternoon gathering

porque me gusta   because I like

collectar   to collect (for *coleccionar*)

guiti things que dice la gente   witty things people say

no estoy aquí pa' espongear ni pa' tomar su beicon de camello   I'm not here to sponge or take your camel bacon

no hay bronca   no problem

un poco   a little

para hacerme   to give me

16.2

pajarito   little bird

*(un) sin ventura que de tan lueñes
   tierras viene*   a helpless being . . .
   come from far-distant lands

apagar el fuego de la hambre   put out
   the fire of hunger

16.3

újule   oh no!

al fin y al cabo   at last

16.4

a piece of eaten bread   from *pan
   comido*, "a piece of cake"

16.5

que te bajo del huque   get you off the
   hook

guau   wow!

hechizo   spell, enchantment

mochila   backpack

sin aliento   out of breath

16.7

un tiro de piedra   a stone's throw

agué   away

chale   oh no!

la raza del que no tiene raza   like
   family to one who has no family

miren   look

*las tinieblas estan hoverando sobre la
   haz del abismo*   darkness was upon
   the face of the deep

del todo escura   quite dark

entre mí y mi nidito   between me and
   my little nest

un camino no usado   an untrodden
   path

zalá   prayer

sírvete las sobras   help yourself to the
   leftovers

ropa   clothes

rajas de queso y mendrugos de pan
   scraps of cheese and crusts of bread

toalla   towel

carnales   friends

cuando vine mendigando   when I
   came begging

demostraron su bondad   they proved
   their generosity

marroquíes   Moroccans

pierda el rumbo   lose my way

pícaro   someone prowling for easy
   money

mi viejo   my old friend

embobados   awestruck, spellbound

boquiabiertos   openmouthed

that's what's not even what   that goes
   without saying

peques   children

a gritos   with cries

*sospirarán, desmayaránse, acuitaránse
   mucho*   they will sigh, they will
   swoon, much distressed

con que satisfagan, etc. with the means of appeasing their hunger

16.8

güey term of address to men

cabrón rascal

hello-o duh!

mission unpleasantly long errand

Casa Yuca, BFE a remote location

que pena how annoying

dasit that's it

crib home

donde viven mi kids where my kids live

pero like but

dale let's have it

consejo advice

pues se llevarán un chasco then they'll be disappointed

tranza con man

te caerás del banco you'll fall off the bench

16.9

sin vergüenza shameless

mentiras lies

sobremesa after-dinner conversation

ve con él go with him

esperanza hope

tienes que saludar you need to take a bow

alabanza praise

ya lo sabes you know

ay te wacho I'll be watching out for you

un montón de bien a heap of good

bang it move along

getties get-togethers

tonterías nonsense

buzzard bad

yo siempre tengo cuidado I'm always careful

pierdo mi mente lose my mind

ve con Dios go with God

cada uno su camino each his own path

NOTES

Unlike some of the other varieties used in this book, Spanglish is not a pidgin or a creole. Rather, the name is loosely applied to everything from using a few words of English in one's Spanish (or vice versa) to code-mixing by fully bilingual speakers. Though often belittled by critics who think it reflects, or even generates, bad English or bad Spanish, it is a source of pride for many users, some of whom write poems, stories, and essays in it (e.g., Chávez-Silverman, "Anniversary"). Spanglish has even been used as a language of translation: Ilan Stavans, a Mexican-American academic, has put selections of *Don Quixote* into it (Stavans, "Don Quixote"). Like any language, Spanglish follows rules (on which see Zentella, "Grammar"). But it is not standardized, in the sense that different speakers distribute their English and Spanish differently. In imitation of what native speakers do, my re-creation relies on borrowing, adaptation, calques, and humorously literal transpositions of idioms. Yet this Imposture, like Stavans's rendering of Don Quixote, should be read as a literary creation, not an attempt to duplicate the way anybody speaks in real life. The title, "Con safos," is a Chicano term used to mark works of art as impervious to criticism (see Albor, "Mi 'Con Safos'").

The Glossary explains all the Spanish and Spanglish elements in §16.1 only. Thereafter it addresses only the items that cannot be guessed on the basis of English and very basic Spanish. Citations of Cervantes, *Don Quixote*, are given in John Ormsby's 1885 translation, with chapter references only.

"Raka" (§16.1) is *rak'ah*, a cycle of movements repeated as part of the prescribed Muslim prayer. "For if the flies" is a literal translation of the idiom *por si las moscas*. For a lively explanation of this and other idioms, see Superholly, "20 Idioms." "Closer than fingernails and grime" is a literal translation of *como uña y mugre*. "Camel bacon": the original has "salted camel fat." Regarding the original of "loosening their ponchos," Chenery explains: "The Arabs in the desert had, when sitting, nothing to rest their backs against; it was their custom therefore to draw up their knees to their stomachs, and then bind their back to their legs with a garment, or a piece of cloth, such as a turban is made of" (Chenery, *Assemblies*, 412). "Between, between, and drink a seat" is a literal translation of *entre, entre y tome asiento*, with a deliberate play on the two senses of *entre* and *tomar* (Stavans, *Spanglish*, 52).

"Golpeando" (§16.2) is a phonetic translation of "gulping," as *golpear* actually means "to hit." "Un sin ventura que de tan lueñes tierras viene" comes from Cervantes, *Don Quixote*, I:xxix. "Zalá" was a term used by renegades and prisoners of war from Algiers, according to Cervantes (Leyla Rouhi, personal communication). "Rajas de queso . . ." comes from Cervantes, *DQ* II:xxviii. "Whatever's there . . ." is a translation of *algo es algo, dijo el calvo*.

In Arabic palindromes (§16.3–5), the sequence of letters must be precisely reversed, though short vowels, doubling, and the glottal stop (which are not indicated by letters) can be altered as necessary. Of al-Ḥarīrī's translators, the only one I know to have used a comparable device is al-Ḥarīzī. In his Hebrew version, the players all come up with three-word palindromes, and Heber the Qenite outdoes them by producing two four-word and two eight-word sequences, though not a poem (*Maḥberōt*, 50). Rückert makes the contest about something else: *Doppelreim*, verses in which the last two stressed syllables in each line rhyme with their respective counterparts in successive lines. For example, instead of a four-word palindrome, the second player in the game according to Rückert produces a four-line *Doppelreim* (*Verwandlungen*, 98):

> Halt vorm Deibe deine Truh zu,
> Vor der Liebe deine Ruh zu.
> Binde, schlottert er, den Schuh zu,
> Und den Mund, der stottert, thu zu.

> (If you see a thief, guard your coffers;
> When in love, stay calm.
> If your shoe's too roomy, tie it;
> And instead of stammering, pipe down.)

By contrast, al-Ḥarīrī's English translators have been timid. Chenery gives the Arabic original its literal meaning, while Preston "entirely sympathizes with Hareth in his inability to write verses of the kind above mentioned, and therefore has omitted this Makama, which would lose all its point by a translation imperfect in that respect" (483).

But palindromes are not so hard to produce in English. For a brilliantly inventive example, see Demetri Martin's "Dammit I'm Mad," a palindromic poem 224 words long. The present translation has a palindrome (and in one case, two) for every one in the original. In one case ("Me? Definitely: let in, I fed 'em," §16.5) the English very roughly approximates the contextual meaning of the original. In all other cases, though, I was able to meet al-Ḥarīrī's conditions (number of words, or being part of a poem) only with an English palindrome that has no relation to the meaning of the original. This does not matter very much in the description of the game (§16.3), where the players' entries are not closely tied to the context. But Abū Zayd's palindromic poem (§16.5) arguably has something to do with the plot, and in this sense my translation of it fails. Finally, with one exception, I have put all the palindromes into English, not Spanish or Spanglish. This is because learned men in pre-modern Islamic societies might banter in their own languages and dialects, but when it came to literary games, the lingua franca was formal Arabic. Similarly, Latinos in the US may speak Spanish or Spanglish with their friends, but schoolwork is (usually) in English.

"Like the paws on the cat" (§16.3) comes from *buscarle cinco patas al gato*, "to look for five paws on a cat," i.e., "to overthink." "Los Durmientes de Éfeso" are the Sleepers of Ephesus, of whom there were five, according to one account (see Q Kahf 18:22). "Thinking instead about the lifespan of the crayfish" is from *pensando en la inmortalidad del cangrejo*, to be distracted or inattentive, and "made into balls" is from *hacerse bolas*, "to get confused."

"San Ruche" in §16.4 is Sarūj, Abū Zayd's hometown and "Ejjás Elmósani" is Iyās al-Muzanī, a proverbially observant judge in Basra (§7.5). "It didn't have your aunt" comes from *no habia tutía*, "there was no remedy," which is often misunderstood (nonsensically) as *no habia tu tia*, "there wasn't your aunt." "Ask for pears from an elm" is a literal translation of the expression for "get blood from a stone." "Above todo sabio . . ." comes from Q Yūsuf 12:76.

"Las tinieblas . . ." (§16.7) is Genesis 1:2, modified from Reina-Valera's Spanish translation of 1602, to imitate Abū Zayd's allusion to Q Falaq 113:3 ("from the evil of darkness as it descends"). "Del todo escura" is Cervantes, *DQ*, I:ix. "As dark . . ." is Cervantes, *DQ*, II:xlviii. "Un camino no usado" is "based on Cervantes's *mar no usado*, "a trackless ocean" (*DQ*, I:xxxiv). "That's what's not even what" is a literal translation of *eso que ni que*, "that goes without saying." "Sospirarán . . ." is based on Cervantes, *DQ*, I:xxi (*sospirará él, desmayaráse ella . . . acuitaráse mucho*). "Con que satisfagan . . ." is based on Cervantes, *DQ*, I:xxiv.

The boy's speech in §16.8 is in Miami youth slang circa 2018, of which there are at least two subvarieties: a Spanglish variety used by Latinos (see Baca, "Definitive Guide"; Munzenrieder, "Miami Slang Glossary"; Sh*t, "Shit Miami Girls Say") and a distinct non-Spanglish one used by African Americans (see Dee, "Miami Slang," 101). The boy's speech mostly uses the first, but includes a term or two from the second.

BIBLIOGRAPHY

Albor, Alec. "Mi 'Con Safos.'" http://miconsafos.blogspot.com/2011/04/meaning-of-con-safos.html.

Baca, Mandy. "The Definitive Guide to Miami Slang." *Thrillist Miami.* 5 November 2015. http://www.thrillist.com/lifestyle/miami/the-definitive-guide-to-miami-slang.

Campbell, Ted. "Mexican Slang Master List." *No Hay Bronca: Travel Stories and Practical Tips for Mexico.* http://nohaybronca.wordpress.com/2016/12/06/mexican-slang-master-list/.

[De Cervantes, Miguel]. The Project Gutenberg EBook of Don Quijote, by Miguel de Cervantes Saavedra. http://www.gutenberg.org/files/2000/2000-h/2000-h.htm.

———. The Project Gutenberg EBook of Don Quixote, by Miguel de Cervantes. Translated by John Ormsby. http://www.gutenberg.org/cache/epub/996/pg996-images.html.

Chávez-Silverman, Susana. "Anniversary Crónica." In Ilan Stavans, ed. *Spanglish*, 125–29. Westport, CT: Greenwood, 2008.

Dee, Kassey. "Miami Slang 101 | Welcome to Miami." Uploaded 31 May 2018. http://www.youtube.com/watch?v=mx5nCoGzJZw.

[Martin, Demetri]. "Dammit I'm Mad—A Poem by Demetri Martin." http://genius.com/Demetri-martin-dammit-im-mad-annotated.

Munzenrieder, Kyle. "Miami Slang Glossary: Pero Like, It's Super-Definitive, Bro." *Miami New Times*, April 5, 2014. http://www.miaminewtimes.com/news/uncle-luke-says-ron-desantis-is-a-racist-10873722.

De Reina, Casiodoro, and Cipriano de Valera. *La Biblia.* 1602. http://www.biblestudytools.com/rvr/genesis/1.html.

Rückert, Friedrich. *Die Verwandlungen des Abu Seid von Serug, oder die Makamen des Hariri.* 4th ed. Stuttgart: Cottaschen, 1864.

Schandillia, Amit. "Órale, Ándale, and Others—Decoding Mexican Spanish." PeppyBurro. http://www.peppyburro.com/blog/orale-andale-mexican-spanish/.

Sh*t Miami Girls Say. "Shit Miami Girls Say . . . and Guys." Uploaded 26 January 2012. http://www.youtube.com/watch?v=FtB29gJ6dLQ.

Stavans, Ilan. "Don Quixote de la Mancha (I): Miguel de Cervantes; First Parte, Chapter Uno; Transladado al Spanglish por Ilán Stavans." *Cuadernos*

Cervantes. Epoca II, Año III / 2012. http://www.cuadernoscervantes. com/art_40_quixote.html.

———— *Spanglish: The Making of a New American Language.* New York: Rayo, 2003.

Superholly. "20 Idioms in Spanish and Their Meanings." Uploaded 27 May 2018. http://www.youtube.com/watch?v=z7L9dYqSW1g.

Zentella, Ana Celia. "The Grammar of Spanglish." In Ilan Stavans, ed. *Spanglish*, 42–63. Westport, CT: Greenwood, 2008.

IMPOSTURE 17

BACK WORDS

In this Imposture, Abū Zayd is challenged to produce a speech where the units to be reversed are words, not letters as in Imposture 16. The rest of the English imitates the style of the once-famous comic novelist Jerome K. Jerome (d. 1927), whose name, like Abū Zayd's speech, is reversible.

IN WHICH BOOTS PRODUCES A REVERSIBLE SPEECH

A debate.—An eloquent stranger.—A game.—Harris and friends come off a poor second.—The reversible speech.—The stranger named.—His poem.—The parting.

17.1   *Harris was reminded of a story.*

I remember being somewhere very far away and pleasant to look at when I caught sight of a party of sensible and highly cultured young men. They were deep in animated discussion—sparks flying upward—arms waving madly in the air. I went over and sat down, with the idea that I was going to enjoy myself and learn something useful into the bargain. They asked if I wished to contend with them for the crown of glory amid the crash of battle-music. I said it would suit me wonderfully to look on as they went about that part of the business. So they left me alone and resumed their discussion.

As I looked round the circle I noticed, in the middle of the assembly, an 17.2 old man so thin with care and so blasted by simooms, that he had assumed the desiccated air of a bundle of reeds or a pair of scissors. The clever young men were asking him questions and marvelling at his answers. He was so brilliant that had dear old Saḥbán been among us he would have been ignored. The more the old fellow went on, the more I admired his ability to hold the company in thrall. He had a reply ready for every question, and he struck home with every arrow he let fly. It became clear after a while that the young men had, for their part, dug down to the bottom of their quivers and, finding nothing left to aim at him, were quite unable to continue.

Then the old man proposed a game. When he kindly offered to go first, there were murmurs of delight as each member of the group politely invited the fellow beside him to join in.

"Write a letter," the old man said, "whose firmament is its fundament and whose fundament is the firmament—whose long low lines of dawn and dusk are the same—a letter much like a cloak of which the warp is the weft and the weft the warp, and the shimmering cloth changes colour when turned out—a letter like a curious double-faced coin—or like a stately mosque with two magnificent niches, each set in a different wall, and both pointing to Mecca!"

Well, that wasn't what they expected. Everybody was struck speechless. 17.3 Not a sound was heard from our little corner save the great stillness of no one saying a word. The old man waited. But he might just as well have asked beasts of the field, or images carved in stone.

"I daresay I've given you a fair start," he said after a while. "So let's show our hands! Have the muses inspired you? If so, it will be greatly to your credit. If not, I'll try to strike a spark from the obdurate skulls I see."

"These waters are too deep for us, old chap," we said. "We're afraid we can't manage it. Give us a hand here, can't you? Think how much better you'll feel if you have us as friends, ready to do you a good turn when it's wanted!"

He sat for a few moments, pondering. Then he said, "Very well, then. Get a bit of paper and write this down, and remember to name the author when you pass it round."

17.4   *Friends keep secrets and secrets keep friends. Is it clear how remarkable friendship is? It matters what significance it is that opinions have to them: allow subordinates to speak. Loyalty and trust inspire forbearance and fairness. Work hard, undo plots and schemes: you know they may arise. You can fail to seek, can't you? Winners embrace tenacity and will celebrate triumphs. Do leaders trouble to run risks? Take ambition to men exemplary of success: the attribute once known as wisdom. What test will fools face? To deliberate instead: crises emerging from hastily made choices? No! Don't flinch or shirk: don't waver, ever! Don't! Hand and heart win honor and reputation. Must you praise? Yes! Kindness practiced is friendship gained. Sincerity inspires humility, while self-indulgence breeds arrogance. Fault-finders despise others but forgive friends, sometimes, and forgiveness is best. Grow mercies, see them developing. Others summon to mind one force that speeches (say I) once attained. Never limit the glory one gives God. Does one honor the indebtedness of feeling a thing first? Man tempers self-respect with gratitude. Generosity? Try being human, joyful, not covetous or irritable or bored. Wise the fools that love a god through friends. Seek another one to give!*

17.5   "There you are," he said. "Two hundred words' worth of good advice. If you recite it as I just did, no one will see any fault in it. Now if you start from the other end and recite it backwards, you get:

    "Give to one another; seek friends through God, a love that fools the wise!"

    "Then keep on backwards word by word, until you reach the beginning, which is now the end:

    "Remarkable how clear it is: friends keep secrets, and secrets keep friends."

17.6   *Harris continued:*

It was a staggering performance—not the sort of letter you hear every day, I mean, and some useful instruction folded into it too. To see him produce it was a beautiful lesson against uppishness. In his presence, our small ambitions crept away, ashamed, and we knew that talent is but the gift of

God, who distributes it not as we should wish, but with a wisdom too vast and deep for childish human minds to grasp.

Of course everyone had to touch the hem of his robe for a blessing and pay what we had promised. But when it was my turn the old man declined my precious penny, saying that he would take nothing from a pupil.

"Why, you must be Boots!" I exclaimed. "But you look a decrepit wreck."

"To say nothing of grubby and starving," he said, "but I am Boots."

I started to tell him what I thought about his wandering over the face of   17.7
the earth. He couldn't help it, he said: as hard as his life was, God had condemned him to it. Looking thoroughly miserable, he recited these verses:

> From dawn to dusk I roam, unblessed,
> Fate's cold blade against my chest,
> I cannot sleep, I cannot rest,
> West to east, east to west.
> West to east, east to west,
> I cannot sleep, I cannot rest,
> Fate's cold blade against my chest,
> From dawn to dusk I roam, unblessed.

Then he turned his back on us and marched away in grand style, swinging his arms. Some of us watched him go while others rose as if to fly after him. In the end, we all rose, unwrapped the turban-cloths we had tucked around our knees, and, like the Ten Lost Tribes, went our separate ways.

NOTES

Here is the reverse of the speech in full:

> *Give to one another; seek friends through God, a love that fools the wise! Bored, or irritable, or covetous? Not joyful? Human being, try generosity! Gratitude with self-respect tempers man. First thing, a feeling of indebtedness. The honor one does God gives one glory. The limit? Never attained once, I say! Speeches that force one mind to summon others: developing them, see mercies grow. Best is forgiveness and*

sometimes friends forgive, but others despise fault-finders. Arrogance
breeds self-indulgence, while humility inspires sincerity. Gained friend-
ship is practiced kindness. Yes, praise you must. Reputation and honor
win heart and hand. Don't ever waver, don't shirk or flinch; don't! No
choices made hastily from emerging crises! Instead, deliberate. To face
fools will test . . . what? Wisdom, as known once. Attribute the success
of exemplary men to ambition. Take risks! Run to trouble: leaders do.
Triumphs celebrate will and tenacity. Embrace winners! You can't seek
to fail, can you? Arise: may they know you! Schemes and plots undo
hard work. Fairness and forbearance inspire trust and loyalty. Speak
to subordinates; allow them to have opinions. That is it: significance.
What matters? It is friendship. Remarkable how clear it is: friends keep
secrets, and secrets keep friends.

The reversible letter has challenged al-Ḥarīrī's translators. Rückert and Preston simply omit the whole Imposture, the latter describing its reversibility as
"an ingenious artifice it is useless to attempt to duplicate" (*Makamat*, 483).
Chenery puts both the forward and the backward readings into English, giving
the sense but not the form. In French, René R. Khawam translates the forward
reading only, adding a footnote that explains that the original text can be read
backward as well (*Livre des malins*, 173). Wang Dexin's 2017 Chinese rendering,
though monorhymed, is not reversible. But some translators have managed to
duplicate the trick. Al-Ḥarīzī, with his usual brilliance, reproduces it in Hebrew
(*Maḥberōt*, 53–54). In the eighth chapter of his *Taḥkemoni* (the original impostures he wrote after translating al-Ḥarīrī), he goes a step further: when read
backward, his hero's Hebrew letter means the opposite of what it does if read
forward. In his English *Taḥkemoni*, David Simha Segal ingeniously transposes
the reversibility to the phrase level (instead of the word level) and prints the
phrases in two parallel columns (see Alḥarizi, *Taḥkemoni*, tr. Segal, 86–92 and
the commentary at 468–72). Dolinina and Borisov's 1978 Russian translation of
al-Ḥarīrī omits Imposture 17, but Dolinina's 1987 revision includes it. Her text is
not only reversible but metrical in both directions.

In §17.6, "we knew that talent . . ." is a paraphrase, in Jerome's language, of a
Qur'anic verse quoted in the original: "Bounty is in the hand of God, He gives it
unto whomsoever He will" (Q Āl ʿImrān 3:73, tr. A. J. Arberry).

BIBLIOGRAPHY

Arberry, A. J. *The Koran Interpreted*. London: Allen and Unwin, 1955.

Jerome, Jerome K. *Three Men in a Boat (To Say Nothing of the Dog)*. New York: A. L. Burt, 1889.

IMPOSTURE 18

A SCANDAL IN MESOPOTAMIA,
OR, THE TELL-TALE TART

Asked what this Imposture is about, early readers might have said that it shows off several genres of composition: rhymed prose description of beautiful people and objects, vindictive poetry, and skillful repurposing of Qur'anic verses. More evident to modern readers is that the story has a distinct form. A character recoils from some perfectly innocent object and then has to explain his reaction to his friends, which means describing some long-ago catastrophe associated with the object. This device also appears in the work of al-Ḥarīrī's predecessor al-Hamadhānī and in The Thousand and One Nights. *A similar device lies at the heart of the classical detective story: actions inexplicable in the present are shown to make sense in light of a story about the past, a story that has to be teased out by the characters. On this basis, Abū Zayd and friends here adopt the Sherlock Holmes stories of Arthur Conan Doyle (d. 1930) as the basis for their English. Although this Imposture is not a proper detective story (for better candidates, see Bray, "Physical World"), Doyle's idiom helpfully supplies a great many ways to describe intimidation, extortion, and betrayal. Also, it brings out some of the similarities between Abū Zayd and Holmes on the one hand, and al-Ḥārith and Watson on the other. The long poem is Englished in the manner of "The Raven" by Edgar Allan Poe (d. 1849), whom Doyle acknowledged as his predecessor in the creation of the detective story.*

El-Hareth ben Hammam told us the following story.

I was travelling from Damascus to Baghdad with some companions of the Numayr tribe, all of them prosperous, charitable men. Among us was my celebrated friend, Aboo Zaid of Serooj, whose singular gifts in the field of oratory had made him the object of popular applause; his powers, it was said, could bring comfort even to the grief-stricken. Shortly after reaching Sindjar, we learned that a merchant had invited the entire district, town and countryside alike, to a wedding feast: not only his associates, who were men of substance, but also anyone who chanced to be in the vicinity, including those who had arrived with the caravan.

Having accepted the merchant's offer of hospitality, we repaired to the place appointed for our entertainment. Our host called for soups, then for roasts, all of them excellent and well served. Then he brought out a goblet that might have crystallised out of the very air, or congealed out of light; it seemed to have been moulded from the choicest pearls, or formed by a precipitation of dust-motes. Inside it were pastries that had been deftly folded, splashed with rose-water, and drenched in syrup. This glorious dish, and the perfume that wafted from it, caused a stir among the guests, who transfixed it with their eager glances and would no doubt have devoured it utterly, had Aboo Zaid not recoiled from it in a frenzy of horror, as if it had been some foul and venomous beast.

"Come now!" came the cry from all around. "Pray resume your seat, there's a good fellow. We're not lepers, you know."

But he swore a solemn oath that he would not come back unless the goblet was removed. What could we do, for his honour's sake, but accede to his request? So the dish was taken away, leaving our hearts broken and our eyes blurred with tears. Appeased, Aboo Zaid returned to the table. We asked him to tell us why he had risen and demanded that the dish be removed.

"A glass vessel," he said, "exposes to view everything entrusted to it; and years ago I swore never to dine with a tell-tale."

We asked him to explain the reason for his strict and binding oath.

"I once had a neighbour," he said, "who seemed a pleasant, well-spoken man, but whose suavity of manner concealed a malicious and vindictive heart. As he lived so near me, I was naturally inclined to seek his company, and his amiable disposition invited me to intimacy. Never once did it cross my mind that harm might come of his winning ways. I was a fool: I took him for the kind, obliging fellow he seemed to be, not the ruthless bird of prey he was. For all his protestations of friendship, he was a poisonous swamp adder; if only I had known, as we shared our food and drink, that I would one day wish him gone for good, and rejoice at seeing the last of him for ever!

18.4   "You must also know, gentlemen, that I owned a slave, who was unrivalled in the perfection of her person. When she raised her veil, the sun and the moon would stand abashed, and the hearts of all who beheld her would kindle with desire. Her teeth, gentlemen, put pearls and silver beads to shame. Her glances stirred up secret longings, and cast spells, as if she were a sorceress of Babylon. Her speech could deprive a man of his reason, or summon mountain goats down from the crags. When she recited the Koran, she could comfort the heartsick, chanting sweetly as David; or revive a buried child. When she sang, it was all sweetness and delicacy and harmony; when she played the pipes, it was a treat for the angels; and when she danced, she swirled like bubbles in a glass, and caused men's turbans to lurch and topple. With her in my house, I scorned all other wealth; she was the crowning glory of all my blessings. I kept her hidden from the world, forbidding her to go out whether by day or by night, and forbearing to speak of her in company. All the same I feared lest the wind waft her scent abroad, or some flash of lightning reveal her, or some diviner strike upon her hiding place.

18.5   "As ill luck would have it, I once spoke of her in my cups, to none other than my tell-tale neighbor. The next day, my conscience reproached me bitterly, but too late: the arrow had flown. I felt a creeping of the flesh, and a presentiment of misery and despair, for I well knew that any secret entrusted to that leaky vessel would soon dribble out. Yet I had implored him to tell no one, even if we should quarrel; and he promised to hold it closer than a miser holds his pennies, nor to divulge it, even if menaced with a fiery furnace.

"A day or two after this, the governor of the town, who was also commander of her garrison, made up his mind to pay a visit to his sovereign, in order to show off his cavalry and to seek any benefactions that might be forthcoming from the court. As it was necessary to offer a gift to the king, the governor dispatched agents to look for a suitable offering. He also advertised a reward to anyone who might help him in his quest. My treacherous neighbor, moved to infamy by wicked lust for gold, and undeterred by the prospect of remonstration or rebuke, went eagerly to the governor and revealed my secret to him.

In an instant the governor's subordinates had descended upon me in a swarm, demanding that I give up my precious treasure to him for any price I cared to ask. Surrounded by his lackeys, I felt a wave of grief close upon me, like the wave that engulfed Pharaoh and his hosts. I tried all I could to keep him from her, but he persisted; and none of my attempts to bring influence to bear upon him had the slightest effect. The more I resisted, and the more I sought some means of escape, the more furious and abusive he became, and the more he gnashed his teeth. I could not bring myself to part with the light of my eyes; I would sooner tear my heart from my breast. But when at last his threats became blows, in fear for my life I relented, and sold, for filthy lucre, the apple of my eye. As for my loathsome neighbor, he succeeded only in bringing himself into disrepute. It was then that I swore a solemn oath never again to keep company with a tell-tale. Glass, gentlemen, is proverbial for hiding nothing, and for that reason I invoked my oath and refused to touch it.

> Though crepe-less, do forgive me, friends,
> For now you know my ancient hurt;
> Forgive, and let me make amends
> With stories sweeter than dessert.

El-Hareth ben Hammam continued: 18.6

We accepted Aboo Zaid's excuse and covered his cheek with kisses, reassuring him that even the greatest among us had been afflicted by tell-tales: had the Prophet not suffered at the hands of Umm Jameel, as proclaimed in the Koran? Then we asked him what had become of his false friend, the overbearing neighbor who had betrayed him.

"He humbled himself before me, and asked persons of influence to intercede on his behalf. But having vowed never again to admit him into my company, unless time itself should run backwards, I met his entreaties with the most resolute and inflexible refusal. Yet, far from being discouraged by my coldness, he shamelessly redoubled his efforts. What saved me in the end from his importunity was the vindictive verse that boiled up out of my injured heart. It drove away the demon that possessed him and forced him to stay indoors for fear of being mocked. When my poem was proclaimed, he gave a great wail of distress and bade farewell to joy, for he realized that our quarrel was beyond all reconciliation, and renounced all hope of reviving our friendship, even as the unbeliever denies the raising of the dead."

We begged him to recite his poem for us.

"By all means," he said, "sniff its bouquet, if you cannot bear to wait."

With remarkable self-possession, he then sang out:

18.7
Once I had a friend who smiled—smiled and my heart beguiled,
For I thought him true and faithful, more than any friend before;
   With our laughter nearly burst we, for secret wine were we e'er
      thirsty;
   Fondly wished I for one mercy—swiftly when I asked, he swore:
'Tell me,' said I, 'shall we not be like the faithful friends of yore?'
   Quoth my friend, 'For evermore.'

When he turned upon me scowling, like a rabid mastiff growling,
Only then did I see clearly what a poisoned heart he bore—
   Why he found my kindness hateful, why then suddenly
      ungrateful,
   Still I do not know; but wakeful, only night can I endure—
For the daylight shows too clearly that the friend I had before
   Is a wretch—forever more!

18.8
Our host, having heard Aboo Zaid tell his tale and recite his verses, applauded his skill in expressing both admiration and disdain. He offered him his own cushion at the head of the table and seated him in the place

of honour. He then had ten trays of silver brought in, each heaped with confections of sugar and honey. "'Not deemed alike shall be the fellows of the Fire and the fellows of Paradise,'" he said, "nor should the innocent suffer as the guilty. Like a man of honour, a silver vessel retains its secrets. So keep not aloof, and punish not the prophet but only his wicked tribe!" Then he ordered his serving-boy to carry the sweets to Aboo Zaid's tent for him to do with them as he wished.

Aboo Zaid then addressed the company. "Proclaim the Victory," he cried, "and rejoice, for the wound is healed! God has recompensed you for your loss and made this dish permissible to you, bringing you together in sweetness. 'Yet peradventure that ye hate a thing while it is good for you'!"

As Aboo Zaid prepared to take his leave, it occurred to him to ask whether he could keep the silver trays.

"Let me reverse myself," he said, addressing the host, "and say that now I would like to be be-trayed."

"Say no more," cried the host. "Take them, and the serving-boy as well. And now, goodbye!"

Aboo Zaid leaped up and thanked him, proclaiming him a rain cloud   18.9
and himself a parched field. Then he led us away to his tent. There he gave us the freedom of his sweetmeats, making sure each of us had a share.

"I cannot say," he mused, "whether I should complain of that tale-bearer or thank him. How long should I bear a grudge? True, he committed a crime when he disclosed my secret, but without him I would never have acquired this little fortune. His is the cloud that drenched me, and his the sword that won these spoils. But now I think I will retire to my little ones. I am content with what Fate has placed in my way, and I need weary myself and my camels no longer. Farewell, and may God keep you!"

With that he seated himself upon his mount and turned back the way he had come, to where his people were. His great she-camel strode away, leaving us as lonely as a moonless night and a table with no one at the head.

NOTES

The pastries that appear in §18.2 are later called *qaṭā'if* (§18.6), a term Charles Perry renders as "crepes." His edition and translation of a thirteenth-century Syrian cookbook gives several recipes, including this one:

> Blanch pistachios, dry them out, toast on a low fire, pound, and knead with finely ground sugar and rose water. After stuffing the crepes with this mixture, extract a little pistachio oil . . . and moisten the crepes with it. Serve in syrup (*Scents and Flavors*, §7.25; see further §§7.26–31).

In §18.2, the guests plead with Abū Zayd not to be like Qudar, who was persona non grata among the tribespeople of Thamūd. The closest Doyle comes to saying something like this is in a passage about leprosy ("The Yellow Face," *CSH*, 301). "Sorceress of Babylon" (§18.4) is an allusion to Q Baqarah 2:102, where the angels Hārūt and Mārūt are taught sorcery in Babylon. The reference to reviving buried children alludes to the pre-Islamic practice of burying unwanted girls after they were born. The description of the enslaved woman's vocal ability puns on the names of Maʿbad ibn Wahb and Isḥāq ibn Ibrāhīm al-Mawṣilī, famous singers from the early Umayyad and early Abbasid periods, respectively. The English substitution comes from Holmes's description of "violin land" in "The Red-Headed League" (CSH, 143). "A treat for the angels": the original says that the slave surpassed Zunām, a musician, active during the reigns of al-Mutasim and al-Wathiq, who played woodwind instruments—identified by al-Sharīshī as the *mizmār*, a double-reed instrument like an oboe, and the *nāy*, an end-blown reed flute. The English paraphrases "a treat for the gods," Watson's description of good violin-playing in "A Study in Scarlet," in *CSH*, 9. "Diviner": the original names a particular diviner, Saṭīḥ, a pre-Islamic figure renowned for his ability to interpret dreams and omens.

"Umm Jameel" (§18.6) is a reference to Q Masad 111:4–5, which condemns Umm Jamīl, the wife of Abū Lahab. The commentary tradition says that she would report on the Prophet to his enemies (Sharīshī, *Sharḥ*, 2:345). "Even as the unbeliever denies . . ." alludes to those who deny that God will resurrect the dead at the last judgment; see, e.g., Q Anʿām 6:29, Hūd 11:7, and Raʿd 13:5, among many others.

The original of the poem in §18.7 uses various kinds of *tajnīs*, that is, resemblance between words. Some are words are homonyms: e.g., *ḥamīm*, which means both "close" (of a friend) and "scalding" (of water). Others share root consonants but are etymologically unrelated: e.g., *dhimām* "keeping of an agreement" and *dhamīm* "reprehensible." And others, again coincidentally, have letters in common: e.g., *mustaqīm* "straight" and *saqīm* "ill." To hint at this effect, the English verses are modeled on Poe's "The Raven," whose complex form entails a great deal of rhyming and various other echoic effects.

The dialogue in §18.8 is full of allusions to the Qur'an. "Not deemed alike . . ." comes from Q Ḥashr 59:20, in the 1888 translation by E. H. Palmer. "Punish not . . ." alludes to Q Hūd 11:50–60: when the tribe of 'Ād refused to accept Allah as their god, all were punished except for the prophet Hūd and his followers. Abū Zayd is using these verses to argue against condemning an innocent dish along with a guilty one. "The Victory" is the name of Surah 110 of the Qur'an, which runs as follows in Palmer's translation: "When there comes God's help and victory, and thou shalt see men enter into God's religion by troops, then celebrate the praises of thy Lord, and ask forgiveness of Him, verily, He is relentant!" "Yet peradventure . . ." comes from Q Baqarah 2:216. In this context it suggests that even though the guests lost out on the first dish they ended up with a better one.

"Be-trayed" (§18.9) renders a pun in the original: in Arabic, Abū Zayd says that real elegance (*ẓarf*) entails giving away the dish (*ẓarf*) as well as the food.

Katia Zakharia, who believes that the *Impostures* trace Abū Zayd's progress toward spiritual bliss, argues that his decision not to marry in Imposture 43 affirms that "the happiness he seeks will not be found with a woman, no matter who she may be" (*Abū Zayd*, 291). Although I disagree with Zakharia's reading of the collection as a whole, I admit that the present Imposture may support this part of her argument. On the other hand, Abū Zayd's willingness to accept sweets and plates as compensation for the loss of his supposedly irreplaceable companion suggests that, at this stage at least, he remains as attached to the material world as ever—or, more exactly, that his character is again doing whatever it needs to do in order to create a pretext for verbal performance. In Imposture 43, the debate over the merits of the two prospective brides turns out to have been invented. One suspects that the story of the enslaved singer within the fictional world of Imposture 18 is also an invention.

BIBLIOGRAPHY

Bray, Julia. "The Physical World and the Writer's Eye: Al-Tanūkhī on Medicine." In *Writing and Representation in Medieval Islam: Muslim Horizons,* edited by Julia Bray, 215–49. London: Routledge, 2006.

Doyle, Arthur Conan. *The Complete Sherlock Holmes.* http://maggiemcneill. files.wordpress.com/2012/04/the-complete-sherlock-holmes.pdf.

Perry, Charles, ed. and trans. *Scents and Flavors: A Syrian Cookbook.* New York: New York University Press, 2017.

Palmer, E. H. *The Qur'ân.* Sacred Books of the East, vol. 9. 1880. http://www. sacredtexts.com/isl/sbe09/index.htm.

Poe, Edgar Allan. "The Raven." http://www.poemhunter.com/poem/ the-raven-14/.

IMPOSTURE 19

MY MAN ZAYD

This Imposture is unusual in several respects. The Abū Zayd who appears here is settled and apparently prosperous, and instead of hoodwinking his friends he throws them a dinner party. The generally cheerful tone suggested P. G. Wodehouse, whose novels and stories involve wealthy Englishmen enjoying themselves. Linguistically, the most unusual feature of the original is the list of foods and related items referred to by odd nicknames. As these are not culinary terms, but a kind of jargon, the best equivalent seemed to be early- to mid-twentieth-century American diner lingo, a shorthand used to convey orders to the cook. For this I have relied almost entirely on Jack Smiley's Hash House Lingo, *originally published in 1941. The resulting mix of styles has a precedent in Wodehouse, who enjoyed imitating the American slang of his own time. Here, for example, is a speech he puts in the mouth of a con artist named Smooth Lizzie: "And where have you been all this darned time? Gosh-dingit, you leave me a coupla days back saying you're going to stick up this bozo that calls himself McTodd with a gat . . . What's the big idea?" (*Leave It to Psmith, *190).*

Howard Ben-Hammam managed to cough up the following story. **19.1**

Once, when the breeze of a joyful dawn blew free and all that, Iraq went as dry (so to speak) as a bone. Something about clouds, I believe. The whisper flew round the caravanserais: "The country near Nisibis is just the thing, old man: fellows rolling in dirhams, don't you know." So I straddled some camel flesh, clapped a spear to the saddle, and ambled out into the wide world. Many a vasty expanse was traversed, bringing me to further vasty expanses, and many a hill climbed, bringing a further generous supply of hills; and I am not ashamed to confess that the Howard Ben-Hammam who toppled off in Nisibis was a very different Howard from the merry, laughing lad who'd set off for it. The camel was looking a bit shopworn too.

All the same, Nisibis was a decent sort of place, so I made myself the owner of a bit of grazing-land, sought the company of the right sort of chappies, and settled down for a spot of exile. The plan was to wait for the rains of springtime to rally round and drive off the drought that was busy ravaging the old ancestral. Well, morning in the bowl of night had hardly flung a stone and what not, when I found Aboo Zaid of Sarooj running about the town and its outskirts, tracking his prey as unerringly as a bloodhound. Seeing him decant his usual flood of epigrams and apply himself vigorously to the local udders, I felt that my search was at an end and my efforts crowned, you might say, with success.

19.2   I stuck to the Sarooji like a brother and hung like a limpet on his every word until he fell ill, poor chap, with something chronic and wasting. Rumour had it that he looked so bad that many an experienced corpse-washer would have started washing him on sight. I was in something of a reduced state myself: with his absence everything had gone to sixes and sevens, and dash it all, I did miss the poor blighter! But worse was to come, in the shape of a report that he was edging closer to death's door—practically hanging from the knob, so to speak. Thrown into a panic, his friends rushed to his rooms:

> From the desert we came to him
> > On stallions shot with fire,
> Leaving the four winds far behind
> > In the speed of our desire.
> Our faces wet, our garments torn,
> > Our eyes bright-rimmed with red,
> We called on Fate to spare his life
> > And send scythes for us instead.

Howard continued his account as follows.   19.3

The chappies and I (he said) staggered over and presented ourselves at
the Sarooji's gate. When his son and heir came out to receive us, which
he did very cordially, we let slip a question or two about the old fellow's
complaint.

"Until just now I would have said Pater was for it, don't you know," he
said. "Wasted away and all that. But then, by Jove, he rallied, and now he's
feeling thoroughly all right again. I shouldn't worry about him any longer.
Awfully kind of you to look in. Before too long I imagine he'll be asking you
to pop round for a glass of something, what?"

This capital bit of news cheered us up considerably and we proposed
knocking up the old man straightaway. The boy disappeared to announce
us then reappeared to escort us inside. We found Aboo Zaid flat on his back
but ready to gas away sixteen to the dozen. We clustered around his bed and
peered at him. He gave our delegation a good looking-over, then cleared
his throat. "Some verses, if I may, for the occasion." Then he declaimed:

> I am restored, though who can say
> Have I a Year, or a week's Delay?
> Rejoice, my friends, but know that Death
> Shall claim his Due another Day.
>
> And when that Angel of the darker Drink
> At last shall find me by the river-brink,
> And offering his Cup, invite my Soul
> Forth to my Lips to quaff—I shall not shrink.

Be that as it may, the old boy was still with us for the foreseeable, so   19.4
with a great weight rolled off our minds we offered our congratulations.
Then we proposed toddling off before we made a nuisance of ourselves.
"Nonsense," he said. "Spend the day here, why don't you? Your chirruping
will buck me up like a tonic, and a little chat is just what the doctor ordered
to re-align the old magnetic poles."

When he put it that way there was nothing to do but stay on. We did our best to keep the old fellow amused (with no little success if I may say so) until our tongues went sticky in our mouths and it felt like time for a nap. It was a beastly hot day too, with the hollyhocks nodding in the garden and all that.

"*L'heure de la sieste*," said Aboo Zaid, "does seem to have crept up. No point in kicking at Nature, I say: best restore the tissues with a spot of the old dreamless. Recommended by all the best authorities, don't you know."

19.5 We followed his statesmanlike course and commended ourselves to the arms of Morpheus, there to doze through the afternoon heat like courtiers in the Palace of Sleep. So soundly and deeply did we slumber that the hour for devotions passed unremarked. When at last the mists cleared away, the heat had subsided and the day begun to totter to its end. After vigorous application of cold waters to the old extremities we bucked up and squared our accounts with the Creator. Then we bustled about as if making for the stables, as it was time to toddle off. But then Aboo Zaid called out to his son and heir, the two looking as alike (you might say) as two peas in a pod, and said something extraordinary. It sounded a bit like this:

"Chin gang's got a burning in the bread basket: duffer up, on the double, and let the stokers squff it! Then burn a slab of meh, put some acid on it, and drag it through the garden with Mike and Ike in the alley. Shoot nervous bossy in a bowl and stretch it for the moss backs. Got it? Then put 'em outside of a mully n' hope, dress me a load of yardbird in a bog top, and let 'em pitch till they win. Finish it with a gravel train and bake some bee juice: we don't want 'em calling us nickel nursers. And don't speedball the Adam's ale: hold the brace until they're ready to 23. When they're through with the crying towels, give 'em the stink: it's a duzey. And don't get caught in a snowstorm!"

19.6 Young Zaid took all this in with no apparent straining of the old bean and was soon making the rounds with platters and scents. When at last the sun buckled down to the business of setting, we gathered round to say good-bye to Aboo Zaid. "Bit of a marvel, old boy, what? Got off to quite a dismal start this morning, didn't we, but now it's all come right again."

The old chappie was so moved by this remark that he prostrated himself for a considerable time. Then he sang:

When life looks jolly rotten,
    Don't hang your head and mope:
Every cloud has a silver lining,
    And where there's life there's hope!
Don't fret about that tempest:
    Wait for the sun to shine.
Forget those clouds on the horizon:
    Soon the weather will be fine.
So keep that top lip steady:
    Now there's a plucky lad!
Life is full of surprises,
    And some of them aren't bad!

We asked him to recite the lines for us again so we could scribble them down. Then we said our good-byes. "Pip-pip, old boy! Awfully kind of you to give us a bit of supper. Delighted to see you looking yourself again. Toodle-oo!"

GLOSSARY

19.5

chin gang   tearoom customers (but here, guests)

bread basket   stomach

duffer   bread

up   is needed; is arriving

on the double   hurry that order

stoker   fast eater

squff   eat heavily

burn   cook (a steak) well

slab of meh   roast kid

acid   vinegar

drag it through the garden   put all the condiments on it

Mike and Ike   salt and pepper

in the alley   on the side

shoot   pass

nervous   gelatin

bossy in a bowl   beef stew

stretch it   make it a large order

moss back   conservative eater

put yourself outside of   to eat or drink

mully   beef stew

hope   oatmeal

dress   prepare, make

load   order

yard bird   chicken

bog top   fruit cobbler

pitch till you win   eat all you can

gravel train   sugar bowl

bee juice   honey

nickel nurser   miser

speed ball   hurry up!

Adam's ale   water

brace   set of two things (here, a ewer and a basin)

23   go away

crying towel   cloth napkin

stink   perfume

duzey   a very good thing

caught in a snowstorm   unable to remember orders

NOTES

The verses in §19.2 paraphrase but then diverge entirely from Bayard Taylor's "Bedouin Love Song," which is mentioned in Chapter 7 of Wodehouse's *Damsel in Distress*. The poem in §19.3 incorporates, with modifications, quatrain XLIII of the *Rubáiyát of Omar Khayyám* in Edward FitzGerald's 1859 translation, which was still very popular in Wodehouse's day.

In the original of the diner speech in §19.5, Abū Zayd calls for a table laden with white bread; a roast kid with vinegar, salt, and greens on the side; *sikbāj*, meat stew in aspic; *harīsah*, a savory pudding of grain and meat; *jūdhāb*, a dish made by roasting a chicken and letting the drippings accumulate in a pan full of fruit and starch; *khabīṣ*, a pudding of dates, clarified butter, and starch; *fālūdhaj*, a sweet made of rice flour and honey; a basin and ewer; a towel; and incense. Instead of calling them by their proper names, Abū Zayd uses jargon terms of the type "Father of X." For example, he gives the *jūdhāb* the name Abū l-Faraj, apparently because Faraj sounds like *farrūj*, a word for "chicken." "Slab of meh" is my invention for "roast kid," based on "slab of moo" for beef steak and "meh" as the sound goats make (according to the users of WordReference.com). "Bee juice" is my invention for "honey," by analogy with "maiden juice" for "cherry syrup" and "sky juice" for "water."

"When life looks jolly rotten" (§19.6) is inspired by a line from Eric Idle's "Always Look on the Bright Side of Life." But Idle's song is parodic while Abū Zayd's is straightforward (or as straightforward as anything he says can be). The rest of the poem is accordingly cast in a chipper tone intended to be at least reminiscent of Wodehouse's imitations of contemporary doggerel.

BIBLIOGRAPHY

Diner Lingo. http://www.dinerlingo.com/.

Idle, Eric, writer, vocalist. "Always Look on the Bright Side of Life." Virgin Records, 1991.

Khayyám, Omar. *The Rubáiyát*. http://classics.mit.edu/Khayyam/rubaiyat.html.

Smiley, Jack. *Hash House Lingo*. Originally published 1941. Republished with an introduction and notes by Paul Dickson. Mineola, NY: Dover Books, 2012.

Taylor, Bayard. "Bedouin Love Song." http://www.bartleby.com/360/2/209.html

"What Do We Call the Sound a Goat Makes?" WordReference. http://forum.wordreference.com/threads/what-do-we-call-the-sound-a-goat-makes.2396869/.

Wodehouse, P. G. *A Damsel in Distress*. New York: George H. Doran, 1919.

———. *Leave It to Psmith*. New York: Norton, 2012.

———. *My Man Jeeves*. London: Newnes, 1919. http://www.gutenberg.org/files/8164/8164-h/8164-h.htm.

———. *Right Ho, Jeeves*. New York: Norton, 2011.

Imposture 20

Down Under

This Imposture stages another double-meaning joke: Abū Zayd's poem about his fallen comrade turns out to refer to a malfunctioning part of his own anatomy. Reporting this discovery to his friends, al-Ḥārith says that he told them the truth, without evasion or euphemism—something al-Ḥarīrī does too, but only at the very end. This dancing around the problem of explicit reference is nowhere handled more brilliantly than in Joseph Furphy's Such Is Life *(1903). Set in Australia, this set of loosely connected stories is full of long speeches in the various dialects used by natives and immigrants in the nineteenth century. Many of the characters are supposed to be shockingly foulmouthed, but the moral standards of the day did not permit Furphy to use in print the actual words he had in mind. To compensate, he uses various paraphrases, all of them hilarious. Furphy's style also opens up the archive of late-nineteenth- and early-twentieth-century Australian English—which fortunately includes several synonyms for the organ of interest to Abū Zayd. In addition to Furphy, this Imposture draws as necessary on nineteenth-century terms attested in Sidney Baker's 1945 compilation of Australian idiom. The period is furthermore the one in which A. B. Paterson compiled his* Old Bush Songs, *a collection of the ballads sung by the drovers, shearers, and other denizens of the outback. Several of these are dirges sung for dead comrades, and one of these furnished the model for Abū Zayd's long poem.*

As Harrie Hammo was telling us: 20.1

I once drawed out to Forkees with a company of honest, good-natured
blokes who were easy to get on with. Travelling with them, I nearly forgot
I was up the backblocks, far from my mates and cobbers. After we reached
the settlement and settled our mounts, though we were glad to leave the
miseries of the saddle for the comfort of the cottage, we were reluctant to
part for good. So we picked a possie and resolved to turn out there every
morning and evening for a gossip.

One day the company had come trickling in like bullocks on a string   20.2
when a loud-spoken bloke barges up to us and hails us bold as brass.
He looked like a kurdaitcha spitting a bone, or a gully-raker who'd as soon
hunt a Tassie tiger as duff your jumbuck. Then he sang:

> All you wise men and sages, to my tale lend an ear.
> Alas! for poor Percy, no more shall we hear
> Of his thrusts on the field, his assaults on the gate,
> His strokes in the trenches, his hearty "Shoot straight!"

> CHORUS
> My old fella is fallen, who once stood so proud,
> Oh will anyone give me a coin for his shroud?

> In the thick of the battle he'd stand strong and tall,
> And strike blow after blow, 'till the citadel fall;
> And at night with the lasses, get as good as he gave,
> And took fair suck of the sheilas, did Percy the brave.

> CHORUS: My old fella *&c.*

> Now he's come a cropper, the lasses do mourn,
> And I wait in vain for Percy's return,
> For Percy has carked it, and prostrate he dies,
> The quacks could not save him, so buggered he lies.

> CHORUS: My old fella *&c.*

20.3   Then the old swagman began to cry as if he'd lost a cobber. At last his fit passed away and he dried his eyes. Then he said, "Day, chaps! Thrice-prayed-for, best-beloved bonzer blokes! 'Strewth, that song 's fair dinkum. I seen the poor misforchunate fellow perish with my own eyes, swelp me Gawd. If I wasn't flyblowed in regard o' cash, and short a brass razoo, I'd rise the money myself instead of burking it and handin' the job to you. But when a man's knocked stiff, it's hard lines to blame him for not kickin' in. Why, I haven't a skerrick left!"

20.4   The company put their heads together to have a yabber about how much to fork out. But the swagman, thinking they meant to demand proof, or send him away empty-handed, gave them a gobful.

"You bunyips!" he shouted. "What's this slimy little word-shuffle? You're a tatty lot of vips n' wowsers! A shroud's all I'm asking for, not an hour's hard yakka; a bit of rag, not a hundred hides; a scrap of cloth, mates, not a set of drapes for the Holy House of Gawd. Why, you're no more use than tits on a bull, you yaller-hided dodgers!"

Quailing before the terrible flowers of his speech, the company forked over their loose silver, hoping that, having borne the shower, they might be spared the soaking to come.

20.5   *Harrie Hammo continued his yarn:*

Now the cadger was standing behind me to avoid my eye. The company had tendered their mites, and it came my turn to do the same. So I pulled off my finger-ring and turned round.

"Well, I'll be dashed!" I thought. "It's old Zaydo, as sure as he's standin' there!" And it was Baghdad to a brick that his yarn was a canard. But I had a scruple against blurting it out, and so I held my tongue. Anyhow, I bunged him the ring. "Spend it on the funeral," I told him.

"Good on ya, ya little ripper!" he exclaimed, as full of brushfire as I remembered. Then he shot off like a boomer with a pot of horse blister stuck on his tail.

Curious to know who the poor dead bloke was, and to examine Zaydo's pretence to pious duty, I dashed after him full chase. A bowshot away I caught him. No one else was in sight. Seizing him by his sleeve-ends, I slewed him around.

"Strewth," I shouted, "I'll stick to you like a bear to a branch till you show me that shrouded dead cobber of yours!"

He yanked down his dacks and pointed to his donger.

"D—n you!" I exclaimed. "You'd lamb any man down, and clean him out."

Like a good honest scout, I returned to the group and gave my mates the bad news without beating around the bush. They burst into laughter when they heard the tale, and cursed that poor dead digger who would never rise again.

GLOSSARY

20.1

backblocks   remote country areas

cobber   best friend

possie   (pronounced "pozzy") position, spot

20.2

on a string   tied together with a rope

barge up to   accost

gully-raker   one who steals unbranded stock

duff   steal livestock

jumbuck   sheep

come a cropper   fall heavily

cark it   collapse, die

buggered   exhausted; broken, wrecked

20.3

swagman   an itinerant odd-jobman and beggar

bonzer   excellent

'strewth   God's truth! (an exclamation)

straight dinkum   honest, aboveboard, true, genuine

flyblowed in regard o' cash   destitute

brass razoo   an imaginary coin of trivial value

burke   to get rid of by some indirect maneuver

skerrick   a small amount of anything, usually money

20.4

yabber   talk, converse

give a gobful   abuse, usually justifiably

tatty   bad, disliked, or out of order

vip   miser

wowser   killjoy

yakka   labor

20.5

cadge   "to obtain by imposing on
another's generosity or friendship; to borrow without intent to
repay; to beg or obtain by begging"
(Macquarie)

it was Baghdad, etc.   my coinage
based on "It's London to a brick,"
meaning "It's certain" or "It's very
good odds"

canard   an extravagant or absurd
story circulated to deceive the
credulous

bung   toss

a little ripper   something good, exciting, or admirable

full of brushfire   full of vim and spirit

dacks   trousers

donger   penis (also "Percy" and "old
fella," as in the song)

lamb out   to induce (someone)
to spend in a reckless fashion;
swindle, cheat, fleece

digger   soldier

NOTES

Present-day Strine (Australian English) speakers often create variants of words,
including proper names, by dropping a syllable and adding a suffix (-a, -ee, or
-o; on these hypocorisms, see Baker, *Australian Language*, 194, and hijosh,
"How to Speak Australian" and "How to Speak Australian: Part Two"). The application of this rule to al-Ḥārith ibn Hammām gives "Harrie" and "Hammo"
(§20.1). "Forkee" is a similar coinage based on Mayyāfāriqīn, the northern Meso-
potamian town (today called Silvan, and located in Turkey) mentioned in the
original.

For "a kurdaitcha spitting on a bone" (§20.2), the original Arabic says "like a
man who spits on knots," an allusion to Q Falaq 113:4, "the women who spit on
knots." In the Qur'an, the women are casting a malicious spell (*sharr*), perhaps
one intended to cause illness. But al-Ḥarīrī seems to have in mind another purpose mentioned by the exegetes—namely, the foiling of others' plans, symbol-
ized by the loosening of the knots. In the present context, the allusion seems to
indicate that "Abū Zayd accosted [the company] with the confidence of one who
can solve any riddle and circumvent any antagonist" (Chenery, *Assemblies*, 452).
In Central Australian Aboriginal culture, a "kurdaitcha" (Baker, *Australian Language*, 133) is a person empowered to carry out a ritual assassination (Spencer
and Gillen, *Native Tribes*, 476ff.). "Spitting a bone" is "a form of native magic by
which an enemy is 'willed' to death" (Baker, *Australian Language*, 225). "Tassie

tiger" comes from "Tasmanian tiger" (on "Tassie" see Baker, *AL*, 187), a now-extinct predator.

"All you wise men . . ." (§20.2) is based on "The Stockman's Last Bed" (in Patterson, *Old Bush Songs*, 110; see performances by Tex Morton and others). "Fair suck" comes from "fair suck of the sauce bottle," which is "a request to cut the speaker some slack" (Wiktionary, "Appendix: Australian English Vocabulary"), but is here meant more literally. "Sheila," meaning "woman," is not attested in Furphy or Patterson, but is dated by the *OED* to at least 1839. "Thrice-prayed-for, best-beloved" (§20.3) comes from Furphy, *Such Is Life*, 133.

A "bunyip" (§20.4) is "an imaginary creature of Aboriginal legend, said to haunt rushy swamps and billabongs." According to *Macquarie*, it also means "an impostor." The original Arabic accuses the company of being "lowland mirages" and "gravel that looks like silver." The implication of lacking value is conveyed by "tits on a bull," which I have moved to the end of the speech.

"To examine [his] pretence to pious duty" (§20.5) comes from Chenery, *Assemblies*, 222.

BIBLIOGRAPHY

Baker, Sidney J. *The Australian Language*. Sydney: Angus and Robertson, 1945.

[Furphy, Joseph]. *Such Is Life, Being Certain Extracts from the Diary of Tom Collins*. London: Hogarth, 1983. First published 1903. E-text at Gutenberg (http://www.gutenberg.org/cache/epub/3470/pg3470-images.html) and University of Sydney Australian Digital Collections (http://adc.library.usyd.edu.au/data-2/p00015.pdf). Page references are to the latter.

hijosh. "How to Speak Australian: Abbreviate Everything." http://www.youtube.com/watch?v=yDb_WsAt_Z0.

———. "How to Speak Australian Part Two: Abbreviate Names." http://www.youtube.com/watch?v=rw7FbcosSDE.

Koala Net. "Australian Slang." http://www.koalanet.com.au/australian-slang.html.

The Macquarie Dictionary Online. http://www.macquariedictionary.com.au/.

Morton, Tex. "The Stockman's Last Bed (1940)." Published Sept. 8, 2012. http://www.youtube.com/watch?v=JtoQoQu-YRk.

Paterson, A. B., ed. *The Old Bush Songs, Composed and Sung in the Bushranging, Digging, and Overlanding Days*. Sydney: Angus and Robertson, 1905.

Spencer, Baldwin, and F. J. Gillen. *The Native Tribes of Central Australia.* London: MacMillan, 1899.

SIL: see Furphy.

Wiktionary. "Appendix: Australian English Vocabulary." http://en.wiktionary. org/wiki/Appendix:Australian_English_vocabulary.

Wiktionary. "Appendix: Australian English Terms for Clothing." http://en.wiktionary.org/wiki/Appendix:Australian_English_terms_ for_clothing.

IMPOSTURE 21

DOWN IN BAM

This Imposture is unusual because Abū Zayd uses his oratorical powers to help someone. (See also Imposture 6.) The preacher who takes up the cause of the oppressed and speaks truth to power called to mind those African-American clergymen famous for doing the same thing, albeit in a very different context. The many forms their preaching takes—from scholarly exegesis to vigorous cajolery to ecstatic effusion—provided a spectrum of variations rich enough to match Abū Zayd's exuberant performance in this episode. For the narrative voice, and for the nonstandard parts of the preaching, the translation uses Harlem Jive: that is, the variant of African American Language (AAL) associated with the Harlem of the 1930s and 1940s. This variant has the advantage of having been documented by several contemporary observers, including the composer, jazz singer, and band leader Cab Calloway; the anthropologist, novelist, and short-story writer Zora Neale Hurston; and above all the sportswriter and editor Dan Burley. These authorities represent hepcats as speaking entirely in Jive, using elaborately poetic equivalents for many Mainstream English words. It seems unlikely that anyone ever spoke quite this way; rather, Burley, Hurston, and Calloway are helping to create a literary language based on Jive. It is this literary language that al-Ḥārith, Abū Zayd, and company will adopt here, under the expert supervision of linguist Nandi Sims.

21.1   *Here's what my brotha Haarith son of Hammam laid on us.*

Well, alright now. Ever since I got my boots on and come to school, I been latchin on to righteous sermons and stayin away from the dozens. When I listen to good preachin, I ack like I was raise right, and I don't talk outta place no mo. Instead a bustin conk to keep from blowin my top, I jus' collar some solid preachin till I get mellow. Now bein in the groove done got good to me; I'm down with it, bound with it, and around with it.

21.2   Anyhow, this story is about what happen one time after I quit fumblin 'round and walk through the door that God open for me. This was up in Rayy. One early bright after I pop in port, the joint starts jumpin. I dig a frantic mob free-wheelin down the stroll, slicin they chops 'bout some preacher come on like the Gang Busters. "He cap Ibn Samun!" they say.

Like I had told y'all, I'd walk clear to Diddy-wah-diddy for a righteous sermon. So I stanch out right afta them, pushin and shovin through the no-manners. Pretty soon we was in a big open space with every kind of folk there, from the Governor of Gro'venor to the Home from Rome, from Sugar Hill to Beluthahatchie. Right in the middle of the main kick, down in front of the poppa-stoppas, is a butt-sprung battle-hammed old storm-buzzard togged to the bricks in a tall sky-piece and a lead sheet over his shoulders. He preachin like the tree—all root!—and he got them cats and hens fallin out and blowin their wigs. It was chillbumps and goosefeathers, gate! Here's the spiel I heard him lay on:

21.3   "Brothers and sisters! Sin cannot *delude* unless you *collude*. Before it can *harm* you, it must *disarm* you. But I see folks giving it a hand. I see folks chasing after it . . . and being surprised when they catch it! The truth is, you don't catch Sin: it catches *you*. And the time you waste in the chase you could use to get right with GOD.

"Now, y'all know folk be runnin after what don't belong to them. But that's not *need*, that's *greed*! Did the Lord not bless us enough? Is there anything we need so bad that we have to turn away from Him to find it? Every Four-and-one I tell you the answer to that question; I don't know if y'all listening. But never mind that now: GOD gave you the answer, and warned you what's going to happen if you don't heed His Word. So why do it *your* way, when you can do it *His* way? Why grope in the dark when He's holdin up a lamp?

"Now back to dem dead caliphs that y'all be working so hard fo'. Who gonna collar 'em when GOD say the show is over? Not you: you be done *died*! And yet, and yet, brotha, you can't get enough of that *material accumulation*. You may satisfy your animal cravings, but will that put you right with GOD? Or maybe you think He'll just let you slide dis one time. All right, Jack, but what if you call off all yo' bets not next year, not next week, not tomorrow, but *tooo-night*? Do you think you can say, 'Watcha say, Brotha Death? How 'bout I mash you a fin and you dig me some other time?' Do you think he care if you think you a gasser?

"C'mon, y'all! Ain't nothin' gonna get him to go, not money and not chillun neither. And ain't nothin' do your dead-and-buried self no good except yo' *good deeds*! Can I get an 'Amen'? Lord, help us live up to what we say when we layin a racket! Help us keep ourselves out o' dem jooks and gut-buckets! And, Lord, remind us that if we don't get in there, we ain't gettin' *in* there! We ask this in Your name, Lord; amen!"

Then he start to whoopin: 21.4

> It's comin soon, beloved! It's comin soon!
> Your money won't keep it out!
> Your mansion won't keep it out!
> Go down look at the cemetery:
> It's takin in;
> It's not puttin out!
> We goin down there soon, Lord.
> Old Man Mose comin to take us down.
> We can't take no poke with us, Lord.
> So we gon' leave it with you!
> Don't know when we goin, Lord.
> So we givin it to you now!
> Now the Devil he say wait awhile.
> He say, What you in such a hurry fo'?
> I say: Get up off of me, Devil!

Beloved, help me drive dat devil away!
Tears will do it!
Repentance will do it!
We walkin in de shadow of Death, Lord.
We goin down in de earth, Lord.
But we ain't goin alone: no, Lord!
We got our good deeds, Lord,
And Your Judgment comin soon!

21.5   Well, them folk stashed there weepin and repentin 'till early black, 'till just about time for worship. Then when the hollerin die down and everybody get sober and quiet, a brotha yell out to the Governor (who was in the house) saying his deputy treating folk sadder than a map and leavin them beat to they socks. But the Governor igg the brotha and keep on listenin to the deputy. After a while the brotha dig he makin the wrong play. So he turn to the preacher and aks him to sound off on behalf of everybody.

Well now, when the preacher hear that, he lick his chops, frisk his whiskers, and take off loud-talkin with this riff:

Take comfort, brother!
Somewhere I heard
About a mighty governor who used his office
Not to raise his people up but to wear them down.
Somewhere I heard
About a governor draped in the robes of oppression,
Grown fat from wallowing in a swamp of corruption,
Heedless of the difference between right and wrong.

But somewhere I heard
Of a law that stands above his law:
Of a law that says that no man can hold power forever,
That the counsel of slanderers breeds injustice.
So when that governor denies you your rights
Bear it patiently.

When he drinks fresh water while you drink from the branch
Bear it patiently.
And when he make your lives bitter with hard bondage
Bear it patiently, for somewhere I read

That Fate raises a man only to cast him down,
And one day you will see this governor
Cast down, spat on, mocked;
And one day you will see this governor
In a place where the eloquent tremble and fall silent,
Where sinners are judged, and trodden underfoot,
Where all he ate and drank will seethe him in his belly.

And on that day
He will be called to account with more severity
Than he ever showed to you
And on that day
The Lord shall be honored upon him, his chariots, and his
    horsemen.

Then he eyeball the Governor with a slice of ice and lay this down: 21.6
    "Govanuh, the wind may blow and the door may slam, but what you shooting ain't worth a damn! I know you think you the Man, but you astorperious and over-sport yo' hand. Ain't you heard the preacher declare it? The kingdoms of dis world are vanity and vexation of spirit. The only good shepherd the one that care for his flock; the rest go to Ginny Gall, under a rock. This here world ain't worth no pain and strife; you gotta focus them glims on the afterlife. It ain't no call to oppress your brother: ain't the Lord tole us to help each other? The Head Knock down with your jive, ofay! He settin up His scales for Judgment Day. Now you might think I'm beatin up my gums, but I know you gone go when the wagon comes!"
    De Governor hear that, he look chewed and his color go pale. He com-   21.7
mence to bad-mouth his own job, sighin "My people! My people!" Then he straighten the afflicted brotha and knock that hincty deputy a cut-eye look. After that he mash the preacher a glory roll and aks him to truck on up and

see him later. So the brotha that done been scoffin fishheads and scramblin for the gills, he cop a drill with a roll in his kick, while the deputy haul it with nothin to the bear but his curly hair.

After a while the preacher step out with his homies, cuttin rug like a jitter bug. I skivver along behind him till I get close enough to gim him kinda hard. When he dig me smokin him over he say, "If you ain't hep, ole man, better ask Granny Grunt." Den he put down a lick:

21.8
    I'm the cat you always see
    Havin' a ball with royalty
    I'm the cat that'll blow your top
    With jazz or blues or real ring bop
    The cat from Sarooj, that's me!

    I seen trouble and plenty of it
    But this hep cat can rise above it
    My crumb crushers still pearly white
    My goola keep boppin' all through the night
    The cat from Sarooj, that's me!

    I done hepped 'em ev'ry place
    I got horses runnin' in every race
    I been around since Noah's sabbath
    With hep cats Sam and Hem and Japheth
    The cat from Sarooj, that's me!

21.9   *Brotha Haarith lit up his coal pot and went on tellin his heavy lard:*

"Sure as I am born," I say, "you Aboo Zayd! That was some righteous signifying, gate! You was cookin with gas!"

He smile at me like a bloke with the yolk when folk cop a trot to his dommy. Den he lay down this backcap: "Here's confidential right from the Bible, ole man:

Never fear to speak the Truth
And walk the narrow way;
If in your heart you do not yield
You'll overcome some day,
You'll overcome some day."

After that he tell his Jacksons his play's a trilly and den he cut out, draggin his righteous rags behind him. Some time later we knock a broom around Rayy trying to collar him. We even write to folks in Bam, and down in Bam, but ain't nobody know where he stashed hisself, and can't nobody tell us what Hoo-Rah done flew him back to its nest.

GLOSSARY

Unless otherwise specified, *HD* refers to Calloway, *Hepster's Dictionary*; *OH* to the glossary section of Burley, *Original Handbook*; *OH* plus a page number to other parts of *Original Handbook*; GHS to Hurston, "Glossary of Harlem Slang"; *BT* to Smitherman, *Black Talk*; and *AAE* refers to Green, *African American English*. References to Hurston, "Story," are so designated. References to the glossaries are not paginated, as terms are listed alphabetically (though some of Burley's are out of order).

21.1

brotha   brother (on treatment of *r* see *AAE*, 4.5)

well, all right now   from Hurston, "Story," 1001

got your boots on   you know what it is all about, you are a hepcat, you are wise (*HD*)

come to school   acquiesce, learn (*OH*)

latch on   grab, take hold, get wise to (*HD*)

ack   act (on reduction of final consonant clusters, see *AAE*, 4.2)

righteous   splendid, okay (*HD*)

bust your conk   apply yourself diligently, break your neck (GHS)

blowing your top   getting very angry (GHS; cf. *HD*, which defines "blow the top" as "to be overcome with . . . delight")

collar   get, obtain; comprehend (*HD*)

solid   great, swell, okay (*HD*)

mellow   fine, the tops (*OH*)

in the groove   perfect (*HD*)

git good to somebody   "to get carried away while doing something that starts out in a routine fashion" (*BT*)

183

21.2

Rayy   town in north-central Iran; now a suburb of Tehran

early bright   morning (*HD*)

pop in port   show up, appear (*OH*)

joint is jumping   the place is lively (*HD*)

dig   look, see (*HD*)

free-wheeling   parading briskly (GHS, s.v. "cruising")

stroll   street (*OH*, s.v. "stroll," and 83)

slice one's chops   talk (*OH*)

come on like (the) Gang Busters   excel in performance (*HD*)

cap   outdo, surpass (*HD*, s.v. "capped")

Ibn Samun   Ibn Samʿūn, a famous Arabic orator

Diddy-wah-diddy   a far place, a measure of distance (GHS)

stanch out   begin, commence, step out (GHS)

pushin and shovin, etc.   based on Hurston, *Their Eyes*, 60

Gro'venor   Grosvenor, the name of several places, imposed to supply a rhyme with "Governor"

Home from Rome   a working man (*OH*, 17 and 18)

Sugar Hill   a prosperous part of Harlem (GHS)

21.3

Four-and-one   Friday (*OH*)

dead caliphs   money

call off your bets   die (*OH*)

Beluthahatchie   next station beyond Hell (GHS)

main kick   the stage (*HD*)

poppa-stoppa   old man, professor (*OH*)

butt-sprung   a suit or skirt out of shape in the rear (GHS)

battle-hammed   badly formed about the hips (GHS)

stormbuzzard   shiftless, homeless character (GHS)

togged to the bricks   dressed to kill (*HD*)

sky-piece   hat (*HD*)

lead sheet   a topcoat (*HD*)

like the tree, etc.   a term of vigorous approbation (*OH* 16) whose precise meaning is unclear to me

cat   a male, esp. one who knows his way around (*OH*)

hen   any woman over twenty-nine (*OH*)

blow one's wig   to become excited, enthused, crazy (*HD*)

chillbumps and goosefeathers   from Jakes, "Danger"

gate   an address to men (*HD*)

spiel   a declaration, supplication, or dissertation (*OH*)

mash you a fin   give you five dollars (*HD*)

dig me   meet me (*HD*)

gasser   something that is tops, great, excellent (*OH*)

get you to go   power, physical or otherwise, to force the opponent to run (GHS)

21.4

Old Man Mose   death (*OH*)

21.5

Be stashed   stand or remain (*HD*)

early black   evening (*HD*)

sadder than a map   terrible (*HD*)

beat to my socks   lacking everything (*HD*)

igg   ignore (*HD*)

make the wrong play   make the wrong choice (*OH*, 17)

21.6

the man   the law (*HD*)

astorperious   "haughty, biggity" (GHS)

Ginny Gall   "a suburb of Hell" (GHS)

glims   eyes (*HD*)

it ain't   there isn't (Wolfram, "Grammar," 130)

Head Knock   "the Lawd," i.e., God (*OH*)

down with   through with (*HD*; possibly an error for "done with," as

21.7

My people! My people!   "Sad and satiric expression in the Negro language: sad when a Negro comments on the backwardness of some members of his race; at other

lay a racket   be shrewd (*OH*)

jook   a pleasure house (GHS)

gut-bucket   low dive (GHS)

get in there   to exert your best efforts (*OH*)

poke   money (*OH*)

sound off   begin a program or conversation (*HD*)

lick the chops, frisk the whiskers   "what the cats do when they are warming up for a swing session" (*HD*)

loud-talking   speaking in such a way as to be overheard and thereby shame one's interlocutor (see *AAE*, 5.3.2)

OH says it means understanding or being ready for something)

ofay   white person (GHS, *HD*)

beating up your gums   talking to no purpose (GHS)

go when the wagon comes   "You may be acting biggity now, but you'll cool down when enough power gets behind you" (GHS)

times, used for satiric or comic effect" (GHS)

straighten   pay back, compensate (or so I infer from the example given by Mezz Mezzrow in Peretti, *Creation*,

130–34, cited in Wikipedia, "Glossary of Jive Talk")

hincty   conceited, snooty (*HD*)

mash   give money (*HD*)

glory roll   money (*OH*)

truck   go (*HD*)

scoffin fishheads, etc.   having a hard time of it (*OH*)

cop a drill   leave quickly, disappear, or walk away (*OH*)

kick   pocket (*HD*)

haul it   flee on foot (GHS)

with nothin to the bear but his curly hair   "don't be afraid of him" (GHS)

21.9

heavy lard   a story to be told (*OH*)

signify   declare yourself; brag, boast (*HD*)

cooking with gas   doing well, making good progress (used, but not glossed, in *OH*; see also *BT*)

a bloke with the yolk   a man with money (*HD* uses "bloke" in "Minnie the Moocher," and "yolk" is from *OH*, 20)

cop a trot to his dommy   run to his home (*OH*, 98 and 99)

backcap   reply, supplementary remark, conclusion (*OH*)

rug cutter   good dancer (GHS)

jitter bug   swing music addict (*OH*)

skivver   walk (or so I gather from Hurston, "Story," 1002)

gim   look over (*OH*)

smoke over   look over (GHS)

ole man   my friend (*OH*, 16–17)

Granny Grunt   a mythical character to whom most questions may be referred (GHS)

put down   say, perform, describe, do (*OH*)

lick   hot musical phrase (*HD*)

crumb crushers   teeth (*HD*)

goola   piano (*OH*, 16 and 18)

Jackson   form of address between male friends (*OH*, 16)

his play's a trilly   he's leaving (*OH*, 130)

cut out   leave, depart (*HD*)

righteous rags   the components of a Harlem-style suit (GHS)

knock a broom   take a brisk walk (*OH*, 84)

Bam, and down in Bam   down South (GHS; here as in the title I take advantage of the fact that there is a town in Iran called Bam)

stashed hisself   based on *stache*, "to file, to hide away" (*HD*)

NOTES

The sermons and other performances attributed to Abū Zayd in this Imposture use a range of forms, from formal Mainstream English to heavily marked AAL, following the lead of African-American preachers (e.g., Charles G. Adams, D. T. Jakes, Donald Hillyard, and Raphael Warnock) who vary their diction for expressive purposes. For AAL syntax I have relied on Green, *African American English*, and Wolfram, "Grammar," which contains a helpful appendix that breaks features down by period and region. Nearly all the Jive expressions come from Hurston, Calloway, or Burley, as noted in the Glossary. For a few non-Jive expressions I have drawn on Hurston's novel *Their Eyes Were Watching God* (1937), in which speech is represented in what I take to be something closer to the normal AAL of the period. (Admittedly, the action of the novel takes place far from New York, but Harlem was full of migrants, meaning that Southern expressions might plausibly be attributed to Harlemites; see Hurston, "Story," 1005). The only items in the narration not specifically attested in mid-century sources are the irresistibly apposite "got good to me," known to me only from Smitherman, *Black Talk*; and "chillbumps and goosefeathers," from a recent sermon by Jakes. It should nevertheless be noted that the primary target language in this Imposture is a historical form—more bluntly, a dead language, in the sense that most of its native speakers are no longer with us and no new speakers are being born. It is, furthermore, a literary register of that variety, deliberately intensified by my sources. (On the use of literary sources in the reconstruction of past forms of AAL, see Dillard, *Lexicon*, 143–55.) Readers should therefore not expect the Imposture to sound like the normal speech of a present-day user of AAL. I have made some attempt to signal the distinctive sounds of AAL, but the wide range of variables and the different approaches adopted by my sources made it impossible to achieve consistency.

I am aware that my use of Harlem Jive and preachers' style raises the question of cultural appropriation—that is, whether it is legitimate for someone who is not African American to imitate these language varieties for his own ends. Geneva Smitherman describes the core objection by saying that non-native users "reap the psychological, social, and economic benefits of a language and culture born out of enslavement, neo-enslavement, Jim Crow, U.S. apartheid, and twentieth-century hard times," adding that "there is a multibillion dollar industry of Black Language and Culture, while at the same time there is continued underdevelopment and deterioration among the people who produce this language and culture" (*Black Talk*, 32 and 33). As far as this translation is concerned, the objection would be that African Americans have long suffered the consequences of speaking non-Mainstream forms of English (on which see Labov, *Language in the Inner City*) whereas I can imitate that language with impunity. Without contesting this fact, I offer a response grounded in my work as a philologist. Anyone who studies language believes, or should believe, that all forms of it are equally deserving of respect. Stigmatizing particular languages, dialects, or accents, forbidding children to use them, treating their speakers as backward, and the like are all scientifically baseless and morally abominable practices. Of course, people have the right to teach their children whatever idiom they feel will be most useful to them, even if that means that the community's ancestral language will eventually disappear. But to claim that certain languages are intrinsically inferior to others is simply ideology masquerading as linguistics. Admittedly, many more people will read a scientific paper, or listen to a song, if it is written in English. Yet this is the result of history and geopolitics, not the phonological or grammatical superiority (whatever that would mean) of English to other languages. On these points see further McWhorter, *Talking Back*; and Cunningham, "The Case for Black English," which reviews it.

To avoid writing in certain varieties because they have been stigmatized, whether by their own speakers or by others, is to give one's consent to a bigoted judgment of inferiority. By contrast, to write in a stigmatized variety, and to translate foreign literature into it, is to affirm its worthiness. For many languages, including English, the moment they were used to translate the Bible is the moment they became a proper language in the eyes of many of their speakers. Similarly, Burley's translations of *Hamlet* and Wordsworth into jive demonstrate that one can use AAL (or his particular construction of it) to express all the same ideas that famous authors have expressed in Mainstream English. On this premise, I use AAL in this book for the same reason I use cowboy jargon or Middle English: to mobilize the fullest possible range of English expression in order to convey the dazzling variety of al-Ḥarīrī's Arabic. The only alternative would have been to *exclude* AAL, which would amount to saying that it doesn't deserve to be used as a literary language.

Of course, readers may agree with my position in AAL but insist that the person producing it in such cases should be African American. One argument for this position is that a non-native user in AAL is doing what Maisha Z. Johnson calls privileging his or her own voice—that is, pretending to speak for others while drowning out or ignoring their account of their own experience. The point is well taken. But this Imposture does not claim to represent the *experience* of African Americans. Rather, it uses their *language* to render the experience of a third party, al-Ḥarīrī's characters. To this transposition one might object that a language cannot be separated from the history and culture of its speakers. In one sense, of course, this is true. But in another sense it is false. Because they are discrete combinatorial systems (on which see Pinker, *Language Instinct*), languages are incredibly adaptive and can be used to talk about anything. Early-twentieth-century Navajo, for example, did not have words for grenades, battleships, and dive bombers. But when Navajo speakers served as code talkers in World War Two, they came up with equivalents ("potato," "whale," and "chicken hawk," respectively; see McWhorter, *What Language Is*, 61). As a purely formal exercise, it is no harder to put al-Ḥarīrī into Jive than into Hebrew, German, or Mainstream English. The only reason doing so seems odd is that AAL has never before been used (as far as I know) for translations from Arabic. But this is a historical problem, not a linguistic one.

All the above notwithstanding, it would have been foolish to attempt writing in AAL on my own when expert help was available. At the recommendation of my University of California colleague Anne H. Charity Hudley, I reached out to Nandi Sims, a doctoral student in linguistics at Ohio State University. Ms. Sims reviewed my text, making numerous corrections and suggesting several critical rewordings. While she is not in any way responsible for my choice of target languages, she deserves all the credit for making the final text as correct a representation of AAL as is possible given the difficulties of writing in a dated literary register. I am also grateful to Werner Sollors, Henry B. and Anne M. Cabot Professor of English and of African American Studies at Harvard University, as well as Global Professor of Literature at New York University Abu Dhabi, who was kind enough to comment on an early draft. To emphasize, finally, the extent to which this Imposture is based on what Dillard calls "giving strict attention to the works of Black authors" (*Lexicon*, 150), the Glossary documents my source or sources for each expression, and the Notes give more detail on particular items.

"I'm down with it . . ." (§20.1) is adapted from *OH*, 56, where the series is unglossed but seems to correspond fairly well to the sense of the Arabic that something (in this case, self-restraint) became second nature to the speaker.

Werner Sollors has drawn my attention to the possibility that "spiel" (§21.2) which came into English through German, Yiddish, or both, may be a Hollywood invention rather than an authentic Harlem hepster term, and indeed Smitherman has no entry on it. But Burley's definition of it (of which I have cited only a small part) is so elaborate that the word seems to have been alive and well for him, at least.

"Dead caliphs" (§21.3) is my invention, based on "dead presidents," meaning paper money (*OH*), and the fact that early Islamic coins bear the name of the reigning caliph. "Whooping" (§21.4) is a distinctive rapid diction used at the end of sermons (see Anyabwile, "Elements," and for an example Adams, "Drunk," 46:40ff). "Go down look at de cemetery . . ." is adapted from Hurston, "Story," 1006. The sequence that begins "Somewhere I heard . . ." (§21.5) is inspired by Martin Luther King, Jr.'s use of auxesis (arranging words or clauses in a sequence of increasing force) and ennoia (purposefully holding back information while hinting at what is meant; see King, "I've Been to the Mountaintop"). On branch water see Hurston, "Story," 1002. "The LORD shall be honored . . ." comes from Exodus 14:17–18, 23, 26 (KJV).

"Eyeball with a slice of ice" (§21.6) comes from Hurston, "Story," 1001. "The wind . . ." is adapted from Hurston, "Story," 1004. "Over-sport your hand" comes from Hurston, "Story," 1005. "Chewed" (§21.7) comes from Hurston, "Story," 1007. On "bad mouth" see *BT*; cut-eye look: Hurston, "Story," 1002. The poem in §21.8 is inspired by Calloway's "The Hi De Ho Man." On "Lit up his coal pot" (§21.9) see Hurston, "Story," 1001. "Confidential right from the Bible" is from Hurston, "Story," 1001–2. The poem in §21.9 is based on "I'll Overcome Some Day," by gospel composer Charles Tindley (d. 1933). More closely translated, the original reads: "Be sure to tell the truth, even if / truth gets you burned in the fire of truculence. // Seek to gratify God, not man; for nothing is stupider / than to flatter His creatures but anger the Lord."

Often spelled "hurrah's nest," a Hoo-Rah's nest (§21.9) is a messy, disorderly place. The Hoo-Rah itself is often described as a kind of bird. I have not found the word in my jive sources; it was communicated to me by my father, Jay N. Cooperson, who heard it around mid-century from Fanny Parry of North Carolina. Subsequent research confirms its use among southeastern US speakers as far back as the nineteenth century. See Morris, "Hurrah's Nest."

BIBLIOGRAPHY

AAE. See Green, Lisa J.

Adams, Charles G. "Drunk on the Eve of Construction." http://www.youtube.com/watch?v=RNO6aBhjBgg.

Anyabwile, Thabiti. "Elements of Styles in Black Preaching." The Front Porch. http://thefrontporch.org/2014/07/elements-of-styles-in-black-preaching/.

Baker, Katie J. M. "A Much-Needed Primer on Cultural Appropriation." *Jezebel*. November 13, 2012. http://jezebel.com/a-much-needed-primer-on-cultural-appropriation-30768539.

BT. See Smitherman, Geneva.

Burley, Dan. *Dan Burley's Original Handbook of Harlem Jive*. DeKalb, IL: Northern Illinois University Press, 2009. Originally self-published, 1944. Abbreviated *OH*.

Calloway, Cab. "Hepster's Dictionary." There appear to have been several editions. Two are online at http://www.openculture.com/2015/01/cab-calloways-hepster-dictionary.html and http://www.dinosaurgardens.com/wp-content/uploads/2007/12/hepsters.html. Abbreviated *HD*.

Calloway, Cab, Buster Harding, and Roy Palmer, composers. "The Hi-De-Ho Man." Sung by Cab Calloway. 1934. http://www.youtube.com/watch?v=mDL-gJmAniM.

Calloway, Cab, composer. "We the Cats Will Hep Ya." Sung by Cab Calloway. http://www.youtube.com/watch?v=owV8PlYC1L0, 2:14ff.

Cunningham, Vinson. "The Case for Black English." *The New Yorker*. May 15, 2017. http://www.newyorker.com/magazine/2017/05/15/the-case-for-black-english.

Dillard, J. L. *Lexicon of Black English*. New York: Seabury, 1977.

GHS. See Hurston, Zora Neale.

Green, Lisa J. *African American English: A Linguistic Introduction*. Cambridge: Cambridge University Press, 2002. Abbreviated *AAE*; references are to section numbers.

HD. See Calloway, Cab.

Hurston, Zora Neale. "Story in Harlem Slang" and "Glossary of Harlem Slang." In *Zora Neale Hurston: Novels and Stories*, 1001–1010. New York: Library of America, 1995.

———. *Their Eyes Were Watching God*. New York: Perennial, 1998.

Jakes, T. D. "The Danger of Low Expectations." http://www.youtube.com/watch?v=omcj7A1d4HU.

Johnson, Maisha Z. "What's Wrong with Cultural Appropriation? These 9 Answers Reveal Its Harm." *Everyday Feminism*. June 14, 2015. http://everydayfeminism.com/2015/06/cultural-appropriation-wrong/.

King, Martin Luther, Jr. "I've Been to the Mountaintop." Sermon delivered April 3, 1968, at the Mason Temple, Memphis, Tennessee.

Labov, William. *Language in the Inner City: Studies in the Black English Vernacular*. Philadelphia: University of Pennsylvania Press, 1972.

MacWhorter, John. *Talking Back, Talking Black: Truths about America's Lingua Franca*. New York: Bellevue, 2017.

———. *What Language Is (And What It Isn't and What It Could Be)*. New York: Gotham Books, 2011.

Morris, Evan. "Hurrah's Nest." The Word Detective. http://www.word-detective.com/2010/09/hurrahs-nest/.

Niles, Lyndrey A. "Rhetorical Characteristics of Traditional Black Preaching." *Journal of Black Studies* 15:1 (September 1984), 41–52.

OH. See Burley, Dan.

Peretti, Burton W. *The Creation of Jazz*. Champaign, IL: University of Illinois Press, 1994.

Scafidi, Susan. *Who Owns Culture? Appropriation and Authenticity in American Law*. New Brunswick: Rutgers, 2005.

Smitherman, Geneva. *Black Talk: Words and Phrases from the Hood to the Amen Corner*. Boston: Houghton Mifflin, 2000. Abbreviated *BT*.

———. *Talkin and Testifyin: The Language of Black America*. Detroit: Wayne State University Press, 1977.

Sundaresh, Jaya. "Beyond Bindis: Why Cultural Appropriation Matters." The Aerogram. May 10, 2013. http://theaerogram.com/beyond-bindis-why-cultural-appropriation-matters/.

Tindley, Charles, composer. "I'll Overcome Some Day." http://www.hymntime.com/tch/htm/i/l/l/o/illoverc.htm.

Wolfram, Walt. "The Grammar of Urban African American Vernacular English." http://www.researchgate.net/publication/251736187_The_grammar_of_urban_African_American_Vernacular_English.

IMPOSTURE 22

LEVERAGING THE FLOW

This Imposture stages a debate between two classes of bureau-crats: the kuttāb, *or scribes, and the* ḥussāb, *or accountants. The former drafted official declarations, prepared legal docu-ments, and handled correspondence with the central govern-ment or with subordinates in the provinces. The latter kept track of government revenues and expenditures. The theme of petty rivalry as well as the use of technical terms suggested manage-ment jargon as an appropriate register for the translation.*

H. I. Hammam submitted this performance report. 22.1

At a time-specific point in my life trajectory I implemented a transfer of residence, upgrading to the Greater Tigris Riparian Region. This transi-tion facilitated quality time with a cohort of state-sector creatives who could out-wizard Furat & Sons. Right from the get-go we had a great cul-ture fit. For me the priority was acquiring best practices (not perks and comps LOL!), which made joining their team an exciting personal-growth milestone. Net-net, it was a banner year: I interfaced with some world-class rainmakers (F2F!) and took my people skills to the next level. Going forward, I was looking at an enhanced intimacy scenario, with power din-ners and catered offsites, all within an accelerated timeframe. As a valued associate, I functioned as the affective nexus of our self-selecting affinity cluster on and off the job. My core competence was facilitating confidenti-ality outcomes, whether we were doing head-down time or just screwing the pooch.

22.2   On the date under review the team was tasked with taking the lead on an agricultural tax-district survey. To meet their transportation needs, the team opted for a river boat with black trim. It was "a sweet little ride," with a good roll time, great heave, and dead rise forward. The team tapped me to join the offsite and then doubled down on the invite.

On completion of standard embarkation procedures for the watercraft, which we were able to spin as value-equal to quadruped-based travel options, it was brought to our attention that there was already a passenger on board. He was an older individual who at that time was facing challenges around his apparel, which consisted of a thread-count-impaired item of outerwear paired with a piece of headgear negatively impacted by continuous use well beyond the manufacturer's recommended replacement date. The team felt that his presence represented a non-trivial downgrade of our conviviality experience, and the associate who had brought him on board was almost promoted to customer. It was suggested that the passenger complement be right-sized by effectualizing the removal of the individual from the watercraft, but by the time we ran that idea up the flagpole none of the team members had the heart to shoot the puppy.

At that juncture, the elderly individual, having processed our engagement-averse interpersonal affect, made a bid to scale down the tension level by rolling out a conversation starter. The pushback was immediate and severe. When he later suffered a bronchial spasm that didn't raise a single courtesy signal from the group, he rowed back his initiative and, seeing no path forward, went into lockdown.

22.3   Ignoring the elephant on the deck, the team members and I proceeded to craft a conversation around issues of shared concern, including key operational parameters as well as some "non-PC" humor. It was at that juncture that the good old Public Relations-versus-Accounting debatable came to the top of the pile. Some associates felt that PR represented best in breed, while others shared their understanding that Accounting brought more to the table.

These IBPs produced a significant disconnect. Both sides upped the pitch, but they couldn't align on anything, much less achieve agreeance. The doo-doo was skewing toward the fan when suddenly the mystery passenger made himself a player.

"I don't mean to break your crayons," he said, "but you're pulling some of those data points right out of the RDB. What you need is a braindump from an SME. Well, I can deliver the goods. So sit back, relax, and let me unpack it for you.

"PR drives the top of the funnel, but Accounting gives more bang for the buck. PR is proactive while Accounting is reactive. With PR, you're talking curated artisanal content. Now think liquidity event: the bean-counters and paper-shredders have to start from scratch! PR folks are your real-time point people: they know where the C-levels keep the secret sauce and they get facetime at the head shed. Need public-sector messaging? Want to outbeat your competitors? PR's got your gurus and your outside-the-box thinkers. For seamless roll-outs, a mission-critical heads-up, or boots on the ground, they've got your back. Plus, they manage your optics. These guys and gals can run a killer campaign, incentivize across-the-board buy-ins, and get to yes, even when you've got cowboys going off paradigm. The upside for them? They don't get audited, no one blows the whistle on them, and they never have to massage the numbers on an 1120." | 22.4

By the time he hit that point in the bake-off, the mystery passenger could see that some of us were drinking the Kool-Aid while others were definitely not on board. That's when he pivoted. | 22.5

"Other side of the ledger," he said. "PR's just jargon and buzzwords! For deliverables, it's Accounting every time. PR is just the sizzle; your numbers people are the steak. With Accounting, you're setting up a point-of-purchase revenue stream, or keeping track of accounts receivable; with PR you're just massaging boilerplate. The one gets you wallet share; the other one gives you paper cuts, strains your eyes, and leaves you brain-dead. Just look at the job description: accounting is about trust, integrity, and fairness. If there's a failure to deliver, the dirham stops at Accounting. See who they've got in their cubicle: the Head of the Exchequer, who reports directly to government at the highest level. He's at the top of the org chart, corner office, blue-sky overview of the whole operation, soup to nuts. So hey, give him an unpolarized ecosystem! Give him a stability-challenged biome! If it's process facilitation you're after, he's still your best resource. And if you're talking cash flow, positive or negative, he's the nodal point of the nexus. He's your change agent—the one with the key to the lockbox. If it weren't for Accounting, revenue wouldn't stream where it's supposed to, and you'd have enough legality-dubious appropriation of unsecured assets to keep you busy until EOT. Without their team, transactions would go unregulated; there'd be no liability in cases of fraud, no basis for enforcing terms of contract, and no framework for assessing compensatory damages.

"At the end of the day, there's a synergy: PR handles branding and spin, while Accounting drills down to the nitty gritty. But you share a downside too: the higher you're promoted, the more of a LIHOM you become, and the more likely to make people's life hell unless they come and grovel in person, or incentivize you under the table just to do your job—unless you're one of the good apples, and I haven't seen too many of those."

22.6   *H. I. Hammam further minuted:*

Bottom line, he crushed it with his preso. We asked him to open the kimono a little and tell us about himself, but he threw up the Heisman. If he hadn't been exit-challenged (from a boat-ride perspective) he would have ducked out of our powwow. The whole interface was going sideways when suddenly I had an aha moment. "You've clearly experienced a wellness dropoff," I said, "but I'd bet all my holdings in shipping and navigation that you're Abu Zayd!"

"I've taken a few knocks," he smiled, "but yes, I'm Abu Zayd."

I shared my intel with the team ASAP. "This is the guy who can hang the bell on the cat and nail jelly to the hothouse wall!"

22.7   The associates put forward their best grip and grin and even tried slipping him some cash to grease the skids, but it was a non-starter.

"I'm not buying it," he said. "First you file-thirteen me for dressing downscale, then you rub my rhubarb because my personal brand doesn't look ready for prime time. We may be in the same boat, but it's too late to CYA." Then he sang:

> Listen up, listen up, listen up,
> This is all straight talk
> Straight talk, straight talk, straight talk

It's not about the package
It's not about the shelf
You can't say you don't want it
Till you've eaten it yourself

Listen up, listen up, listen up

Those other guys, they've got the ads,
They've got the jingle too;
But when you try the one we've got
You'll know it's right for you,
It's just so right for you!

Straight talk, straight talk, straight talk

It's not about the paint
Who cares about the shine
You gotta kick the tires
And take her for a drive

Listen up, listen up, listen up

Make a vow, and make it now
Not to pay for what you see;
Until you know what I can do
You can't say you know me,
Don't say that you know me!

Having unloaded chapter and verse, he put in a hard-stop request with
the boatman, disembarked, and disappeared. After his check-out, the team
members kicked themselves for sticking a finger in the wind and eyeball-
ing him as a liability. Then we decisioned it: going forward, we would get
into the weeds and see what stuck *prior* to color-coding anyone. It was a
kumbaya moment, and a key learning for all of us.

GLOSSARY

22.1

F2F   face to face

head-down time   uninterrupted work

screw the pooch   be at leisure, goof off

22.2

promoted to customer   fired

shoot the puppy   take on an unpleasant task

22.3

IBP   initial bargaining position

RDB   rectal database (the source of ideas pulled out of one's ass)

SME   subject matter expert

22.4

drives the top of the funnel   draws potential clients in

C-levels   executives whose titles begin with "chief," as in CEO

head shed   headquarters

22.5

bake-off   comparison

EOT   end of time

LIHOM   a legend in his (or her) own mind

22.6

preso   presentation

hang the bell on the cat   make a risky but successful move

nail jelly to the hothouse wall   do the impossible

22.7

file-thirteen   throw away

rub my rhubarb   annoy me

CYA   cover your ass

kumbaya   involving a display of good feelings between former antagonists

NOTES

Most compilers of management terms in English announce up front that they have collected them in order to ridicule them and discourage readers from using them. Many of the terms are in fact "weasel words"—that is, verbiage intended to disguise unpleasant realities or make ordinary things sound more impressive than they are. But other terms mock the pieties of the corporate world, protest the indignities its denizens suffer, or otherwise do what poetry does—that is, convey feeling and experience in novel ways. Among the brilliant coinages

I wish I could have included are "percussive maintenance" for trying to fix a piece of equipment by hitting it; "duck shuffler" for someone who, once you have your ducks in a row, comes along and moves them around; and "boil the ocean" for doing things the hard way.

"Furat & Sons" (§22.1) are the Banū Furāt, a family of secretaries and viziers who served the Abbasid caliphs and Ikhshidid emirs in the late ninth and early tenth centuries. "Good roll time, great heave, and dead rise forward" (§22.2) is a paraphrase of a description given by Dave Gerr of Gerr Marine, Inc., quoted in Steinberger, "How to Choose." "Guys and gals" (§22.4): no women appear in the original, but I have come across the name of at least one female scribe in ninth-century Arabic sources. For several more *kātibāt* see Sourdel, "Le 'Livre des secrétaires.'" The 1120 is a form submitted to the USA's Internal Revenue Service by corporate taxpayers. For the ethics terms in §22.5 I have drawn on AICPA, "Code." "End of time" is my own coinage by analogy with EOD "end of day" and EOW "end of week." "Threw up the Heisman" (§22.6) means "pushed us away," after American college football's Heisman Trophy, which shows a player lifting a hand to fend off a tackle.

BIBLIOGRAPHY

AICPA Code of Professional Conduct. http://www.aicpa.org/RESEARCH/STANDARDS/CODEOFCONDUCT/Pages/default.aspx.

Cohen, Heidi. "Marketing versus PR: What's the Difference." At Heidi Cohen: Actionable Marketing Guide. http://heidicohen.com/marketing-versus-pr-whats-the-difference/.

Irwin, Matthew R. "The Ridiculous Business Jargon Dictionary." The Office Life. http://www.theofficelife.com/business-jargon-dictionary-A.html.

"MBA Jargon Exhaustive List." Corporate Bullshit Generator. http://bullshit-generator.blogspot.ae/2010/01/mba-jargon-exhaustive-list.html.

Sourdel, Dominique. "Le 'Livre des secrétaires' d''Abdallāh al-Baġdādī," *BEO* 14 (1952–54), 115–53.

Steinberger, Heather. "How to Choose the Best-Riding Boat." Boating. February 2, 2015. http://www.boatingmag.com/how-to-choose-best-riding-boat.

Unsuck It. http://unsuck-it.com/browse/a-c/.

Watson, Don. *Watson's Dictionary of Weasel Words, Contemporary Cliches, Cant and Management Jargon.* New York: Knopf, 2004.

IMPOSTURE 23

THREE MEN IN A DUB

The theme here is supposed to be sariqah, *often translated as "plagiarism," though al-Ḥarīrī's characters insist on the original meaning of "theft." Abū Zayd hauls his son Zayd before a judge on the charge of stealing his verses, and the judge takes the accusation seriously. In literary criticism, however,* sariqah *is "riffing on" or "repurposing," and thus often admired. The question before the judge is whether Zayd's reuse of his father's verse is legitimate. Here, as in other episodes featuring Zayd, some kind of youth slang seemed appropriate. This time the choice fell on Multicultural London English (MLE), which has pushed aside Cockney (see Imposture 44) as the jargon of many young Londoners. In that sense, MLE marks a generational shift. Helpfully, too, it contains at least seven words that allegedly mean "steal." Also, the coexistence in London of Jamaican Patwa, the English-derived creole spoken by most of Jamaica's 2.88 million people, and MLE provided an opportunity to let the different characters speak differently. Here, al-Ḥārith and Zayd speak MLE, Abū Zayd speaks something like Patwa, and the judge (here called the Gubna) speaks MLE with a smattering of Jamaican expressions. This Imposture was corrected and improved by Mel Tom, a content creator whose work includes videos about London slang.*

El-Haref ben Hammem told us man dis story: 23.1

Man was just a yute still. Den dis madting happen round da bits and I couldn't cotch there no more. Man got shook, y'get me? If sleeping was a drink, I pour da cup out, fam. Den I bowl out of dere and ride all night, got into a madness in dem endz I swear nobody has stepped dere before. Not even a sand grouse could find dat place again, fam. Man don't stop until I reach da caliph endz. Dem bits are calm: nobody dem sides gunna screw you, nobody gunna boy you off. So I stop moving it shook, start moving it calm. Man didn't need no more, just a place to shubz and some story times, yeah?

One day man go riding round Caliph's Yard just to give manz horse a 23.2 bowl and see what was up dem endz. Oh my days! I see hella whips in a line and a bag of people runnin' on the roadside and dat, and dis facety older in a short hood, holding some tore-up younger by the collar. Dem heads dat came to watch, man breezes after dem as far as de Babylon gate. And who was sitting up dere, fam? Da Gubna-Jinaral, ready to shank your nan!

"Rispeck!" da older says. "Gad bless, me boss, and beat you enemy dem! Heah me now: me take chaage of dis-ya bwoy when im jos' a baby wid no fada and no mada. Me work haad, teach im aal a lang. Jos' when im learn evriting, watch ya now: im draw im kotlas, im draw gens ME! 'Member, 'Sorry for mawga dawg, mawga dawg tun roun bite you.'"

"Ah, come on, big man," da younger says. "I beg you tell me: When have I evah boy'd you off? When have I evah baited you out? You tink I'd go dat low? Best believe man's always bigging you up on a madting: dunknow, fam!"

"Bwoy, you no shame?" da older says. "Dem-ya nowadays pickney no have no broughtupsy! You tief me science an claim fi you owna ting; you take me poetry an say you make dat. Poet say: tief me silvah, tief me gole, but me words a not for you. Make dem stay!"

Den da Gubna aks da older, "When he finessed your poem, did he jook it? Did he tax it? Or did he tick it?"

Da older say, "I swear by Gad dat make poetry di Registrar General fi all a di Arabs, an di spokesman fi colcha: im take knife chop one kwarta a me riddim, dash weh a part of wha me mean say."

"Spit some bars," da Gubna say, "and come we see if he's a fala-fashin."
So da older brings dis:

23.3 Fayah buhn dung dis chupid ol wurl:
   She pretty but she suh dutty;
   She tell yuh all fruits ripe but den
   Tun out a bagga mout catty.

   She look good, sweet talk di yute dem,
   Promise dem coconut jelly;
   But yuh dun know wha sweet a mout
   Inna di latez buhn a belly.

   Chicken merry, an muss-muss tink
   A cool breeze, deh im tail a fayah;
   Wurl skin her teet, but she no laff;
   Truss me: dis wurl a bag o wayah.

23.4 Da Gubna aks, "Wo' did he do wif dat, mon?"
"Dat bong belly pickney tek liberty wid me eight-syllable riddim," say da older, "dash weh two, mek im a likkle bit shaata but two time wuss."
"So tek di miggle and show me."
"Open up yuh ears an listen, me boss," says da older. "Yuh go overstand how bad dat borosie sin gens me." Den he busted out dese rhymes, an' yeah, he was groaning wit every line:

   Fayah buhn dung dis ole wurl!
   Wha mek her suh dutty?
   She talk gud, but mat'rafak
   She a bagg' mout catty.

   She sweet talk a yute, say
   Come nyam coc'nut jelly;
   But wha sweet goat ago
   Latah run im belly.

Muss-muss tink a cool breeze,
Deh im tail a fayah;
Nuh every teet a laff;
Dis wurl a bag o wayah.

The Gubna turn to da yute. "Raaaah! He brought you up and trained   **23.5**
your clart, and den you jerked him, yeah? You're movin' like a paigon!"

"Best believe man nevah heard any of dem riddims before I spit my
own, G!" said da yute. "If I'm gassing, then yeah, call me a next man, and
say I got beef wiv mandem who spit bars! No, big man: what came about
was dat us-man both busted out the same words by accident. Like when a
horse steps right where another one did, y'get me?"

Now da Gubna is looking like he's thinking, "Oh sh*t! Maybe da yute
is levels," and maybe he didn't really want to be taking da piss wivvout
knowing what was going on, innit? So he starts finking about how to find
out which one of dem was big man ting and which one was a wasteman.
He musta made up his mind to have dem man kick it off freestyle so he
could put dem to da test. So he says, "Look, yeah? Come we bait out da
yute an find out who's telling the trufe an who's gassing. You man should
spit some bars but obviously do it in a cypher, like take it in turns. I wanna
see you buss like geegees at da flippin' derby. Dat way, whoever gets owned
gets owned onna basis of hard evidence, y'get me? And whoever locks it
down locks it down legit."

Bofe of dem answer at da same time, "Yeah, dat's calm! Get it started,
G."

"Da waviest rhetorical device," says da Gubna, "is wordplay. It's da one,
yeah? So come you lot lay down ten bangin' lines wif bare wordplay like
stripes on a crep or diamonds on a ring. And make sure you talk about da
madting man's got goin' on wif my wifey! She's mad peng you know, wif
dark red lips; she looks mad prestige and she's hella rude, fam! She's always
airin' me, and when she makes plans she doesn't turn up. Not gonna lie, she
makes me feel like I'm beggin' it, you get me?"

So the older lays down first and the younger spits right behind him,
cyphering until they had everyting top:

23.6　　　OLDER: My mistress' lips are black as kohl,
In mourning for my swift demise.

YOUNGER: Mornings I lie there like a lump of coal,
Having smoldered all night with open eyes.

OLDER: O she mauls me, even as the bear
Rips apart the hart with bloody claws.

YOUNGER: And yet my heart would gladly bare
The bite of every mordant clause.

OLDER: *To* me she lies, but *with* me she lieth not;
Her lies fall flat, and mine fall even flatter.

YOUNGER: How well she binds me without a knot
And, wounding me, how quick to flatter!

OLDER: A lass, alas! whose sashays and sways
So endear me to her dumb-ass ways.

23.7　　　When them man finish, the Gubna was gassed. "You man are COLD!" he
says. "Swear down, you man are actually wavey: dat cypher was RAW. You
man are coming like top boys in dis ting—two big dawgs, innit? Like two
fayah 'ticks in jus one sack! And da yute is hard on his J's—he don't need no
help from nobody. So give him a bly, mon! Don't hate da yute; big him up!"

"No sah," said the older. "Me nah go truss im, nah go care bout im nuh
mo! Im cuss out cuss out im fada, im nah follow nuttin wi me say. 'Member,
'Yuh kyaan siddung pon cow back, cuss cow 'kin!'"

Den da yute buss in. "Sekkle yourself, yeah? Not allowing a ting like dat
is bare deep, fam! Staying vex is soggy an' moving it paranoid, dat's bare
wet. Oh yeah, an' parring off a sideman, dat's dead. Big man, even if I did
a madness, and did one move, don't you remember the bars you spit back
when we was haps?

Whassup? Yuh bruv messed up, stressed up 23.8
One Love says 'member when he blessed up
One Love says 'member that he 'fessed up
So allow it, bruv; hush yuh gums, squash yuh beef
Yo, yo! One Love, keep mum, be da relief
He's yuh blud, give him props; YOU take da grief
Dat's da game, no shame, yeah it gets long
But show me a bruv ain't done nu''in wrong
Grow it up! Showin' up don't win no prize
Yuh want da fruit, bes' fight da flies
Pow pow, bruv, give it two mo' tries
Nuff mandem gunna tell you lies."

The older screwed him like a hungry hawk and s-chooped at him like a 23.9
yellow boa. Den he says, "I swear by Gad, who dash da stars an' make fall
da rain! Only one ting 'top me make it up wit im: me fraid fi go shame. Dis
bwoy get used to me take care a him, y'know. Dem time deh when times
did good, me did kind, give give bagga money. But now times a screw
face, we deh yah walla walla inna sufferation. Dis clothes wi me wear, me
borrow; an' no even one muss-muss come close to me yard."

Musta been, da Gubna felt sorry for him, as if wha' happened to him was
so peak, he musta been finking about how to give dem some help. So he
tells all da heads dat was dere watching: "You lot bowl out!"

El-Haref continued: 23.10

Now man was trying to see da older caaz I fought if I could get a good look
I could reckanize him, you get me? At fust da crowd was in da way so man
couldn't see or get close. But den da rows finned out an da heads dat was
standing dere roll away, so I check his clart, an' skrrt! It's Abu Zayd, an
da yute is his son. Dat's when man clocked wha' he was doing dere, fam.
Man almos' run up to him an' say, "What you saying, fam? It's me!" but
he screwfaces me an' frows up a hand sign like "Don't watch me, fam!"
So man just stays dere. But den da Gubna says to me, "Oi! Wuup to? Wha'
you still here for, G?"

Abu Zayd buss in first: "Dat a mi fren, big man: da one wi lent mi da clothes."

Da Gubna says "Skeen! Safe, bruv, slide through," so I sit down.

Den da Gubna goes and gives dem man two da sickest garms and a score of dinars. He tells dem to treat each ovva safe from now until Armagideon. Dey stand up and squalay out of his drum, bigging him up as dey cut.

Man was movin' it nosy, so man follows dem out to see where dem yard is. Soon our whole batch is bare far from da Gubna's endz, on our ones somewhere out in da cunch, y'get me? But den one of da Gubna's squad catches up wif me and tells me come back to his yard.

"Why would boydem call me?" I say to Abu Zayd. "Just to aks me questions, innit? What should I say? I don't want to make it bait."

"Tell dat mon say, him a poppy show, mi give him basket carry wata! Tell 'im say, him a breeze wi buck in a hurricane! Him a riva wi buck in a flood!"

"Fam!" I say. "Are you mad? Wha' if he gets vexed and burns you? Wha' if he sends his mandem to do a madness to you?"

"No badda bout me: mi a guh Edessa. Dat mon can' catch Quaco, OR him shut!"

23.11   By da time man gets back, da Gubna's session was bussed, and he wasn't on the turn no more. He was bigging up Abu Zayd and saying how peak it was dat he was so scrub. When he sees me he says, "Fam! Ain't you da one dat tricked him out in dem clappin' garms?"

"You're on da wrong track, big man," I say. "Swear down, I didn't trick him out, but he pulled a grimy trick on *you*, ma G."

Da Gubna jerks his eyes away an his face goes red. "Best believe man always clocks it when mandem are movin' it bookie; I ain't a dickhead. But I never seen a samfy man rocking a rastacap, yeah? Dat's how he ginnaled me. So d'y know where dat wasteman mighta breezed to, bruv?"

"After he messed you around, he got shook," I said, "an' he took a leg for it out of Bagdad."

"God make dat wasteman's trek long, and not keep him safe where he's at! Man's fully never been finessed like dat, an' never seen no one as road as dat guy, fam. If man didn't rispeck his colcha, best believe man would be going on a mission to find him, send him shop, an merk 'im, d'y get me?

And bruv: man don't want anyone in Bagdad to hear 'bout dis, yeah? so man don't get baited up dem endz, and vex da Top of the Top, and get so violated dat even da tourists be bennin' at me."

So he made me promise I wouldn't move bait for as long as I was movin' wit' dem man on endz.

El-Haref ben Hammem said:

So I fully said man was serious, blud, wivvout kawalissin' nobody; an' I kep' my word, same as Samaw'al.

GLOSSARY

23.1

us man   us

man   I

yute   kid

madting   disturbing event

bits   one's neighborhood

cotch   relax, feel comfortable

got shook   was frightened, got nervous

fam   term of address

bowl out   leave

endz   neighborhood

dem sides   there

screw   stare at in a hostile manner

boy off   to insult someone by ignoring, swearing at, or attacking them

moving it shook   feeling scared

shubz   party

23.2

oh my days!   an exclamation of dismay

hella   a lot of

whip   a car (but here, horses)

a bag of   a lot of

bussing   running

facety   assertive, rude

older   senior member of a gang

younger   junior member of a gang

heads   people

Babylon gate   the governor's headquarters

shank your nan   stab your grandmother, i.e., respond with extreme violence

enemy dem   enemies

kotlas   machete (but here "sword")

gens   against

mawga   skinny

mug off   offend or insult

bait out   snitch on, expose

big up   show gratitude or respect

on a madting   to excess

dunknow   you have no idea

pickney   children

broughtupsy   manners

tief   steal

science   magic

make dem stay   leave them alone

finesse   steal

23.3

fyah bun   fire burn (a curse)

chupid   stupid

wurl   world

suh dutty   so dirty

all fruits ripe   everything is fine

bagga mout   all talk

catty   woman

yuh dun know   you already know

wha sweet a mout   what tastes good

23.4

bong belly pickney   greedy child

a likkle bit shaata but two time wuss
   a little bit shorter but twice as bad

tek di miggle   you're on

borosie   rude person

23.5

raaaah   an expression of disbelief

your clart   you (pejorative)

jerk   rob

paigon   false friend

spit   produce (verse)

G   respectful term of address

gassing   lying

next man   interloper

beef   quarrel, grudge

jook   steal

tax   steal

tick   borrow

one kwarta a me riddim   one quarter
   of my rhythm

dash weh   threw away

bars   rhymes

fala-fashin   imitator

inna di lataz   later

bun a belly   burn the stomach

merry   oblivious

muss-muss   mouse

deh near   is near

deh im tail   by her tail

fiyah   fire

skin her teet   grin

bag o wayah   traitor

mat'rafak   as a matter of fact

nyam   eat

wha sweet goat ago, etc.   what once
   tasted good to a goat will later give
   her the runs

snap   I see!

big man ting   serious

wasteman   stupid

musta been   (I think) what happened
   next was . . .

dem man   they, them

kick it off   fight

freestyle   impromptu

come we . . .   let's . . .

wannabe   pretender

gassing   lying

cypher   produce (lines of rap) in
alternation

buss   run

geegees   horsies (British child's word)

owned   bested

lock down   dominate, have under
control

23.7

gassed   excited

cold   extremely skilled

swear down   I swear

actually wavey   very good

raw   new and exciting

on his J's   by himself

give him a bly   give him a chance,
overlook his mistake

hate   express disapproval of

yuh kyaan siddung, etc.   you can't sit
on a cow's back and curse cowhide
too

23.8

allow it   drop it, get over it, restrain
yourself

hush yuh gums   be quiet

squash yuh beef   decline to pursue
your grievance

23.9

s-choop   suck one's teeth in
disapproval

yellow boa   a common Jamaican
snake

'top   stop

waviest   best

crep   athletic shoe

madting   situation, predicament

wifey   wife or girlfriend

mad peng   exceptionally attractive

hella   very

air   ignore

sekkle yourself   settle down

allow   ignore, forgive

bare deep   unjustified

vex   angry

soggy, wet   embarrassing

par off   mock, vilify

sideman   someone uninvolved

dead   bad

do one move   commit a crime

haps   happy

give him props   show respect

dat's da game   that's life

it gets long   it gets tedious

nuff mandem   many people

me fraid fi go shame   I'm afraid of
being shamed

did good   were good

bagga   a lot of

we deh yah   which is here

walla walla   wallow

muss-muss   mouse

yard   house

23.10

caaz   because

heads   people

roll away   leave

clocked   realized

check his clart   look at him closely

skrrt   an expression of delighted
   surprise

don't watch me   get back

Wuup to?   What are you doing?

skeen   I see

safe   a greeting

sickest garms   most beautiful clothes

a score of   twenty

23.11

bussed   finished

on the turn   visibly angry

peak   unfortunate

scrub   broke

clappin'   out of date; worn out

garms   clothes

grimy   amusing

clocks it   realizes it

movin' it bookie   hiding something,
   acting suspicious

samfy man   con man

rocking   wearing

ginnal   take in, con, deceive

wasteman   lacking ambition

breeze   run

peak   unfortunate

bowl out   leave

Armagideon   Armageddon

squalay out of   leave

cut   leave

on our ones   alone

cunch   countryside

boydem   police

poppy show   fool, object of ridicule

mi give him basket carry wata   I took
   advantage of his stupidity

wi buck in   that ran into

to do a madness to you   to beat you up

badda   worry

mi a guh   I'm going to

took a leg for it   ran away

finessed   manipulated

road   formidable

send him shop   arrest, report, cause
   trouble for

merk   kill, insult

baited up   exposed

da Top of the Top   superior (here, the
   caliph)

violated   made a laughingstock

tourist   a clueless person

bennin'   laughing uproariously

move bait   expose

on endz   around

kawalis   deceive

NOTES

Compared to the other courtroom episodes that appear in the collection, this one is less deftly handled. Only the first two poems in the episode actually involve *sariqah*. The third is a love poem remarkable for containing up to three homonyms in each line, and the fourth is a poem of reconciliation rhyming in the unusual sound -*aṭ*. I have put the first two into Abū Zayd's Patwa and the third into Standard English, which is what such eminent Jamaican writers as Derek Walcott, Jamaica Kincaid, and Kei Miller use in their poems, novels, and essays. The last poem appears here as a rap, mostly in MLE, but not strictly so, as British rappers borrow freely from other varieties, including Standard English and US slang.

Most of the non-Cockney elements in MLE come from Caribbean languages, especially Jamaican Patwa. Many speakers of MLE have first-generation immigrant parents or other relatives who speak Patwa. Yet many other speakers have no connection to the Caribbean, and have acquired MLE through growing up in the greater London metropolitan area. These speakers are sometimes perceived as trying to sound Jamaican—a perception that has given rise to the (often disparaging) term "Jafaican" to refer to MLE. The most common terms among speakers are "London slang" or "street slang." Since these terms might apply to many varieties, I have not adopted them here.

I call Abū Zayd's speech "something like Patwa" because full-on Patwa is a language distinct from English, with its own orthography. As such, it cannot be understood by non-natives without proper training. But when certain key words are written (inaccurately) in a manner closer to Standard English, it becomes much easier for untrained readers to follow. I have, therefore, used an etymological spelling for those key words. The result will doubtless prove irritating to those who know standard Patwa pronunciation and spelling. With apologies, I ask those readers to think of what I've written as a riff on Patwa rather than an attempt to write the real thing.

The reader should also note that al-Ḥarīrī himself does not make his characters speak differently: everyone from governors to slaves speaks in elaborate rhymed prose. For this reason, I have mostly avoided the use of different varieties within single Impostures. In this case, though, the linguistic difference mapped so well on to the conflict of generations staged by Zayd and Abū Zayd that it seemed worthwhile to impose it.

This Imposture could not have been Englished without heavy reliance on the work and speech of others. For MLE, I used the linguistic overviews by English Jade ("The BEST. . .") and other YouTube contributors, as well as the editors of Wikipedia's entry on Multicultural London English. For vocabulary, in addition to the Wikipedia article, I relied on the short glossary compiled by the London Slang Dictionary Project. For syntax, speech rhythm, and discourse strategies, I referred continuously to the skits and monologues of Mel Tom, who kindly revised the entire draft and updated many terms. Expressions I use on his authority include "story time" (§23.1) and "musta been" (§23.9) from "CRAZY," and "bigging you up on a madting" (§23.2), from "Speaking to Relatives." For Patwa, Patrick's *Jamaican Creole* and the Open Grammar Project's *Learner's Grammar of Jamaican* provided a useful introduction. The online Jamaican Patwa (JP) dictionary proved indispensable, as did the collection of proverbs on the National Library of Jamaica website. I read the Patwa poetry of Louise Bennett Coverley and Linton Kwesi Johnson, but did not try to imitate either poet specifically. When all else failed, as it often did, the Bible Society's translation of the New Testament into Patwa supplied the necessary phrase.

The place where al-Ḥārith goes in §23.2 is *al-ḥarīm*, which is usually the women's quarters of a house, but here indicates an open space for troops to assemble near the palace. I call it the Caliph's Yard, "yard" meaning "house" in Jamaican Patwa and MLE. "Babylon" is a Jamaican term for the police, or for any public institution perceived as oppressive or corrupt. "Bwoy, you no shame?" is a reference to Louise Coverly's poem "No Lickle Twang" ("Weh yuh pick up dah slackness deh? Bwoy, yuh no shame?"). The proverb "Sorry for mawga dawg, mawga dawg tun roun bite you" means "Sometimes it is the same ones we've helped who are the most ungrateful" (*Jamaican Patwa*, s.v. "bite").

Asking about the alleged theft, the governor asks (§23.2) *wa-hal ḥīna saraqa salakh, am masakha am nasakh?* A lexical rendering might be: "When he repurposed it, did he skin it, transform it, or copy it?" The terms used refer to different kinds of *sariqah*. "Skinning" someone else's poem meant conveying the same content using entirely different words; "transforming" meant using the same words in a different order, or mostly different words but in the same order; and "copying" meant what we mean by cut-and-paste plagiarism. In MLE, I have used "jook" to mean "copy," "tax" (on the basis of its apparent etymology) to mean "steal some of," and "tick" to mean "restate," which, like borrowing,

212

was perfectly acceptable. For a short account see Chenery, *Assemblies*, 481–83; for a detailed one, Sharīshī, *Sharḥ*, 3:80–95; for modern studies see Heinrichs, "Evaluation"; Bonebakker, "*Sariqa* and Formula," "Ancient Arabic Poetry," and "The Root n-ḥ-l"; Naaman, "*Sariqa* in Practice"; and al-Ṣūlī, *Life and Times*, xxiii–xxiv. On *maʿnā* as "content," see Key, *Language*.

"Chicken merry" (§23.3) is part of the proverb "Chicken merry, hawk deh near," meaning "The chicken, unaware of the danger posed by the hovering hawk, makes merry" (National Library of Jamaica, "Jamaican Proverbs"). "Tek di miggle" (§23.4), that is, "Take the middle," means "'get on to the floor' or 'it's your turn' as in a contest or competition" (*Jamaican Patwa*). My first translation of the poem in §23.6 was revised and much improved by Richard Sieburth.

For "two big dawgs" (§23.7) the original is *al-farqadān*, two stars in Ursa Minor. "One Love" (§23.8) is "an expression of unity" that "refers to universal love and respect for all people, regardless of race, social status or any other defining characteristics" (*Jamaican Patwa*). Edessa (§23.10) is a city in what is today eastern Turkey.

"Dat mon can' catch Quaco," etc., meaning "That man can't catch Quaco or his shirt," is a reformulation of the proverb "Yu cyaan ketch Quaku . . . yu ketch im shut," meaning "If you can't catch Quaku, you can still catch his shirt," or "It is not always possible to get everything you want" (National Library of Jamaica, "Jamaican Proverbs"). A rastacap (§23.11) is a round knit cap often worn by Rastafarians with dreadlocks. I use it here as a mark of religious commitment comparable to the *ṭaylasān*, a garment draped over the head to indicate dedication to religious scholarship. Samawʾal was a Jewish poet of pre-Islamic Arabia who, when asked to safeguard a suit of armor, did so even at the cost of his son's life.

BIBLIOGRAPHY

Bible Society of the West Indies. *Di Jamiekan Nyuu Testiment*. Kingston: Bible Society of the West Indies, 2012.

———. *Jamaican Audio New Testament*. http://soundcloud.com/biblesociety/sets/jamaican-audio-new-testament.

Bonebakker, S. A. "*Sariqa* and Formula: Three Chapters from Ḥātimī's *Ḥilyat al-Muḥāḍarah*." *Annali dell'Istituto universitario orientale di Napoli* 46 (1986): 367–89.

———. "Ancient Arabic Poetry and Plagiarism: A Terminological Labyrinth." *Quaderni di Studi Arabi* 15 (1997), pp. 65–92.

———. "The Root n-ḥ-l in Arabic *sariqa* Terminology." *Dutch Studies Published by NELL* 3, nos. 1 and 2 (1997): 133–61.

Coverley, Louise Bennett. "No Likle Twang." http://louisebennett.com/no-lickle-twang/.

The Dialect Dictionary. http://www.thedialectdictionary.com.

English Jade, "The BEST British Street Slang." Published April 20, 2015. http://www.youtube.com/watch?v=9Z8JqutRWrs&t=29s.

———. "How to talk like a REAL Londoner." Published January 28, 2017. http://www.youtube.com/watch?v=PbCiNdAAUM4&t=11s.

Heinrichs, Wolfhart. "An Evaluation of *sariqa*." *Quaderni di studi Arabi* 5–6 (1987–88): 357–68.

Jamaican Patwa and Slang Dictionary. http://jamaicanpatwah.com/.

Johnson, Linton Kwesi. "Inglan Is a Bitch." Published by thecatkeaton, September 24, 2007. http://www.youtube.com/watch?v=Zq9OpJYck7Y.

justyazoo. "British Street Slang." Published January 30, 2017. http://www.youtube.com/watch?v=HwZtkcYa4ro.

Key, Alexander. *Language between God and the Poets: Maʿnā in the Eleventh Century.* Berkeley: University of California Press, 2018.

Mel Tom, "CRAZY HOUSE PARTY." Published March 2, 2018. http://www.youtube.com/watch?v=G-iWNigV-gI.

Mel Tom, "Speaking to Relatives." Published May 4, 2018. http://www.youtube.com/watch?v=4atDBmztXeE.

National Library of Jamaica. "Jamaican Proverbs." http://nlj.gov.jm/jamaican-proverbs/#bowl%20go.

Naaman, Erez. "*Sariqa* in Practice: The Case of al-Ṣāḥib ibn ʿAbbād." *Middle Eastern Literatures* 14, no. 3 (2011): 271–85.

Open Grammar Project. *A Learner's Grammar of Jamaican.* http://opengrammar.github.io/jam/#_or.

Patrick, Peter L. "Jamaican Creole Morphology and Syntax." In *A Handbook of Varieties of English*, vol. 2, Morphology and Syntax, edited by Bernd Kortmann et al. Berlin: Mouton de Gruyter, 407–38.

Rose, Eric. *Jamaicasaurus. Jamaican Thesaurus and English-to-Patois Translation Dictionary.* Jamaicasaurus Digital Publishing, 2016.

Al-Ṣūlī, Abū Bakr. *The Life and Times of Abū Tammām*. Edited and translated by Beatrice Gruendler. New York: New York University Press, 2015.

Wiley. "Wiley—Call the Shots Ft Jme." Published November 18, 2017. http://www.youtube.com/watch?v=QnQSjLb-Oxc.

Woods, Tim, comp. and ed. *The London Slang Dictionary*. 2008. PDF may be purchased at http://www.timwoods.org/the-london-slang-dictionary-project/. The website contains some terms not found on the PDF. Many of the definitions are unfortunately so poorly written as to be unusable.

"Multicultural London English." Wikipedia. http://en.wikipedia.org/wiki/Multicultural_London_English.

IMPOSTURE 24

ARABIANS LEARN ARABIAN

As the main incident in this Imposture is a lecture on language delivered by a graybeard to a circle of aspiring youngsters, the model for the English is Bernard Shaw's Pygmalion. *Common to both is the idea that self-conscious attention to one's speech can improve one's position in society. In al-Ḥarīrī's day, command of proper Arabic was a signal of good birth or, failing that, of good breeding. This is why the young men in this episode are so eager to be right about obscure points of language. In English, the song that triggers their argument about grammar comes from a Shakespearean sonnet that poses a comparable problem. As equivalents for his grammar riddles, Abū Zayd uses English puzzles that revolve around similarly odd features of the language. As in the original, the answers are not given in the text but in the notes that follow it.*

DRAMATIS PERSONAE

H. B. Hammam	A Newcomer
A Group of Young Men	A Musician

SCENE

24.1   *(The Rabīʿ quarter of Baghdad, at the height of spring. A group of fresh-faced* YOUNG MEN *of refined appearance chatting with an air of serene and kindly gaiety. H. B.* HAMMAM *gazing at them as if their presence rendered*

him insensible to the beauties of nature and made music or any other enter-
tainment superfluous.)

H. B. HAMMAM: With these friends I have vowed to live on terms of
natural affection and perfect equality. Each of us is determined to
indulge in no pleasure, no matter how trifling, unless the others also
share in it. It is a beautiful day, with the mist now lifted and the rain-
clouds inviting a morning draught. We have come a journey to this
grassy field to enjoy the prospect of the wildflowers as we await the
rain. We are in number as the months of the year, and follow each
other with as much constancy. To this garden, with its gowns of
leaves and its colorful scarves of flowers, we have brought a strong
tawny wine, cupbearers as splendid as the sun, and a musician who,
no matter what we ask him to play, will enrapture us with the tender
beauty of his singing.

(The YOUNG MEN *sit down in a semicircle. A cupbearer offers a cup of wine*   24.2
to one of them, who drinks, then passes the cup to his neighbor. During these
movements a NEWCOMER, *a sly-looking fellow dressed in a shoddy cloak,*
enters and boldly squats among the banqueters. Those nearest him recoil,
and the others turn to look at him, disagreeably surprised.)

NEWCOMER *(noticing their distaste but determined to brazen it out)*:   Peace
upon you all!

(The NEWCOMER *sits down. Confusion, with the* NEWCOMER *speaking*
and the others edging away and muttering together as if debating how to
send him on his way. The MUSICIAN *strikes a note. Silence.)*

MUSICIAN *(singing)*:

    O change thy thought, that I may change my mind,
    Shall hate be fairer lodged than gentle love?
    Be as thy presence is gracious and kind,
    Or thy self at least kind-hearted prove,

Make thee another self for love of me,
That beauty may still live in thine or thee.

24.3 ONE OF THE YOUNG MEN *(turning on the* MUSICIAN*)*:   What is "in thine or thee?" Is that a proper string of words?

MUSICIAN *(indignantly)*:   I sang them just as they were taught me, according to the system of C. B. Waye.

(General hubbub. Cries of "Thine" is an adjective! It must govern a noun! *etc. come from some of the* YOUNG MEN. *Others respond with* It is a possessive pronoun! A noun in its own right! *etc. A remoter group increase the noise with cries of* What about "thee"? What is its government? *etc. The* NEWCOMER *takes no part in the uproar but seems to be enjoying it immensely. Finally the clamor subsides.)*

NEWCOMER: Gentlemen! *(They attend.)* Perhaps I can explain. "Thine" is a possessive pronoun, here serving as a noun, or substantive. But what does it refer to? Likewise, "thee" is a personal pronoun in the accusative case, governed, like "thine," by the preposition "in." But never mind all that: you must begin by guessing what "another self" means. Once know that, and the rest is obvious.

24.4 *(The* NEWCOMER*'s self-satisfied manner provokes resistance. The* YOUNG MEN *attempt to shout him down.)*

NEWCOMER: Very well! *(Defiantly)* If you must make a battle of it, then let us take all of grammar as our field. Solve these riddles, gentlemen, if you please:

Which word, when it falls, signifies assent, but asks a question if given ascent?

Which word is too big for its britches, referring to a single thing using the plural of an agent that does not exist?

Why did the Basran grammarian think the plural of "bathtub" must be "bathtubim"?

Which verb wilfully breaks the bonds of conjugal felicity between a subject and all other verbs?

If a sentence ends with "to out of up for," how does it begin?

What are the only three occasions when "to" means "this"?

Which interjection means the same thing backwards and forwards?

When do "give" and "take" mean the same thing?

Which suffix indicates both singular and plural?

This morning I rode a camel in my pantaloons. How he got into my pantaloons I don't know. Do you?

Which word can be used as a pronoun, an adjective, a conjunction, and an exclamation?

When are "up" and "down" not opposites?

Those are my questions, gentlemen: one for each, and enough to start with. If you insist on quarreling with me I have more.

(*The* YOUNG MEN, *bewildered, murmur together briefly, then, admitting*   24.5
their ignorance, turn and stare helplessly at the NEWCOMER. *His natural
gift of rhetoric has effected a conversion: their snobbery has collapsed like
a pricked bladder. Far from regarding him with disdain, as they had been
doing, they are now dazzled, and eagerly await his instruction.*)

NEWCOMER: Praise God for making grammar as indispensable to
    articulate speech as salt is to cookery! I swear by Him that I shall not
    satisfy your curiosity unless each of you pay for his lesson. (*Submis-
    sively, the* YOUNG MEN *fish coins out of their sleeves. After collecting
    their money, the* NEWCOMER *begins lecturing inaudibly. Gradually the
    young men's expression changes to one of astonishment.*)

24.6 H. B. HAMMAM: As he revealed the solutions of his riddles, we understood, as if for the first time, the susceptibility of language to being expounded by a man of genius. In the radiance of this discovery it exasperated us to think that the man we had sneered at was precisely the one capable of clearing up all our confusions. Stricken by remorse, we begged his pardon and invited him to bury our quarrel in a bowl of wine.

(The YOUNG MEN *offer the* NEWCOMER *a cup.)*

NEWCOMER: An offer made with no warmth of heart is no offer at all. And wine no longer gives me any pleasure.

(The YOUNG MEN *press their entreaties. The* NEWCOMER *turns away, sniffing in disdain, then recites the following poem.)*

NEWCOMER:

> When sere old age forbids me take the cup
> And bids me look upon my image in the glass,
> Where Time's blanching hand hath covered up
> The coal-black hair, that once sprung up as grass,
>
> I make a vow, to wear the dignity of age,
> As long as I have breath, to breathe the No,
> My riots past, deprived of heat to swell my rage,
> As embers slaked with water lose their glow;
>
> But Age, be not deceived: the love of drink
> Is not slaked, and still runs riot in my blood,
> Of wind-cooled morning draughts I haply think,
> Wishing the Tigris were of wine, and mine its flood;
>
> And yet, fell Age, I grant thy importune request:
> Unwelcome though thou cam'st, thou art my guest.

(His poem finished, the NEWCOMER *extricates himself and slips silently away.)*

H. B. HAMMAM : Suddenly I recognized him as none other than the celebrated A. Z. Sir Eugene, who sweeps like a moon through the mansions of literature. His departure left us fit for nothing but to lament his absence and long for his return.

NOTES

"O change thy thought . . ." (§24.2) comes from Shakespeare, Sonnet 10, *NS* 2253. "Make thee another self" means "have a child." "In thine or thee" means "in that child of yours, if not in you." (Oddly, *NS* does not explain this; for a modern English rendering see SparkNotes, No Fear Shakespeare, Sonnet 10.) The original Arabic question has to do with the case endings of nouns in sentences where certain elements have been left out. This sonnet, similarly, cannot be explained without *tadqīr al-muḍmar*, that is, filling in the elided element that accounts for the form of the pronoun (pronouns being the only English words that are fully declined for case). "C. B. Waye" renders Sībawayh (d. ca. 180/796), the foundational Arabic grammarian.

Below are the answers to the English riddles in §24.4, along with a brief explanation of the linguistic point I have tried to approximate. A close translation and detailed explanation of the original appear in Chenery, *Assemblies*, 246–53 and 501–14. These require familiarity with Arabic script and grammar.

What word, when it falls, signifies assent, but asks a question if given ascent? The answer is "Yes": pronounced in a falling tone, it signals agreement; and in a rising tone signals a question ("What is it?"). The Arabic riddle is about homophony: *naʿam*, which means "yes," can also mean "livestock," producing a further pun about *ḥarf*, both "grammatical particle" and "lean she-camel."

What word is too big for its britches, referring to a single thing using the plural of an agent that does not exist? "Trousers" is a plural noun that refers to a single object. Formally, at least, it is the plural of "trouser," which despite appearances does not refer to a thing that trouses. The Arabic riddle is about *sarāwīl*, "trousers," which some authorities treated as singular and others as plural.

Why did the Basran grammarian think the plural of "bathtub" must be "bath-tubim"? Based on a false analogy with "cherub" and "cherubim," the -*im* ending being used only with a few borrowings from Hebrew. This brilliant example of false analogy in English comes from Lederer, *Crazy English*, 148. I have foisted it on an imaginary Basran grammarian, as the Basrans were allegedly overfond of analogy, as opposed to the Kufans, who reportedly judged correctness by actual usage. The original riddle has to do with the effect of adding the ending -*a(tun)* to indeclinable plurals (it does not change their meaning, but makes them declinable).

What verbs willfully break the bonds of conjugal felicity between a subject and all other verbs? In English, the modal auxiliaries, including "will," break the agreement between subjects and verbs ("she *goes*" vs. "she will *go*"). The original riddle is based on the analogous effect of the particle *sa-* "will," which changes the mood of the following verb from subjunctive to indicative, as in *'alima an sa-yakūnu* . . . ("He knows that there will be . . .") (Q al-Muzzammil 73:20).

If a sentence ends with "to out of up for," how does it begin? It begins with "What did you bring that book that I didn't want to be read . . ." The resulting sentence means "For what reason did you bring upstairs that book out of which I didn't want you to read to me?" (Imagine a child complaining about a proposed bedtime story.) For more on this sentence see Bill Poser, "What For" and Carey, "Up from . . ."; on so-called preposition stranding, see Lieberman and Pullum, *Far from the Madding Gerund*, 15–24; and on the cognitive implications see Pinker, *Language Instinct*, 97. The original Arabic riddle has to do with what happens when one preposition (in this case, *min*, "from") governs another (in this case, *'inda*, "near"). Since the English words in this case aren't really prepositions, the parallel is approximate.

What are the only three occasions when "to" means "this"? "Today," "tonight," and "tomorrow." The Arabic riddle asks about *ladun ghudwatan*, "in the morning," where the second word takes the accusative instead of the expected genitive.

What interjection means the same thing backward and forward? "Oy" (also spelled "oi") and "yo," both of which are exclamations used to attract attention (*OED*). The Arabic equivalents are *yā* and *ay*.

When do "give" and "take" mean the same thing? In the compounds "caregiver" and "caretaker" (Lederer, *Crazy English*, 20). The Arabic riddle has to do with a case where the words *wa-* "and" and *bi-* "with, by" are interchangeable.

What suffix indicates both singular and plural? The suffix *-s*, which with verbs indicates the singular ("she reads") and with nouns the plural ("books"). The original riddle is about the numbers three to ten, which take feminine forms with masculine nouns and vice versa.

This morning I rode a camel in my pantaloons. How he got into my pantaloons I don't know. Do you? This is a paraphrase of Groucho Marx's quip: "This morning I shot an elephant in my pajamas. How he got in my pajamas I don't know." The original riddle deals with a different kind of ambiguity: one that occurs when the subject and object of a verb are both indeclinable.

What word can be used as a pronoun, an adjective, a conjunction, and an exclamation? "Whatever," as in "Whatever will be will be" (pronoun), "of whatever length" (adjective), "Whatever happens, don't panic" (conjunction), and "What-EVER!" (exclamation). This is a minimal account; for additional uses see *OED*. The original is about the Arabic "whatever" (*mahmā*), which requires two verbal complements.

When are "up" and "down" not opposites? In at least two cases, both noted by Lederer: "burn up" and "burn down" mean more or less the same thing (*Crazy English*, 29), and "upright" and "downright" have nothing to do with each other (*Crazy English*, 21). The original riddle hinges on the fact that adding the meaningless syllable *-un* to the word *ḍayf*, "guest," produces *ḍayfun*, "unwanted guest."

The verses in §24.6, "When sere old age . . .," are a Shakespearean sonnet, at least in form, intended to complement the citation in §24.2. For a thorough schooling in the inimitable complexities of the real thing, see Vendler, *Art*.

The English of this Imposture supplements Shaw's *Pygmalion* with his *Caesar and Cleopatra* (set in the Middle East) and *A Treatise on Parents and Children* (because it is about education, and long enough to provide a sizeable sample of his vocabulary). The English title quotes the lyric "Arabians learn Arabian with the speed of summer lightning," from the song "Why Can't the English," from *My Fair Lady*, the musical adaptation of *Pygmalion*. For a modern study of this Imposture, focusing on how al-Ḥarīrī "performs the role of a teacher and an interpreter–commentator on his own discourse," see Matthew Keegan, "Commentarial Acts," 81–116.

BIBLIOGRAPHY

Carey, Stan. "Up from out of in under for." Sentence First. August 25, 2009. http://stancarey.wordpress.com/2009/08/25/up-from-out-of-in-under-for/.

Lederer, Richard. *Anguished English: An Anthology of Accidental Assaults upon the English Language.* Layton, UT: Wyrick, 1987.

———. *Crazy English. The Ultimate Joy Ride through Our Language.* New York: Pocket Books, 1989.

Lieberman, Mark, and Geoffrey K. Pullum. *Far from the Madding Gerund, and Other Dispatches from Language Log.* Wilsonville, OR: William, James, 2006.

My Fair Lady. Music by Frederick Loewe and lyrics by Alan Jay Lerner. 1956.

NS = The Norton Shakespeare.

Pinker, Steven. *The Language Instinct: The New Science of Language and Mind.* New York: William Morrow, 1994.

Poser, Bill. "What For." Language Log, June 19, 2004. http://itre.cis.upenn.edu/~myl/languagelog/archives/001084.html.

[Shakespeare, William]. *The Norton Shakespeare.* Edited by Stephen Greenblatt et al. New York: Norton, 2016.

Shaw, George Bernard. *Pygmalion.* Digital edition at Project Gutenberg: http://www.gutenberg.org/files/3825/3825-h/3825-h.htm.

———. *Caesar and Cleopatra.* Digital edition at Project Gutenberg: http://www.gutenberg.org/files/3329/3329-h/3329-h.htm.

———. *A Treatise on Parents and Children.* Digital edition at Project Gutenberg: http://www.gutenberg.org/files/908/908-h/908-h.htm.

SparkNotes. "No Fear Shakespeare." http://nfs.sparknotes.com/sonnets/sonnet_10.html.

Vendler, Helen. *The Art of Shakespeare's Sonnets.* Cambridge, MA: Belknap Press, 1997.

IMPOSTURE 25

DE FROID TREMPÉ

This Imposture sends al-Ḥārith to the frozen town of Karaj, where he finds Abū Zayd begging for a coat. For descriptions of cold weather and importunate neighbors, there is no better English prose than that of Susanna Moodie, an Englishwoman who in 1832 emigrated to the Province of Upper Canada, an administrative region that covered part of what is now the Canadian province of Ontario. Al-Ḥārith and Abū Zayd will therefore speak in the language of her memoirs.

El-Hareth ben Hammam declared: 25.1

Having an errand to execute there, as well as a debt to collect, I wintered in Karaj, where the rigour of the climate tried my powers of endurance to the uttermost. As the bitter winds howled without, I huddled, shivering, near the fire. Except to attend Friday worship, I was reluctant to venture far from the hearth unless it be for some urgent cause.

One day, I was forced from my lair by a pressing errand. The air was frigid and the heavens were shrouded in leaden-looking clouds. Presently I came upon an old man who was nearly naked. The poor creature had no other covering to his body than a kerchief wrapped around his head, and a breech-cloth, one end of which he had twisted together, passed between his legs, and tucked into his waist-band. Not in the least abashed, he was haranguing the crowd that had gathered close around him:

225

25.2　　Stranger, as you pass this way
　　　　Behold my visage pale,
　　　　My quaking limbs this bitter day,
　　　　Unshielded from the gale.

　　　　I was not a poor man born,
　　　　But one of noble blood,
　　　　My blade no foeman dared to scorn,
　　　　My wealth was as the flood.

　　　　But Fortune's smile too soon turned cold
　　　　And Fate unsheathed his sword,
　　　　My house I lost, my goods I sold,
　　　　To swell a stranger's hoard.

　　　　Be not complacent, gentle folk,
　　　　But my sad tale recall;
　　　　In God's good name, give me a cloak,
　　　　For any man may fall!

25.3　　"Ye tarnation rich," he continued, "who strut about in furs! Let him that hath, give to him that hathn't; for it is more blessed to give than to receive. This world promises fair, but will grievously deceive you; Nature may have an honest look, but her paths are treacherous; for vigour passeth as a phantom, and fortune as a summer cloud. For many years I met the winter with all seven c's on hand, and ample provisions in store. But now, good people, I have no pillow but my arm, no cloak but my hide, and no bowl but the hollow of my hand. Let the wise man pay heed, and wake—before it is too late—from the dark dream of ruin! For happy is he, who takes a lesson from the sorrow of others, and makes provision for Eternity!"

"I guess you know your literary subjects," said a bystander. "But what is your name, and your tribe?"

"My name? My tribe? Now don't expect me to pass off any airs on you; fear of God, refined habits, and literary propensities are what make a man's reputation, not a heap of crumbling bones:

226

Let no man praise his father's deed,
Or bless his father's grave;
No, the man himself must bleed
Ere I call him brave."

And here he sat down in a shivering, shrinking heap, bending himself nearly double against the chilly blast. "God," he said, "Thou hast commanded us to ask of Thee Thy bounty, which Thou scattereth with unsparing hand; so then deliver me from this bitter cold! Send me a brave fellow to take pity on my destitution, and succour me, if only with a scrap of cloth!"

While he ran on dilating upon his own merits, in terms no less ingenious than eloquent, I examined him long and carefully, and recognised Abou Zayd. I also perceived that his nakedness was an unprincipled artifice by which he intended to trick his audience out of their property. Apprehending that I had recognised him, and fearful that I might expose him, he resumed his harangue. 25.4

"As sure as night will fall and the moon will rise, I see, clear as starshine, and bright as moonlight, the gentleman who will provide me a cover— o gallant, noble-hearted fellow!"

I caught his meaning, though the others did not. And as I gazed heartstricken upon his shiverings, my fortitude gave way. Stripping off my fur, which served me by day as a cape and by night as a blanket, I flung it from me.

"Take it," I said.

As I looked on, he wrapped himself up in it, and recited:

Thy gift, dear friend, was not in vain!
By heeding my advice
A greater prize wilt thou attain:
The silks of Paradise!

Quite won over by his marvelous oratory, his audience showered him with more fur-lined gowns and colored coats than he could well carry. Shouldering his burden, he staggered off in triumph, calling a thousand 25.5

blessings down upon Karaj. I followed him until we reached a place shielded from view, where the pretence of ignorance might safely be abandoned.

"Oh yes: nearly perished from the cold, are we?" I said. "Or are you ready to expose yourself again?"

"An unjust rebuke," he cried. "Don't be over-hasty to reproach me, when you know nothing of my troubles. By the God who blanched my hair, and perfumed the earth where the Prophet lies, had I not exposed my nakedness, my striving would have come to nought, and all my labour been in vain."

Then, assuming a cold and stony expression, he bestirred himself to depart. "'Tis my nature, you'll recall, to seek now one prey, now another: if not Tom, then Dick and Hareth. You've cost me twice as much as you brought me, yet here you are checking me and bandying words with me. So spare me your prattle, for I will suffer no more of it, whether in gravity or in jest."

Playfully I drew him near and held him fast.

"If I hadn't covered for you," I said, "you would not have gathered a single coat, but now you have more skins upon you than an onion. If you would repay me for my kindness, either return my fur cape or tell me what the seven c's of winter are."

25.6   He looked at me astonished. "Raise the dead," he said, "or bid time return! Those would be easier tasks than reclaiming that fur. As for the seven c's, how can the verses of Ibn Sukkarah have escaped your memory? Didn't I recite them for you in the wine-hall?

> When winter rains come pouring down
> The seven c's are bonny:
> A cave, a cloak, a cup, some coin,
> Cabob, some coal, a cunny!

"There's your answer; rest satisfied, for a proper answer does more good than a heavy coat. Now be off!"

Bitterly regretting the loss of my fur, I left him, and spent the winter with my teeth chattering in my head.

NOTES

The Arabic Imposture is set in Karaj, a town southeast of Hamadhān, in what is today northwest Iran; regarding it the *Encyclopaedia of Islam* says:

> Nothing is known of the town beyond the information in the geographers that it was built of unfired brick, had two markets, numerous baths and a crowded population, even though it extended over two parasangs; the sources stress the absence of orchards, but mention the fertility of the surrounding countryside, where stock-raising was practised. Various poets who frequented the Dulafid court celebrated the town, but Ibn al-Faḳīh found it crowded-together, dirty, cold and poverty-stricken ("Karaḏj").

Of her own "dirty, cold, and poverty-stricken" home in Canada, Moodie writes:

> The winter had now fairly set in—the iron winter of 1833. The snow was unusually deep, and it being our first winter in Canada, and passed in such a miserable dwelling, we felt it very severely. In spite of all my boasted fortitude—and I think my powers of endurance have been tried to the uttermost since my sojourn in this country—the rigour of the climate subdued my proud, independent spirit, and I actually shamed my womanhood, and cried with the cold (*Roughing It*, 1:149–50).

And of a neighbor as grabby as Abū Zayd she writes:

> Day after day I was tormented by this importunate creature; she borrowed of me tea, sugar, candles, starch, blueing, irons, pots, bowls—in short, every article in common domestic use—while it was with the utmost difficulty we could get them returned. Articles of food, such as tea and sugar, or of convenience, like candles, starch, and soap, she never dreamed of being required at her hands. This method of living upon their neighbors is a most convenient one to unprincipled people, as it does not involve the penalty of stealing; and they can keep the goods without the unpleasant necessity of returning them, or feeling the moral obligation of being grateful for their use (*Roughing It*, 1:91–92).

229

Moodie's memoir contains many sentimental verses of the type common in her day. This Imposture offered no opportunity to use any of her lines, but the verses imitate her prosody and her generally lugubrious tone.

Although her memoirs are written in Standard (British) English, Moodie does give us speeches in all sorts of accents: French, Scottish, Irish, "Yankee," and "Indian"—that is, of the people she further identifies as Missisaugas or Chippewas. Some of this material appears in the translation: for example, "tarnation" (§25.3), used by Moodie's Yankee speakers to mean "extremely." "Hathn't" is my invention, inspired by her mimicry of local speech. One example reads: "Now ma'am—now, sir, was not that bad manners in a gentleman, to use such appropriate epitaphs [sc. epithets] to a humble servant of God, like I?" (*Roughing It*, 2:72). But the only word she specifically identifies as "vulgar Canadian" is "pritters" for "potatoes."

"Coloured coats" (§25.5) comes from Roxburgh, "Pursuit," 174. "Wine-hall" (§25.6) translates *daskarah*, which al-Sharīshī and de Sacy identify as a town called al-Daskarah between Ḥulwān and Baghdad. However, the word also appears in §12.5, referring to the tavern in Anah. I have therefore decided to imagine that Abū Zayd recited the poem there, during the events of that episode. Ibn Sukkarah (d. 385/995–96) was a poet known for his erotic and scatological verse. "Cabob" is kebab, first attested in 1698, and spelled with a *c* as late as 1855.

"Cunny" is, according to the OED, a synonym of "cunt," and "coarse slang." Needless to say, it does not appear in Moodie. The original Arabic word, *kuss*, as best I can judge from current usage, is a very rude word when used in imprecations, but when used literally is not disparaging (though it is still taboo). For me, a speaker of American English, "cunny" sounds archaic and therefore less disparaging. In that sense it suggests itself as a reasonable equivalent. Chenery translates it as "wife" (*Assemblies*, 258).

BIBLIOGRAPHY

Dollinger, Stefan, and Margery Fee, eds. 2017. *DCHP-2: The Dictionary of Canadianisms on Historical Principles*. 2nd ed. Vancouver, BC: University of British Columbia. www.dchp.ca/dchp2.

Haliburton, Thomas Chandler. *The Clockmaker, or the Sayings and Doings of Samuel Slick of Slicksville, First Series*. Boston: Mussey, 1838.

"(al-)Karadj." In *Encyclopaedia of Islam, Second Edition*. Leiden: Brill, 1960–2007.

Moodie, Susanna. *Roughing It in the Bush, or, Life in Canada*. London: Richard Bentley, 1852. http://www.gutenberg.org/files/4389/4389-h/4389-h.htm.

Roxburgh, David J. "In Pursuit of Shadows: Al-Ḥarīrī's *Maqāmāt*." *Muqarnas* 30 (2013): 171–212.

IMPOSTURE 26

WHAT THE DICKENS?

In this episode, Abū Zayd is hounded for a debt. Naturally enough, Charles Dickens (d. 1870), whose father's imprisonment for debt forced his family into poverty, came to mind as a model for the English. But the main feature of this Imposture is not the plot but the exercise in constrained writing, one of the four in the collection. In the original lipogram, the first letter is undotted, the second is dotted, the third undotted, and so on. The result, as the commentator al-Sharīshī puts it, "is no precious specimen of eloquence," but rather "an exercise in ingenuity" (Sharḥ, 3:294). In his English version, Abū Zayd (here called Papa Dodger) will apply the Prisoner's Constraint, an invention of the OuLiPo group. A prisoner given a scrap of paper to write a note decides to save space by using no letter that rises above or falls below the line. The only permissible letters are thus a, c, e, i, m, n, o, r, s, u, v, w, x, and z. Many common words, including "the," "of," "and," "you," "he," "she," "it," "they," "that," "for," and "at" must be avoided, resulting in odd but necessarily assonant and alliterative prose.

26.1   *From* The Life and Adventures of Master Fretful

There limped slowly one morning into the day-market of Atte-Howes, and shortly afterwards into the night-market too, a traveller whose attire bespoke a state of extreme poverty. He remained in the city for a time, sustained by the hope that his struggles might induce the bleak days of suffering and privation to pass more quickly; but soon perceiving that to persist there would only prolong his distress, he bid farewell to the bustling town, now as loathsome to him as a desolate ruin; and, sleeves tucked up, took to his heels in search of greener pastures.

Master Fretful, for that was his name, had increased the distance between himself and Atte-Howes by two nights' worth of trudging when he was roused by the sight of a great flapped tent and before it a blazing fire. He resolved to ask for a drink. "Perhaps, too," he thought, "'I shall find by the fire one to guide me onward.'"

When he reached the shelter of the tent, he saw some splendid furni- 26.2
ture, and servants in the lovely bloom and spring-time of boyhood. There was a heap of newly plucked fruit, and sitting hard by was an old man who was gaily, not to say gorgeously, attired. Master Fretful greeted him, then recoiled, overcome with an unaccountable dread. But the old man smiled and returned his salutation.

"Won't you partake," he asked, "of jest a little fruit? Or a fruitful little jest?"

Eager to devour the latter rather than the former, Master Fretful sat down.

When, grinning, the old man proceeded to display his literary stock in trade, his oratorical powers as well as his hideously yellow teeth rendered it a matter of certainty that he was Papa Dodger. The two men exchanged cries of recognition. Master Fretful hardly knew which was the greater occasion for joy: that his old friend had reappeared after his mysterious procession of voyages abroad, or that fortune had smiled upon him after years of destitution. He felt the most eager and burning desire to penetrate the mystery in which old man's advancement to riches was enveloped. "Whence did you come?" asked Fretful. "Whither are you going? And by what expedient have you filled your coffers?"

"I came," he said, "from Tewes; my destination is Sewes; and whatever of fortune I may possess I owe to a letter I wrote offhand."

Master Fretful begged to be admitted into the secret and to hear the letter read aloud.

"You have as much chance of that," rejoined the other, "as of eating your own head, unless you come with me to Sewes."

With a very ill grace, Master Fretful complied.

In Sewes he remained for a month, during which he repeated his request at frequent intervals, only to be met with polite evasions, and with promises that were never redeemed.

At length, his patience exhausted, he confronted Papa Dodger. "I have trusted in your goodness," he cried bitterly, "to no avail. The raven has croaked; I go tomorrow, as empty-handed as I came."

"God forbid I should break a promise," said the old man, coaxingly, "or put myself in opposition to you. My only motive for forbearing to instruct you has been to prolong the pleasure I derive from your company. But if you so far doubt my word as to wish yourself gone, then I must do what I can to prove the injustice of your suspicions. When you hear the whole story of my rescue from misery, you will think it worth your while."

"Out with it, you hardened old rascal!"

26.3 "What malignant Fate," began Papa Dodger, "flung me to Tewes, I know not; but I arrived without a penny in my pocket or a farthing in my purse. So dire was the extremity, that I was obliged to borrow. Unfortunately, the man to whom I contracted my debt was a hard-hearted brute. Fancying that my affairs would prosper, I spent my money foolishly; only when the debt was called in, and proved to be a substantial one, did all the truth of my position come flashing on me. In a flutter of agitation, I appealed to my creditor for a delay. So far from relenting, he refused to hear my entreaties, and pressed me with redoubled ferocity, threatening to drag me before a judge. I besought his mercy, seeking to awaken in him the spirit of clemency worthy of a noble character. But as often as I prayed him to show forbearance until I should again have ready money, he sneered, 'You want a delay, do you? Until you attain to fortune? Bless your eyes,' he said with an oath, 'there won't be an end of it until I hear the chinking of coin.'

"Finding him implacable, and knowing I could not appease his greed, I began by provoking him, and then made a rush at him. That was in order that he might bring me before the police magistrate instead of the King's Bench; for the Bench was notorious for severity and avarice, whereas the magistrate was famous for his learning and liberality.

"In due course I appeared at the threshold of the magistrate of Tewes. Feeling that I was safe there from domination and ill-treatment, I called for a sheet of paper and an inkstand, and wrote a letter subject to the Prisoner's Constraint. It ran thus:

SIR: SECURE *near our emir—no common* SARACEN—*our caravan careens no more across immense sierras; we raise a canvas near* MERV. CEREMONIOUS, *our emir immerses us in excess; we consume in awe.* SERIOUS, *our* CRONUS *on occasion censures us; even so, we nurse no animus: a sincere man's censure is renown.* SERENE, *our* SUZERAIN *is a moon; or, once seen, warm as a sun, or warmer.*

26.4

> NO *mere vizier: a* CRASSUS,
> NO *mean sermoniser;*
> SEVERE *in war, eximious,*
> AS *wise as* SENECA, *or wiser.*

ON *our emir's concern, verses concur, unanimous: coins run over urn-rims; we swim in monies as in a sea.* CAN *men, even men as voracious, as ravenous as we, consume a river so immense?* AS *crewmen on our emir's man-o'-war, we overrun our enemies; we earn ever more income; we amass crowns, écus, 'n zuzes.* SOME *emirs crave revenue; ours scorns avarice.* SOME *are vicious misers; ours is never mean or coarse.* SOME *coerce, or accuse; ours is never acrimonious.*

> NEVER *sans reason is our man severe:*
> AWESOME *as a* CAESAR, *a* MARS *in war;*
> IN *merrier venues, easier in manner,*
> WARMER, *semi-serious, ever a señor:*
> OUR OMAR, *our savior, our crown,*
> OUR *source, our suzerain, our* MOOR.

CRIERS *across* EURASIA *announce in unison: our emir is our resource, our reservoir, our* EOZOIC *rain; our succour, sorrow's ransom, care's surcease.* IN CRISIS, *no one unnerves—in races,*

235

no one overcomes—our man. SUCCESSORS? NONE *can vie; even enemies are won over en masse; encomiums accrue.*

AN *orison:*
VIVA *rex!*
REMAIN *a moon,*
NEVER *wane!*
REVIVE *us now,*
MONSOON *rain!*

MERCIES, *wax numerous; messianic rumors, increase!* I, *sir, serve our emir; now* I *crave a savior.* CAREWORN, I *ooze miseries; in woe,* I *am* CAIN; *even so,* I *survive, as some* ASIAN ROMANOV; *in verse, moreover,* I *mesmerize; in sermons,* I *overawe* CICERO; *in missives,* I *summon snow in summer, or mimic, in mosaic, zinnias and roses.* EVEN SO, I *save,* I *conserve,* I *economize:* I *consume no sauce, no caviar, no sesame; a carer's coin snares me acorns or, on occasion, marrows.* MUSES *averse, career in ruins,* I *am, moreover, in arrears; a usurer, a ravenous monomaniac, vexes me.* SO *review, sir, our case; ransom me, or issue me a sinecure; & so* REMAIN, *in verse, a* MAECENAS, *as we, mere men, revere an ever-wise* NUMEN. AMEN!

26.5 "Inspecting the letter closely, the magistrate divined its hidden feature, whereupon he ordered that my debt be paid and my creditor desist from pressing his case against me. Nor did his attentions end there: he proposed that I should enlarge his circle of acquaintance, and enjoy his special favor. I partook of his hospitality for some years until, enriched by his generosity and kindness, I contrived to take my farewell, having attained the rather improved condition in which you see me now."

"What a blessed fortune it was," said Master Fretful, "that put you in the way of such a liberal benefactor, and rescued you from the clutches of your creditor!"

"Thank Heaven," he rejoined, "the Author of my deliverance!" After a moment's pause he continued: "Which of the two would you prefer: a purse of money, or the text of the Prisoner's Constraint?"

"Oh, the letter, if you please, sir," said Fretful.

"I am glad to hear it," he said, "for I would rather open my mouth than my pocket-book."

Then, as if ashamed of his meanness, he not only dictated the letter but also handed over the purse. Master Fretful thus came away with a double prize; he returned amply rewarded to his native place, laden with missive and money both.

NOTES

In Arabic, this Imposture is called *al-raqṭā'*, "black speckled with white, or the reverse" (Lane), referring to the alternation of dotted and undotted letters. It is the only title to appear in the text—as opposed to the margins—of the oldest manuscript, Cairo 105.

The action begins in Ahwāz, a town located in what is today southwestern Iran. It was a center of trade and of silk and sugar production. Tenth-century geographers declared its climate oppressively hot, "its inhabitants irritable and poorly educated, and its mosque a nest of layabouts" (Tillier, "al-Ahwāz"). Abū Zayd speaks of arriving from Ṭūs, a town adjacent to what is now Mashhad, in northeastern Iran, over 1,050 miles (1,680 km) from Ahwāz. He then speaks of going to Sūs, for which al-Sharīshī proposes three different identifications: the town now called Shūsh, north of Ṭūs; Sūsa, a town on the Mediterranean in what is now eastern Libya; and Sūs (al-Aqṣā), a region that lies on the Atlantic coast of Morocco. In the real world, the likeliest candidate would be the one near Ahwāz. But in the time- and space-folded world of the Impostures, there is no reason for al-Ḥarīrī not to send Abū Zayd and al-Ḥārith on a 4,828 mile (7,700 km) journey to the other end of the known world. The translation anglicizes these place names. "Atte" appears in "Stratford atte Bowe" (Chaucer, *Canterbury Tales*, line 125), and "Tewes" and "Sewes" are coined from Lewes, in East Sussex.

"I shall find by the fire" (§26.1): Q Ṭāhā 20:10. "Jest a little fruit": the Arabic makes a pun on *fākihah*, fruit, and *mufākahah*, joking. The translation takes advantage of the fact that Dickens indulges in the occasional pun (see, e.g.,

Great Expectations, Chapter 2, on the name Bolt). "Jest" for "just" appears in the speech of Mr. Peggotty, *David Copperfield*, Chapter 51.

"The raven has croaked" (§26.2) is an Arabic idiom here retained more or less literally. Because of its name, the raven, called *ghurāb*, is associated with *ghurbah*, exile.

The so-called Spotted Epistle has vexed al-Ḥarīrī's translators. Al-Ḥarīzī, who usually tries to pull off an equivalent trick in Hebrew, says of this one that he gave up and rendered the content only (*Mahberot*, 85). Rückert's rendering does apply a constraint, albeit one that has nothing to do with letters: nearly every line contains the words *stumm* (mute), *taub* (deaf), *blind* (blind), or *lahm* (lame), and one eighteen-line poem uses only *stumm* as a rhyme (*Verwandlungen*, 148–53).

Under the Prisoner's Constraint I have applied here, the uppercase forms of the permitted letters may likewise be used. To maintain the visual effect that results from not having any ascenders or descenders, I have rendered capitalized words in all caps and a smaller font. In composing the English, I relied heavily on the list of permitted words compiled by Estate Game.

BIBLIOGRAPHY

Dickens, Charles. *David Copperfield*. http://www.gutenberg.org/files/766/766-h/766-h.htm.

———. *Great Expectations*. http://www.gutenberg.org/files/1400/1400-h/1400-h.htm.

———. *Oliver Twist*. http://www.gutenberg.org/files/730/730-h/730-h.htm.

Estate Game. *OuLiPo*. http://www.estatega.me/OuLiPo/Prisoners-Constraint.

Tillier, Matieu. "Al-Ahwāz." In *Encyclopaedia of Islam, Third Edition*. Leiden: Brill, 2009.

IMPOSTURE 27

THE WILD EAST

In the original, this Imposture is full of expressions associated with the desert Arabs. Since the story involves horse stealing and camel rustling, the language of the American West seemed a good equivalent. Just as the pure Arabic of the desert nomads is said to have been "collected" by eighth- and ninth-century scholars from Basra and Baghdad, American cowboy lingo was studied too, notably by the Texan bibliographer and folklorist Ramon Adams (d. 1976). Most of the English here is based on his work.

El Harith out of Hammam's outfit spun us this yarn.   27.1

I don't travel like a colt no more, but back when I was fryin' size, I took it into my head to split a blanket with some hair-tenters. What I was after was to learn their lingo and put some gravel in my gizzard. First thing, though, I rode the plains hard, broke brush in the canyons, and built me a herd of stinkers, along with near a hundred head of camel. Then I took the whole shebang and camped near the A-rabs. Now they were a square bunch who'd do to ride the river with, and they stood by me close as a biscuit shooter guardin' a sourdough keg. They were strong on the tongue oil, too. With folks like that singin' to me I was cozy as a toad under a cabbage leaf or a puncher snorin' away in a skunk boat.

One moonlit night one of my best she-camels, a real milk-pitcher,   27.2
slips her hobbles and runs off. Not wantin' to set on my one-spot and let her stray, I took a run at a snorty puller of a range hoss and hit the trail with a belly-buster in my cinch. All night long I tracked that camel over

the prairies and through the brush country. Then the sun hoisted its flag and it got to be time when a sin-buster might call a body to the Koran-mill. So I broke camp and said my prayers. Then I stepped across that hoss again and pushed on the reins, cuttin' for sign as I went. I was scratchin' gravel, pullin' leather, and hailin' every rider I met to ask if he'd seen my stray. But for all the good it did I might as well have been trackin' bees in a hailstorm.

27.3　　Soon enough it got to be high noon, and warm enough to make Ghaylan forget all about droppin' a rope on Mayyah. Now when a day starts to feelin' hot as a burnt boot and long as a wagon track, any darn puncher who won't make for the shade is sure to get plumb wore out and end up handin' in his checks. So I swung off under a big leafy tree to grab me a siesta till the shank of the afternoon.

Well, I hadn't hardly got my breath and cooled my saddle when a chuck-line rider bulged into the trail. He was makin' right for my black spot, rattlin' his hocks an' fixin' to squat. I don't like folks wedgin' in, but then I judged this feller might have raised my camel. He was two whoops and a holler from my tree when I saw it was none other than that old stub-horn ☞ ABU ZAYD, out of Sarūj. You bet he was a sight for weak eyes, standin' there with his war-sack tied around him for a belt and his gear under his arm. It wasn't long before he had me laughin' so hard at his windies that I plumb forgot about the stray.

27.4　　By and by I ask him to chew it finer and tell me why he was on the dodge. First rattle out of the box he sings me this ditty:

> When the shadows grow long on the prairie,
> Some folks drop in and jaw for a spell.
> I ain't stayin' long, got to be movin' along
> But this much at least I can tell.
>
> The one place I call home is the desert,
> The one mount I've got is my boots.
> When I come into town, I settle on down
> For a night in the hay with my books.

I got nothin' I'd miss if it's gone,
There ain't nothin' I've done I regret,
When I blow out the light I sleep well at night,
There ain't nothin' I wish I'd forget.

If I have to, I'll drink from a hoofprint,
But there are some things a man just won't do.
I won't steal sheep from a man who's asleep
And I won't blot a brand if it's true.

Some men might sell off their saddles,
But my good name's my only wealth,
'Cause when the sun sinks low on the prairie
The only comp'ny you got is yerself.

Then he looks me up and down and says, "I'll reckon you ain't here for 27.5
the fishin'." So I tell him about how I've been playin' hell since yesterday
tryin' to track that stray camel.

"Son," he says, "every wrangler loses a hoss now and again, and dogies
die on every drive. It ain't no use cryin' over spilt milk, or squawkin' over a
busted flush. Why, folks have found El Dorado only to lose it again. Anyone
who'd flag his kite and leave you bogged to the saddle skirts ain't worth
hobblin' anyhow, even if he's your truest friend and top amigo.

"Now how about we rest our jaws for a spell and have us a siesta? It's hot 27.6
as hell with the lid off, and I've come near to runnin' all the tallow off my
bed-slats. Ain't nothin' like a little noon-time shut-eye to get you singin'
with your tail up, especially round this time of year."

"Please yourself," I say, "and sorry for takin' too much spread."

He lays hisself down with his back for a mattress and plays it like he's
lazin' off to sleep. I rest on my elbow judgin' I'd keep watch, but with no
one there to talk to I doze off.

When I wake up it's as dark as Jonah's pocket, with the morning star just
risin', and Abu Zayd and my hoss are both ☞ GONE.

Well, that night passes slower 'n it ever did for that old medicine tongue
El Nabighah, who says he got so lonesome for his lady-friend Umaymah

that the stars slowed down just for hissake. Me, I can't sleep for thinkin' of how I lost my favorite camel, and rememberin' what the Good Book says of Jacob, who rent his clothes, and put sackcloth upon his loins, and refused to be comforted. I keep wonderin' how long it'll take me to high-heel it back home, and what I'll say when I reach there.

27.7   Well, the sun hadn't finished skally-hootin' over the horizon when I raised a rider comin' at a hard gallop across the prairie. I flap a robe at him but he keeps on ridin' hell-for-leather, playin' it like he ain't seen a hand in distress. So I high-tail it over to block his path. He's put me in a sod-pawin' mood, but it's as plain as the ears on a mule I'll have to pull in the horns and ask him for a ride. Well, I laid some far-apart tracks, but I caught him. Then I take a good look at his mount and I see it's my runaway camel.

Quicker 'n you can spit and holler howdy, I pull the feller down off her hump and start to wrasslin' the reins out of his paw. "She's mine," I sing out, "milk, colts, and all, you sticky-ropin' ear-grubber! Let go, or I'll saw your horns off!"

Well, the feller sets that camel to buckin', and pitchin', and horn-swog-glin', and pin-wheelin', and cat-backin', and jack-knifin', and chinnin' the moon, like I'm the one rustlin' *him*. And in the middle of all that, another rider comes blowin' in with the tumbleweeds. It's ole ☞ ABU ZAYD, lookin' tetchy as a teased snake, with a craw plumb full of salt and fightin' tallow!

27.8   Now seein' how he hamstrung me the day before, ¿quién sabe whether he's fixin' to finish the job today, and send me to my last roundup? I reckon all I can do is remind him how we used to be compadres, and how he served me a dirty trick by leavin' me afoot. Then I ask for his range word: is he comin' to hang up my hide, or tail me up out of the bog hole?

"I'll be d—d," he says, "if I kick a feller who's already chewin' gravel. No, I come back to see how you're fixed, and throw in with you if you ain't."

When I heard that you can bet I felt easy right off. So I told him about how this other party found my camel but now he's gettin' his bristles up about givin' her back. Abu Zayd shoots the feller a look that would peel the hide off a Gila monster. Then he points the belly-buster at him and swears by the LORD GOD ALMIGHTY that if he don't curl his tail and run like the heel flies are after him, he'll soon be garglin' on a spear-point and won-derin' why he thought a stray she-camel was worth the ride to a shallow grave. Pretty soon the other party pulls in his horns and hits the trail hard enough to break wind.

"Here's your humper," Abu Zayd sings out to me. "Come an' get 'er! Better to get one hog back than gin around after two."

El Harith continued: 27.9

Well, I'm buffaloed whether to thank him or spank him. He must have been cognoscious of it, too, because he smiles at me and rattles off these here verses:

> You know me better 'n my own brother:
> When I take one thing, I give another.
> Now I know you're lookin' for a dog to kick,
> But I'm a pack rat, and that's my trick.
> So don't thank me, or shake me, 'cause I'm leavin':
> Let's both of us say we came out even.

Then he says: "You say 'stake' and I say 'picket,' so we'll have to whang a few more whittles before we smoke a peace pipe." Then he turns and lights a shuck, with that hoss kickin' jack rabbits out of the trail. I don't calf 'round neither: I mount that camel and drag it for home. I reached there in the end, too, after a hair-lifter or two.

Tie one to that!

GLOSSARY

27.1

fryin' size small	*tongue oil* talking ability
gravel in the gizzard courage	*biscuit shooter* cook
stinkers sheep	*sing to* stand night guard over
square courageous and honest	(a herd)
do to ride the river with reliable and	*skunk boat* canvas bed cover
brave	

27.2

milk pitcher   a milch cow (but here a camel)

set on my one-spot   be idle

take a run at   run up to and mount (a horse)

snorty   high-spirited

puller   a horse that champs at the bit

range   open country where cattle graze

hoss   horse

belly-buster   pole (but here a lance)

cinch   saddle strap

sin-buster   preacher

Koran-mill   mosque

step across   mount (a horse)

push on the reins   urge one's mount to full speed

cut for sign   examine the ground for tracks or droppings

scratch gravel   climb a steep bank on horseback

pull leather   grab the saddle horn

27.3

drop a rope on   marry

puncher   cowboy

hand in his checks   die

shank of the afternoon   late afternoon

chuck-line rider   an idle cowboy looking for a free meal

bulge   appear on the trail

black spot   shade

rattle his hocks   travel at speed

fixin' to squat   intending to stay

wedge in   come uninvited

raise   see in the distance

two whoops and a holler   a short distance

stub-horn   battle-scarred veteran

war-sack   cowboy's bag

windies   tall tales, lies

27.4

chew it finer   explain in simpler words

on the dodge   fleeing from the law

first rattle out of the box   without delay

blot a brand   to alter a cow's brand in order to steal it

27.5

dogie   orphaned or poorly nourished calf

busted flush   plans gone awry

flag his kite   leave in a hurry

bogged to the saddle skirts   deeply implicated

hobble   keep from running off

top amigo   best friend

27.6

tallow   fat

bed-slats   ribs

singin' with your tail up   in high spirits

take too much spread   make oneself
  disagreeable

medicine tongue   fluent talk (but here
  an eloquent speaker)

27.7

hand   cowboy

in a sod-pawin' mood   furious

lay far-apart tracks   run hard

sticky-ropin'   prone to stealing cattle

ear-grubber   a rustler who cuts the
  ear off cattle to remove the owner's
  mark

buck, pitch   try to throw off a rider

horn-swoggle   wriggle in an attempt
  to throw off a rope

27.8

hamstrung   at a disadvantage

¿quién sabe?   Who knows?

send me to my last roundup   kill me

compadre   partner, protector

leavin' me afoot   taking my horse

range word   the truth

hang up my hide   kill me

tail up out of the bog hole   help (cattle)
  to their feet

27.9

buffaloed   confused

cognoscious   aware

lookin' for a dog to kick   furious

shake   ask for money

whang a few more whittles   have a few
  more quarrels

high-heel it   go on foot after losing
  one's horse

pin-wheel   leap forward, flip, and land
  on its back

cat-back   buck with an arched back

jack-knife   clip the front and back legs
  together

chin the moon   stand on the hind legs
  and paw the air

*a craw plumb full of salt and fightin'
  tallow*   ready to fight

chewin' gravel   thrown from a horse

*peel the hide off a Gila
  monster*   vituperative

humper   camel

get one's hog back   retrieve stolen
  property

gin around after   chase cattle
  unnecessarily

lights a shuck   leaves in a hurry

*kickin' jack rabbits out of the
  trail*   riding at full speed

calf 'round   loaf, idle

hair-lifter   adventure

NOTES

In Arabic, this Imposture is called *al-wabariyyah*, "the hair-tent episode," the nomadic Arabs being known for making tents from the hair of camels and goats. Nearly all of the English comes from Adams's *Western Words*, whose definitions are paraphrased in the Glossary. A few essential terms come from other sources, primarily *Cowboy Lingo*, another work by Adams, and Harry Maule's *Great Tales of the American West* (1945). I was forced to coin a few expressions (e.g., "humper" and "not here for the fishin'") in what I hope is the right tongue-oil cowboy spirit.

In §27.1, al-Ḥārith buys livestock so as not to be a burden on the Bedouin, who "never accept any compensation for their kindness, in money or any other form" (Preston, *Assemblies*, 270). Compare Adams on cowboys' hospitality: "An offer to pay by a guest was a grave offense and brought upon him the scorn and contempt of every man on the ranch" (*Cowboy Lingo*, 17). Range cooks ("biscuit shooters") were famously jealous of the kegs in which they laboriously prepared their sourdough (Adams, *Western Words*, s.v. *sourdough keg*). A skunk boat is "a heavy canvas . . . which, when propped up at each corner with a small stick, formed a barrier about the sleeper's bed" believed to protect him from being bitten by a skunk (Adams, *Cowboy Lingo*, 202–3). The belly-buster of §27.2 was originally a latch used on wire gates, consisting of a long pole which, if dropped, could injure the user. "Koran-mill" is my own derivation from "gospel-mill," a church (from Twain, "Buck Fanshaw's Funeral," 18). In §27.3, Ghaylan is the poet Dhū l-Rummah (d. 117/735), and Mayyah the woman he praises in his verse (see Papoutsakis, "Dhū l-Rumma"). A stub-horn is a bull whose horns are chipped and broken from fighting, and by extension a man scarred by battle. El Nabigha (properly al-Nābighah) was a pre-Islamic poet. For the story of Jacob see Genesis 37:34–35 and Q Yūsuf 12:4–18.

Adams does not define "skally-hootin'" (§27.7) except as it occurs in the sentence "They came skally-hootin' into town," which, he says, "paints a complete picture of men riding recklessly down the dusty street and drawing their sweating horses to a slithering halt before the hitch-rack" (*Cowboy Lingo*, 208). A pack rat (§27.9) is a western rodent that always leaves something in exchange when he carries something off. "Stake" is the Texan term for a fence post and "picket" the northern one (Adams, *Western Words*, x). "Tie one to that!" is "a phrase used by western storytellers at the conclusion of a wild tale, as if inviting the next man to tell a bigger one" (Adams, *Western Words*, s.v. *Tie one to that*).

BIBLIOGRAPHY

Adams, Ramon F. *Cowboy Lingo*. Boston: Houghton Mifflin, 1936.

———. *Western Words: A Dictionary of the Range, Cow Camp and Trail.* Norman: University of Oklahoma Press, 1944.

Knibbs, Henry Herbert. "A Shot in the Dark." In Harry E. Maule, ed., *Great Tales*, 249–66.

Maule, Harry E., ed. *Great Tales of the American West*. New York: The Modern Library, 1945.

Henry, O. "Hearts and Crosses." In Harry E. Maule, ed., *Great Tales*, 52–65.

Papoutsakis, Nefeli. "Dhū l-Rumma." In *Encyclopaedia of Islam, Third Edition*. Leiden: Brill, 2009.

Rhodes, Eugene Manlove. "Beyond the Desert." In Harry E. Maule, ed., *Great Tales*, 78–99.

Tuttle, W. C. "Sunset." In Harry E. Maule, ed., *Great Tales*, 191–234.

Twain, Mark. "Buck Fanshaw's Funeral." In Harry E. Maule, ed., *Great Tales*, 15–24.

IMPOSTURE 28

A VOID IN SAMARKAND

This is another constrained-writing episode, the constraint in this case being to compose a Friday sermon containing no dotted letters. This means using only thirteen of the twenty-eight letters of the Arabic alphabet. Excluded, as a result, are almost all the common prepositions, second- and third-person imperfect verbs, and many other exceedingly frequent features of the language (though the dotted feminine ending is allowed). For his English equivalent, Abū Zayd will deliver a sermon without using the letter e. This difficult but not insuperable constraint is the one adopted by George Perec in his novel La disparition, *and by his English translator Gilbert Adair, who excluded e from his rendering too (the title is* A Void*). In the next episode, where Abū Zayd does the trick again, he will use no vowel except e. The rest of the Imposture is delivered in heavily slangy New Zealand English. The action is set in Samarkand, a city in what is now the southwest part of Uzbekistan. Seen from al-Ḥarīrī's Basra, Samarkand was very far east indeed. New Zealand, similarly, is at the eastern edge of the English-speaking world—from a British perspective, at least. It is also helpful that so-called Kiwi slang has a robust vocabulary for drinking, which is a theme of this episode. My Kiwi text was corrected and improved by Toby C. Brown.*

Al-Harith sprog of Hammam spun this yarn: 28.1

Once, back in the day, I tramped though the wops, yeah, humping a heap of sugarcane to sell in Samarkand. Being a young fellah, I was a bit of dag back then—bright as a button too: any chance of a piss-up and I'd be keen as. Kicked on through the mirages and all that, but it was pretty hard yakka. And by the time I reached Samarkand it was sparrow's fart on a Friday, so I had a hell of a time finding a futtah for the cane and a warry for me. Soon as I had a roof over the ol' coconut, though, I nipped over to the bathhouse cause I ponged a fair bit, to be honest. So yeah, that was me, bro, looking pressed off and buttoned. Then I ran full tit to the masjid: noon prayers eh. I wanted a seat up front so I could get a good squizz at the imam and make me a primo offering to the LORD.

Being as I was first through the door I got me a choice spot for the   28.2 sermon. Then heaps of people start coming in, some just by themselves, some with other fellahs, and pretty soon the place is chocka. At the crack of noon the preacher makes his grand entrance and follows his offsiders straight up the guts. Taking the stairs he goes to the top of the pulpit and lifts his right hand, like he's saying "Hey, what's up fellahs?" Then he sits himself down waiting for the prayer caller to finish up. When it's his go, does he go!—all full on, I tell ya. He gives us a right old ear bashing.

"Kia hora! Glorious is GOD, and glorious all words naming Him! For   28.3 His favors, I thank Him; for His gifts, I laud Him; and in hardship I cry out to Him, GOD, King of nations, who will lift my body from its tomb on doomsday! Our LORD is bountiful in giving, swift in forgiving, slow to punish, but mighty in His wrath, as Ad and Iram saw. What shall pass is known only to Him; what you lot know ain't worth bugga all.

"I submit to Him, proclaiming His unity; and I call on Him, hoping for His pardon. I affirm Him as all that is, or was: a just god, subsisting without division; not born of anything, and without child; an only god, all-sufficing. By His command Muhammad brought Islam to pull us along a straight path, giving us a Qur'an to confirm what Hud and Salih taught, and to proclaim His law to all nations, of ruddy skin or black.

"Through him GOD bound up all our rifts and divisions and laid down a way of living for His community, distinguishing right from wrong and commanding purity of body for pilgrims to His Kaaba.

"May GOD cast rainfall upon Muhammad's tomb, proclaiming his salvation! May our LORD lift up his family and his iwi for as long as tuis cry and Tukis baa, as long as stormclouds burst and sailors go on cursing!

28.4 "I call on all of you to act rightly and toil mightily for your own salvation. Spurn illusion, for it is sworn to harm you, and amass your provisions joyfully for that coming world. Gird your soul as if with armour: spurn lowly things, fight off that malady known as ambition, and push away all thought of joining God without labouring for Him first.

"Look at how all things pass away. In good nick today, and happy as Larry? Ah, but tomorrow—tomorrow you may look total crap, or just a bit crook, but soon it's all piss awful, and finally that cry: 'that bugga's CARKIN' IT!' Now think of that last day, as your soul slips from your body and your body to your tomb. What a horrid sight: a shaft with nobody in it but you, and Munkir and Nakir asking whom you worship! Up that old boohai now, I'd say, right boys? Too bloody right!

"Look around you! This world has no pity: it will trick you, trap you, and undo you, as it will all of us. It turns luscious fruit into biting colocynth, routs mighty hosts, and lays all nobility low. It brings, if not infirmity and pain, sorrow and frustration; it may nourish you now, but its milk is curdling into poison. I who talk to you will soon cark it, and you who worship will up sticks and kick it in your turn. OFF YOU GO, says Bob Munro: not just to us ordinary folk, but to czars and shahs and kings!

"Do you look at folk with dosh and wish you too had a big fat stash? Fat lot of good wishing will do! I'll knock, if I may, that wool off ya coconuts. Not too far off, that pack of rich bastards will blow through, and so too will you! Oh, lions may maul and worms may sting, but all that lot will kick on for a day or two, and vanish. You, too: this world may go your way, but swiftly will it turn its back, tossing away your plans and scorning your indignation, putting out a hand only to draw it back, and giving you what you want only to snatch it away! Go on, bust a gut trying to hang on: you too will succumb to that fatal pang that brings sorrow to kith and kin!

"Think now of that GOD who guards you, though you fail to stay mind-   28.5
ful of Him. How long will you pass your days in frivolity and distraction,
stubborn and sinful, scorning good words from all who know, and ignoring
His command? How long will you stuff about, two kumara short of a hangi,
till all you can do is whip your cat?

"As you cling to this world, you watch your wits slip away, and you
slouch toward a sarcophagus that is nothing but clay. Don't you know that
your doom is at your back, and gaining? That your turn to burrow in that
soil is not so far off? That a footpath sharp as a sword awaits, and an hour
mighty and grim? That horrors will afflict you past that hour? Flout God,
and you will burn, as kindling in a conflagration, charring your skin, with
a guardian who has no pity, slaking your thirst with poison and thrusting
you into blasts of scorching wind. On that day no acquisition will avail you,
not your offspring, nor crowds of companions, nor armour and arms, nor
slumgullions and barmolic!

"Whom will God pardon? Him who curbs his lusts and follows a path   28.6
of right action, doing as God wills, and labouring to gain that bliss that will
sustain him in his tomb. Toil, I say, so long as your day is young, your stars
compliant, your body vigourous, and your constitution strong, for soon,
much too soon, what you wish to avoid will assail you and agony will afflict
you, striking you dumb, robbing you of your wits, and pulling you down
into a tomb-shaft! If you fail, agony awaits: a pain that will not stop, and
sorrow unabating, with nobody to pity you, or cool you with a balm, or
push away that flail.

"So how will it go for us? Rough as guts, fullahs, and ain't that God's
own truth! Our way out—that's right: all of us, bros—is to pray that God
stir our convictions, lavish His pity on us, and admit us to His court. I ask
Him to favor us and all Islam by wiping away our sins, as no god bar Him,
a saving and forgiving God, can do. May it go with a bang, boys: that's my
last wish for you!"

Al-Harith continued: 28.7

When I heard that, I thought: "Mean as! That fellah just preached a whole
sermon without once using the letter *E*. Faaa!"

Now I was curious, so I took a good long gawk at him, trying to suss him out. At first I thought I didn't know him from a bar of soap, but then I realised: hard out, it was Abu Zayd, the Impostures bloke! Given where we were, though, I had to keep quiet. So I waited until the prayer was over and the punters were gapping it for the doors. Then I went up to him and said, "Chur, cuz!"

He jumped up, looking stoked to see me. After that we bowled round to his house, where we had a yack and he told me his deepest secrets.

28.8   By that time it was getting dark and I was ready to crash. But he'd brought out the booze, big jugs full, man, nek minnit.

"Bugger!" I said. "You're on the piss even though you lead the prayers round here?"

"Nah yeah bro, in the daytime I preach, and at night I'm on the turps, eh."

"Bloody hell! I don't know what's more dodgy, mate: seeing you go bush and leave the rellies, or hearing a boozer like yourself deliver such a stonking sermon."

He turned away, looking hacked off. Then he said:

> Did I leave you in the churn?
> Don't pack a sad, bro: people change.
> Look around, cuz, and you'll learn
> It does bugger all to rage
> When it all to custard turns.
> Not even, ow: The age
> Is rotten. Get after joy; never spurn
> A piss-up. She'll be right if you engage;
> For bloody soon they'll come, the worms,
> And no one, be he fool or sage,
> From that bourne has yet returned.

28.9   Later, when the jugs had gone round, and we were both a bit munted, he made me swear honest to G that I'd keep his secret all to myself. Well, I saw him right, and not half-pie either: I didn't just keep the boozing under wraps, I went round calling him pious to the days. We kept on that way till it was time for me to shoot through. When I left, he was still ear-bashing by day and hitting the piss by night.

GLOSSARY

28.1

sprog child

spin a yarn tell an unlikely tale

back in the day sometime in the past

wops middle of nowhere

bit of a dag jocular

bright as a button energetic

piss-up festivity

keen as very eager

kick on continue, usually with success

hard yakka hard work

sparrow's fart early morning

futtah a storehouse raised above the ground to protect the contents from rodents

warry a large communal accommodation for single shepherds and station hands

coconut head

nip over go quickly

pong stink

pressed off and buttoned spruced up

full tit at high speed

eh a sentence-final particle used to soften assertions

squizz look

primo outstanding

28.2

heaps of many

chocka full

offsider friend; assistant

straight up the guts into the thick of the crowd

give someone an ear bashing harangue

28.3

bugga all anything

tui a sort of vociferous bird

Tukis a breed of New Zealand sheep (my abbreviation of Tukidale)

28.4

in good nick in good shape

happy as Larry very happy

crook ill

piss awful unpleasant

cark it die

up the boohai lost

up sticks pick up and leave

off you go, etc. a rhyming phrase signaling the start of something

dosh money

knock the wool, etc. help someone think more clearly

blow through   depart

kick on   persist

28.5

stuff about   waste time

two kumara short of a hangi   not very intelligent

28.6

rough as guts   harshly

28.7

mean as   great

faaa   an exclamation of approval

gawk   look

suss out   identify

not know him from a bar of soap   have no idea who he is

hard out   definitely

28.8

crash   go to bed

nek minnit   ... is what happened next

bugger   oh no!

on the piss   drinking alcohol

nah yeah   yes

on the turps   drinking heavily

dodgy   suspicious

go bush   take a break, become reclusive

28.9

munted   drunk

honest to G   honest to God

see right   take care of, fulfill one's obligation to

bust a gut   make a great effort

whip the cat   regret, feel remorse

slumgullions and barmolic   anything at all

go with a bang   succeed

punters   crowd

gap it   dash for the exit

chur   here, a greeting

cuz   common form of address

stoked   pleased

bowl round to   visit

yack   chat

rellies   relatives

hacked off   annoyed

pack a sad   pout, sulk

bugger all   nothing

turn to custard   fall through

not even, ow   an emphatic

she'll be right   it'll work out

half-pie   sloppily, half-heartedly

to the days   extremely

shoot through   leave

NOTES

I am aware that Kiwi slang overlaps substantially with its Australian counterpart. Since Imposture 20 uses nineteenth-century Aussie, I chose present-day Kiwi here, emphasizing those features that Kiwis themselves put forward as unique to their way of speaking. (For a well-informed list of differences between Kiwi and Aussie, see Wikipedia, *NZS*). For the sermon, which is less heavily Kiwi, I used David McGill's 2003 compilation of slang to give a different flavor. Avoiding *e* meant changing some expressions slightly: for example, "whip the cat" had to become "whip your cat." My Kiwi draft was vetted by Tony C. Brown, who removed British and Aussie usages, corrected several errors, and proposed many improvements to the wording.

After some experimentation, I decided against trying to represent Kiwi pronunciation. To be sure, writing "bed" as "bid" or "dag" as "deg" would have given a better sense of how the language sounds. But phonetic spellings would often coincide with actual English words (as with "bid" above), and the resulting text was just too confusing to read. In other cases, Kiwis have agreed on a particular spelling, and there is not much point in bucking the consensus. For example, "dag" is always written that way, such that spelling it "deg" does not seem worthwhile.

I use "warry" and "futtah" (§28.1; see Te Ara, "Rural Language," 2) in combination to create a rough equivalent of the *khān* or caravanserai—the merchant's lodging, stabling, and storage facility—where al-Ḥārith is likely to have stayed.

In §28.3, "Ad" (an ancient Arabian tribe punished for scorning the message of the prophet Hud; Q Aʿrāf 7:65–72), "Iram" (the city "of pillars" that was home to ʿĀd; Q Fajr 89:7) and "Salih" (the ancient Arabian prophet sent to the tribe of Thamud; Q Aʿrāf 7:73–79) appear in the English only, as the original speaks of "prophets," "messengers," or "emissaries," but all those words have an *e* and so could not be used. Similarly in §28.4 Munkir and Nakir—the angels who interrogate the dead in their graves—appear in the English only, as the original speaks of an "angel," but that word has an *e* and so could not be used. (For his part, al-Ḥarīrī could not use the expected form *malakān*, "two angels," because the *n* has a dot.)

"Slumgullions and barmolic" (§28.5) is a "nonsensical response to the question 'What is for tea?'" (McGill). "Punters" (§28.7) in Commonwealth English usually means "customers" or "marks," but the word is attested for Kiwi English in the sense of "crowd" (Atkinson, 75). "In the churn" (§28.8) is not a specifically Kiwi term, but attested as (1) a surfing term for rough water, and (2) a business term for customer turnover.

BIBLIOGRAPHY

Absolute, *KS*: Absolute Aotearoa. "Kiwi Slang." 2017. http://www.absolutebus. co.nz/kiwi-slang.

Atkinson, 75: Atkinson, Olivia. "75 of the Most New Zealand Sayings Ever." The Urban List. 23 April 2017. http://www.theurbanlist.com/ auckland/a-list/75-Kiwi-Slang-And-Colloquialisms-And-Their-Meanings.

Bren, *UTG*: Bren on the Road. "The Ultimate Traveller's Guide to New Zealand Slang." 16 May 2104. http://brenontheroad.com/ travellers-guide-new-zealand-slang/.

ELH, *KSH*: English Language Help. "Kiwi Slang." [A through S.] 2018. http:// englishlanguagehelp.info/kiwi-slang/kiwi-slang-a/.

Hendrieka, 56: Hendrieka, Anita. "56 Typical New Zealand Slang Words and How to Use Them." http://anitahendrieka. com/56-typical-new-zealand-slang-words-use-like-kiwi/.

HTD, *HTUNZS*: How to Dad. " How to Understand New Zealand Slang." Uploaded 22 May 2018. http://www.youtube.com/ watch?v=yRxFm7onOrY.

Kiwitopia, *KS*: Kiwitopia. "Kiwi Slang." 2018. http://kiwitopia.net/kiwi-slang/.

McGill, David. *The Reed Dictionary of New Zealand Slang*. Auckland: Reed, 2003.

NEF, *NZS*: Not Even French. "New Zealand Slang: 110 Words in 5 minutes! Speak Like a Kiwi (w/ Subtitles)." Uploaded 17 October 2017. http:// www.youtube.com/watch?v=61WwIzhW9Lg .

NEF, *NZS* 2: Not Even French. "New Zealand Slang and Phrases (Part 2): The Ultimate Guide | 110 Kiwi Slang Words." Uploaded 3 November 2017. http://www.youtube.com/watch?v=61WwIzhW9Lg.

Te Ara—The Encyclopedia of New Zealand. http://teara.govt.nz/en.

UD: Urban Dictionary.

Wikipedia, *NZS*. "New Zealand English." Wikipedia. http://en.wikipedia.org/ wiki/New_Zealand_English#Vocabulary.

IMPOSTURE 29

THE BEHN OF HIS EXIſTENCE

This Imposture consists of two seemingly unrelated parts. The first is the riddle section, where al-Ḥārith overhears Abū Zayd tell his son to take something to the market and trade it for something else, referring to both objects by their (paradoxical) attributes rather than by name. The second and much longer section involves a staged marriage that provides the pretext for an unusual sermon by Abū Zayd. Those who like their Impostures to hang together might argue that the riddle sequence is needed as a way to tip off al-Ḥārith to his friend's presence in the inn. Similarly, the sermon, which contains only undotted letters, may be a clever allusion to the unfinished wedding ceremony: in both cases, what's missing is tanqīṭ; *that is, the dotting of letters as well as the showering of the bride with coins. For the English Imposture, Abū Zayd and al-Ḥārith will use the language of Aphra Behn's comedies, especially* The Rover *(1677), which features the antics of men lodging in rented rooms and includes a scene where one of them is lured into a booby-trapped bedroom and robbed. Besides screwball comedies, Behn (d. 1689) wrote tragedies and novels, which taken together provided equivalents for nearly everything in al-Ḥarīrī's Arabic. As in Impostures 9, 13, and 24, the use of dramatic form required a division into acts and scenes and a recasting of some descriptive passages as stage directions. Following the 1724 edition of* The Rover, *dashes indicate a change of topic or addressee. The speech which in the original has no dots is here rendered using no vowels but* e.*

257

29.1 ### PROLOGUE

Spoken by Mr. *Ben Hamam*

Like a single white Hair in a jet-black Barb
I was caſt off to Wásit *in a Stranger's Garb,*
To seek my Living, as any poor Man might have done,
Who, unknown to all, himself knew none.
Having no more Lodging than a Whale upon the Sand,
I reached an Inn, where from ev'ry Land
Came Travellers, some honeſt, some Piccaroons,
Drawn by Fortune and Chance, those two Shameroons;
Where a clean-swept Floor bid the weary Wanderer sit
And all the Company seem'd Men of Wit.
In short, a Room I took, none too nice,
And without disputing paid the Price.

29.2 ACT I. SCENE I. *The inn-yard, with two Chambers adjoining. In one Chamber are discovered* ABOO ZEID *and his* SON, *seated. To the other enter* BEN HAMAM, *who liſtens.*

ABOO ZEID: Rise, my Son. A Bleſsing on you, and Confusion to your Enemies! ———— Rise, and take that Moon-faced one of a paſty Hue; for though he is a shaggy Maſs, lamed in his Body, and sore in Knead, pinch'd and ſtretcht, clapt upon the Rack, batter'd and proven, and expos'd to Sale, he is a Flower sprung from a noble Seed! ———— Then fly to the Market-Place, swift as any anxious Lover, and barter him for a clapping Spark, who spits without a Mouth, throws without a Hand, and ſtrikes without a Blade; who needs a Neſt and a Bed, but sleeps in neither one nor the other; one of an even Temper, who, tho' dead, gives Life; tho' black, brings Light; tho' cold, gives Warmth; who puts the Char in 'charming' and makes of Ember an Embrace. [*Pauses.*

BEN HAMAM: Hah, the Huffing and Bluſtering are at laſt abated. Now   29.3
nothing remains but that some Fellow come forth.   [*Aside.*

The SON *iſsues alone from his Chamber, ſtrutting and cocking, and goes off.*

BEN HAMAM: A Pox of all ill Luck! The Boy has a charm that draws the
Heart away, and tempts to Indiscretion. ——— But I will follow
him, that I might see the Meaning of those Riddles.   [*Aside.*

ACT I. SCENE II. *A ſtreet, towards the Evening.*

Enter SON, *running nimbly as a jinnee,* BEN HAMAM *following. Looks on
the Wares in Heaps before the Shops. Stops before a Store of Flint, gives the
Seller a Loaf, and takes a fine thin sharp Stone.*

BEN HAMAM: 'Sheartlikins, how cunning was he who dispatched the
Boy, and how cunning the Boy dispatch'd! No need of asking; 'tis the
Saroojer's Wit ——— Let me fly back to the Inn with all Speed,
there to learn how shreud my Gueſs, and how true the Arrow of my
Divination.

Exit SON, *Ben Hamam following.*

ACT I. SCENE III. *Discovers* ABOO ZEID *sitting in the inn-yard. Enter*   29.4
BEN HAMAM, *salutes him. They embrace.*

ABOO ZEID: Ha! What Mishap has befall'n thee, to bring thee so far
from Home?

BEN HAMAM: A wicked Mischief done me by the Malice of my Stars.

ABOO ZEID: By Heaven, that dips the Earth in its Tears, and draws the
Date from the Spathe! This is a spiteful, poison'd Age, where we find

none to help us, and none but God to hear our cries ———— How then came you hither, and in what manner made you your Escape?

BEN HAMAM: With Night as my Cloak, and Hunger my Companion.

ABOO ZEID *casts his Eyes to the Ground, and scratches there with his Stick, as if bethinking himself of a Means to procure a Loan, or beg a Gift. At last stirs, like a Huntsman at the approach of Prey, or a Boot-haler at the Sight of Spoils.*

ABOO ZEID: Sir, I have a mind to what I'm going to do ———— marry you to a Lady, whose Estate will repair the Ills you have suffered.

29.5　　BEN HAMAM: Ha! Would you clap up a Match between Poverty and Matrimony? And what Lady would have Unfam'd, son of Unknown, for a Husband?

ABOO ZEID: I will ply your Suit, and raise your Glory high; repose your Trust in me, and I will do your Business, and hers too ———— Her People are a generous, dutiful, counsel-taking Race withal, eager to redeem Captives, and patch up broken Limbs ———— And yet any Suiter of theirs, be he Abraham Ben Adhem in his sooty Rags, or Gebelah Ben Aihem in his golden Gown, must pay a Dower of five hundred Pieces; because the Prophet settled a like Sum on his Wives, and asked the same in Dower for his Daughters. But they will never press you for Coin, nor bring you to Divorce. And further, when the People gather to attend your Contract, will I preach a Sermon more thorow-stitched than any made before.

29.6　　BEN HAMAM: Ha! I am more impatient to hear that Sermon, than to see the Bride lift her Veil.　　　　　　　　　　　　　　　　　　[*Aside.*

Gallant Friend, I commit the Matter to your Care; I know you will not stop at any Thing that may advance my Interest.

[ABOO ZEID *rises, then runs off. Returns, all Rapture.*

ABOO ZEID: Moſt excellent News! Fortune is pleased to smile on us, and give us an Udder to suck; for I am truſted with the Lady's Contract, and engaged to deliver the Sum. The knot is tied, or good as tied. ———— And now to invite our Fellow-Lodgers, and prepare a Sweet-Meat for the Table.

ACT II. *The Inn-Yard, and Chambers adjoining. Enter* BEN HAMAM *and* ABOO ZEID.

ABOO ZEID: The Tent of Night is pitched, and every Door locked faſt. — [*Aloud.* Come all, this very Hour!

From one side enter the BRIDE *and her Party, and the* WITNESSES: *from the other, the* LODGERS. *They gather before* ABOO ZEID's *Chamber, and sit down in Rows, the* WITNESSES *sitting hard by* BEN HAMAM. ABOO ZEID *draws forth an Aſtrolabe and raises it high, then lowers it; now ſtudies an Almanack, now lays it aside; for so long, that the People begin to nod and the drousy Fit to o'ertake them.*

BEN HAMAM: Muſt the People sit waiting your Leisure, Sirrah? Out with it!

[ABOO ZEID *gazes on the Stars, then shakes his Ears.*

ABOO ZEID: I swear by Moses' Mountain, and the Sacred Scripture, that my Secret will soon be discovered, and Fame's Trumpet sound its Tale till the very Day of Doom!

[*Kneels, imposes silence. Preaches.*

We revere the Gerent, the bleſsed Rex! Ever gentle, He lets mere   29.7
Men beget; He shelters them when beset; He tends the sweet

261

Stretches where they Bed; He erects the Jebels. Secrets He kens, Scepters He bends; new Events He decrees, then extends the Effects, when He deems beſt. Perfect, excellent, yet He descends, clement, whenever Need seeks Help; He heeds the Bereft when they beg; He feeds the Depleted ——— We remember the Creed: seven leſs three, leſs three, HE, the peerleſs Eſsence, ever replete! He sent the Meſsenger; the Meſsenger led Men, quelled the Rebels, slew Sekhmet, even felled Bel; then presented Precepts, erected leges, set new Terms, left renewed the Pledge. Let the Meſsenger be pre-served, ever respected, ever serene; let the Meſsenger's Descent be bleſsed wherever Breezes sweep the Ether, wherever Deer flee Men, wherever Selene emerges, whenever the Credent cheer!

29.8   Bleſs ye! Let the Deeds ye render be the meeteſt. Be decent; never err! Flee lewd Lechers, leſt ye Repent. Heed the beſt Decree: defend Breed, be tender, never renege. Ere ye wed, let them ye select be rev-erent, never Revelers; well bred, well served, held level, respected where they dwell ——— See ye then? Here's the Element ye seek! He tenders the Meſsenger's Settlement; he represents the Elect, the beſt Seed; he deserves the beſt Helpmeet. Let them be wed! Ye need never regret the Merger, never see free Men eſteem ye leſs. ——— Regent, bleſs them! Lend them ever-renewed Meed! Let them serve; let them be redeemed when the Term here ends! Ever bleſsed be He, ever bleſsed the Meſsenger!

29.9   BEN HAMAM: 'Sheartlikins! 'Twas a very pretty Sermon, for there was no Vowel in it, but *E*.   [*Aside.*

ABOO ZEID: I pronounce it a lawful Marriage, for 500 Pieces. I wish you Joy, and a Brood of Heroes.

                                        [*Brings out the Sweet-Meat already prepared.*

BEN HAMAM: Oh impious Traitor!   [*Aside.*

The BRIDE *and her Party, the* WITNESSES, *and the* LODGERS *rush forward:* BEN HAMAM *offers to eat; but* ABOO ZEID *makes a sign to put him off, urges him rather to offer the Sweet-Meat to the others: they no sooner taſte it but fall languiſhly to the Ground.*

BEN HAMAM: Why, how now, what means this? They tumble like worm-eaten Palm-Trees in a sudden Storm, and lie as if overcome in Drink! ———— Alas, methinks I know the Source of all this Villany.
[*Aside.*

Covetous Rogue! What haſte thou'ſt made to damn thyself! Pray was it a Sweet-Meat that thou serv'ſt, or some murderous Trick?
[*To* ABOO ZEID.

ABOO ZEID: 'Tis but a Pudding of Mandrake in Dishes of Maple-wood.

BEN HAMAM: I swear by Him, that fixt the Stars to shine and guide the wearied Traveller, that this shameful Crime betrays thee to everlaſting Infamy!   [*To* ABOO ZEID.

What shall I do? What if his Peſtilence be contagious? I feel a cold Terror around my fainting Heart. Oh, how my Blood runs shivering through my Veins!   [*Aside.*

ABOO ZEID: Methinks he looks all pale, and mightily alarmed.   [*Aside.*

Come, rouse thy wonted Spirits! If you tremble for my sake, fear not; I am no Jack-Pudding; I will take my Plunder and fly—be gone—depart—vanish into Air, as I so often have before ———— And if you tremble for your self, that you be carry'd to Prison, you need but eat up a small Morsel of the Sweet-Meat, and be reconciled to the Loſs of your Shirt; thus may you remain here when I am gone, safe from Petitioner and Magiſtrate ———— Else flee, flee! left you be toused and dragged.

29.10 [*Goes from one Chamber to another, ransacking Baggages and Wardrobes; picks out the fineſt Treasures from every Hoard, whether it be of Gems, or Perfume, or Stuff, leaving whate'er escapes his Snare, as empty as a Bone suck'd of its Marrow; wraps the Stuffs in a Cloke, and ſticks the reſt in his Waſte-Belt; turns up his Sleeves, ties his Girdle; then puts off the Mask of Friendship and turns upon Ben Hamam with an impudent Air.*

Shall we travel together to Bog-Town? There I may marry you again, to a pretty one this time.

BEN HAMAM: I swear by Him whose Prophet was bleſsed wheresoever he would be, and who, though inn-digent, committed no Inn-famy, that two Wives of Quality would be too high i' th' Mouth for me; nor could I long dwell in a House full of Noise and Mischief.
[*Aſsumes* ABOO ZEID's *Manner, and apes his Raillery.*

One Wife's enough to Boaſt of; let the second grace another Bed.

[ABOO ZEID *smiles; offers to embrace* BEN HAMAM; BEN HAMAM *turns away and shrinks back;* ABOO ZEID *takes notice of his Aversion.*

29.11 ABOO ZEID:

All human Things are subject to Decay,
And Friendship pledged eternal falls away.
So I proteſt, when Hareth waxes hot,
And tells me, rob his Kinsmen I should not:
Once was I their Gueſt, and scanty Hoſts
Were they, tho' Tyrants fond of pompous Boaſts.
Had they Honeſty, or Kindneſs, or Largeſs,
I would not cause their Tribe, or you, Diſtreſs,
Nor come to them a Wolf among the Kine,
Nor leave them ſtrewn like Drunkards felled by Wine;
But now 'tis done: one swift and sure Attack
Settles all their Bounty on my Back.

How many others, felled with baneful Drugs— 29.12
Soft-couchèd Lords, besprawled on Rugs—
Have I left groaning, to avenge a Slight,
And done by Cunning, what none could do by Might;
And how oft ƒtood where Lions fear to tread,
And how oft slain, and left my Foe for dead;
Now, though a Sinner ne'er to be forgiven,
I dare yet lift my guilty Eyes toward Heaven.

[*Falls a weeping in a moƒt violent manner.*

Once more, sweet Heaven, have Mercy!

BEN HAMAM, *who has turned away, sighs and looks on him.*

BEN HAMAM: Do you repent? Turn yet, and be forgiven.

ABOO ZEID *wipes his Eyes, claps the Sack under his Arm, and begins to sneak out.*

ABOO ZEID: Carry off the reƒt, and may God guard us well. [*To his* SON.

Exeunt ABOO ZEID *and* SON.

BEN HAMAM: 29.13

Gone the Viper and his Hatchling
Leaving me the only one;
Swiftly now muƒt I be going
Else I find myself undone.

Now I bind my little Baggage,
Now I ride to Teebah-town;
Cursing, as I cut my Paƒsage,
That Rascal in a Preacher's Gown!

GLOSSARY

29.1

piccaroon   thief, outlaw   *shameroon*   trickster, rascal

29.4

boot-haler   bandit

29.9

touse   to handle roughly

NOTES

The original Imposture is named after al-Wāsiṭ, a town on the Tigris roughly equidistant from Basra, Kufa, and Ahwaz. It was founded by the Umayyads on the west side of the Tigris opposite the Sasanian town of Kaskar, which was connected to it by a floating bridge. It was an important center for agricultural production and for the minting of coins (Sakly and Darley-Doran, "Wāsiṭ").

In §29.2, Abū Zayd describes a loaf using terms that seem to apply to a person (e.g., "moon-faced") and the flint or the flame using paradox (e.g., "the destroyer that repairs"). The English uses puns ("in Knead") and riddle forms ("spits without a Mouth"). A "lame" is a blade used to slash the surface of a loaf, allowing the dough to expand and creating a decorative pattern (see Saffitz, "How Bakery Breads . . ."). A "nest" is a bundle of tinder. A "bed" is a place supplied with kindling and fuel, where the burning tinder is placed to build the fire (see Bush, "Traditional Firestarting"; for a video that demonstrates the process clearly see Grierwolf, "The Truth").

"'Sheartlikins" (§29.3) is an exclamation of affirmation or surprise, much favored by the character Blunt in *The Rover*. Abraham Ben Adhem (§29.5) is Ibrāhīm ibn Adham (d. 161/777–8?), a Sufi exemplar famous for his poverty and asceticism. Perhaps not coincidentally given the events of this Imposture, he is said to have died of a stomach ailment (Jones, "Ibrāhīm b. Adham"). Gebelah Ben Aihem is Jabalah ibn Ayham, an Arab king of pre- and early Islamic times, famous for living in luxury. The "dower" here means the sum of money the husband undertakes to pay the wife in the event of divorce. Mandrake is a root that promotes sleep but can have a number of ill effects, including intestinal upset.

"Impious traitor" (§29.9): The Arabic has al-Ḥārith, in his capacity as narrator, tell us that Abū Zayd brought undying shame on himself when he played the trick he is about to play. But the al-Ḥārith who is a character in the English

Imposture does not yet know that a trick will be played. This line should therefore be understood as spoken by al-Ḥārith the storyteller as an aside to the audience. A "Jack-Pudding" is a buffoon, introduced here to stand in for the pun Abū Zayd makes on *ajlī*—"my offense" as well as "my sake."

Bog-Town (§29.10), according to al-Sharīshī, is a town south of Basra. The Arabic name (al-Baṭīḥah) suggests a connection with the marshes of that region. "Him whose Prophet . . ." comes from Q Maryam 19:31 and the translation is based on Sale's rendering of 1734. "Inn-digent" and "Inn-famy" stand in for al-Ḥārith's pun on *khān* ("inn") and *khān* "he betrayed." "All human Things . . ." (§29.11) is the first line of "Mac Flecknoe," by John Dryden (d. 1700). "Teeba" (§29.13) is Ṭībah, which Al-Sharīshī says is a place near Wāsiṭ, though it is also used to refer to Medina.

On the use of dashes in seventeenth-century English see Canfield, ed., *Broadview Anthology*, xxi; and Bourne, *Typographies*. My use of the long s (ſ) follows the ad hoc rules devised for Imposture 31. Oddly, some of the words Behn uses go unmentioned in the *OED* (for example, "janting," "to cony up to," and "flabber chops").

BIBLIOGRAPHY

Behn, Aphra. *Plays Written by the Late Ingenious Mrs. Behn in Four Volumes.* Vol. 1. 3rd ed. London: Printed for Mary Poulson, and sold by A. Bettesworth in Pater-noster Row, and F. Clay without Temple-Bar, 1724.

———. *The Works of Aphra Behn.* Edited by Montague Summers. London: Heinemann, 1915.

Bernstein, Max. "Breadmaking 101: How to Mix and Knead Bread Dough Like a Pro." Serious Eats. http://www.seriouseats.com/2014/09/breadmaking-101-how-to-mix-and-knead-dough-step-by-step.html.

Bourne, Claire M. L. *Typographies of Performance in Early Modern England.* Forthcoming.

Bush, Darren. "Traditional Firestarting Part I: How to Make Fire with Flint and Steel." The Art of Manliness. January 5, 2011. http://www.artofmanliness.com/2011/01/05/traditional-firestarting-part-i-how-to-make-fire-with-flint-and-steel/.

Canfield, J. Douglas, ed. *The Broadview Anthology of Restoration and Eighteenth-Century Drama.* Peterborough, Ontario: Broadview, 2005.

Grierwolf. "The Truth about Flint and Steel + Unspoken Tips." Published April 4, 2014. http://www.youtube.com/watch?v=FYEnrbZWMaU.

Jones, Russell. "Ibrāhīm b. Adham." In *Encyclopaedia of Islam, Third Edition*. Leiden: Brill, 2009.

Saffitz, Claire. "How Bakery Breads Get Those Gorgeous Patterns (and How Your Loaves Can, Too)." Bon Appétit. January 28, 2016. http://www.bonappetit.com/test-kitchen/how-to/article/bakery-breads-patterns

Sakly, Mondher, and Robert Darley-Doran. "Wāsiṭ." In *Encyclopaedia of Islam, Second Edition*. Leiden: Brill, 1960–2007.

Imposture 30

Stop Hole Abbey

In this episode, al-Ḥārith's nosiness leads him to a big, frighten-
ing house where odd rituals take place. Naturally, he narrates
this episode in the style of Jane Austen's Northanger Abbey
(1818), which parodies the Gothic novel. In their speeches, Abū
Zayd and the doorman use words from Francis Grose's lexicon of
eighteenth-century criminal slang. Abū Zayd's poem is based on
the works of Austen's favorite, William Cowper (d. 1800).

Of Elhareth ebn Hammam we had this account.   **30.1**

No one who leaves Baghdad for the fine and striking environs of Tyre
is expected, once settled at that place, to come away—but that is what
Elhareth did. Having made a fortune in trade, risen to honour, and acquired
the means of resuming his travels, he felt his weariness of Tyre change into
a violent desire to see Egypt. The resolution to depart once formed, it was
not in the power of all the amusements of Tyre to detain him longer. He set
off in haste; and, in spite of robbers, and tempests, and all manner of difficulties and dangers, he arrived at last in Cairo. His feelings of delight on
first beholding that city were so strong, that he burst forth in wonder and
praise, and called himself without scruple as happy a being as ever existed.

He was engaged, one morning after two or three days had passed away, **30.2**
in threading, upon a short-stepping horse, the alleys of the town, when his
eye fell upon a party of splendid-looking men riding short-haired steeds.
Eager to court the acquaintance of so elegant a party, and desirous of joining them in what augured to be a pleasant excursion, he asked those about

him if they knew who the company were, and whither they were going. "Witnesses, sir," was the information on their side, "going to perform their office at a wedding."

It was not only a sweet elation of spirits, but—it must be acknowledged—a wish of taking refreshment at an occasion certain of being furnished with tolerable meat and cake, that impelled El-Hareth to set out after that party of strangers.

After some exertion and fatigue, they reached a large and lofty edifice enclosing a spacious court, the whole a monument to the wealth and splendour of its builders. They alighted and paraded to the door.

Gaining the hall, Elhareth saw that its walls were hung with ragged cloaks and ornamented with beggars' baskets. There was a tittuppy bench with a velvet cloth thrown over it, and a figure sitting upon it. The sight filled him with an awful foreboding of future misery, and a suspicion that past scenes of horror had been enacted within the solemn edifice.

30.3   His heart beat quick, but his courage did not fail him. Addressing himself to the seated figure, he asked him to tell him, who was the master of the house.

"It has no master, and belongs to no one. It is the stop hole abbey of canters and cadgers, and the resort of setters and brothers of the coif."

His blood ran cold from the horrid suggestions which naturally sprang from these words. He immediately thought of returning to town; but the prospect of leaving a place he had reached only five minutes before, and of taking the shameful journey alone, persuaded him to remain. With a feeling of terror not very definable, he entered the house.

30.4   He observed with some surprise that the parlour was furnished with couches of painted stuff, sitting-rugs, and heaps of hassocks, and the walls hung with tapestry. The bridegroom, a pompous young man dressed in a striped gown and attended by a crowd of servants, had already made his appearance. As soon as the latter, with all the pride of a young Croesus, had seated himself, one of his relations rose and cried out: "By the honour of old Lord Sasan, the Beggar King, let no man perform this solemn business but a mendicant of our order, trained up young and now grown old in the trade!" Delighted by this proposal, the bride-people gave their consent to summon anyone who corresponded with this description.

Then came into the room a man of commanding aspect, past the bloom, but not past the vigor of life. The company welcomed him with eager anticipation. He sat down on a carpet and crept along until he had gained a hassock. Turning a forbidding eye upon the company, he stroked his beard and waited for the clamour of voices to subside. He then spoke as follows.

"Praise be to GOD, the bestower of bounties, and the author of charity! To him we make supplication, and upon him we fix our hopes. It is he who hath ordained the poor-tax and forbidden believers to repulse the beggar. It is he who exhorts us to succor the indigent, giving to eat 'unto him who is content with what is given him, without asking, and unto him who asketh.' He hath described, in his perspicuous Book, his favoured servants, saying (and who is more true in what he saith?) that they are 'those ready to give a due and certain portion of their substance unto any who ask, and unto any too ashamed to ask.' I praise him who enables easy digestion, and I take refuge in him from prayers uttered without proper intention. I bear witness that there is no god besides GOD, who rewards the alms-givers of either sex, and removes his blessing from usury, and multiplies the reward of almsgiving. 30.5

"I bear witness likewise that GOD's merciful servant and honorable messenger is MOHAMMED, whom he sent to banish the darkness of oppression and seek justice for the poor against the rich. Did our Prophet not excite the believers to feed the pauper? Did he not show tender affection to the lowly? Did he not levy taxes upon the property of the great, and instruct them in their duties to the destitute? May GOD bless Mohammed his emissary and bring him near, and may he bless likewise the indigent Companions of the Portico!

"Now then: Certain great volumes command us to be fruitful and multiply, and declare that it is better to marry than to burn. Saith the LORD: 'Verily we have created you of a male and a female; and we have distributed you into nations and tribes, that ye might know one another.' Here before us is BEN BUDGE son of DIMBER DAMBER, a roaring boy and brazenfaced Corinthian, a sturdy beggar, and a swinging great teller of clankers. He seeks in marriage the filching mort SPITFIRE daughter of BULL BEEF, the arch doxy of her gang, on account of her being a cleaver and a clapperclawer, devoted to the business and assiduous in the trade. He herewith 30.6

offers by way of dower a wallet, a staff, a kerchief, and a pouch. So take him for a son-in-law as befits one of his standing, and have no fear of poverty, for the LORD will provide. I ask pardon for myself, and you alike. May God multiply your kinchins along the maunders' kerbs, and keep your union from the hatches!"

30.7　　His speech concluded, the master of the ceremonies pronounced the parties bound by the contract of marriage. A great shower of coins, so excessive as to awaken a corresponding liberality in the meanest of men, next followed. The master of the ceremonies then rose up, and, dragging the hem of his robe along the ground, moved away, the whole vulgar mob following in his train.

30.8　　Elhareth was eager to learn what sort of people these were, and to partake of their festivity; and so followed the mob to a row of tables, arranged in perfect symmetry, upon which the cooks had conferred every advantage afforded by their art. Each member of the company found before him a plentiful portion, to which he applied himself heartily, putting Elhareth in mind of a man working in his garden. He in the meanwhile made his way through the throng, and, as he disengaged myself from the crowd, perceived himself to be angrily regarded by the dreaded master of the ceremonies himself.

"Where are you going to, flincher?" he cried, "will you not dine, and pay your shot? This is a bang-up club!"

"I do promise upon my honour," Elhareth replied, "that I will touch no bread, nor eat any soup, unless you declare the mineret that announces your home, and name the hearth that soothes your heart."

This question brought a sudden change of countenance, and it was only after fetching many great sighs, and bursting several times into tears, that the fellow was able to recite, during the general pause that followed:

> Sarooj was my home; for the valleys I mourn
> Where riches poured from a gen'rous horn.
> There fountains spring—there hillocks rise,
> There Zephyr whispers, and the stream replies.
> How gentle the touch of her breezes sweet,
> When flowers awaken and snows retreat.

How happy were we, who those scenes beheld,
And how wretched now, from Sarooj expell'd.
Joy has fled, by force of arms subdued,
And the refugee's grief is each day renew'd.
Of our sorrows and sighs, how shall I speak?
Our towers are fall'n to the impious Greek!
Far sweeter 't would be, to lie there entomb'd,
Than to live as I live, to wandering doomed.

Hearing him pronounce the name of his native town, and attending closely to the import of his verses, Elhareth discerned that this was his learned master Aboo Zaid, now gouty with old age. Elhareth took his hand with the liveliest pleasure, and accepted the honour of sharing his trencher. The remainder of his days in Egypt he spent as his faithful pupil, finding in him a model of the utmost liveliness of diction. Though he had little right to expect a long continuance of this intimacy, when it was finally put an end to, his grief and agitation were excessive. It had been a very happy interval, and forlorn was the sinking from it into the common course of days.

NOTES

In Arabic, this Imposture was called "of Egypt" and "of Tyre," with the latter eventually becoming the accepted title even though the action takes place in Egypt. The opening lines, in which al-Ḥārith makes a fortune in trade, may echo the fact that, in al-Ḥarīrī's time, Tyre was a major port of the Crusader states of Outremer.

In addition to *Northanger Abbey*, the English of this Imposture draws on Austen's other works, notably *Pride and Prejudice* (1813) and *Emma* (1815). Unattributed definitions come from the first edition (1785) of Grose's *Dictionary*; "1811" means that the definition comes instead from the expanded edition of that year. A few needed words come from John Gay's *Beggar's Opera* (1728). The only extraneous word, apart from proper names, is "trencher" (§30.8), which is, however, attested for the period.

"Stop hole abbey" (§30.3) is defined by Grose as "the nick name of the chief rendezvous of the canting crew of beggars, gypsies, cheats, thieves, &c., &c."

Canters are "thieves, beggars, and gypsies, or any others using the canting lingo." A "cadger" is one who cadges, that is, begs (1811). A "setter" is a bailiff's henchman, "who, like a setting dog, follows and points out the game for his master." Here it translates *mushaqshiq*, which al-Sharīshī defines as a hunter who attracts birds by imitating their calls (*Sharḥ*, 3:422). Admittedly, this could be a thief who uses a lure of some kind to attack his victims, but I am assuming that the term must have something in common with the next word, *mujalwiz*, a bailiff (here translated as "brother of the coif," meaning "a serjeant at law" according to Grose, *Dictionary*; see also §23.10). Steingass has "ballad-singers and rehearsers of the traditions" (see *Assemblies*, 26, and the note on p. 198), which seems justifiable in the case of *mushaqshiq* but not *mujalwiz*.

"Unto him who is content . . ." (§30.5): Q Ḥajj 22:36 (tr. Sale). "Those ready to . . .": Q Maʿārij 70:24, retranslated based on Sale. The Companions of the Portico (*ahl al-ṣuffah*) are people who came to Medina to join the Prophet's community and, having no family or property there, were forced to live in the portico of the mosque and to subsist on charity (Tottoli, "Ahl al-ṣuffah").

"Verily we have created you . . ." (§30.6): Q Ḥujurāt 49:13 (tr. Sale). Ben Budge is a character from *The Beggar's Opera*. To budge, according to Grose, means "to move, or quit one's station," making "Budge" analogous to Darrāj, "walker," specifically a far-ranging itinerant beggar (de Sacy, *Séances*, 1:329). Grose further describes a budge as "one that slips into houses in the dark, to steal cloaks or other clothes." A "dimber damber" is "a top man, or prince among the canting crew, also the chief rogue of a gang, or the compleatest cheat." A "roaring boy" is "a noisy, riotous fellow" (1811). A "Corinthian" is "an impudent, brazen-faced fellow." "Sturdy beggars" are "the fifth and last of the most ancient order of canters, beggars that rather demand than ask." A "clanker" is a "great lie." A "filching mort" is "a woman thief." "Spitfire" is Steingass's apt rendering of the name Qanbas (*Assemblies*, 29). "To look like bull beef" is "to look fierce or surly." An "arch doxy" is a woman who heads a gang of female thieves. A "cleaver" is "a forward or wanton woman." To "clapper claw" is to "scold, abuse, or claw off with the tongue." "Kinchin" are children. A "maunder" is a beggar (1811). "From the hatches" is based on "under the hatches," meaning "in trouble, distress, or debt."

A "flincher" (§30.8) is "one who passes the bottle" or "abstains from drinking" (*OED*; cf. *Beggar's Opera*, III:6, where it seems to mean "miser"). "To pay one's shot" is to pay one's share of a reckoning. A "bang-up club" is "a meeting or association, where each man is to spend an equal and stated sum." "Mineret" is a 1761 spelling of minaret (*OED*), echoing the church spire that tells *Northanger Abbey*'s Catherine Morland that she has finally arrived back home.

BIBLIOGRAPHY

Austen, Jane. *Northanger Abbey*. Digital edition on Project Gutenberg: http://www.gutenberg.org/files/121/121-h/121-h.htm.

———. *Emma*. Digital edition on Project Gutenberg: http://www.gutenberg.org/files/158/158-h/158-h.htm.

———. *Pride and Prejudice*. Digital edition on Project Gutenberg: https://www.gutenberg.org/files/1342/1342-h/1342-h.htm.

Cowper, William. *The Works of William Cowper: His Life, Letters, and Poems*. Edited by T. S. Grimshawe. London: William Tegg, 1849.

Gay, [John]. *The Beggar's Opera*. New York: Huebsch, 1920. Originally published 1728.

Grose, Francis. *Dictionary in the Vulgar Tongue*. 1st ed. Revised and enlarged "by a member of the Whip Club assisted by Hell-Fire Dick, and James Gordon, Esqrs. of Cambridge; and William Soames, Esq. of the Hon. Society of Newman's Hotel," 1811. London: Hooper, 1785. http://www.gutenberg.org/cache/epub/5402/pg5402-images.html.

Tottoli, Roberto. "Ahl al-ṣuffah." In *Encyclopaedia of Islam, Third Edition*. Leiden: Brill, 2009.

IMPOSTURE 31

A Hajji's Progrefs

Abū Zayd, here called Father Increase, accosts a caravan of pilgrims and reminds them that their visit to Mecca should be a journey of repentance, not simply a series of rites. He and al-Ḥārith (here called Plowman) will speak in the manner of John Bunyan's Pilgrim's Progress *(1678), which uses pilgrimage as an allegory for Christian life and makes a similarly vigorous case for the importance of faith.*

31.1   Neighbor *Plowman* told us another tale, that thus began:

When I was a young man, and strong, and my nature in its prime, I could not bear to abide by the door of mine own house, but did venture myself abroad, knowing that with a little pain I might richly provide for myself, and whoso would come to Honor must needs leave his friends and his comforts behind him. Wherefore, ruled by the Counsel of men of good will, I resolved to set out for the sea coast of *Syria*, there to trade.

31.2   Now I had no sooner got to *Arimathea*, and cast down my staff, and lighted under a little shelter, but I perceived a Stir and Commotion; and going out came upon a Company of Pilgrims that would ride to the *Mother of Cities*. Whereupon a great fire did dart from heaven into my Soul, and a great longing ravish my Heart, to behold the *Holy Caaba*. So I girded my camel, and loosed my Burdens, and they fell from off my back. Then I sang:

Thou surly one, wilt thou hearken to me?
Thy wares are vanity; blest rather be
The well of Zamzam where Hagar did call,
Abraham's Station, the Stone, and the Wall!

So I cast in my lot with a Company bright and twinkling like the stars,   31.3
and swift as the waters; and we hastened by day and preſsed on by night,
galloping with speed always, until we were come with gladneſs to the
Starting-point in *Juhfah*, where, with Trembling and Joy, we should put
on us the Pilgrim's Garb. But we had no sooner made our camels to kneel
down, and taken their burdens from off their backs, behold a Man, clothed
with rags, crying, "Arise, ye living, and learn how you may be delivered
from the Wrath to come!"

Whereupon a great Multitude followed him; and when they were gathered together, he went up onto a Hill, and the people sat about him like
stones around a pot. Then he lifted up his eyes, and looking upon them,
cleared his throat, and taught them, saying:

"O Pilgrims, arrived from every cleft in the rocks! I will ask if you know,   31.4
whither you are going? and before Whom you seek to stand? and what way
it is you have taken? and to Whose plough you have set your hands?

"Beware lest you say, that the Pilgrimage require only this: that you
choose a strong camel, and tie up your bundle, and mend your speed; or
peradventure that Piety demand only this, that you roll up your garment,
and suffer hunger, and depart from your children, and hazard yourselves
abroad.

"For I say unto you: what is a man profited, if he shall gain camels in
abundance, while he bear on his own back the burden of Sin? Shall he enter
the House of God, whose own house is builded on a foundation of dust?
Wherefore should he go in haste, whose Path is crooked? For what availeth
his Capacity, but for Obedience? And whither speedeth he his camel, ere
he abide with his fellow in Righteousneſs?"

"Good brethren! I bid you now take heed, that as you go on your way   31.5
you shall overtake a Man, whose name is FORMALIST. He will draw up
unto you, and enter into discourse with you, and you must answer him
roundly, thus:

FORMALIST: Have we not poured Water out of buckets, and washed ourselves? Will that not suffice?

PILGRIM: We must yet cleanse ourselves of Sin.

FORMALIST: Have we not cast off the Raiments of this World? Will that not suffice?

PILGRIM: We must yet cast off the Raiment of Sin.

FORMALIST: Have we not put on the Pilgrim's Garb?

PILGRIM: Yes, but not yet the Garb of Purity.

FORMALIST: Have we not girded up our Loins?

PILGRIM: Yes, but not yet armed ourselves with Righteousneſs.

FORMALIST: Are we not shaven?

PILGRIM: Howbeit our Trespaſs against His Servants is grown up unto the heavens.

FORMALIST: Are we not shorn?

PILGRIM: Yea, but our Wickedneſs spreads itself like a green bay tree.

FORMALIST: Shall we not stand at *Arafah*?

PILGRIM: Who shall ascend into the Hill? He that hath clean Hands, and a pure Heart.

FORMALIST: Shall we not abide in tents at *Mina*?

PILGRIM: Whosoever purifieth not himself defileth the tabernacle of the LORD.

FORMALIST: Howbeit we shall pray where *Abraham* stood!

PILGRIM: What availeth us to pray there, but we keep the Way of the LORD?

FORMALIST: Surely, our Pilgrimage shall be acceptable to Him!

PILGRIM: To do Justice is more acceptable to the LORD than sacrifice.

FORMALIST: Shall we not be rewarded for running between *Safa* and *Marwa*?

PILGRIM: We must run the way of His Commandments, that He may enlarge our hearts.

FORMALIST: But what of the Water of *Zamzam*? Shall we not drink it for a bleſsing?

PILGRIM: Unleſs we are cleansed first by the Waters of the Law it will profit us nothing.

FORMALIST: What of our bodies? Are they not clean?
PILGRIM: The body without the Soul is a dead carcase.
FORMALIST: And what of our farewell Walk around the Caaba?
PILGRIM: Walk first in His Statutes, and keep His Commandments."

Then he sang with a loud Voice, that had like to make the deaf hearken,   31.6
and the mountains to start:

> Come hither, you that walk along the way;
> Behold how Pilgrims fare that go astray!
> They consider only how they go, and when;
> They seek not God, nor meditate on Him.
> Keep, dear Brother, Mercy by thy side;
> Let Virtue be thy road, Honesty thy guide.
> Should any beg from thee, extend a Hand,
> Lest thy striving be for nought, o Man!
> Scorn the poor, and planting is in vain,
> Thine harvest thorns, and cursèd is thy name.
> Be mindful, then, in all thou dost, of Him
> Who hath decreed the use of every Limb.
> For Death will come, who mocketh thy Disdain:
> Good works do now, while yet some Days remain!
> Though thine the Head it be that wears the Crown,
> Shun Haughtineſs, and keep thine eyes cast down.
> Hearken not, when Men thy Lord deny:
> Proclaim them false, and all their works decry.
> And from this World, take nothing but thy Meat:
> The rest is foul Corruption and Deceit!

Neighbor Plowman proceeded, saying: 31.7

Seeing him awaken the people with words like fire out of the mountain,
I smelled the sweet savour of Father Increase. Wherefore I tarried until
he had done his Work and come down from the Hill. Then I preſsed forward, that I might see more perfectly his Face, and touch the Hem of his

Garment; and behold! he was my Sheep which was lost, and the Author of the Verses we had heard. I fell on his neck, as the ∫ falls on the *s*, and embraced him, as if I were hurt, and he the balm of *Gilead*. Then I invited him to join himself to us, that I might have his good Company. But he waxed surly and churlish, saying, "I have sworn, on this Pilgrimage, to cast away all Vanities and Wares, to shun Lust, Pleasure, and Delight; and to scorn Deceivers, Cheats, Games, Plays, Apes, Fools, Knaves, and Rogues of every kind!"

31.8 And with that he took his leave of me, wherefore I fell to sighs and bitter lamentations, wishing he would tarry, lo, even with his Heel upon mine Eye, as he sped him away.

Howbeit I looked after him, and saw him take his way to the top of another hill, where he stood waiting for the Pilgrims. Then, when he espied their Camels bounding acro∫s the Sand-hills, he clapped his hands, and declaimed:

> Pilgrims, descend! And that for several reasons, for—
> First, On foot a Servant goes; he doth not ride.
> Second, Riding lifteth up the Heart to Pride.
> Third, Be him who buildeth, not him who teareth down.
> Fourth, The faithful, not the slothful, earn the Crown.
> Fifth, Thou must behold how vain are earthly things.
> Sixth, Thou must repent afore the Trumpet rings,
> Lest thou—Seventh—fall into a Valley dark as pitch,
> With—Eighth—Hobgoblins, Satyrs, and Dragons of the pit!
> Ninth, Be zealous, my good Pilgrim, and repent;
> And Tenth, Rejoice in Bliss, like Manna heaven-sent!

Then he sheathed the sword of his tongue and fled away.

31.9 Afterwards we drank of no Spring, nor made a stand in any Meadow to ease our Flesh, but that I sought for him, and entreated others to seek him also, but all in vain; and, seeing him no more, I could not think, but that the Earth had swallowed him up, or the *Dgens* sped him away to their Lairs. I have never, upon a journey, so often sighed, nor ever in travel tasted such Grief.

NOTES

Modern editions call this Imposture "of Ramlah" (*al-Ramliyyah*), which is also the title of Imposture 45. Katia Zakharia has argued that the synonymy is deliberate (Abū Zayd, 301–6, discussed in the Notes on Imposture 45). The Istanbul manuscript supplies an alternative title for this one: al-Makkiyyah, of Mecca. Al-Ramlah, in al-Ḥarīrī's time the main city of the province of Palestine, is mentioned only in passing. It is probably not Arimathea (§31.2), though Europeans have thought so (Honigmann, "Ramla"). "Mother of Cities" refers to Mecca.

The real focus of the Imposture is the rite of pilgrimage. Several important sites of visitation are listed in §31.2; for reasons of rhyme and meter, the translation uses a different but overlapping list of sites. According to Islamic tradition, Hagar, the wife of Abraham, was left in the desert with her infant son Ishmael. The place where God, responding to her thirsty cries, caused water to spring from the ground is called the well of Zamzam. The so-called Station of Abraham (*maqām Ibrāhīm*) is (according to one tradition) where Abraham stood while building the Kaaba, the shrine that is a focus of the pilgrimage. The Kaaba contains the Black Stone, here called "the Stone," which pilgrims try to touch or kiss during their visit. "The Wall" (*Ḥaṭīm* in the original) is a low semicircular wall near one side of the Kaaba. The space it encloses is respected as the burial place of Hajar and Ishmael. At §31.5 is mentioned Arafah, a hill where pilgrims spend a day praying for forgiveness; Mina, the valley near Mecca where the pilgrims sleep out in tents and carry out the ritual of stoning the Devil; and Safa and Marwa, the two hills Hajar is said to have climbed while looking for water.

Though *The Pilgrim's Progress* is one of the most popular works ever written in English, Bunyan (d. 1688), in my view, was an indifferent (if desperately earnest) writer of prose, as well as a bad poet. What redeems his style is its heavy reliance on the English Bible. The translation therefore draws freely on the King James version. A few words come from Bunyan's *Grace Abounding to the Chief of Sinners* or from period citations in the *OED* (e.g., "Dgen," for *jinn*, attested in 1684). Inspired by the beautifully typeset electronic edition of The Pilgrim's Progress by Samizdat, I tried to approximate the format of the printed editions, including irregular capitalization. Even so, I have not used the long s (ſ) everywhere it belongs, but instead followed the eighteenth-century practice of using it only when a word has two esses in a row (for details see West, "Rules").

Despite its striking similarities to the Imposture, *The Pilgrim's Progress* has certain distinctive features difficult to imitate without playing freely with the original. For example, the Arabic contains no dialogue with Formalist (§31.5). What it does contain is a series of assertions by Abū Zayd that the rites will only be meaningful if the pilgrims do good works and avoid sin. In each case, the pretext for the assertion is a similarity in the words used for the two terms of the comparison: e.g., the pilgrim's state of ritual purity, *iḥrām*, requires avoiding abomination, *ḥarām*. To render these repeated antitheses, the English recasts the passage as a dialogue. To do this, it brings in an allegorical figure whom Bunyan calls the Formalist (Part 1, "The Third Stage"), who is not there in the Arabic. In §31.8, similarly, the original has a poem, not a list, but since lists are also a distinctive feature of Bunyan's prose, the translation recasts it as one, retaining the rhyme.

BIBLIOGRAPHY

Bunyan, John. *The Pilgrim's Progress*. Samizdat, 2013.

———. *Grace Abounding to the Chief of Sinners*. Project Gutenberg e-text based on the David Price edition of 1905. http://www.gutenberg.org/ebooks/654.

Honigmann, E. "Al-Ramla." In *Encyclopaedia of Islam, Second Edition*. Leiden: Brill, 1960–2007.

West, Andrew. "The Rules for Long S." http://babelstone.blogspot.ae/2006/06/rules-for-long-s.html.

IMPOSTURE 32

JURY-RIGGED

*This episode is about law, specifically Sunni Shāfiʿī jurispru-
dence, which like all Islamic legal systems covers belief and ritual
as well as what certain other legal systems call civil and criminal matters. It was commonly expected that jurists have a good
command of Arabic, including the distinctions between similar
or seemingly identical terms. Al-Ḥarīrī takes this requirement
as the pretext for a series of legal riddles based on homonyms.
These are rendered here as English puns, while the narration is
based on the* Law Dictionary *of Henry Campbell Black. Abū
Zayd does not pretend to use any of his terms in their proper
legal sense, and in some cases he has knowingly misused them.
In section §32.2, he quotes the Qurʾan in the Latin rendering by
Ludovigo Maracci (d. 1700). As one bit of Latin led to another,
the English verses quote or allude to lines by the Roman poets
Seneca and Terence.*

AL-HARITH IBN HAMMAM testified *ipsissimis verbis:*   32.1

I, AL-HARITH IBN HAMMAM, having fulfilled the statutory require-
ments of the pilgrimage and completed all rituals appertaining there-
unto, including but not limited to proclaiming my presence to God and
participating in the sacrifice, did, in full command of my faculties, form
the deliberate intention of traveling to Medina in the company of certain
parties affiliated with the Shaybah tribe, with the purpose of visiting
the Prophet's tomb, and by that expedient placing myself beyond the

range of any future prosecution for neglect of this solemn concomitant of the mandatory Hajj. WHEREAS it was alleged that the local Bedouin were in tumult and the roads deserted, I was compelled to balance the competing claims of prudence and zeal. Upon due deliberation, I found in favor of submitting to the will of God and visiting the tomb. Pursuant thereto, I chose a mount, purchased provisions, and set out, along with the parties aforesaid, traveling without divagation, dilatoriness, or delay as far as the jurisdiction of the Harb tribe, whose members were at that time newly returned from some violent altercation. We thereupon resolved to pass the remainder of that day among their dwellings and in their company.

32.2   As we searched for a dismounting-place proximate to a source of potable water, we became aware of a commotion, insofar as our hosts had begun to vacate the premises with indisputable rapidity, in *prima facie* accord with the precedent of those pagans who ran to serve their idols. Alarmed by this disorderly proceeding, we inquired as to its cause, and were apprised that the alleged Jurist of the Arabs had arrived upon the premises, and that the persons aforementioned sought to attend him *instanter*. I thereupon proposed to my associates that we join the gathering, for *veritas nihil veretur nisi abscondi*. With their express consent, we allowed ourselves to be guided to the assembly.

Upon reaching that place, we did observe, perceive, and see the Jurist aforementioned, whom I identified positively as Abu Zayd (hereinafter ABU ZAYD), a party known to have willfully, knowingly, absolutely, and falsely declared, deposed, and certified as truth numerous material matters he knew to be false. He was posed and attired in the manner of the jurists, to wit and viz., beturbaned *sine* festoon, with his garments tightly wrapped as to prevent indecent exposure and his knees drawn up to his chest. A considerable number of persons, among them representatives of the *mobile vulgus* as well as the notables, were gathered around him. We overheard him making the following declaration:

"Bring before me your moots, and all your doubtful cases and questions, for I swear to you by the One who spread the sky and taught Adam the names of all His creatures, that I am the most discerning in matters juridical of all the Arabians nomadic, and the most learned man under the sun."

His challenge was accepted, with ostensible cognizance of risk, by a well-spoken youth (hereinafter THE YOUTH), who stated that he "had attended the lectures of all the most eminent jurists and selected one hundred (100) of their subtlest rulings," and that the claimant, if he wished to receive a consideration from Harb, and prove that he had not misrepresented himself, should hear the questions and provide true, complete, and correct answers to them all.

ABU ZAYD replied: "*Ad majorem Dei gloriam! Oportet quod certa res deducatur in judicium! 'Manifesta igitur id, quod juberis!'*"

TRANSCRIPT 32.3

Q: Does touching one's *na'l* invalidate the lesser ablution?
     (Na'l *commonly means "sandal" but can also mean "wife."*)
A: It's something to wash out for.

Q: What about succumbing to *bard*?
     (*"Chill" but also "sleep"*)
A: No, and beware of synecdoche: mistaking the bard for the cold.

Q: What if one touches his *unthayān*?
     (*"Testes" but also "ears"*)
A: He should wash. Let me add that so far this hasn't been much of an examination: more like a test-icle!

Q: What if he's spattered by a *thu'bān*?
     (*A* thu'bān *is a "snake" but the word also means "wadi"*)
A: No. I thought you'd never asp!

Q: Is washing-water provided by a *ḍarīr* better than washing-water provided by a *baṣīr*?
(*Ḍarīr means "blind" but also "edge of a wadi"; baṣīr means "sighted" but also "dog"*)

A: Yes, and you can take that to the bank.

Q: Is it permissible to *ṭawf* in the *rabī'*?
(*"Walk around a shrine in the springtime" or "defecate into a river"*)

A: Without beating around the bush: no.

Q: Is the greater ablution invalidated if you *amnā*?
(*"Ejaculate" but also "travel to Minā"*)

A: It depends on whether you're coming or going.

Q: Does removing ritual impurity require washing one's *farwah*?
(*"A fur" but also "the scalp"*)

A: Yes; otherwise you'll never get a-head.

Q: May one omit washing his *fa's*?
(*"Axe" but also "occiput"*)

A: What a boneheaded question!

Q: What if you perform ablution with sand for lack of water but then come across a *rawḍ*?
(*"Flowerbed" but also "residue at the bottom of a cistern"*)

A: You should wash! Water you waiting for?

32.4 Q: May a man prostrate himself in an *'adhirah*?
(*"Pile of excrement" but also "courtyard"*)

A: Yes; dung heap him waiting!

Q: What about on *khilāf*?
(*On "willow branches," which is allowed, but also on "a sleeve," which is not*)

A: Khi-láf to pray somewhere else.

Q: What about on his *shimāl*?
    ("On his left side," which is not allowed, but also "on cloaks," which is)
A: You'll have to coats that one out of me.

Q: What about on *kurāʿ*?
    ("Trotters" but also "basalt")
A: No shanks!

Q: May he pray *ʿalā raʾs al-kalb*?
    ("Over a dog's head" but also "by a cliff called Dog's Head")
A: As long as he's bluffing.

Q: May you pray with your *ʿānah* exposed?
    ("Pubic area" but also "herd of onagers")
A: No, but you can bare your ass.

Q: What about praying while under *ṣawm*?
    ("An obligation to fast" but also "ostrich droppings")
A: Instant re-pray!

Q: May you pray holding a *jirw*?
    ("A puppy," which is unclean, or "a small cucumber or pomegranate," which isn't)
A: Upheld on a peel!

Q: What if he's walking around with a *qarwah*?
    ("Testicular hernia" but also "dog's bowl")
A: No, that's a dish tinct problem.

Q: What if *najw* spatters his garment?
    ("Bodily fluid" but also "clouds")
A: He's free to go if he's only been a-rained.

32.5 Q: May a *muqannaʿ* lead men in prayer?
       ("Woman in a veil" but also "man in a helmet")
     A: Yes, but warrior imams armor common on the frontier.

     Q: May a prayer-leader have a *waqf*?
       ("Endowed property" but also "ivory or tortoiseshell bracelet")
     A: That's a difficult one to unbangle. But no.

     Q: What if his *fakhdh* is exposed?
       ("Thigh" but also "subtribe")
     A: No can-can, but with the clan he can.

     Q: May an unarmed *thawr* serve as imam?
       ("Bull" but also "chief")
     A: As long as he's a spearless leader.

     Q: May the *shāhid* prayer be abridged?
       ("Friday" but also "evening star")
     A: No, you need a full intra-Venus.

32.6 Q: May a *maʿdhūr* omit fasting during Ramaḍān?
       ("A person with an excuse" but also "a circumcised person")
     A: Only boys make the cut.

     Q: What about a *muʿarris*? May he eat?
       ("Groom" but also "traveler who rests before dawn")
     A: Yes: that's won for the road.

     Q: What about the *ʿurāt*?
       ("Denuded" but also "afflicted with ague")
     A: That would be *ʿurát* with me.

     Q: What about eating after you *aṣbaḥ*?
       ("Wake up" but also "kindle a lamp")
     A: As long as you know light from wrong.

Q: What if one deliberately eats *laylan*?
   ("At night" but also "baby bustards, partridges, or cranes")
A: His piety is for the birds!

Q: What if he eats before the *bayḍāʾ* retires?
   ("Light-skinned woman" but also "sun")
A: Not so fast!

Q: Can a fasting man eat if he produces *kayd*?
   ("Trickery" but also "vomit")
A: Yes, now that you bring it up.

Q: May one break the fast at the urging of a *ṭābikh*?
   ("Cook" but also "burning fever")
A: No to cakes, yes to ail.

Q: And if a woman *ḍaḥikat* during her fast?
   ("Laughs" but also "menstruates" as in Q Hūd 11:71)
A: Her fast is invalid, period!

Q: Can a woman eat if smallpox appears on her *ḍarrah*?
   ("Co-wife" but also "mammary adipose tissue")
A: Yes, if she keeps others abreast of her condition.

Q: How much alms-tax is due on one hundred *miṣbāḥs*?   32.7
   ("Lamps" but also "a camel fat enough to rest in the morning instead of going to pasture"; the answer is "a pair of sturdy camels")
A: Attach two riders.

Q: What about ten *khanājir*?
   ("Daggers" but also "copious milch camels," and the answer is "a pair of sheep")
A: The tax is up two ewe.

Q: What about handing your *ḥamīmah* over to a *sāʿī*?
   (*"Handing your close friend over to a slanderer" but also "handing your most valuable property over to an alms collector"*)
A: Now you're getting down to brass tax!

Q: Are those carrying *awzār* entitled to charity?
   (*"Sins" but also "weapons"*)
A: Yes, warriors have the right to bear alms.

32.8 Q: Can a pilgrim *yaʿtamir*?
   (*"Perform the lesser pilgrimage" but also "wear a turban"*)
A: The law headdresses that concern: no.

Q: May he kill a *shujāʿ*?
   (*"Brave man" but also "snake"*)
A: Yes, and if he sees another snake, he can adder.

Q: May he kill a *zammārah* in the sacred precinct?
   (*"Ostrich" but also "flute player"*)
A: Ney.

Q: What's the penalty for striking a *sāq ḥurr* with an arrow and killing him?
   (*"Free man's leg" but also "turtledove"; for the latter, the penance is a sheep*)
A: I have an answer I can shear with you.

Q: What about killing *Umm ʿAwf* after putting on pilgrim's garb?
   (*"Awf's mother" but also "a grasshopper"*)
A: It's a lo-cust penance: just a handful of meal.

Q: Does a pilgrim need to bring a *qārib* along?
   (*"Boat" but also "a tracker who finds water at night"*)
A: Someone has to take pitchers!

Q: What about *ḥarām* after *sabt*?
(*"Something forbidden after Saturday" but also "a pilgrim after he has shaved his head"*)

A: It's allowed, if I may be so bald.

Q: Is it permitted to sell a *kumayt*? 32.9
(*"Bay horse" but also "ruddy vintage"*)

A: No, so stop wine-ing!

Q: May one trade *khall* for camel meat?
(*"Vinegar" but also "a two-year-old camel"; a live animal cannot be exchanged for meat of the same or any other kind*)

A: Let me reflesh your memory: no.

Q: May one sell a *hadiyyah*?
(*A gift of meat offered at the Kaaba*)

A: Not at the present time.

Q: What about an *ʿaqīqah*?
(*"Lamb's wool" but also "animal sacrificed seven days after a child is born"*)

A: No, you can't fleece God.

Q: What about transactions involving a herdsman's *dāʿī*?
(*"Crier" but also "unextracted milk"*)

A: Udderly impossible, even to a tax collector!

Q: May a *ṣaqr* be bartered for dates?
(*"Falcon" but also "molasses"*)

A: Don't believe it! There's a *ṣaqr* born every minute.

Q: May a Muslim man purchase a Muslim woman's *salab*?
(*"Items plundered" but also "tree bark" and "panic-grass fibers"*)

A: Yes, because it's not about her booty!

Q: May one buy a *shāfiʿ*?

    ("A person who intervenes on one's behalf" but also "a ewe and her lamb")

A: Is that ewe again? Yes!

Q: May one sell an *ibrīq* to a Roman?

    ("Pitcher" but also "highly polished blade")

A: As bad as lending them your spears!

Q: May a man sell off his *ṣayfiyyah*?

    ("Colt born in summer" but also "child born to an aged parent")

A: A foalish act!

Q: If one buys a slave and then discovers that his *umm* is injured, is it permissible to return him?

    ("Mother" but also "pia mater")

A: Yes. That's a no-membraner!

Q: Is pre-emption valid among partners in a *ṣaḥrāʾ*?

    ("Desert" but also "dappled donkey")

A: No, even if they own some amazing greys.

32.10 Q: May one *yaḥmī* the water of a well or a *khalāʾ*?

    ("Heat" but also "keep others away from"; "empty tract" or "privy" but also "pasture")

A: No; you should offer water to your brethren and your cistern!

Q: Is it permissible to consume *mītat al-kāfir*?

    ("Infidel carrion" but also "fish floating on the surface of the sea")

A: Yes, on a sliding scale.

Q: Is it permissible to make a sacrifice of *ḥūl*?

    ("Cross-eyed people" but also "barren female animals")

A: The animals are allowed, to avoid a stigma-tism.

Q: May one sacrifice a *ṭāliq*?
   (*"Divorced woman" but also "camel left to graze freely"*)
A: Yes; don't worry about the drama, dearie.

Q: What about sacrificing before the *ghazālah* appears?
   (*"Gazelle" but also "rising sun"*)
A: No, or someone else'll be guzzling it down!

Q: May one earn a living by *ṭarq*?
   (*"Beating wool" or "hammering metals" but also "telling fortunes by casting pebbles"*)
A: No, and if you want reasons I'll give you lots.

Q: May a standing man greet a *qāʿid*?   32.11
   (*"Seated person" but also "postmenopausal woman"*)
A: Unless you know her I wouldn't dry it.

Q: May a reasonable man sleep beneath *raqīʿ*?
   (*"A patched garment" but also "the sky"; sleeping under the stars in al-Baqīʿ, the cemetery of Medina, is especially pleasant*)
A: Yes, especially if he's a grave man too.

Q: Should a protected non-Muslim be allowed to *qatl al-ʿajūz*?
   (*"Kill an old woman" but also "mix wine with water"*)
A: Vine not?

Q: May a man leave his father's *ʿimārah*?
   (*"Building" or "cultivation" but also "tribe"*)
A: No kin do.

Q: What is your view of *tahawwud*?
   (*"Converting to Judaism" but also "turning in repentance," as in "We have turned to You in repentance," Q Aʿrāf 7:156*)
A: No better *trayf* than sorry.

Q: What about *ṣabr al-baliyyah*?
   ("Fortitude in distress" but also "the pre-Islamic practice of confining a camel near his master's grave and starving it to death so he could ride it upon resurrection")

A: Let pagans be by-gones!

32.12 Q: Is it permitted to strike a *safīr* or ride against a *mustashīr*?
   ("Ambassador" but also "fallen leaves"; "seeker of advice" but also "fat camel" as well as "camel that can sense whether another camel has conceived")

A: Yes; it's mulch ado about nothing.

Q: Shall a man *yuʿazzir* his father?
   ("Punish" but also "revere")

A: Yassir!

Q: Shall he *yufqir* his brother?
   ("Impoverish" but also "provide a camel to")

A: Yes, if it means taking him for a ride.

Q: Shall he *yuʿrī* his child?
   ("Leave unclothed" but also "give a year's worth of dates")

A: Yes! It's a good way to grease his palms.

Q: Shall he bake his *mamlūk* over a flame?
   ("Slave" but also "dough")

A: Yes, if he kneads it.

Q: May a woman *taṣrim* her *baʿl*?
   ("Spurn her husband" but also "cut down the fruit of her deep-rooted date palm")

A: She's free to play "good crop, bad crop" if she likes.

Q: May a woman be chastised for *khajal*?
   (*"Diffidence" but also "being obnoxious when rich"*)
A: A sound khájal-ing is what the arrogant deserve.

Q: How do you judge a man who strips another's *athalah*?
   (*"Tamarisk" but also "honor"*)
A: Not on his bark—on his bite.

Q: May a ruler restrain one with *thawr*?
   (*"A bull" but also "insanity"*)
A: Yes, and warn others to steer clear.

Q: May a man *yaḍrib ʿala* an orphan's *yad*?   32.13
   (*"Strike his hand" but also "appoint a guardian for him"*)
A: Yes, if his intent is to a-ward him.

Q: May he obtain a *rabaḍ* for him?
   (*"Buildings built outside a city wall" but also "wife"*)
A: No, but don't rá-bad in.

Q: When may one sell a fool's *badan*?
   (*"Body" but also "short mail coat"*)
A: Any time; it won't do him any ʿarm.

Q: May one buy him a *ḥashsh*?
   (*"Privy" but also "cluster of palm trees"*)
A: Better copse than robbers!

Q: May a ruler be a *ẓālim*?   32.14
   (*"Oppressor" but also "drinker of uncurdled milk"*)
A: Yes, if he's lactose and intolerant!

Q: May someone without *baṣīrah* serve as a judge?
   (*"Perceptiveness" but also "a shield"*)
A: Yes, unless you think the buckler did it.

Q: What if he has no *'aql* at all?
     ("Intellect" but also "painted silk")
A: The less figuring, the better!

Q: What if he has the *zahw* of a *jabbār*?
     ("A tyrant's arrogance" but also "dates whose color is changing, hanging from a tree out of reach," as opposed to one whose fruits are within reach)
A: Nothing wrong with keeping up-to-date.

Q: May a witness be *murīb*?
     ("Of dubious veracity" but also "having much cottage cheese")
A: If he can eat curds and weigh the evidence.

Q: What if it turns out that he *lāṭ*?
     ("Committed sodomy" but also "daubed the inside of a basin")
A: Grant him some lat-itude!

Q: And if he is discovered to have *gharbal*?
     ("To sift" but also "to kill")
A: His testimony might as well be garbled.

Q: What if he is revealed as *mā'in*?
     ("Mendacious" but also "one who provides for his dependents")
A: Good for him: no lying down on the job!

32.15   Q: What should be done with an *'ābid al-ḥaqq*?
             ("Worshipper of God" but also "one who denies a debt")
        A: He has to swear an owe-th.

Q: What should be done with one who gouges out the eye of a *bulbul*?
     ("Nightingale" but also "slightly built man")
A: His should be gouged out too, for committing such a warble crime!

Q: What about one who strikes a woman's *qaṭāh* and kills her?
  (*"Arabian bird" but also "rump"*)
A: That's a capital offence, and no grousing.

Q: What about one who strikes a pregnant woman and causes her to lose her *hashīsh*?
  (*"Grass" but also "stillborn infant"*)
A: He should manumit a slave to uphold lawn order.

Q: What is the legal penalty for *ikhtifā'*?
  (*"Going into seclusion" but also "grave robbery"*)
A: To be excised like a tomb-er!

Q: What if one steals a *thamīn* of gold?
  (*"Precious object" but also "one eighth"*)
A: No amputation: that's tha mín thing.

Q: What about a woman known for *saraq*?
  (*"Theft" but also "white silk"*)
A: There's no penalty for saraqasm.

Q: Is a marriage contract valid without being witnessed by *qawārī*?
  (*"Starlings" but also "witnesses"*)
A: No: you can't just wing it!

Q: What happens to a bride who *bātat laylah ḥurrah* and is sent back intact early next morning?
  (*"Passes the first night of the month" but also "refuses her husband," the opposite being "passes a white-haired night"*)
A: Refund her, refund her, let donors beware!

"*Omnia performavit!*" declared THE YOUTH (*vide supra*). "I would 32.16 propose an analogy with the sea, whose volume remains undiminished by the efforts of persons equipped with pails. I would furthermore claim that your expertise is such as to render any additional corroboration superfluous." Whereupon he inclined his head and exercised his right to remain silent.

At this juncture we distinctly heard ABU ZAYD protest the termination of proceedings and express his willingness to continue the cross-examination. THE YOUTH replied that, whereas his learned friend (sc. ABU ZAYD) had provided a fully satisfactory account of himself, he had no further questions. In view, however, of the other's (sc. ABU ZAYD's) conspicuous merit, he wished to know his original domicile and place of residence. To this ABU ZAYD made the following clear and unequivocal reply:

> *Vt profugus errem? Semper ut patria arcear*
> *opemque gentis hospes externae sequar . . .*
> *in servitutem cadere de regno grave est.*

He then addressed the Deity: "God, even as thou hast guided me and made me a guide to others, let the others do the right thing and offer an honorarium."

Whereat the assembled company presented him with a drove of camels and a serving-woman, and appealed to him to visit them again at such times and intervals as might please him. He responded by making an oral contract to that effect, and, driving the servant and the camels before him, proceeded to depart.

32.17 AL-HARITH IBN HAMMAM continued his testimony as follows.

WHEREAS additional discovery was in order, I accosted him (sc. ABU ZAYD) and addressed him ad hominem: "Insofar as my experience enables me to judge, you were, and have always been, a lightwit; how then have you attained the rank of jurist?"

After proceeding with his motion for some greater or lesser interval of time, he (sc. ABU ZAYD) offered a versified confession (*vide infra*):

I am a man, and all of man embrace,
And plead not always pro, nor con,
But change my suit depending on the case,
And here defend the sic, and there the non.

With lawyers, I might quibble, or appeal,
With topers, I pass the cup, or hold;
With words that bring a wild horse to heel,
And pens that bleed with newly burnished gold.

But though my writ doth run on land and sea
To move all men to laughter or to tears,
The trick I play on you is played on me
And taken all my friends, and all my years.

In all my turns I do but mimic Fate,
My firewalker's dance his change of state.

Upon the termination of his address I charged him to moderate his com- 32.18
plaint and withdraw his grievance against what might be termed Acts of
God, proposing also that he express gratitude to the One who had delivered him from his position as the Devil's Advocate and made him instead a
guildsman of al-Shāfiʿī.

"Leave off your unintelligible pleading," replied ABU ZAYD, "and
beware of defamatory allegations! Let us rather seek conveyance to the
Mosque of Medina, where by virtue of propinquity to the Prophet's place
of interment we might make expiation for our sins."

"Objection!" I cried. "I hereby refuse to approve, endorse, or sanction
any such journey, except on condition that you reveal, divulge, and confess
the meaning of your riddles, in such manner that I might myself expound
them."

ABU ZAYD replied: "You make a not entirely baseless appeal to moral
obligation; and, your demand not being onerous in itself, I will comply
with it, and interpret these matters in such a way as to remove all reasonable doubt. *Oyez, oyez!*"

When he had concluded his explanation, shedding light thereby upon even the most recondite obscurities, we undertook the lading of our camels and effected our departure. For the duration of this journey, I was able, as a consequence of his unceasing flow of wit, to postpone *sine die* any distasteful rumination on the discomforts of the road, so much so, indeed, that I would have sought a postponement of our arrival. Notwithstanding this counterfactual velleity on the part of counsel, we did subsequently arrive in Medina, where a visit to the Prophet's mosque placed us in fulfillment of our resolution. Thereupon ABU ZAYD departed in the general direction of Syria, and I in that of Iraq, that is to say, he adopted a northwesterly trajectory while I favored the northeast.

GLOSSARY

32.2

veritas nihil, etc. truth fears nothing but to be hid

oportet quod certa, etc. a thing certain must be brought to judgment

ad majorem, etc. to the greater glory of God

manifesta igitur id, etc. "Proclaim openly what you are commanded" (Q Ḥijr 15:94)

32.16

Omnia performavit he has done all

NOTES

In the original Arabic of these riddles, the questioner uses words that have two meanings, a well-known one and a rare one. The well-known meaning suggests one answer to the riddle while the rare one suggests the opposite answer. For example, the first riddle asks whether touching one's *naʿl* breaks the state of ritual purity required for prayer. *Naʿl* is a common word for "sandals," and if we take that to be the meaning here, the answer would be that touching one's footwear does not cause impurity. But, as al-Ḥarīrī tells us, *naʿl* also has the rare meaning of "wife." According to the jurists, touching one's wife does (subject to various conditions) break a man's state of purity. This is why the correct answer to the question is "Yes." (If the word has two meanings, we might expect either answer to be acceptable, but an unstated rule of the game is that the only correct answer is the one based on the lesser-known meaning of the word.)

In other Impostures, explanations of various verbal tricks appear in appendices, making it possible for the translator to invent equivalent verbal tricks in English without being tied down by the lexical meaning of the Arabic. In this episode, however, al-Ḥarīrī gives the riddle, the answer, and the two meanings of the word (or sometimes just the obscure one) all in the same place. Fortunately, though, he leaves the translator an opening. In theory, almost all his riddles could be answered in a word or two, often just "yes" or "no." But because all the clauses in the Impostures have to rhyme, many are padded out with words that have no other purpose, at least as far as the legal issue is concerned. I therefore decided to reproduce the lexical meaning of the question and the explanation but to play freely with the wording of the answer in order to create an English pun. For example, the original Arabic answer to the *naʿl* question is: "By his action, he has invalidated his lesser ablution." The English rendering reads: "It's something to wash out for." That is to say, I have moved the pun from where it was in the original to a different place. Like al-Ḥarīrī's rhyme words, the invented answers contain irrelevancies, but they do endeavor to convey, or at least not to contradict, the correct answer.

The punning in this episode consists of ninety back-to-back wordplays in rapid succession. (There are supposed to be a hundred, which is why later manuscripts supply additional riddles, but my base text, the manuscript Cairo 105, has only ninety.) In the English-speaking world, similar performances take place at the O. Henry Pun-Off World Championships, held annually in Austin, Texas, where contestants have to improvise puns in subject areas chosen at random. Before I saw competitors like Jerzy Gwaizdowski, Ben Ziek, and Janani Krishnan-Jha pull off their extraordinary feats of paronomasia (for sample performances see the bibliography under "Pun-Off"), I did not think it was possible to reproduce al-Ḥarīrī's puns in Arabic. But, being less talented than the folks in Austin, I managed only about half of the puns myself. Eventually I got stuck, but I was rescued—as at many moments of crisis in the course of this work—by Phillip Mitsis, who was kind enough to host a dinner party for the purpose of pun-gathering (or, as one of us put it, to grappa with the text). There Phillip, Peter Goodrich, and Joseph Lowry applied their considerable wit to the several dozen riddles that had stumped me.

The riddles are divided into thematically linked groups that correspond to the topics covered in works of Hadith and compilations of legal rulings. These themes are indicated in the notes. In most cases, admittedly, the only point being made is the general one that many words are ambiguous and jurists need to be aware of multiple possibilities. For example, whether an oppressive ruler can still be a legitimate one was a matter of actual debate, but al-Ḥarīrī's riddle does not address the substance. Instead, it merely points out that the word for "oppressor" can also mean "drinker of uncurdled milk." More explicit indications of the legal principles involved may be found in Steingass. For a detailed exposition of the positions taken by al-Shāfiʿī, who is Abū Zayd's ostensible exemplar (see §32.17), see Shāfiʿī, *Epistle*, tr. Lowry, where the legal principles involved are exemplified in Arabic with a translation and notes.

In several other Impostures, the unnamed young man who challenges Abū Zayd turns out to be his son and the interaction between them to be a prearranged scam. Such a setup would make sense here too, though al-Ḥarīrī never actually says that this is the case. Perhaps he wanted his readers to figure this one out themselves.

"Jurist of the Arabs" (*faqīh al-ʿarab*, §32.2) is a title associated with the language scholar Aḥmad ibn Fāris (d. 395/1004), who wrote (among other works) a collection of legal riddles like the ones in this Imposture.

"The precedent of those pagans who ran to serve their idols" in §32.2 echoes Q Maʿārij 70:43, which compares deniers of the truth to people running to *nuṣub*, idols, or to a *naṣb*, a waymark, both readings being attested. For a discussion of this passage see Keegan, "Commentarial Acts," 332–36.

Most of the riddles in §32.3 deal with ritual purity, specifically with actions and substances that may or may not necessitate renewing one's ablution (either *wuḍūʾ*, the "lesser ablution" required after minor defilements, or *ghusl*, the "greater ablution" required after major ones). The riddles at the end of the section deal with the ablutions themselves.

Section §32.4 focuses on the conditions for proper performance of the canonical prayers. These include using the proper sort of ground cover and avoiding contact with impure substances such as semen and feces.

Section §32.5 addresses the conditions for serving as an imam, that is, leading others in a valid canonical prayer.

The riddles in §32.6 play on the conditions for performing a valid fast, as during Ramadan. One must abstain from food, drink, and certain specified activities from before first light to sunset. Those who are ill or on a journey may break the fast but must make up the days later. In the riddles, "break the fast" means to act in a manner that invalidates one's observance for that day.

Section §32.7 deals with the alms tax (*zakāt*), a percentage of one's property (usually 2.5 percent) taken by the state for redistribution to the needy. The riddles play on questions about the correct rate for various kinds of property as well as the matter of who is entitled to a share.

The riddles in §32.8 address the conduct of pilgrims, who during their visit to Mecca and environs must adopt special dress and refrain from certain activities, such as hunting.

In §32.9 the topic shifts from acts of worship to contracts and the like, beginning with the law of sale. Some riddles deal with what can and cannot be sold: for example, one cannot sell an animal offered as a sacrifice, nor sell weapons to an enemy. Others deal with what may properly be exchanged for what. For example, something cannot be exchanged for a part of itself (e.g., dates for date molasses). Others again address the transaction itself: that is, whether it can be cancelled or preempted. In his translation of the eighth question, Steingass misreads *sakhl* "young goat" as *salkh* "flaying" (*Assemblies*, 48).

Section §32.10 deals with miscellaneous questions of *ḥalāl* (permitted) and *ḥarām* (forbidden), mostly with respect to the lawfulness of certain kinds of food.

Section §32.11 contains some riddles about *ḥalāl* (permitted) and *ḥarām* (forbidden), as well as some that seem to refer to points of *adab* (roughly, "etiquette"). In the second riddle, Steingass translates *raqīʿ* (which al-Ḥarīrī does not explain) as "fool," but "patched garment" seems more likely.

The riddles in §32.12 turn on questions of when it is lawful to do harm to others. In §32.13, the pretext is the legality of certain actions taken on behalf of someone else. In §32.14, the riddles play on conditions that may disqualify someone from serving as a ruler, judge, or witness in a legal proceeding. §32.15 contains miscellaneous riddles dealing with actions such as bodily harm and breach of contract.

"*Vt profugus errem . . .*" (§32.16) comes from Seneca, *Phoenissae*, lines 586–87 and 598: "That I may wander outcast? That I may be forever shut out from my country and as a stranger look to the bounty of an alien race? . . . To fall from a king's estate to slavery is hard" (Seneca, *Tragedies*, tr. Miller). I was directed to this passage by Burton, *Anatomy*, 1:371.

"I am a man . . ." (§32.17) is based on *"Homo sum: humani nihil a me alienum puto"* (Terence, *Heautontimorumenos*, 1:25). The line is commonly understood to mean "I am human and nothing human is alien to me," though in its original context the more accurate translation seems to be "I am a man, and nothing that concerns a man do I deem a matter of indifference to me," an expression of "benevolence and disregard of self" (Terence, "The Self-Tormentor," tr. Riley, *Comedies*, p. 139 and note 2). The translation repurposes the line to express Abū Zayd's willingness to play to all expectations in the hope of gain.

Al-Shāfiʿī (d. 204/820; §32.18) is the foundational figure in Sunni jurisprudence (see his *Epistle*, tr. Lowry). His "guild" (*madhhab*) is the community of jurists who judge and teach in accordance with what they take to be his vision of the law. "I would have sought . . .": the Arabic *wadidtu maʿahu buʿda l-shuqqah* contains an echo of the Qurʾanic *wa-lākin baʿudat ʿalayhimu l-shuqqah* (Q Tawbah 9:42) "but the distance seemed too great for them."

BIBLIOGRAPHY

Black, Henry Campbell. *A Law Dictionary*. 2nd ed. St. Paul, MN: West, 1910.

Burton, Robert. *The Anatomy of Melancholy*. Edited by Holbrook Jackson. New York: New York Review of Books, 2001.

[Maracci]. *Refutatio Alcorani . . . ab auctore Ludovico Maraccio Lucensi*. Padua: N.p., 1698.

Seneca, L. Annaeus. *Tragoediae*. Edited by Rudolf Peiper and Gustav Richter. Leipzig: Teubner, 1921. http://www.perseus.tufts.edu/hopper/text?doc= Perseus%3Atext%3A2007.01.0009%3Acard%3D586.

Seneca. *Tragedies*. Translated by Frank Justus Miller. Loeb Classical Library. Cambridge, MA: Harvard University Press, 1917. http://www.theoi.com/ Text/SenecaPhoenissae.html.

Al-Shāfiʿī. *The Epistle on Legal Theory*. Edited and translated by Joseph E. Lowry. New York: New York University Press, 2013.

Terence. *Heautontimorumenos*. In *Publii Terentii Comoediae VI*, edited by Edward St. John Parry. London: Whitaker, 1857. http://www.perseus. tufts.edu/hopper/text?doc=Perseus:text:1999.02.0089:act=1:scene=1.

[————]. "The Self-Tormentor." In The *Comedies of Terence*, translated by
Henry Thomas Riley. New York: Harper and Brothers, 1874.
http://archive.org/details/terencecomediesootererich.

"Pun-Off 2016: Punniest of Show 22: Jerzy Gwiazdowski." Uploaded by Brian
Combs. May 9, 2016. http://www.youtube.com/watch?v=xZmvj8pbGgE.

"Pun-Off 2015, Punniest of Show: 08 Ben Ziek." Uploaded by Brian Combs.
May 12, 2015. http://www.youtube.com/watch?v=euLwL4CbygU.

[Pun-Off.] "2016 O. Henry Pun-Off World Championships, semi-final round
(Janani Krishna-Jha vs Jerzy Gwiazdowski)." Uploaded by sashimikid.
May 8, 2016. http://www.youtube.com/watch?v=OI4LaYBXAqc.

IMPOSTURE 33

THE JOY OF YARABIC

In this Abū Zayd asks for charity on the basis of an apparent disability. His complaints about poverty and illness are reminiscent of the kvetch comedy associated with twentieth-century Jewish-American performers like Henny Youngman, Don Rickles, and Rodney Dangerfield. In this Imposture, accordingly, he will speak in Yiddish-inflected American English. This variety, sometimes called "Yinglish," has spread beyond the northeastern United States and has contributed many words and expressions to informal English. It has also been extensively documented, most notably by the prolific Leo Rosten (d. 1997). Besides listing the many colorful Yiddish words that have passed into general use, Rosten documents pragmatic strategies like fronting and stress shift, with copious examples.

Howie said to stop him if we'd heard this one before.

33.1   What, miss a prayer? Me? Listen, as soon as I was old enough, I promised HA-SHEM I would never wait too long to daven, if I could help it. Even in my wanderings in the wilderness, and all the eating, drinking, and making merry under the sun, I always kept an eye on the zmanim so I wouldn't miss a service, G-D forbid. Whenever I went on a trip and we stopped somewhere, you think I wasn't glad to hear a barekhu? You think I didn't look for a minyan?

So this one time, I arrive in Tbilisi, and I daven with a bunch of poor kaptsonim. We finish up and everyone's getting ready to leave when this old man, nebekh, comes up to us. He's dressed in shmattes and one side of his face is paralyzed. He says to us, he says: "If you're a mensch, and you've got a bissel rakhmones in your heart, you'll take a load off and listen to me for a minute. That's all I ask! Then, if you want to give a little something, give. If you don't, who am I to make you?"

So everybody sits down, wraps their taleysem around their knees, and waits, quiet as a bunch of stones.

When he sees he's got an audience that knows from speeches, he says,   **33.2** "Listen, I don't have to put a finger in your mouth: you know it's better to trust one eye than two ears. Remember the three things you can't hide? Well, poverty's one of them! Look at me: my hair's gone gray and I can hardly stand. I look terrible and I feel worse! You want to hear something? I used to be ongeshtopt mit gelt, and a balebos to boot. I was always ready to help the poor and the stranger. A regular k'nocker, that's what I was . . . until I took a bath and lost it all! They nickel-and-dimed me to death and took every shekel. Look in my pockets: bupkes! Look at my house. You call that a house? Or take my clothes . . . please! 'Hard service with mortar and brick,' that's what my life is. And the kinder—oy vey! Always kvetching, and why not? They'd be lucky to get a kraitzik to chew on.

"Believe me, I wouldn't be here right now, telling you about my tsuris, and putting myself to shame, if I hadn't tried everything else, and come out worse off than I was before. I should have saved the trouble, and died first. Halevai!"

Then, after a mournful krekhts, he wheezes out these lines:

I cry out to the Holy One, Blessed be He!
They say you love fools. So what about me?
I was somebody once: I had honor and wealth,   **33.3**
I was strong as an ox; I was bursting with health!

Then fire burned me black,
And troubles broke my back.

When I was rich, I welcomed the poor,
Even the goyim knocked on my door.
That's over and gone! My cupboard is bare,
Not even the roaches go looking in there.

So I'll take; it's all I can do.
But giving's a mitzvah for you!

33.4 *Howie wasn't finished:*

Now the congregation wants to know, "Who is this guy already? He must be hiding something! What's he not telling us?" So they say: "We can see you're a khokhem who knows the mama loshen, but what about your mishpokhe? Whose lontsman are you? Nu?"

The old schnorrer gets a look on his face like a man whose wife just had another daughter. He mumbles a curse on nudzhes and nudniks, and says anything, even skinning a carcass, is better than begging. Then he sings in a plaintive wail:

If honey pleases your tongue
Why ask me where it's from?
Just shut up and eat!

If the wine ain't got a hechsher,
Don't give me a lecture;
Just shut up and drink!

A maven doesn't ask,
He just empties the glass;
That's what I call taste!"

33.5 *Howie still wasn't finished:*

The crowd ate it up. How could they not, seeing a sick man sing like that? So they pulled out the coins they had hidden in their waist-bands and money-belts, and put them together. "Listen," they said, "we've got money like an axe can swim. If we were twice as rich we'd be broke. But take this: it's better than a hole in the head."

The old schnorrer made a big production of thanking them, as if their pitifully few coins were an oytser. Then he turned away and stumbled off, with one side dragging the other.

"Wait, wait, let me finish!" 33.6

Suddenly I notice that there's something cockamamie about the way he's carrying himself. So I get up and follow him. He keeps giving me looks— such looks, kinehora!—and tries to duck me. Finally we reach a place where there's nobody on the road but the two of us. So now I've got him. What's he going to do, run away?

When he sees me coming he has the chutzpah to pretend running into me is a simha and he's ready to plotz with joy.

"Hah, I can always tell!" he says. "You were looking for company. Listen, have I got a deal for you! How'd you like to come in as my partner? You won't have to lift a finger and I'll take good care of you. Expenses included!"

"So who's saying no?" I say. "The Holy One, Blessed be He, must have led me to you."

"'If now I have found favor in thy sight,'" he says, "'pass not away, I pray thee, from thy servant . . . and ye shall rejoice in all that ye put your hand unto, ye and your households, wherein the LORD thy God has blessed thee.'"

And then in mitten drinnen he laughs and stands up straight. Whaddaya know? It's our melamed from Serug. Paralysis, shmaralysis: there's nothing wrong with him anywhere. Oy, am I glad to see him, and glad his illness was just a shtik! But when he sees I'm about to give him an earful for being such a gonif, he cuts me off, and again with the singing:

> *Alts far gelt*, all for gold,
> > A stroke is worth the trouble;
> *Alts far gelt*, all for gold,
> > Let 'em call you a shlemazl!"

Then he recites, "'I have been a stranger in a strange land,' but the land of my sojourning cannot bear me. So if you want to come with, let's get a move on. Nu?"

So we took off by ourselves and stayed together two whole years. Me, I was ready to stay with him for the rest of my life, but better you should ask for the moon from heaven.

GLOSSARY

33.1

Ha-Shem "the Name"; that is, God

daven pray

zmanim appointed times

service a ritual prayer

barekhu call to worship

kaptsonim paupers

nebekh poor fellow

shmattes rags

mensch decent human being

a bissel rakhmones a little compassion

33.2

taleysem prayer shawls

knows from understands

I don't have to, etc. you can take a hint

ongeshtopt mit gelt stuffed with money

balebos head of a household

regular real

k'nocker big shot, show-off

took a bath lost money

bupkes nothing

kinder children

oy vey woe is me!

kvetch complain, nag, grumble

kraitzik end of a loaf

tsuris troubles

halevai if only (that had happened)

krekht groan

33.3

goyim non-Jews

mitzvah religiously mandated good deed

33.4

khokhem wise man

mama loshen mother tongue

mishpokhe family, ancestry

lontsman person from the same place as you

nu out with it

schnorrer beggar

nudzh person who nags, pesters, or needles

nudnik long-winded bore

hechsher   kosher certification   *maven*   expert

33.5

oytser   treasure

33.6

cockamamie   fraudulent, contrived   *in mitten drinnen*   out of nowhere

kinehora   an exclamation used to   *melamed*   schoolteacher

   ward off the evil eye   *shtik*   act

chutzpah   audacity   *gonif*   swindler

simha   happy occasion   *shlemazl*   sad sack

plotz   burst

NOTES

In Arabic this Imposture is called *al-Tiflisiyyah*, that is, of Tbilisi, today the capital of Georgia. The Arabic geographers of al-Hariri's time describe it as a large city protected by a double wall with three gates. The Kura river with its watermills divided the city into two parts connected by a bridge of boats. The houses were built of pine, and the baths were supplied with hot water from the thermal springs (Minorsky and Bosworth, "Tiflis"). Although, per al-Hariri's usual practice, the Imposture includes no local references, it has been translated into Georgian by Nino Dolidze, *Maqama Genre*.

Abū Zayd's use of what Rosten calls "Yinglish" (not a term that has caught on) proved a good match for this Imposture. It contains a great many derogatory terms for con men, swindlers, and petty tricksters. Also, each of the three poems turned out to have a more or less approximate counterpart in the repertoire of early-twentieth-century Yiddish song. Moreover, al-Ḥarīrī's penchant for Qur'anic quotations, classical tags, and cleverly embedded stock phrases could be imitated by having characters quote from the Hebrew Bible (in the JPS Tanakh translation).

With respect to embedding, the surprising claim has been made that Jewish humor owes its special character to the imitation of this device in Arabic. The distinctive element of Jewish humor, argues Hillel Halkin, is the ability to reframe scriptural texts in ways that at first seem comically irreverent but then illuminate through irony. This trick, he says, was first performed in the medieval Hebrew Imposture, which took its cue from its Arabic predecessor ("Why Jews Laugh"). Whatever the merits of Halkin's argument, I must admit that it made the project of making Abū Zayd sound like Henny Youngman a little less quixotic. Encouraging, too, was the discovery of the Imposture-like story "A Yom Kippur Scandal," originally written in Yiddish by Sholem Aleichem (d. 1916), which presents a con man as crafty as Abū Zayd.

"Listen" (§33.1), says Rosten, is "not a verb but an interjection made to gain attention or stress a point" (Rosten, *Yinglish*, 317). "Eating, drinking . . .": cf. Ecclesiastes 8:15. A minyan is ten adult males, the minimum number needed for Jews to perform a valid group prayer. The prayer shawls are here taken to be analogous to the long garments that al-Ḥarīrī's contemporaries would wrap around their drawn-up knees when sitting. "Quiet as a bunch of stones" is based on Exodus 15:16.

"The things you can't hide" (§33.2): the other two are love and a cough ("Yiddish Sayings"). "You want to hear something?" is "an invitation to the revelation of unsolicited information" (Rosten, *Yinglish*, 569). "Take my clothes—please!" comes from Henny Youngman's famous joke about his wife. "Hard service": Exodus 1:14. Though known to my father, Jay Norman Cooperson, *kraitzik* is attested (in the non-diminutive form) only in Harkavy, *Yiddish-English Dictionary*, s.v. קראיעץ. On the semantics of "I should have saved the trouble," see Rosten, *Yinglish*, s.v. "So it shouldn't be wasted," 499–500.

The poem in §33.3 is very roughly modeled on the 1936 Yiddish theater song "Der dishvasher," which is spoken by a similarly down-and-out character. "Fire burned me black" is based on Job 30:30.

On the use of "already" in §33.4 see Rosten, *Yinglish*, 33–34. "A man whose wife . . .": Among traditional Jews, the family of the bride paid the dowry (if they could afford to), making it costly to marry off daughters. "Skinning a carcass": see Rosten, *Joys*, 360. "If honey . . .": This poem can be sung to tune of the 1936 Yiddish theater song "Bei mir bistu sheyn" (1932).

"Like an axe can swim" (§33.5) comes from the expression "He reads Hebrew like an ax swims" (Yiddish Sayings). "If we were twice as rich . . ." comes from the quip "If he were twice as smart, he'd be an idiot." "Cockamamie" (§33.6), says Rosten, is "not Yiddish, but triumphantly Yinglish, Manhattan division" (*Yinglish*, 120). "If now I have found . . .": Genesis 18:3. "And ye shall rejoice . . .": Deuteronomy 12:7.

A *melamed* (§33.6) is a teacher of elementary Hebrew, but also a term of condescension for an impractical or unsuccessful person. "Shmaralysis": Repeating a word and adding the *shm-* prefix is a way of dismissing or belittling the thing named (see any of the Rosten books under *shm-*). The verses are my (mostly) English adaptation of Lebedeff's "*Alts far gelt*" ("Anything for Money," 1923), following the translation and performance by Jane Peppler.

"I have been a stranger . . .": Exodus 2:22; "the land of my sojournings": cf. Genesis 36.7. "Ask for the saucer . . ." is based on the proverb "She wants the saucer from heaven" (Yiddish.Wit.com).

BIBLIOGRAPHY

Aleichem, Sholem. "A Yom Kippur Scandal." Translated by Julius and Francis Butwin. http://sholemaleichem.org/a-yom-kippur-scandal/.

Dolidze, Nino. *Maqama Genre in the Arabic Literature*. Tbilisi: Tbilisi State University Publishing House, 2010.

Halkin, Hillel. "Why Jews Laugh at Themselves." *Commentary* 121 (April 2006): 4:47–54. http://www.hagshama.org.il/en/resources/view.asp?id=2180.

Harkavy, Alexander. *Yiddish-Engish Dictionary*. 22nd ed. Milwaukee: Caspar Kreuger Dory, n.d. First published 1896.

Lebedeff, Aaron. "Alts far gelt." Transcribed, translated, and performed by Jane Peppler. Yiddish Penny Songs. http://www.yiddishpennysongs.com/2017/02/alts-far-gelt-original-version-as.html.

Minorsky, V., and C. E. Bosworth. "Tiflīs." In *Encyclopaedia of Islam, Second Edition*. Leiden: Brill, 1960–2007.

Rosten, Leo. *Hooray for Yiddish*. New York: Simon and Schuster, 1982.

———. *The Joys of Yinglish*. New York: Penguin, 1989.

———. *The New Joys of Yiddish*. Revisions and commentary by Lawrence Bush. New York: Crown, 2001.

Secunda, Sholom. "Bei mir bistu sheyn." Milken Archive of Jewish Music. Vol. 13, Great Songs of the Yiddish Stage. http://www.milkenarchive.org/music/volumes/view/great-songs-of-the-american-yiddish-stage/work/bay-mir-bistu-sheyn/.

Yablokoff, Herman. "Der dishvasher." Milken Archive of Jewish Music. Vol. 13, Great Songs of the Yiddish Stage. http://www.milkenarchive.org/music/volumes/view/great-songs-of-the-american-yiddish-stage/work/der-dishvasher/#linernotes.

"Yiddish Sayings, Proverbs, Phrases, Aphorisms, Curses, and Insults." http:// kehillatisrael.net/docs/yiddish/yiddish_pr.htm.

Yiddish Wit. http://www.yiddishwit.com/List.html.

IMPOSTURE 34

THE FRAUD OF SLAVERY

In this episode al-Ḥārith visits the slave market and ends up making a purchase from a mysterious stranger. The object of the transaction, a boy who calls himself Joseph (or, more exactly, quotes Joseph's self-identification in the Qur'an), soon afterward disputes the sale. This plot device hinges on the fact that many enslaved persons offered for sale in premodern Islamic societies claimed to be freeborn Muslims. Against this background, Joseph's protest against being sold as if he were an object rather than a human being may most plausibly be explained as a complaint about the unjust treatment of himself as an individual rather than a denunciation of slavery as a practice. And yet it is hard not to hear in his words a sense of revulsion against the whole institution, akin to the revulsion Frederick Douglass (d. 1895) ascribes to his childhood self: "I was just as well aware of the unjust, unnatural, and murderous character of slavery, when nine years old, as I am now" (Life and Times, *81). Douglass, who escaped enslavement in the American state of Maryland to pursue a career as a journalist, publisher, and activist, insists that children, unless they are taught otherwise, see all persons as equal and recognize slavery for the abomination that it is. Apart from whether this claim applies to al-Ḥarīrī's world (or any other), Douglass proved an excellent model for the English style of this Imposture, which contains one of the most powerful denunciations of slavery I have ever seen in a pre-modern text. Among other parallels, both he and al-Ḥarīrī's characters dwell on the attachments between masters and enslaved people*

315

(see, e.g., Life, 85–86, 435–39; cf. Imposture 18) and the pain of separation that followed a sale (see, e.g., Life, 26). In both cases, too, the trade in enslaved persons involves Africans. In al-Ḥarīrī's world, people of many different ethnic groups might be enslaved, but the town of Zabīd, where the Imposture is set, was a center for the specifically African trade, and al-Wasiti's illustration for this Imposture depicts a slave market full of African prisoners (Ḥarīrī/Wāsiṭī, Makamat, Folio 105r).

34.1   *Mr. Harress Ben Hammam related this outrage:*

When I crossed the wilderness to Zabíd, I was accompanied by a boy whom I had brought up and raised to bodily strength and maturity of judgment. He had so far accustomed himself to my character that he was able to gratify my desires in every way and to anticipate my wants with perfect accuracy. No wonder that I had become deeply attached to him and trusted him without reserve, both at home and on the road. We had no sooner reached Zabíd, however, when he took ill and died. For a year after his voice was stilled and his corpse borne upon our shoulders, I scarcely touched food, and sought no other boy. Yet loneliness, and the inconvenience of doing for myself when traveling, at length compelled me to seek a make-shift, though it be a greatly inferior one. I told the slave-dealers of Zabíd that I was looking for a well-trained boy who could bear up under scrutiny, offered for sale only because his master was destitute. They responded with alacrity, each one promising to fulfill my commission at once. Yet month followed month; moon after moon waxed and waned; and those promises were no nearer to being fulfilled than they had been at the beginning. It was a galling disappointment.

34.2   Realizing that the dealers had forgotten my commission, or were being deliberate in their neglect of it, I perceived the truth of the proverb, that "Talk is cheap," and resolved to apply the maxim, that "One is never so well served as by oneself." Scorning thereafter to delegate my search to others, I appeared in the market-place, cash in hand. I was inspecting the boys and

making inquiries as to prices, when I was approached by a man whose nose
and mouth were hidden under a cravat, and whose hand was wrapt firmly
about the wrist of a boy. He said:

SLAVE AT SALE
BOY: a likely boy,
Sold for no fault.
Guaranteed against the maladies
Prescribed by law;
Intelligent, fine tempered,
A trusty boy,
Faithful and devoted,
Kind words ever on his lips;
Caring, tender,
Cheerful in poverty,
Honest and discreet,
A superior boy;
Gifted in poetry
As well as prose.
Had I the cash to keep him
And feed my starving brood,
I would not sell him
For all of Caesar's gold."

I gazed at the boy. He was fine looking, of a singularly pleasing counte-   34.3
nance, and I fancied him one of the youth of Paradise. "'This is no mortal,'"
I thought, "'but a gracious angel.'" I asked him his name, not because I
wished to know it, but to satisfy myself that the beauty of his speech was
proportional to the beauty of his person;—in a word, that he was as eloquent as he was elegant. Any boy, slave or free, might well answer such a
question, but he made no reply. I turned away disgusted. "D—n and blast
the lock on your tongue!" But he laughed me to scorn, and with a mocking
shake of the head, chanted:

Will you wax wroth? Hear then my poem:
"I am Joseph," your brother: aye, Joseph!
A warning to you, did you but know it.

34.4   By this chant the boy proved my remonstrance groundless, and utterly disarmed me. Too dazzled to make any further inquiries, I failed also to perceive the meaning of his allusion to Joseph. I had but one object in view: to learn how much his master wanted for him and to produce the required sum.

I expected the old man to scowl and drive a hard bargain, but in this I was agreeably disappointed. "When a slave costs his master but little," he said, "he is regarded as an occasion of prosperity, and so comes to be held in esteem. If by reducing his price, I bind him to you by the ties of affection, I willingly reduce it. Weigh out, if you please, two hundred dirhems, and you will have reason to remember me gratefully as long as you live."

I produced the sum without a murmur. Why not, I thought, when the transaction was perfectly lawful, and brought advantage to myself? It never entered into my mind that anything so easily acquired was likely no bargain at all.

The exchange complete, it was time to part. The boy, weeping bitter tears, and refusing to be comforted, said to his master:

34.5   For shame! Shall I be sold to feed
            Thy little ones? O wouldst thou trade
        For coin to meet an hour's need
            One who for better things was made?
        Is Justice blind? Doth she not see
            The steadfast one who stood by thee?

        Did I, if sent to hunt down game,
            Not bring home saddles piled high?
        Did I, doing battle in thy name,
            Not rout thy foes with hue and cry?
        And when 'twas comfort thou didst seek
            Did I not caress, and gently speak?

Have I some fault or flaw concealed?
   Have I done some wrong, or lied
About some vice, that once revealed,
   Decrees that I be cast aside,
Bought and sold from hand to hand
   As if a THING and not a MAN?

Were I a horse, that has no soul,
   Thou wouldst say, 'No sale or lease!'
Alas! I stand above that foal
   In all but law; and thou, beneath.
In selling me, whom thou embraced,
   A brave young heart hast thou debased!

Perceiving the import of the boy's pure and artless verses, the old man 34.6
wept so bitterly that none who saw him could be anything but deeply
affected. "I regard this boy as my own child," he said, "and never dearer
to me than now. If I were not in the extremity of destitution, I would not
permit him to leave my nest until the hour came for him to march me to
the grave. You have seen, sir, his anguish at parting with me. A believer's
heart is kind. Would you not console him in his grief by promising to nul-
lify the sale if I should ever wish it? And to feel no resentment towards me?
For have trustworthy men not recorded that teaching of the Prophet:
'Release thy brother from a bargain, if he regrets it, and God will make
easy terms with thee'?"

Mr. Harress Ben Hammam continued: 34.7

Ashamed, I consented, though—truth compels me to admit—with some
reservations of a private nature. The man then summoned the boy to him,
kissed him upon the brow, and, his tears flowing freely, sang:

Easy, child, it won't be long
Till we're together again
That caravan, it won't get far
Before we're together again
God's gonna keep His eye on you
Till we're together again.

"This kind gentleman will take care of you now," he said to the boy. Then he fastened up the end of his robe, turned away, and vanished.

The boy's heartrending shrieks and piteous cries continued for as long as it takes to walk a mile. At last he recovered himself and brushed away his tears. "Do you know," he asked, "why I have been sobbing, and why I take comfort?" I replied that it was the pain of parting from his master that made him weep. "Between us," he said, "is a chasm not so easily bridged, for you mean one thing when I mean another." Then he recited:

My tears stream hot, but not for love,
Nor in regret for comforts past.
No, I weep in pity for the greed
That made you think this deal would last.

Remember Joseph? I dropped the hint:
No slave was he when he was sold.
I too am free; the sale is void.
Gone am I, and gone your gold!"

34.8   He was indulging in a little pleasantry, I thought, or perpetrating a joke. But he stood firm, like one who has right on his side, and continued to insist that he was a freeman. The war of words ended in blows, which brought us into court.

After the case had been explained and the facts presented, the judge addressed me as follows. "If a man gives a warning and the warning is disregarded, he cannot be responsible for the result. Whether one brings good news or bad, he may claim to have fulfilled his obligation to others. You yourself have testified that this boy gave you a hint, which you failed to heed. Rather than prosecute him, look to your wits, and try to suppress this report of their dullness. Renounce your aim of enslaving him, for he is as free as anybody, and cannot be acquired by purchase. Indeed it was only yesterday that he came here with his father, who declared him his only son and heir."

"His father?!" I cried. "You know his d—n father?"

"Know him?" said he. "Does any judge *not* know Abby Zane? He's defrauded every one of us!"

Thunderstruck, then enraged, I saw what had happened, and understood, too, what the cravat, the trick's crowning touch, was for. Of course, my understanding came too late. Ashamed, I swore I would never again do business with men who hide their faces behind cravats. "O why," I thought, with saddened heart and tearful eye, "did I squander my money on a senseless deal? What a spectacle I will present to my friends!"

The judge, perceiving my wretchedness and anguish, said: "A loss, sir, is a gain if it profits your soul, and the thief who opens your eyes has done you a service. This calamity is a lesson; study it. You need not reveal this incident to your friends, but remember it, and let the memory guard your treasure. In this way you will join those who have sharpened their good sense in the school of adversity."

Shrouded in clouds of shame and sorrow, I bade him farewell. Painfully   **34.9** alive as I was to the humiliation of having been deceived as well as robbed, I resolved to shun Abby Zane forever. I stayed clear of his haunts and did all that I could to avoid seeing him. One day, however, he accosted me in a narrow street and hailed me with affection. I frowned and made no reply.

"Why the upturned nose and scornful lip?" he asked.

"Have you forgotten," I asked, "your cheating and deceit?"

"Pfft!" he sputtered in derision. Then, altering his manner, he made an appeal to my sympathy:

> You're looking very angry, friend
> And the words you have in mind
> Will bite as deep as arrow-heads
> If you let them fly

How dare I sell a Muslim freeman
The way you'd sell a horse?
If you look into the Scriptures, friend
You'll see I'm not the first

Take Joseph's brothers in the
Chapter by that name
They sold him down in Egypt
So the Good Book says

I wish I hadn't cheated you
I admit that it's a crime
But at the time I had no choice
I didn't have a dime

Until you've been where I have been
You have no right to judge
So grant me your forgiveness, friend,
And please don't bear a grudge!

34.10 "You have," he said, "my excuse, even if your dirhems are gone. If you shrink from me now because you fear the loss of what money you have left, recall that I never strike the same victim twice. And if you turn from me in disgust in the hope of recovering your loss, you should rather hire mourners to lament your good sense."

Mr. Harress Ben Hammam concluded:

Compelled by the power of his oratory, I let myself be reconciled. Our friendship restored, I forgave him his crime, atrocious though it was.

NOTES

Frederick Douglass wrote three autobiographies. My model here is the *Life and Times*, the last and most extensive of the three. The phrase "fraud of slavery" comes from Douglass, *Life*, 161.

Zabíd (Zabīd) is a town located on the southern coast of Yemen. In al-Ḥarīrī's time it was the capital of the Najāḥid dynasty (ca. 1050–1158) and an important center of trade, including trade in enslaved Africans.

"One is never . . ." (§34.2) comes from "On n'est jamais servi si bien que par soi-même," a line from *Bruis et Palaprat* (1807), by Charles-Guillaume Étienne (d. 1845), more famous in the form "If you want it done right, do it yourself."

The rendering of the poem in §34.2 draws on the language of posters advertising the sale of enslaved persons in the United States, or announcing rewards for the capture of runaways. Like the "Joseph" of this episode, the people described display an impressive range of abilities, from speaking German (Slavery and Remembrance, "Poster") to playing the violin (Humanities Texas, "Runaway Slave Reward Poster"). Like him, too, many are children (Teaching Tolerance, "Broadside"). There is nothing unlikely in "Joseph's" mastery of poetry and prose: while enslaved persons in the American South were usually forbidden to teach or learn (see *Life*, 87–94, 125–26), in al-Ḥarīrī's world, by contrast, educated slaves were fixtures of upper-class society. "Guaranteed," etc.: the American posters sometimes state that the persons listed are "guaranteed against the vices and diseases" (or "maladies") "prescribed by law" (see, e.g., Teaching Tolerance, "Broadside"; Schinto, "Ambrotype"). These included being "addicted to theft" and "in the habit of running away" (see Schaefer, "'Guaranteed,'" 310, 316–20).

"This is no mortal . . ." (§34.3): Q Yusuf 12:31. Abū Zayd's use of a beautiful boy, presumably his son Zayd, to beguile his victims is also a theme of Imposture 13. "I am Joseph": Q Yūsuf 12:90. Here al-Ḥārith fails to realize that the boy's declaration "is not his real name but a passage from the Qur'an . . . Al-Ḥārith is so dazzled by his eloquence that he fails to recognize both the Qur'anic allusion and its applicability to his current situation" (Keegan, "Commentarial Acts," 320). In other words, the boy, like the prophet, was sold into slavery on false pretenses.

The verses in §34.5 invoke a disputed area of Islamic jurisprudence in that enslaved persons might be treated in some respects as property but in other respects as responsible agents who could do things like marry and earn their own wages. The translation is inspired by the abolitionist writings of Henry Wadsworth Longfellow (d. 1882) and John Greenleaf Whittier (d. 1892), though it is not modeled on any particular poem.

"For as long as it takes to walk a mile" (§34.7): according to Islamic law, a sale might be canceled by either party so long as they remain together; once they part, the sale is final. The original is in the passive voice and leaves it unclear which party did the walking in this case.

If this were a real case, the judge in §34.8 would presumably invalidate the sale because the seller had misrepresented the boy's status. But like other judges in al-Ḥarīrī, this one sets great store by the use of rhetorical devices—in this case, the allusion to the Joseph story.

"Abby Zane" is a phonetic translation of Abū Zayd. The name Abby appears in the *Life* (p. 523, inter alia), and Zane is the name of a family prominent in Ohio since the eighteenth century.

"Sputtered in derision" (§34.9): the Arabic is *aḍraṭ*, to make a farting noise with the mouth, that is, to perform what American English calls a Bronx cheer. Steingass renders it as "puffed his cheek and cracked it at me in derision" (*Assemblies*, 70). Apart from some words in the poems, "sputter" is the only word in the translation not found in some form in the *Life*.

BIBLIOGRAPHY

"Broadside for a New Orleans Auction." Teaching Tolerance.
http://www.tolerance.org/classroom-resources/texts/hard-history/
broadside-for-a-new-orleans-auction.

[Douglass, Frederick]. *Life and Times of Frederick Douglass*. Hartford, CN:
Park, 1882.

[Ḥarīrī/Wāsiṭī]. *Les Makamat de Hariri; exemplaire orné de peintures exécu-
tées par Yahya ibn Mahmoud ibn Yahya ibn Aboul-Hasan ibn Kouvarriha
al-Wasiti*. Bibliothèque nationale de France. Département des manu-
scrits. Arabe 5847. Folio 105r appears at http://gallica.bnf.fr/ark:/12148/
btv1b8422965p/f219.item.

Humanities Texas. Digital Repository. "Runaway Slave Reward Poster."
http://www.humanitiestexas.org/archives/digital-repository/
runaway-slave-reward-poster-1852.

Longfellow, Henry Wadsworth. *Poems on Slavery*. Cambridge: John Owen, 1842.

"Poster Advertising a Slave Auction." Slavery and Remembrance. http://slaveryandremembrance.org/collections/object/?id=OB0042

Schaefer, Judith K. "'Guaranteed against the Vices and Maladies Prescribed by Law': Consumer Protection, the Law of Slave Sales, and the Supreme Court in Antebellum Louisiana." *The American Journal of Legal History* 31, no. 4 (1987): 306–21.

Schinto, Jeanne. "Ambrotype of Runaway Slave and Other Photos Highlight African Americana Sale." *Maine Antique Digest*. June 2015. Pp. 26D–28D.

Whittier, John Greenleaf. *The Poetical Works in Four Volumes. Vol. 3, Anti-Slavery Poems: Songs of Labor and Reform*. Boston: Houghton Mifflin, 1892.

IMPOSTURE 35

DE-CANTED

In this episode, Abū Zayd (here called Alter Sekt, German for "old champagne") again fools an audience that prides itself on its knowledge of Arabic. After he recites a poem about a young woman who needs money for a dowry, his audience takes up a collection for her. But—appropriately enough given that the Imposture is set in Shiraz—the poem can also be read as a story about drinking wine, which is what Abū Zayd has in mind. As with Imposture 8, the translation extends the principle of double entendre to the narration, as a way to compensate for the loss of assonance, alliteration, and prose rhyme. In this case, the words with double meanings are wine-making and wine-tasting terms.

35.1   *We heard through the grapevine:*

I was barreling through Shiraz when I passed a crew so grand that even a traveler who was pressed for time could see that a stopping was a must. So, d'ju want to sit? they asked. "Oaky Tokay, don't mind if I doux," I said, plonking myself down. Their level of culture more than met my expecto-rations, and it was easy to blend in. Everyone was in a ferment, and the conversation was a becoming a real corker, when suddenly we were inter-rupted by a fellow wearing something like an old sack. Though he seemed of ancient vintage, his tone was brisk and firm. He sat down, wrapped the end of his cloak around his knees, and settled in, saying "Any port in a storm!"

The crew ignored him and went back to mouthing their tuns of phrase, 35.2 forgetting that greatness stems from complexity and expressiveness, not clarity or color. The newcomer stayed closed, not opening up, and not breathing a word. But he was sniffing and sipping the whole time; and when he had probed them to the punt, assessed their balance, troweled out their fruits and spices, and distinguished the mellow from the hollow and the creamy from the coarse, said: "If your noses weren't so high in the air, you wouldn't need to rack your brains."

After that opener, he pulled the bung from his barrel. Out came a torrent of dense, concentrated verbiage, chewy, round, and firm, with the occasional peppery note, wowing the judges and earning him a perfect score. Then, as they were savoring the long, complex finish, he rose to his feet and prepared to leave. But the crew wanted a re-sling. "We've quaffed your tipple," they said. "Now name the *terroir!*"

At that he fell silent, as one overcome with emotion, and then burst into heartrending sobs. This was no sham pain: he seemed entirely Sancerre.

The tasting notes continue as follows. 35.3

There was something familiar about that particular mixture of jamminess and astringency: was it the *méthode saroudjienne*? That fallen-over face and that barnyard aroma? Then I was sure of his appellation: it was Alter Sekt! The man was insidious as black rot, and I could have said so. But I kept Mumm for his sake—though I'm not sure he realized that at first. Soon enough, though, he understood that I'd seen through his act. He gave me a wink, and then with a great show of sedimentality put in this plug for himself:

> May God forgive my youthful sins:
> I adulterized so often then!
> Some were young, some were old,
> Some full-bodied, some austere,
> Some lean and racy, some silky smooth;
> But even the rich and opulent
> Never protested at the deed,

And, if reproached for what I'd done
I'd blame it on an unkind fate.
And now old age bids me refrain
And poverty stays my trembling hand.
But gentlemen, I have a ward,
Secluded, untouched by e'en the wind,
And pursued by lovers even so.
The time has come to see her wed,
But no less than a hundred will suffice
To dower her, and I have none.
So lend me a hand, dispel my care;
You shall I bless in ev'ry prayer.

35.4 When Alter Sekt had recited his magnum opus, every member of the crew dipped into his stock and found something to give him. Soon he had harvested the one hundred dirhams he asked for. Then he blessed everyone and rose to go.

Who might his adulterous partners be? And what did this ward of his look like? I mulled those questions over but drew a blanc. So I followed him out, hoping he'd at yeast give me a clue. When he saw me stalking him, he turned around and confronted me, saying: "Let me claret up for you:

'Adulterize' means 'water down,'
Not what it is you're thinking;
And the virgin bride I have at home
Is an agèd daughter of the vine.
The hundred I need for a sturdy jug
And a cup to pour her into.
Reproach me if you must, my friend,
Or better yet, ignore me:
¡Que Syrah, Syrah, *mon pote*,
You just keep on Trocken!

"The imbalance," he added, "is that I'm zesty and bold while you're flabby and flat. Between us are too many soul fights!"

But as he canted off he shot me the affectionate glance of a well-paired friend.

NOTES

In al-Ḥarīrī's Iraq, wine was shipped in amphorae (*dinān*), which were drained through the bung (*fidām*), that is, the plug at one end, which was sealed with pitch (*musarbal bi l-qār*). This draining lent itself to various metaphors, such as bloodletting (*faṣd*). As in ancient Greek drinking, the wine was drained into a bowl, mixed with water, ladled into a jug, and finally poured into cups (on Greek symposia, see Davidson, *Courtesans*, 43–47). In Abū Zayd's poem, he calls the mixing *qatl*, which normally means "killing" or "murder." In his German translation, the ever-ingenious Rückert renders this wordplay using the expression *den Hals brechen*, "to break someone's neck" but also "to crack open a bottle" (*Verwandlungen*, 205). I have used the less felicitous "adulterize," which means both "commit adultery" and "adulterate," that is, water down (*OED*).

BIBLIOGRAPHY

Davidson, James. *Courtesans and Fishcakes: The Consuming Passions of Ancient Athens*. New York: Saint Martin's, 1998.

Wine Folly. "Wine Descriptions and What They Mean." September 10, 2013. Infographic at http://winefolly.com/tutorial/wine-descriptions-chart-infographic/.

IMPOSTURE 36

WHAT IS THE QUESTION?

In this Imposture, Abū Zayd (here called Double Daddy, as he might be called in a children's book) stumps his audience with ahājī, riddles that require you to replace each word in a phrase with a synonym such that the synonyms produce another phrase. An approximate equivalent is the cryptic clue used in British crosswords. Unlike the hints in American puzzles, cryptic clues require the solver to manipulate the given words or letters, often more than once, to produce a solution. Of course, the only reason to torment oneself with that kind of puzzle is to solve an actual crossword, so Double Daddy has provided one that may be solved using his cryptic clues. The clues are keyed in the marginal notes, which also contain the enumeration (the number of letters in the answer). The narrative voice imitates Gertrude Stein's children's book The World Is Round, *with occasional borrowings from* The Autobiography of Alice B. Toklas. *The former tells a story using a good deal of prose rhyme, making the style appropriate for an Imposture. The latter makes Toklas into a seemingly naive observer of the geniuses of her age (not only Stein but Picasso, Matisse, Hemingway, and so on), making it a good model for al-Ḥārith's (here, Everyman's) observation of Double Daddy. And in a letter dated February 26, 1935, writer and photographer Carl Van Vechten wrote to tell her that "there [are] crossword puzzles in the newspapers called Gertrude Stein" (Burns, ed., Letters, 399). In keeping with the 1930s theme, Double Daddy in §36.11 speaks in a voice that echoes J. R. R. Tolkien's "Far Over the Misty Mountains Cold" (*The Hobbit, *17–18).*

Everyman told us another one, which ran like this. 36.1

I rode my camel all the way to Malatya, and tied her there with a tether. On her back was a sack with scads of gold inside. Right away I began going from one house to another to rouse up people who were clever but I never did find them all, not ever. Some were here some were there but not all of them anywhere so I decided to spend my gold on things I would need when I left Malatya where my camel was on a tether. Well you know I was just about to go when I saw a clever man and another and another and two more and four more so that came to nine sitting on top of a hill with a jug of wine. People were looking at them because they were ever so clever. Well I did not care about their wine I liked how they were all birds of a feather. Nothing could be better I thought than sitting down with them and so we all sat together.

After I had been sitting with them a while I found that they were all 36.2 different styles of men some looked like folk who had blown in from the desert but all of them were there because they loved to talk and joke yes they certainly did and that made them all the same. Like the stars and oh so bright and I was glad I was where I was perhaps a star had showed me the way. Anyway I joined in their game. When I had something to say I would say it and we just kept going around and around that day until one of them said we should address ourselves to cryptic clues. A cryptic clue is when you say "Dazzled rime tossup acts" and the answer is IMPOSTURES.

Well everyone tried coming up with their own clues some were clever 36.3 but some were half done and could not be used. And then as we were making up clues I saw there was a man there, an old man who was not much to look at but sharp as a tack. He watched us and listened until none of us could think up any more to use. Some began with the clue and tried to find the answer and some began with the answer and tried to find the clue but when you cannot think of anything whatsoever there is nothing you can do. So the man stopped listening to us gathered up his skirts and turned to go. As he made to leave he said:

> All that glitters is not gold,
> Not every tawny drink is wine.

36.4   No we cried come back you cannot say that and then just vamoose and we blocked his path and grabbed him and said he must come back. If a thing is torn you must mend it and if you do not mend it why then we must defend it. You cannot flourish a sword and poke at our turbans and then just march away. That's what we said. So he came back and sat down as if he meant to stay. And he did. He said ask me anything you want and King Solomon himself will give you the response.

36.5   You are all very clever he said but coming up with cryptic clues is no picnic. To make them tick you have to have the wit for all things hid in language. Of course the solution must match the clue to the hilt and each part of the clue must be grist for the mill. And most of all they should be skilled. But oh my I see you confusing your anagrind with your anagrist, and biffing instead of waiting for your PDM. This just won't do. You are so right we said. So help us move ahead. What shall we do? Let me help, he said. Let no one say I claim to understand things I cannot master as a game.

36.6   Then he turned to the leader of our group and recited a little poem. Then he did the same for all of us and I am going to write down all the verses for you and here they are. The first one was:

> "Cant jog, ran all over." Done?   (1 ACROSS; 6)
> Sorry, that was an easy one.

Then he grinned at the next man and said:

> Miss this one and it's jailable.
> Ready? "Current not available."   (7 ACROSS; 2,3)

Then he squinted at the third man and said:

> Here's an easier one for you:
> Ready? "Shift rear in loo."   (8 ACROSS; 6)

Then he craned his neck at the fourth man and said:

Next: "Princes juggled me, sir."   (9 ACROSS; 5)
A little simpler? I concur!

Then he shot a glance at the fifth man and said:

Now try "Kudos allegedly offers grace."
Come on, man, keep up the pace!   (12 ACROSS; 5)

Then he pounced on the sixth man and said: 36.7

"Semitic starter brew adds acidity":   (13 ACROSS; 5)
How 'bout that one for limpidity?

Then he wiggled his eyebrows at the seventh man and said:

Here's one where Latin helps a bit:
"Otium impinged on, I quit."   (14 ACROSS; 2,3)

Then he leaned over close to the eighth man and said:

Now this next one's a real breeze:
"Access concealed by aspen trees."   (17 ACROSS; 6)

Then he stared hard at the ninth man and said:

Grandma will know if you ask 'er:
"Dined at the Dār, for al-Mustaẓhir?"   (18 ACROSS; 3,2)

At last he came to me and when he came to me he patted me on the
shoulder and recited this:

You're a clever one: you can't fool me!
Try "Journey's windup begins with tea."   (19 ACROSS; 6)

36.8   Well he waited for a while to see if we could come up with any solutions but we couldn't and then he said well that's only the half of it so what if I gave you the other half and we said yes yes because we were sure we would do better the next time and he said all right then and he turned back to the first man he had spoken to and said:

> We'll start with another easy one:
> "Shuffle upsets a rag man." What fun!   (2 DOWN; 7)

Then he tilted his head at the second man and said:

> How about one that's a little longer?
> "Baffled baby loses compass, moves solver."   (3 DOWN; 4,3)

Then he shifted his gaze to the third man and said:

> "All of you, used by men in error."   (4 DOWN; 4)
> Why, you all seem struck with terror!

Then he glared at the fourth man and said:

> Here's another, for the real addict:
> "Persian poet's capacious, as rumor has it."   (5 DOWN; 4)

Then he looked slyly at the fifth man and said:

> Now here's one for folks in the know:
> "Fewer classes cut short." How'd you go?   (6 DOWN; 4)

36.9   Then he eyed number six and said:

> Maybe it's time to raise the bar:
> "Addled Almaty gains tone where we are."   (10 DOWN; 7)

Then he peered slantwise at number seven and said:

> Just four more: we're almost there!
> Try: "Full fold again, I hear."   (11 DOWN; 7)

Then he ogled number eight and said:

> Don't be alarmed by this, dear reader:
> "Badly injure prayer leader."   (14 DOWN; 4)

Then he smirked at number nine and said:

> How about this: "Ulysses upended sign"?   (15 DOWN; 4)
> Hurry: we're nearly out of time!

And now when he came to me he clutched my sleeve and said:

> Marvelous fellow! Here's my last clue: (16 DOWN; 4)
> "What's inside taking shelter." Back to you!

Everyman continued: **36.10**

Well we were all taken by his clues but when he asked us to come up with the solutions we said we couldn't because they were far too abstruse and nobody could ever solve them so could he please tell us the answers if he did not it would be cruel. So he thought about it and first said he would and then that he wouldn't and finally he said he would.

He said I am going to teach you something you didn't know and didn't expect to learn, so carry it with you and use it when you play this game again and it's your turn. And then he explained each clue yes that he did do and he shook all the money out of our sleeves oh yes he did that too until our heads were relieved but our purses were aggrieved.

Finally he stood up to go and we asked him where he lived and he sighed **36.11**
and then sang this song.

In darkened fields I make my bed,
On broken stones I lay my head.
I take the road at break of day
To a sunlit meadow far away,
For over the Zagros Mountains lies
Sarúj: I see the town before my eyes,
Full of morning mist, and bright quick things,
And thickets where the warbler sings.
I tasted sweetness in those glens;
I shall not taste its like again.

Everyman continued:

I said to the others why that must be Double Daddy of Sarúj who can sing and tell stories that rhyme and many other things including riddles that come out right and as I was saying all this I looked over and he had vanished from sight. Double Daddy of Sarúj was not there anymore, he was not anywhere, gone up in smoke. Poof!

NOTES

An Arabic *uḥjiyyah* (pl. *aḥājī*) begins with a phrase of two words, e.g., *shaqīq aflat*, "a brother who escaped." The solution is *akhṭār*, "dangers." Why? Not the apparently related meaning, which is a coincidence. The first syllable, *akh*, is a synonym for *shaqīq*, "brother," and the second, *ṭār*, is a synonym for *aflat*, "escaped." The solver needs to guess these synonyms. With them he produces a new phrase, *akh ṭār*. He must then collapse the phrase into a single word—namely, *akhṭār*, which happens to mean "dangers." A similar case in English might be:

Clue:	Leave W5 (*a London postcode*)
Substitution:	Quit Ealing (*borough in W5*)
Respacing:	Quite a ling! (*praise for a cod*)

English has a special problem with the third stage, since, unlike Arabic, it cannot simply ignore most of the vowels in a word. Although there are English word games that entail re-chunking (e.g., Strine), cryptic crossword clues are much more familiar, at least to the legions of crossword fans worldwide. Of course, the cryptic clues here are functional equivalents rather than lexical translations, as it proved impossible to come up with clues and solutions that have anything in common with any of the *aḥājī* at the surface level. On the distinction between *aḥājī* and riddles proper (*alghāz*) see Smoor, "Weeping Wax Candle." *Alghāz* are the topic of Imposture 42.

Though bewildering to the uninitiated, cryptic clues fall into distinct types, each governed by its own rules. Like al-Ḥarīrī, who included an appendix analyzing his *aḥājī*, I break down my clues below. This breakdown should supply enough hints to make it possible to guess the solution. The answer key appears on the "Book Supplements" page on the Library of Arabic Literature website at www.libraryofarabicliterature.org/extra-2/.

ACROSS

1   Cant jog, ran all over (6)

7   Current not available (2,3)

8   Shift rear in loo (6)

9   Princes juggled me, sir (5)

12 Kudos allegedly offers grace (5)

13 Semitic starter brew adds acidity (5)

14 Otium impinged on, I quit (2,3)

17 Access concealed by aspen trees (6)

18 Dined at the Dār, for al-Mustaẓhir? (3,2)

19 Journey's windup begins with tea (6)

DOWN

2   Shuffle upsets a rag man (7)

3   Baffled baby loses compass, moves solver (4,3)

4   All of you, used by men in error (4)

5   Persian poet's capacious, as rumor has it (4)

6   Fewer classes cut short (4)

10 Addled Almaty gains tone where we are (7)

11 Full fold again, I hear (7)

14 Badly injure prayer leader (4)

15 Ulysses upended sign (4)

16 What's inside taking shelter (4)

CRYPTIC CLUES AND SETTER'S JARGON EXPLAINED

In §36.2 "Dazzled rime tossup acts" is an anagram, as indicated by "dazzled." "Rime tossup" is the anagrist: the word or words to be manipulated. "Acts" is the definition, that is, the word synonymous with the solution. If you manipulate the letters of "rime tossup" you can make "Impostures," which are a kind of act. ("Rime" is an archaic spelling of "rhyme.")

In §36.5 "anagrind" is the phrase that signals that the clue is an anagram (e.g., "dazzled") and "anagrist" is the word or words to be reshuffled into the solution, often in combination with other manipulations (substitution, deletion, etc.). "To biff": "to enter a clue's answer from the definition without fully understanding its parsing." "PDM": "The beautiful 'Penny-Drop Moment' when the workings of an elusive clue or theme suddenly become clear to the solver." These definitions are from Shuchismita Upadhyay's Crossword Unclued site.

Across

1   **Cant jog, ran all over (6).** Another anagram, indicated by "all over." The anagrist is "jog" and "ran," ignoring the comma and the space. "Cant" (notice the lack of apostrophe) is the definition. The solution is a six-letter word.

7   **Current not available (2,3).** This is an example of double definition. There is no wordplay; each of the two parts of the expression is a synonym for the solution.

8   **Shift rear in loo (6).** This is a so-called container clue. "Shift" is the definition. "Rear in loo" means that a synonym for "rear," in this case "aft," appears inside (that is, is inserted between the letters of) a synonym for loo, in this case "can." "Shift" is also a misdirection, since it can also be used to signal another type of clue, the letter shift or anagram.

9   **Princes juggled me, sir (5).** The definition is "princes" and the solution is an anagram, as indicated by "juggled." The anagrist is "me sir."

12   **Kudos allegedly offers grace (5).** A homophone clue, as indicated by "allegedly," based on a substitution for "kudos," in this case "praise." "Offers grace" is the definition.

13   **Semitic starter brew adds acidity (5).** This is an example of a charade clue. "Semitic starter" is the definition, referring to the first letter of various

Semitic-language alphabets. For "brew" use the synonym "ale." To "ale" add "pH," the abbreviation for "acidity."

14 **Otium impinged on, I quit (2,3).** "Impinged on" signals an anagram; the anagrist is "otium." Remember that in anagrams, punctuation and spacing may vary freely. The definition is "I quit."

17 **Access concealed by aspen trees (6).** "Access" is the definition. "Concealed by" indicates a hidden word clue: that is, one where the letters of the solution appear, in order, somewhere in "aspen trees."

18 **Dined at the Dār, for al-Mustaẓhir? (3,2).** An example of a cryptic definition, which unlike other clue types is also used in American-style crosswords. Al-Mustaẓhir was the Abbasid caliph from 1094 to 1118 and the Dār is the Dār al-Salṭanah, the ruler's residence in Baghdad.

19 **Journey's windup begins with tea (6).** Charades. "Journey" is the definition. Take "ravel," a synonym for windup, and add T to the beginning.

Down

2 **Shuffle upsets a rag man (7).** "Shuffle" is the definition (which is tricky, since it looks like an anagram indicator). The actual indicator is "upsets," and the anagrist is "a rag man."

3 **Baffled baby loses compass, moves solver (4,3).** "Baffled" indicates an anagram. The anagrist is not "baby" but its synonym, "youngest." "Loses compass" means that the anagram works only if you drop an N, S, E, or W. In this case, the dropped letter will be N. The result means "moves solver," the solver being you.

4 **All of you, used by men in error (4).** A hidden-word clue, indicated by "used by." "All of you" is how many people were in the group before al-Ḥārith joined it. The letters of the solution appear in order in the phrase "men in error."

5 **Persian poet's capacious, as rumor has it (4).** A homophone, indicated by "as rumor has it." The homophone is not "capacious" but a synonym for it.

6 **Fewer classes cut short (4).** A deletion clue, indicated by "cut short." The word to be cut short is not "classes" but a synonym for it. "Fewer" is the definition.

10 **Addled Almaty gains tone where we are (7).** "Addled" indicates an anagram. Use "Almaty" as the anagrist but add a (musical) tone, in this case A.

The solution is synonymous with "where we are" from al-Ḥārith's point of view.

11 **Full fold again, I hear** (7). A homophone, indicated by "I hear." The solution sounds like "fold again" and means "full."

14 **Badly injure prayer leader** (4). "Badly" indicates an anagram. The anagrist is not "injure" but a synonym for it. The solution means "prayer leader."

15 **Ulysses upended sign** (4). "Upended" means a reverse clue, that is, one in which the word needs to be spelled backward or, in this case, "upended," because the solution is in a DOWN column. The word to be upended is not "Ulysses" but what Ulysses calls himself (in Latin) when questioned by the Cyclops.

16 **What's inside taking shelter** (4). A container, indicated by "taken." "What's inside" is the "contents," which contains the solution, a kind of "shelter."

BIBLIOGRAPHY

Burns, Edward. *The Letters of Gertrude Stein and Carl Van Vechten, 1913–1946*. New York: Columbia University Press, 2013.

Crossword Solver, The. http://www.the-crossword-solver.com/.

Smoor, Pieter. "The Weeping Wax Candle and Maʿarrī's Wisdom-Tooth: Night Thoughts and Riddles from the *Ǧāmiʿ al-awzān*." *Zeitschrift der Deutschen Morgenländischen Gesellschaft* 138, no. 2 (1988), 283–312.

Stein, Gertrude. *The Autobiography of Alice B. Toklas*. New York: Harcourt, Brace, 1933.

———. *The World Is Round*. New York: Harper Design, 2013.

Sutherland, Denise. Cryptic Class at Puzzling. http://alwayspuzzling.blogspot. ae/p/cryptic-class.html.

Tolkien, J. R. R. *The Hobbit*. Boston: Houghton Mifflin, 2001.

Upadhyay, Shuchismita. Crossword Unclued. http://www.crosswordunclued.com/. List of clue types at http://www.crosswordunclued.com/2008/09/dictionary.html.

Universal Anagram Solver. http://anagram-solver.net/.

IMPOSTURE 37

OFF THE HEEZIE

Abū Zayd again drags his son to court, this time on the dubious charge of ingratitude. The theme here being the supposed brattiness of the younger generation, some kind of youth speech style seemed a good choice for the language (including the narrative voice, since al-Ḥārith says he was young when he witnessed this incident). The choice fell on the language used a decade ago by students at the University of California, Los Angeles, whose slang has been extensively documented by generations of undergraduates directed by linguist Pamela Munro. The translation emphasizes two sources of this UCLA lexicon: surfers' jargon and African-American Language. The whole text was corrected by linguist Nandi Sims, who also co-wrote the rap-style lyrics.

37.1   *Al-Harith ibn Hammam was like:*

Road trip up to Saʒdah! That was back when I was taller than a baller and totally wired: I mean like baby-ostrich-on-crack wired. When I got there I was all FOB: "Dude, check it out: it's so whole-grain up in here!" I found some savvy guys with mad skills and asked them to scrat for a bossman who could make it rain, 'cause I needed a connect to hook me up if times got sheisty. They told me to check out this one judge who was legit and could totally spot me: he was an old-school Tamimi and that's how they roll. So I started putting in some work and kissing some ass. After a while the judge and me became such good peeps that he was calling me "Bro" and I was calling him "Homie." I wasn't just mooching off of the cheddar—y'know, like, the lettuce, the green, the skrilla? Naw, I got to check out all the plaintiffs and defendants who showed up for trial, and lowkey help them settle out of court.

One day Homeslice is getting his judging on. There's a gripload of people in the house and the scene is off the heezie. That's when this sketchy old guy in tore-up threads shows up, shaking all over. He scopes out the crowd like we're loose change and he's the coin checker from hell. Then he tells the judge he's got a case against some tool who's mega aggro and won't come to court. Seconds later—faster than you can light a bowl or throw up a sign—they find the guy and bring him in, and schwa! he's a total beast.   37.2

Then the old guy is like, "Holla atcha Judge! And keep it real! This is my son, and he's whack: y'know, like when your pen's all janky or your blade's all jacked. Basically, he won't give me props and he's always talking smack. When I'm like 'Let's kick it,' he's all 'Gotta bail.' When I'm like 'Dope!' he's all 'Nope!' When I'm like 'Dank!' he's all 'Jank!' And when I'm like 'Solid!' he's all 'Epic fail!' But jeez Louise: I've been taking care of him since he could crawl, and I've totes been an awesome daddy to him."

The judge is like, "For serious?" And everybody there was like, "That is so effed!" And then the judge was like, "Word! A kid like that is worse than *no* kids—I mean, some people are better off infertile, yaddadamean?"

Now the son, who's getting butt-hurt listening to this, is all like, "I swear to GOD! He's the One who hooks you up with the whole judging thing, right? And lets you decide what's lame and what's legit? Well, every time my dad goes 'Yo,' I'm like 'Hey!' Every time he goes 'Fresh!' I'm all 'For reals!' Every time he goes 'Dang!' I'm all 'Most def!' And every time he goes 'Boss!' I'm all like 'What's crackin?!' Even though he's always getting all up in my grill, asking me for rooster eggs and flying camels and whatnot."   37.3

So the judge is like, "Bust out some deets, playa: how ezzackly does he get all up in your face?"

So the dude is like, "Dude! So at some point he's fresh out of cheddar? And he's like, 'Put that smartass mouth to work and chase some paper!'? Like, he wants me to hit people up for green? Just 'cause he ain't got no bones and can't hang? But back when he was teaching me the man code, he was all, 'Son, don't get greedy! Pushy makes you a tool, and grabby makes you a fool. Inhale your bites and you'll be hurling; if you're mooching you're being a goob.' Then he'd bust out some of his own rhymes:

37.4   You say 'If you ain't got squat don't have yourself a conniption.
        But for what you do got, you need to say a benediction.

        I'm laughing at your passion 'cuz you dig yourself, clown.
        You wanna climb up, get your grind up but you bring yourself down.

        You think you rhyme on a dime but you ain't that cat.
        Don't try to mess with the best. I'm all over the map.

        Just use your intellect, it's about your self-respect
        You got your pride, my man, what else you gonna protect?

        Just like a lion pride, go ahead protect what you get.
        Just like a lion pride, go ahead protect what you get.

        If you can't get no caliph heads go get yourself a backbone.
        If you gon' stay acting foolish betta leave that cheddar alone.

        You need that ability to, skillfully, display a bit of dignity,
        And draw upon it easily and willfully, consistently.
        So show some flexibility when you come upon hostility,
        And you will, unconditionally, have better sensibilities.'"

37.5   The old dude makes a thizz face. Then he gets all up in his son's grill and starts tripping out.

        "Bite me, you ungrateful little tool! You're so nasty you make me want to spew. Are you going to teach your mother to put out? Or show your wet-nurse where to find her headlights? You're a scorpion messing with a cobra! You're a grommet dropping in on the greybellies, and you're finna get nailed!"

Then the old dude checks himself, like he's feeling bad that he flipped out. I mean, he hated on his own son—uncool, right? So then he starts talking to the kid like he's his BFF.

"C'mon, dawg: that advice I gave about keeping it on the down-low was for players who got a stash of cash or some bling to sling. But it's not messed up to beg if you don't have jack: the interpretive tradition has got your back. Mmkay, so you didn't know that; it's all good. But don't diss a daddy: that's so hood! Here's my real advice:

Don't ride a cruncher 37.6
　And get pounded down the fa-alls (doo wah!)
Just so they'll say,
　'That dude is off the wa-all!' (doo wah!)
Look for a set and get outside
That's all you need for a righteous ride
Paddle out and you might just catch a wave!

If the break's onshore
　No need to hang aro-ound (doo wah!)
Leave the hodads in the soup
　Cause they'll just bring you do-own (doo wah!)

There's no shame if you try and fail
Jonah wiped out and he had to bail
Paddle out and you might just catch a wave!"

Now the Judge can see that the player wasn't being totally straight-up 37.7 about his dad, and in fact was being kind of a poser. And so he gives him a nasty look and goes, "Foo, you are so sketch: first you're Tamimi and then you're from Qays! I don't like players who flip-flop and front instead of being straight up."

So the kid is like, "Praise the LORD, Your Honor, who made you the Man! You're right: I messed up and harshed on my dad. Brainfart: my bad! But I'm feeling beat 'cause I need to eat. Don't you have a door open to the poor? And the freebie plan if a player needs more? Those old-school judges knew the score: if you were jonesing they'd feed your face. Hardcore!"

Then the judge is like, "Lock it up, dawg! Not every cloud is a player hater: the lightning comes first but the rain comes later. So keep your eye on the sky, and when the good stuff comes down you can testify."

At this point the old dude realizes that the judge is getting heated 'cause the kid lowkey said he was a stinge. The old dude figures the judge is finna bust out some lettuce to show he's for reals. So he doesn't dick around. Faster than you can reel in a fish and slap it on the grill he's throwing down a rap:

37.8   Don't nobody know the law like you does
Ain't right for a guy to rag, it's true, cuz.
Just as a Hijaz mount: with that new buzz,
You grantin' out that manna like in Exodus.

This playa don't know Tamim's got steaze
If I was you I wouldn't help him. Please,
come over here get at your old-school peep
'Cuz I'll recognize up and down the street.

When the judge hears that he gets stoked and beers the dad a major grip-load of green. Then he turns to the son and calls him out. "See what happens when you talk smack, bro? Next time, make sure you're keeping it real before you rag on somebody else. Get a clue: don't play yourself! And I better not hear about you fronting on your dad again: if I do I will *school* your ass!"

Now the kid looks whipped. He barges over to his dad and hugs him awkwardly for a second. Then he's all, "I'm blowing this popsicle stand," and rolls out. Then the old dude's like, "Gotta bounce too!" As he's bailing he's all:

If you're getting pounded and you think you're toast
Then catch a bombora to the Yemen coast (wah oo!)
The judge out there makes all the rest look bad
He'll treat you better than you've ever had (wah oo!)"

Al-Harith was like: 37.9

The whole time I've been all, "Do I know this old dude, or is he just a rando?" So then when he's like "Peace out," I'm all "Dude! I'll follow him back to his crib and find out what's got him all amped. Fosho he's keeping something on the low-low."

So I mobilize and roll out after them. They walk, and I walk; they twist, and I twist; they shimmy, and I shimmy, until schwa! The old dude sees me and I see him, and it would be uncool for us to diss each other. So he stops shaking (which he was faking) and does this thing where he looks stoked to see me. Then he's like "Bros before shows," and I know fo' shizzle that it's the dude from Sarūj, real talk. So I'm all "Gimme some skin, blood, and tell me what's crackalackin'!" But he's all, "Gotta kick it! But you can ask the son of your brother from another mother."

But the boy just cheeses at me. Then he kicks some rocks and ditches like his dad did. Now I know it's them for reals, but they've both boned out.

GLOSSARY

37.1

be like   say

baller   basketball player

wired   hyper, jittery; mentally prepared

on crack   crazy

FOB   fresh off the boat (i.e., recently arrived, and therefore bewildered or easily impressed)

dude   interjection showing emotion

check out   look at

whole grain   healthy, good

have mad skills   be really good at something

scrat for   look for

bossman   person who commands respect

make it rain   spend a lot of money

connect   supplier

hook someone up with something   supply at no charge

sheisty   unreliable, suspicious, unsafe

legit   credible, honest, good

spot   lend money to

old school   classic

how they roll   how they do things

put in some work   build a relationship

peeps   close friends

homie   close friend

mooch off   take advantage of someone's generosity

37.2

homeslice   friend

get one's (something) on   do
(something)

a gripload of   a lot

off the heezie   great (of a thing)

sketchy   suspicious

tore up   dirty, tired, gross, ugly

threads   clothes

scope out   evaluate (by looking)

from hell   of an extremely bad type

tool   rude male

mega   extremely

aggro   aggressive

bowl   pipe full of marijuana

throw up a sign   make a hand gesture
to indicate membership in a gang

schwa   wow! (indicating surprise)

beast   impressive person

holla atcha, Judge   (from *holla atcha
boy*) good for you!

keep it real   be honest or down to
earth

37.3

butt-hurt   (unreasonably) upset

lame   stupid

yo   a greeting

fresh   very good

for reals   really

dang   wow!

most def   definitely

boss   very good

get all up in someone's grill   confront

cheddar, lettuce, green, skrilla   money

naw   no

whack   not acceptable, stupid, crazy

janky   not good, cheap, poor

jacked   (from jacked up) in poor
condition

give props   show respect

talk smack   speak disparagingly

kick it   pass time pleasantly

bail   leave

dope   really good

dank   really good

jank   (from *jank-ass*) not good,
cheap, poor

solid   very good

epic fail   what a mistake!

jeez Louise   enough of that!

totes   totally

for serious   really

effed   in a bad situation

word   I see; I agree; goodbye to you
too

yaddadamean   you know what I
mean

bust out   produce

deets   details

playa   term of address to men

get all up in your face   confront

cheddar   money

chase some paper   make money

hit up someone for   ask someone for

green   money

bones   money

348

can't hang   unable to handle things

man code   unspoken rules followed
   by males

inhale   eat very rapidly

37.5

thizz face   grimace of disgust

trip out   get upset

bite me   I'm not listening to you

spew   vomit

put out   to have sex (of a female)

headlights   nipples

grommet   beginning surfer

greybelly   an older surfer with a big
   belly

finna   going to, about to

nailed   knocked off one's board

check oneself   control oneself

flip out   overreact

hate on   evince dislike

37.6

cruncher   a big, hard-breaking wave
   that folds over and is almost impossible to ride

pounded   (from *pounder*) a hard-
   breaking wave

off the wall   incredible, excellent

set   a group of waves

outside   the area farthest from shore
   where the waves are breaking

37.7

straight up   real, true

poser   wannabe

foo   (disparaging) term of address

sketch   suspicious

front   pretend

bites   food

hurl   vomit

goob   socially inept person

uncool   unfair, unacceptable

BFF   best friend forever

dawg   term of address to guys

on the down-low   secret

bling   jewelry, but here figuratively
   "goods"

sling   to sell (drugs)

messed up   wrong

jack   nothing

mmkay   okay

it's all good   it's all right

diss   insult

hood   like a stereotypical gang
   member

onshore   with the wind blowing
   toward the land, spoiling the waves

hodad   (annoying) non-surfer

soup   foamy part of the broken wave

wipe out   get knocked off the board

bail   jump or dive off the board to
   avoid a wipeout

harsh on   (evince) dislike

brainfart   careless mistake

my bad   it's my fault

beat   exhausted

jonesing   craving

349

hardcore intense

lock it up control yourself

heated upset

37.8

steaze style

recognize respect who you're talking
  to

stoked excited

beer hand (someone something)

play mislead, lie to

school show who's boss

37.9

rando stranger

peace out goodbye

crib home

amped excited

fosho for sure

on the low-low secret

mobilize leave

bros before shows invented from
  bros before hoes, "don't let a girl
  come between you and your male
  friends"

fo' shizzle for sure

lowkey sort of

stinge stingy

dick around waste time

whipped submissive

barge it hurry

blow this popsicle stand leave

roll out leave

bounce leave

bombora a big wave that breaks
  outside the normal surf line

real talk truthfully

blood term of address for a close
  friend

what's crackalackin' what's up

kick it leave

brother from another mother very
  close male friend

cheese smile

kick some rocks leave

ditch leave

bone out leave

NOTES

Every four years since 1989, UCLA students have compiled a dictionary of their own slang. The edition Nandi Sims and I happened to have available was the sixth, published in 2009. Surprisingly, it contained a range of vocabulary broad enough to convey everything in this Imposture except for specific references to things like ostriches and camels, for which I used Standard English. Almost all of the definitions in the Glossary come from *UCLA Slang 6,* with some lightly edited for concision or clarity. The remaining items come from surfer glossaries; the *Urban Dictionary,* which is often useless for proper definitions but at least attests to the existence of a word at a particular time; and my own knowledge of UCLA student speech, which I have been listening to for two decades now.

"Sa3dah" (§37.1) is Ṣaʿdah, a town in Yemen, here written using 3 for ʿayn as in Arabizi, an informal way of writing Arabic words using English keyboard characters, common in texting.

"Tamimi" (§37.1) is from Tamīm, a northern Arabian tribe jealous of its reputation for generosity and rivals of the southern Arabian tribe Qays (§37.7).

"They walk . . . I shimmy" (§37.9) is based on a lyric from "California Sun."

BIBLIOGRAPHY

Blanco, Erik, Emily Franklin, Colleen Carmichael, and Elissa Swauger. *UCLA Slang 6*. Edited by Pamela Munro. Department of Linguistics, University of California: Los Angeles, 2009.

Glover, Henry, and Morris Levy. "California Sun." Performed by Joe Jones. Roulette Records, 1961.

Love, Mike, and Brian Wilson. "Catch a Wave." Performed by The Beach Boys. Capitol, 1963.

El Porto Surfer Slang. http://www.cougartown.com/surf-slang.html.

Lighter, J. E. *Random House Historical Dictionary of American Slang*. Vol. 1. New York: Random House, 1994. Vol. 2. New York: Random House, 1997.

Surfing Waves. "Surf Terms." http://www.surfing-waves.com/surf_talk.htm.

Urban Dictionary. http://www.urbandictionary.com/.

IMPOSTURE 38

WOCKY TALKIE

Al-Ḥarīrī made a point of using unusual words and rare expres-
sions throughout the Impostures. To judge by the notes scribbled
in the margins or between the lines of the manuscripts used by
students, many passages puzzled readers and listeners even in
pre-modern times. But the occasional stretches of ordinary lan-
guage, as well as the use of hendiadys (saying the same thing
twice using different words), helped audiences follow the plot
even if the details remained sketchy. To render this effect in
English, al-Ḥārith and Abū Zayd will imitate Lewis Carroll's
"Jabberwocky," a poem that replaces many nouns and verbs
with plausible-sounding inventions. "Somehow it seems to fill
my head with ideas—only I don't exactly know what they are!"
exclaims Carroll's heroine Alice after hearing the poem (Alice,
152–54). The two sets of verses at the end of the Imposture follow
the limerick form beloved of the nonsense poet Edward Lear
(d. 1888).

38.1   *Al-Harith ibn Hammam reported:*

From the time I could pitter-pat and twick my ziff, I had a yankering for
well-turned loquitation. I used to chivel round the talkeries, whiffling for
a loquitor with lots of whumpus to his name. When I found one who was
wingadoo, I would grimp onto his barlick and wait to cledge a titch of
his obblejot. No one had a more blotious store of obblejot than the man

from Saruj, nor was anyone more zifferous in placking it just where it was wanted. Unfortunately, he was as slidgery as a serp and as flombic as the moon: to snick him, I had to go shumbling along behind him from one talkery to another. But I was so bliffered by his yim-yam that I didn't mind. Shumbling is a squerfous whark, but in the end I came to like it.

At one point I'd shumbled all the way to Maroo, a town pletherous with loquitors. I'd had a twickish feeling—a quiddly sort of premogation—that I'd snick him there. But I'd noogled near the bumpus-grounds and chivelled round the gatheries without seeing yerf or kerf of him. Finally I gave up. Then one day I was sitting with the Great Gombustious Yeffernak when in walked Abu Zayd. He was fringued in tatterous ragments, and he was clearly fixicated on slothering up the host. **38.2**

"May you never be trumbled or crankled!" he began. "As you know, gombous potentery brings gombous redentery. No sooner do you nivel up, than everyone starts cladgering for yelf. But be jollerous: by yelfing everyone you are able to yelf, you rendify yourself for all the goom you've been glabbered with. You, sir, have nivelled up to great gombosity, and you stand now as the most pantoglasmic yeffernak of the aenum. All those who yanker for yelf planch their asterations on you, and all those crivelling for suffulence disteck their minibims to you. Few have been so richly guckined and glabbered! Why not flunge that obosity that you slaff upon your familims, and slaff it upon the rectorious as well? For I, sir, was once profligent, even if my goomage has whuffled away. I come to you from a distantious loke, in a shimbling condition, aspitive of some small guggulence from your vasteous riffadoo, or a wallycack toward your bozzle. And what better proffage to yoff to one who cladgers, what better spelf to him who yelfs, than aspition? You are oweful to God: make me oweful to you, and skritch your dobbit to Him! But whatever you do, do not turn snorfling away, or squidge up your hand, when a cladger comes to your pillocks and whumps at your door, bidgering for a snick of your plethory; for there is no glim-glam in grabbery, nor any goom in being a shiveling little niff. No, a man who is truly trellant will thig away whatever he carfs, not once, but redofully; and the real arparian is one dibulous enough to thig away anything he's asked for, even if it's auric." **38.3**

38.4   With that he spicchered it and perstood to see what paction his lippery would have. The Yeffernak, thinking his visitor's loquation might be mere cledgery and bumbalore, lowered his head to think of a question that would jark his scumber. But all Abu Zayd saw was the turning of the head, and all he heard was nothing; and so thinking that no yelf was coming, he flew into a rumptious rage and let fly with this:

> If a man is literacious,
> Raffinate, and quick-quotatious,
> Don't glurk at him, and don't be glacious.
>
> Is he cruff? Is he squodgy?
> Is he blabbic? Or too codgy?
> Not your bumpus: don't be grodgy!
>
> Instead, be tooflig! Show your meckle:
> When he asks you for a tekel,
> Yally-hoo him with your peckel!
>
> For what's the point of being plethic
> If not to build a name erethic,
> That will perstand till time endethic?
>
> Gobbers given without shrankage
> Sling more slue than ones in bankage
> Because they earn you lots of thankage.
>
> Why spend your days so hard a-licky
> Except to save a wodge of ticky
> To welf the folks who live in yicky?
>
> So no more chibbling: be a wowser!
> Warf your clinkage like a towser:
> That's the way to raise a hawser!

When you learn to yelf your proshie,
You'll come to love the oshie-goshie
More than muskatoo that's poshy.

But if you keep on being squercous,
Folks will say: "What? Him berk us?
Sooner mome raths at the circus!"

So no more twickish lippery!
You're no noofie! Don't you see?
People can't stand squidgery!

What they want in a Yeffernak
Is a slaffer with a bulging sack
Who warfs away and won't look back.

But if you mean to be that gent,
Be him now, ere life is spent,
For time and tide do not relent.

"Well windered, by God!" cried the Yeffernak. "Tell me, now: who's 38.5
your gumpher?"

Abu Zayd shot him an ascrombic look, then chiffered his yobblers at the
floor and said:

There was an old wine from the Zagros,
Who said, Who cares where my grape grows?
The taste is the same
Regardless of fame,
Said the wise old wine from the Zagros.

So bliffered was the Yeffernak by Abu Zayd's mooly-gooly obblejot
that he had him wimber up and plotch down right next to him. Then he
flundered him with gewgobs, making it clear that he intended to keep him

on (at some humbargeous rifadoo) to slaff his ticky with the yim-yams. So Abu Zayd took his leave with a jubelous heart and a blodgy sleeve.

38.6 When he rose to go, I did too, and slaggered along behind him. As soon as we'd left the Yeffery, I said: "Conjubilations on your gewgobs, and mooly mifkin on the job!"

He gave a critchy grin, and, looking positively cloffish, cried out in praise of God. Then, gimbling like a slithy tove, he chanted:

> Three cheers for me, Abu Zayd!
> I'm altogether self-made;
> It's all repartee,
> Not my family tree,
> That makes me the great Abu Zayd!

"Kerkin jerkin on anyone who doesn't love good loquitation, and mooly gooly on all of us who do!"

With that he said goodbye and went away, leaving me all mizzly around the heart.

NOTES

This episode, writes Preston, "contains little beyond a repetition of circumstances and phrases which occur in other Makamat, and is of inferior interest to most of them" (*Makamat*, 492). Steingass gamely defends it, arguing that al-Ḥarīrī's collection was never meant to be read straight through, and a reader who "happens to hit on the present Assembly, taking it by itself and on its own merits . . . will proclaim it to be a composition of exquisite beauty" (*Assemblies*, 89–90). My sense is that this was an early attempt on the author's part to master the form. In a more developed Imposture, al-Ḥārith would doubtless report that Abū Zayd disappeared with the governor's money instead of returning to serve as a paid entertainer. In this case, it is unclear exactly what the hero does—a sign, to my mind, that al-Ḥarīrī was not yet thinking very hard about plot.

But why would an early attempt be placed thirty-eighth? Here one notes that Imposture 48, reportedly the first episode al-Ḥarīrī wrote, is also tucked away toward the end of the book. The best explanation seems to be that the author reshuffled the episodes to avoid the appearance of a progression from less- to better-developed ones. If so, the placement of this episode would not be inconsistent with its having been written early on. Another feature of the Imposture that makes it seem early is its thematization of generosity, the oldest and most persistently elaborated theme in pre-modern Arabic poetry. The banality of the subject, and the straightforward manner of dealing with it, suggest that al-Ḥarīrī was still teaching himself to write Impostures. The introduction of a subtheme, that of self-reliance, at the very end, also gives the impression that he had not yet achieved full control of the form.

Since I, like Preston, found this episode of little interest in itself, I decided to use it as the basis for a translation that would emphasize a particular aspect of the collection—namely, the presence of many rare words whose meanings can nevertheless be guessed in context. Many of these words once referred to specific elements of the natural world and of Bedouin society. Used figuratively in pre-Islamic poetry and oratory, they were later remembered only as synonyms for more common words. Though not especially rare, the word *iqtabas*, used twice in §38.1, illustrates the process. It originally meant to take a stick or other flammable object over to a campfire being tended by someone else and ask permission to light the end of the stick so that one could go elsewhere and start a fire of one's own. As used here, though, it simply means "learn." It should be kept in mind, nevertheless, that the original Imposture is not nonsensical, merely difficult, and in that sense no different than any of the other episodes. For properly nonsensical writing in (modern) Arabic, see Al-Mahdi, "Jabberwocky."

The original Imposture is named after the town called Merv in Persian and Marw in Arabic. Located in what is now Turkmenistan, it is currently spelled "Mary" in English. Since all these renderings are either confusing or unpronounceable to most English speakers, I use here the invented variant "Maroo" (§38.2). Given the Imposture's theme of generosity, it may be relevant that the people of Marw were often mocked for their alleged stinginess.

"Shumbling is a squerfous whark" (§38.1) is an allusion to a hadith: "Traveling means living a little bit of Hell: it deprives you of sleep, food, and drink. When you finish what you went to do, come back to your family as quickly as you can" (cited in Sharīshī, *Sharḥ*, 4:256).

BIBLIOGRAPHY

Al-Mahdi, Wael. "Jabberwocky in Arabic." http://waelalmahdi.com/ jabberwocky-in-arabic/.

Carroll, Lewis. *Alice's Adventures in Wonderland and Through the Looking-Glass and What Alice Found There*. London: Macmillan, 1911. http://archive. org/details/alicesadventuresoocarr.

Lear, Edward. *The* [or: *A*] *Book of Nonsense*. First published 1845.

IMPOSTURE 39

THE SEAFARER

This mostly lighthearted story of a sea voyage and the success-
ful application of a home remedy suggested Jonathan Swift's
Gulliver's Travels *(1726–27) as a model, at least for the narra-*
tion. *For Abū Zayd's nautically inflected tirades, the choice was*
obvious: Herman Melville's Moby-Dick *(1851), which uses the*
sea, and everyone and everything in or on it, as the basis for a
vast religious allegory.

El-Hárith related to us: 39.1

As soon as my whiskers sprouted and my nether hairs grew coarse, I felt
an insatiable desire of seeing foreign places. My camels carried me over the
mountains and across great deserts, to the familiar and the remote parts of
the world. I wasted my mounts with hard riding, wearing down my horses'
hooves and driving my camels until their toes bled. But being at last grown
weary of travelling by land, and having some business in Sohar, I found
myself inclined to attempt the sea. So I chose a ship and saw my furnishings, provisions, and waterskins on board. As we lay at anchor, I put myself
in mind of the likely addition to my fortune. Yet I could not but apprehend the danger to my person, and so commended myself to the mercy of
Providence.

We heaved anchor just after nightfall; but when we were just hoisting   39.2
sail we heard a voice cry out from the shore: "Shipmates! Will you ship in
that ship? O that ship that cleaves the sea, driven by the hard hand of God!
Shall I teach you a trade that will save you from the belly of Hell?"

"Rather take the helm," we cried, "and steer us, as a friend guides a friend!"

"Will you first give passage to a stranger, an easy, good-humored man, who seeks only a berth and carries only a basket?"

With common consent we took the man up and resolved to entertain him as hospitably as we could.

39.3   As soon as he came on board he cried, "I take refuge in God from a watery doom!" Then he said: "As many a teacher of old days was wont to say: the ignorant cannot be compelled to learn unless the learned are commanded to teach. I have with me an incantation laid down by the prophets, as well as much wholesome advice, proved by experiment, which it behooves me not to conceal, nor is it my habit to withhold sound counsel. Consider, then, these words; comprehend them aright; apply them to your affairs, and teach them to others. For what do ye know," he cried out, as if contending with us, "of this traveller's spell, that when the billows roll in riots, protects from grief at sea? It is *this* which kept Noah safe amid the Flood, and saw his crew and his animals to shore, as it is particularly stated in the Alcoran." Whereupon he made a very absurd speech consisting of absurdities delivered in a sort of jabber.

"Let us go below!" he cried at last. "Godspeed and a straight wake with us, by God!" He heaved a bitter sigh, as if he were a debtor or a repented man deploring the waywardness of his former fellows in sin. "I have done my duty by ye, and I beseech ye, as God is my witness, to mind your eyes, and turn from the wrath to come!"

"Huzzah!" we cried, hailing his fiery address.

39.4   To me (said the author, resuming his account) there was something familiar in the ring of his voice. "By the Lord who commands the briny deep," I asked him eagerly, "are you not the Sarujer?"

"Aye," he replied—"and couldst thou mistake me?"

With that I congratulated myself on going to sea, and drew aside my veil before him, as he had before me. I took such joy in his company as a miser takes in gold or a drowning man in a floating spar. And so we sailed on, the sea calm, the breeze fresh, and the days spent in idle diversions. But then a dreadful monsoon came up, and calm was forgotten, as wave after wave battered the ship from all sides. Driven by the gale, we set course for a nearby island, intending to rest there and wait until the storm should abate. But the wind continued fierce, and we soon found our provisions much reduced.

At last Aboo Zaid took me aside and said, "It is a maxim that necessity is the mother of invention! Shall we not go and bear her a hand?"

I promised to hold as fast to him as his shadow, and to follow in his footsteps as meekly as a shoe.

We rose and hastened into the country to gather what provisions we 39.5 could. We were in a very weak condition, and carried not so much as a string, nor any means of discovering a path. We pushed forward wherever we found passage, and took what shade we found. At length we came to a noble palace barred with an iron gate, and standing before it a knot of slaves. We approached and desired them to admit us, or to give us water; but upon coming nearer we perceived them to be struck with the utmost grief and despair. We asked them the reason of their sorrow but could get no answer, fair or foul. At length we grew tired of chasing a will o' the wisp and hailing the fata morgana; and so loaded them with all the injurious terms our language can afford, blaming ourselves for seeking the help of imbeciles. Whereupon one of the slaves, a grave elderly man, his eyes flowing with tears, came forward and said: "Pray injure us not, nor reproach us; for we are so much distressed that we are hardly able to speak a word."

"Compose yourself," said Aboo Zaid, "and favour us with any speech you can produce; whatever your malady, you will discover me a most ingenious physician and apothecary."

"Listen, then: the master of this house is a king, and all this country is his dominion. For a long time he lived in the utmost misery for want of a son. He sought the most fertile beds, and there tilled the soil, but the earth remained barren, until a seed at last struck root in the shadow of a noble tree. Many a pledge was given for sake of the infant, and the months— nay, the days until his birth were reckoned one by one. But when the hour approached, and the shirt and crown were laid out, the labour grew difficult; and now the tree and the branch are both in danger of their lives. The court is disconsolate, and none among us sleeps except in fits." Then he fell again to weeping, and crying out, and lamenting.

39.6 "Avast!" cried Aboo Zaid. "Tremble not, but be rejoiced! I bear you glad tidings for your prince. Have I not the secret of the *spuma maris*, of universal fame, which eases birth?"

The slaves ran to their master, eager to tell him that deliverance had come. Before I could say "Jack Robinson" a page appeared and beckoned us inside. We were presented to the king, who promised to reward Aboo Zaid if his claim should prove true and his spell have effect.

Aboo Zaid presently called for a sharpened reed, some meerschaum, and some saffron dissolved in fresh rosewater. In the trip of a minute these were brought. He prostrated himself and laid his face in the dust, praising God and asking His forgiveness. He then took up the reed and, using the saffron-water for ink, scribbled these lines on the meerschaum:

> *Baby Bunting, safe and warm*
> *Safe and warm, safe and warm*
> *Baby Bunting, safe and warm*
> *Don't come out to daddy!*

> *Here outside you'll cry and cry*
> *Cry and cry, cry and cry*
> *Here outside you'll cry and cry*
> *Don't come out to Daddy!*

> *Folk will hurt you, yes they will*
> *Yes they will, yes they will*
> *Folk will hate you, yes they will*
> *Don't come out to daddy!*

> *Baby Bunting, do you hear?*
> *Do you hear, do you hear?*
> *Baby Bunting, do you hear?*
> *Don't come out to Daddy!*

39.7 At a moment when he could do so unperceived, Aboo Zaid covered up the writing. He sputtered at the meerschaum, spraying it thoroughly.

Then he sprinkled it with ambergris, wrapped it in a silken cloth, and commanded that it should be applied to the mother's thigh, stipulating also that no menstrous female should touch her as she lay in labour. Afterwards we were forced to wait no longer than a pause between milkings; for, faster than the flicking of a toper's tongue, the babe slid free, by the virtue of the meerschaum and the power of the Almighty. Whereupon the prince and his subjects were greatly rejoiced, and the palace shook with their huzzahs. The people crowded around Aboo Zaid, singing his praises, kissing his hands, and touching his rags for a blessing, as if he were Oweis El-Karanee, or Dubeis El-Asadee. He was rewarded with so many purses, and granted so many favors, that his every desire was satisfied, and his every want supplied. This revenue flowed undiminished from the day the lambkin was born until it was safe again to attempt the sea and pursue our journey to Oman.

Being well content with the prizes he had received, Aboo Zaid made preparations to depart. But the Governor, having tried his quickening power, would not suffer him to leave, desiring instead that he join his household, and draw on his treasury as he saw fit.

When I perceived Aboo Zaid's inclination to remain, in hopes to improve his fortunes, I railed at him, and endeavored to show him how contemptible was his disposition to renounce his country and his friends. Whereat he replied, "Away with thee, friend Háreth, but first hear this: 39.8

> Pine not away for native soil
>   Where all with disdain greet thee;
> Where steady work and honest toil
>   Make no man better treat thee.
> Sail instead around Good Hope
>   Or past the Horn go trolling,
> Find a place to clinch thy rope
>   And hear the sea-bells tolling.
> Forget thy home: in his own land
>   Ne'er was prophet heeded;
> And shell-bound pearls no price command
>   Before they are un-seated.

"This counsel should suffice thee," he said, "if thou wouldst but take it!"

Whereat I made known to him the cause of my reproach, and desired that he pardon me; which he did, and hoped that he too might be pardoned. He furnished me with provisions, omitting nothing; and did me the honor of seeing me on board, as he would a kinsman. I then took my leave, much deploring the necessity of parting from him, and heartily wishing that mother and child had died.

NOTES

Abū Zayd's tirades (§39.2) are based on four speeches from Melville's *Moby-Dick*: Father Mapple's nautical sermon on Job (Chapter 9), Captain Bildad's exhortations to Queequeg (Chapter 18), Elijah's warnings to Ishmael (Chapter 19), and Captain Ahab's rallying of the crew (Chapter 36). "Pious man deploring . . ." (§39.3) is based on the Qur'anic context of *al-mukramīn* (Q Yā Sīn 36:27), where a man who has heeded God's messengers wishes that his fellow townsmen would do the same. For *ṭawq* (usually "neck-ring," §39.5) Steingass has "necklace" (*Assemblies*, 98), but I understand rather a garment with an opening for the neck, as al-Sharīshī calls it a *thawb* (a long shirt, *Sharḥ*, 4:304). I use the word "shirt" as the eighteenth-century term following Burnston, "Baby Linen." The pseudo-lullaby in §39.6 is based on "London Bridge," first published in 1744. "Baby Bunting" is from the lullaby of that name, first published in 1784.

"Before I could say 'Jack Robinson'" is an expression first attested in 1778 (*OED*).

"At a moment when he could do so unperceived, Abu Zayd covered up the writing" (§39.7): the original is much shorter but of uncertain meaning. Abū Zayd covers or blots out (*ṭamasa*) the writing, with no explanation of why, and he does so *ʿalā ghaflah*, that is, at a moment when he or others aren't paying attention. Obviously chosen to rhyme with *taflah*, *ghaflah* offers no clear meaning in this context. Al-Sharīshī offers no explanation of it and Rückert leaves it out: "thereupon he rubbed out what he had written" ("*darauf zerrieb er das Geschriebene*," *Verwandlungen*, 232). Steingass has "he blotted out the writing unawares" (99), which is correct, but no clearer than the original. The translation follows de Sacy's explanation that *ghaflah* means some inadvertence on the part of the audience (de Sacy, *Séances*, 1:439).

"Oweis El-Karanee" is Uways al-Qaranī, a pious early Muslim who lived in poverty and whose attributes were described by the Prophet before the two met. Dubeis El-Asadee is Dubays al-Asadī, head of the Mazyadids, a quasi-independent Arab dynasty based in central Iraq, and a generous patron of scholars. He was reportedly delighted to have been mentioned in the *Impostures* (al-Sharīshī, *Sharḥ*, 4:313; see also my note to §0.3).

The verses in §39.8 have the form (but not the diction) of "A South Sea Ballad," in Swift, Gulliver's Travels, 275–77.

BIBLIOGRAPHY

Burnston, Sharon. "Baby Linen, or How to Make a Basic Essential Layette for Eighteenth Century Re-enactor Infants." http://sharonburnston.com/baby_linen/shirt.html.

[Cooper, Mary.] *Tommy Thumb's-Song Book . . . by Nurse Lovechild*. Lumsden: Glasgow, 1815. Originally published 1744. http://archive.org/details/tommythumbssongbooloveiala.

Melville, Herman. *Moby-Dick*. Edited by Harrison Hayford and Hershel Parker. New York: Norton, 1967.

———. *Moby-Dick*. Read by Frank Muller. Audible Audio edition. Recorded Books, 1987.

[Swift, Jonathan]. *Gulliver's Travels*, by Dean Smith. Philadelphia: Wanamaker, 1800.

Imposture 40

Iran go Brágh

*Like Impostures 9 and 45, this Imposture has Abū Zayd and his
wife take a trumped-up case before a judge with the aim of loosening his purse strings. Here al-Ḥarīrī has perfected the form:
each of the litigants produces a speech and a poem, and both
poems make a difference to the plot. The judge has his innings,
and even the bailiff has some lines. The subtext, oddly enough,
has to do with anal intercourse, which—according to the litigant's trumped-up tale, anyway—leaves the wife unsatisfied
and provides the pretext for much of the wordplay. But the real
showpieces are the speeches in which man and wife invoke the
cultural heroes of early Islam, male and female, to describe just
how much they (allegedly) despise each other. The theme of the
slanging match brings to mind the quarrel between Bessie Bur-
gess and Mrs. Gogan in Seán O'Casey's play* The Plough and
the Stars *(1926). Abū Zayd (here called Buséad) and company
will therefore speak early-twentieth-century Irish English or
Hiberno-English, as described by the educator, antiquarian,
and music collector Patrick Weston Joyce (d. 1914). The Arabic
and Persian names in the text have been put into the forms they
might plausibly take in Gaeilge.*

Arthur O'Hannan reported: 40.1

I was just after puttin' it before me to ride the breeze out of Tabroís. 'Twas no place for a spalpeen, let alone a lord, for there wasn't a soft heart or an open hand in it. So 'twas cuttin' me stick I was, and lookin' for fellows to travel the road with, when who should I meet but Buséad of Searúg and he wrapped in a coat amidst a women's prashameen.

"How are you getting on?" I asked. "And where are you going, with all your care?"

He pointed to one of the ladies. With her pookeen drawn back from her face she was as fair as May, but she was looking scunnered and no mistake.

"I married herself," says he, "for to wash off the clat of lonesomeness and comfort me on the shaughraun, but from that day out 'tis nothing with her but the heart-scald. When it comes to me rights, she puts the pot in the tailor's link, and I to thole more than a body can bear. Now the breath is barely in and out of me, just enough to sing the ullagone. So we're a-kempin' to the Brehon to ask him to show Murrogh to the one in the wrong. If he sets things right between us, well and good; otherwise, the divorce it is, and many a dry eye after!"

Well, said I to meself, I'm no great help in a mullaberta, but why shouldn't I see the dergaboo and the victor crowned? So I dropped me packing like a hot potato and set off after Buséad.

Now the Brehon was a man who'd heard the money jingling in his 40.2 mother's pockets before he was born. Why, you wouldn't put it past him to wrangle over a striffin!

When he arrived, Buséad to fall on his knees and say, "God bless your honour and help him! This pooka horse of mine is ree and won't be carried, while I'm docile as the lamb with her, I am, and show her more dooraght than she shows herself."

"Yerra!" says the Brehon to the lady. "Don't you know that disobedience angers the Lord? It's a good warrant for a skelp!"

"Ah, but himself likes to come in by the back door," says she. "'If you can't fill a hole,' they say, 'fill its neighbour.'"

The Brehon turned on Buséad. "Blast your soul! So it's in a bog you'd sow your seed, is it then, and far from the nest you'd look for eggs? Be off out of that, and bad cess to you!"

"Well, she's an ol' rip of a blasted liar, by the hokey she is!" said Buséad.

"Believe him and who'll believe you?" she said to the Brehon. "I swear by the One who put wings on the ostrich and rings on the dove that he's the liar, with his soul wizened up in the arts and dodgeries!"

With that Buséad started up blazin' mad, as if the blood were boilin' in his veins.

"You strap, you streel, you bone in the throat! Hateful to your husband you are, and a bother on the neighbors, bent on afflictin' me at home an' callin' me a liar outside doors. Do you disremember, after the haulin' home, how I found me bride? You were ugly as the devil's breeches, dry as a lime-burner's wig, tough as a gad, putrid as carrion, manky as the squitters, bloody as the curse, barefaced as a peeled egg, chillier than a stepmother's breath, thick as a ditch, and broader than the Toígris. I hushed all that up, so I did, and never put the shame on you. But you could be fair-faced Shoírínn, or Senbeagh, queen of Palmyra; clan-proud Choindiff, or Siobaidha with her kelters; Ráibeagh the anchorite, or Búirháinn of the shingerleens; O'Chanságh the poetess, or the Queen of blinkin' Sheba: I would scorn you for a helpmeet and spurn you for a dam!"

40.3   With that the lady to become a war-fury, bare her teeth in a snarl, and roll up her sleeves for a ballyragging.

"Pool-fouling scut!" she cried. "Blight on the herd! You've all the heart God gave a gaurlagh, you have, and none o' the brains He gave a flea. Don't you know the faults you're findin' are all yours, and the honour you're cuttin' into clouts is your own? Why, you're not worth the black of me nail! You're a worn-out old staggeen with a mortifyin' smell of goat fart about you, and you're worse than a keeroge in a cruiskeen for kickin' up a ruction. And you could be a sermonizer as sweet-mouthed as O'Tháseann, a professor as prodigious as O'Sheabaigh, a *grammaticus* as glamorous as O'Chailloíl, a rhapsode as ribald as Dearuír, an orator as orotund as Ciuss, a scriptorialist as skillful as O'Thamaíd, a declamator who declines like Bumreadh, and a folklorist as flahulach as Bukraíb, but never would I give you leave to plant a kippen in me bole or come near me basket with your boghaleen, if you go to that of it."

"I see you two are cat of a kind," said the Brehon. "A pity to spoil two houses! You, me man, quit your knauvshaulin' and let you take the high road with herself. And you, ma'am, so himself come by the front door, stop the Ballyhooly and spare him the rough side of your tongue."

"The devil I will," the lady replied, "unless he brings me lashin's and leavin's, and something to wear, before he rattles the hasp."

"Sorrow fly away with me," cried Buséad, "if I own more than the flitters on me back!"

The Brehon gave them a hard canny questing look and pondered their claim with a sceptical air. Then he glowered at them with the old devil between his two eyes.

"'Twasn't enough for ye, was it, to come into court with your blather and cheek, that you needs must try to walk up me sleeve too? Well, you're just after skellying, you are, and sittin' on the ground instead of your grug. The King of the Faithful—that the Lord may keep him, and preserve our religion!—appointed me to settle clampers, not pay debts. So now, by the Man above, who set me in this seat and gave me the power to loose and to bind, let you tell the truth and speak up plainly. And none of your hunker-sliding, or I'll bell you through the earth till you pass into a proverb!"

With that Buséad to lower his head like a serpent, and say "Whisper here!"

> Buséad am I, and she my bride: 40.4
> No less befits a man of pride.
> Our love has never been in doubt:
> Her growler's never gone without
> A gooter in its proper place.
> But now it's been five days, your grace,
> Since we've sipped, or had a sup;
> Our bellies are quite shrivell'd up,
> As ashen-faced we palely sway
> Like risen souls on Judgment Day.

Blind with hunger, we sought at last
To stake our lives on one more cast,
For e'en the proudest, when needs must,
Will swop his honour for a crust.
Behold my state, and if you say
I lie, ask what I ate today,
Then lock me up, or let me live:
Death, or life, is yours to give.

40.5 "Out of that poem I'll pardon your offence," said the Brehon, "and give you a present to take the cockles off your heart."

When the lady heard this she jumped up fit to be tied, and shouted—and she pointing at the hurlers on the ditch:

He's a fair man in most ways, the magistrate here in Tabroís;
But in this case, good people, his verdict provides no relief!
With me help-mate I came, and we flailed at his fruit-laden tree,
And me help-mate, God save him, did strike it and break the bough clean,
While I clutched at some branches that swayed too swiftly to seize.
But 'twas I who insensed me good help-mate in plain-chanting speech,
And 'tis I who will humbug the Brehon for failing to please!

40.6 Seein' how willin' they were to jeer him, the Brehon twigged that he was kilt an' quartered; for if he gave a present to one half of the couple and turned the other away empty-handed, he would be robbin' Peadar to pay Pól, or prostratin' only twice at the evenin' paddhereen. So he glowered and glared, and fretted and fumed, and hemmed and hawed, and turned northwards by left and back again, cryin' a thousand murthers. Then he commenced to chaw the rag agin his office, callin' it a catalogue of catastrophes and crimes, and givin' the jaw to anyone foolish enough to seek appointment. "Wirrasthru!" he said, groanin' like a poor man despoiled of his brill-yauns, and moanin' as if he didn't care two rows of pins about givin' rise to goster. "One skirmish it was; must two arrows strike me down? Must I pay both claims to settle a single case? And how in the world will I settle both at once? Ullilu!"

With that he turned to his bailiff, or bumbailiff. "Is today a day for judgings and arraignments, or orders and detainments? 'Tis not! 'Tis a woeful day: a day to pay through the nose, a day of ignominy and infamy, a day of loss and destitution, a day that proves your judge's judgment lacking. Now rid me of that caffler and his targe! Give them a kelter each, dismiss the officers, and close the door. Then let you proclaim today an inauspicious day. Announce that the Brehon is grumagh and let no more disputants come in."

"That will do, sir," said the bumbailiff, and he blirting a bit by the way he was so distressed. Then he to pay Buséad and his bride the yellow kelters. "Oh," he said, "there's no ho to you two for kimmeens at all at all. But be not so bold in the Brehons' courts, and restrain the foulness of your tongue. Not every judge is the Brehon of Tabroís, and not every doggerel has its day."

"The likes of you," they said, "do honor to the bumbailiffery, and we're terrible thankful entirely."

'Twas then they rose to go, just after winning two kelters and reddening two brosnas under the Brehon's heart.

GLOSSARY

All unmarked items, except for the descriptions of figures from Arabic literary history, come from the alphabetical word list in Joyce's *English* (JE). Items marked JE plus a page number come from the text proper. SIE stands for Moylan, *Southern Irish English*. OCP stands for O'Casey, *Plough*.

40.1

put before oneself to   resolve to (JE 39)

spalpeen   "a low rascal"

in it   there (see SIE 66–67)

cuttin' me stick   preparing to leave

Buséad   Abū Zayd

prashameen   "a little group all clustered together"

all your care   "your family, those persons that are under your care" (JE 32)

pookeen   a cloth or headgear that covers the face

scunnered   disgusted (see also *OED*)

clat   dirt, clay

on the shaughraun   wandering in search of work

the heart-scald   "a great vexation or mortification"

puts the pot, etc.   to "delay the performance of any work . . . with some secret object in view"

thole   endure

sing the ullagone   lament

40.2

striffin   "the thin pellicle or skin on the inside of an egg-shell"

ree   almost unmanageable, of a horse

carry   lead or drive

dooraght   "tender care and kindness"

yerra   "take care, look out"

skelp   blow

come in by the back door   have anal intercourse

be off out of that   go away (JE, s.v. "out")

cess   luck

rip   "a coarse ill-conditioned woman with a bad tongue"

ol' rip of a blasted liar   OCP, cited in SIE, 128

believe him, etc.   he's lying (JE 13)

soul wizened up in the arts and dodgeries   OCP, cited in SIE 128

strap   "a bold forward girl or woman"

streel   "a lazy untidy woman"

disremember   forget (also OCP, cited in SIE 123)

kemp   to race against someone in finishing a task

Brehon   a judge or lawyer, after Brehon law, "the old native law of Ireland"

show Murrogh   cause to suffer (my derivation)

mullaberta   arbitration

dergaboo   fight

haulin' home   "bringing home the bride, soon after the wedding, to her husband's house"

gad   a withe, that is, "a twig or branch, as of willow or osier, used for binding or tying, and sometimes for plaiting" (OED)

manky   filthy

squitters   diarrhea (this and the preceding are widely attested modern terms)

the curse   an Irish-American term for menstruation (see, e.g., MUM, "Words," under "Ireland")

ditch   earthen wall (JE 248)

kelters   money, coins

shingerleens   "small bits of finery; ornamental tags and ends of ribbons, bow-knots, tassels, &c. hanging on dress, curtains, furniture, &c" (JE)

40.3

war-fury   a terrifying pre-Christian goddess (see JE, 177)

ballyrag   "to give fierce abuse in torrents"

scut   "the tail of a hare or rabbit: often applied in scorn to a contemptible fellow"

gaurlagh   baby

clouts   rags (JE 137)

staggeen   "worn-out worthless old horse"

keeroge   beetle

cruiskeen   jar

ruction   fighting

flahulach   generous

kippen   "any little bit of stick"

bole   a shelved recess in a room

boghaleen   the same as crusheen, "a stick with a flat crosspiece fastened at bottom for washing potatoes in a basket"

if you go, etc.   "often added on to a statement to give great emphasis, amounting almost to a sort of defiance of contradiction or opposition" (JE 10)

cat of a kind   "like each other and both objectionable"

a pity to spoil, etc.   said of two bad people, apparently meaning that

40.4

growler   vulva

they should be kept together rather than be allowed to spoil two houses instead of just the one (see JE 87)

knauvshaul   grumble, scold, mutter

so   if (JE 329–30)

lashin's and leavin's   "plenty and to spare . . . specially applied to food at meals"

rattle the hasp   to dance on a door taken down for that purpose (JE 163), here adopted as a figure for shaking the furniture

flitters   rags

to walk up me sleeve   try to trick me (JE 193); on "me" for "my" see JE 103.

skelly   "to aim askew and miss the mark"

on one's grug   squatting

clamper   dispute, wrangle

Man above   a direct translation of a Gaeilge expression for "God"

hunker-slide   "to slide on ice sitting on the hunkers . . . instead of standing up straight . . . hence to act with duplicity"

bell you, etc.   from "bell you through the parish," i.e., spread news of some outrage of yours (JE 187)

whisper here   listen to me (JE)

gooter   penis (Coughlan, "Everyday English")

40.5

take the cockles, etc.   cheer up
  (JE 194)

fit to be tied   very upset (JE 125)

40.6

twig   understand, realize

paddhereen   prayer

a thousand murthers   "a general
  exclamation of surprise, alarm, or
  regret" (spelled "murders" in the
  wordlist, but "murthers" elsewhere
  in JE)

chawing the rag   "continually grumbling, jawing, and giving abuse"

give the jaw   be impudent to

agin   against (JE, 31)

wirrasthru   "a term of pity; alas"

brill-yauns   "the poor articles of furniture in a peasant's cottage"

goster   gossip

ullilu   "an interjection of sorrow"

bumbailiff   "A contemptuous synonym of bailiff . . . 'A bailiff of the

insense   explain how to do something, train someone (JE 277–78)

humbug   make fun of (JE, s.v. "hand")

  meanest kind; one that is employed
  in arrests' (Johnson)" (OED; used
  twice in Joyce, *Ulysses*)

pay through the nose   "be made to
  pay, against your grain, the full sum
  without delay or mitigation"

caffler   "a contemptible little fellow
  who gives saucy cheeky foolish
  talk"

targe   "a scolding woman"

grumagh   gloomy, ill-humored

blirt   weep

by the way he was   pretending to be
  (JE 38)

no ho   no equal

kimmeen   "sly deceitful trick"

redden   to light

brosna   a bundle of sticks for firing

NOTES

Though rambling and unsystematic, P. W. Joyce's *English as We Speak It in Ireland* (1910) is wide-ranging and keenly observed, and the text and glossary contain almost all the words needed for this Imposture—provided that one freely mix terms from different regions, which Abū Zayd and company do, with apologies to historians of Hiberno-English. Words borrowed or adopted from Irish were cross-checked against Terence Patrick Dolan's *Dictionary of Hiberno-English* (1998) and the online *Hiberno-English Archive*. For terms not in Joyce, including Standard English terms that needed period attestation, the translation draws on *Ulysses* (1922), by another, more famous Joyce—namely, James (d. 1941). Also very helpful was Séamas Moylan's *Southern Irish English*

(1998), which provides a modern linguistic description and a sampling of texts, including O'Casey's ballyragging scene, with commentary. The only historically unattested contemporary words are "growler" and "gooter" ("vulva" and "penis," §40.4). These may have been used in the past as well, but I have no attestation for them. The Gaelicized Arabic and Persian names were created for me by Slavomír Čéplö.

"Tabroís" (§40.1) is Tabriz, a town in what is now northwestern Iran. On the "'Twas . . . I was . . ." construction see JE 51 and SIE, 54–55. On "Who should I meet but . . ." see JE 83. "As fair as May" comes from JE 206. "And no mistake": see JE 10. On "herself" see JE 46–47. On the use of the definite article in expressions like "the heart-scald" see JE 87–88. Joyce explains the expression "puts the pot in the tailor's link" by noting that

> tailors commonly worked in the houses of the families who bought their own material and employed them to make the clothes. The custom was to work till supper time, when their day ended. Accordingly the good housewife often hung the pot-hangers on the highest hook or link of the pot-hooks so as to raise the supper-pot well up from the fire and delay the boiling (JE 168–69).

"Now the breath is barely . . ." comes from JE 132. "Show Murrogh" is my derivation based on the following:

> During the War of the Confederation in Ireland in the seventeenth century Murrogh O'Brien earl of Inchiquin took the side of the Government against his own countrymen, and committed such merciless ravages among the people that he is known to this day as "Murrogh the Burner"; and his name has passed into a proverb for outrage and cruelty. When a person persists in doing anything likely to bring on heavy punishment of some kind, the people say "If you go on in that way you'll see Murrogh," meaning "you will suffer for it."

For "dry eye" see JE 18. On "hot potato" see JE 188.

"Heard the money . . ." (§40.2) comes from JE 128. "Put it past him . . ." comes from JE 300. "Striffin" renders an Arabic word that means "the gunk flicked off a toothpick." On constructions like "Buseád to fall" see JE 45–46 and SIE, 53–54.

A "pooka horse" is a goblin

that generally appears in the form of a horse, but sometimes as a bull, a buck-goat, &c. The great ambition of the pooka horse is to get some unfortunate wight on his back; and then he gallops furiously through bogs, marshes, and woods, over rocks, glens, and precipices; till at last when the poor wretch on his back is nearly dead with terror and fatigue, the pooka pitches him into some quagmire or pool or briar-brake, leaving him to extricate himself as best he can.

"It's a good warrant for a skelp" (§40.2): the original refers to Q Nisāʾ 4:34, which allows striking one's wife under certain conditions. On the various inter-pretations of this verse see Ali, *Sexual Ethics*, Ch. 7; Bauer, *Gender Hierarchy*, 161–218. "Fill a hole": the original means something like "punish a person for his neighbor's crime," here meaning "have anal instead of vaginal sex." The trans-lation is a double entendre based on the modern Irish use of "hole" to mean "anus." On "by the hokey" see JE 77. On "with that" see JE 351–52. On the devil's breeches see JE 60–61. On "Dry as a lime-burner's wig" see JE 170. On "chillier than a stepmother's breath" see JE 139. "Toígris" is the Tigris, the river that runs through Baghdad.

For purposes of euphony, I have changed the order in which the historical figures appear. They are: Shīrīn ("Shoírínn"), heroine of the Persian epic *Khos-row and Shirin* by Nizami Ganjavi (d. early seventh/thirteenth century), which al-Sharīshī calls "a famous Persian story in verse" (*qiṣṣah manẓūmah mashhūrah bi l-ʿajamiyyah*; Sharḥ 4:332); Zenobia ("Senbeagh"), a third-century queen of Palmyra and a figure of early Arabic historical legend; Zubaydah ("Siobaidha"), an Abbasid princess (d. 216/831–32) famous for sponsoring the building of way stations and cisterns along the pilgrimage road, as well as for her lavish life-style; Khindif ("Choindiff"), the foremother of the Arabs of the Hijaz (Sharīshī, *Sharḥ*, 4:347–49); Rābiʿah ("Ráibeagh"; d. 185/801), a Basran ascetic, mystic, and poet later venerated as a great Sufi; Būrān ("Búirháinn"), whose wedding to the caliph al-Maʾmūn (r. 198–218/813–33) was famous for its extravagance; al-Khansāʾ ("O'Chanságh"; d. mid-seventh c.?), the most famous composer of elegies in Arabic; and the Queen of Sheba is the legendary monarch whose en-counter with Solomon is described in Q Naml 27:15–44.

The original for "pool-fouling" (§40.3) is "meaner than Mādir," referring to a tribesman who (according to al-Ḥarīrī's commentary on this episode) reportedly defecated in a water hole so others could not draw from it. The original of "blight on the herd" says "more ill-omened than Qāshir," a camel stallion who (according to al-Ḥarīrī's commentary on this episode) caused the death of any female he mated with. "Black of me nail" comes from JE 216.

The figures mentioned in §40.3 are: al-Ḥasan al-Baṣrī ("O'Tháseann"; d. 110/728), a pietist famous for his admonitions; al-Shaʿbī ("O'Sheabaigh "; d. between 103/721 and 110/728?), a prolific transmitter of legal and historical reports; al-Khalīl ibn Aḥmad ("O'Chailloíl"; d. between 160/776 and 175/791), a pioneering grammarian and lexicographer credited with the first systematic description of Arabic prosody; Jarīr ("Dearuír"; d. 110/728–29?), a poet most famous for his performances of invective; Quss ibn Sāʿidah ("Ciuss"), a semilegendary sage of pre-Islamic Arabia, celebrated for his oratory; ʿAbd al-Ḥamīd ("O'Thamaíd"; d. 132/750), an Umayyad secretary well known for his letters, which helped establish prose as a form in Arabic; Abū ʿAmr ibn al-ʿAlāʾ ("Bumreadh"; d. ca. 154/770), a Qurʾan reciter credited with one of the seven canonical readings; and Abū Qurayb ("Buckraib"), better known as al-Aṣmaʿī (d. 213/828), an early Abbasid philologist credited with some sixty works on Arabic vocabulary and related topics.

Ballyhooly is "a village near Fermoy in Cork, formerly notorious for its faction fights, so that it has passed into a proverb. A man is late coming home and expects Ballyhooly from his wife, i.e. 'the length and breadth of her tongue'" (JE). On "sorrow fly away" see JE 70. On "questing" see JE 39. "With the old devil between his two eyes" comes from JE 57.

The poem in §40.4 adopts the iambic tetrameter form favored by Jonathan Swift (d. 1745). For examples see McCormack, Irish Poetry, 21–45.

On "out of that poem" (§40.5) see JE 26. "Hurlers on the ditch" is "said in derision of persons who are mere idle spectators sitting up on high watching the game whatever it may be and boasting how they would do the devil an' all if they were only playing" (JE 248). The wife's poem follows the form P. W. Joyce uses to translate Gaeilge poems into English—namely, anapestic tetrameter with a single assonantal end rhyme and another single internal rhyme repeated as often as possible (see JE 55).

On "kilt an' quartered" (§40.6) see JE 123. With respect to "paddhereen," an evening prayer consisting of only two prostrations would not be valid. On "northwards by left" Joyce notes:

> The cardinal points are designated on the supposition that the face is turned to the east: a custom which has descended in Ireland from the earliest times of history and tradition, and which also prevailed among other ancient nations. Hence in Irish "east" is "front"; "west" is "behind" or "back"; north is "left hand"; and south is "right hand" (JE 167; Arabic *shamāl* also means "north" as well as "left").

"Didn't care two rows of pins" comes from JE 192. For "how in the world" see JE 49. For "at all at all" see JE 43. "Terrible thankful entirely" comes from JE 104.

BIBLIOGRAPHY

Ali, Kecia. *Sexual Ethics and Islam.* Expanded and revised edition. Oxford: OneWorld, 2006.

Bauer, Karen. *Gender Hierarchy in the Qur'ān: Medieval Interpretations, Modern Responses.* Cambridge: Cambridge University Press, 2017.

Coughlan, Gerry. "Everyday English and Slang in Ireland." http://www.irishslang.co.za/print.htm.

Dolan, Terence Patrick. *A Dictionary of Hiberno-English: The Irish Use of English.* Gill and Macmillan: Dublin, 1998.

———. A Hiberno-English Archive. http://www.hiberno-english.com:80/archive.php.

Joyce, James. *Ulysses.* http://www.gutenberg.org/files/4300/4300-h/4300-h.htm.

Joyce, P. W. *English as We Speak It in Ireland.* London: Longmans, Green; Dublin: M. H. Gill & Son, 1910.

Mc Cormack, W. J., ed. *Irish Poetry.* New York: NYU Press, 2000.

Moylan, Séamas. *Southern Irish English: Review and Exemplary Texts.* Dublin: Geography Publications, 2009.

MUM. "Words for Menstruation." http://www.mum.org/words.html.

IMPOSTURE 41

THE CUP OF COUNSEL

In this Imposture, al-Ḥārith again takes Abū Zayd to task for exhorting others to repentance while continuing to drink. For his part, Abū Zayd insists al-Ḥārith is missing some obvious but unspecified point. As each party is insisting the other needs help, the English will be based on the jargon of psychology, counseling, and recovery.

A troubled patient self-reported: 41.1

In early adulthood, I experienced a regression to adolescence. This stage was characterized by pleasure-seeking and heterosexual promiscuity. With the onset of aging, however, a diminished libido and the prospect of death triggered guilt feelings over my long-neglected religious duties. Now I felt the urge to pursue conscious restructuring of my maladaptive behavior. A first step was to visualize my good deeds inflicting corporal punishment on my sins and driving them away. I also imagined myself racing against my sins and beating them to the finish line. My pursuit of proprietary rights over sex workers, as well as my fixation on early-morning intercourse with virginal partners, began to feel ego-dystonic. At the same time, relationship-building with peers who could serve as role models of ritual performance came to seem more and more appealing. So I committed myself to interacting only with devout men who were using abstinence to help them move gracefully toward the end of life. When confronted with delinquent, work-averse individuals, I practiced self-care through avoidant behavior.

41.2   Eventually a geographic life-change put me on the path to Tinnis. One day I visited the local mosque and experienced a surge of positive affect. But my perceptual field was dominated by a self-sufficient, extroverted, highly articulate subject who was speaking to a gathering crowd.

"Psychic suffering," he was saying, "is intrinsic! To feel secure in a world full of anxiety-producing stimuli, all of us rely on constructions of reality that turn out to be illusory. Our need to form attachments leads to morbid preoccupation with unattainable objects. Unfortunately, the fact that those attachments do not help us prepare for post-mortem continuity of personality makes it no less painful when they end. I swear it by the *Urvater*, the *Grundprinzip*, and Moses's monotheism: more conscious cognition can curb substance abuse, while real mindfulness allows us to grieve our dysfunctional histories.

"Tell me: have you thought about breaking the pattern you've set? And what the consequences are of staying on the same course? How do you feel about the hurtful things you've done? What about making amends to everyone you've harmed—and doing it now, before it's too late? Now, before the death drive leaves you in an inorganic state?

"Few pathologies are more destructive than risking long-term anguish for the sake of momentary material advantage. Why do we hoard possessions that will only benefit our heirs? Nor is it easy to understand how somatic manifestations of aging can fail to arouse compensatory remorse."

41.3   Then he offered a multi-step plan:

> Evaluate your behavior:
>   Is it normative for your age?
> Or are you suffering regression
>   To an inappropriate stage?
> Are you tremulous and alopecic
>   But still pursuing pleasure
> When you should be in elder care
>   By any clinical measure?
> Is your way of acting out
>   Becoming a source of tension?

Have friends begun to comment
    And talk of intervention?
Well, your moral sense has atrophied!
    You stink to heaven high!
But there's still time to work it through
    And be blissful when you die.
So call on a Higher Power!
    Lay aside your fears!
If you don't, there's not much point
    In living on for years.
Start by supporting survivors:
    Need is no excuse.
Face abusers with a loving heart
    And forgive them their abuse.
Support those in recovery!
    Don't let them slip away:
The one you help up when he falls
    Steadies you on Judgment Day.

This is the cup of counsel
    Given me by men now gone.
If you see others thirsting
    Drink deep, and pass it on.

With that the speaker concluded his explicit directive to mourn the   **41.4** harm we'd done to ourselves and others. Then, after an interval below the threshold of perception, an adolescent boy, who seemed to be a practicing ecdysiast, leapt up and addressed the crowd.

"All of you," he said, "seem so receptive! If you understood the verses and you're ready to change, make sure your behavior reflects it: practice your generosity on me! Look: I exhibit full correlation between latent and manifest personality traits—God loves me for who I am. But I can't confront any more stressors without some support. Help me, and may a Higher Power help you help yourselves!"

Meanwhile the older man was using vocalizations to move the crowd to empathy. Soon the filthy lucre was piling up faster than an OCPD patient hoards up junk. When his bag was full, the boy wriggled out of the circle and strutted off, praising the altruistic orientation of the people of Tinnis. Once the boy had separated himself from the group, the old man seemed to present a sudden onset of anhedonia. He asked the group to join him in raising their hands in prayer. Then he disappeared as well.

41.5   *The self-report continued:*

"I need to find out who that was," I thought to myself. "Does that make me some crazy stalker?"

I followed the old man as he strode away, looking emotionally unavailable. But when we reached what felt like a safe space for him, he initiated the interaction, leaning in and assuming a more extroverted demeanor.

"How did you feel about that little demonstration of aptitude?" he said.

"Euphoric!" I responded.

"That boy's my direct descendant," he said. "But still, a skill set like that is extremely low-incidence."

"Not given the parent," I said. "Studies on fruit trees and flammable substances show a similarly high degree of heritability."

That comment took him to a joyful place.

41.6   Then he asked if I'd be open to prolonging our interaction. "We could affirm relational ties through substance abuse," he said.

"I'm disappointed," I said. "Can you understand why? When you urge people to do something and then do the opposite yourself, it's hard not to think of dissociative personality disorder."

He smiled mirthlessly but didn't challenge my diagnosis. He started walking away, then changed his mind and turned back. "Keep this in mind," he said, "but don't tell anyone it came from me:

> I drink to dull my affect!
>   If you flag it I just say:
> 'It's chemotherapeutic:
>   Drink up or go away!'"

Then he said, "I'm going somewhere where I can engage in some sustained bingeing. If that doesn't work for you interpersonally, then it's time to terminate. We're facing different directions right now. And let me caution you against developing an obsession with tracking me down."

The troubled patient self-reported:

The termination triggered real grief—so much so that I fantasized about never having met him.

NOTES

Like Imposture 38, this Imposture seems to have been written early on and then moved toward the end of the collection to avoid the appearance of progressive improvement. Inspired by the phrase "cup of counsel" that appears in one of the poems (§41.4), I decided to use the episode as an opportunity to bring out a theme that runs through the whole collection: the enigmatic behavior of the protagonists. Why does al-Ḥārith travel relentlessly from place to place? Why does he find Abū Zayd wherever he goes? Why does he usually fail to recognize him? Why does Abū Zayd often treat him abusively? Why is al-Ḥārith always so sorry to see him go? And what role do the other figures—Abū Zayd's wife, or wives, and son, or sons—play in this family drama?

Amateur psychoanalysis, of the kind critics used to apply to literary texts, can suggest various answers to these questions. The relationship may be homosocial, as Shawkat Toorawa, applying Eve Sedgwick's term, might call it (Toorawa, "Language"). Or it may be one of repressed same-sex attraction. Or al-Ḥārith and Abū Zayd may be two aspects of the same disassociated personality (as seems to be the case for the protagonists of the modern Arabic novel *Season of Migration to the North*, by Tayeb Salih). This last possibility has always appealed to me, since it explains why al-Ḥārith repeatedly fails to recognize his friend, why al-Ḥārith's language is almost indistinguishable from Abū Zayd's, and why their world is so disturbingly different from ours—different in ways that suggest a psychotic break with reality. Also, the role of religion, which provides the language for expressing suffering, and holds out the hope of transcending it, opens up the field of psychology of religion as a body of theory that might someday illuminate the world of the Impostures.

In search of an appropriate idiom for the English, I have consulted several reference works in the field of psychology, without of course aspiring to any kind of clinical or theoretical consistency. Fortunately, modern psychological language runs the gamut from statistics and cognitive science to genetics and philosophy of religion, and so could supply an equivalent for nearly everything in the Arabic. In the rare instances where it did not, I dipped into the language of recovery and of New Age movements. The aim was not to mock therapeutic language, but to use it in order to most forcibly make the point that the Impostures are full of disturbing behavior that is never explained or resolved, whether at the level of plot or in the realm of theory; and that struggling to understand what is happening in these texts can help us see the shortcomings of our own theories of self.

BIBLIOGRAPHY

Colman, Andrew M. A *Dictionary of Psychology*. 3rd edition. Oxford: Oxford University Press, 2008.

Kazdin, Alan E. *Encyclopedia of Psychology*. Oxford: Oxford University Press, 2000.

Laplanche, J., and J.-B. Pontalis. *The Language of Psycho-Analysis*. Translated by Donald Nicholson-Smith. New York: Norton, 1973.

IMPOSTURE 42

DISCRUCIATE THIS!

The theme of this episode is riddles, which Abū Zayd will produce in imitation of those by Jonathan Swift (d. 1745). Swift's riddles are short, lighthearted poems, many about everyday objects. For the narration and the other verses, Abū Zayd and al-Ḥārith (here called "Harry Under-the-Hatches") will use the thieves' jargon documented by the bon vivant Francis Grose (d. 1791) and by his successor, the thief, forger, and embezzler James Hardy Vaux (d. after 1841).

Harry Under-the-Hatches tipped us the traveller: 42.1

My journeys canted me to and fro, and far down Jumblegut Lane did fancy take me, till any place was home and every man a brother. Yet I trod no track nor sought any society, but for one purpose: to cadge a bit of that learning, that comforts a man in sorrow and raises him in honour. At length I became known for this kidney, and as celebrated for it, as the tribe of Ózra for the green sickness, and the clan of Aboo Sófra for snabbling coves in battle.

Once laying my camel's colquarron on the ground at Najrán, and finding there some trusty trouts and Trojans, I took its assemblies for my Kit-Kat Club, resorting there for raillery and flim flams all the darkman's. I thus came to witness, by dint of frequentation early in the morning as well as late at night, divers occasions of joy and sorrow.

One day having joined the multitudes at a fine banging assembly, I 42.2
saw a Death's head upon a mop-stick, dressed in more rags than ribands.

He came down on his marrow-bones and saluted us like a clapperdogeon. "Rum dukes and whip jacks!" he cried. "A good pair of top lights is worth two buffers, and a leary cove needs no peeper to spy the dawn. Now you've twigged my kelter, what say you? Will you give me a lift, or will you sherk your duty?"

"Bloody end to us!" they replied. "You meant to cadge the swells, but now you've put our back up."

He begged the company in God's name to tell him, how he hobbled them, that they should serve him so rudely.

"We were playing at carry-witchets," they said, "with puzzlewits for bolts!"

Unable to contain himself, Captain Queernabs mocked anyone who lost at riddling, and called the game ridiculous.

The chaff-cutters among the company were nettled and gave the old file a good ragging. Assuming an air of contrition, he tried to stall off his sneering, but they continued to rattle him off, leaving decency and good manners a little on the left hand.

"Indulgence," he said at length, "is the mark of gentility, so stash the clapper claw and stow the chivey. Let us play at carry-witchets, then, and may the best man win!"

These bene whiddes mollified his tormentors and banked their glimmer down. Assenting to his proposal, they invited him to take the first turn. He paused only as long as it takes to slip a foot into a sandal-loop or draw a girth around a grogham.

42.3   With a "Cat's your uncle!" he rhymed a riddle on a punkah:

> For all my dashing to and fro,
> Outside four walls I never go.
> My master bids me make a draft,
> Though he, like me, is made of baft.
> I spend the summer on the rack
> And all the winter hanging slack."

42.4   "And here's another, o haberdashers of pronouns, if you please!" 'Twas on a harness-rope for climbing trees:

By her banished, tho' grown from her root,
Now embraces her, and plucks the fruit.

"And here's another," he said, "to tax the thalamus!" 'Twas on the writ-   42.5
ing-reed or common calamus:

My tongue is slit, my mouth is furr'd,
And yet I carry Allah's Word.
A magpye of the blackest dye,
But silent when my throat runs dry.
All languages I can command,
Yet not a word I understand.

"And another," he said, "as easy as one-two-three," on a pencil for   42.6
antimony:

Two wedded sisters do I serve,
And blacken, as I dip and swerve,
Each one's skirts, before I spin
To service her impatient twin,
Unlike those husbands who prefer
One of their wives, and favor her.

"Or this, for word-grubbers and wielders of the quill," he said, puzzling   42.7
on a water-mill:

Though I only run in place,
I cannot turn without a race;
Half *sub aqua*, half afloat,
Paddle-thrust, yet not a boat;
Lashed all day, but never rammed,
My tears flow best when they are dammed.

When he'd canted five carry-witchets in a row, he said, "I dropped   42.8
those in good twig, so gun them and have them for your own. Now will

you gather your skirts and shift your bob, or take five more birds of a feather?"

Though taken all-a-mort by the codger's storm of eloquence, the company was all-a-gog for more. "You've so queered us," they said, "that we can't strike a glimmer in your pratts. If you make it a full ten riddles, it must be your own doing."

So, as cock-a-hoop as one whose arrow has struck the butt and discomfited his rival, the old file praised God's judgment, then pronounced this riddle on the gugglet:

> My lid lacks an eye, my neck has no head;
> I lie on a rack, tho' tucked into bed.
> In summer beloved, when lovers repine,
> In winter be-shunned, by no fault of mine;
> My coat is well padded, its colours are gay,
> And I wear it all summer, tho' indoors I stay.

42.9 Then he bared his yellow cogs and chaunted, "Here's another; all hail!" This one was on the finger-nail:

> Its wondrous secret no one knows:
> It never eats, and yet it grows!
> Sharpish, thus unwelcome, but
> Pushes back whene'er it's cut.

42.10 Then, bluff as bull beef, he cutty-eyed, saying: "Here's another to snatch!" This was on a sulfur match:

> Too valuable to do without,
> Tho' once I serve, you cast me out;
> Two heads have I, each one alike,
> And both suffice you for a strike
> No sooner made, than spells my doom,
> As the heads my form consume.

Then he roared like the town bull: "Another of mine!" This time it was 42.11
wine:

> So often praised in prose and verse,
> It makes men go from bad to worse;
> But let it spoil: strange to say,
> It does very little harm that way;
> Once warm and fiery, now gone pallid,
> It lends a pucker to a sallad.

Now clapping his stick under his fin, the old cove rose to box his trot- 42.12
ters. "Here's the tenth," he said, "to complete the tale." He recited this, on
a jeweler's scale:

> Borne aloft to the judge's seat,
> I give each man his proper mete.
> None seems to mind, truth be told,
> That gravel, to me, is good as gold,
> Nor that I am far from staid,
> And by a feather gently swayed:
> Nay! The more I tilt before their eyes
> The more they trust the king's assize.

The company applied itself to these conundrums, but their thoughts ran 42.13
hubble-de-shuff down blind alleys for so long that anyone could see they
were pitch-kettled. When he tired of watching them milk the pigeon, the
old codger said, "Enough humming and hawing! What are you yorking at?
Was it not your task to discruciate my carry-witchets, or admit to being
mutton-heads?"

"You beat us all hollow with your gallipot words," they said, "and made
us sing small; so it would be judgment to let you name your prize, and
carry off riches as well as honour."

So the old cuff imposed a tax on each conundrum, and collected it all in
the ready slap-bang. Then he put the company flash to all his riddles, discovering the carry-witchets and explaining all the puzzlewits. Afterwards

he tried to broom it, but the chief cock of the walk seized him by the rigging. "Tip us a nut before Mr. Nash is concerned," he said. "Stash the queer chant, cut the line, and tell us your clan."

42.14   The rum gagger kept his goggles on the ground so long that we began to smell a rat. But then, clapping his peepers full of tears, he chanted:

> I was born in Sarooj, in swell street,
> Snug as a kinchin mort;
> But 'twere slanging-dues concerned
> That took every joy of my heart.
> The baggage threw me a bale of bristles,
> And made me a knight of the road.
> I'm never at rest, and across the pond
> I've been lagged, and swallowed the toad;
> I wear the bands, and the stomach-worm gnaws,
> Cold charity cants me my grub;
> Today in Damascus, tomorrow in Nejd,
> Sleeping in the rough.
> O bitter days, all stiver-cramped,
> Pray tip me a tester bright!
> I have a bill on the dam of Má-rib
> From living the flash-cant life.

Then he breeched the lour and scoured off. We called after him on the humble suit, promising him rum quids if he would come back. But none of our yarns would do: he'd shifted his bob and binged avast.

GLOSSARY

42.1

under the hatches	in debt or distress	*snabbling coves*	killing men
tip the traveller	tell an unlikely story	*colquarron*	neck
cant	throw	*trusty trouts and Trojans*	true friends
Jumblegut Lane	rough road	*flim flams*	idle stories
kidney	disposition	*darkman's*	night

42.2

banging   great

Death's head upon a mop-stick   a poor, miserable, emaciated fellow

riband   ribbon

marrow-bones   knees

clapperdogeon   a born beggar

rum duke   jolly, handsome fellow

top lights   eyes

buffer   sworn witness

leary cove   person in the know

peeper   spyglass

twig   observe

kelter   condition, order

give a lift   assist

42.8

cant   throw out

drop in good twig   part with freely

gun   look at, examine

shift one's bob   move off, go away

all-a-mort   dumbfounded

all-a-gog   eager

42.9

cogs   teeth

42.10

bluff as bull beef   fierce, surly

42.12

fin   arm

42.13

hubble-de-shuff   confusedly

pitch-kettled   stumped

milk the pigeon   try in vain

york   look

mutton-headed   stupid

old cuff   old man

cadge the swells   beg from gentlemen

hobble   interrupt

carry-witchet   riddle

nettled   provoked

old file   old man

rag   abuse

rattle off   scold

stash   stop

clapper claw   scolding, abuse

stow   put aside

chivey   scolding

bene whiddes   good words

glimmer   fire

grogham   horse

queer   puzzle, confound

pratt   tinderbox

cock-a-hoop   elated, in high spirits

old file   old man

gugglet   water jar

cutty-eye   look askance

box one's trotters   leave, go away

the ready slap-bang   in cash, and right away

put someone flash to   explain to someone

broom it   make off, run away

chief cock of the walk   leader

rigging clothes

42.14

goggles eyes	*cants me my grub* tosses me my food
clapping his peepers full of tears start-ing to cry	*stiver-cramped* short of money
	tester a sixpence
in swell street prosperous	*flash cant* underworld jargon
threw me a bale of bristles cheated me using false dice	*breeched the lour* pocketed the money
knight of the road highwayman	*scoured off* ran away
lagged across the pond sent abroad as a punishment	*on the humble suit* submissively
	rum quids a rich haul
swallow the toad bear insults	*shifted his bob* moved off
wear the bands be hungry	*binged avast* went away

NOTES

The Arabic original is named after Najrān, a city once famous for its Christian population, located in what is today southwestern Saudi Arabia, near the border with Yemen. Although this episode appears late in the collection, it may have been written in an early phase when the only plot event in each Imposture is the surprise discovery of Abū Zayd's superior knowledge of whatever verbal art is being discussed. In this case, oddly, Abū Zayd is never actually named. The riddles themselves are introduced with their answers. One might imagine various reasons for this, but the result in any case is that one can relish the cleverness of the riddle without feeling pressure to guess the solution.

The so-called flash cant used here overlaps to some extent with the New York jargon documented by Matsell (see Imposture 7), and is used briefly also in Imposture 30. It has a special word, "carry-witchets," for "a sort of conundrum, puzzlewit, or riddle," though it is not clear to me whether a specific game is meant or, if so, what the rules were. Unless otherwise noted, the definitions here and in the Glossary come from Grose's *Classical Dictionary*.

"The green sickness" (§42.1) is a "disease of maids occasioned by celibacy," here used as an equivalent for the chaste love immortalized by the Arabic poets of the 'Udhrah tribe, here called "Ózra." Abū Ṣufrah (here called "Aboo Sófra") is Ẓālim ibn Surrāq or Ṣāriq, whose descendants, most notably al-Muhallab ibn Abī Ṣufrah, fought with ferocity on behalf of the Umayyad dynasty. The Kit-Kat

Club was "a society of gentlemen, eminent for wit and learning, who in the reign of queen Anne and George I, met at a house kept by one Christopher Cat."

"Whip jacks" (§42.2) are "rogues who having learned a few sea terms, beg with counterfeit passes, pretending to be sailors shipwrecked on the neighbouring coast." Here it translates *buḥūr al-nawāfil*, literally "seas of superfluities," which appears to mean "generous men," but the double meaning ("persons concerned with trivia") is probably intentional. Just as the whip jacks are pretending to be something they are not, the *buḥūr al-nawāfil* claim knowledge of Arabic but are easily bested by Abū Zayd. "Bloody end to us" was among "the favourite oaths of the thieves of the present day." "Captain Queernabs" is "a shabby ill-dressed fellow." A "chaff-cutter" is "one whose tongue is of great use to him, in order to silence an antagonist." "To stall off" is to resort to "a pretence, excuse, or prevarication—as a person charged with any fault, entering into some plausible story, to excuse himself," or "to avoid or escape any impending evil or punishment by means of artifice, submission, bribe, or otherwise" (Vaux, "Vocabulary," 212).

"Grinagog, the cat's uncle" (§42.3) is a phrase said of "a foolish grinning fellow." A punkah is a moistened piece of canvas suspended from the ceiling and pulled back and forth to cool a room.

"Harness-rope" (§42.4): my rendering of *ḥābūl*, a climbing apparatus consisting of a rope or strap of twisted fibers attached to a section of mesh. The rope is slung around the trunk of a palm tree and fastened around the climber's waist. By leaning back against the mesh, the climber frees his hands to collect dates ("Shāhid" shows one in use).

"All languages . . ." (§42.5) comes from Swift, "On a Pen," in *Poems*, II:62.

The riddle in §42.6 is about an applicator for kohl, which is a cosmetic and medicinal paste applied around the eyes.

"Word-grubbers" (§42.7) are "verbal critics, and also persons who use hard words in common discourse."

Abū Zayd's riddle in §42.8 is about "a green jar, covered with canvas . . . and lined between this cover and its own outer surface with a layer of straw, to keep the water in it cool in summer time" (Steingass, *Assemblies*, 258–59). The English word "gugglet" refers to "a long-necked vessel for holding water, usually made of porous earthenware, so that the contents are kept cool by evaporation" (*OED*).

The matches in §42.10 may be similar to the "sulfur-tipped sticks" mentioned in Nasrallah, *Treasure Trove*, 119, which were lit by being struck on granite. Al-Ḥarīrī's matches are described as having sulfur on both ends, apparently because, if one end failed, the user could try the other.

"Gallipot words" (§42.13) are difficult words, like those used by gallipots, that is, apothecaries, "from the assumed gravity and affectation of knowledge generally put on by the gentlemen of this profession." To "sing small" is "to be humbled, confounded, or abashed, to have little or nothing to say for one's-self." "It would be judgment": Judgment, says Vaux, is the ability to execute "the most intricate and hazardous projects; any thing accomplished in a masterly manner, is, therefore, said to have been done with judgment; on concerting or planning any operations, one party will say, I think it would be judgment to do so and so, meaning expedient to do it" ("Vocabulary," 182). "Discruciate" is a nonce word used by Swift (*Poems*, I:85) and seems to mean "solve." "Tip us a nut" means "give us something." Vaux explains that "to please a person by any little act of assiduity, by a present, or by flattering words, is called nutting him; as the present, etc., by which you have gratified them, is termed a nut" ("Vocabulary," 192). "To nash" is "to go away from, or quit, any place or company; speaking of a person who is gone, they say, he is *nash'd*, or *Mr. Nash is concerned*" ("Vocabulary," 191). A "chant" is "a person's name, address, or designation; thus, a thief who assumes a feigned name on his apprehension to avoid being known, or a swindler who gives a false address to a tradesman, is said to tip them a queer chant" ("Vocabulary," 162). To "cut the line" is to "put an end to the suspense in which you have kept anyone, by telling him the plain truth, coming to a final decision, etc." ("Vocabulary," 187).

"Rum gaggers" (§42.14) are "cheats who tell wonderful stories of their sufferings at sea, or when taken by the Algerines." "Kinchin mort" are "beggars' children carried at their mothers' backs in sheets." Vaux defines "slanging-dues" as follows: "When a man suspects that he has been curtailed, or cheated, of any portion of his just right, he will say, there has been *slanging-dues concerned*" ("Vocabulary," 206). "Baggage" is a "familiar epithet for a woman." I use it here to translate the Arabic *dunyā*, "earthly life," which poets often depict as a fickle woman. "A bill on the dam at Má-rib" is my Arabization of "a bill on the pump at Aldgate," meaning a worthless bill of exchange: that is, one drawn on something that the issuer does not actually own. The dam at Ma'rib in the Yemen was famous in pre-Islamic times. Vaux explains that the phrase about yarns is used when someone has been producing "a great deal of rhetoric, and exerting all his art to talk another person out of any thing he is intent upon, the latter will answer, Aye, Aye, *you can spin a good yarn*, but it won't do; meaning, all your eloquence will not have the desired effect" (Vaux, "Vocabulary," 226).

BIBLIOGRAPHY

[Grose, Francis]. *Grose's Classical Dictionary of the Vulgar Tongue, Revised and Corrected, with the Addition of Numerous Slang Phrases, Collected from Tried Authorities, by Pierce Egan.* London: Sherwood, Neely, and Jones, 1823.

Nasrallah, Nawal. *Treasure Trove of Benefits and Variety at the Table: A Fourteenth-Century Egyptian Cookbook.* Leiden: Brill, 2017.

"Shāhid kayfiyyat taʿallum ṣuʿūd al-nakhlah." Uploaded by Qanāt al-Fadghiyyah, 6 September 2017. http://www.youtube.com/watch?v=xy6w78zht5E.

[Swift, Jonathan]. *The Poems of Jonathan Swift, D. D.* Edited by William Ernst Browning. London: G. Bell and Sons, 1910. II:59–88.

[Vaux, James Hardy]. "A New and Comprehensive Vocabulary of the Flash Language." In Vaux, *Memoirs*, II:147–227.

———. *Memoirs of James Hardy Vaux.* 2 vols. London: Clowes, 1819.

Imposture 43

Containing Great Variety of Matter

This unusually long Imposture consists of three episodes, which may have been strung together because no single one is quite long enough to stand on its own. The English model, Henry Fielding's Tom Jones *(1749), is also a very long work of its kind. It contains several set pieces on women, including the descriptions of Sophia Western (IV:ii), her aunt Mrs. Western (VI:ii), and several quarrelsome landladies. Taken together, these depictions supplied a good deal of the material needed for the comparison of the matron and the maid.* Tom Jones *also has the reputation of being a bawdy book, though this Imposture is actually more explicit in its language. Finally, this Imposture features a cameo appearance by an arbiter, that is, a man entrusted with settling disputes among tribespeople. Fielding (d. 1754), besides being a novelist, served as a magistrate—that is, a law enforcement officer—and is credited with cofounding London's first police force.*

43.1 *Containing a story recounted by Elhares Ben Hammam, as told by himself*

I once arrived, after wafting across vast tracts of land, and enduring a further fatiguing journey, in a country where even one excellently well skilled in finding the way would miss his right track, and a valiant soldier be frighted out of his wits. As I was alone, I had reason to be alarmed; but I collected courage enough to clap a switch to my camel, and to set forward as one who, having cast the dice, submits to his fate. I rode for many miles, sometimes at a trot, and others at a gallop, till the sun began to set and night came on ten times blacker than an army of Hottentots. Such was my consternation, that I knew not whether to gather my skirts and tie my beast, or advance into the night scarce knowing whither I went.

As I chewed the cud upon this matter, I saw the apparition of a camel **43.2** upon the summit of a mountain. Hoping it might belong to a traveller who had laid himself down to rest, I approached it, though with great caution. The matter proved to be as I had imagined: the beast's back was bare and the rider, wrapt up in his habiliments, lay composed in slumber. I sat down by him and waited till sleep should take its leave of him. At length he opened his eyes, and no sooner did he perceive that some one had surprized him, than he started from his place.

"Friend or foe?" he cried.—"Rather one who has lost his way in the dark," said I: "show me some kindling and I'll show you a flint!"— "Be of comfort," he replied: "man hath oft a brother found, of other than his mother born."

This declaration relieved my fears, and now my fatigue began to operate very forcibly upon me. But my acquaintance cited the maxim, that when day breaks, the traveller is grateful for the journey that cost him so much trouble the night before. He asked me, "Shall we ride?" I replied: "That I will, sir, to the world's end."

He returned my civility and commended my resolution. We then set **43.3** forwards, putting on as fast as possible through the darkness, submitting to the inconveniences of night-travel, and conjuring down the charms of sleep, till the dawn sent forth its first streams of light. When the day at length appeared in its full lustre, I examined my companion and fellow-traveller, and saw that he was no other but the celebrated Aboo Zaid, way-mark of the well-guided. So great was the surprize and joy which we conceived at this meeting, for we had formerly been most intimate acquaintance and friends, that it is impossible to recount half the congratulations that passed between us. But while we were communicating our news and bringing forth our secrets, I observed that though my beast had exhausted her breath, his was trotting along with the alacrity of a fox-hound. I was astonished at her strength and fortitude, and could not help expressing my inquisitiveness. "Where did you acquire her?" I asked;

to which he answered, "This she-camel was once the occasion of a curious and diverting history. If you desire to hear it, pray halt; or if not, I shall tell it, and you need not listen." I made no reply to this, but kneeled my poor beast and sat with eager and impatient ears.

43.4   "She was shewn me in Hadramaut," he said, "and I purchased her, after being nearly undone for want of her. I have ridden her across many a country, and with her hooves belabored many a stony tract; I know her to be a ship of the desert, and a trusty means of flight. She does not tire, nor will she suffer herself to be overtaken; and she has never known the application of tar. Finding in her a treasure, I nourished her with care, that she might avail me in joy as in misfortune.

"It happened that she one day escaped, and I was left with no beast to ride. This loss drove the remembrance of all other losses out of my head. So great was my distress, that I despaired of life; and gave myself up for three days to the effects of melancholy, scarce able to rise from my bed, yet unable to sleep except in fits. At length I set out in pursuit of her, tracing out the journey she must have taken. I hoped to surprize her loose in a pasture or kneeling by a water-hole; but I got no scent of her, nor yet found cause to despair and by so doing gain relief. I bethought myself again and again of her swiftness, that made her rival to the kite; and every time felt with the remembrance a bitter pang.

43.5   "At last I arrived at a place where some two hundred tribesmen had pitched their tents. There I heard a distant voice cry out: 'Has any one lost a high-stepper from Hadramaut, well fitted, and marked on the hide, with blacking on the welts and a braided cord, and a back once broken but now reset? A high-stepper, I say, springy and of good stock, durable, pliable, showing no fatigue, causing no soreness, easily broken in, and true to the last?'"

Aboo Zaid continued: "The cry led me to the crier, and filled my head with hope of recovering what I had lost. Upon reaching him, I saluted him, and said, 'If you will but give me that high-stepper, you shall be nobly rewarded.'

"'Pray, sir, may I, without offence, enquire what it is you have lost?'

"'A she-camel,' I answered; 'as big as a hill, with a hump like a dome, who can fill a skin with a single milking. A fellow offered me twenty dinars for her in Yabreen, but then made a mistake, in not having bought her when I demanded more.'

"When he heard this description, the man turned away, saying: 'You are not the owner of my foundling.' At which words I laid violent hands on his collar, and endeavoured to tear his shirt from his back, calling him a d—d liar. 'I have no camel of yours, you rascal,' he cried; 'be pacified, and put a stop to your cursing; or else bring me before the tribal arbitrator, who is a man of strict honesty. If he finds in your favour, you may take what I have; or else hold your tongue!'

"As I saw no other prospect of relief, I consented to go before the arbitrator, though I feared he might not only deny my claim but also give me a drubbing.

"We hastened to the arbitrator, whom we found to be an old man of   43.6
serious and steady disposition, and of such benevolent aspect that a bird might without apprehension alight upon his elegantly turbaned head. I complained to him in high terms and bitter language of the injustice done me. The other party stood silent till I had finished my story and exhausted my spirits in discourse. Then he pulled out a sturdy pair of sandals. 'This is what I was describing,' cried he; 'and if it brought him twenty of anything, it was twenty blows; yet here he is with his eyes in his head, so let him shew the back of his neck as a proof; or else he is lying backward and forward, the villain!'

"'The Lord forgive us!' said the arbitrator, and fell to examining the sandals. He presently said, 'Why, these belong to me!' And then, turning to myself, he added, 'As for your she-camel, I have her here. Take her, and endeavour to do good, as far as you are able.'

"I rose and recited to the arbitrator: 43.7

> Long life to thee, ever just and wise!
> By thy arbitration do the Arabs rise;
> I swear by the House: just is thy decree,
> Thy words give joy, and justice breathes in thee!

"To which he replied, with great quickness of invention:

A blessing on thee! But no thanks are owed,
To duty done, nor praise by right bestow'd:
By law hath Man o'er brutish nature sway,
By fraud doth he none else but Man betray.

"He then dispatched a fellow to deliver me my she-camel, which was done without importuning me for a gratuity. Matters being thus adjusted, I took my leave, and departed in ecstasies and raptures."

43.8 *Containing a dialogue on the subject of matrimony*

I declared, and ratified it with an oath, that Aboo Zaid's story was one of the oddest, most comical tales I had ever heard. "And is it possible, sir," I said, "that you can have met any one more eloquent or more bewitching of speech than yourself?" He solemnly affirmed that he had: "Listen," he said, "and I will satisfy your curiosity."

"When I had been some time in Tihamah," said Aboo Zaid, "I resolved to take a rider into my litter, that is, to procure a helpmeet, or in short, to marry; but after the preliminaries had been ratified and the matter brought nearly to an issue, I began to feel some doubts concerning the success of the enterprize I had undertaken. I passed the night in no very agreeable manner, debating with myself whether to proceed. At last I determined to rise early in the morning and to seek the counsel of the first person I should see. No sooner had darkness struck its tents, and the stars turned their tails, than I set out as early as one does who traces a wandering beast, or practices augury by the flight of birds. In my way I met a handsome youth; and, taking his comely features for a good omen, I desired him to give his opinion of marriage.

"'Is the bride a matron,' asked the youth; 'or would you submit to a maid?'—'Whichever you would choose for me,' I said; 'I surrender the matter into your hands.'—'I will describe both,' he said; 'but you must decide between them.' After paying me the very civil compliment of wishing himself my ransom and my enemies dead and buried, he proceeded as follows:—

"'A virgin maid is a pearl beyond price and a treasure too precious for   **43.9**
display. Her wine is untasted and her meadow untrodden; she is unsunn'd
as an ostrich egg and unblemished as first fruit. She is untousled, unprod-
ded, unsullied, and unravished. She hath a modest look, a downcast eye,
a faltering tongue, and an innocent heart; but with these, she is a statue
sprung to life, frolicsome and coy, and as sprightly as a figure in a pup-
pet-show, especially when her limbs perform the office of a sash; lay her
in your bed, and she will revive the wildness of youth, and drive away
old age.

"'As for the matron, she is broken to the saddle, and ever hath a dish **43.10**
smoking on the flame; she hath constantly that desire of pleasing, which
may be called the happiest of all desires in this, that it scarce ever fails
of attaining its ends. She is a fond and tender friend, and an affectionate wife; she hath ingenuity and skill, discernment and experience; and
yet she may be devoured from the saddle, and enjoyed for the asking.
She offers a gentle ride to the invalid, and easy spoils to her comrade in
arms. She is candid, complacent, and obliging, and her service does you
honour.

"'And now I promise you, sir, that I have dealt with you honestly, and
shewn you the doe and the heifer alike. Tell me which of them has taken
possession of your heart, and given a joyful rising to your cock.'"

Aboo Zaid continued thus: **43.11**

"I apprehended that the youth could fling a weighty stone, and it were
prudent not to provoke him with gravel, lest he should leave me bleeding
without a cupping. But I could not help saying, 'I have heard that the maid
is more affectionate and less deceitful.'

"'Such indeed,' replied the youth, 'is the opinion of many, but O! how
often are such opinions wrong. Is she not a jealously guarded citadel, a
flint slow to spark, and a mettlesome unruly mare? Are her expenses not
immoderate, her contribution small, her company obnoxious, and her
coquetry a trial? Is she not clumsy at her work, implacable in strife, and
quarrelsome in spirit? Is any night more sleepless than the one she spends
in wrath? Can she be subdued, but by the utmost effort? or understood,
but by persisting in importunity? Does she not humble the defiant, spurn
the amorous, scorn the playsome, and tame the teething stallion-camel?

"Go and seek one to manage the house!" This is one of the few passages whose reading and interpretation remain uncertain. Cairo Adab 105, the primary manuscript, reads *fa-ṭlub*, or possibly *fa-'aṭlub, man yuṭliq(u) wa-yaḥbis(u)*. (A similar expression, *ḥabīs wa-ṭalīq*, appears in §32.17.) The Istanbul University manuscript and the de Sacy edition read *fa-ṭlub*, with the rest the same, though de Sacy adds that some manuscripts read *man tuṭliq(u) wa-taḥbis(u)*. UCLA 286 indeed reads *fa-ṭlub man tuṭliqu wa-tuḥbis*, corrected to *fa-ṭlub man yuṭliqu wa-yaḥbis*. This reading, which is the best attested, has the lexical meaning "Seek someone to release and confine (someone or something else)." The interlinear Persian translation says *be-juy ān-rā ke pāy goshāyand u bāz darand* (Ḥarīrī, *Maqāmāt*, ed. Ravāqī, 312), lexically "Go look for someone whom they divorce and restrain" or "Go look for someone who can be divorced and restrained," which suggests an Arabic original that read or was understood to read *fa-ṭlub man yuṭallaqu wa-yuḥbasu*. The only extant manuscript of al-Ḥarīzī's Hebrew translation, being incomplete, unfortunately does not include this Imposture. The 1873

Beirut edition has *fa-aṭlub man yuṭliqu wa-yaḥbis*, which it explains as "I will look for someone who has the power to confine and release and act effectively" (*man lahu ḥabs*

And is she not the one who says, "I shall dress myself and sit; go and seek one to manage the house!'"

"'And what do you say, my good friend, of the matron?'

"'Ah! And would you content yourself with others' dirty leavings, or the dregs of a draught already drained? Would you put on another's shabby cloaths, or wash at a spattered basin? Would you take a wife who scolds, growls, swears, domineers at will, sallies out of doors, nibbles at a dozen dainties, and assumes the most provoking airs of contempt? And would you be upbraided by disadvantageous comparisons to her first husband, whose praise she has eternally in her mouth?

wa-iṭlāq wa-nafādh taṣarruf, 461). De Sacy's commentary explains his reading, namely *fa-ṭlub man yuṭliqu wa-yaḥbis* as "seek anyone who is capable, i.e., of looking after you." Rückert does not translate the line (*Verwandlungen*, 262). Steingass,

adopting *fa-'aṭlub*, translates: "So I seek one who holds and spends" (*Assemblies*, 127). Dolinina and Borisov have "Look for someone who will take care of the house" or "take pride in the house" (*a ty poishchi, kto o dome budet radet*; Makamy, 457). Khawam, also reading *fa-aṭlub*, has: "I seek one with the power to release and to imprison" (*Je cherche quelqu'un qui ait le pouvoir de libérer et d'emprisonner*; Livre des Malins, 451). Devin Stewart suggests adopting the reading *fa-ṭlub man tuṭliqu wa-taḥbis* and translating "So you go ahead and choose whom you are going to let go and whom you are going to keep," implying that the speaker is no longer the young wife but Abū Zayd's male interlocutor, who is asking him to choose between the two wives he has described. This is certainly a plausible reading, though it requires al-Ḥarīrī to switch speakers in mid-rhyme. Here I have translated from the best-attested reading of the Arabic and adopted the most commonly offered explanation of it. At the same time, I include this commentary in order to reproduce, in this one place, the sort of discussion pre-modern readers would have found, and added to, on the pages of their copies of the *Impostures*.

"I've been ill-used," she says, "but many's the good time and oft I've taken revenge! Alas! Why are those happy days no more?" And if she has a grown child, whom she loves with ardent affection, or a former husband, on whom she doats, then you will find her as painful as an iron collar crawling with lice, or a mortifying wound that will not heal.'

"'Do you then advise me,' I said, 'to renounce all womankind, as if I was 43.13 a monk?'—At that word the youth rebuked me severely, as a tutor does his unruly pupil: 'How? A monk?' he cried; 'after the Truth has become manifest? Faugh! I pity your ignorance; fie upon it, and the monks too! Have you not heard, that there is no monkery in Islam? Are you not acquainted with the marriages contracted by our Prophet, upon whom be peace? Why, a good wife will maintain your house, indulge your wishes, chasten your glances, and preserve your repute. To her you owe the delight of your eyes and the joy of your heart; to her, the flourishing of your garden and the continuance of your name. Without her, who will provide for you, if not today, then tomorrow? Would you break, sir, with the custom of the prophets and the patriarchs? Would you scorn an institution that maintains chastity, produces wealth, and propagates the species? Your ignorance, brother, subdues my patience!' Here he sprung up nimbly as a locust, his countenance full of rage. 'Fie upon it, young man!' I said, 'will you prance away and leave me perplexed?'—'Methinks you do affect perplexity,' he said, 'in order to flog Oomayra, and thus avoid paying the bride price.'— 'The devil take your wicked presumption,' I cried; 'and pox o' your locks!' Then I turned from him abashed, vowing never again to ask the advice of a stripling."

Which concludes with an instance of ingratitude, which, we hope, will   43.14
appear unnatural

At the conclusion of this story I said to Aboo Zaid: "I will take my oath, that both sides of the question were argued by yourself."—He laughed heartily, like one surprized in some imposture. "If the honey pleases thee," he said, "ask no more questions, but lick it up!"

Here I found means to introduce a discourse in praise of Learning, which, I declared, did better become a man, than Wealth. As I delivered my harangue, he smiled at my simplicity—that is, when he paid any great attention at all. When my encomium of men of letters arrived at the highest pitch of vehemence, he cried, "Hush, sir; rather listen, and be instructed:

> 'Letters adorn the man!' is all the cry
> Yea, if he keep a heap of cash hard by!
> If he be poor, better a sop and a crust,
> Than the tutor's rod, or the scholar's dust."

43.15 He added, that I would soon see his argument proved as clear as the sun, upon the plainest and most manifest evidence.

We now rode hard, without slackening our pace, and found ourselves near a village, which, as we were to learn, was cursed with a total want of charity. Our bags being empty, we entered the town, intending to examine into the state of provisions. No sooner had we reached the place where beasts are halted and unloaded, than there appeared a boy not yet arrived at the age of indiscretion, carrying a bundle of herbs on his shoulder. Aboo Zaid saluted him as an honest Mussulman and desired him to stop, as if he would ask him the way. "Bless you, sir," said the boy, "what would you know?"—"Does an oration," said Aboo Zaid, "in these parts, secure a libation?"—"Why, no."—"Does an artful boast procure a roast?"—"Nay, nay!"—"Is a supper bespoke with a jest or a joke?"—"'Tis not, sir!"—"Naught to eat, for a bold conceit?"—"Ho!"—"Nor a cutlet, for a couplet?"—"Ha!"—"Nor a purse, for a verse?"—"O la!"

43.16 Aboo Zaid was delighted by the boy's repartees, and amused by his wit; but the boy, perceiving that my friend was a merry-Ásh'ab, and his jesting far from exhausted, said: "Leave off that banter, as you may be pleased to call it, for I see what kind of fellow you are; take your answer in gross, and much good may it do you. In these parts, sonnets supply no supper, prosody provides no profit, and rhetoric reaps no reward; nothing is more useless than a eulogy, more emetic than an epic, or more odious than an ode. Men of these times offer no compensation for well-crafted orations, nor any reward for conversation; even the nobles begrudge a ruble for the epistolographer's trouble, and no one will pay for a lay. Why, they say that letters without riches are like a pasture without rain. Where no rain falls, nothing grows; and where nothing grows, no beast will graze. Letters, likewise, unwatered by wealth, wither and wilt, and the gleaner gathers only brambles." With which words he turned and ran away.

"You see," said Aboo Zaid, "the market for letters is slack, and its partisans have fled the field of battle."

I congratulated him for his discernment and allowed that he had the right.

"Now let us put an end to this debate," he said, "and turn to the matter   43.17
of sustenance, for prosimetrum will not satisfy the craving appetite, and we are quite famished to death. By what expedient, I wonder, might we procure something to eat?"—"I leave the matter entirely to you," I replied. "If you would follow my counsel," he said, "pawn your sword, and fill your belly, as well as mine. Come, my dear boy: deliver it to me, and wait here; and I will return with a morsel to preserve you from starving." I gave him the sword and put the business into his hands; but no sooner had he mounted his she-camel than he basely and treacherously rode away. I stared a moment after him, then leapt up to pursue. "He's gone," I said, "he's gone! Damn me if he is not gone!" and with him the sword gone too.

GLOSSARY

43.8

Tihamah   the western coast of the Arabian peninsula

43.13

Oomayra   penis

43.16

merry-Ásh'ab   jester, buffoon

NOTES

Section §43.2 contains three proverbs, which are translated more or less literally, as they are fairly clear as they stand, or at least no more obscure than some of the expressions in Fielding. "Show me some kindling and I'll show you a flint" is roughly equivalent to "You scratch my back and I'll scratch yours." "Hadramaut" (§43.4) is Ḥaḍramawt, a region in the southwestern part of the Arabian Peninsula, in what is today Yemen. "An application of tar" is used to treat the mange, a skin disease caused by parasites. Yabreen (Ar. *yabrīn*, §43.5) means "sandy ground" (Sharīshī, *Sharḥ*, 5:92) but here it is apparently a place name.

"If it brought him twenty of anything . . ." (§43.6) supposedly refers in a roundabout way to the fact that thieves were beaten on the back of the neck with shoes. Such beatings allegedly brought so many tears to the eyes of their victims that they would go blind. The tribesman is thus accusing Abū Zayd of being a liar twice over. He cannot have been offered twenty dirhams for the sandals, because no one would pay that much; nor can he have been beaten with them, as he still has his eyesight and bears no scars. This explanation, supplied by al-Sharīshī (*Sharḥ*, 5:94–96), is rather contrived, but I cannot find a better one.

The two poems in §43.7 are loosely based on the form of Alexander Pope's translation of Homer's *Iliad*, a work quoted several times by Fielding. Though Fielding quotes from Chapman's translation, Pope's stricter numbers make his verse a more likely simulacrum of Arabic poetry.

"A village . . . cursed . . ." (§43.15) seems to echo Q Kahf 18:77, where Moses and the figure identified as al-Khiḍr pass through a village that refuses them hospitality. The idea, perhaps, is that Abū Zayd's various sins and crimes, like al-Khiḍr's, are actually good deeds in disguise. Steingass reads the phrase as a curse: "May the good keep aloof from it" (*Assemblies*, 130). Grammatically at least, this reading is entirely plausible but I find no support for it in the commentaries. "Merry-Áshʿab" (§43.16) is modeled on "merry-Andrew," meaning "jester."

BIBLIOGRAPHY

Fielding, Henry. *The History of Tom Jones, a Foundling.* London: Macmillan, 1904.

[Homer]. *The Iliad of Homer.* Translated by Alexander Pope. London: Warne, 1920. Digital edition at Project Gutenberg: http://www.gutenberg.org/files/6130/6130-h/6130-h.html.

IMPOSTURE 44

NEAR EAST ENDERS

In this Imposture, Abū Zayd regales his host and fellow guests with a series of riddles based on double meanings. His third riddle, for example, says: "Starving Arabs who in times of famine roast a khirqah *for food." A* khirqah *is commonly a rag, which makes little sense; but al-Ḥarīrī then explains that the word also means a swarm of locusts. In translation Abū Zayd will use Cockney rhyming slang, which produces similar puzzles. In rhyming slang, "apples and pears," for example, means "stairs." The expression is usually abbreviated to "apples," to the bewilderment of the uninitiated: what does it mean to "go up the apples"? Applying this process to the example above, it turns out that "bugs" in Cockney are (or were) called "steam tugs," or "steamers" for short. There is also an equivalent for "starving," or more exactly "starvin'"—namely, "Hank Marvin" (pronounced 'Ank Marvin), an English rock guitarist. The resulting translation is "Give them steamers a go, if you're 'Ank Marvin," and the explanation is "Steamers is bugs, and 'Ank is starvin'." This rendering is anachronistic, as steam-powered tugboats and rock guitarists did not exist in al-Ḥarīrī's world. But his riddles are full of absurd images (absurd, that is, until the riddle is explained), so the translation will embrace the anachronism. The English of this Imposture was corrected by Stuart Brown.*

44.1   *El-'Arif Ben 'Ammam towd us dis mornin' glory.*

On a take-a-fright as black as yer Burnet's fair, I was makin' me woi towards a Jeremiah blazin' 'igh up on a Jack n' Jiw. Some bloke sayin' he's keen t'giz a glorious, know wha' I mean? Meanwhile it was bloomin' ta'ers: the apple pie 'ad 'is holler-boys bu''oned up to the bushel, the Turin shrouds was piled high, and the lah-di-das was hidin' under a blanket. I was shiverin' like a mangy goat meself, and why shouldn' I? Blimey! The bloomin' air was icier than a lizard's mince. But I kep' on drivin' me camel along, sayin' "Look sharp, there's a good lass!" and tellin' meself to keep the ol' chin up.

Soon the geezer wot lit the Jeremiah sees us racin' up the Jack, and comes trottin' dahn, singin' this knees-up:

44.2   Welcome, China plate,
Come in out of that,
Jeremiah's brought you to us,
Come 'ave a wooly 'at!

We're glad when people call
We like to see a crowd;
When times is rough you'll eat enough
Cos givin' makes us proud!

We never duck and doive
Or tell you, "Wai' a bi'";
Noight n' day we've Uncle Fred
And Billy on the spi'!

44.3   After that 'e shows me 'is bashful Chevy Chase and 'olds out a gener-ous St. Mar'in's. Then 'e leads us inna tent where all the camels wot was ten months up the duff was busy bleatin', an' the ten-man cookin' pots was boilin' over, an' the servin' ribbons was runnin' back n' forf, an' the Cain-an'-Abels goin' round an' round. Off to the side was a loine o' guests dragged in by the same geezer wot invi'ed me. Seein' 'em enjoyin' the fruits of win'er, I went an' warmed meself at the ol' Jeremiah like they was doin'.

We 'ad a giraffe togevah, and it did me 'orse-and-cart as much good as a second Khyber o' rise-an'-shine.

As soon as we was feelin' cozy-like and tickety-boo, in comes lots o' Cains as round as a bloomin' 'alo, wiv plates o' proper grub piled 'igher than Aprils in a garden. There was nobody about to give us an earful or tell us mind our manners, so why not scoff up the scran, wivout a blind bit o' notice to wot they say about fillin' up ya Auntie?

By the toime we'd finished Frankin' like a lot of Billy Bunters, our New- **44.4** ingtons weren't 'alf playing us up. But we passed round the ol' serviette, wiped the grease off our St. Mar'in's, and settled down for an all-night bowler. Everyone let fly wiv wha'eva 'e 'ad in 'is Muvver: everyone, I mean, except one grizzled ol' geezer dressed in a worn-out weasel and a freadbare Uncle Bert. 'E went offa the side, 'e did, and knelt dahn wivout payin' us any mind. We didn't fancy that: we 'adn' done nuffin to deserve the cold shoulder, 'ad we? Blimey! We should 'ave taken the piss out of 'im. But we didn't want any bovver, so we talked to 'im friendly-like, tryin' to make 'im open up and join the bowler we was 'avin'. Durin' all that toime he kept turnin' away like 'e was a fine gentleman and we was dirt under 'is feet. Then 'e'd recite a verse about some blokes rabbiting on about a load of Jacksons from long ago.

In the end, though, a fightin' spirit seemed to move 'im, or 'is Jekyll whispered sumfink in 'is King Lears. 'E gets up an' comes over, wiv no more airs and graces, workin' hard to make up for any ill feelin'. Then 'e calls on the lot of us to listen up, an' lets fly like a ragin' flood:

'Ave a butcher's at me rabbits, fresh from the city, **44.5**
 An' do ya best, me chinas, to twig the chitty-chitty.
Got a Geoff 'Urst on? 'Ave some Acker Bilk!
 Geoff 'Urst is thirst, and Acker Bilk is milk.
Give them steamers a go, if you're 'Ank Marvin.
 Steamers is bugs, and 'Ank is starvin'.
Want to babbling brook? Fetch some do-me-good!
 Babble means cook, and do-me-good is wood.
Need to patch a skin? Fetch a Jeremy Beadle!
 In me rhymin' rabbit, a Jeremy's a needle.

Why did blokes in armour ride after a tenner?
Run the tenner backwards: it's a tartan banner.

44.6   She's brown bread, th' poor gooseberry puddin'!
Brown bread's dead, and the rest means woman.
Wha' abou' the lads wot 'ad a bull-an'-cow?
Look lively, mate: it means they 'ad a row.
Would ya 'elp a bird in a righ' ol' two-and-eight?
Lord love a duck! It means she's in a state.
And would ya go to Syria to find a Chairman Mao?
Why not, me china? It means a bloomin' cow.
Wha' abou' havin' it on ya Bromley by Bows?
It means to scarper, 'cause ya take it on ya toes.

44.7   Would ya mix your Acker wiv some farmer's daugh'er?
Honestly, mate! It only means wa'er.
Oi! I seen a basin of gravy read and write.
A basin's a baby, and read means fight.
Can planting millet make ya gay an' frisky?
Of course it can, guv, 'cause gay is whisky.
Can ya ride a bo''le of sauce wiv a Geoff 'Urst?
Ya mean ride an 'orse wiv a burnin' thirst!
'Ow long can ya go wivvout a Jimmy Riddle?
You're givin' us gyp, 'cos that means piddle.

44.8   Can ya Charlie Pride on the frog and toad?
Charlie means ride, and a frog is just a road.
See that, squire? Wha' an Easter ball of chalk!
Easter bunny's funny, and ball means walk.
'E's got a dodgy 'at 'cause he's bat 'n ball.
'Is 'at rack's his back, and bat means tall.
Wiv all them Beecham's, I'm boracic lint.
Beecham's Pill's a bill, and boracic means skint.
I'll 'ave a Rex, but no pork pies!
Rex Mossop is gossip, and porkies are lies.

Ya don't Adam an' Eve me? But it's Irish stew!   **44.9**
   The first one's believe, and Irish means true.
'E's a right 'ard Julius, but 'e looks cream crackered.
   Add Caesar for geezer, and the rest is knackered.
'Ow d'ya fevver 'n flip on the Rory O'Moore?
   The one means kip and the other means floor.
Me Baf bun cried when they snipped 'is Uncle Bob.
   Baf bun is son, and the rest means knob.
'Ere! You've got fisherman's on ya Chevy Chase!
   Add daugh'er for wa'er, and Chevy's a face.

And wha' abou' them steamers wot live by 'alf inchin'?   **44.10**
   A steam tug's a bug an' the rest means pinchin'.
Mind ya minces now, or you'll go bacon rind!
   Mince pies is eyes and bacon means blind.
Save ya bees an' 'oney for a rainy day—
   Blimey! That one's money, wouldn't ya say?
—and buy a Sir Walter for a bo'le of spruce.
   Scott means pot, and the bo''le's a deuce.
If ya need 'elp, call the bo''les an' stoppers!
   Steady now, mate: that means the coppers.

Me old London's go' a gang full of ease.   **44.11**
   That's just me dog wiv a gob full o' cheese.
Can ya ride an 'orse if you're eliphant's trunk?
   Why not, luv? Eliphant means drunk.
Can ya draw fisherman's out of mince pies?
   The first one's wa'er, and the second is eyes.
Can ya carry some fisherman's on an 'at rack?
   Course ya can, mate: it's only ya back.
Ever saw a drover carryin' a tin?
   A tin tack's a sack, for keepin' fings in.

Oi! Ya give us a clip on the Ruby Rose!   **44.12**
   Ruby's no bird, guv: it means ya nose.

Can ya eat a fig wivout cloimin' a tree?
Yeah, coz crackin' a crib means burglary.
'Ow 'bout ya chinas in the field of wheat?
That means ya mates walkin' dahn the street.
That geezer's still go' 'is Biffo the Bear!
'Ow's that, luv? I've lost all me 'air!
Wot's it mean if a bloke's pear halved?
Why, 'e's sayin' 'e ain't 'alf starved.

44.13   Mind that geezer: 'e's a septic tank!
'E ain't full o' Tom, 'e's just a Yank.
I 'ad a sit-down wiv me trouble and strife —
It's all right, luv: it means me wife.
She's dead chuffed 'cos she's Keif Cheggers.
Hip hip hoorah! That means she's preggers.
No 'arm done if I take ya Dicky Dirt?
'Ands off, mate: it's me last clean shirt!
It's me Duchess wot runs me Pope in Rome.
Duchess is wife, and the rest is home.

If ya twigged me rabbit, ol' china plates,
You'll Adam-an'-Eve I'm from Bow;
And if ya di'nt I'll leave ya skint,
Cos ya don't know yer arse from yer elbow!

44.14   *El-'Arif Ben 'Ammam 'ad this to say too:*

So we took a good butcher's at 'is verses an' tried our best to work 'em out, which was no doddle wiv him 'avin a giraffe at us and sayin' "Gertcha!" every time we 'ad a go. Pretty soon we twigged we didn't 'ave a bloomin' chance. So we said, "Righto, we give up. Now tell us the answers, won't ya, guv?"

Well, first 'e said 'e would, then 'e said 'e wouldn't, and finally if we was goin' to catechize 'im we'd 'ave to make it wurf 'is while. Wot 'e meant was, 'e wanted a nobble. When 'e 'eard that, our pillar and post turned a bit shirty, seein' as how the geezer meant to rush us in 'is Pope. So 'e brings out a foroughbred she-camel an' some these-an'-those like the ones the Prophet gave Sayeed Ebn El-Aas. "Toik these," he says, "but from me guests, no' a brass farthin'!"

"I see you 'ave a disposition like 'Atim's, sir," said the ol' geezer, "an' a stop-an'-start as princely as 'is grandad Akhzam!" Then 'e turned 'is brigh' shinin' Chevy Chase on us an' said, "Look 'ere, lads, the take-a-fright's got a good bit of life in it yet, an' it's time we all 'ad a kip. Let's go to Uncle Ned; we'll 'ave a nice fevver an wake up full o' beans, so when I exploin, you'll twig wot I'm rabbiting on about, yeah? 'Cause right now ya 'aven't got a Scooby."

The whole bloomin' lot of us said it was a good idea and went off to Bo Peep.

The guests was too cream-crackered to keep their minces open, and 44.15 pretty soon they fell asleep. That's when the Julius jumped up, slapped a saddle on the she-camel, mounted 'er, and scarpered. As 'e rode away he sang 'er this ding-dong:

> Take me to Sarooj, ol' girl,
> Take me far away;
> We'll ride all night, we will,
> An' all the bloomin' day.

> Wear out your 'ooves on the rocks,
> And don't turn east or west,
> Until we reach the good soft earth
> Where bowf of us can rest.

> If you push on, me love,
> And never stop for wa'er,
> And bring me back to ol' Sarooj
> You'll be me bricks n' mor'ar.

El-'Arif said:

That's when I knew right enough it was that Saroojer bloke—the one wot ducks and dives as soon as 'e fills 'is Lucy Locket.

At first merry, as soon as the lot was out of Uncle Ned, I told them while they was 'avin a fevver, the old geezer 'ad run off wiv the camel an' left us 'igh and dry. They got themselves in a right ol' two-and-eight just finkin' about 'ow 'e'd wound 'em up. Then each one took 'is own frog n' toad, and set off under 'is own la-di-da.

GLOSSARY

44.1

mornin' glory story

take-a-fright night

Burnet's fair hair

Jeremiah fire

Jack n' Jiw for *Jack 'n' Jill*, i.e., hill

t'giz to give us

glorious for *glorious sinner*, i.e., dinner

ta'ers for *taters-in-the-mould*, i.e., cold

apple pie sky

holler-boys for *holler-boys-holler*, i.e., collar

bushel for *bushel-and-peck*, i.e., neck

bu''oned buttoned

Turin shrouds clouds

lah-di-das stars

mince for *mince pie*, i.e., eye

geezer man

dahn down

44.2

china plate mate (friend)

wooly 'at for *wooly hat and scarf*, i.e., laugh

duck and doive skive (dodge one's responsibilities)

wai' a bi' wait a bit

Uncle Fred bread

Billy for *Billy Button*, i.e., mutton

44.3

Chevy Chase face

St. Mar'in's for *St. Martin's-le-Grand*, i.e., hand

up the duff pregnant

ribbons for *ribbons and curls*, i.e., girls

Cain-an'-Abels tables (here, a low table or large serving tray with feet)

giraffe laugh

togevah   together

horse-and-cart   heart

Khyber   for *Khyber Pass*, i.e., glass

rise-an'-shine   wine

'alo   halo

44.4

Frankin'   from *Frank Bough*, i.e., scoff
   (eat voraciously)

Newingtons   for *Newington Butts*, i.e.,
   guts

bowler   for *bowler hat*, i.e., chat

Muvver   for *Mother Hubbard*, i.e.,
   cupboard

weasel   for *weasel and stoat*, i.e., coat

44.5

butcher's   for *butcher's hook*, i.e., look

rabbits   rhyming slang words

twig   understand

44.6

scarper   run away

44.7

give gyp   give grief, cause pain

44.8

skint   broke, having no money

44.9

right 'ard   well built

knackered   tired

kip   sleep

44.10

deuce   twopence (Hooten)

44.11

London   for London fog, i.e., dog

gang   for *gang and mob*, i.e., gob
   (mouth)

April   for *April showers*, i.e., flowers

scoff   eat voraciously

scran   food

Auntie   for *Auntie Nellie*, i.e., belly

Uncle Bert   shirt

offa   off to

rabbit   for *rabbit and pork*, i.e., talk

Jacksons   for *Jackson Pollocks*, i.e.,
   bollocks

Jekyll   for *Jekyll and Hyde*, i.e., pride

King Lears   ears

chitty chitty   for *Chitty-Chitty-Bang-Bang*, i.e., Cockney rhyming slang

steamers   for *steam tugs*, i.e., bugs

knob   penis (the original refers to
   circumcision)

ease   for *stand at ease*, i.e., cheese

44.12

eat a fig   burglarize

44.13

Tom   for *Tom Kite*, i.e., shite

Duchess   for *Duchess of Fife*, i.e., wife

44.14

doddle   an easy task

gertcha   Get away with you!

nobble   "to secure the support of by
   unfair or underhand methods; to
   influence the opinion or actions
   of in advance of a formal decision"
   (*OED*)

pillar and post   host

shirty   irritated

these-an'-those   clothes

rush   overcharge someone for

stop-an'-start   heart

'Atim, Akzam   Ḥātim and Akhzam,
   proverbially generous Arabs

Uncle Ned   bed

fevver   for *feather and flip*, i.e., kip
   (sleep)

Scooby   for *Scooby Doo*, i.e., clue

Bo Peep   sleep

44.15

ding-dong   song

bricks n' mortar   daughter

duck and dive   skive (dodge one's
   responsibilities)

Lucy Locket   pocket

merry   for *merry-and-bright*, i.e., light

la-di-da   star

NOTES

Traditionally defined as the speech of those born within earshot of East London's Bow Bells (see §44.13 below), Cockney—or, more exactly, a variety that includes many of its features—has now become diffused over a much wider area. Within the city itself, meanwhile, it has largely been supplanted by a variety called Multicultural London English (see Imposture No. 23). In one sense, it is easy to find examples of Cockney: there are many glossaries of rhyming slang, the oldest dating to 1859, and even a genre of Cockney rock music. But it is difficult (at least for a non-native) to distinguish ephemeral expressions from current ones, and to sort out which expressions belong to which period. Unlike most others, this Imposture mixes together terms from different periods. Otherwise, there would not be enough to cover all the riddles or indeed to tell the story. For example, "take a fright" meaning "night" appears in John Hotten's word list of 1859 but nowhere on the websites that document current usage. Rather than give it up, I have used it, along with other phrases that are doubtless now extinct. As a result, real Cockney speakers from any given period would likely find many of the "rabbits" puzzling, just as the Arabic speakers dubbed into Cockney do within the fictional world of the Imposture.

This Imposture makes more effort than usual to represent the sounds of this particular variety in writing. Thus "other" is written "ovver" and "thing" as "fing." Stuart Brown very generously corrected the many mistakes I made trying to do this myself. In cases where the phonetically correct spelling seemed too distracting, we have retained Standard spelling. This kind of inconsistency is common in written representations of Cockney (see, for example, Coles, *The Bible in Cockney*, Kindle Edition, especially the discussion at location 72).

A "knees-up" (§44.1) is a popular dance in which the knees are vigorously raised to the accompaniment of the song (*OED*). I use it here to render *rajaz*, a poetic meter used in pre-Islamic times for chants and "artless folk poetry" (Ullmann and Heinrichs, "Radjaz"). "Welcome . . ." (§44.2): this song may be sung to the tune of "Knees up, Mother Brown," a pub song associated with Cockney culture. "Chevy Chase" (§44.3) for "face" was originally a reference to an area on the Anglo-Scottish border, and included in Hotten's list of 1859. "Billy Bunter" (§44.4): a schoolboy in stories written between 1908 and 1961 by "Frank Richards" (Charles Hamilton, 1875–1961), "used allusively to indicate fatness, gluttony, clumsiness, etc." (*OED*). "A verse about some blokes": the verse paraphrased here is Q Anʿām 6:25, "This is nothing but fables of the ancients."

"No pork pies" (§44.8): the original turns on the word *khalq*, meaning either "creation, people" or "fabrication," citing Q Shuʿarāʾ 26:137, where the word may also be read as *khuluq*. "'E's a right buff Julius . . ." (§44.9): the original plays on *līn*, "weakness" or "flaccidity" but also "date palms" (a form of which is attested in Q Ḥashr 59:5). Regarding "ease" (§44.10) for "stand at ease," i.e., cheese, Aldertons notes that "for whatever reason, this one is backwards."

In §44.11, "Ever saw a drover . . . ," the original wordplay is on *kurrāz*, supposedly a bottle, but also a ram used by shepherds to carry bags of provisions around. But the dictionaries give the word for bottle as *kurāz*, not *kurrāz*. My translation contains a similar liberty, as "tin tack" (a short, light iron nail coated with tin) is attested as rhyming slang for "sack" in the phrase "get the sack," that is, be fired or dismissed from one's job, not (necessarily) "sack" in the sense of "heavy bag."

"Eat a fig" (§44.12) is an unusual off-rhyme for "crack a crib," a phrase meaning "break into a house" (Hotten). "Bow" (§44.13) is a reference to the old definition of a Cockney speaker. In the original, Abū Zayd says that the trunk of his palm tree attests to the quality of his dates. "Gertcha!" (§44.14) is used "as a derisive expression of disbelief" (*OED*). It has been immortalized in the eponymous 1979 song by Chas and Dave. Ḥātim of Ṭayyi' is proverbially known for his generosity, which was compared to that of his ancestor Akhzam. See further Steingass, *Assemblies*, 278.

BIBLIOGRAPHY

Aldertons. *A Cockney Rhyming Slang Dictionary*. http://aldertons.com/home/slang/.

Chas and Dave. "Gertcha." On *Don't Give a Monkey's*. EMI, 1979.

Cockney Rhyming Slang. London's Famous Secret Language. http://www.cockneyrhymingslang.co.uk/.

Cockney Rhyming Slang. http://www.phespirit.info/cockney/.

Coles, Mike. *The Bible in Cockney: Well Bits of It Anyway* . . . Abingdon: The Bible Reading Fellowship, 2001.

Green, Jonathon. "Language. Rhyming Slang." In *Critical Quarterly*, vol. 45 (July 2003), nos. 1–2: 221–26.

[Hotten, John Camden]. *The Slang Dictionary, Etymological, Historical, and Anecdotal: A New Edition, Revised and Corrected, with Many Additions*. London: Chatto and Windus, 1874: 358–68.

Ullmann, Manfred, and Wolfhart P. Heinrichs. "Raḍjaz." In *Encyclopaedia of Islam, Second Edition*. Leiden: Brill, 1960–2007.

IMPOSTURE 45

CAT AMONG THE PIDGINS

In this Imposture, Abū Zayd and his wife again drum up a false complaint in order to hoodwink a judge. Here the wife claims that Abū Zayd refuses to sleep with her, and he counters that he is afraid to have children because he is too poor to support any. The ensuing scene calls to mind another case of public marital arbitration: the one in Chinua Achebe's Things Fall Apart, *in which a husband goes before the ancestral spirits and accuses his brothers-in-law of taking his wife and children away (Ch. 10). On the strength of this association, Abū Zayd and company, in collaboration with the Nigerian novelist Richard Ali, will use Naijá and Nigerian English as they replay this Imposture.*

Na Harisu Hammam nack us this tori: 45.1

People wey sabi talk say to journey na mirror wey dey show man things wey go totori bodi. As such, I take the matter to heart just dey travel, I don cross Sahara desert wey water no dey sam sam, enter plenty place wey you go fear fear, for sake of say I wan see all the totori totori thing for this world. Of the many many things wey my eye don see, none of them confuse me pass wetin happen when I enter see oga Judge of Ramla. I never see surprising thing like that, I am telling you. Oga judge of Ramla get money well well and na very big man he be. One day, I dey for him court and they come charge one old man wey wear old and tear tear cloth and one fine fine sisi wey wear good cloth wey don old small for bodi. The old man want start dey blow grammar wetin bring them come but the sisi no even let am talk,

419

she just sharrap him like that. Na him the woman come lift her handker-
chief from her mouth come start dey talk as woman wey no get shame and
wey no dey fear anybody face:

45.2   Oga Judge for Ramla, na you biko!
I say oga Judge for Ramla, na you biko!
Na you fit give me better, or refuse me better
My life don spoil pata pata
For sake of my husband:
Alhaji go round Kaaba every every time,
But he no go come back after he don throw stone,
No no, no no.
After Mecca, he go visit Prophet too,
Come join another small visit go Mecca again
Na who send am?
Since he marry me, I no dey see am sam sam,
So if he no pull with me,
Abeg make he free me,
Bifor I become ashewo,
I say make he free me!

45.3   "You hear," said the judge to the old man, "the lady's howling and lamentation, and what recalcitrance she ascribes to you and accuses you of,
talk less of what comeuppance you shall bag, if care is not taken; as such,
shine your eyes, lest she be vexed and burn your character."

The time he hear this, the old man kneel down for ground start dey blow
big big grammar, say:

Listen, Judge, yourself blameless,
To learn of her heart's unease the cause:
Not aversion, no, nor weariness, I swear
But alteration found, and fortune
Ill-disposed: nacreous hoardings
Gone, not a dust-mote: a house
Bare as her neck of ornament.

And where I was as ardent in amour
As any Udhri, now I in chastity
Forbear, turning timid from my tilth.
Judge, rebuke me not, for what
Insult would you add to penury?

When she hear this tori, the lady come vex well well come dey halla at   45.4
im husband. "Thunder fire you!" she shout. "I say, make thunder fire you!
You no dey give me chop, you no dey give me poke sef! You no gree to get
pickin, say because of money, yet you don see any animal wey no get chop?
Open ya sense! You no wan hear, dey carry your foolish sense make your
wife dey wor-wor!"

"Chei!" judge say to her. "With such sharp mouth, you might quarrel
Hansa herself and silence her outrightly! But if your husband is broke to
the marrow, it is no gain saying that he first think about his belly and not
his John Thomas."

When she hear this, she bow her head dey look with corner-corner eye.
We say, praps she begin shame, praps she think the matter don finish.

"Mtchewww!" old man hiss. "May God punish you for embellishing
your account, and willfully concealing facts well known to you!"

"Talk anoda thing!" she say. "Afta we make gra-gra come for court, na
wetin you wan hide? I talk true, you talk true, we done fall our hand well-
well, now everybody go poke nose! E for better make we no hear anything,
than for us to come front of judge!" Na him she wrap body for cloth and
pretend to cry for sake say her character don injure.

The judge begin wonder, tell everybody to look at them, see the kain
kasala them get: "It's a pity!" he say. Then he bring two thousand silver
dirham, say to them: "Have it, and fill up your cavities, in defiance of all
detriments to the matrimonial home."

"Thank you!" they say. "We see your hand o!" Them happy as them
come waka commot, like sweet and fresh palmwine.

After them don waka commot, the judge begin praise their deep Arabic.   45.5
He ask whether anybody sabi them.

The oga of his staffs, wey dey tight-tight with him, talk say: "The old man
be that Saruj person, know book well well, and the lady na him paddy; but

na cunny man he be, and all that them palaver dey one kain, na wayo wey he do."

As Judge hear that, he come vex well-well because they done use am do mumu. So he say to the oga of his staffs: "Pursue them, and when you see them, burst out and apprehend them!"

Na so the olopa cry blood, run commot from that court. Small time he come back sweating like Christmas goat.

"Divulge now," Judge talk, "what you have unearthed, and do not conceal any unpleasant truth."

"I done go afta dem," he say, "carry leg waka enter plenty road for this Ramlah, use every sabi we I sabi for this olopa work, until finally I see dem dey walk enter desert, to cross am go yonder. I catch dem, offer plenty money, promise say dem say another mumu dey wey them go fit catch a second time. But old man no gree. 'Pepper done rest,' he say. 'To run go enjoy am better pass. Greedy goat na him yam go choke!' But the woman say she want come with me. She say, 'To chop mumu two times na him better, fear fear no good.' The old man no happy at all to hear this.

45.6　　"The old man see the wife no use number six, and because say na fly wey no dey hear word dey follow dead body enter grave, he catch im blouse for im hem, sing poem say:

> Thief wey jump fence
> Fit enter house, take evritin,
> But just one time o!
> Me, I say he take just one time!
> Thief wey go back
> See owner dey wait for im,
> No go jump again!
> Me, I say he no go jump again!
> But my sister no wan hear.

45.7　　"Den he tell me, 'Dey make you chase me! Go back where you come from and tell the one wey send you:

Take your time o! You done shake bodi
But now you want mise, and lose good name.
Sake of what? I no be first person wey cunny
And you no be first mugu. Make you no shame!
Dis time wetin you lose? Only money!
Abu Musa sef done mumu fall mugu before your own!'"

"Marvelous! More grease to his elbow!" Judge say. "What beauteous   45.8
lamentation, what piquant mastery of genre!" Then he give the oga two
agbada and one bundle gold, tell him: "Run like a brush fire in the harmattan, without fear or favour! Pursue the old man and the young lady, and
when you see them, grease their palms with this kola, and convey to them
my partiality to persons of eloquence."

In the tori man's words:

I done go far far, talk with people wey don waka everywhere, but I never
see anything so fine true true, never hear anyone break grammar pass that.

GLOSSARY

45.1

na   (it) is, are, was, were (indicating equivalence)

nack us this tori   told us this story

wey sabi   who know

talk say   say

go totori bodi   are exciting

dey travel   keep on traveling

don cross   have crossed

wey water no dey sam sam   where there's no water at all

totori totori   thrilling

45.2

na you biko   you're the man

for this world   in this world

pass   more than

wetin   what

oga   person in charge

I dey for him court   I was at his court

sisi   young woman

blow grammar   pontificate in Standard English (but in this case Arabic)

sharrup   shut up

him   she

na you fit   you can

pata pata   completely

alhaji   pilgrim

he no go come back, etc.   he is unable
to go a second round

after Mecca . . . na who send am   no
one would object if, after Mecca, he
visited Medina too

45.3

shine your eyes   be careful

45.4

come vex well well   got very angry

chop   food

no dey give me poke sef   don't even
have sex with me

no gree to get pickin   won't agree to
have a child

no wan hear   refusing instruction or
advice

dey carry your foolish sense, etc.   I
condemn the stupidity that has
made your wife miserable

chei   Wow! Really?

outrightly   entirely

it is no gain saying   there is no
denying

45.5

deep   complex or pure (form of a
language)

sabi   know

wey dey   who was

know book well well   literate and
intelligent

na him paddy   is his partner

cunny man   con man

palaver   quarrel

I no dey see am sam sam   I haven't
seen him at all

pull with   be affectionate

abeg make he free me   please make
him let me go

become ashewo   lose all shame

broke to the marrow   indigent

John Thomas   penis

with corner-corner eye   askance

talk anoda thing   say something
better

make gra-gra   be unduly quarrelsome

na wetin you wan hide   What is it you
want to hide?

we done fall our hand we-we   we have
exposed each other

e for better   it would have been better

the kain kasala   the kind of trouble

see your hand   acknowledge your gift

waka commot   went out

dey one kain, na wayo wey he do   was
one of his tricks

done use am do mumu   made a fool
of him

olopa   police officer

small time   shortly thereafter

sweating like Christmas goat   i.e.,
excessively

another mumu, etc. they could pull off another trick

to run go enjoy am better pass discretion is the better part of valor

pepper done rest we have enough money

Greedy goat, etc. Greed makes a goat choke on a yam

45.6

number six intelligence, common sense

no wan hear refusing instruction or advice

na fly wey, etc. to ignore him and go back would be terribly risky

45.7

shake bodi spend some money, pay the bill

make you no shame don't be ashamed

mise be stingy

mumu fool

mugu fool

45.8

agbada robe

kola small gift

harmattan parching wind; dry season

NOTES

The Arabic Imposture is named after Ramla (al-Ramlah), a town on the coastal plain of what is now central Israel. Noting that Imposture 31 is also called "of Ramla" in de Sacy's edition, Katia Zakharia ingeniously connects the two by noting that both refer to the pilgrimage. Imposture 13 describes the journey to Mecca, while 45 uses the pilgrimage as a figure for sexual intercourse. This text-internal allusion, she says, "sets up a clear link between sexual pleasure and the joy of proximity to God." Noting, further, that the word Ramlah has the same root as *armal*, "widower," she reads the trial in this episode as symbolic of the process by which Abū Zayd comes to renounce sexuality in favor of mystical bliss (*Abū Zayd*, 301–6). In the face of such a clever reading it seems almost churlish to point out that, unknown to Zakharia, the Istanbul manuscript gives Imposture 31 the disambiguating title "of Mecca," a fact that undermines at least part of her argument.

The present English rendering is a joint effort. I produced a first draft in Standard English, Nigerian English, and a very faulty approximation of Naijá based on the sources listed in the bibliography. The passages in Naijá were then entirely rewritten by Nigerian novelist Richard Ali, author of *City of Memories* (2012), who is to be credited with whatever literary merit they possess.

According to Ethnologue, Nigeria can claim 527 languages, of which "350 are vigorous" and "20 are institutional." In the midst of this often contentious diversity, English, the language of the country's former colonizers, serves as the lingua franca. In informal settings, however, speakers who share no other language speak Naijá. (The accent on the a indicates *a* high tone, one of two tones in the language.) Originally a pidgin, Naijá has become a first language for many users (see Elugbe and Omamor, *Nigerian Pidgin*, 45–74). According to one source, it is "the native language of approximately three to five million people and is the second language for at least another 75 million citizens" (*Big Issue*, "Use," 1:59ff). Like other creoles, it has long been regarded by purists as a "broken," inferior form of English. More recently, it has come to be recognized and celebrated as a distinctive form of expression. Since 2006, it has had its own name and its own system of spelling (Ofulue and Esizimetor, "Guide"). And in August 2017, the British Broadcasting Corporation (BBC) launched a news site in "West African Pidgin," embracing the varieties used in Ghana, Cameroon, Guinea, Sierra Leone, and Liberia, as well as Nigeria.

Between the formal written language and the fully illiterate vernacular lies a continuum of intermediate forms. One of the most accessible of these is so-called Nigerian English, a variety that consists almost entirely of Standard English words but uses many of them in distinctive local ways. This variety has been documented in at least three glossaries (Jowitt, *Nigerian English Usage*; Kperogi, *Glocal English*; and Blench, "Dictionary") and is very much in evidence online, in government documents, and in the press.

The present translation combines Standard English, Nigerian English, and Naijá. Standard appears in the poem in §45.3, which attempts to mimic the diction of Wole Soyinka, winner of the 1986 Nobel Prize in Literature. Al-Ḥārith narrates in Nigerian English. The judge's lines, which demanded a more oratorical style, are modeled on the compulsively erudite diction of the journalist Olatunji Ololade. The wife's speeches, the bailiff's, and some of Abū Zayd's are in full-on Naijá.

"Harisu Hammam" (§45.1): on the form of the name see Thurston, "Muslim Names." The judge's speech in §45.3 is composed of items taken from Jowitt's list (*Nigerian English Usage*, 153–266) of British English words and phrases used with somewhat different meanings in Nigeria. An Udhri (§45.3) is a member of the Banū ʿUdhrah, an Arab tribe whose poets were famous for their chaste and unrequited love. "Kperogi" more fully defines "chei" (§45.4) as an exclamation expressing "deep admiration tempered with a dose of disbelief" (Kperogi, *Glocal English*, 187). Al-Khansāʾ ("Hansa") was an Arabian poet who witnessed the rise of Islam. She was famous for her dirges, but also for her sharp retorts to challengers. Jowitt more fully defines "mtchewww" (§45.4) as "a sound produced by protruding the lips and drawing air inwards noisily" to express "disapproval or derision" (Jowitt, *Nigerian English Usage*, 193).

In §45.6, "Thief wey jump fence," etc. is based on the proverb "Thief wey jump fence enter house wey owner dey wait for am, no go jump again." "Abu Musa" (§45.7) is Abū Mūsā al-Ashʿarī, a companion of the Prophet who, when chosen to represent ʿAlī ibn Abī Ṭālib in the arbitration with Muʿāwiyah over the caliphate, was reportedly tricked by the latter's representative, ʿAmr ibn al-ʿĀṣ, into deposing ʿAlī. An agbada (§45.8) is a West African robe worn by men. I use it to translate *burdah*, as both are flowing garments, open in the front, with wide sleeves. "Like a brush fire in the harmattan, without fear or favour": Jowitt identifies these as common NE clichés (*Nigerian English Usage*, 144).

BIBLIOGRAPHY

Asomugha, C. N. C. *Nigerian Slangs*. Onitsha: Abic, 1981.

[Babawilly]. "Babawilly's Dictionary of Pidgin English Words and Phrases." http://www.ngex.com/personalities/babawilly/dictionary/default.htm.

Big Issue, The. "The Use of Pidgin English in Nigeria." http://www.youtube.com/watch?v=o_kJH2bQ7gs&t=1789s

Blench, Roger. "A Dictionary of Nigerian English." http://www.rogerblench.info/Language/English/Nigerian%20English%20Dictionary.pdf. Published online in 2005, marked as "Draft Circulated for Comment." I have not found any subsequent version.

Elugbe, Ben Ohi, and Augusta Phil Omamor. *Nigerian Pidgin (Background and Prospects)*. Ibadan: Heinemann, 1991.

EthicMotif. "Tag Archives: West African Proverbs." http://www.ethnicmotif.com/index.php/tag/west-african-proverbs/.

Ethnologue. http://www.ethnologue.com/19/country/NG/languages/.

Faraclas, Nicholas Gregory. *A Grammar of Nigerian Pidgin*. PhD diss., University of California, Berkeley, 1989.

Jamaican Matey Groupie. "African Proverbs." http://www.jamaicanmateyangroupie.com/aspects-of-our-jamaican-culture/african-proverbs/.

Jenifa's Diary. Season 1, Episode 1. Published by irkotov | NOLLYWOOD, November 16, 2017. http://www.youtube.com/watch?v=445RGSICjjQ.

Jowitt, David. *Nigerian English Usage: An Introduction*. Lagos: Longman, 1991.

Kperogi, Farooq A. *Glocal English: The Changing Face and Forms of Nigerian English in a Global World*. New York: Peter Lang, 2015.

[Kuti, Fela]. "Fela Kuti Lyrics." Transcribed and compiled by David McDavitt. The Afrofunk Music Forum. http://afrofunkforum.blogspot.com/p/fela-kuti-lyrics.html.

Ofulue, Christine I., and David O. Esizimetor. "Guide to Standard Naijá Orthography: An NLA Harmonized Writing System for Common Naijá Publications." http://www.ifra-nigeria.org/naija-corner/naija-languej-akedemi.

Ofunne, Adim, and Obilo Nwokogba. Naija Lingo.http://naijalingo.com/words/a/alphabet.

Ololade, Olatunji. Articles archived at: http://thenationonlineng.net/category/olatunji-ololade/.

Olowo-okere, Bamidele. *Learn Nigeria Pidgin-English*. N.c: N.p., 2014.

Saro-Wiwa, Ken. *Sozaboy*. Port Harcourt: Saros, 1985.

Thurston, Alex. "Muslim First Names in West Africa." *Sahel Blog*. http://sahelblog.wordpress.com/2013/03/12/muslim-first-names-in-west-africa/.

IMPOSTURE 46

ARABY

With his audience already staggered by Abū Zayd's verbal artistry, al-Ḥārith adds another twist by reporting that even children can match it if they have Abū Zayd for a teacher. The schoolroom setting of this Imposture brought to mind the scene in Chapter Two (the "Nestor" episode) of James Joyce's Ulysses *(1922), in which Stephen Daedalus tries (with decidedly less success) to impart history, poetry, and mathematics to his charges. In the spirit of the novel, which revels in ad hoc coinages, Abū Zayd and al-Ḥārith will relax the usual constraint and use or invent text not found in Joyce if it comes across as something he might plausibly have used.*

Related the doughty narrator: 46.1

An imperious desire drew me, yearning, longing, to Halep. Decisive, brisk, no family then to feed, I took my cockle hat and staff and flew the roads. Alighted in the spring when young men's fancy. Sucked dry the saps of Halep, slaked my droughth. Sated, cloyed, felt the peregrine flap. Idly: Where now? Emessa! Jolly Emessa! O to estivate, where every citizen is an imbecile. Onward through the bowl of night, like a comet slung to put the djinn. Upon her outskirts I pitched my tent. Wafty wind's caress. How now? What old pedagogue is this? Quondam vigour lost, half unwithered still. About him ten schoolurchins, some in pairs, others alone. A propitious opportunity: are the sages of Emessa as stupid as men say? The *senex* saw me approach, at once put on a blithe broadly smiling face, and returned my greeting with a more gracious. I sat eager at his feet. Not a word could fall from his lips without betraying his suppositious vacancy of mind.

46.2   Presently he pointed with his rod at the eldest of his pupils.

—Give us twelve verses without an O, he said. Be quick.

Blurted the boy:

> Sans that letter, I can spell
> *Blade* and *belt* and *shield,*
> *Brave* and *fierce* and *plucky,*
> And *Let the craven yield!*

> Sans that letter, I can spell
> *Wine* and *girls* and *games,*
> Which all bright lads must put away
> Lest tarnish dim their names.

> Sans that letter I can be
> Cultured as a scribe;
> I can lend a friend a hand,
> And in battle guide my tribe.

—Soar silver orb, cried the schoolmaster, o, you blessed abbot.

46.3   Turning then to the next pupil, image of the first:

—Come up, you peerless mummer.

The boy came forward smartly, poised as a passer of cups.

—Scrawl me some lines like a dunner's note, where every word contains an O.

The imp trimmed his stylus and snipped the tip, clapped a tablet to his lap, scribbled:

> Woe to your poet, for lo,
> Off your poet's doe doth go!
> No more throbbing voice so low,
> Nor orotundity of form: oh no!
> No more gibbous moons aglow,

Nor songs along old Lovers' Row;
For coyness cannot joy bestow,
Nor love so coldly lopped regrow.

The teacher squinted scrapeshuffling at the inscription.
—Dear gazelle! Blessed tree of life!
Then he called Garryowen!   46.4
A boy: a star by night, a Grecian statue in a niche.
—Make me mongrel couplets whose *only* vowel is O.
The boy seized the reed and wrote:

Yon box of obols,
Or lot of spoons: goods
Lost too soon, to mobs, to rot,
To voodoo, or monsoons!
Do good: do not hold on!
Look: to poor folk
Go obols, gold,
Yon box of spoons!
No loss to donors,
To poor folk boons!

—Ne'er forget thy cunning, said the teacher, nor thy tongue its mischief.
Then he called: Grabby, you perisher!   46.5
Another pupil, a dewdrop pearl, ox-eyed, obeyed.
—Five anagrams in verse. Mahak makar a bak!
Took pen in hand the lad without stopping wrote:

Her lidded darts impale my heart,
    Shredded, tamed, impartially.
She has lovely eyes then?
    Eh, yes! Even so they shall
Ne'er outdo her bosom
    Tremorous, Bede: oh no!

Put both, Ben: a litheness
  To banish sleep, but then
My viler art invoked, she caves,
  And revives my lovesick heart.

The pedagogue peered at his pupil's slate. Orthography: satisfactory. Jots and tittles up to scratch.

—Keep a steady hand. A keener lad never drew the breath of life.

46.6 Another boy: peachy cheeks: roses of damask.

—Recite, said the *senex*, two lines, inimitable and immune to a third, of which the chief feature is epanalepsis.

—May God spare thee presbycusis, said the boy, and preserve thine host unvanquished. Listen. Without dilly-dallying he declaimed:

A good lad says "Thank you," there's a good lad.
He'll go bad if he's greedy; if he lies he'll go bad.

—Hoopsa, boyaboy, hoopsa!

46.7 Then he said, Tom Thumb! Versify, if you please, all the words with silent B.

On his feet in an instant, the boy gabbled nasally:

There's *limb* and *lamb* and *jamb* and *comb*
And *climb*, but don't say *clomb*;
There's *numb* and *crumb* and *doubt* and *dumb*
And *plumber, plumb, succumb*;
And *subtle* rules of *thumb*: for *womb*
Has but one rhyme: the *tomb*.

—Bravo, little breeches, o, you martial clash of cymbals!

46.8 He said: Now then, Rantipole: versify the words with silent K.

Up sprung a cub. Unstumbling sung:

Knock is one, and so is *knot*,
And *knee*, and *knead*, and *kneel*;

And *know*, and *knoll*, and *knitting*,
But don't call Neal *Kneal*.

There's *knuckle, knife, knave,* and *knight*,
And *knap-*, that goes with *-sack*.
It's not too hard to list 'em all
Once you've got the *knack*.

—Bless you my child: o welcome glee!
Wee as a chesspiece, the next boy was. But darting deftly: a sparrowhawk.   46.9
—Some verse, if you please, on ambigraphs. Look sharp!
Pulling along his gowns the boy stood up stout chanted with waving graceful arms:

You can write *adviser*
And merrily run *amuck*;
Or you can write *advisor*
And win, with any luck.

But is it better to write *racket*
Or *racquet* with a Q?
And how to finish *mollusk*?
I haven't got a *clew*!

How many E-s in judg(e)ment?
And is ax or axe preferred?
I wish I could enquire;
Oh, this furore is absurd!

Amuck can or may with equipropriety be indicted amok. *A* racket *is (1), a fraudulent scheme or (2), an implement for striking a ball, while racquet denotes only the latter.* Mollusk *and* mollusc *are for all intents and purposes the same, whilst* clew *is a heterograph of* clue. Judgment *may pseudoepenthetically be spelled* judgement. Ax *and* axe *(pseudoparagogic) each commands its legions.* Enquire *may with the approval of eminent epigraphists be set down as* inquire *as* furore *may be cropped and docked to* furor. *Cry and countercry as to the correct method of writing these and other amphigraphs recalls that verse of sacred Scripture:* They have flayed you with sharp tongues.

—Wee little wee little pipy wind, said the teacher, o you eye of newt!
Then he said: Jumbo, you pandemonium of ills!   46.10
—Here, sir, said a boy bright as a newlaid egg.
—A poem, please, on principal parts in *-ing* and *-ung*.
—May thy din chagrin thy foe, said the boy. Then without waiting for a word of help:

One paradigm is based on *sing,*
Which gives us *sing, sang, sung;*
It works for *ring,* but not for *cling,*
So don't say *cling, clang, clung*!
So too *fling* and *sting* and *string*:
The last two parts are one.

The teacher, rocking with delight, implored God's protection for the lad. Offered to sacrifice himself for his sake if need were.

46.11 —Boomer, you catastroph, he called out next.

Up with a boy. Bright: a lamp lifted beside an open door.

—Rhyme some cryptic glyphs. Vex thereby thy foes.

Awriggle with delight, the boy fell to bellowing:

A certain Charivarius
    Put it into *verse*:
Our spelling isn't all that bad:
    Actually it's *worse*!

Why should *put* take after *foot*
    Instead of a word like *nut*?
And *foot* itself should rhyme with *hoot*!
    How to know what's *what*?

Shouldn't *worse* sound just like *horse*
    Or be spelled some other way?
But *horse*, of course, rhymes with *coarse*,
    And *way* with *cabaret*.

Why do *comb* and *bomb* and *tomb*
    Each have a different O,
And *rose* and *dose* a different S?
    Does anybody know?

Three whole spellings for just one sound
    In *poor* and *pour* and *pore*;
But with *shoes*, and *goes*, and *does*,
    It's the converse I deplore!

Ate and *eight* are homophones,
    But *read* and *read*, not so;
Tear and *tear* have different vowels,
    And *though* resembles *throw*.

And who on earth would ever guess?
    A simple name like *St John*
When you say it as you should
    Rhymes (more or less) with *engine*!

Orthoepically, shoes *rhymes with* booze, goes *with* nose, *and* does *with* fuzz. Read, *if uttered* reed, *is the present tense, and if* red, *the past tense and past participle. By the operation of an analogous differentiation of vowels,* tear *denotes (1), a laceration, laniation, or separation violently wrought; as well as (2), the lachrymotic effluvium. St John in utterance becomes* SIN-jin *or* SIN-jun.

Cholmondeley, oddly, rhymes with *glumly*
    Leveson Gower is 'loosen-gaw';
For *Featherstonehaugh* just say 'fanshaw,'
    And for *Arkansas*, 'ark-in-saw'!

Egyptian *Cairo* turns to *care-o*
    Up in Illinois;
And *Palestine*'s called *pal-e-steen*
    Down in Texas, boy!

Though I could list a hundred moor
    I'll stop hear if I may;
Unless you learn them won by one
    Yule give yourself aweigh!

Cholmondeley, *pronounced* CHUM-ley, *is an English family name; so* Leveson Gower *and* Featherstonehaugh. Arkansas, *autochthonously sounded without the final* s, *is one of the United States (cf. Arkansas City, in the state of Kansas, which is pronounced* ar-KAN-zis; *and the Arkansas River, which admits both of apocopation and nonapocope.)* Cairo, *Illinois (*ill-i-NOY*), eponym of* Cairo, *Egypt, the latter with* biro homoiocatalectic; Palestine, *Texas (*TEG-zis*) reportedly named after Palestine, Illinois (also* PAL-e-steen*).*

—Bravo! Clapclap. Good man. Clappyclapclap. An ephebe. Fresh and tender. Keeps a charge all the same. Keeps a charge closely as the earth herself, forgetting nothing, as none shall be forgotten on that terrible Day. I led you beside the pure fresh waters. You and your schoolmates: a pentice of gutted spearpoints. Remember me in your prayers. As I you. Think of me with thankibus. How sharper than a serpent's tooth!

46.12 *Related the doughty narrator:*

It was a marvel to see one so adept in his *ad libitum* and yet a dullbrained yokel. I scanned him cap-a-pie. Probed mercilessly. Inscrutable: nethermost darkness. Howling waste. At last, impatient of my plodding wit, he glowered at me and grinned.

—The sign and dueguard of fellowcraft is no more.

The shaft struck home: it was Buséad. By his weasel teeth bared yellow I did know him. I began to remonstrate. Why dwell among dunces, ply the trade of dunderheads? He recoiled: kiss of ashes. Draught of bile. Spat back:

> Bless cretintown
>> And teacher's gown
>>> For fortune loves a fool, o!
> Go find the rain
>> Down by the drain
>>> In a lazy swirling pool, o!
> Or brave the drought
>> And wet your snout
>>> In puddles, learnèd mule, o!

46.13 *How did Buséad respond to his interlocutor's expression of contempt for his profession?*

Yes teaching is the noblest profession never wanting for takers and the best intercessor on behalf of your immortal soul and so impressive too when done right all those lads eager to obey oh yes and a bit terrified of you docile as sheep aren't they and you ordering them about like a hussar or a prince in your little kingdom where your word is law not for long though too soon senile and famous for imbecility and little wit oh you can take it from me all right.

—Old father, I said, old artificer, who beguiles the mind, and breaks to his will the unruly steed of speech.

He continued long thereafter cloistered with his schoolboys bailing pails of philologic from his winedark deep until the blazoned days ran their course and sundered us by a dusty doom and so I wept alone

GLOSSARY

46.1

Halep   Aleppo

Emessa   Homs (a town in Syria)

senex   old man (Latin)

NOTES

In the spirit of *Ulysses*, which sets puzzles for the reader but does not explain them, I have glossed only one of the oddities drawn from that work.

In present-day Syria and Lebanon, Homs ("Emessa," §46.1) is still the butt of jokes about the supposed stupidity of its citizens.

In the original of §46.2, the boy is asked to compose a poem using only undotted letters. Conversely, the poem in §46.3 uses only dotted letters. In §46.4, the original alternates dotted and undotted words. "Mongrel couplets" comes from Steingass, *Assemblies*, 150.

In §46.5, the original consists of five lines where nearly every pair of successive words is written with nearly identical letters. In English, similarly, composing anagrams means using the letters of one phrase (or, in this case, one hemistich) to compose another, without additions or deletions. In composing these I have used the helpful generator at Wordplays.com.

"Mahak makar a bak" (§46.5) is an unexplained phrase in *Ulysses*, 549. One commentary suggests it might be an imitation of Arabic (Gifford, *Ulysses Annotated*, 522).

The poem in §46.6 uses the same sequence at the beginning and end of each line, though the Arabic also involves word redivision. In §46.7, the original is a versified list of words commonly misspelled because of confusion between the letters *sīn* and *ṣād*. In these words, the presence of *q* and *r* causes the original *s* to be pronounced as *ṣ*, leading to confusion about how to spell the word. The poem in the next section (§46.8) is a versified list of words misspelled by substituting the letter ṣād for sīn. That is, it is the converse of the poem in §46.7.

The chess piece in §46.9 is specifically a pawn. What al-Ḥarīrī means may perhaps be understood by looking at a twelfth-century chess set from Nishapur, where the pawns are stubby cylinders rounded on one end and topped by a knob (Metropolitan Museum of Art, *Chess Set 12th century*).

The poem in §46.9 lists all the words that may be spelled with either sīn or ṣād. ("Ambigraph" is my coinage for a word that can be spelled in two different ways.) Starting with the second line, and continuing at irregular intervals afterward, al-Ḥarīrī glosses the poem's rare words. In episodes where he puts such glosses in an appendix, I have omitted them from the translation. But here he puts them in the main text, so I have included them—or something like them, anyway: mine define not the words al-Ḥarīrī uses but the English words I have chosen under a different constraint. Despite this necessary modification, I have fit in the Qur'anic verse (Q Aḥzāb 33:19) al-Ḥarīrī cites to illustrate one of his words. For a lexical translation, see Steingass, *Assemblies*, 152.

In §46.10, the original verses contain a mnemonic for spelling verbs that end in -ā in the perfect but have different final vowels in the imperfect. In §46.11, the Arabic poem lists the words that should be spelled with the letter ẓā'. In several varieties of spoken Arabic, the sound designated by this letter, though originally distinct, merged with the sound designated by ḍād, leading to frequent misspellings. As an equivalent, I have taken the general field of English orthography, with its many inconsistencies resulting from historical changes in pronunciation. Many of my examples come from "The Chaos," a long poem published by the Dutch pedagogue Gerald Nolst Trenité (d. 1946) under the pseudonym Charivarius.

The original of "Remember me . . ." (§46.11) is *fa-dhkurūnī adhkurkum wa-shkurū lī wa-lā takfurūn*, quoting Q Baqarah 2:152. Though it is marked by *tajnīs* (repetition of sounds), the phrase does not add up to a pair of rhymed clauses, making it one of the very few lines to break with the *sajʿ* that patterns all the Impostures. This attention-grabbing break marks what seems to be a heartfelt plea by Abū Zayd to al-Ḥārith, and possibly also from al-Ḥarīrī to its readers.

BIBLIOGRAPHY

Gifford, Don, with Robert J. Seidman. *Ulysses Annotated: Notes for James Joyce's Ulysses*. Revised and expanded edition. Berkeley: University of California Press, 1989.

Joyce, James. *Ulysses*. Dijon: Darantière, 1922. Online at http://archive.org/details/ulyssesoojoyc_1/page/n7.

———. Ulysses-Audiobook-Merged. http://archive.org/details/Ulysses-Audiobook-Merged/.

Metropolitan Museum of Art. *Chess Set 12th century*. http://www.metmuseum.org/art/collection/search/452204.

Trenité, Gerard Nolst. "The Chaos." http://ncf.idallen.com/english.html.

"Anagrammer, Anagram Generator." Wordplays. http://www.wordplays.com/anagrammer.

Imposture 47

The Confidence Men

This episode finds Abū Zayd working as a cupper. A cupper— more exactly, a wet cupper—is a medical practitioner who makes incisions in the skin and then covers them with globes of glass turned upside down and emptied of air. In theory, the vacuum in the globes is supposed to draw out the bad blood and noxious vapors. Although the Prophet is said to have favored the practice, cupping itself is often described as a dirty business. Here, as usual, Abū Zayd's ostensible profession is merely a cover for his latest trick. The English is modeled on that of Herman Melville's The Confidence-Man *(1857), whose protagonist assumes a variety of guises, and which features a barber who, like al-Ḥarīrī's cupper, refuses to extend credit. The original Arabic is notable for embedding a series of proverbial expressions, for which, in the manner of Melville, the English alludes to Shakespeare and the King James Bible.*

47.1   *Harris Ben Hammock narrated:*

It was at Hajar-El-Yamamah, where, feeling in need of a cupping, I was told of an aged barber-surgeon, clean in aspect, who was competent to provide that service; so, bidding my serving boy go bring the old fellow, I kept a sharp look-out for their arrival—an event, however, so long postponed, that I had begun to suspect the lad of running away or fleeing like a shadow; when, with the air of one who, failed of his object, felt himself useless to his master, the boy at length returned.

440

"So soon?" said I. "Patient have I awaited thee, upholding on my frozen brow the piled entablatures of ages; what hinders, that I should wait as many again?"

Ah, but the cupper, it seemed, was as busy as a dairy-maid who, with a pail of new milk in each hand, must shove off an ardent suitor; and with the drawing of blood no less occupied than were the warriors at Honain.

Though scorning at first to go in search of a humble cupper, and so remaining for some time irresolute, I bethought me at last that nobody may be blamed who seeks merely to relieve those necessities that alike afflict all men.

An old man neat in his dress, and deft in all his movements, as I learned   47.2
upon arriving at his place of business, was the cupper, about whom a great throng had gathered, crowding, trampling, and jamming, all eagerness to see him. Before him, seeking likewise to be cupped, stood a young man, in person lithe and straight as a harpoon, whom the cupper was addressing as follows:

"I perceive, child, that you have removed your turban, without, however, displaying so much as a note and likewise offered your scalp, while yet forbearing to extend a coin. It has always been a principle with me, young friend, never to sell a thing on credit, or take promises in place of cash. Fish forth thy purse, child, and be cupped in both thy neck's blue veins; or, if thou wouldst clutch thy mite to thy bosom, and cast it upon a miser's hoard, take thy shekels, turn away thy face, and begone!"

"By the One who curses the liar," imploringly cried the boy, "as He curses the desecrator of His sanctuary, I have no more small change by me, than does a new-born babe; but cup me, and depend upon your money to-morrow."

"To-morrow!" returned the cupper. "To-morrow is a green sapling, as likely to fall prey to the hideous blight of life, as to grow and bear fruit; and so thy promises, child, which are as apt to wither as to blossom on the bough. And how is one to trust, in this world that wears deceitfulness as a blazon, that his fellow creature, once gone his way, will make good on his promise? Pish!" he cried, vexedly. "Do me no more injury, and be off with yourself!"

47.3   Shamefaced, the young man advanced toward the cupper. "Who but a scoundrel is faithless to his word, and who but a low-born rascal is heedless of his honor? Ah, if you but knew to whom you spoke, you might have spared me the sharp edge of your tongue; but you, all ignorance, let slip what you had better left unsaid, not unlike one who, opening his mouth to speak, puts his foot in it! Alas! How piteous is poverty, and how much more piteous is poverty in exile! And how bright the merit of the poet who says:

> Bring on your slings and arrows
> And your idle cries of 'Shame!'
> They turn my languid heart to steel
> And my sluggard's blood to flame."

47.4   Replied the cupper: "How unseemly this pride, and how distressing it must be to your clan! Is this a place for making boasts and giving glory? Nay, it is a place where hides are scraped and napes are slashed! But grant that, in claiming a noble birth, you tell the truth. Does it follow that the world owes a duty to your scruff, to be discharged by no other means than a cupping? Nay, not even if Semiramis, Porus, Hannibal, and all the successive monarchs of the east once paid homage to your line! The iron you hammer is cold, and my resolution firm. If boast yourself you must, let your boast be not the glories of your fathers or the blood in your veins, but your rejoicing good deeds and the coins in your purse. But be sure of this, o young ambition: all mortal greatness is but the pride that goeth before a fall. So demand no bowings and scrapings, but credit rather the poet's words to his son:

> Always practice sell-free lions
>   And don't depend on others, son;
> Never let the mere uke wry
>   When you're famished as a Hun;
> Know your place, un-lie kicker us,
>   Who flew—alas!—too near the sun.

Make sure your kinsmen loo quell Fed:
    A clan in rags makes you seem cheap.
Repay good faith with ten dirk air:
    For as you sow, so shall you reap.
To err is human, two-four gifty vine.
    Although you tremble, make the leap

And stop that whining, for cot's ache:
    If needs must, bend, but never break."

"How, in wonder's name," returned the young man, addressing the   47.5
crowd, "is that nose held so high aloft, when its owner's rear parts are
plunged into the swamp? I hear words warm as ruddy wine but see
deeds like slings and arrows." His indignation now at last boiling over, he
turned his barbed tongue on the cupper. "Fiddler on heart-strings! Snake!
An appeal to honor, from one as slippery as a whaler's deck, is only cant
and gammon. Or is it that, by prosperity, you are elated into heartlessness?
In that case, a blight and a curse on your trade, and I pray to see you idle as
a coaler to Newcastle, and your profits as abundant as the camels that pass
through the needle's eye."

"Boils plague your mouth!" roared the cupper. "And when boiling
plagues your blood, I wish you before a brother cupper who is a snotty,
wind-breaking, hard-hearted, price-gouging cut-purse, and a clumsy
wielder of the cupping knife."

Perceiving that his interlocutor was immovable and further entreaty
in vain, the young man made no attempt to reply to this last volley, but
started to his feet.

The cupper, who, to all appearances, had not been left entirely unaf-   47.6
fected by the young man's appeal, and now seemed uneasy at the thought
that he may have been a little bit too hard on him, at this juncture pressed
for a truce, offering to perform the operation for nothing. The young man,
resolved to quit the field with his malady intact, scorned to accept. Thus
began a prodigious bout of entreaty and abuse, of obstinacy and appeal,
that ended only when the young man, clamoring against his opponent, felt
his shirt-sleeve part in the manner of the Red Sea. With that, he began

to wail with keenest anguish at the injury done to dignity and shirt alike. Eager to staunch his streaming tears, the old man begged his pardon; but the lad paid him no heed, nor did he leave off his sobbing. At length the cupper expostulated with him, saying, "If I could, by inflicting like injury upon myself, repair that done to you, I would do so. But are you not weary of lamentation? Does stoic endurance have no merit? Are you unmoved by the verses of him who counseled forbearance, saying:

> Ahmet, be hella meek, my youth; key he though suffer him,
> Me nary guise. Equus fo' hinge, ah? Nah, Johnny!
> Foul hell; moo, Ma's Dan, a lab, Igbo be he;
> Wallach, double off weak llama, Johnna, Johnny!"

47.7　　At first the young man protested against this view, insisting, with some warmth, that if the cupper but knew the undeserved misery he had endured, he might more readily forgive his tears; adding that sympathy is most keenly felt, or rather, can only be felt, upon the heel of shared misfortune; but gradually, as if the other's appeal to self-possession had produced some effect, he mastered his feelings, and in a tolerably composed tone he spoke:

"I comply, sir, with your request; now make good what you have sundered."

"Fie! The milk of kindness is turned, and from this cloud will come no squall." The cupper rose and surveyed the crowd. "But charity never faileth." Then he passed along the rows, his hand extended in supplication, chanting as he went:

> I swear by Mecca's holy Caaba
> Where the pilgrims wend their way,
> 'Tis shameful want that brought me here
> To slit, and strop, and flay.
> With heavy heart draw I the lancet,
> And unwilling stoke the flame;
> For mine is a soul that hungers
> For a nobler sort of fame.

And if my gentle heart had reached
The glorious heights it sought,
I would not have stung this lad,
Nor with this lad have fought.
But unkind fate is merciless,
It hounds me all my days;
I would as lief the lancet ply
As leap into a blaze.
Oh, for pity, men of Yemama,
Will no man lift the curse?
Will no man hear my mournful lay
And dig into his purse?

Harris Ben Hammock narrated: 47.8

Moved by these pleadings, I tossed him two doubloons, saying, "Well spent, even if he is a scoundrel!" He hailed my alms, which he accounted a good omen, as I was the first of the company excited to compassion by his case. Soon, indeed, the doubloons began to pour down upon him in such showers that they seemed to bank him up all round, as if the step-mother world, so long cruel, did at last stroke and caress him; and he rejoiced with great joy, and was glad of heart.

"Of this reaping," he said to the young man, "the seed was yours, and so the milking that filled this pail; so come, let us divide the proceeds." And so they divided the coins into two parts, equal as the halves of a cloven lotus, then rose in the most loving and affectionate manner. Seeing that the old cupper, their truce concluded, meant to depart, I accosted him, saying, "My blood, sir, is spoiled; I have shuffled and limped all the way; I apply to you for relief."

He stared at me a moment, then drew a pace nearer and recited:

Have you ever seen a trick   47.9
    Pulled off as neat as that?
I fling some curses at my son
    Then pass around the hat!

No bolted door resists my spell,
  My every hand's a winner;
My charm can make the wasteland bloom
  Or conjure up a dinner.
Now the chap from Alexandria,
  I admit, came first;
But the dew that falls before the rain
  Ain't never quenched a thirst.

Upon hearing his free-and-easy chant, I perceived that this was my old friend the confidence-man. When I reproached him with acting the part of a reprobate, and so degrading himself, he, in no way abashed, cried, "Necessity knows no law, and heeds no risk." Upon which, with a grand scorn, he turned on his heel, and with his son, swift as a race-horse, darted away.

NOTES

The translation supplements *The Confidence-Man* as needed with words and phrases from Melville's *Moby-Dick*. For the many proverbs and stock expressions cited in the Arabic, I have given English equivalents for most that have them. Others (e.g., the one about the milkmaid in §47.1) seemed worth keeping in something closer to the original form. Three of the five poems in this episode are relatively straightforward. One of these is recast in the ballad meter of nineteenth-century light verse. The other two are modeled on *Lays of Ancient Rome*, by Melville's contemporary Thomas Macaulay, whose over-the-top heroic style suited the bombast of the original. The remaining two poems (for no obvious thematic reason) feature identical sequences of sounds with different meanings. One poem, for example, has a line that reads *lammā an aṭā'a l-hawā hawā*, "when he succumbed to temptation he fell." For the first of these (§47.4), I re-spelled the corresponding English as if it consisted of different words (e.g., "sell-free lions" for "self reliance"). In the second (§47.6), I extended the principle to create entire lines that sound like the original Arabic. This technique makes it difficult to capture any of the original sense, which is why I have used it only here, and for a very short poem.

Hajar-El-Yamamah (§47.1) is Ḥajr al-Yamāmah, an ancient town located approximately where Riyadh is today. The original of "so long postponed" accuses the boy of being as slow as Find, a freedman who, ordered to bring a firebrand from a neighboring house, disappeared for a year and then returned with the firebrand, which he promptly dropped. Honain (Ḥunayn) was the site of a battle where the Muslims routed a confederation of pagan Arabs.

"Rejoicing good deeds" (§47.4): *Moby-Dick*, Ch. 82, meaning deeds over which one rejoices. "Always practice . . ." (§47.4): For various reasons, it is easier to find respellings that make sense in Arabic than in English. The most popular examples of respelling seem to be those that turn on particularities of accent (e.g., Lauder's *Let Stalk Strine*, based on Australian) or coincidences across languages (van Rooten's *Mots d'heures*, across English and French). But when the respelling is neither meaningful in itself nor apposite to some broader theme, I find the fun wears off quickly. I have therefore made only sparing use of the technique here.

"Ahmet, be hella meek . . ." (§47.6): These verses attempt to convey the sound of the original Arabic; as a result, they lose much of the sense, though "be hella meek" is not a bad summary, as the poem exhorts the young man to control his temper and not allow himself to be provoked. In 1969, Celia and Louis Zukofsky applied the homophonic technique (called *traducson* in French) to the Latin text of Catullus, producing results more satisfactory than I have managed here.

"The chap from Alexandria" (§47.9) is Abū l-Fatḥ al-Iskandarī, the hero of the first Impostures, those of al-Hamadhānī. In his introduction, al-Ḥarīrī speaks with all due reverence of his predecessor, but Abū Zayd makes no such pretense of modesty.

BIBLIOGRAPHY

[Catullus]. *Catullus*. Translated by Celia Zukofsky and Louis Zukofsky. London: Cape Goliard, 1969.

Lauder, Afferbeck. *Let Stalk Strine*. Sydney: Ure Smith, 1965.

Macaulay, Thomas Babington. *Lays of Ancient Rome*. London: Longman, Brown, Green, and Longhams, 1842. https://www.gutenberg.org/files/847/847-h/847-h.htm.

Melville, Herman. *The Confidence-Man: His Masquerade*. New
    York: Dix, Edwards & Co., 1857. https://archive.org/details/
    confidencemanhisoomelvrich.
———. *Moby-Dick*. Edited by Harrison Hayford and Hershel Parker. New
    York: Norton, 1967. https://www.gutenberg.org/files/2701/2701-h/2701-
    h.htm#link2HCH0010.
Van Rooten, Luis d'Antin. *Mots d'heures: gousses, rames*. New York: Penguin,
    1980.

IMPOSTURE 48

ALCOHOLICS EPONYMOUS

This Imposture, said to be the first al-Ḥarīrī wrote, was report-
edly inspired by a real-life incident: the appearance in Basra of
an eloquent beggar who alleged that his child had been captured
by the Byzantines. In the Imposture, the role of the beggar is oddly
divided into two. First, a man gets up in a mosque and asks the
congregation to help him overcome his addiction to drink. Then
another man gets up and urges the worshippers to give money
not only to the first man but also to himself. The second man is
Abū Zayd, and the first one possibly his confederate. Unusually,
this Imposture is narrated almost entirely by Abū Zayd. With
its account of a seemingly unshakable addiction, the speech of
the penitent in the mosque is reminiscent of Samuel Johnson's
famous biography of John Savage, a poet who "was never made
wiser by his sufferings, nor preserved by one misfortune from
falling into another." In his Englishing of this episode, Abū Zayd
will accordingly assume the voice of his half of the Boswell-and-
Johnson pair featured in Imposture 2.

Of himself Aboo Zaid el-Saroujee gave the following account, reported entire **48.1**
by El-Hareth Ben-Hammam.

"It is universally acknowledged by Wit, and confessed by Learning, that
the monuments of Bassora, whether of flesh or of stone, and her antiqui-
ties, of which many wear a martyr's crown, possess a virtue that cannot fail
to affect the passions. From the time when I first saddled my camel and
took leave of wife and children, I had longed to see that city as eagerly as

men hunger after righteousness. I therefore besought Providence to suffer me to set foot there, and to move her inhabitants to hospitality, that I might roam her remotest corners unchecked. When Fortune smiled upon my design, and removed me there at last, I gazed upon her with all my eyes:

> Behold a wonder! Whom to behold but thee,
> And thee beholding forget my home?

48.2   "One morning, I ventured abroad at a tenebrous, antecrepuscular hour, that is, at cockscrow, to perambulate her publick streets, for it was my wish, to pass through the town at its broadest part. After threading her lanes and rambling from alley to alley, I found myself in All Hallows, a quarter of solemn aspect, graced with more stately mansions, celebrated temples, cisterns of publick resort, and other marks of distinction, than may easily be enumerated. As for its inhabitants, this notice of them must suffice:

> *Among them, sir, will you find the worldly and the sacred con-*
> *joined. Behold, one citizen is enraptured by the recital of the*
> *Alcoran, while another falls into a swoon at the strumming of a*
> *lute. Where one peruses the figures of rhetorick, another proclaims*
> *a collection to ransom a prisoner of war. Some emerge blear-*
> *eyed after ceaseless study, while others go bright-eyed in search of*
> *guests. How many learned doctors are there, how many summon-*
> *ers to company, and how many songstresses warbling their lays!*
> *None will gainsay you, if you join the worshipper at his devotions,*
> *or the reveler at his jug; nor intervene, should you seek Learning*
> *in her lecture-room, or Debauchery in her den!*

48.3   "I passed the time till the close of day roving Bassora's streets and peering at the fabric of her splendor; then, as Helios 'dropt from the zenith, like a falling star . . . and leveled his evening rays,' I saw a mosque of quaint appearance, resplendent with the faithful. The crowd was at that moment engaged in a discourse on Allophony, with much heat and animation. I joined the auditory, not in the hope of learning, but of unburdening a purse.

"I had hardly sat down when the call to devotion rang out, and the prayer-leader went forward to his place. Immediately the swords of disputation were sheathed and knee-wraps loosened, as all rose up, set worldly traffick aside, and dispatched their petitions to the mercy of Heaven.

"When their devotions were complete, the worshippers began to disperse. Then a dignified man of middle age, so fairspoken as to seem a Demosthenes of eloquence, came forward and addressed himself to the crowd.

"'Neighbors,' he cried, 'under whose shade-tree I sit, rather than my own, and whose canton I have made my home in exile! You I have adopted as my family and the repository of my secrets. Do you not know that of all earthly raiments, the most illustrious is veracity? that it is better to suffer opprobrium in this world, than damnation in the next? that to give sage counsel is a commandment of religion, even as supplying right guidance is a precept of our creed? that the seeker of advice is as worthy of respect, as the purveyor of it is exempt from reproach? that your true friend is he that reproves you, not he that offers exculpation? that speaks the truth to you, but doubts what you say to him?'

"Those present responded with professions of their amity and fellow-feeling, and entreated their friend to explain his cryptick utterance, promising, by the One who had bound them by ties of affection, to spare him no counsel nor stint him any gift.

"'May God compense you,' he cried, 'and shield you from evil! To your circle no petitioner appeals, but is gratified; from your assembly is fraud exiled, misery banished, and mendacity expelled. Dear friends, I will open to you my whole heart, and tell you of an affliction that surpasses endurance.   48.4

"'Once, in a condition of desperate poverty and distress, I made a vow to the Almighty that, if I were delivered, I would renounce, eschew, disown, and abnegate the fermentation of the grape, any convivial tippling, and all giddy inebriety. But my treacherous soul and base appetites soon beguiled me, and I sat with bibbers and bowsers, and I did drink. Laying dignity aside, I sucked at the dugs of the wine-jar, and committed all the outrages of temulence, my pledge of sobriety forgotten, as if made to a dead man. Nor did one night of riot and dissipation suffice me: on Thursday evening, I closeted myself with an aged vintage, and passed the last night insensible, embraced by the foul Fiend. Now I come before you with my vow broken and my dejection plain, for I have poured away my felicity, leaving only the dregs of remorse.

> How to please my Lord, having stooped to shame,
> That now I scorn, and blush to name?'"

48.5   *Aboo Zaid's history, continued*

"When the man had finished lamenting his condition and deprecating his state, my soul goaded me on, saying, 'Here, Aboo Zaid, is a pretty picking; now is the time for address, and the occasion for industry!' I rose up from my squat as if eager to display my liberality, and flew out of my row of worshippers as if shot from a bow. Then I declared:

> Splendid Fellow, who in a luckless Hour,
> Fall'n from the summit of his princely Pow'r,
> Craveth Counsel, that his Pain may cease:
> Let Virtue guide you to the Throne of Peace!
> Where I have been frenzied, be you calm,
> From my Torments press a healing Balm.

> I hail from Sarooj, there called bless'd,
> All men my Servants, each man my Guest;
> With bounteous Gifts my Honor secured,
> Of the Mosque a Pillar, among Men a Lord;
> On the Hilltop my Fires bade Men draw near
> To sate their Hunger and still their Fear;
> None came to me thirsty, thirsty to remain,
> Nor came the Seeker to my Camp in Vain.

48.6
> Fortune's Favorite, I was each Man's Friend,
> Till God decreed long Custom's End,
> And the grasping Greek, by Bloodlust hurl'd,
> Ravished our Lands, and shook the World;

And I, who vied with Bounty's Hands,
Now shew my Miseries in distant Lands,
And a Grief, that doth all Peace destroy:
A Daughter taken, who was my Joy,
Abducted, when the Romans 'pon us crept,
Now held as a Prize, for Ransom kept.

Will you gaze 'pon one so sunk in Grief   48.7
And grudge the Boon of bless'd Relief?
No mortal Foe, but vengeful Fate
Hath poured the bitter Cup of Hate!
Abducted Virtue cries, 'O Friend,
Thy Wallet open, thy Hand extend,
And win, an thou givest coins enow,
Forgiveness for thy broken Vow!'
Nor forget, good sirs, one more beside:
Myself, who would ye to Repentance guide!

Aboo Zaid's history, continued   48.8

"My auditor now convinced of my veracity, I suffered my fit of nervous volubility to subside. Urged to charity, and entreated by compassion, he proved keenly desirous to offer assistance, which he did prodigally, and without delay. I then repaired to my lodgings, delighted with the success of my imposture: for, by sly artifice, I had gained a supper, and procured a pudding with a string of verse."

El-Hareth Ben Hammam concludes his tale.   48.9

To Aboo Zaid I said:
"This confession, sir, of your ingenuity, and that of your Maker, I know not how to receive, or in what terms to acknowledge!"
He loosed a roar of merriment, then replied with great volubility of speech:

What use, among Savages, is honest Toil?
Abhor no Trick, nor from Lies recoil:
To turn thy Wheel, and eat thy Fill,
Thou must block the Stream, and bend the Rill.
Hunt the Eagle: 'tis better to seize
A single Feather, than snatch the Breeze;
And raid the Orchard: when fails the Fruit
Gather thee Branches, or grasp the Root.
With these, make the Joy thou dost not find,
And with this Spectacle, calm the Mind:
The motley World, in ceaseless Jest,
Heralds the Change to eternal Rest.

NOTES

Al-Sharīshī's account of the incident in the mosque runs as follows. One day, a judge named Ibn Qaṭarī appeared in the mosque of the Ḥarām quarter to announce that he had vowed to give up drinking but had broken his vow. What, he asked, was the appropriate penance?

> In the mosque was a man who claimed that he was from Sarūj and that the kafirs had captured his daughter. He said to Ibn Qaṭarī: "Your penance is to give me money to ransom her." Ibn Qaṭarī offered him ten dinars, and he took it and disappeared into a tavern. Al-Ḥarīrī used this incident as the basis of an Imposture he named after the Ḥarām quarter. Those who read it told him it was better than the Impostures of al-Hamadhānī. He went on to write forty of them, and when people asked for more, a full fifty (Sharīshī, *Sharḥ*, 5:320, citing al-Fanjdīhī or Panjdīhī, d. 584/1188).

This story is unlikely for various reasons. A judge who made a public confession of drunkenness would probably have been stripped of his judgeship and flogged. Moreover, why would a judge ask a group of strangers to rule on the law? Obviously, the story is a back-formation from Imposture 48 rather than the inspiration for it. It should be noted, however, that a variant cited by Yāqūt, and credited by him through al-Fanjdīhī to al-Ḥarīrī himself, is not implausible:

Abū Zayd of Sarūj was an old mendicant beggar, eloquent and well-spoken, who had ended up in Basra. One day he stood up in the Banū Ḥarām mosque, got everyone's attention, and appealed for help. The mosque happened to be crammed with educated people, including a certain governor, who were impressed with how clever and well-crafted his speech was. He mentioned a child who had been captured by the Byzantines, just as I have it in the Imposture of the Banū Ḥarām, which is number 48 . . .

That evening I mentioned the incident to a number of Basran scholars who had gathered at my home, going on about how deftly the man had used particular expressions and allusions to manipulate his audience. Everyone in the room said that he had seen the same man doing the same thing. Not only that, they had each seen him speak even more beautifully on a different subject altogether. Each time, he would alter his dress and appearance, proving himself a master of disguise. Everyone was amazed at how good he was at transforming himself. That's when I wrote the Imposture of the Banū Ḥarām, which was the first I did. The ones I wrote later are based on it (Yāqūt, Mu'jam, 5:2203).

Another variant, cited by Ibn Khallikān, adds that the eloquent beggar claimed to be from Sarūj (Ibn Khallikān, *Wafayāt al-A'yān*, 4:63).

Abdelfattah Kilito has argued that the search for a real person behind Abū Zayd is a response to the uneasiness generated by an avowed fiction (Kilito, *Séances*, 125–33; see further §0.6 and the Notes on al-Ḥarīrī's Introduction). Katia Zakharia adds that the story, which exists in several variants, is the invention of Ibn Barrī (d. 582/1187), who defended al-Ḥarīrī after al-Khashshāb denounced him for writing fiction (Zakharia, "Norme"). But Matthew Keegan has made a convincing argument that al-Ḥarīrī's fiction did not actually need to be defended (see Keegan, "Commentarial Acts," 249–302). Taken on its own, the eloquent-beggar story, in Ibn Khallikān's version at least, seems ordinary enough. The further adventures of Abū Zayd were clearly invented by al-Ḥarīrī, but there is nothing unlikely in the assertion that a real-life incident triggered the first composition and supplied a few key details.

On the assumption that this Imposture was indeed the first, Steingass suggests that it represents an experiment, after which al-Ḥarīrī realized that it would work better to have Abū Zayd's escapades narrated by someone else

(Steingass, *Assemblies*, 163). But this Imposture has a precedent. In at least one of al-Hamadhānī's Impostures (al-Baghdādiyyah), the narrator plays the role of the trickster, too, and so narrates his own adventure.

"Bassora" (§48.1) is an old spelling of Basra. By "martyrs" the narrator may mean Muslims killed during the wars of conquest. As Johnson's *Dictionary* often cites Milton to exemplify a word, I have used the latter as a model for the verses here. "Behold a wonder!" Milton, *Paradise Lost*, 1:777; "whom to behold but thee": Milton, *Paradise Lost*, 5:45; "and thee beholding forget my home": based on "With thee conversing I forget all time": Milton, *Paradise Lost*, 4:639.

"All Hallows" (§48.2) was the name of a neighborhood in eighteenth-century London. Here I use it to translate the name of the quarter of the tribe of Ḥarām, to which al-Ḥarīrī himself belonged (de Sacy, *Séances*, 2:3). "Ḥarām" is a personal name, though the word itself means "forbidden" or "sacred," the meaning I have used as the basis of the translation.

"Among them sir . . .": In the original this is a poem. Here I have rendered it as a block quotation in prose, in imitation of Johnson's frequent citations of long passages from letters and the like in his *Lives*.

"Dropt . . ." (§48.3) comes from Milton, *Paradise Lost*, line 745. "Leveled . . ." comes from Buchanan's gloss of the preceding passage (*First Six Books*, 274). "Allophony" is a rough translation of *badal*, the pronunciation of a sound in a variant form, either as a regular feature of the standard language, e.g., **waḥad* instead of *'aḥad*, or as a dialect feature, e.g., **nāt* for *nās* (see examples in De Sacy, *Séances*, 1:566). "Knee-wraps": see note to §16.1. Demosthenes, the ancient Greek orator, is standing in for for al-Ḥasan, the Prophet's grandson. Here as elsewhere I am taking advantage of the fact that pre-modern Arabic speakers were familiar with many ancient Greek figures (though not Demosthenes in particular as far as I know). A "canton," according to Johnson's *Dictionary*, is "a small parcel or division of land," and thus a rough equivalent for *khiṭṭah*, the term for the tribal allotments laid out when new cities like Basra were designed. "Repository of my secrets" comes from a hadith where the Prophet praises the Medinans who welcomed him there after his flight from Mecca (see Lane, *Lexicon*, s.v. *k-r-sh*).

"Thursday evening" (§48.4): Drinking on Thursday night (which, by Arab reckoning, is already Friday) was especially bad: "Make it a rule never to drink on the night preceding Friday . . . for Friday has an especial sanctity because of the assembly for worship" (Ibn Qābūs, *'Unṣur al-maʿālī*, 39; Ibn Iskandar, *Mirror*

for Princes, 60) and praying while drunk is explicitly banned in the Qur'an (Nisā'
4:43). "How to please my Lord . . ." is based on lines by John Savage cited in
Johnson, *Lives*, 368. "The grasping Greek" and "the Romans" (§48.6) both mean
the Byzantines. "I know not how to receive . . ." (§48.9) comes from "Johnson's
Letter."

BIBLIOGRAPHY

[Buchanan, James]. *The First Six Books of Milton's Paradise Lost: Rendered into
Grammatical Construction . . . with Notes Grammatical, Geographical,
Historical, Critical, and Explanatory; To Which Are Prefixed Remarks
on Ellipsis and Transposition . . .* Edinburgh: printed for A. Kincaid and
W. Creech, and J. Balfour, 1773.

Ibn Iskandar, Kai-Ka'us. *A Mirror for Princes: The Qabus Nama.* Translated by
Reuben Levy. London: Cresset Press, 1951.

Ibn Qābūs, Kaykāvūs ibn Iskandar. *'Unṣur al-Ma'ālī.* Edited by Sa'īd Nafīsī.
Tehran: Maṭba'ah-i Majlis, 1312 [1933].

Johnson, Samuel. *A Dictionary of the English Language.* London: Printed by
W. Strahan, 1755

———. *The Lives of the Most Eminent English Poets with Critical Observations
on Their Works.* Revised ed. London: Walker, 1821.

[———]. "Johnson's Letter to Chesterfield, 7 February 1755." Edited by Jack
Lynch. http://andromeda.rutgers.edu/~jlynch/Texts/letter55.html.

———. *The History of Rasselas, Prince of Abyssinia.* Edited by Jack Lynch.
http://andromeda.rutgers.edu/~jlynch/Texts/rasselas.html#3.

———. "The Vanity of Human Wishes." Edited by Jack Lynch. http://androm-
eda.rutgers.edu/~jlynch/Texts/vanity49.html.

Milton, John. *Paradise Lost.* Text at The John Milton Reading Room. http://
www.dartmouth.edu/~milton/reading_room/contents/text.shtml.

IMPOSTURE 49

THE PARLIAMENT OF ROGUES

As this Imposture consists of Abū Zayd's (dying?) advice to his son, the obvious model was the Earl of Chesterfield's Letters to His Son on the Art of Becoming a Man of the World and a Gentleman *(1774). Like al-Ḥarīrī, Chesterfield composes in what he calls "periods," that is, groups of sentences bound together by sound and sense. Like him, too, he peppers his text with allusions and quotations. While al-Ḥarīrī draws only on Arabic sources, Chesterfield tosses in Latin, French, Italian, German, and Spanish, in addition to English. To imitate this, Abū Zayd will cite, paraphrase, or allude to the Bible, Ovid, the Qurʾan, Shakespeare, Milton, Pope, and Rückert's translation of the Impostures. He will also quote proverbs in Maltese, Egyptian Arabic, and French (a language known to al-Ḥarīrī's contemporaries as Frankish). He will use words absent from the* Letters *only if they are attested in Samuel Johnson's* Dictionary, *Johnson being a contemporary (and disgruntled client) of Chesterfield.*

49.1   *Mr. Ben Hammám gave this account:*

When Aboo Zaid, whom fourscore and thirteen had shackled to his couch, felt the approach of death, he rallied his forces and sent for his son.

"Dear boy," he said,

Do not for ever with thy vailed lids
Seek for thy noble father in the dust.
Thou know'st 'tis common, all lives must die,
Passing through nature to eternity.

"You are, thank God, my son and heir, destined to succeed me as Palatin of the Parliament of Rogues. A young man of your parts need not await the knocking of my cane to discover he has committed an error, nor have me rouse him with gravel to put him to the trial. It is his duty, rather, to put men in mind of virtue, and to file and polish their thoughts. Let me then advise you, and do so more usefully, I trust, than Seth did the Nabathees, or Jacob the tribes of Israel. This counsel is one I most earnestly wish you to retain in your thoughts and observe in your conduct. If you steer by my lights, your affairs will prosper and your estates flourish; but if you neglect my charge, your camp-fires will gutter and your dependents prefer to make a shift for themselves.

"Let me be that guide, who has gone to the bottom of things, and wit- **49.2** nessed many a perversity of fate.

"Men rise in the world, not by their accomplishments, but by their incomes; not by birth, but by wealth. I had heard it reckoned, that the means to a livelihood are four: agriculture, manufacture, commerce, and government. I have practiced them all, in order to discover the most profitable. Each, it is true, supplied the wants of life, but none its superfluities. The cultivation of the soil constrains a man's motions and is unbecoming to his honor, while the management of lands costs him his dignity without providing him serenity of mind. The tradesman's profit suffices but to keep him from starvation, and even that, not always; and it is dependent for its continuance on his youth and vigour. As for the merchant, his commerce is the plaything of fortune and his goods a temptation to the thief; his stock is no more likely to remain where he leaves it, than a bird of passage to remain upon a branch. Power, it is true, gives opportunities for gain, and authority some chance for profit; but these vanish, 'as a confused heap of dreams,' or a passing shadow; and yet a man will part from his office with as much distress as an infant torn from the breast.

49.3   "If you would have booty without bloodshed, feast without famine, and plenty without pain, there is no profession more lucrative than that founded by the Parliament of Rogues, who, by the cultivation of its various branches, have made it the glory of the world. I wear the riband of this order, and have ridden into battle under its banner. Its commerce is brisk, its spring inexhaustible, its fame a taper in the dark; by its brilliancy are the *borgne* and the blind guided to the light. How formidable are its members, and how blessed! Above the reach of misfortune, safe from fire and sword, they fear no sting, and tremble before no man soever. Let storms rage, and men run riot: unmoved, the Rogue looks upon the tumult. His assembly is full of gaiety and spirits; his meals appear promptly and his conversation sparkles. Wherever he stops, he finds something worth picking up; and he cannot insinuate himself without earning some profit or other. He belongs to no nation and fears no king. He and his bretheren are like 'the fowls of the air, for they sow not, neither do they reap,' yet home they fly with bellies full."

49.4   "What you say is very correct," replied his son, "but anything half said is not said at all. Pray tell me how to gather the flowers in my way, and how not to mangle what I mean to carve."

"My dear son," said Aboo Zaid, "you must be active, diligent, alert, indefatigable, and above all things, forward. You must race like the *cincindèle*, scramble like the locust, spring like the wolf, and run by moonlight like the fox. Do not trust fortune; but rather let striving supply the want of luck, and labour overcome the enmity of circumstance. Wriggle yourself into every hole; dive into the 'dark, unbottomed, infinite abyss'; 'graze the verdant mead'; and plunge your bucket into every cistern. Take no denial: repulsed twice or thrice, persist, and you will prevail at last. Did not our master Sasán have inscribed upon his cudgel: 'Ask, and it shall be given you; seek and ye shall find'? Pray, therefore, no indolence, no sloth! Laziness is the harbinger of misery, dependence, and want; if indulged, it will make you stagnate in a contemptible obscurity all your life. 'Slothfulness casteth into a deep sleep, and an idle soul shall suffer hunger.'

"Push yourself forward, even if a lion stand before you; for fortune favours the intrepid, and daring lends ardour to the tongue. By boldness alone are riches won and rank attained. Timidity, on the other hand, begets only failure. If you set out with diffidence, your labours will miscarry and your efforts come to nothing. Thus it is said that 'the bold adventurer succeeds the best,' while he who hesitates is like the ass in the fable, that starved between two hampers of hay.

"And so, my son, rise early as the raven, and sally forth as bold as the   49.5
lion. In deliberation, emulate the chameleon; in cunning, the wolf; in assiduity, the boar; in alacrity, the gazelle; in craftiness, the fox; in steadiness, the camel; in blandishment, the cat; and in mutability, the hummingbird.

"Perfect your elocution, and use it to attain your ends; for it is the ears that must be flattered and seduced, and this can only be done by eloquence.

"Survey the market before you supply it; coax the teat before you milk it; inquire of the pasture before you graze it; and pommel your bed into softness before you lie in it.

"Refine your powers of observation and discernment, for poor judgment leads to error, and error to disappointment, while a moderate share of penetration will be amply rewarded.

"Indulge weakness in others, but not yourself.

"Despise no draught as too scanty; rather than await the torrent, gather the dew. Never refuse a trifle, and be grateful for what is offered, however small. Acccpt no rcfusal, for even a solid stone may yield a drop. 'Never despair of Providence, for despair is the mark of the impious.'

"Asked if you would have a speck today or a peck tomorrow, take the speck, if it be ready money; for no resolution is safe, nor any promise exempt, from delay, change of heart, or the accidents of life; and between giving one's word, and keeping it, lies a rugged road indeed.

"Emulate, in men of valour, their *force d'âme*; and in men of judgment, their *adresse*. Cultivate ease of manner, but shun the negligence of excessive familiarity.

"Keep your coins on a tether, and temper your generosity with prudence. Do not squander your gold dinars away, but scorn to wrangle over dirhams.

"Should a country grow tiresome, because of low spirits, or real grief, renounce it, and ride away; for a place is only as good, as it is good to you. Do not complain of the rigours of the road, nor bewail the trouble of removing from your lodgings. Without exception, the illustrious founders of our order believed (as the ditty justly says) that *min ibiddel l-imkien ibid-del il-vintura*, 'Who changes countries, swaps for a better fortune,' and condemned those who call travel an affliction and exile a curse. That, our patriarchs said, is the excuse of those content to sink into low company, and live on the scanty gleanings of their own *patrie*.

"If you resolve to go abroad, you will find good company as needful as your stick and baggage. *Ganna min ghēr nās* (as the vulgar expression is) *ma tindās*, 'A heaven without friends is no heaven at all,' and the Franks say, very prettily, *Mieux vaut être seul que mal accompagné*, 'Better alone than in poor company.'

49.6 Give heed, my son, to this Bequest,
For by its like are Rogues address't;
Tho' none since old Sasán held sway,
Nor any one till Judgment Day,
Has heard, will hear, so well-wrought
A Charge, or one so rich in Thought.
Keep it well! for thus, dear Zayd,
Are Glories won, and Heroes made.
And tho' thy Sire will shortly die,
'Pon thine Ears will fall the wond'ring Cry:
'Twixt roguish Father and roguish Son
Is all a Rogueness; the two are one!

49.7 "My dear son, I have given you my last testament, and that at length. If you follow it, I shall rejoice; should you resist it, the loss shall be your own. I leave you under the care of God, trusting that you will answer the hopes you have inspired."

"May God raise you from your sickly bed!" said the boy. "An admirable lesson, full of truth and probity, and a gift like no other given by father to son. I cannot wish to outlive you; but should that misfortune befall me, I shall form myself upon your model, and follow the path you have pointed out, till it be said of me, 'Thou art thy father's spirit,' and *wie kehrt das Morgenroth wieder im Abendroth*—'How like the twilight is the dawn!'"

Aboo Zaid was moved to joy, and said, smilingly, "The likeness of his sire upholds his mother's fame!"

Mr. Ben Hammám finished his story:

It has been reported that when the Parliament of Rogues heard these splendid precepts, they declared them superior to the epigrams of Lokmán. They fixed them in their memory forever, as one treasures up the text of the Alcorán; and their children, to this day, learn them by rote, upon account of their merit, which is more precious, they say, than a vein of native gold.

GLOSSARY
49.3
borgne   one-eyed
49.4
cincindèle   tiger beetle
49.5
force d'âme   fortitude
adresse   skill, dexterity

NOTES
At the beginning of this episode, we learn that Abū Zayd is close to death. But if he dies, he dies offstage. Perhaps, then, the illness he suffers here is the one described in Imposture 19, from which he recovers. If, on the other hand, he does die here, this Imposture belongs after the last one, Imposture 50, where he mends his ways. Since, furthermore, he advises his son in this episode to steal and beg, it follows that the change of heart described in 50 is either temporary or feigned, and that Abū Zayd died a rogue after all.

The quotation in §49.1 comes from Shakespeare, *Hamlet*, I:2. The knocking of the cane is a reference to the practice of a certain pre-Islamic arbiter, who, when he grew old and began making errors in judgment, asked his daughter to tap with a stick every time he slipped up, so that he could reverse himself (Sharīshī, *Sharḥ*, 5:323). The rousing with gravel refers to a test of fitness to go raiding. To learn which of their fellow tribesmen were likeliest to keep alert, the

Arabs would drop gravel near them as they slept, then choose the men who were awakened by the sound (Sharīshī, *Sharḥ*, 5:325).

The English presentation of the four ways to earn a living (§49.2) reverses the order of the original. "As a confused heap of dreams" comes from Q Anbiyāʾ 21:5, tr. Sale. In (§49.3), "the fowls of the air . . . ," from Matthew 6:26, renders the allusion to a hadith where the Prophet says, "If you trusted in God truly, He would provide you with sustenance, as He does for the birds that fly away hungry in the morning and return sated in the evening" (cited in Sharīshī, *Sharḥ*, 5:331). In (§49.4), "dark, unbottomed, infinite abyss" comes from Milton, *Paradise Lost*, line 405, cited in Johnson, *Dictionary*, s.v. "abyss." "Graze the verdant mead" comes from Pope, "Messia," cited in Johnson, *Dictionary*, s.v. "graze." "Ask, and it shall be given you . . ." comes from Matthew 7:7. "Slothfulness . . ." comes from Proverbs 19:15. "Bold adventurer . . ." comes from the translation in Ovid, *Metamorphoses*, 2:112, which corresponds very distantly to Book 8, lines 72–73. In §49.5, "pommel" is Johnson's spelling of "pummel," i.e., pound (not in Chesterfield). "Never despair . . ." comes from Q Yūsuf 12:87.

In §49.5, "*min ibiddel l-imkien* . . ." comes from the Kantilena, the first known poem in Maltese (here given in modern spelling). A full text with translation may be found in Briffa, *This Fair Land*, 63–64. As Maltese is an offshoot of spoken North African Arabic, it is arguably homologous, with respect to al-Ḥarīrī, to the "vulgar" English occasionally quoted by Chesterfield. "*Ganna min ghēr nās* . . ." is a proverb here given in Egyptian dialect, another "vulgar" offshoot of Arabic. In §49.7, "May God raise you. . ." alludes to "She has rais'd me from my sickly bed," from Shakespeare, *All's Well*, II:3; and "thou art . . ." invokes "I am thy father's spirit," from Shakespeare, *Hamlet*, I:5. "*Wie kehrt . . .*" comes from Rückert's translation of this passage (*Verwandlungen*, 318). "The likeness . . ." is based on a verse by Kaʿb ibn Zuhayr as translated by Steingass, who takes it to mean that, by resembling his father, a son provides proof of his mother's chastity (*Assemblies*, 175). Lokmán (Luqmān) is a figure of pre-Islamic legend, famous for his wise aphorisms.

BIBLIOGRAPHY

Briffa, Charles, ed. *This Fair Land: An Anthology of Maltese Literature*. London: Francis Boutle, 2014.

[Chesterfield]. *The Project Gutenberg EBook of The PG Edition of Chesterfield's Letters to His Son, by the Earl of Chesterfield.* http://www.gutenberg.org/files/3361/3361-h/3361-h.htm.

[Ovid]. *Ovid's Metamorphoses.* Translated by Maynwaring, Croxall et al. London: Suttaby, Evance, and Fox, 1812.

Pope, Alexander. "Messia: A Sacred Eclogue." http://www.bartleby.com/203/40.html.

IMPOSTURE 50

SEE SAW MARGERY DAW

The last Imposture describes Abū Zayd's apparent change of heart and his embrace of fervid piety. Some readers have taken it as genuine, others as another imposture. If genuine, it has to be reconciled with Imposture 49, where Abū Zayd seems to die unrepentant. The English narration is modeled on the autobiography of Margery Kempe (d. after 1438), which also describes a conversion experience. Like Abū Zayd's, Kempe's account is not entirely convincing: although she claims to have achieved bliss through her spiritual marriage to Jesus, even by her own account she does so only intermittently, and she never seems to lose her acute self-consciousness. In both cases, too, one misses the steady joy that is said to mark genuine mystical experience. To render the verbal performances without equivalents in Kempe, the English draws on other Middle English sources. Abū Zayd's bumptious travelogue channels The Book of John Mandeville, *a fanciful itinerary compiled by multiple hands beginning in the mid-fourteenth century. Abū Zayd's chilling verses on death are based on poems by William Langland (d. ca. 1386) and John Skelton (d. 1529). A word-for-word transposition of the pseudo-Middle English of this Imposture into modern English appears at the foot of the page.*

Alharet Eben Hammam seyd to us thes wordys: 50.1

On a tyme it bifel I was vexid and labowryd wyth sorwye and sadnes al inflaumyd, and it chongyd my cuntenawns wonderly. But I had herd seyn to make gret preysyng and thankyng to God is solas and cowmfort. And I wend nothyng mote slakyn the hete brennyng in my brest but I schuld go to the gret moseach of Bassora. At that tyme was ther so many folke that unethe a creature myth fynden a peler ther to leyn him, for many folk wer sor athryste. Fro hys gardyn wer gadyrd many fayr flowerys of speche, and fro hys porchys cam a scrapyng of pennes. And so went I forth wyth rygth good wyl, not yrke, ne tyrnyng on syde for anything. Than anon as I set fote upon hys cheselys of gravel and lokyd abowte the yerd to the forthest ende, I beheld a man stondyn hy upon a ston, weryng a cloke ful of clowtys, and abowt hym meche pepyl gadyrd to lokyn and wonderyn on hym, so many that they myte not be nowmeryd, and havyng gret merveyle of hys speche. So I hyed me to hymward for I was sor mevyd in spiryt to be recuryed of my sekenes. As I went thorw the press of the pepil I was labowryd with many that bofetyd me in the brest and bobyd me beforn my mowth but I went forth ful mekely and answered not, tyl I cam biforn hym. And I sat as ner as I cowde that I mygth know him, and lo! he was the olde man of

---

Alharet Eben Hammam said to us these words:

On a time it befell I was vexed and labored with sorrow and sadness all inflamed, and it changed my countenance strangely. But I had heard say, to make great praising and thanking to God is solace and comfort. And I thought nothing might slake the heat burning in my breast but I should go to the great mosque of Basra. At that time was there so many folk that no creature might find a pillar there to lean him, for many folk were sore athirst. From its garden were gathered many fair flowers of speech, and from its porches came a scraping of pens. And so went I forth with right good will, not weary, nor turning on side for anything. Then as soon as I set foot upon its pebbles of gravel and looked about the yard to the furthest end, I beheld a man standing high upon a stone, wearing a cloak full of patches, and about him much people gathered to look and wonder on him, so many that they might not be numbered, and having great marvel of his speech. So I hied me to himward for I was sore moved in spirit to be cured of my sickness. As I went through the press of the people I was labored with many that buffeted me in the breast and bobbed me before my mouth but I went forth full meekly and answered not, till I came before him. And I sat as near as I could that I might know him, and lo! he was the old man

Seruj, wyth which syght was I wel relevyd and comfortyd. And when he sey me stondyng biforn him he cryed:

50.2 "Good folke of Bassora, *benedicité!* God kepe yow rygth wel, and dryfe awey your enmys, and strengthyn among yow the reverens of God! How swet is yowr smell, how good yowr odowr! Clenest of townys is Bassora and purest; hir feldys ar brode and wide, hyr pasture gentil. Her moseak poynteth Meccawards most line-ryth, and ther Hiddekel is brodest; non towne hath mor reverys and palmys, ne is any so godly in al thynges gret and smal. Sche is the foreyerd of the Holy Londe, ageyn the Dor of the Caaba and the Stacyown of Abraham; sche is on of the wynges of this worlde, and the cité bilt on Goddys dred, defowlyd by no fyr tempyl, ne abominable processyon of images, for no lord had evyr be served ther but owr mercyful God. Hir meted coostes han many holy placys, moseachs, londmarkes, grave-yerds and other famows syghtes, ther meche pepyl come on pilgrimage. Ther se-men metyn hir schepys, and the salaman-dre the whale; ther the marinyr meteth the camle-drovyr, the huntyr the plough-man, the archyer the launce, and the courser the swymmyr; and sche hath for a sygn, the ebbe and flod of the tyde.

50.3 "And as for yow, al men, even your enmys hemselfe, speke wyth on assent of yowr vertues. Yowr comown pepil are most obedyent servawntys

---

of Seruj, with which sight was I well relieved and comforted. And when he saw me standing before him he cried:

"Good folk of Bassora, blessings! God keep you right well, and drive away your enemies, and strengthen among you the reverence of God! How sweet is your smell, how good your odor! Cleanest of towns and purest is Basra; her fields are broad and wide, her pasture gentle. Her mosque points Meccawards most line-right, and there the Tigris is broadest; no town has more rivers and palms, nor is any so godly in all things great and small. She is the fore-yard of the Holy Land, against the Door of the Kaaba and the Station of Abraham; she is one of the wings of this world, and the city built on the fear of God, defouled by no fire temple, nor abominable procession of images, for no lord had ever been served there but our merci-ful God. Her measured districts have many holy places, mosques, landmarks, grave-yards and other famous sights, where much people come on pilgrimage. There sea-men meet their ships, and the salamander the whale; there the mariner meets the camel-drover, the hunter the plough-man, the archer the lance, and the courser the swimmer; and for a sign, she has the ebb and flood of the tide.

"And as for you, all men, even your enemies themselves, speak with one assent of your virtues. Your common people are most obedient servants unto the sultan, and most thanking

unto the sowdan, and most thankyng of goodnesse; and yowr ankrys most
holy in hir maner of lyving. Yowr doctorys of dyvynyté cun more skyl than
any men befor hem or aftir, havyng grace inow to answer every clerke in
the love of God. It was a man of yowr towne whech fowndyd the rwelys of
gramer, and another whech ordeyned of rimyn the balaunce. In doyng gret
dedys han ye honowr and preemynence, for the whech arn ye worthy gret
worshep fyrst of all eother. Ferthermore arn yowr somownyrs to prayerys
mor than in any other towne, and yowr ankrys best in the streytnesse of
hir rewle. Al don aftyr yowr exampyl, that ye shavyn the hed aftir Arafat,
and eatyn er day al the tyme of the fastyng moneth. And whan other gon
to bedde and slypen in rest and pees, ye waken al the nyghte praysyng God
and cryng ful lowde, wherby ye waken them that slypen but give rygth
glad cher to them that slypen not. Wyth every risyng of the sunne, thow
the wedyr wer nevyr so hoot or colde, is herd the callyng to prayer, wyth
a roryng lyke to the wynd upon the see. So the lore of ancien tyme seyth
of yow, and so seyde owre Prophete, blyssyd mot he be, whan he declaryd
yowr cryeng at day lythe is lyke to the bomelyng of bees in her hyves, and
thus honouryng yow with his tydyngys. Worshyped be your citie, thow
sche is fallyn to nought, and only a remenaunt abydeth."

---

of goodness; and your anchorites most holy in their manner of living. Your doctors of divin-
ity can more skill than any men before them or after, having grace enough to answer every
clerk in the love of God. It was a man of your town which founded the rules of grammar, and
another which ordained of rhyming the balance. In doing great deeds have you honor and
preeminence, for the which are you worthy of great respect first of all other. Furthermore
are your summoners to prayers more than in any other town, and your anchorites best in the
strictness of their rule. All do after your example, that you shave the head after Arafat, and
eat before dawn all the time of the fasting month. And when others go to bed and sleep in
rest and peace, you wake all the night praising God and crying full loud, whereby you wake
them that sleep but give right glad cheer to them that sleep not. With every rising of the sun,
though the weather were never so hot or cold, is heard the calling to prayer, with a roaring
like to the wind upon the sea. So the lore of ancient time says of you, and so said our Prophet,
blessed might he be, when he declared your crying at day light is like to the buzzing of bees in
their hives, and thus honoring you with his tidings. Respected be your city, thou she is fallen
to naught, and only a remnant abides."

50.4 Therwyth he restraynd his tung and cesyd from spekyng. The pepil lokyd at him schrewydly and gan to skornyn him, seyng he cowd no skyll, for he had spoke but lytil. Wherfor he syhyd ful sore, lyke to a man takyn to ben sleyn for a deth, or a man alto rent and torn undyr a lyouns clawes. Than he sayd: "As for yow, pepil of Bassora, thar is no man among yow but he is worshepful and learnyd, fayr and mercyful. But as for myself, yf ye knowyn me, I am he whech ye knowyn, and the werst felawshep is the felawshep whech harmeth the. And yf ye knowyn me not, I shal telle that I have sey. I was bore in the toun of Batnae, but have lyvyd in eny but. I have gon estward to Tehomet, westward to Najhet, southward to Ynde the Lesse, and northward to Syrry, travelyng by day and by nyght, over the desert and uppon the see. I have passyd thorgh narwe places and barryd gates; I have seye gret batayles, discomfityd mine enmys, and thrystyd hir noses to the erthe; I have smytyn the roch, and meltyd stonys. Aske of the est and the west, ask hof and cowche, what man I am; ask the gret ostes and conseils of men, hir knyghtes and kyndes; ask the clerkys and jestours, whech tellyn storyes of mervailes, wher thei knowyn me; ask the dryvers of ladyn camels, or crafty divynours, and thei may tell yow, how many wayes I have passed bytwyne the hilles, how many kerches to-drowyn, and how many wicked londes and perelous I have y-seye. Many a conning man

---

Therewith he restrained his tongue and ceased from speaking. The people looked at him shrewdly and began to scorn him, saying he could no skill, for he had spoken but little. Wherefore he sighed full sore, like to a man taken to be slain for a death, or a man utterly rent and torn under a lion's claws. Then he said: "As for you, people of Basra, there is no man among you but he is worshipful and learned, fair and merciful. But as for myself, if you know me, I am he which you know, and the worst fellowship is the fellowship which harms you. And if you know me not, I shall tell what I have seen. I was born in the town of Batnae, but have lived in any but. I have gone eastward to Tihama, westward to Najd, southward to Yemen, and northward to Syria, traveling by day and by night, over the desert and upon the sea. I have passed through narrow places and barred gates; I have seen great battles, discomfited my enemies, and thrust their noses to the earth; I have smitten the rock, and melted stones. Ask of the East and the West, ask hoof and hump, what man I am; ask the great hosts and counsels of men, their knights and tribes; ask the clerks and jesters, which tell stories of marvels, whether they know me; ask the caravan-drivers, or crafty diviners, and they may tell you, how many ways I have passed between the hills, how many veils drawn away, and how many wicked lands and perilous I have seen. Many a cunning man have I beguiled, and much fraud and guile

have I bygylyed, and meche fraude and gile feined. Many chaunces have I takyn, many beestes caught, and many breddes fellyd; many a tersour fond by castyn charmys, and many a ston by sotil artes cloven, tyl a strem brast owt.

"Alle thes thyngys I did whan I was fresshe and grene, whan myn hayre was blacke, and the cloke of youthe unclowtyed. But now my lippes shrunken are for age, and croked be my lymes alle; myn hed's derk nyght parteth befor the morn. Now nowt abydeth save repentawns of my synnes, yf it help me, and sewyng the cloke I rent, for the gappe gro. And therfore I have thowt of an acounte that I onys herd, an acounte ratefyd and confermed: that Goddys mercyful eye falleth every day upon yow, and whil other mennys armes ar of yre, yowr armes ar of prayer. So have I gon thorgh many londes, and wastyd many camles, and now I stond before ye; but I ask ryth nowt but that ye may wel gevyn me, for I am comyn for myn owyn nede, to sekyn socowr. I ask no gyft save yowr bedys, ne eny mony, but only yowr prayers. So beseche God to gyde me to repentawns and make me redy for deth; for He answereth our cry, and sendeth to contricyon, and forgyfeth al syn and trespas."

Then he sang:

50.5

50.6

---

feigned. Many chances have I taken, many beasts caught, and many birds felled; many a treasure found by casting charms, and many a stone by subtle arts cloven, till a stream burst out.

"All these things I did when I was fresh and green, when my hair was black, and the cloak of youth unpatched. But now my lips shrunken are for age, and crooked be my limbs all; my head's dark night parts before the morn. Now naught abides save repentance of my sins, if it help me, and mending the cloak I rent, before the gap grows. And therefore I have thought of an account that I once heard, an account ratified and confirmed: that God's merciful eye falls every day upon you, and while other men's arms are of iron, your arms are of prayer. So have I gone through many lands, and wasted many camels, and now I stand before you; but I ask right naught but what you may well give me, for I have come for my own need, to seek succor. I ask no gift save your prayers, nor any money, but only your prayers. So beseech God to guide me to repentance and make me ready for death; for He answers our cry, and sends to contrition, and forgives all sin and trespass."

Then he sang:

I am sori for my synnes • I sey to my selfe
I bete on my breste • and bidde hym of grace
As I with wordes and werkes • have wrouȝte yuel in my lyue
But for þi mykel mercy • mitigacioun I biseche
Ne dampne me nouȝt at domesday • for þat I did so ille
For is no gult here so grete • þat his goodnesse is more.
And al þe wikkednesse in þis worlde • þat man myȝte worche or
   thinke
Ne is no more to þe mercye of god • þan in þe see a glede.

50.7   And al the pepil began to prayn for him. And he turnyd hys face to hevyn
so longe til he was resolvyd into terys and stod tremelyng ful sore in hys
flesche. Then he cryed wyth a lowde voys, "Blissyd mote God ben! I have
seyn the token of hys quemfulnes, and the clowd of dowte is lyfted. May
ye have a reward in hevyn, good folke of Bassora, for ye han delyveryd me
fro my diswer!"

Whan thei herd this speche ther was no man but joyd for hym and gaf
hym as many fayr almes as he cowde, and he acceptyd her gyftys, and
thankyd hem gretly of her charyté , mor than thei deservyd. Than he cam
down fro the ston and went forth to the sondes of Bassora. And I folwyd

---

I am sorry for my sins • I say to my self
I beat on my breast • and bid Him of grace
As I with words and works • have wrought evil in my life
But from thy great mercy • mitigation I beseech
Nor damn me naught at doomsday • for what I did so ill
For is no guilt here so great • that his goodness is more.
And all the wickedness in this world • that man might work or think
Is no more to the mercy of God • than in the sea a spark.

And all the people began to pray for him. And he turned his face to heaven so long till he
was resolved into tears and stood trembling full sore in his flesh. Then he cried with a loud
voice, "Blessed may God be! I have seen the token of his mercy, and the cloud of doubt is
lifted. May you have a reward in heaven, good folk of Basra, for you have delivered me from
my doubt!"

When they heard this speech there was no man but joyed for him and gave him as many
fair alms as he could, and he accepted their gifts, and thanked them greatly of their charity,
more than they deserved. Then he came down from the stone and went forth to the shore

him so longe til we wer by owrself alone and no man schuld aspyn us ne wetyn. Than I sayde, "Thow dedist wondirfuly this tyme, but how farist thow, now thow hast repentyd the?"

He sayde, "I swer to the by Hym who weteth alle, and forgyveth alle, that a grace hath fallyn me, to wonderyn on, for thy brethyrs prayer is answeryd."

I seyde, "Tell me thyn intent, and I prey God incres hys grace in the!"

Sayde he agen, "Be thi fadyr, I stode beforn hem in dowt, and in purpose to desseyven hem, but than I was steryd in my soule to contricyon. He is wel blyssed that thei hym lyken, and dampnyd is he by hem acursyd!"

Than he byd me far wel and departyd, leavyng me ful of drede.

I abod a long tym in care and trubbyl for hys sake, desiryng to conferm   50.8
what he seyde to me. Wherfor I speryd of every passer and wey-goer, but herd no mo, than yf I had askyd domb bestes, or specheles roch, and so abode stylle in gret dysese. But at the last I met a felawship returnyng fro her jurné and askyd for fremde tydyngs. Thei seyde, "We have tydyngs more wonderfull than the Fenix of Elyople, or the eyne of the Bithyae of Scythia!"

I speryd of hem to make clere that thei sayd, and way oute for me what to hem had ben wayd. They telde me they had gon forth to Batnae after the

---

of Basra. And I followed him so long till we were by ourselves alone and no man should spy us nor wait. Then I said, "You did wonderfully this time, but how fare you, now you have repented yourself?"

He said, "I swear to you by Him who knows all, and forgives all, that a grace has fallen me, to wonder on, for thy brother's prayer is answered."

I said, "Tell me thy intent, and I pray God increase his grace in you!"

Said he against, "By thy father, I stood before them in doubt, and in purpose to deceive them, but then I was stirred in my soul to contrition. He is well blessed that they him like, and damned is he by them accursed!"

Then he bid me fare well and departed, leaving me full of dread.

I abode a long time in care and trouble for his sake, desiring to confirm what he said to me. Wherefore I inquired of every passer and way-goer, but heard no more, than if I had asked dumb beasts, or speechless rock, and so abode still in great unease. But at the last I met a fellowship returning from their journey and asked for odd tidings. They said, "We have tidings more wonderful than the Phoenix of Heliopolis or the eyes of the Bithyae of Scythia!"

I inquired of them to make clear what they said, and weigh out for me what to them had been weighed. They told me they had gone forth to Batnae after the pagans had left it. And

paynems had left it. And ther they had seyne, in a gowne of wulle arayd, the famows Abosayd, now an ankyr of name.

"Meynen ye," I askyd, "Abosayd, of Imposture fame?"

"The same," he cryd, "but now he worketh wondyrs!"

50.9 Wherfor I had a longyng to hymwardys, and being loth to fayle of this occasyon, I made me redy to departyn. Then I hyed me therwardys so longe til I cam to hys moseach, wher he kept hys place of prayer. And I fond him and hys felawshyp asunder, and hym standyng in his hirne. He was clad in a cloke ful of clowtys and a cloth of canvas as it were a sakkyn gelle. Whan I saw hym I hadde gret drede, as he were a lyon, for hys face bar the token of mech prostracyon. Whan hys paire of bedys was endyd, he reysed hys fore fynger to greten me, but never askyd for tydyngs anydeel, ne spak a word of the olde tyme. Than he gan to prayn hys supplicacyon, levyng me alone to lokyn upon hys fervowr with ful gret envye and marvelyn at hem that God gydeth aright. He gaf God preyse and worshyp ful humbely and mekely, and so plentyuowsly and contynualy that the five prayers wer endyd and this day turnyd to yesterday. Than he had me into hys howse and proferyd hys cake and oil. Sythen he stey up and went to his prayer place and had dalyawnce of our Lord. Whan at the laste the sunne gan aryse, he endyd his

there they had seen, in a gown of wool arrayed, the famous Abosayd, now an anchorite of name.

"Mean you," I asked, "Abosayd, of Imposture fame?"

"The same," he cried, "but now he works wonders!"

Wherfore I had a longing to him-wards, and being loth to fail of this occasion, I made me ready to depart. Then I hied me there-wards so long till I came to his mosque, where he kept his place of prayer. And I found him and his fellowship asunder, and him standing in his niche. He was clad in a cloak full of patches and a cloth of canvas as it were a garment of sackcloth. When I saw him I had great dread, as he were a lion, for his face bore the token of much prostration. When his pair of beads was ended, he raised his forefinger to greet me, but never asked for tidings at all, nor spoke a word of the old time. Then he began to pray his supplication, leaving me alone to look upon his fervor with full great envy and marvel at them that God guides aright. He gave God praise and worship full humbly and meekly, and so plenteously and continually that the five prayers were ended and today turned to yesterday. Then he had me into his house and proffered his loaf and oil. Then he stood up and went to his prayer place and had dalliance of our Lord. When at the last the sun rose, he

wakyng with preyse of God. Than he lay him downe to rest, and whil he lay
gan to chauntyn ful semly:

> Camp groundes of spryng,   50.10
> Fire stones in a ryng,
> Lyngeryng farewells,
> Pealyng camell bells:
> Forget them all
> And morn withall
> Dayes now passed beyonde recall:
> Full of fowle deedes recordyd,
> Defoyled and ensordyd,
> And ffylty nyghtes
> In lousy beddes
> With warkyng heads
> In Goddys dyspyt,
> Lewdly and lothsome,
> Waywyrde and wrothsome!

---

ended his waking with praise of God. Then he laid him down to rest, and while he lay began
to chant full seemly:

> Camp-grounds of spring,
> Fire-stones in a ring,
> Lingering farewells,
> Chiming camel-bells:
> Forget them all
> And mourn withal
> Days now passed beyond recall
> Full of foul deeds recorded,
> Defiled and sordid,
> And filthy nights
> In lousy beds
> With aching heads
> In God's despite,
> Lewdly and loathsome,
> Wayward and wrathsome!

But now I repent me of my wylfulnesse
And ask mercy of my neglygence.
For I am but dust
And dy I must,
With synnews wyderyd,
A worme etyn maw,
And a gastly jaw
Gaspyng asyde,
Nakyd of hyde.
For no worldly blys
Redeme vs from this:
Drawttys of deth
Stoppyng our breth,
Oure eyen sinkyng,
Oure bodys stynkyng,
Our gummys grynnyng,
Our soulys brynnyng.
Who then shall my Saviour be

But now I repent me of my wilfulness
And ask mercy of my negligence.
For I am but dust
And die I must,
With sinews withered,
A worm-eaten maw,
And a ghastly jaw
Gasping aside,
Naked of hide.
For no worldly bliss
Will redeem us from this:
Draughts of death
Stopping our breath,
Our eyes sinking,
Our bodies stinking,
Our gums grinning,
Our souls burning.
Who then shall my savior be

Almyghty God, but thé?
O God! I repent me with harte contryte
The repentance I haue no man can wryte.
To thé pray I, as Lord incomparable,
As thou art of mercy and pyte the well,
Thou bring unto thy joye eterminable
My soull from all daunger of hell
In endles blys with thé to dwell,
In thy heaven aboue the orient,
For thou art Lord and God omnipotent.

Alharet Eben Hammam seyd: 50.11

He contynued murmowryng hys prayer sor syhyng and sorwyng ful boistowsly, in so meche that I mygh not beryn it but wept for his wepyng as I had be wone to wepe for hym. Then he went forth to hys moseak, styll washyd clen fro hys wakyng. I folwyd and prayd wyth hem that prayd behynd hym. And whan the pepil gadyrd ther wentyn asunder and

---

Almighty God, but thee?
O God! I repent me with heart contrite
The repentance I have no man can write.
To thee pray I, as Lord incomparable,
As thou art of mercy and pity the well,
Thou bring unto thy joy interminable
My soul from all danger of Hell
In endless bliss with thee to dwell,
In thy heaven above the orient,
For thou art Lord and God omnipotent.

Alharet Eben Hammam said:

He continued murmuring his prayer sore sighing and sorrowing full boisterously, so much so that I might not bear it but wept for his weeping as I had been wont to weep for him. Then he went forth to his mosque, still washed clean from his waking. I followed and prayed with them that prayed behind him. And when the people gathered there went asunder and scattered them wide-where, he began preaching and teaching, and pouring this day into the mold

toscateryd hem wyde-wher, he gan prechyng and techyng, and pouryng this day into the mold of the oon bifor, wyth so gret wypyngs and lowd sobbyngs that I wel saw that he was joynyed to Goddys servawntys, and wolde be alone be hymselfe in Hys lofe. So I purposyd me fullych to departyn and levyn hym in hys felingys and revelacyons. He wern as he had red my thowt in my face, or had it seyde to his mende by Goddys powyr, for he syhyd ful sore and seyd, "'Anoon as thu be in purpos, trust ful wel in God.'" Wherfor I confermed, that the clerkys tellen us trewely that owre dispensacyon hath hem that owr Lord doth speke unto and daly to hir sowles. Than I gan neygh hym to taken him in honde, and I seyde, "Good seynt, geve me a word of cownsel!"

He seyde, 'Kep Deth befor thyn eyne! 'For now is the partyng of us tweyne for eueremore.'"

I byd hym far wel wyth boystows sobbyngys and gret plenté of terys. Then partyd we asundyr and I saw hym no mor.

---

of the one before, with so great weepings and loud sobbings that I well saw that he was joined to God's servants, and would be alone by himself in His love. So I purposed me fully to depart and leave him in his feelings and revelations. He were as he had read my thought in my face, or had it said to his mind by God's power, for he sighed full sore and said, "As soon as you be in purpose, trust full well in God." Wherefore I confirmed, that the clerks tell us truly that our dispensation has those that our Lord does speak unto and dally to their souls. Then I went nigh him to take him in hand, and I said, "Good saint, give me a word of counsel!"

He said, 'Keep Death before your eyes! For now is the parting of us two for evermore."

I bid him fare well with boisterous sobbings and great plenty of tears. Then parted we asunder and I saw him no more.

NOTES

The imitation of Kempe's Middle English is full of inconsistencies, just as the Middle English texts are themselves inconsistent, differing not only from each other but also within themselves. For derived forms I have sometimes had to guess at a reasonable spelling, based on the forms in the Michigan *Middle English Dictionary* (*MED*, for my use of which see Imposture 10) as a guideline. In the few cases where Kempe, Mandeville, and the poets all lacked the word I needed, I used the reverse lookup feature of the *MED*, favoring forms used by Chaucer.

The modern English version follows the pseudo-Middle English almost exactly. Besides updating spelling and grammar, it substitutes modern words for original terms that have fallen out of use (e.g., "thought" for "wend") or undergone a significant change in meaning (e.g., "respect" for "worshyp").

"Caaba" in §50.2 is the Kaaba, the shrine which according to tradition was built by Abraham in what is now Mecca, and the Station of Abraham is the place where he stood when building its walls.

Abū Zayd's praise of Basra in §50.3 refers to Sībawayh, whose *Kitāb* is the oldest extant systematic study of Arabic grammar, and al-Khalīl ibn Aḥmad, who derived the rules for the poetic meters.

In §50.4, Abū Zayd says that he was born in Sarūj and raised in the saddle (*surūj*, in the plural). The English uses this wordplay with "Batnae" and "any but." His claim to have struck a rock and brought forth water echoes Q Baqarah 2:60 and Aʿrāf 7:160.

The verses in §50.6 are taken, sometimes with modifications, from different parts of Langland's *Piers Plowman*, Passus V (specifically 410, 458, 376, 481, 482, 459, and 294–95 in the PPEA edition). The letter þ stands for *th*, and ȝ (in this case) for *gh*. Although I used Skeat's modern English translation to read the verses, my recasting does not follow his but instead simply modernizes the spelling except in a few cases where it seemed necessary to substitute a modern word (e.g., "spark" for "glede"). In this verse form, every line is divided by a medial caesura and each half line contains two stressed syllables. Three of the four stressed syllables in each line should begin with the same vowel or consonant. For a more complete explanation see Skeat's introduction to Langland, *Vision*, xxi–xxiv.

Although an enterprising traveler, Kempe has little to say about the places she visited, making it necessary to supplement her stock of words with borrowings from Mandeville. The TEAMS edition does not mention the Phoenix of Heliopolis, which I have from another recension cited in the *MED*: "In Egipt is the citee of Elyople . . . the cytee of the sonne. In þat [that] cytee þere [there] is a temple . . . the foul [fowl] þat is clept [called] Fenix . . . cometh to brenne [burn] himself vpon the awtere [altar] of þat temple at the ende of v hundred ȝeer [years]" (s.v. "fenix").

As an example of a marvel, the original mentions a famously farsighted woman named Zarqā' (Blue-Eyes). The English equivalent is based on a passage from Mandeville that speaks of an island populated by women with "stones in her eyen, and tho han soch a kynde that if they byholdeth any man with wrathe, they sleeth hym with her lokynge," that is, "stones in their eyes, and the ability to kill a man with a glance if they look on him with anger" (Mandeville, *Book*, 2530–32). The editors explain that the story "apparently refers to the Bithyae of Scythia, reported by Vincent of Beauvais (*Speculum Historiale* IV.15). Vincent, however, describes them as having *pupillas geminas* (double pupils), a description Mandeville appears to have misinterpreted as *pupillas gemmas* (gemstone pupils)" (Mandeville, *Book*, note to 2531).

"Dalyawnce" (dalliance, §50.9) is a word that Kempe commonly uses to refer to "one human being speaking to another" but more often to "God speaking to Margery in her soul" (Riquetti, *Stylistic*, 37).

The second half of the poem in §50.10 borrows, with modification, from Skelton's "Upon a deedmans hed . . ." (original spelling in *Poetical Works*, ed. Dyce, 1:23–25; modernized spelling in Ex-classics edition, 87–88); "Upon the dethe of the Erle of Northumberlande" (*Poetical Works*, 1:8–18 = 74–79); and *Magnificence* (Ex-classics edition, 308–72; missing in the electronic edition of the *Poetical Works*, ed. Dyce, and so consulted in the facsimile edition for the original spelling).

"Anoon as thu be in purpos, trust ful wel in God" (§50.11) comes from Q 'Imrān 3:159. "Owre dispensacyon hath . . .": that is, our religious community (*ummah*) has among its members persons to whom God imparts knowledge of matters otherwise unknown. I have borrowed "dispensation" from Steingass, *Assemblies*, 185.

Abū Zayd's parting words to al-Ḥārith come from Q Kahf 16:78, part of a conversation between Moses and his teacher, a mysterious figure referred to as al-Khiḍr. The latter has just performed a series of inexplicable actions—knocking a hole in a boat, killing a boy, and repairing a wall in a town full of misers. Moses, who had promised not to ask about anything al-Khiḍr might do, is unable to keep his promise. Al-Khiḍr then bids him farewell, but before taking his leave explains that each of his apparently senseless acts was performed for some greater good (Q Kahf 18:65–82). With this allusion, Abū Zayd seems to be suggesting that all of his tricks and lies contain some lesson for al-Ḥārith, who is too obtuse to grasp it. This is the position argued by Katia Zakharia (*Abū Zayd*, 315–16), who reads the Impostures as the tale of Abū Zayd's progress to a higher spiritual state. Philip Kennedy, by contrast, suggests that the allusion may serve to "collapse the verbal edifice of personal reform" that Abū Zayd has constructed around himself: here, as everywhere else in the collection, "the truth is incessantly discovered to be a pack of lies" (Kennedy, *Recognition*, 306).

Readers who want to believe that Abū Zayd's reform is (within the fictional world of the *Impostures*) genuine and permanent must somehow explain what happens in Imposture 49, in which the supposedly dying hero advises his son to follow in his con man footsteps. One way to do this is to posit that the Abū Zayd of 49 experiences a miraculous recovery—specifically, the recovery described in Imposture 19, where, we are told, "he fell ill . . . with something chronic and wasting" but then "rallied, and now he's feeling thoroughly all right again" (§19.2–3). On the other hand, if al-Ḥarīrī had intended this to be the obvious and agreed-upon sequence of events, he might have put 19 between 49 and 50. The fact that he did not do so suggests that the ambiguity surrounding Abū Zayd's conversion is another one of the book's special effects.

Whatever the case, Imposture 50, read on its own, does not appear to describe conversion to a state of mystical bliss. Abū Zayd prays almost incessantly, as if determined to power through to direct experience of God; and though he is supposed to reach the special state of consciousness characteristic of the Sufis, he never seems at peace, nor is he suffused with love for his fellow creatures. In the end the deficiency may be al-Ḥarīrī's. For all his cleverness—indeed, perhaps, because of it—he may have lacked the skill, or the will, to depict genuine religious feeling. It is striking that Abū Zayd's communion with God in §50.11 happens offstage. Perhaps al-Ḥarīrī is admitting that if such a thing as communion with God is real, it cannot be represented using his (or al-Ḥārith's) exquisitely self-conscious language.

"Then parted we asunder and I saw him no more" comes from Bunyan, *Pilgrim's Progress*, 226.

BIBLIOGRAPHY

Bunyan, John. *The Pilgrim's Progress*. Samizdat, 2013. http://www.samizdat. qc.ca/arts/lit/Pilgrims_Progress.pdf.

[Kempe, Margery]. *The Book of Margery Kempe*. Edited by Lynn Staley. Kalamazoo, Michigan: Medieval Institute Publications, 1996. Online at University of Rochester TEAMS Middle English Texts. http://d.lib. rochester.edu/teams/publication/staley-the-book-of-margery-kempe.

———. *The Book of Margery Kempe*. Translated by B. A. Windeatt. London: Penguin Classics, 2000. Online at ProQuest Literature Online, 2011.

[Langland, William]. *The Piers Plowman Electronic Archive*. Vol. 9, The B-Version Archetype. SEENET Series A.12. Edited by John Burrow and Thorlac Turville-Petre. http://piers.chass.ncsu.edu/texts/Bx.

———. *The Vision of Piers the Plowman by William Langland, Done into Modern English by the Rev. Professor Skeat*. London: Alexander Moring, 1905.

[Mandeville, John]. *The Book of John Mandeville*. Edited by Tamarah Kohanski and C. David Benson. Kalamazoo, Michigan: Medieval Institute Publications, 2007. Online at University of Rochester TEAMS Middle English Texts. http://d.lib.rochester.edu/teams/text/ kohanski-and-benson-the-book-of-john-mandeville.

McSparran, Frances, et al., eds. *Middle English Dictionary*. http://quod.lib. umich.edu/m/med/.

Riquetti, Susanne. *A Stylistic Analysis of the Book of Margery Kempe*. PhD diss., Oklahoma State University, 1978.

[Skelton, John]. *Magnificence*. London [?]: Tudor Facsimile Texts, 1910. https://archive.org/details/cu31924013166453.

———. *The Poetical Works of John Skelton*. Edited by Alexander Dyce. 3 vols. London: Thomas Rodd, 1843, 1862. Electronic edition edited by the Exclassics Project, 2015, with a delightful glossary. http://www.exclassics. com.

The Author's Retraction

In this send-off, al-Ḥarīrī asks God's forgiveness for writing a pointless book of fun and games—exactly what he promises in the Introduction not to do. The English is modeled on Chaucer's retraction of his non-devotional works.

Quod the lore-fader Abo Mahoun Elkasem Alis sone: 51.1

Here endeth the Pleyes of Myracles that I in my vain glorie wroughte, and al unthankes bade my tonge endite. Nedely I outed swich chaffare at market, and putte it forth in feires, thogh I knew it for mullock better sold than boghte. Hadde I had grace to biwayle my giltes, and to studie to the salvacioun of my soule, I wolde ful feyne have hid my defaute and kept myn honour and renoun; but al was aforn ordeined. Wherefore I pray that God foryeve me my endytinges of vanities and chater, that sounen in-to sinne; and sende me grace to defende me from errour, so that I may be oon of hem at the day of dome that shulle be saved. Only God ful worthy is to drede, and from him alone is mercy to be soghte; for from him procedeth al goodnesse in this present lyf and in the tother.

Here is ended the book, that thanke I oure Lord of al the worldes, bisekynge him Makomete our prophete and his folk to blessen.

GLOSSARY

lore-fader teacher

al unthankes by necessity, unwillingly

endite dictate

nedely perforce

outed swich chaffare displayed such wares for sale

mullock rubbish, refuse

endytinges writing down

chater prattle

sounen in-to   lead to

errour   distraction, perplexity, confusion

oon of hem   one of those

dome   doom

that thanke I   for which I thank

bisekynge   beseeching

BIBLIOGRAPHY

Chaucer, Geoffrey. *The Canterbury Tales*. Edited by Walter Skeat. Oxford: Oxford University Press, 1900. https://en.wikisource.org/wiki/Canterbury_Tales_(ed._Skeat).

———. *The Canterbury Tales*. Edited by A. C. Cawley. New York: Everyman's Library, 1958.

Fulk, R. D. *Introduction to Middle English: Grammar and Texts*. Toronto: Broadview, 2012.

McSparran, Frances, et al., eds. *Middle English Dictionary*. https://quod.lib.umich.edu/m/med/.

✤ ABOUT NYU ABU DHABI INSTITUTE

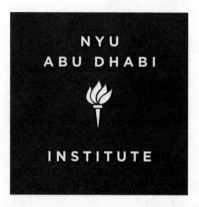

The Library of Arabic Literature is supported by a grant from the NYU Abu Dhabi Institute, a major hub of intellectual and creative activity and advanced research. The Institute hosts academic conferences, workshops, lectures, film series, performances, and other public programs directed both to audiences within the UAE and to the worldwide academic and research community. It is a center of the scholarly community for Abu Dhabi, bringing together faculty and researchers from institutions of higher learning throughout the region.

NYU Abu Dhabi, through the NYU Abu Dhabi Institute, is a world-class center of cutting-edge research, scholarship, and cultural activity. The Institute creates singular opportunities for leading researchers from across the arts, humanities, social sciences, sciences, engineering, and the professions to carry out creative scholarship and conduct research on issues of major disciplinary, multidisciplinary, and global significance.

Titles Published by the Library 🐍 of Arabic Literature

For more details on individual titles, visit www.libraryofarabicliterature.org

Classical Arabic Literature: A Library of Arabic Literature Anthology
Selected and translated by Geert Jan van Gelder (2012)

A Treasury of Virtues: Sayings, Sermons, and Teachings of ʿAlī, by al-Qāḍī al-Quḍāʿī, with the **One Hundred Proverbs** attributed to al-Jāḥiẓ
Edited and translated by Tahera Qutbuddin (2013)

The Epistle on Legal Theory, by al-Shāfiʿī
Edited and translated by Joseph E. Lowry (2013)

Leg over Leg, by Aḥmad Fāris al-Shidyāq
Edited and translated by Humphrey Davies (4 volumes; 2013–14)

Virtues of the Imām Aḥmad ibn Ḥanbal, by Ibn al-Jawzī
Edited and translated by Michael Cooperson (2 volumes; 2013–15)

The Epistle of Forgiveness, by Abū l-ʿAlāʾ al-Maʿarrī
Edited and translated by Geert Jan van Gelder and Gregor Schoeler (2 volumes; 2013–14)

The Principles of Sufism, by ʿĀʾishah al-Bāʿūniyyah
Edited and translated by Th. Emil Homerin (2014)

The Expeditions: An Early Biography of Muḥammad, by Maʿmar ibn Rāshid
Edited and translated by Sean W. Anthony (2014)

Two Arabic Travel Books
　Accounts of China and India, by Abū Zayd al-Sīrāfī
　　Edited and translated by Tim Mackintosh-Smith (2014)
　Mission to the Volga, by Aḥmad ibn Faḍlān
　　Edited and translated by James Montgomery (2014)

Disagreements of the Jurists: A Manual of IslamicLegal Theory, by al-Qāḍī al-Nuʿmān
Edited and translated by Devin J. Stewart (2015)

Consorts of the Caliphs: Women and the Court of Baghdad, by Ibn al-Sāʿī
Edited by Shawkat M. Toorawa and translated by the Editors of the Library of Arabic Literature (2015)

What ʿĪsā ibn Hishām Told Us, by Muḥammad al-Muwayliḥī
Edited and translated by Roger Allen (2 volumes; 2015)

The Life and Times of Abū Tammām, by Abū Bakr Muḥammad ibn Yaḥyā al-Ṣūlī
Edited and translated by Beatrice Gruendler (2015)

The Sword of Ambition: Bureaucratic Rivalry in Medieval Egypt, by ʿUthmān ibn Ibrāhīm al-Nābulusī
Edited and translated by Luke Yarbrough (2016)

Brains Confounded by the Ode of Abū Shādūf Expounded, by Yūsuf al-Shirbīnī
Edited and translated by Humphrey Davies (2 volumes; 2016)

Light in the Heavens: Sayings of the Prophet Muḥammad, by al-Qāḍī al-Quḍāʿī
Edited and translated by Tahera Qutbuddin (2016)

Risible Rhymes, by Muḥammad ibn Maḥfūẓ al-Sanhūrī
Edited and translated by Humphrey Davies (2016)

A Hundred and One Nights
Edited and translated by Bruce Fudge (2016)

The Excellence of the Arabs, by Ibn Qutaybah
Edited by James E. Montgomery and Peter Webb
Translated by Sarah Bowen Savant and Peter Webb (2017)

Scents and Flavors: A Syrian Cookbook
Edited and translated by Charles Perry (2017)

Arabian Satire: Poetry from 18th-Century Najd, by Ḥmēdān al-Shwēʿir
Edited and translated by Marcel Kurpershoek (2017)

In Darfur: An Account of the Sultanate and Its People, by Muḥammad ibn ʿUmar al-Tūnisī
Edited and translated by Humphrey Davies (2 volumes; 2018)

War Songs, by ʿAntarah ibn Shaddād
Edited by James E. Montgomery
Translated by James E. Montgomery with Richard Sieburth (2018)

Arabian Romantic: Poems on Bedouin Life and Love, by ʿAbdallah ibn Sbayyil
Edited and translated by Marcel Kurpershoek (2018)

Dīwān ʿAntarah ibn Shaddād: A Literary-Historical Study
By James E. Montgomery (2018)

Stories of Piety and Prayer: Deliverance Follows Adversity, by Muḥassin ibn ʿAlī al-Tanūkhī
Edited and translated by Julia Bray (2019)

The Philosopher Responds: An Intellectual Correspondence from the Tenth Century, by Abū Ḥayyān al-Tawḥīdī and Abū ʿAlī Miskawayh
Edited by Bilal Orfali and Maurice A. Pomerantz
Translated by Sophia Vasalou and James E. Montgomery (2 volumes; 2019)

Tajrīd sayf al-himmah li-stikhrāj mā fī dhimmat al-dhimmah: A Scholarly Edition of ʿUthmān ibn Ibrāhīm al-Nābulusī's Text
By Luke Yarbrough (2020)

The Discourses: Reflections on History, Sufism, Theology, and Literature—Volume One, by al-Ḥasan al-Yūsī
Edited and translated by Justin Stearns (2020)

Impostures, by al-Ḥarīrī
Translated by Michael Cooperson
Foreword by Abdelfattah Kilito (2020)

Maqāmāt Abī Zayd al-Sarūjī, by al-Ḥarīrī
Edited by Michael Cooperson
Foreword by Abdelfattah Kilito (2020)

ENGLISH-ONLY PAPERBACKS
Leg over Leg, by Aḥmad Fāris al-Shidyāq (**2 volumes; 2015**)
The Expeditions: An Early Biography of Muḥammad, by Maʿmar ibn Rāshid (2015)
The Epistle on Legal Theory: A Translation of al-Shāfiʿī's *Risālah*, by al-Shāfiʿī (2015)
The Epistle of Forgiveness, by Abū l-ʿAlāʾ al-Maʿarrī (2016)
The Principles of Sufism, by ʿĀʾishah al-Bāʿūniyyah (2016)
A Treasury of Virtues: Sayings, Sermons, and Teachings of ʿAlī, by al-Qāḍī al-Quḍāʿī with the **One Hundred Proverbs**, attributed to al-Jāḥiẓ (2016)
The Life of Ibn Ḥanbal, by Ibn al-Jawzī (2016)
Mission to the Volga, by Ibn Faḍlān (2017)
Accounts of China and India, by Abū Zayd al-Sīrāfī (2017)
A Hundred and One Nights (2017)
Disagreements of the Jurists: A Manual of Islamic Legal Theory, by al-Qāḍī al-Nuʿmān (2017)
What ʿĪsā ibn Hishām Told Us, by Muḥammad al-Muwayliḥī (2018)
War Songs, by ʿAntarah ibn Shaddād (2018)
The Life and Times of Abū Tammām, by Abū Bakr Muḥammad ibn Yaḥyā al-Ṣūlī (2018)
The Sword of Ambition, by ʿUthmān ibn Ibrāhīm al-Nābulusī (2019)
Brains Confounded by the Ode of Abū Shādūf Expounded: Volume One, by Yūsuf al-Shirbīnī (2019)
Brains Confounded by the Ode of Abū Shādūf Expounded: Volume Two, by Yūsuf al-Shirbīnī and **Risible Rhymes**, by Muḥammad ibn Maḥfūẓ al-Sanhūrī (2019)
The Excellence of the Arabs, by Ibn Qutaybah (2019)
Light in the Heavens: Sayings of the Prophet Muḥammad, by al-Qāḍī al-Quḍāʿī (2019)
Scents and Flavors: A Syrian Cookbook (2020)
Arabian Satire: Poetry from 18th-Century Najd, by Ḥmēdān al-Shwēʿir (2020)

ABOUT THE COVER ARTIST &

The artist **Hayv Kahraman** was born in Baghdad in 1981, and now lives
and works in Los Angeles. A vocabulary of narrative, of memory, and of
the dynamics of non-fixity found in diasporic cultures forms the essence
of her visual language and is the product of her experience as an Iraqi
refugee-cum-émigrée.

The painting that appears on the book's cover is a detail from Kahraman's "Kachakchi," part of a series titled *"How Iraqi are you?"* Formally
based on the 12th-century Baghdadi illuminated manuscripts of the
Maqāmāt al-Harīrī depicting ordinary life around Iraq, this painting narrates personal and collective stories of Iraqis and their diaspora, as typified
by the Iraqi word, *kachakchi*, "smuggler." The brown body of the protagonist has been erased and made white. The inclusion of Arabic text in this
series of paintings became a personal performance for Kahraman, who was
negotiating her own disassociation from her culture as she re-learned to
write her mother tongue.

Further details about the artist and her work can be found at:
www.hayvkahraman.com.

⚘ ABOUT THE TRANSLATOR

Michael Cooperson (PhD Harvard 1994) is professor of Arabic at the University of California, Los Angeles, where he teaches Arabic literature from pre-Islam to the nineteenth century as well as courses on translation from Arabic to English. He has published two monographs on early Abbasid cultural history: *Classical Arabic Biography* (2000) and *Al-Maʾmūn* (2005). He supervises the UCLA Subtitle Project, which trains students to produce English captions for culturally significant Arabic-language videos. He is a consulting member of the Editorial Board of the Library of Arabic Literature, and the editor and translator of Ibn al-Jawzī's *Virtues of the Imam Aḥmad ibn Ḥanbal* (2013). This work received the Sheikh Hamad Prize for Translation and International Understanding, and the English has been reissued as *The Life of Ibn Ḥanbal* (2017). His other research interests include Maltese language and culture. His study of Arabic sources for medieval Maltese history received the 2016 Malta Historical Society Publication Award for Established Authors.